THE NEW IRISH AMERICANS

To Lisa, Kate and Liz

THE NEW IRISH AMERICANS

RAY O'HANLON

ROBERTS RINEHART PUBLISHERS

Published in the United States and Canada by Roberts Rinehart Publishers,
6309 Monarch Park Place, Niwot, Colorado 80503, USA
TEL 303.652.2685 • FAX 303.652.2689
Visit our web site: www.robertsrinehart.com

Distributed to the trade by Publishers Group West

Published in Ireland and the UK by Roberts Rinehart Publishers,
Trinity House, Charleston Road, Ranelagh, Dublin 6

Library of Congress Cataloging-in-Publication Data

O'Hanlon, Ray
    The New Irish Americans / by Ray O'Hanlon.
        p.   cm.
    Includes index.
    ISBN 1–57098–212–0 (softcover)
    1. Irish-Americans—History—20th century. 2. Irish-Americans—
Cultural assimilation. 3. United States—Emigration and Immigration—
History—20th century. 4. Immigrants—United States—History—20th
century.   I. Title.
    E184.I6047 1998
    973'.049162–dc21   97–52317
                                                                CIP

10 9 8 7 6 5 4 3 2 1

Cover design:
Ann W. Douden
Interior design:
Pauline Brown, pebble graphics, Denver, Colorado
Typesetting:
Red Barn Publishing, Skeagh, Skibbereen, Co. Cork, Ireland

Printed in the United States of America

CONTENTS

)

ACKNOWLEDGMENTS

A decade is a long time that has flown by. Irish immigrants invariably remember the day they arrived in the United States. Given the pace of life, much of what follows can be a bit of a blur. It is easier to attach memories to people, and in the now more than ten years that I have worked as an Irish journalist in America, it has been my privilege to encounter outstanding and extraordinary people on an enviably frequent basis. Some of them are named in the pages of this book. Others are not, but their work yet forms part of this book's still evolving story.

I would like to pay particular thanks to all those who have battled, and continue to battle, on behalf of the right of Irish people to settle in the United States: Pat Hurley, Sean Minihane and the other founders of the Irish Immigration Reform Movement, Paul Finnegan, Trish O'Callaghan, Rep. Chuck Schumer, Debbie McGoldrick and the many others who work the immigration coalface to this day. Bruce Morrison and Brian Donnelly were especially helpful in opening the often mystery-shrouded doors of Congress for those chapters dealing with the congressional debates during the 1980s.

I am particularly indebted to my colleagues over the years at the *Irish Echo* and in the gone but never to be forgotten *Irish Press* Group. A paycheck might satisfy the stomach, but the camaraderie in papers such as these is what truly nourishes the soul. Equally, the small band of Irish journalists in the U.S. has been a constant source of aid and comfort. Thanks especially to John O'Mahony for his razor-edged enthusiasm, Seán Cronin for his deep well of knowledge, Jack Holland for his Belfast-born skepticism, Patrick Farrelly for blowing lids off things and Conor O'Clery for his advice and insight. Thanks also to Irish American standard bearers, including Jim Mulvaney, Kevin Cullen, Terry Golway, Tom Connelly, John Thornton and Pete Hamill. America might be a relatively open book, but it sure helps to have interpreters.

A particular debt is owed to Dermot Brangan, formerly of the Irish Consulate General in New York, for his ability to read instantly the newspaper mind. Others in the Irish diplomatic service who have helped significantly over the years include Adrian O'Neill, Anne Barrington and Noel Kilkenny. My thanks also to those British diplomats who have been invariably courteous and helpful, even when their country has been the recipient of critical comment.

A special mention should be made of the *Irish Echo*'s readers, never shy about making their opinions known. There are some who could show Woodward and Bernstein a thing or two. Particular thanks to Tom Ruane, Tom Maher, and James Mullin.

I would like to thank publisher Claire O'Gara Grimes and publishers Roberts Rinehart, for making my work far easier to accomplish than might have been the case, my wife Lisa and my parents, Frank and Phyllis O'Hanlon, for not letting me off the hook when I announced the intention to write this book . . . but oh someday, maybe in a few years.

Finally, in a most special sense, this book is dedicated to Conor O'Brien (1928–1985), editor, mentor and friend.

New York
January 1998

FOREWORD

This is an important book. Over the past twenty years, more Irish men and women have arrived in the United States than at any time since the 1920s, and they are making a significant impact on American life. In one way, they are part of a continuing process, not unique to the Irish. But they are also something very new. To begin with, they are the best-educated Irish immigrants in history. More than a few have found their way into journalism, publishing, television and film, where their presence is having a ripple effect far beyond their actual numbers. Others are practicing in the medical and legal professions or attending universities or teaching in their classrooms. They have reached this level of accomplishment with greater speed than any previous generation of Irish immigrants, most of whom settled for hard work and marginal living conditions in order that their children would have better lives. Many members of this new generation are not living a postponement or a sacrifice; they are having their American lives now. This book recounts many of their stories.

There are, of course, large differences between these Irish immigrants and those of a century ago. Technology has changed the lives of all immigrants, and the Irish are not unique among the Mexicans, Koreans, Dominicans, Russians and others who are part of the largest immigration wave in a century. For all of them, the Old Country is not some distant spot on a vast map. For the Irish, the days of the American Wake are long over; nobody waves goodbye forever from the rocky shores of Donegal. Some of the Irish come for a short time, "to try America," and if they are unlucky or disappointed or even hurt, they go home. Others stay in touch with friends and family by telephone, fax and e-mail. Several superb weekly newspapers complete the sense of remaining connected, preventing Ireland from becoming a permanent part of the past. In addition, the airplane has shortened the Atlantic passage to a few hours and those huge jets travel in both directions. This has drastically altered the psychology of the immigrant, whether he or she is from Oaxaca, Santa Domingo, St. Petersburg or Mayo.

These newest Irish Americans are part of another phenomenon. The old tale of immigrants and their American children was based on an interrupted narrative. That explained the often dreadful gap between Irish fathers and American sons, Irish mothers and American daughters. The Irish American, for example, had the confident sense of having come in at the beginning of a story. The immigrant, however, had left behind another country – its places, weather, legends and myths – and had left it behind forever. For the immigrant, a story that had its beginnings in the fogs of history had been permanently broken. A new identity was impossible; only a system of masks could bring comfort and safety. The Stage Irishman was the creation of people who needed masks.

The new Irish immigrants don't require masks. They can be themselves, create their own American narratives, and with the help of technology, maintain a powerful connection to the old. This is something new. The influence of Irishness is today, as it was before, cultural, from U2 to Seamus Heaney. But even those examples are part of a transatlantic exchange, as influenced by Harvard or the blues as they are by the tales of the Black and Tans. The Irish embrace of the American sense of irony, derived in its turn from the great Jewish immigration waves, has also altered contemporary Irish culture; it is now more secular, modern and urban than at any point in Irish history. This historic exchange is enriching both nations. New York and Dublin are now suburbs of each other.

Ray O'Hanlon in this book tells the tale of this new Irish immigration, without in any way romanticizing its players. His account of the struggle for immigration reform is the most complete now in existence. He doesn't leave out the darker side of the story either, and makes clear that story is not yet over. This is a situation report. Much more will be written about all this in the coming century, by novelists and sociologists, by poets and historians, by the immigrants and their children. For now, O'Hanlon has given us a superb opening chapter.

Pete Hamill
New York
January 1998

INTRODUCTION

"When the soul of a man is born in this country there are
nets flung at it to hold it back from flight. You talk to me
of nationality, language, religion. I shall try to fly by
those nets."

James Joyce, *A Portrait of the Artist as a Young Man.*

On a warm summer's evening in 1987 a visitor leaned over the velvet rope hung across the door of the Oval Office. The room was bathed in light even though it was almost midnight. You could have said that not a creature was stirring, not even a President of the United States who, by that hour, was likely dreaming of jelly beans, chopping logs or troublesome Communist insurgents in Central America.

The Oval Office is familiar to people around the world. It has been recreated in countless movies and television dramas and, during daylight hours, is often filled by the cameras of the press. The visitor was, however, profoundly impressed by this sneak peek at the real thing, its relatively modest size and location, in a wing of the White House, not at its center. A pre-revolutionary French king would not have been impressed. But who needs to impress when you can destroy the world at the touch of a button.

The visitor took a last look, admired the works of Frederic Remington, briefly imagined a scene with JFK sitting in his rocking chair, and turned to the right down some steps into a small hallway. It was here that the visitor stopped. The walls were dotted with photographs—all featuring President Ronald Reagan. Pictures of Reagan raising a beer, wearing a green derby hat, joking with well known Irish American political leaders and lesser known diplomats from a small country three thousand miles away that would barely satisfy the acreage appetite of a bewigged absolute monarch.

The Irish American President was clearly having a good time. The photographs had been taken many weeks earlier, on St. Patrick's Day. And yet, there they were, still hanging in the West Wing on a sultry night in June. Here, clearly, was a president who was "Irish" 365 days a year.

The photos spoke of a warm and relaxed relationship between the island so far away and the court of the sun president. Here were friends gathered in a common celebration of Irishness. They represented an old, very special relationship, forged by ties of history, heritage and family. The scenes depicted in the photos bore witness to a bond that, on one level at least, was cordial, chummy, intimate, almost loving.

But they had nothing to do with the world outside, where bonds of kith and kin were being sorely tested in the market-driven America of the 1980s. Ronald Reagan hoisted his beer. Back in Ireland thousands were doing the same thing, but for a very different reason. Not a night passed in the Ireland of that decade without family and friends gathering in a home or pub to sink a few and bid farewell to another son, daughter, brother, sister, friend, who were packing bags and heading down the well-worn trail to New York, Boston, Chicago, San Francisco, Toronto or a thousand other places on the map of North America.

The midnight visitor to the White House could rely on the favors of an administration friend with highest level security clearance. But what of the thousands back across the ocean in Mayo and Donegal, Kerry and Roscommon? No White House passes or Washington pals; no social security numbers, jobs or visas; rather, a series of immigration laws designed to keep them well and truly outside the new, trans-Atlantic Pale. But just try and stop them. No muskets, no nuclear missiles, no law, no frontier, no president of the New Rome could. It was midnight. The Irish were coming— again!

All very dramatic stuff. But just ask anyone who has been following the affairs of Irish America over the past dozen years or so and they will quickly tell you that the period roughly extending from the early 1980s to the late 1990s has been quite extraordinary, even by the turbulent standards of the last couple of centuries. These were the years of "Legalize the Irish," "Free Joe Doherty," "We're Here, We're Queer, We're Irish," a woman in Ireland's White House, and a young American president who told the world, "I am Irish, I look Irish." It eventually reached a point where the *New York Times* decided that "The Irish Are Ascendant Again."

So how did this come to pass? Sure, the Irish political machine in America isn't what it was. But being ascendant is no longer just about controlling city halls in Boston or Chicago. As the twentieth century draws to a close, it is more to do with being recognized as having all the offshoots of a unique and powerful heritage and being confident enough to proclaim loudly these attributes to the rest of America and the wider world.

For centuries, the Irish have been roaming the earth in search of new places to establish and express their Irishness. But the idea of "Irishness" being a global phenomenon, not necessarily joined at the hip to Ireland itself, is something quite new. And it can spring up just about anywhere. Ireland's emergence as a truly modern European nation has been mirrored by an Irish cultural revival that has roots in the United States and other countries where the Irish have taken up residence in significant numbers. If Riverdance was Ireland proudly presenting its culture anew to a global audience, it should be remembered that the feet that really kicked the show into prominence were American. Yes, the Irish are coming. But they are not just coming from that small island on the fringe of Europe. And Ireland's relationship with America has progressed well beyond that established in years past by generations who knew only the one way ticket.

One thing immediately evident when looking back over the last ten or fifteen years is that, to say the least, there was rarely a dull moment. In fact, there never seemed to be enough time to cover all the stories, never mind write a book. But that's precisely the reason why a book has to be written. And so here it is.

This is a story about the Irish generation that came into the world largely in the 1950s; the generation that became the children of the 1960s, came of age in the 1970s, emigrated in large numbers to America in the 1980s and came through, one way or another, in the 1990s. It is also a story of that generation's encounter with Irish America, an established and expanding fraction of the new world's epic story.

The New Irish Americans is, additionally, a story about Ireland itself, a country that is finally managing to shed some of the historical burdens it has carried for too long and that can now offer its ideas and solutions to other cultures on more or less its own terms. And, finally, it is a story that touches upon the relationship between the Irish in America and those who live in Ireland itself. "Ireland" refers to the entire island although the politically generated distinctions between North and South are acknowledged in these pages whenever necessary.

This is not a definitive history, more a personal retrospective. But if it is a tale highlighting the endeavors of a relative handful of individuals and groups, it is also one to which countless people have contributed, in major ways and small. For every name mentioned in these pages there are many more who, while worthy of acknowledgment, were destined to contribute anonymously to the latest chapter in the saga of the Irish in America. To paraphrase the commercial: This book's for you!

1

THE NEXT PARISH

*"...a land whose countryside would be bright with cozy
homesteads, whose fields and villages would be joyous with
the sounds of industry, with the romping of sturdy children,
the contests of athletic youths and the laughter of comely
maidens, whose firesides would be forums for the wisdom of
serene old age."*

Eamon de Valera, radio address, St. Patrick's Day, 1943.

By 1975, the year of Eamon de Valera's death, few Irish people, athletic, comely or otherwise, were particularly interested in trying to grasp the essence of the former leader's vision. If it ever was that way it sure wasn't now. Many homesteads were being deserted in the rush to the expanding cities. Irish women, whose perceived capacity to bear sturdy children, hordes of them, was the marvel of the western world, were now loudly uttering a word that would never have made a de Valera radio address: contraception. The comely maidens of Dev's dreamland were, by the mid 1970s, increasingly disinclined to sit by the fireside awaiting the cold beckoning shadow of old age, serene or otherwise.

De Valera's final passing took place some years after his vision of an Ireland, largely self-sustaining and perfectly balanced between the wheels of native industry and agriculture, had inevitably succumbed to the advance of a global economy and mass urban culture. The emerging new Ireland was driven more by the need to throw multi-lane bypass roads around de Valera's now traffic-choked villages than by a desire to make them warm and cozy places in which to pass a lifetime.

Ireland in the closing quarter of the twentieth century was a place where change was a word used minimally because the sheer pace of it almost wasn't noticed, or paid much heed. But change there was. The population was growing younger on average by the day and the me-first culture, which had wrapped itself python-like around the youth of North America and western Europe in the 1960s, was sinking its amplified roots into the sturdy Irish at a rate which, on the surface at least, seemed at odds with the widely held view that Ireland was an easy going place, not given much to frivolous change or godless alien pleasures. Dev's death at the age of ninety-two that August was of course big news. But it hardly plunged the bell bottom generation into deep mourning. The passing of Elvis or Thin Lizzy's Philip Lynott would soon do that to a far greater extent. By 1975, Dev's vision was already gone and in the grave, keeping it cozy for the long fella's formal arrival.

But at least de Valera had dreams. What of this new generation, brought up on a diet of American soap and British pop with an occasional "Oirish" twist? Ireland in the 1970s was of the west but had yet to stamp its own pronounced mark on western popular culture. For much of the country's youth it was a matter of sit tight and let it fall in your lap, job or dole. The idea of projecting a specific Irish view, the thought of saying to the world, hey, we can do it even better, was an invitation to be labeled a daydreaming fool. Social commentators might talk long into the night about the colonial hangover or a nation born with an apology on its lips, but how could you shed something so rarely acknowledged, something of which you were hardly even aware?

Occasionally, it was an interesting idea to contemplate the idea of an Ireland geographically as well as politically removed from the much larger and dominant neighbor next door, the kind of Ireland that might have evolved if the men and women of 1916 had been able to tow the thirty-two counties far away to some oceanic warm spot half a world away from Britain.

No Black and Tans and apart from suntans, would these theoretical Irish, sixty years after the Rising, have been any different from those who now witnessed the Northern Ireland Troubles, daily absorbing large dollops of human tragedy and the relentless British spin on the "Irish Question;" feigning apathy and indifference to all the problems "up there" while rarely if ever admitting to a near total sense of national impotence.

But mostly it was a matter of passing exams, getting a trade, establishing a professional career and can I afford a car and a couple of weeks in the Costa Del whatever. Jobs, in increasing variety, were cropping up for the later arriving Irish boomers. But still not enough of them. Unemployment, always a fact of life for a significant proportion of the population since the founding of the State, was becoming a regular item in the national newspapers and on the television news. There was always the boat to England. Dublin was closer to London than most Scottish cities and of course Liverpool was the "real capital of Ireland." Moving across the water could mean many things: Opportunity, an escape from the suffocating life of small town Ireland, being close to your favorite soccer team, a job or more dole money. England was not so much a place as it was part of a logical process. If you didn't stay here you went there. It was that simple. Nobody ever talked much about America.

That's not to say that the generation that came of age post-Beatles, pre-punk, was entirely indifferent to America. Nothing of the sort. America was so familiar in all its tempting worldly offerings that it almost wrapped itself around the Irish psyche like a big star spangled blanket. Ireland was never so prickly towards American cultural dominance as, say, France. By historical circumstance, Ireland and the United States conversed in much the same language and the Irish of the immediate post-war era grew up on a diet of Humphrey Bogart, John Wayne and Jimmy Stewart, just as their far off cousins did in Southie or South Dakota.

Irish television, born at the dawn of the 1960s, was both financially limited and uncertain of its mission and relied heavily on imported American shows. A photo of a group of kids in suburban Dublin and outlying Boston in the mid '60s would portray children who, at first glance, appeared virtually indistinguishable. And while the two cities diverged in many ways, both sides converged again courtesy of television. All were lost in space, singing along with the Monkees, voyaging to the bottom of the sea and sorting out the weekly batch of villains who disturbed the peace and tranquillity of the Ponderosa.

America's immeasurable achievements and sweet small screen offerings simply couldn't be ignored. The Apollo missions held Ireland in thrall. And were they not launched by an Irish president?

America's woes were also pumped through the tube wires into Irish homes. JFK's assassination, Vietnam, the burning of Watts. But there was also that sense of being there, shoulder to shoulder with America, the good guys. When Kennedy was laid to rest in Arlington National Cemetery, the armed forces of the United

States and one other country stood guard at the graveside. Alongside the sentinels representing the might of America's military was
a small, solemn detachment of Irish Army cadets. Kennedy had
been impressed by the cadets during his visit to Ireland only a few
months before his death. The dead president's admiration had been
conveyed to his family and with its consent, Joe Kennedy's second
son went to his final resting place under the gaze of tall young men
in green and tan uniforms taking orders in Irish. There was a powerful symbolism here that would find echoes thirty years in the
future, when another young president with Irish roots walked
through the front doors of the White House.

Pictures like this, the sight of de Valera, almost totally blind,
striding out with the leaders of the world that morning in Washington were yet more reminders to Irish people of all ages that there
was another place, not quite like ours but then again not quite
entirely different, where Irish destinies were being played out to the
very end.

It was hard at times like this to maintain the Republic of Ireland's facade of political and military neutrality. Despite all the
familial feeling for America, Ireland, specifically the twenty-six
counties of the Republic, was nobody's official base of operations
during the Cold War. Irish foreign policy was, as Minister for External Affairs Frank Aiken once told the Dáil (Irish Parliament): " A
combination of selective indignation and diplomatic discretion."
Ireland was the mouse that contemplated an occasional, rather
muted roar. And most of the time said little or nothing.

Established Ireland winced at the horrors of Vietnam and while
most Irish harbored a deep-rooted antipathy towards "godless Communism" the general view at government level was that it wasn't a
matter for Irish concern, one way or another.

Neil Sheehan, who covered the conflict for United Press International and the *New York Times*, would, years later, reach back to
his Irish roots and draw comparisons between the struggle of Ireland to free itself from the control of more powerful neighbors and
that of Vietnam's centuries-long effort to escape the clutches of
powerful invaders. In his book *A Bright Shining Lie*, Sheehan would
portray the Vietnamese as a people whom foreigners have repeatedly sought and failed to conquer and pacify. "There are a small
number of such peoples on the earth," he would write. "The Irish
are one. The Vietnamese are another."

But few in Ireland could clearly see the parallel in 1968 as Lyndon Johnson, looking sad most nights on the evening news, threw in the presidential towel and walked away from America's most divisive ever foreign adventure.

There were some in Ireland, mostly of the native grown left, who decried the American presence in a country known mostly to kids with stamp albums. But Ireland at the end of the '60s was not seething like much of the rest of western Europe. Huge crowds of angry protesters would lay siege to U.S. embassies in London, Paris and elsewhere, but not in Dublin. The Tet offensive in 1968 came two years after Ireland, for the last time, marked the 1916 Rising with fervor and a sense of national purpose. But independence had brought with it new burdens and a legion of practical considerations. Ho Chi Minh and his comrades could expect little sympathy, even from a country striving to forget its own recently shed foreign colonial yoke.

Throughout the decade of lunar shots and countless more earthly ones, Ireland was dominated politically by two men, Sean Lemass, who was Taoiseach up to 1966, and the aging but still larger than life figure of de Valera. Dev's formal role, as President, was limited by the constitution he himself drew up in the 1930s. But his guiding hand was still seen, a little shaky now perhaps, as Ireland's efforts to modernize at last began to catch up with long stated ambition.

For years, de Valera had nurtured the idea of an Ireland economically divorced from its traditional over-dependency on Britain. To that end, it was clear that the emerging Irish economy could not be nakedly exposed to uncontrolled emigration. The seepage of people from Ireland had to be curtailed. Unrestricted entry to Britain was an established right for citizens of the Republic. Indeed, anyone in the twenty-six counties born prior to the birth of the Irish Republic in 1949 was entitled to a British passport. Britain remained the primary destination for those who could not be provided for by the still infant Irish industrial economy. But the United States, which had also been a magnet for countless thousands of Irish throughout the century, was not a door so open as Britain. If access to Britain could not be stopped, partially plugging the sporadic leak, and periodic flood, of young men and woman to America was at least possible. By the time JFK and Dev huddled together in the Irish White House, Áras an Uachtaráin, in June 1963, the founder of Fianna Fáil and the Lemass-led Fianna Fáil government were keenly aware that a renewed surge of Irish emigration to America could be a severe hindrance to newly minted plans for Irish economic development. In order to foster Ireland's belated industrial revolution, such migration had to be bottled up. It's a stretch to say that Irish wishes were specifically reflected in the U.S. immigration reform act passed in Washington in 1965. By the mid 1960s, the sustained surge of Irish emigration which had so dominated Ireland a decade before had largely tailed off. Irish emigration was cyclical in nature and now, two years after de Valera and Kennedy had conferred, the cycle had come almost full circle, from flood to spate. The new law which emerged from the often turbulent process of debate and horse trading on Capitol Hill would restrict entry to the U.S. to almost all but those who had direct family ties to legal aliens or U.S. citizens. In effect, the policy of attracting largely European immigrants was being dropped in favor of a new plan to broaden and diversify the face of immigration. However, the most stringent effects of the new laws would not be felt in Ireland for almost twenty years when, in the early 1980s, the emigration cycle was to turn full circle again.

In Ireland, the 1970s were akin to a period between great wars. When de Valera finally passed away it was ten years since the once open golden door to America had been reduced to a mere slit. But it hardly seemed to matter. The rising numbers of kids leaving Irish schools every year expected jobs, a place in third level education or a boat ticket to England. Either way, there seemed to be alternatives. Heading for Britain was par for the course, lengths of stay varied and while it undoubtedly counted as emigration, London wasn't all that far away, geographically or psychologically. Some people were going to Australia and that was goodbye big time. The troubles in Northern Ireland were not much of a factor when it came to making the decision to move to England, especially if you came from the Republic. For those who stayed back in Ireland, prospects seemed to be improving. The country was definitely on the move in every way that mattered.

America was never entirely out of the loop though. While emigration to the U.S. had slowed to a comparative trickle, every summer saw several thousand Irish students heading for the U.S. and returning home a few months later in exotic t-shirts with stories about how big and amazing "the States" was. For most, however,

America was a supposedly familiar but still faraway place, dissected and explained for the most part on TV or in the movies; a country full of people to envy and sometimes resent. Americans, it was widely felt, were incredibly dynamic and go-ahead sorts but also a little daft in the head sometimes. The stereotypical Yank was never far from mind. Graham Greene, English but a convert to Catholicism, had written a book called *The Quiet American* and was obviously taking the mick.

But despite the sometimes less than flattering portrayals of Americans, Ireland, as the 1970s drew to a close, was still leading in the Fifty-first State stakes. Or at least that's what many thought. Sometimes it seemed that it suited to be closely identified with all that passed for normality across the water, sometimes it did not. When it came to measuring economic and social progress at home, America was Ireland's benchmark.

Twenty years on, Ireland is more dependent than ever on U.S. investment to prop up the illusion of national solvency if not actual economic independence. But at the same time, Ireland is now a "gateway to Europe," a stepping stone to the reborn old world. Green Ireland is now a field of investment dreams and if you can think of a good angle, a catchy slogan—while throwing in some hefty financial incentives—they will most assuredly come.

But effective public relations and slick selling don't quite explain away the Irish dilemma. Unlike, say, Japan, Ireland is not a noticeably introspective culture intent on maintaining at almost any cost some cherished notion of national historical purity. Ireland has neither the means nor the inclination to be some sort of self-sustaining and inward looking nativist state. Besides, geography and history have combined to present the Irish with certain inescapable facts of life—not least being the fact that any Irish state could never hope to function free of outside economic intervention, benign or otherwise. Ireland would or could never be an Albania surrounded by water. The country, despite periodic internal outbursts of exaggerated self-importance, is forever destined to be a small nation in a part of the world where big nations hold sway. Others largely decide what Ireland is, while the Irish themselves are allowed to apply the gloss coat. The Irish, depending on circumstances, might feel they are on the edge of the world or a kind of North Atlantic middle kingdom. But from a British perspective—particularly during the Second World War—Ireland, no matter how de Valera felt, was little more than the fortress guarding the western approaches.

To this day, Ireland is a front door to Europe if you're viewing it from the west, and a back door if you are looking from the east. Ireland is both the Fifty-first State and the first stepping stone, a land of Euro-American facilitators, surviving on its wits and understanding of the rules of political and economic expediency. It is a country not unlike those small birds that pluck ticks from the hides of rhinos and elephants. Is the rhino really a friend, or does it simply not pay heed to its small, fleet-winged companion?

Some are a little alarmed by the shape of things that have come to pass in the modern "New Ireland." The gloomier observers see a country with its left hand holding the door ajar for the latest American corporate bigshot with computer chips to build and golf courses to conquer, while the right hand twitches nervously for the next, and now diminishing, European Union regional fund handout. Irish journalist Fintan O'Toole, in his 1994 book *Black Hole, Green Card*, argued that there is no longer an Irish economy, just a "Black Hole" through which profits and jobs vanish, that there is no longer an Irish nation, just a scattered people who still hold a country in their heads, that there is no longer an Irish history, just a supermarket of reconstructed memories for tourist consumption—that the Ireland invented by nationalists in the early years of this century has ceased to exist.

But the idea of Ireland as a 32,000 square mile piece of flotsam in a turbulent market driven sea is not the entire story. Whatever the source of bread, it is a fact that there is more bread to go around than ever before, lots more. A mere one hundred and fifty years ago, the Irish were starving by the million. The glass is half empty or half full, but at least now, as the 1990s dip to their conclusion, it is definitely half something.

Yes, it seems at times that Ireland twists in the geopolitical wind like some demented weathercock. But there are moments in time when the collective Irish mind gathers itself and decides that better fortune is to be found this way or that. The years of, and those immediately following, the Great Famine saw that sense of destiny firmly rest on the western horizon. Hundreds of thousands of Irish did not flee to Europe and by the strict political definitions of the time, migration to England was an internal matter just as moving from Oklahoma to California was never officially termed what it actually was in the dustbowl days—emigration.

More than anywhere else on earth, North America became the repository for a collective Irish destiny during those desperate years. When it mattered most, America was there, broad-shouldered and inviting. It has been little different ever since.

The Irish "discovered" America. And they "built" it. The White House was designed by one Irishman and the U.S. Navy founded by another. And if all this was not sufficient to shore up Irish sensitivities in uncertain times, there was further statistical comfort for the Fifty-first State boosters in the 1990 U.S. Census. It threw up the now almost daily quoted figure of forty-four million Americans claiming their primary ethnic links to the old sod. So even if the Irish hadn't placed every brick upon every brick, they must have knocked more than their expected share together. America wouldn't be America without Ireland.

The concept of discovery, however, is more remote and harder to grasp than a brick. Take a straight course from Ireland's Atlantic shore, follow the curve of the watery earth for roughly 2,000 miles and, assuming your mode of travel is soundly constructed, you will arrive eventually on the shore of what is now the Canadian province of Newfoundland, an island which, ironically, sundered its final political ties with Britain the same year that the Irish Free State became a republic.

Explorer Tim Severin made such a landfall in the summer of 1977 by means of a cowhide boat named after St. Brendan, the sixth century Irish monk who is believed by many to have voyaged to the new world at a time when the old world was still quite new itself. Severin's account of the journey, *The Brendan Voyage*, became a best selling book and reminded the Irish of the logic of their geographical position as a jumping off point for all stops west of, well, Kerry. The account of Brendan's supposed sixth century voyage is contained in a Latin manuscript entitled *Navigatio Sancti Brendani Abbatis*, or more simply, the *Navigatio*.

Severin was deeply impressed by the tale recounted in the *Navigatio*. As well he might. It described how St. Brendan (489–570ish AD) was approached by another monk while living in the west of Ireland. The monk told Brendan of a beautiful land far to the west where the word of God ruled supreme. Brendan was impressed and decided to build an oxhide boat and go see for himself.

Using all available scholarly material, Severin constructed a boat that corresponded to the kind of vessels which plied the seas in

Brendan's day. His voyage, not without some scary moments, was a complete success. Like the Norwegian Thor Heyerdahl, Severin demonstrated that, assuming the will and inclination, ancient people had the means to make long distance sea voyages. Ironically, Heyerdahl had also "proved" that the ancient Egyptians could have crossed the Atlantic from east to west in papyrus boats long before even Brendan the Navigator. But the who-discovered-America-first debate is a competitive business. He who speaks loudest sinks last and the Brendan advocates have continued to slug it out, usually in reasonably good-natured fashion, with the Columbus and Pilgrim supporters.

Then again, it would be wrong to suggest that there is no edge at all to the debate.

"The definitive claim that Christopher Columbus discovered America in 1492 is, to put it mildly, open to question," Irish Ambassador to the United Nations Noel Dorr told the General Assembly in 1982 during a debate on a resolution proposing a series of celebrations in 1992 marking the five hundredth anniversary of the Columbus landing in San Salvador.

While never straying too far from the diplomatic shoreline, Dorr went on to lecture the nations of the world as to the details of the *Navigatio*, which were themselves written sometime in the ninth century. The mouse wasn't quite roaring but it was making a point.

All the nations listening to Dorr had a toehold in America; at the very least a mission to the U.N. if not a large ethnic bloc with which to hold hands. The ambassador, very diplomatically, was emphasizing that the Irish had rather more than a toehold. Never mind building the place, we had found it first, so there!

Feeling part of the place before you even arrive is an advantage for any immigrant. The Irish wasted little time in going as far as they could in remolding America in an Irish image when they began arriving in large numbers, post-famine. And this didn't go unnoticed. In a message to the U.S. Secretary of State in February, 1881, the U.S. minister to Great Britain James Russell Lowell wrote of an "Irish nation in America."

Sean Cronin, journalist and author, has attributed this formation of an effective nation in exile to the political situation in Ireland, pointing out that while immigrants from most countries in the nineteenth century had tended to pay little heed to the political situations in their motherlands, the Irish were different, due partly to the fact that many of the first Irish arrivals in the new world were as much political exiles as anything else. From the time of its independence, America had become an inspiration and refuge for Irish revolutionaries such as Wolfe Tone and Napper Tandy. Most Irish stepping off the immigrant ships harbored at least some degree of resentment against England. America was the one place in the world where just about anything could take root and flower, even extreme bitterness.

The idea of recreating an ideal Ireland in the new country could well be the basis for explaining why so many nineteenth and early twentieth century Irish were one way travelers. At the same time, not all Irish stayed put in the traditional host cities such as Boston, New York and Philadelphia. Many were to push deeper into the American hinterland, at times inspired by Catholic clerics intent on establishing Irish Catholic settlements in the vast empty spaces of the west, particularly Dakota Territory.

But no matter where they finally came to a stop, the vast majority of Irish arrivals were absorbed by America on a permanent basis. Whether it was Boston or Butte, there was hardly ever any going back. In their study of the Irish immigrant story in America, *Out of Ireland*, Kerby Miller and Paul Wagner point to the fact that in the peak immigration years, more than forty percent of Italian immigrants eventually returned to Italy. The percentage rose to fifty in the case of Poles and Hungarians and exceeded sixty percent among Greeks. *Out of Ireland* is a truly modern piece of work, complete with accompanying video. The tale concludes with the return to Ireland in 1925 of Tim Cashman who had just retired from his job in the Roxbury section of Boston. Cashman wanted to visit the village of his youth in Co. Cork now that his own corner of Ireland had been freed of British rule. His journey, so full of expectation at the start, was to be a sad disappointment at its end. So much had changed and many things had not. The Free State, at the dawn of its independent existence, remained an economic backwater, a reality with which Cashman was more than familiar. This, allied to the fact that the more sentimental links to his youth, friends, his old home, had largely vanished, left Cashman profoundly depressed. Both the book and the video conclude with unforgettable words: "Timothy Cashman spent only a few weeks in Ireland revisiting the haunts of his youth. Before he left, he walked again in Glenbower Wood, the place that was, for him, the embodiment of Mother Ireland. There, in the stone of an old bridge, he carved his name in Gaelic script. Then he left and came home. . .home to America."

The final three words succinctly isolate what is a private dilemma facing every Irish immigrant to America to one degree or another. Where or what is called home will ultimately define the course of every immigrant's life. Some have little problem in calling America home the moment they arrive. Some never will admit to it in an entire lifetime. And there are some who don't care too much one way or another. Tim Cashman's choices were starker. He was a rare event in the Ireland of his day, a visiting emigrant, although he was probably called a Yank by the locals behind his back. In his own way he was a pioneer in his own lifetime—twice.

Today, the choices facing Ireland's emigrants seem unlimited although the waters are correspondingly muddier. Ireland is a spur-of-the-moment phone call away or a few hours on a plane. You can order Irish food products in the mail or, in some parts of the U.S., buy them off the shelves in your local supermarket. Irish newspapers are physically available in some major U.S. cities or everywhere on the web. This new closeness can be a comfort, a tease or a curse. For some, it is better to be cut off completely from what was. For others, all the snippets of the past can serve to confuse, while others again will snatch at everything in sight that can be conceivably defined as Irish. A nation in exile yet again, only this time one at least partly based on the sentimental desires of a new type of expatriate, one who has already imbibed deeply from consumerism's potent trans-national cup. The world talks about the global village. The Irish have long spoken of the next parish. The world is finally catching up.

By the early 1980s, Ireland's industrial coming of age was advancing rapidly. But the lofty employment targets of successive governments could never quite match demographics. It seemed that for every new factory, another would bite the dust. The low-level drift to America had continued through the years since the 1965 act. Few of the emerging generation of Irish were, however, particularly aware of its implications and most paid little attention to the barriers created by U.S. immigration law. The formal boundaries of the United States, were, in fact, more of a nuisance than anything else. America continued to pull the Irish in its direction regardless of Washington's wishes and many Irish simply viewed the U.S. as a logical extension of what was already familiar, native soil.

And why should Americans be surprised that the Irish were about to start coming again in large numbers? If you talk loud and long about being the greatest country in the world, don't feign shock when the world comes knocking on your door!

And so they came, by the tens of thousand. Almost unnoticed at first, the Irish began landing at Kennedy and Logan to attend weddings, funerals, visit long lost relatives or to work for the summer on student visas. They came with return tickets and no return in mind. The labor market quickly soaked up the new arrivals as the go-go eighties began to shed the oil inspired recession of the late Carter and early Reagan years. Mostly, they were single individuals, less often they were entire families. The majority of newcomers were in their early and mid-twenties. They quickly found jobs, money and in most places a social life that mirrored what they had left behind. Overstaying one's visa was a fact of life but it seemed to bring with it few immediate consequences. The occasional individual was nabbed unceremoniously by the INS and flown back to Ireland, but like a herd under attack from a lone predator, the vast majority could be certain of avoiding the claws of the immigration authorities. Life for a while was good, at least in a material sense.

But this was a restless generation, born and raised in great expectation. It had ambition and desire, wants and needs that were not all that easily satisfied. The Ireland of the 1950s, the era of the last great surge across the ocean, had little material largesse to offer its emerging citizens. Thirty years on, Ireland aspired to offer everything to its young, as much as any other developed western economy. But falling short was neither uncommon nor unexpected; like America, Ireland too could be the victim of its own hype.

No matter how many dollars were being earned in a week, no matter how the social "*craic*" of back home could be recreated on a Saturday night in the local Irish bar, the reality of sudden displacement and uncertainty was no less the case for this generation than for any other in years past. The more politically conscious emigrants were immediately aware of their disenfranchisement. They had neither a say in the country they were attempting to adopt, nor in the country they had just left behind. Irish citizens living abroad cannot vote in Irish elections, a factor that was to prove a serious handicap as the 1980s wore on.

As their numbers grew, it was inevitable that some would step forward and begin defining the shortcomings of this new life in

America. As their ambitions grew, fueled by the material prosperity now on offer, almost at the tips of their fingers, it was inevitable that the sharp limits imposed by being "illegal" or "undocumented" were going to be sorely felt. America might be the next parish, but that was fine only so long as you were content with the most parochial existence. As so many were discovering, as soon as you began to obey the demands of the ambition that brought you here in the first place, serious problems arose. Paying taxes, opening a bank account, securing health insurance, mortgages, or changing jobs. All such necessary goals suddenly became insurmountable obstacles to the fresh-off-the-boat undocumented.

The party had lasted only the briefest of moments. These "new Irish" were really no different from their forebears. Economic security and raising a family free of the fears of being discovered would gradually become the priorities of those who had been so recently the envy of less prosperous, but more settled, brothers and sisters back in Ireland. Over here, in America, it was now clearly impossible ever to reach the state of domestic normality so prized by those siblings who had remained behind "at home."

By the middle of the decade it had become serious reality check time for the undocumented Irish. A century before, official America had parted the way for a young Irish woman, Annie Moore, who had become the first official arrival at Ellis Island, on January 1, 1892. Annie was not in fact the first. Several Russian men stepped ashore ahead of her, but it was the plan at the time to mark the occasion with a commemorative china plate. A depiction of a bearded Russian did not quite suit the nascent marketing strategies of the 1890s. But Annie was just right for stepping up to and onto the plate and so became a lasting symbol of the island and the beckoning promise of America beyond.

But now, almost a hundred years later, the Irish were no longer fitting the picture; neither were the Russians for that matter. This was something altogether new for the Irish, a people who had imagined themselves for well over two centuries to be part owners and originators of the great American experiment. The very idea that the United States would slam the door in the face of thousands of young, talented, ambitious, white, English-speaking Irish was as humiliating as it was unexpected. Perhaps it was partly due to a cockiness, indeed arrogance, which the Irish were no less guilty of displaying than others born in western Europe. No matter what it was, it was difficult to explain to the few who cared to listen. Back in Ireland, it was the inevitable view that anyone who had gone to America was on the pig's back. Everyone in America was beavering away on their first million and some had already made it, only they weren't saying because of the taxman, here, there or wherever.

Neither Ireland, nor Irish America, was prepared for the story that began to reach the light of day in 1986-87. How could the Irish be in trouble, in America of all places? The explanation was about to be delivered—and rather loudly. The new Irish had been born into expectation and being bluntly denied their due was simply not good enough. Their collective voice would be heard from coasts to coasts, from both of America's to both of Ireland's. The first to hear it might be the mothers and fathers an ocean away, but the first to absorb the message, whether they were prepared for it or not, were the Irish government and what one report described as the "sleeping giant of Irish American opinion."

The Irish had arrived in America again but, as it turned out, under highly unfavorable circumstances. Now they were going to change those terms by any legal means necessary. The phones began to ring in Washington. When they were answered, the accents would sound a little odd at first, familiar but largely unheard in a while. They were voices from another land, or the next parish, depending on your perspective.

But they were voices that would be heard above the great American din. And they were recounting an alarming tale.

2

THE NUMBERS GAME

*"This time it was different. The boys left pell-mell, with
the cows unmilked, the kindling unbundled, the horse
untethered. No forwarding address. No sign they would
ever return."*

Peter Quinn, *Banished Children of Eve*.

Ted Kennedy was in his element: A corridor of power in Washington. He had just emerged from public hearings staged by the House Immigration Sub-Committee. It was early September 1988, the tail end of a long hot summer of frustration and discontent. Kennedy, looking tanned and a little large for his suit, was offering hope laced with caution.

"The key is to get into conference where we can certainly work things out," he told a small assembly of Irish and Irish Americans who had made the journey to the Rayburn Building on behalf of an unknown number of undocumented, technically unwelcome U.S. residents of Irish origin. The small group of lobbyists and immigration reform campaigners was uncertain. They were putting a lot of trust in the senior senator from Massachusetts and in a system of political horse trading that, by trial and error, they were only slowly getting to grips with themselves. But the Irish understood the essence of the political deal and in Kennedy they had been landed with a master in the art. Nobody was quite sure how Kennedy had become involved, although most had an idea the Irish government's hand was not a million miles away. Either way, it didn't much matter. Kennedy was in. The fix would surely follow.

The road to Washington had started in thousands of Irish homes. From roughly 1982 onwards, a steady flow of young Irish had made the Atlantic crossing in search of work, fatter paychecks, expanded opportunity and, for many, the kind of personal liberation only possible in a big, anonymous society such as America.

Their exact numbers were uncertain and it took a while before Irish officialdom even noticed they had gone. This was because they had never officially departed at all, at least not in the traditionally accepted manner—that in which emigrants had always tidied up their affairs while declaring to all and sundry their intentions to try for another life in another country.

The stories of hardship, frustrated dreams and economic restriction had been shared at first only within families. The exchanges between those who had gone to America and those back in Ireland were frequently tinged with a desire to assure: Yes, America was fantastic but there was a little problem with work. Yes, I had managed to get a job but it was all off the books. No problems really but you'd wonder about the taxman here. Isn't that how they nailed Al Capone?

There probably was a first "illegal," a kind of alpha immigrant, 1980s style. This individual matched all the variables that were to become common factors in the coming months and years throughout the rapidly expanding population of undocumented Irish immigrants. He or she probably left Ireland in the summer of 1982 or 1983 with a return ticket on Aer Lingus and a yarn about a long lost aunt in Philadelphia, a family funeral in Boston or a wedding in the Bronx. He or she might have been a university graduate and most certainly would have completed high school. An interview at the American embassy in Dublin would have been the initial hurdle, but the embassy wasn't too much of a hassle. Just show them that you had a job and convince them that you had good prospects in Ireland and that was sufficient. Very often there was an actual Irish job, but the pay didn't quite match the aspirations generated by the commercials on TV or in the glossy magazines—especially after your pay packet was virtually looted by the Irish version of the IRS, the Revenue Commissioners. Either way, you only had to satisfy U.S. officials that you were gainfully employed on pieces of paper. They didn't come down to check you out with a boss who was about to get your notice or worse, an employer who had never even heard of you. The person behind the bullet proof screen might have sounded tough, but getting the multiple entry visa wasn't too much trouble in the end for most. Off to America we go.

For those in their late teens and early twenties, everything that America had to offer was simply sensational—at least at the outset. But the novelty of minding someone else's baby or clearing tables can soon wear off—especially if such tasks are the only ones where no questions are asked and if the only alternatives are simply someone else's child or dirty tables in another restaurant down the street. Late night conversations in cramped apartments or Irish watering holes from Boston to San Francisco were soon turning to the future, one that was distinctly murky and uncertain.

But more often, as the months passed into a year and later into two, the undocumented Irish—illegal was something of a taboo word—would gather in their favorite haunts in Queens or Dorchester and consider the options. What initially seemed as the widest possible option, simply coming to America, was beginning to noticeably narrow as the deep-rooted Irish urge to "settle down," combined with the more lately acquired ambition to "do well," began to take stronger hold.

The numbers of undocumented Irish kept rising during 1983 and 1984. Ronald Reagan, a descendant of more traditional Irish immigrants, made it back to his roots in Ballyporeen, Co. Tipperary in that latter year. Some of the local kids weren't around to wave at him. They were back in the States giving his government agents the slip.

1985 and 1986 saw no slacking in the east to west migration across the ocean. A few Irish didn't like America and were packing their bags again. But there was work for just about anyone who wanted it, unlike back home in Ireland where the dole queues beckoned. And those still in Ireland who suffered from restless feet were hearing stories. So and so was pulling six hundred a week, into the pocket mind. Mary was going to Florida for a holiday in the winter, money no problem. See you for a pint tonight and we can talk about it. Regardless of the real difficulties being experienced by their brothers, sisters and cousins, the early day tales of the gone aways failed to tarnish the greener American grass in the eyes of those still stuck on the Irish sod. Those who remained behind were being pulled by those already gone. America was well worth the chance.

Still, it soon became clear to those taking the chance that while rapid economic reward was there for the taking, the potential for dramatic failure was also ever present. It wasn't that the new Irish arrivals were facing the kind of systematic discrimination which was the lot of earlier generations, particularly in the mid-nineteenth century; rather it was a sense that lack of status could shatter both achievement and dreams in a mere instant. "No Irish Need Apply" might have sounded prehistoric in a time of noticeable Irish American success and affluence, but the term was being heard again, widely and frequently. It topped an editorial in the October, 1986 issue of *Irish America* magazine, a glossy window into the world of the new Irish, and was followed below by a stinging attack on U.S. immigration laws, codes of practice which, in the eyes of the magazine, were quite simply "a disgrace." The same issue of the magazine revealed a previously suspected but largely unseen hand in the origins of this disgrace, the '65 immigration reform act. In an interview with House Speaker Tip O'Neill, the venerable Irish American legislator recalled that as the debate over immigration reform had reached a climax more than twenty years previously, the then Irish Ambassador in Washington (O'Neill couldn't actually recall his name during the interview but it was William Fay) had paid visits to leading Irish American politicians on Capitol Hill urging them to vote in favor of the measure. The idea behind this ploy was noble enough, at least from the Irish government's point of view. Ireland had finally picked up its pace of economic development by the mid-1960s. Bodies were needed to throw the switches and pull the levers of growth. But that was then and this was now. The suspicion that de Valera had somehow got to John Kennedy was always there in the background. Here was more fuel in the fire. "Irish America" decided that the Lemass-led government of that time had been "short-sighted in the extreme," that the bodies were held back for "an-all-too temporary economic renaissance" and that the Irish government, "with the subtlety of a sledgehammer and no thought for future generations" had "actually acquiesced in the closing of the American frontier, perhaps for ever, to their own p\eople."

It certainly seemed that way. But in politics, nothing is for ever. 1986 was to prove a turning point in the twenty-year U.S. position regarding the who, why and how of immigration. Some legislators had been glaring critically at the family reunification-based 1965 act for years. The notion of reuniting families down to the umpteenth cousin ten times removed was far from what some members of Congress believed was the purpose of allowing new blood into the United States in the first place. The demands of a diversifying labor market and the increasingly technical skills required by many employers were drawing responses from leading critics of the status quo such as Republican Senator Alan Simpson from Wyoming and, as it turned out, Brian Donnelly, an Irish-

American member of the House of Representatives, whose district just happened to include the aforementioned Dorchester.

In 1986, Congress passed the Immigration Reform and Control Act, a broad-based reform package aimed squarely at reversing the effects of its 1965 predecessor. The act provided the first lifeline to the Irish but was at the same time a two-edged sword. It contained tough new labor laws aimed at discouraging employers from hiring illegals. These laws had an immediate and highly restrictive effect. They would make changing a job a very hazardous mission for an undocumented alien, Irish or otherwise. The revised labor codes resulted in thousands of Irish suspending their plans to move on or up in the world. There followed an almost claustrophobic sense of frustration as entire communities of undocumented Irish battened down the hatches, fearful of what even the present, never mind the future, might bring.

But the act also offered some hope. It included an amnesty provision for the undocumented and 40,000 visas to immigrants from the thirty-five mostly European countries considered disadvantaged under the 1965 act. These visas had an official tag. They came under the auspices of the NP-5 visa program. But they also had a human face provided by their primary House of Representatives sponsor, Brian Donnelly. The Donnelly Visas became the first escape route for the undocumented Irish, or at least some of them. They would be issued in batches over a five year period from 1987 to 1991. It all seemed very hopeful. But as change moved at the pace dictated by Washington and not by the countless mostly young immigrants on whose behalf the new law was devised, a dire situation steadily grew worse.

The Donnelly Visas were aimed at over thirty countries whereas, by the dawn of 1987, there were more than enough Irish in the U.S., and on the way from Ireland, to snatch up each and every one of them—and then some.

By the first weeks of 1987, some who considered themselves in the know were beginning to recognize that there was a real crisis brewing. The sheer numbers of newly arrived Irish were beginning to attract attention, not all of it welcome or helpful. A handful of Irish, even a few thousand, could always elude the clutches of the Immigration and Naturalization Service. But it was getting to a point where the INS could enter parts of some cities and scoop up Irish by the dozen, like fish in a net, if the agency so chose. The fact that this hadn't happened was possibly fortuitous, call it the luck of the Irish, and it was certainly due in large part to the limited resources of the INS being tied up by illegals from countries whose exiled populations far outweighed that of tiny Ireland.

But few could expect such apparent restraint to last. The Irish were now attracting greater attention because they were sending up distress signals to others—politicians in Washington, their own government, established Irish American organizations and an Irish American media that was only beginning to notice a suddenly rather expanded pool of potential new customers. It was a bit like being lost at sea. You see the rescue ship and start waving and splashing. The ship might or might not spot you. But the cruising shark most certainly will.

In generations past, the Irish emigrant was always gone but not forgotten, especially if the family left behind was depending on dollars from America or wherever—the famed "emigrant's remittance." The emigrant might be particularly fondly remembered if the remittance was regular and fat. Either way, both sides adapted to the pain of separation as best they could. It was the way things were in Ireland for as long as anyone could remember.

But the emigrants of the 1980s were never quite gone. They seemed to linger in the mind's eye and the habit of sending money back to Ireland was not quite what it was. The gone aways would sometimes take a trip back home to Ireland, even if they were undocumented and risked being stopped on the way back to the U.S. But most of the undocumented were destined not to make the journey home for years, unlike Irish emigrants in Britain who could arrive home for breakfast virtually at the drop of the proverbial hat.

Being denied what was now all of a sudden the luxury of free movement prompted the first complaints to family members. Sometimes a family would pass on the sad story to local politicians. The question was now being asked: Were these kids emigrants in the true sense, or convicts in some kind of economic Van Diemen's land?

The Irish back in Ireland were becoming familiar, thanks to a torrent of political spin speak, with the idea of "voluntary" or "discretionary" emigration, as opposed to forced or involuntary emigration. But no matter the category at the beginning, there was consistently a belief that no matter the reason for departure, life would be better at the destination. But the undocumented in America were now presenting themselves as having been forced out of Ireland and were telling all who would listen that the situation they now faced was in many ways worse—even despite the availability of jobs.

The attitude of those who stay behind towards the emigrant invariably changes. Occasionally, the change is pronounced and can include a tinge of bitterness or feelings of betrayal. At other times it is barely perceptible. The exile, home for a couple of weeks, can be placed in the odd situation of being spoken to, politely, as if he or she was some kind of stranger. But almost always there is a change in relationship, subtle or marked, even between the closest of family members.

Where no personal relationship is involved the attitude towards the emigrants can be harsh as illustrated in this extract from a letter to the *Irish Times* published towards the end of 1996: "Ten years ago, not to put too fine a point on it, this country was in the doldrums. People couldn't wait to get out, like rats off a sinking ship. Now Ireland has pulled itself up by the bootlaces....And the rats are suddenly awakening to their Irish heritage! They wish to partake of all things Irish, including meddling in our internal affairs by voting . . ."

Again, not to put too fine a point on it, that kind of attitude is not confined to a single letter writer to Ireland's main paper of letters.

As the tidal rush of emigration to America gathered momentum, successive governments in Dublin, Garret FitzGerald's coalition administration and, subsequently, Charles Haughey's Fianna Fáil government, were attempting, as governments are often inclined, to both define and confine the issue. The situation was entirely new in modern times. The idea of America rejecting Ireland's youth was unprecedented. Irish political leaders were regular trans-Atlantic travelers and it was impossible to avoid the issue of the illegal Irish once landfall was made in New York and Boston in particular. Mass emigration, coupled with an economic slump and high unemployment, ensured defeat for FitzGerald's government in the general election on February 14, 1987. Fianna Fáil had been able to make political hay from this calamitous combination but no sooner were in power when they too discovered that it would take rather more than a polemical finger in the dyke to halt the outward flow of the nation's lifeblood. Opposition has its comfort zone. By late summer of 1987, Alan Dukes, the professorial FitzGerald's successor as leader of Fine Gael, was urging the Haughey government to negotiate directly with Washington over the issue of visa denial. That was easier said than done and just who did he mean by Washington? President Reagan, the lame duck from Ballyporeen? The gaggle of geese that was Congress? The very idea of a single political entity in the U.S. capital deciding the future course of U.S. immigration law smacked of absurdity. If there was any negotiation to be carried out it would have to be well out of official Washington's gaze. The immigration issue was quite simply dynamite and any overt move by Dublin risked an avalanche of opprobrium from others, not least the powerful immigration lobbies representing those nationalities who were doing well by the family reunification system.

Brian Lenihan was the Tánaiste (deputy prime minister) and Minister for Foreign Affairs in the new Haughey-led administration. Lenihan, who died in 1995, was a popular politician in Ireland. He was approachable, affable, intensely loyal to Haughey and inclined to shoot his mouth off a bit. Journalists loved him for that.

At the end of September of that year, Lenihan was in New York for the opening session of the United Nations General Assembly. Fianna Fáil had been in power for only six months and had inherited a dire situation which included high—almost twenty percent—unemployment and emigration running into the tens of thousands annually.

Lenihan was interviewed by *Newsweek* magazine. Like some old volcano he was about to blow his top again, with, as was his wont, the best possible intentions.

In his answers, given to *Newsweek*'s Paul Keating, Lenihan readily acknowledged the problem of Irish illegals and outlined possible remedial steps, including the latest efforts in Congress and an Irish government plan to set up an immigrant advice bureau in New York.

Keating then asked Lenihan if he thought emigration was a defeat for the Irish Republic.

Lenihan's reply was to unleash a storm: "I don't look on the type of emigration we have today as being of the same category as the terrible emigration in the last century. What we have now is a very literate emigrant who thinks nothing of coming to the United States and going back to Ireland and maybe on to Germany and back to Ireland again. The younger people in Ireland today are very much in that mode. And it's very refreshing to see it. If future legislation in the Congress will acknowledge the skills and the capacities of Irish emigrants and grant legal status to allow entry to qualified jobs, we will have a mobile labor market stretching from the U.S. to Ireland to the European Community where we can participate and contribute fully.

"It's not a defeat because the more (Irish emigrants) hone their skills and their talents in another environment, the more they develop a work ethic in a country like Germany or the U.S., the better it can be applied in Ireland when they return."

Lenihan was then asked what these same emigrants could offer Ireland.

"They should," he said, "do what they have to do. The world is now one world and they can always return to Ireland with the skills they have developed. We regard them as part of a global generation of Irish people. We shouldn't be defeatist or pessimistic about it. We should be proud of it. After all, we can't all live on a small island."

But just who were the "we"? The "global generation" was not amused. Lenihan's remarks, while candid and probably honestly felt, were not appropriate for the moment. His words to *Newsweek* amounted to no Gettysburg address. At the very least he seemed to be washing his hands of Ireland's "lost generation" and leaving its fate to a roll of the dice on Capitol Hill. There was uproar back in Ireland and angry howls of discontent in the United States. Lenihan was pursued by journalists on a subsequent trip to Brussels where he tried to bluff and bluster his way out of it. But his words were set in stone. Ireland was too small, the young would have to fly and that was that.

Irish newspapers, fully aware now that the emigration story was exposing raw nerves, published rebuttals from actual emigrants alongside the usual chorus from rival politicians, ready as always to pounce on one of their own who had so clearly thrown himself bodily on a banana skin. Much of what Lenihan said was factually correct. The world was becoming more of a single labor market and many Irish were eager to tap its potential. But that wasn't quite emigration in the true sense and the laws of the free flow of labor were not applying to the Irish in the U.S. Thousands of undocumented Irish felt as if they had been forced out of Ireland in the first place by circumstances beyond their control, and Brian Lenihan's for that matter. But instead of being an escape, America was throwing up new obstacles, again seemingly beyond anyone's capacity to negotiate.

Lenihan's final line, an almost casual embracing of what had been viewed for generations as a singular Irish tragedy, was like a red rag to a bull. As one emigrant wrote in the *Irish Independent*, the Tánaiste was "smug in the knowledge that he won't be the first to have to go. But if this is true, it's politicians who should shape up or ship out, not young people."

But even those who most despise politicians often find at one point or another that they need their services. Lenihan's overflow Irish in America needed politicians now like they never had before. These politicians would have Irish names too, but they would turn out to be more careful users of the language of politics.

Brian Donnelly was one of the first to rise above the horizon. Encouraged by Irish diplomats based in his native Boston, Donnelly threw his weight behind the 1986 act but at an angle that would attempt to salvage some solace for those Irish it would otherwise run over. That act had included an amnesty provision for all illegals in the U.S. But while it would prove beneficial to illegals from a number of countries, mainly Latin American, the Irish mostly missed out on the amnesty because it applied only to illegals who had entered the U.S. prior to January 1, 1982. The vast bulk of the undocumented Irish had arrived in the U.S. after that cutoff date. As a result, no more than a few hundred Irish secured greencards by the amnesty route.

The NP-5 visa program, which offered the so-called Donnelly Visas, was to prove a far more fruitful avenue. While the Irish were slow to take advantage of these visas at first, the degree of Irish interest would pick up as the four-year Donnelly Visa period progressed and the new labor laws began to bite. By 1990, when all 40,000 NP-5s had been issued, the Irish had secured over 16,000 of that total or just over forty percent. It was an impressive result, one made easier by the fact that Donnelly applicants did not have to possess special job skills nor actual job offers in the U.S. Fully a third of the Irish visa winners were already in the U.S. working under the burden of illegality. At first glance, the Donnelly program had apparently made a significant dent in the undocumented Irish problem. Or had it?

That depended on who was doing the talking. By 1987, the new kind of Irish were speaking and being spoken of with increasing regularity. The American press had latched on to an old story, illegal immigration, but with an irresistible new angle to play up—red hair, freckles, brogues and open defiance of American immigration law.

The secret of the new Irish had been largely kept by the more established Irish community, particularly in New York. There was a strong awareness of the thousands of new arrivals but a tendency to bury the issues they were fast coming to represent. The mood was one of nervous concern but little public action. Many felt that if the new arrivals could be provided with jobs and money all would be well. And there was certainly no shortage of work.

However, the employer sanctions were to prove a catalyst in blowing the lid off the Irish secret. The actual explosives were provided by the *New York Times*.

In March, 1987, the *Times* had heard word on the wind. A reporter had contacted the *Irish Echo* and had been referred by *Echo* writer Anne Canty to an undocumented Irish immigrant named Patrick Hurley.

Hurley, a native of Skibbereen in Co. Cork, was working on a construction site at the time. The *Times* story brought "Patrick" the Irish illegal to the attention of the wider world. As far as future media coverage of the undocumented Irish crisis was concerned, this particular item of news that America's paper of record had deemed "fit to print" was to prove the push that opened the floodgates.

Hurley remembers the *Times* reporter's reaction to the story he laid before her. "She was astonished at the very idea of an Irish illegal."

The *Times* report settled over what had been the overtly calm surface of New York's native Irish community with all the soothing comfort of a horsehair blanket. Some of the more established were annoyed by its revelations, some were a little ashamed, while others were angry and wanted to see something done.

Hurley was a member of the city's Cork Association, one of a group of such societies which tied themselves to each of Ireland's thirty-two counties. The usual business of the association meeting that April was shunted aside with all eyes turning to Pat the illegal and others who spoke of a time of peril for traditional Irish migration to America.

Hurley remembers it as a time when the first sparks began to fly between newly arrived Irish and their elder kin, most of whom had settled legally in the U.S. thirty or so years before. Says Hurley: "Some of the older Irish thought they were still back in the days of James Michael Curley, the mayor of Boston who could make or break presidential dreams. But those days were gone."

The first contacts made by illegals like Hurley were generally with older Irish-born U.S. citizens. The latter group, while initially uncertain over what to do about the new arrivals, were, however, to prove invaluable because of their already strong links to a third arm of the U.S. Irish—that enormous slice of the country's population called Irish America.

The new Irish were impatient. Hurley and others who saw the coming collision between soaring numbers of young undocumented Irish and U.S. law realized that some kind of public platform would have to be created in order to fight the battles that were surely coming. The idea of the Irish organizing in America was as old as the nation itself. But few Irish organizations were founded in a kitchen.

But it was in a kitchen, in the apartment of Sean Minihane, a school friend of Hurley from Skibbereen days, that a campaign was launched to "legalize the Irish." On a Saturday morning in early May, 1987, Hurley and Minihane sat down to a full Irish breakfast. Somewhere between the sausages and brown bread the boyhood pals—even then they were only in their early twenties—came up with a name. It, too, was something of a mouthful. They would call this latest manifestation of the age-old Irish lust for fighting the good fight, the Irish Immigration Reform Movement.

Still, while the name didn't exactly roll off the tongue it had all the essential ingredients for attracting the attention of politicians. It had "Irish" and that was potentially instant access to a large and influential grouping of Irish Americans on Capitol Hill. It had "immigration," always a hot button issue in Washington. Another political buzzword, "reform" made up the third leg of the IIRM table. And the newly concocted *nom de guerre* of the illegal Irish was rounded off by a word that always made politicians a little nervous, "movement."

The emergence of the IIRM into public view was, nevertheless, steady rather than spectacular. The first full meeting of the group took place on May 20 with the blessing, and the meeting room, provided by the Cork Association. The event was reported in the June 6 edition of the *Irish Echo* under the somewhat innocuous heading: "Immigration reform group gears up."

Throughout 1987, as it had done in previous years, the *Echo* gave extensive coverage to the immigration debate in Washington. In the same June 6 edition, the paper, which had been founded in

1928 by an Irish immigrant, led its front page with a story on the U.S. Senate voting to delay "alien curbs." The IIRM story was on an inside page.

But as former *Echo* editor John Thornton remembers it, this was a deliberate move on his part to attract attention to the new organization, but not too much of the wrong kind.

Thornton recalls that there were strong indications at the time of a pending crackdown by federal authorities against illegal immigrants, Irish included. This had evolved into open fear of Immigration and Naturalization Service raids against undocumented Irish with mass deportations to follow.

"I felt the undocumented needed protection from the established Irish community and this would take time. Playing up the immigration debate in Washington was a warning to the same established community that serious and potentially threatening change was emerging in the debate there," Thornton later told this author.

The tensions between those who employed a steady-as-she-goes approach and those who wanted to throw buckets of water on the crisis fire only added to a general feeling that summer of a situation taking shape that could quickly advance beyond anyone's control.

For the IIRM pioneers it was a summer of virtually constant work. Hurley, at first view something of a firebrand, would soon emerge as a man who could draw up workable battle plans and rally others to the IIRM's standard. As he recalls it: "We used to eat, drink and sleep the IIRM." Minihane, in turn, would also turn out to be a detailed organizer with a knack of generating the right kind of press attention. He was also good at projecting positive images to a wary American public. He was clean cut and well dressed. He looked like an Irish version of an all American boy.

Right from the start, the IIRM took on the shape of a classic Washington-based political action committee or lobby group. Its intention was to work with the system while challenging it. The IIRM would function as a quasi-political party but, at the same time, would not be shy if it came to more traditional forms of "movement" action such as street demonstrations.

The first *Echo* story strongly hinted at an organization that would not hesitate to use all resources available to get its message across. The paper reported the setting up of six internal IIRM action groups dealing with areas such as public relations, fundraising and communication with the Irish government. The emergence of the IIRM did not take long to generate headlines back in Ireland where the electronic media was particularly aware that it was dealing with a population that was younger on average than any in Europe. Anybody under thirty was a potential story simply for being under thirty and the vast majority of undocumented Irish fell into this age group. The popular radio and TV journalist Pat Kenny was the first to give the new upstarts a big splash with an hour long segment on RTE, Ireland's national radio and television network.

Back in New York, the IIRM was splicing together the need for work and money and the desire of Irish exiles to meet on a social level. Concerts, sing-alongs and, according to a June 13 *Echo* report, a "cocktail hour" were being planned. It all seemed a little incongruous to some. Drink a Martini, eat the olive, win a green-card!

But behind the scenes a clear political strategy was fast taking shape. Others were coming on board to help, including additional Cork Association members Mae O'Driscoll and Father Matt Fitzgerald, also both, as it turned out, from Skibbereen. Beyond Cork, appropriately known to all Irish as the "rebel county," there were other Irish immigrants, legal and illegal, moving fast into the IIRM's rapidly expanding circle of friends. One was Dubliner Michael Aherne who would later make a name for himself as the piano player in the movie *The Commitments*. Established Irish American help came from the like of radio hosts Adrian Flannelly and Dorothy Hayden Cudahy, who herself was soon to be a story in her own right as first ever woman grand marshal of the New York St. Patrick's Day Parade. *Irish Echo* journalists Julianne O'Riordan, Anne Canty and Mike Devlin found time to help as well as write. Niall O'Dowd, publisher of *Irish America* magazine, was part of the early days publicity arm of the "double-I-R-M," as it was generally dubbed in the group's campaign vernacular. O'Dowd not only sensed an unfolding major story, but also felt there was a need for a new Irish American newspaper to reflect, in detail, the new and extraordinary circumstances surrounding Irish immigration.

From people came plans. Hurley, who was later to join the *Echo* as a copy editor and immigration affairs writer—under a disguised Irish language name, Minihane and others drew up a series of objectives and plans to achieve them. Firstly, the IIRM would work to win an amnesty for all illegals in the U.S., a smart move which illustrated clear recognition of the fact that little or nothing would be secured for the Irish in Washington if other ethnic groups took the view that the Irish were attempting to secure legality all on their lonesome.

The second objective, which again paid heed to the need to forge alliances and avoid making unnecessary enemies, was aimed at securing a large number of annual visas for Ireland and the other thirty-five mainly European and African countries disadvantaged by the 1965 act.

The third objective was a general one. It was a stated intention to address the needs and problems being faced by the recent Irish arrivals, those lucky enough to have visas and those who did not. The IIRM was keenly aware of many such needs and problems, but at this early stage of its existence such awareness was largely of a general nature. The Irish government, on the other hand, was already being informed of some of the more grim details by its diplomatic representatives in the cities where it had diplomatic outposts: Washington, New York, Boston, Chicago and San Francisco. Irish politicians were also about to be told, in rather less than diplospeak, what the facts of life were on the ground for the undocumented Irish. It was decided at an early IIRM meeting to gather a petition for Irish citizens to sign and present to elected political representatives. "We the (exiled Irish) people" were finding their voice.

Against the backdrop of a constant departure of young people from Ireland, the government, elected politicians and civil servants alike, was looking a little like a floundering boat by 1987. Brian Lenihan's remarks concerning population and geographic size were a blunt assessment but at least dispelled some of the widespread naiveté that could often be discerned in official Irish thinking about the United States and the manner in which the world's greatest power actually conducted its daily business. Sentiment could not be depended upon as an engine for change. If anything, what the new Irish could build in the future with the kind of skills they undoubtedly possessed, was the key to reform. But it was a chicken and egg situation. They could not thrive without reform and if they were not thriving, how could they persuade official America that there was advantage in admitting them as fully legitimate new Americans.

The notion that Irish people were somehow entitled to a share of the American pie because "we built the place" had no standing in U.S. law, but it apparently had a firm hold on the minds of some Dublin bureaucrats.

Years later, an example of such misty-eyed wishful thinking would be revealed in a Dublin *Sunday Independent* story written by George Dempsey, by then a retired American diplomat who had been for several years the political officer at the U.S. Embassy in Dublin.

Dempsey described an encounter between a visiting senior official from the State Department's Bureau of European Affairs and a high ranking official from the Irish Department of Foreign Affairs. The Irish official, wrote Dempsey, "raised the neuralgic problem of visa denials and argued that the Irish had the right to work in the U.S. if they wished since the Irish had largely built the United States. My abiding memory is of the American official trying not to look in my direction for fear he would burst out laughing."

As the American desperately tried to keep a straight face, another couple of plane loads of young Irish men and women were heading that very day to the United States. They were all too aware of their lack of status. But most were likely repeating a variation on the "we built the place" mantra. If you're going to bluff, it does well to believe in the bluff to some degree. Yeah, we built the place and don't you forget it pal.

Whatever about the cloud nine aspects of the official view from Dublin, it was not shared by Irish diplomats, especially those based in the country that Paddy and Mary did so much to build. They knew full well that building the place didn't entitle you to habitation rights. Problem was, the kids were coming anyway.

An Irish diplomat, reacting to the Dempsey story, confirmed what the more down to earth officials on both sides of the Atlantic had known for years: "There is a big difference in the Irish and American mentalities when it comes to issues such as immigration, legal or otherwise. With the Irish it's a matter of yes, the law is all very well, but what can we do for so and so. But the American attitude is very different. It's based in law and the application of the law. There's no nod and a wink as the Irish might have it. American officials were always pulling out a book which defined their immigration law. This book would deal with every possible scenario and they would quote from it all the time. There was no leeway. When it came to Irish and U.S. officialdom dealing with the plight of the Irish illegals it was like two ships passing in the night."

As Americans celebrated another year of independence on July 4, 1987, the *Irish Echo* reported on its front page that the harsh labor laws contained in the 1986 act were now being phased in. The undocumented Irish, along with illegals from just about every other country on earth, were facing the possibility of being so much legal grill kill. The 1986 act had been a raised hand, now it was about to become a cold hard slap on the face.

For the IIRM and its friends the main issue was fast boiling down to numbers. Any attempt drastically to reform existing law would certainly raise the hackles of other ethnic groups, particularly those representing Asian and Latin American nationalities who were benefiting from family reunification codes.

To drown out these anticipated objections, it became necessary to single out the plight of the Irish, raise its visibility in Washington and not spare the rod when it came to the numbers game. A small number of undocumented Irish was not a crisis on Capitol Hill. But try, let's say half a million. While entire villages and towns back in Ireland would have been bereft of people to make this figure stand up, it was uttered within earshot of journalists on one or two occasions. More often it would settle in the region of anywhere between 100,000 and 200,000. There were howls of indignation from some who accused the IIRM lobbyists—who were the ones most often asked the question how many—of taking the Irish tendency towards hyperbole to previously unscaled heights.

But knocking down these numbers was no easy task for Irish diplomats who were charged by agitated Irish politicians with addressing the undocumented crisis, attempting to hustle in some solution behind the scenes, while, at the same time, keeping a lid on the wilder claims of the increasingly media savvy IIRM.

Diplomacy is all about striking a balance. In this case it was a matter of persuading "friends" of Ireland in Washington that there was a serious problem and that it required immediate as opposed to down-the-road attention. The issue of numbers was delicate. Politicians think in numbers all the time. If the number of Irish requiring visas was small it would be easy enough to slip through an amendment in Washington on their behalf; the reward in terms of future votes might be limited but, hey, we can do it for the old country. If the total of Irish was up in the hundreds of thousands, slipping them in would be all but impossible, never mind future potential votes. So who was right on the numbers, the Irish government and its diplomats or the Irish kids who kept ending up on TV and in the *New York Times*?

Anne Barrington was press and information officer at the Irish Consulate in New York from 1986 to 1991 and in that capacity found herself right in the middle of the numbers muddle.

"The numbers game went out of control. The figures being quoted bore no relation to reality," she would later recall.

"We in the Irish government had to work on the basis of more realistic numbers. When it came to the crunch some people should not have believed their own propaganda. But they did."

Propaganda or not, the fact was that at the end of 1987 the number of undocumented Irish was still rising and nobody could say for sure when the figures for new arrivals would peak. Those who were beginning to gather themselves around the banner of the IIRM knew they were playing a dangerous game with numbers. But how else could you attract the attention of the media, and through the press buttonhole the right people in Washington?

Pat Hurley, who was not entirely innocent of hyperbole himself at times, remains adamant that there were more than enough undocumented Irish in the U.S. to warrant the word "crisis."

"I remember one congressional hearing at the time. There were all these congressmen going on and on about the evils of illegal immigration. Sure half the people in the room were illegal. It was like Michael Collins getting into Dublin Castle."

And it was true that the growing Irish immigrant lobby had one or two Ned Broys inside the Capitol. The next task at hand was to transform the undoubted degree of Irish American political sympathy into legislative action, because without a package with more visas for the Irish, the numbers would eventually catch up with the propaganda, no matter how far out of the ballpark that propaganda was. As 1987 turned into 1988, the lid was beginning to blow off a problem that was apparently spinning out of control and the press, Irish American and mainstream, was beginning to sniff a story with real legs.

3

THE IRISH ARE COMING

"When your objective is nearby, make it appear as if distant; when far away, create the illusion of being nearby."

Sun Tzu, *Art of War.*

By the end of the 1980s, the Irish who had built America were being kicked out of the country in handcuffs. Their crime? Well, for some it was simply a case of wanting to build America up a little bit more while earning the kind of living that was proving to be sadly elusive back in Ireland. From the U.S. government's point of view it was, of course, far removed from that. It was a matter of U.S. immigration law, of upholding that law and defending the integrity of the frontiers of a sovereign superpower. As with the generations before them, the young Irish who came to America in the 1980s—as a result of what journalist and author Tim Pat Coogan would describe as Ireland's "recurring scourge" of emigration—didn't dwell too much on high falutin' notions such as the integrity of national frontiers. Borders, the U.S. version at the top of the list, were mere impediments along the way, obstacles to overcome, barriers to circumvent. The Irish were not being forced to swim across rivers in the dead of night. That at least was an indignity being spared the new builders. Instead, they would find themselves having to answer a lot of perfunctory but sometimes probing questions. Often they lied, or at least mingled truth with fiction to present a plausible story to the frontier inquisitor. When they did set foot in America they were, for a few months anyway, welcome guests of the nation, relieved holders of six-month holiday visas which were, in effect, potential passports to a new life. Thousands of these Irish guests were intent on overstaying their official welcome and using up all official blessing. There seemed to be no other choice.

The Irish in Ireland expect much of their own in the United States. At least some discernible degree of material success is assumed to be the logical end to an Irish person's American odyssey. Returning home for a visit, aglow with the trappings of success in "Amerikay" is a time worn cliché. Handcuffs and prison garb, however, were not part of the fable. That's the way it was when the Irish of the nineteenth century were all shipped off to Australia! Surely these were very different times? And wasn't America the land of the free, home of the brave and all that and by God we Irish are free and not a little brave?

More surprising then to read stories in the Irish papers of Ireland's best educated generation fleeing as fast as their legs could carry them from the armed agents of a supposedly friendly government. But that's the way it was for the new builders—a life of concocted or "borrowed" social security numbers, sometimes even fake U.S. birth certificates, made-up names, a good story and always, always, an eye on the door or over the shoulder. It was a kind of war really, one in which the INS hounds were always seen to be on the hunt for the Irish fox. That's how it looked from an Irish perspective in the last three or four years of the decade long made famous by George Orwell. All immigrants were equal, but some were definitely more equal than others.

In truth, the Irish were less pursued than some other nationalities because they were fewer in number and blended more easily into the general fuzz and buzz of the American background. But symbols mattered too. Every single Irish illegal who was detained added to a sense of hurt and, for more than a few, the feeling that American officialdom was somehow callous and ungrateful. It was neither for the most part. Officialdom was just doing its job.

But there are jobs and jobs. For Irish diplomats in the Washington embassy or the various consulates in New York, Boston, Chicago and San Francisco, the initial career description began to take on a different shape as the clamor over the situation facing the new Irish in America began growing louder back in Ireland itself.

James Farrell, a quiet spoken man not long in the diplomatic service, was given new orders in the fall of 1987 just after the headline-making visit to the U.S. by Deputy Prime Minister Brian Lenihan. Lenihan's "small island" statements had caused uproar and embarrassment to Taoiseach Charles Haughey. Haughey, known widely in Ireland as simply "the boss," was not a politician who easily tolerated an image of hapless irrelevance, especially when his reputation as a Mr. fixit politician with solutions to all ills was challenged. The stories coming back from America about young Irish being carted off in the INS version of "paddywagons," were causing acute discomfort, especially when they appeared in the Irish daily papers, not least the *Irish Press*, the supposed voice of Haughey's Fianna Fáil party. On top of this, Haughey, on February 11, 1987, had given an election campaign promise of a "major initiative to secure legal status for the large number of young Irish emigrants in the United States who have not got such status at present."

Haughey's "major initiative" wasn't going to be a declaration of war on the immigration laws of the United States. But he did pledge his party "to use every diplomatic and political means available to us to secure legal status for all these young Irish people."

This would entail mobilizing Irish American opinion "to bring the maximum political pressure to bear on Congress and the White House." No, certainly not a war, at least not in the strict sense of the word. But Haughey was never a politician given to understatement and he had an air about him that never quite matched Ireland's rather humble place in the global power balance. He was, at the very least, throwing down a challenge to the status quo as it pertained in another country.

While there was clearly much to do at the federal level, a lot of the early work on behalf of the undocumented Irish took root in city halls in the several cities where the Irish were most concentrated. James Farrell recalls a time when there was considerable concern about the daily welfare of the new Irish but little coordination between interested agencies. The Catholic Church had been in the forefront of initial efforts to meet the more worldly needs of those who had just arrived in the "next parish." The church had existing programs already being applied and even before being elected, Haughey had made contact with Monsignor James Murray, Executive Director of Catholic Charities in the Archdiocese of New York. When the Haughey "major initiative" statement emerged three days before Irish voters went to the polls, Murray's response was immediate. That same day he issued a statement saying that it was "encouraging" to learn that Fianna Fáil's leaders had taken note of "the serious situation their undocumented people are facing in the United States."

One of Farrell's first tasks was to establish a level of dialogue with Catholic Charities. The idea of separating church and state might be a lofty constitutional principle, but this was no time to get hung up on such niceties. Catholic Church and Irish State were long familiar with each other's thinking back in Ireland. It was to be little different in urban America.

Farrell remembers being unprepared for the sheer volume of work that was about to land on his desk. "I remember weeks on end just answering the phone regarding the first batch of Donnelly visas. And there were these church hall gatherings. There was one in the Bronx and I was astonished at the number of people who turned up."

But while all appeared chaotic on the surface, Farrell later recalled another particularly salient factor: "It became unusual for an Irish effort. There was considerable cooperation and little friction."

But "little" does not mean a total absence. There was some. The Irish government, like governments everywhere, was wary of street movements seemingly beyond its area of direct control. The IIRM was just such a group. There is no doubt that Irish diplomats felt on safer ground when dealing with Catholic agencies such as Project Irish Outreach in New York, an offshoot of Catholic Charities established in October, 1987 and headed by Cork City native Patricia O'Callaghan. The IIRM was making noise when Dublin preferred backroom diplomacy. There was a public standoff at one point between the IIRM and the Irish Consulate in New York, with Consulate Press Officer Anne Barrington in the front line. The imbroglio was over the question of funding for advice centers. The IIRM had met both Haughey and Lenihan during visits to the U.S. in 1988 and had submitted oral requests for funding of IIRM run information centers. Dublin wanted "detailed costed proposals" in writing "which would be considered on their merits." The IIRM felt it had little time for composing detailed proposals. What it required was immediate help.

The *demarché* was compounded by a not entirely surprising sense of antipathy towards Irish politicians by IIRM leaders who had sensed hesitation at a time when local politicians such as New York Mayor Ed Koch and Boston's Ray Flynn seemed only too eager to ride over the hill, cavalry-like, to rescue the besieged Irish.

But such spats did not halt the overall momentum. Even if the IIRM said there were 150,000 illegals while Irish diplomats, as they were at the end of 1988, were settling for INS estimates of less than 40,000, the establishment of new safety nets proceeded rapidly.

Lenihan's fall 1987 visit had seen the setting up of a Consulate-based "Irish Immigration Working Committee" in New York which brought all available interested parties together: Irish government, the archdiocese, Irish American labor and business leaders, the Ancient Order of Hibernians and last but not least, the upstart Irish Immigration Reform Movement. Similar committees were soon up and running in Boston, Chicago and San Francisco, cities which were themselves quick off the mark when it came to putting out the welcome mat for the newcomers from a land which had given these same towns the very style of their politics.

In New York, Comptroller Harrison "Jay" Goldin authorized a "Guide for Irish Immigrants." As far as City Hall was concerned, being Irish and undocumented should not imply being fearful of city agencies such as the police or hospitals. The city was, of course, saying the same thing to immigrants of every nationality; but at times it seemed that the Irish were getting a little extra attention. Not that they minded very much. Many were sticking to the old story: "We built the place" etc. A helping hand from the host city was simply well deserved payback.

Before long, the bulk of the undocumented Irish in these cities were up to their necks in information. There was *A Guide For The New Irish In Chicago*, a *Guide For The New Irish*, published in Boston. Back in Ireland the Catholic Church had published *Emigrating USA* and its U.S. counterpart, *Immigrating USA*, soon followed. The Irish weeklies, *Echo* and *Voice* in particular, were full of advice and phone numbers. The *Irish Voice* ran a "Greencard" column and the *Echo* at one point produced a leaflet full of relevant phone numbers and addresses headed "Irish Immigrant Support Network," which ended up on refrigerator doors from Woodside to the Mission District. The Irish were fast becoming the most officially briefed and municipally accepted lawbreakers on the North American continent since the signatories of the Declaration of Independence. They were also being written about in papers and magazines, not just in the U.S. and Ireland, but around the world.

The electronic press too, though a little later, had found a story with fresh young faces and lilting brogues ready and willing to be unleashed at a time of the year, the weeks running up to St. Patrick's Day, when "everyone," to be sure, was "Irish." St. Patrick had long ago saved the Irish from pagan ignorance. More than 1,500 years on he was still drawing attention to himself. Once a year, in the days before and including March 17th, the high kings of American politics and press would look his way and bow in studied and calculated homage—for a few hours. Ireland's national saint had also become, *de facto*, America's leading holy man, a one-time prophet who had been repackaged for twentieth-century profit. In a singularly American twist on an old story, he was an unwitting salesman fronting an annual splurge on all things green. St. Patrick's Day, like Christmas and Easter, was now another yearly heaven meets bottom dollar and Nielsen Ratings day. And no other ethnic group had a day quite like it. It wasn't even an official holiday, but that didn't matter a whit. St. Patrick's Day was one on which Irish eyes might be smiling. But millions more, by no means all of them Irish American, were also watching and buying. By St. Patrick's Day, 1987, the lid was close to being blown off a story which had been, up until then, only a whisper on the jet contrails floating between Shannon and Kennedy.

Stories with an Irish twist are a hardy annual for U.S. journalists in the first half of the month of March. But this one was not to be of the corned beef and cabbage variety. It also came out a few weeks after the usual fuss, on April 17, although the interviews that formed its base had been conducted in March. No matter. The story was in the paper of record, the *New York Times*. And it was to prove to be the first grand scale unveiling of that story with those aforementioned legs.

The *Times* presented "Patrick" the illegal Irishman under the heading: "Invisible Aliens: Irish Fear Effect of New Immigration Law." Patrick, reporter Marvine Howe told the paper's readers in the first paragraph, lived in the country illegally and resented being called an undocumented alien.

"His grandfather," wrote Howe, "was an American who fought with the United States Army in France in World War I. One sister is a nurse in the United States Army in England and is married to an American. Another sister works on a horse farm in New Jersey; a brother has a job in a warehouse in Connecticut. His American relatives include a retired Army colonel, an F.B.I. agent and a Boston police officer."

"It's part of the Irish identity to become an American citizen," Patrick "Pat" Hurley told her.

Howe had spoken to the Immigration and Naturalization Service, a conversation which had thrown up two rather contrasting statistics. In 1986, a mere 1,839 Irish had been admitted as permanent residents but 98,188 had entered the U.S. with temporary visas.

"Officials," Howe reported, "noted recent research showing that the Irish are one of the leading nationalities that tend to overstay the terms of temporary visas." From that the reader could quickly deduce that a significant proportion of the 98,000 were still "temporarily" somewhere in the fifty states. The INS certainly had an idea that the Irish were out there. But how many, and where? "If you could count them you could catch them," Duke Austin, a press spokesman wryly observed in a story carried by the *Jersey Journal* at the time.

The *Times* story did point out the pertinent fact that all these Irish were indeed doing a fairly good job of not attracting INS attention. In fact, only eight Irish illegals had been deported in 1985 compared to 3,034 Salvadoreans and 11,368 Mexicans. Ironically, one of the reasons for relative Irish invisibility was that, unlike Latin Americans, they tended not to congregate in large numbers in work activities such as agriculture, despite the fact that they had fled a country which touted itself—in a well known Irish TV commercial—as "the world's greenest dairy land."

Not that the Irish were shy when it came to working with their hands. Hurley himself, with his political science degree tucked away in the socks drawer, was working on a construction site when the *Times* came calling in search of a good St. Patrick's Day yarn.

"If they get rid of the illegals, who'll do the hard jobs? Most Americans don't want to do what we're doing," Dermot, an illegal from County Carlow, told Howe for the same story. Who indeed?

Patrick and Dermot were not alone in doing the hard jobs. By the morning that the illegal Irish story hit the streets, thousands of Irish hands were at work adding to the labors of earlier generations, only this time off the books. Nobody is quite sure where Dermot ended up, but Patrick's anonymity was soon to be shattered, at least within the confines of the Irish-born community.

The Irish Immigration Reform Movement was the handiwork of a number of people but Hurley and his boyhood friend, Sean Minihane, were to be its most public figures. "They were the Yin and Yang of the movement," is how one early member put it years later. Some would even see comparisons between the two and Eamon de Valera and Michael Collins with Hurley being the guerrilla orga-

nizer and street orator and Minihane playing the role of the calcu-
lating, politically astute and silver-tongued frontman. Certainly,
Hurley possessed something in common with Collins in the early
days of the "Legalize the Irish" campaign: A known name and an
anonymous face.

But anonymity was not to be Hurley's lot for long, nor that of the
budding organization whose public personae he and his pal Sean
were destined to be in such large measure.

In May, 1997, as the IIRM was taking root in and branching out
of New York's Cork Association, Hurley wrote a letter to the *Irish
Echo*. It was headed "Plea from an undocumented alien" and
signed "Patrick, an undocumented alien from County Cork." The
concept of an Irish immigrant being described as an undocumented
alien was something almost entirely new for most of the paper's
readers.

In the letter, published in the *Echo*'s May 16 edition, Hurley
drew a sketch of economic conditions in Ireland, conditions which,
he wrote, were so bad by 1987 that various Catholic Church agencies had started distributing "emigration kits" in secondary schools.

"It is estimated," he continued, "that over 100,000 of us young
Irish are now working and living illegally in the U.S. For us the hour
of decision approaches, before the full force of the recently passed
immigration act is brought to bear.

"Our choice is one of two unattractive options—to return to
poverty and hopelessness in Ireland, or to remain on here, in the
hope that employment opportunities will not be completely oblit-
erated, and in apprehension of being hunted down and ultimately
deported. For the vast majority of us, return is out of the question.
There is no future for us back in the 'old country.'"

Hurley's words did not fall short of the dramatic but those who
knew him never doubted that they were written with serious intent
and heartfelt concern. He wrote of not standing idly by and
"allowing ourselves to be become a lost generation, destined to
wander a world that is no longer made up of wide-open, welcoming continents."

He spoke of a "right of sanctuary" for the Irish in America, a
right "earned by the committed contributions of countless Irishmen in the building of this great country."

And addressing a large proportion of the *Echo*'s readership of
that time directly, Patrick, the undocumented alien, made his bot-

tom line appeal: "We are no different in nature to you immigrants who came before us. We cherish the same hopes and dreams that you once cherished. However, it seems that, for us, this welcoming sanctuary no longer exists.

"Immigrants of the past, do not forget us. Do what you can to help us in our plight. Help us to regain a necessary refuge in this country, not only for ourselves, but also for those who will follow. For remember, if you deny us, you deny that from which you came."

And just for good measure, Hurley offered a vision of what hopefully lay ahead: "And maybe on a St. Patrick's Day in better times to come, we will proudly march side by side. We, proud that we did not fail and that we won through against the odds, and you, proud that you did not forget the 'old country,' or your people, in their hour of need."

There is no doubt that Hurley, in his declaration of both independence and dependence, could be accused of laying things on a bit thick. But it didn't seem so to those illegal Irish who read it, each of whom were living every day as either their first of a new life in America or their last.

Regardless of its heavy emphasis on sentiment, Hurley's from-the-gut approach was an easy sell to journalists, both in the likes of the *New York Times* and the *Echo* which, by the summer of 1987 was about to go through a once-in-a-generation-or-two transformation that was as unanticipated as it was inevitable.

A story in the *Times* was an impressive beginning but it would take sustained and detailed coverage to persuade the established Irish community and elected politicians that the new arrivals were both large in number, serious in intent and in dire need of help. The *Echo* was the primary Irish American weekly. It styled itself as the community's paper of record. But merely recording the arrival of a new Irish wave on American shores would not quite be enough to spark the desired response from a readership that was well dug into American soil and increasingly well-heeled to boot.

Mike Devlin, a weekly columnist for the paper, was the sort of journalist who responded to the near visceral sentiments which were now, out of the blue it seemed, being expressed loudly and persistently. Devlin, according to John Thornton, the *Echo*'s editor at the time, was an "intense" man but one who had a winning way with words if his mood matched the situation.

In his "Cityside" column, Devlin was to introduce *Echo* readers to the lives of Irish illegals as they were being played out from day to day. Devlin had little time for theory, statistics or abstractions. His strength was in writing about people and their struggles in life. One of his columns uncovered the life of an unusual group of Irish illegals—an entire family. Most of the undocumented Irish were single. While there might often be brothers, sisters or cousins in the same predicament complete family units were comparatively rare. Devlin's "Family in the Basement," which saw the light of day in this year of the illegals, 1987, depicted a hidden life of poverty and near hopelessness for an Irish immigrant family in Queens, New York. The story stood in grim contrast to the widely perceived Irish version of the American dream.

Devlin, who died while still in his forties in February, 1990, was impressed by Pat Hurley. In his column in the June 27, 1987, issue of the *Echo* he added a little more to Patrick, the illegal's alien's identity. Devlin called him "Patrick H." Hurley was destined to carry the sobriquet for years.

"Illegal lives: Patrick H. is off and running" was a color story. It began with Hurley leaning over to Sean Minihane at a Cork Association meeting in early May and saying: "What is the bloody point of this club?"

Hurley continued to mutter to Minihane. It was noticed and the club president asked "Brother H," as Devlin described him, if he would like to say something.

Devlin wrote: "Patrick's face kind of went slack, as the faces of children sometimes do when they are called on in a classroom. His mouth opened a bit, and his lower lip fell toward the floor. He turned to his friend Sean, who gave him one of those glances that said 'you can do it mate, go get 'em.'

"Then Patrick H. looked around the room. Everyone was waiting. He stood up. Cleared his throat. 'Well. . .,' he said. And stopped. In future times, when people look back on that moment, they might say they saw his eyes roll heavenward.

'Steady,' Sean whispered.

'Well, let me say this.'

"Patrick's eyes came down and focused on the officers of the club and suddenly, like a switch being thrown, the words started rolling out of him. In the beginning his accent was like a band tuning up. But it also had the effect of forcing people to listen closely to what he was saying. After a few minutes he found the voice most suited to the subject—of being young, educated, and illegal in the world's biggest city—and soon no one in the room had any trouble understanding exactly what he was talking about.

"He described in painful detail the small apartments crammed with Irish men and women; six, eight, a dozen people living in a space not big enough for two. He outlined a life lived in constant fear of being arrested and deported. He told of exploitative employers who would threaten young Irish people with a call to the immigration authorities if they dared complain about the conditions of their labor. It didn't seem possible he was talking about America in 1987.

"It seemed, to everyone, that he had to be talking about another time, or another people. Not, after all, the Irish. Those days were long, long past. Out of another century.

"But Patrick H. was talking about the present. And those ancestral memories of crowded ships, the filthy rooms, the threatening authorities, the back-breaking and low-paying labor, came up from who knows where in the minds that had been, for so long, sleeping. Once again, it seemed, no Irish need apply.

"He spoke for half an hour. No one interrupted him. After describing the lives of the illegals he pointed out that it wasn't just a handful of people he was talking about. It was a very large group."

Hurley had not quite matched the brevity of the Gettysburg address. Nor had he spoken with quite the eloquence of an Abraham Lincoln. But as with what was arguably the sixteenth President's finest moment, Hurley's speech had struck a deep chord. It was less a call for action as an illustration of why action was needed. He didn't cry "charge" or "follow me." But he did make it abundantly plain, even to the ostriches in the meeting room, that standing by and doing nothing was no longer acceptable. Hurley dredged up long gone images which, in truth, all in the room had not really forgotten. They only needed reminding.

While in some respects there was a discernible generation gap between the illegals and the more established Irish, by no means all of the older immigrants were disinclined to listen to what the new arrivals were saying. Some were very quick to grasp the fact that this latest living link to Ireland was extremely tenuous. Natural sympathy for fellow Irish men and women in a difficult situation was the immediate response of individuals such as Mae O'Driscoll, who recorded the minutes of the May meetings and was to make a little history of her own by being the Cork Association's first woman president.

In the early May meeting, following Hurley's torrent of words, members present, according to Devlin, became very excited and began quickly to offer suggestions as to how to deal with the undocumented crisis. Hurley and Minihane were not alone that night. More than twenty other illegals had also attended with a view to joining the Cork Association and harnessing its influence and connections to the new cause. The association's own newsletter was eager to paint a picture of itself as being sensitive and action-minded. "From the moment Patrick H. stood up at the May membership meeting and asked what was being done to help the undocumented Irish in New York, the County Cork Association has been busy devising ways to help these young people," the June issue stated on its front page under the banner headline: "Cork Club takes lead in immigration reform." Not without a bit of nudging in the back. One concerned individual had challenged the association to "get off its backside." To its credit, it did in large measure.

By the time the association gathered again for the May 20th meeting there were more than just members present. Word had traveled fast and the press was now in on the secret big time; not just the likes of the *Echo* and *Irish America* magazine, but also the *Daily News*, *Village Voice* and *New York Times*. Local Irish radio show hosts Adrian Flannelly and Dorothy Hayden Cudahy turned up as did a representative of Congressman Tom Manton and a diplomat from the Irish Consulate.

Niall O'Dowd, publisher of *Irish America* magazine and a correspondent in New York for the *Irish Press* group of newspapers in Dublin, described the meeting as an "extraordinary gathering" in his *Irish Press* column, "The Irish in America."

O'Dowd, whose plans for a newspaper heavily devoted to the new immigrants were by that time well advanced, described the meeting as one where the new arrivals met face to face with the "old guard."

The Cork Association, he wrote, had, like many other Irish organizations, a reputation for conservatism and a tendency to appear out of touch. "This meeting belied that assumption."

O'Dowd went on to describe a three-hour encounter between the new and old guards in which a frank and forthcoming exchange of views mirrored the gap in perception between two groups which were, on average, a quarter century apart in age.

"There was some acrimony, something easily detectable when young and old Irish meet in America these days. But, overall, a tremendous spirit of cooperation prevailed."

It would take more than tremendous spirit to change U.S. law. But the Irish Immigration Reform Movement, publicly unveiled that early summer's evening, was to prove a provocative agent of change. The Cork Association newsletter described the new arrival as an "umbrella organization." It was to prove to be that in the way it gathered the generations closely together in pursuit of a single goal. But it was to be more than just a convivial debating club, something which Sean Minihane thought it might be at the outset. It would prove to be a sharp-tipped umbrella with a startling talent for spinning the right kind of story to an eager and hungry press.

According to Minihane, he was not alone at the beginning in viewing the emerging IIRM as a social forum where young undocumented Irish could meet and discuss their common problems. "But the organization evolved into a political machine instead. This wasn't due to any particular vision on my part. It was simply due to the energy and goodwill of a core group of people."

Minihane could be forgiven his slightly less than obvious sense of urgency in the early stages. He was working legally in the U.S., for the New York City health department's engineering division.

He had come to New York in May, 1985. He returned to Ireland in January, 1991. His almost six years in America were to prove rather more exciting than he had anticipated.

It started to get exciting on one memorable work day. His office number had found its way into the *Irish Echo* as a contact line for the new immigration organization.

"My office was flooded with calls from all over the country. It was embarrassing and unbelievable. It was a deluge. My colleagues thought I was in some subversive group." In a way he was.

Minihane, in reflecting on his own role in the IIRM, describes himself as an organizer, someone who saw potential chaos and attempted to counter this with efficiency. In large part, his efforts would be successful but there were times when restraining the sheer passion and emotion that formed the heart of the IIRM would turn out to be no easy task.

"The organization," according to Minihane, "took on a life of its own. We might have been holding the reins but the horses were bolting anyway."

The hands holding the reins were not all of Minihane's generation. The "old guard," as they were perhaps a little unfairly described, were not monolithic by any means. The notion of generational conflict between the new Irish and the established Irish was sometimes overplayed. Some of the most trenchant criticism of the establishment came from individuals who, as far as the newcomers were concerned, could only be described as cornerstones of that same establishment.

Fr. Matt Fitzgerald had been in the U.S. since 1968 and had detected the first whiff of a potential crisis well before the emergence of the IIRM. In the early 1980s, he found himself dealing with undocumented Irish immigrants, mostly in his assigned working area of Suffolk County on Long Island.

As a cleric, Fitzgerald was well placed to make contact with people in influential positions but his experiences with the likes of the Irish hierarchy, Dublin government and, in America, the Ancient Order of Hibernians, were to prove, he would later recall, frequently frustrating. As his frustration grew in tandem with the influx of young Irish by the planeload, Fitzgerald began thinking of a national lobby organization which would operate beyond the traditional enclave that was the greater New York area. He became more than ever convinced of the need for this after his first encounter with Sean Minihane.

Mae O'Driscoll was one of the more dynamic members of the Cork Association. She was one of the 1950s arrivals who had flown at high speed to America at the very dawn of the trans-Atlantic jet age in 1958. Destined, as mentioned, to be the first ever woman president of the Cork Association and an individual well used to the organizational demands of Wall Street, where she worked, O'Driscoll hadn't slowed down appreciably by 1987. While she would later point to Pat Hurley as a driving force behind the IIRM, others would someday be describing her in exactly the same terms.

O'Driscoll soon found that it was personally easier working with the rather more measured Sean Minihane, but years on, she would throw out adjective after adjective when describing Pat Hurley: "Funny, full of life, a speaker with a blue collar kind of appeal who could reach out to everyone. But also a tough customer, stubborn, obstinate and inflexible at times."

Debbie McGoldrick, who worked as an immigration writer for
the *Irish Echo* between 1987 and 1991, the year she moved to the
Irish Voice, described Hurley in the early IIRM days as someone
who was very intense and almost obsessive about the cause of legalizing the Irish. "He had no social life and was totally driven. He was
such a contrast to Sean Minihane who was suave and businesslike."

The mix that went into the IIRM would be volatile from the
start. But it worked, for a while at least. O'Driscoll and Minihane
went about the legal business of incorporating the IIRM. Hurley,
meanwhile, was rallying people to the new cause by virtue of force
of personality and passionate attachment to a struggle which
seemed hopeless to many at the outset. But if the idea of the fighting Irish was something of an Irish American stereotype, at least in
the eyes of the newcomers, the events that were soon to follow
would merely reinforce the view in Washington that these latest
Irish immigrants would either have to be kicked out of the country
or integrated fully into American society. One way or another, there
was going to be a fight, one that was to roll back and forth across
the land before ending up on Capitol Hill.

"It was wonderful," O'Driscoll would later say. "Such energy,
commitment and creativity despite our differences. The IIRM was
the catalyst. We were helped by individual members of the AOH
(Ancient Order of Hibernians) and the Irish government. It
(Reform) would not have happened without them. They treated us
with disrespect initially but later they took us seriously. They had
to because we screamed."

Screaming tends to attract attention. The months immediately
following the founding of the IIRM were filled with meetings,
fundraisers and attempts to attract the right kind of attention and
publicity. The right kind came in the form of friendly Irish Americans, journalists and politicians. The INS, needless to say, was the
wrong kind. But the government's immigration enforcers seemed to
be keeping their distance, at least for the time being.

The journalists, meanwhile, were mostly friendly even if they got
a little carried away with all the brogue stuff.

"'What'll ye be eatin' for dinner?' warbles the waitress in one
of Boston's best restaurants, speaking in the deep rapid-fire
brogue of County Donegal. Indeed, with little public attention,
this city has become a magnet over the past five years for a new
wave of Irish immigration to this country." Thus began a *Wall*

Street story on September 30, 1987. The *Journal* story, written by John A. Barnes, related the increasingly familiar tale which had bad parts: Fear of the INS, problems getting driving licenses or opening bank accounts, and good parts: Construction companies owned by Irish Americans who were willing to "forget" about asking for greencards.

Mayor Raymond Flynn was also inclined to forget. His adviser on Irish affairs at the time, Frank Costello, told the *Journal* that the city was missing out on new Irish entrepreneurial talents because they couldn't start their own businesses. The city was ready to take the Irish any which way, as fully legal immigrants, legal guest workers or fully-fledged citizens as a result of military service. This was of course Boston, where being simply American was slightly less par-for-the-course than being "Irish."

The *Journal*'s concluding paragraph summed up the general feeling of the illegal Irish in this city and the rest: "Listen, dad," a young illegal Irishman told his father, "I don't feel that I'm doing anything illegal. I'm trying to make a future for myself." He was anything but alone.

It would probably be just a little short of fully accurate to say that the flood of undocumented Irish immigrants and the rise of the IIRM resulted in one of the more dramatic developments witnessed by Irish America in some years. Setting up a new newspaper is not an easy task. It involves multiple and often varying calculations. It is an act of faith, particularly in the television age. But the process is never less than exciting, always certainly nerve tingling and, if everything works out, rewarding in more than one sense of the word.

The *Irish Voice* was born a few weeks before 1987 passed into history. Its founding publisher, Niall O'Dowd, had already worked in the U.S. for some years, in Chicago and San Francisco. New York was his final stop just as it was now the end of the emigrant road for thousands of Irish newcomers. It was in New York that O'Dowd had launched *Irish America*, a glossy magazine with up-market ambitions which first saw the light of day in October, 1985. O'Dowd had quickly become embroiled in the numbers game. He wrote about there being 65,000 illegals and was quickly contacted by a perturbed Irish diplomat. Surely, the diplomat suggested, he had meant 6,500. The magazine had survived into its third year by 1987, but to reach the broader expanse of the new, emerging Irish

America, a general interest newspaper was now clearly necessary. The planned and oft-rumored new paper became reality in the first week of December with the premier issue of the *Irish Voice* and its "We'll Never Return—Young Illegals" front page headline.

The new paper had conducted an "exclusive survey" and the bottom-line finding was that the majority of young Irish people living illegally in the U.S. were possibly lost to Ireland "forever." The poll of illegals in New York had found that fifty-eight percent of respondents had no plans to ever return to Ireland and that seventy-five percent were committed to staying in the U.S. for at least three years.

The survey uncovered a deep running antipathy in the new illegal community towards successive Irish governments but, oddly enough, also found that most of the newcomers actually had jobs back in Ireland. Soaring unemployment in Ireland, while certainly a factor in the mass emigration of the 1980s, was not, it now turned out, the entire story. For many, America was still the sum of its own myths. The American dream was simply bigger and better than the Irish version.

The sample survey in the *Voice* poll was not large, 198 individuals, and it became smaller still when matched with the paper's printed estimate of "135,000 illegals Irish in the U.S. at present." But in one way the survey did not have to cover enormous ground. The Irish were a pretty homogeneous lot and they had come from a small country. The reasons for leaving Ballina did not, could not, vary all that much from the reasons for leaving Tralee.

The first *Voice* editorial explained the birth of the new paper in terms of inevitability due to "the pace of Irish American activities in recent times."

While mentioning other concerns such as Northern Ireland, the editorial made it clear that the campaign to legalize the Irish would be receiving priority coverage. "This newspaper," it announced, "will be forthright in its attempts to win for the estimated 135,000 Irish illegals, their proper places as full members of this society. The Irish in the U.S. contributed too much to stand back now and accept the permanent reality that 'No Irish Need Apply' signs are once again ensconced over this nation's borders."

It was a statement of noble intent. But it takes more than lofty words to sell newspapers, particularly newborn ones. The front page banner headline in the *Voice*'s third issue, dated January 2,

1988, was a screamer indeed: "Slave Labor Girl Scandal." The notion that some Irish illegals could be taken advantage of to the extent of being virtual domestic slaves, in this case reportedly working a 90-hour week for $65 dollars, sounded like something out of Charles Dickens. But the story behind the eye-grabbing headline was fact and nobody could accurately calculate just how many young Irish were so vulnerable to exploitation that the American dream, to them, had become something of a perverse joke. If 1987 had been the year when the new Irish had cried "enough," 1988 and 1989 were to be the years when their cries of anger and frustration would become the stuff of front page news. Stories about slave girls was only the start.

Of course, even as things were getting worse they were getting better for some. Irish arrivals were scooping up visas being offered under the 1986 legislation, although not yet at a rate sufficient to reverse the growth of the now far-flung undocumented Irish population.

The jury was still out—in fact would never quite return—when it came to the argument over numbers. But as the Irish and their backers in Washington and various city halls were sharpening their swords for the coming battle, the Immigration and Naturalization Service could be forgiven for wondering what all the big Irish fuss was about.

INS Spokesman Duke Austin, reacting to a bill introduced in Congress in early 1988 by Senator Edward Kennedy and Congressman Brian Donnelly, summed it up thus: "If you call Kennedy and Donnelly they'll tell you it's not an Irish immigration bill, but if you look at the world situation you'll say it benefits the Irish.

"Once you start becoming internationally specific you run into all sorts of problems. You've got two million people waiting to emigrate to the United States from the Philippines, India, Mexico and Korea."

Two million was no exaggeration. Indeed the number of people arriving in the U.S. at the time the IIRM was born—from any one of these countries—was enough to shove the Irish clean over the edge of the map. Over 27,000 Indians, 35,000 Koreans, and 50,000 Filipinos arrived in 1987 alone. Mexico was a country with enough people eyeing the U.S. to keep the INS working overtime all by itself. An official study on immigration presented to Congress once described illegal immigration from Mexico as nothing less than a "geometric progression."

So how was it that the Irish, with their far smaller numbers, could see to it that flustered INS officials had to keep answering questions by reporters about thousands of Irish as opposed to millions of others? There were several reasons, not least the fact that the Irish were English speaking, educated and, as a result, an easily understood story for reporters to present and both readers and viewers to grasp. They didn't appear "foreign" to the average English speaking American. The Irish were accorded the privilege—and it was a privilege—of being described in terms of national or ethnic rather than racial terms. This helped when it came to tapping the very tangible goodwill factor as so many Americans considered themselves at least part Irish too. The hefty representation that Irish America had in the media was another factor. There was, quite simply, a lot of Irish Americans producing and directing the segments, speaking to camera, assigning the reporters, writing the stories, editing them and pushing them into prime spots on page this or that. There were sympathetic politicians, particularly in the House of Representatives. Individuals such as Brian Donnelly, Bruce Morrison and Joe Moakley were to attain considerable prominence as Irish boosters. And then there was Ted Kennedy.

4

A LITTLE IRISH VOODOO

*"When you have cleared immigration, you need to know
where you are going and how to get there."*

Catholic Church guide for Irish immigrants to the U.S.

It is a not an entirely infrequent Irish view that the 1965 Immigration and Nationality Act was somehow concocted by presidents Eamon de Valera and John F. Kennedy to keep the Irish at home in a country that was just beginning to lay claim to the bounty of mid-twentieth century economic progress. Certainly, de Valera and Taoiseach Sean Lemass, might have been quite happy to see emigration tail off as the 1960s advanced. But other forces were deciding the outcome of immigration law reform in Washington. The act was as much an extension of the spirit behind U.S. civil rights reform as it was a means to change the very foundation upon which the world's greatest nation of immigrants was laid. Lyndon Johnson's concept of a "Great Society" wasn't destined to apply just to those born within its apparent geographic boundaries.

John F. Kennedy had himself acknowledged his and America's immigrant past on numerous occasions. In his book, *A Nation of Immigrants*, first published in 1958, Kennedy wrote that the Irish had been the first to endure "the scorn and discrimination later to be inflicted, to some degree at least, on each successive wave of immigrants by already settled 'Americans.'" (Kennedy's feelings on immigration apparently made an impression on Jackie. When the widowed former First Lady visited Ireland in 1967, she secretly attended a performance of the John B. Keane play *Many Young Men of Twenty* in the village hall in Dunhill, Co. Waterford.)

The story of the post-famine Irish is one of struggling to push the discrimination Kennedy wrote about aside. By the early part of the twentieth century, America's Irish had largely won that fight. But World War One would turn America away from the idea of mass immigration from any source. 1921 saw the U.S., for the first time, reversing its traditional role as a haven for the huddled masses from other, foreign shores. There had been some restrictive laws already enacted. "Lunatics, idiots, convicts and those likely to become a public charge" had been barred under the first federally enacted immigration law in 1882. That same year, the Chinese Exclusion Act was enforced to stem the flow of Chinese labor. Far earlier than that, the alien and sedition laws passed by President John Adams in 1798 were largely designed to keep out the Irish, specifically members of the rebellious United Irishmen.

But it was the 1921 Immigration Act, signed into law by President Warren Harding, which could be construed as being the first mostly sane piece of restrictive immigration legislation in both conception and practical effect. It would not please everyone—no single example of immigration law ever has—but it held in it the idea of lowering the overall numbers of new arrivals, an idea which has prevailed more or less to this day. The 1921 act established a quota system based on the national origins of the U.S. population in 1910. The act was revised in 1924 with a new point of reference being the 1920 census. Both pieces of legislation placed a ceiling on the number of immigrants permitted to enter the United States in any one year. But given the huge proportion of Irish in the now "native" U.S. population in both 1910 and 1920, Ireland would continue to do well under the quota plan confirmed again in 1929 legislation—at least as long as Irish people saw America as the most compelling alternative to their own economically backward land.

But by the mid-1960s, there was another way out and it was much closer to home. It was home. For the first time in living memory and beyond, Ireland was offering possibilities to those who stayed behind. The quota system was still in operation across the western ocean and Irish were still migrating to the United States but the great 1950s surge had sharply tailed off. The annual emigrant number totals were now consistently falling short of Ireland's yearly quota and those unused quota visas were not transferable. Meanwhile, other countries, Poland, Italy and Greece, to name but three, had far smaller quotas than Ireland yet huge numbers of people who had applied for U.S. residence who were being held back in waiting lines that would take many years to process.

The pressure for changes in U.S. law built up noticeably during the late 1950s. But the reformers were battling deeply entrenched views. The 1952 Immigration and Nationality Act had added new cement to the quota system wall, so much so that President Truman had attempted, unsuccessfully, to kill it with a veto. Truman's reaction: "The idea behind this discriminatory policy was, to put it boldly, that Americans with English or Irish names were better people and better citizens than Americans with Italian or Greek or Polish names." Such a concept, Truman added ruefully, was "utterly unworthy of our traditions and our ideals." The soon-to-be greatest living hero of the Irish everywhere, John F. Kennedy, agreed with Truman. Kennedy's pre-White House congressional activities included a 1957 amendment which allowed limited family reunification without reference to national origin. By the decade's end the quota system was seen by Kennedy and others to be entirely inadequate when it came to dealing with divided families, survivors of natural disasters and, perhaps most importantly in the context of the day, political refugees fleeing oppression, not least that imposed by Washington's global enemy number one: Communism. Unlike some groups, the Irish had avoided the Communist yoke and their country was blessedly free of large scale death dealing natural disasters. The game was almost up.

To Kennedy, it seemed only logical and fair. The times had absolutely changed and Cold War America had to base its intake of newcomers on entirely new criteria. On July 23, 1963, four months before his death, Kennedy submitted to the eighty-eighth Congress proposals for "revising and modernizing our immigration law." This entailed elimination of the national quota system after a five-year phase-out period. President Johnson, during his State of the Union Address on January 8th, 1964, took up where his late predecessor had already been. "In establishing preferences," said LBJ, "a nation that was built by the immigrants of all lands can ask those who now seek admission: 'What can you do for your country?' But we should not be asking: 'In what country were you born?'"

Irish Americans were prominent in the subsequent congressional debate. At first glance, the idea of family reunification seemed to pose no threat to Irish immigration so long as the Irish kept coming. The chief sponsor of the bill in the Senate was Senator Philip Hart. The chairman of the House Judiciary Committee was Congressman Michael Feighan.

Feighan had problems with some aspects of the new bill but was not opposed to the elimination of the national quota system. When the dead president's legislative legacy was first submitted for congressional debate, the acting chairman of the Senate Judiciary Committee was for just about every last word. The acting chairman was Ted Kennedy. It would now fall heavily on the youngest brother to ensure that JFK's views, as expressed in *A Nation of Immigrants*, found meaning in new laws. By virtue of his growing skills as a bipartisan weaver of deals, the brother would not fail in this task. As the bill was being debated in 1965, Kennedy, as Senate floor leader with responsibility for presiding over the bill's amendments, gave advance notice of his talents as a broker of compromise. As with all legislation, the bill that finally emerged was indeed a compromise arrangement, or an arrangement of compromises depending on one's point of view. The bill not only did away with national quotas, but it also introduced a controversial ceiling on migration from the western hemisphere. Against the overall backdrop of change, Ireland looked like just another dot in the ocean.

Kennedy summed up the outcome thus: "There is little doubt that of key importance was the unusual parliamentary situation in Congress, where the large Democratic majority was generally responsive to the spirit, if not the letter, of the administration's proposal. Republican leaders were also ready to act on the issue. Moreover, in the Judiciary Committees of both Houses, the balance of power lay with those who long worked for reform, or who readily recognized the need for changes in policy governing the admission of immigrants. And in the executive branch, for the first time in more than a decade, the White House, under both President Kennedy and President Johnson, was deeply committed to basic reform and actively mobilized its forces to see it through.

"The legislative history of the bill," said Kennedy, "especially the drawing of a consensus which, in effect, neutralized any significant opposition both within and without the Congress, generated an atmosphere receptive to reform which was consonant with changing attitudes among our citizens on questions of race and national origin. And not to be forgotten in any list of reason is the tremendous effort put forth by the several private organizations, whose many years of work throughout the country were helping to bring the hope of reform into reality."

Back in Ireland, very few had the slightest notion about what this new "reality" would someday mean. But twenty years on, with the "Great Society" crumbling in the face of the "Reagan Revolution" there would again be cries for "reform"—but a different type of reform when the crying voice was Irish. And there were new private organizations to be reckoned with, not least the IIRM. Ted Kennedy, on the other hand, was still there, a constant in a sea of change. He would be asked by the new Irish to find a way around his own handiwork of twenty years before. And he would oblige in large measure, blood being thicker at times than even legislative ink.

But Kennedy's support would only follow a little cajoling and to some degree at least, a process of education courtesy of fellow Massachusetts politicians, not least Congressman Brian Donnelly.

As a Senator, Kennedy was representing the entire state of Massachusetts. Donnelly, by contrast, covered a smaller area, his district centered in Dorchester on the fringes of Boston. As congressional districts go, Dorchester was as Irish as they come. Donnelly, a member of the House of Representatives from 1979 to 1993, was aware of a problem with the Irish from the beginning of the 1980s. He would hear it from constituents, favors asked on behalf of a cousin or friend from Ireland who was undocumented but eager to obtain a greencard.

Donnelly quickly came to believe that the '65 act had unintended consequences for the Irish, that the bill was effectively discriminating against those Irish who wanted to follow the traditional route to a new life in America.

Donnelly was no expert on immigration but he was hearing things on the street, the kind of things that would always make a Boston politician take notice. "Immigrant" was one of those political do-not-ignore! words in Beantown. Donnelly would later say that he "bullied" his way onto the House Judiciary Sub-Committee on Immigration, Refugees and International Law which, by the time the IIRM was being founded, was chaired by a Kentucky representative with unmistakable immigrant roots, Roman Mazzoli.

What became the 1986 Immigration Reform and Control Act started out as the Simpson/Mazzoli bill in early 1983. In addition to Mazzoli and Senator Alan Simpson, the bill would gather a third name, that of House Judiciary Chairman Peter Rodino, before finding itself poised for final House/Senate approval in late 1986. Immigration, always a contentious issue, was not a matter to be dealt with speedily.

The legislation proposed to deal exclusively with illegal immigration. The argument to exclude legal immigration from the measure was based on the contention that to avoid a national backlash against the legal variety it was necessary to be strong and appear strong in opposition to illegal penetration of the country's borders. Donnelly wasn't impressed. He had an amendment lined up designed for all the cousins and what not in Dorchester and wherever else they might be currently hiding out. The amendment contained the Donnelly Visas. But how would it pass?

Donnelly felt he was getting the runaround. "Next year Brian, we'll deal with your idea next year." As far as Donnelly was concerned that meant never.

The Simpson/Rodino/Mazzoli bill, employer sanctions and all, went on its merry way through various committees and both House and Senate. It passed through the House/Senate Conference phase before returning to the House for what should have been pro-forma approval. Donnelly had other ideas. He was going to get his visas, of that he was certain.

"The vote began, he would later relate, with mostly green lights of approval. But I had worked things out with other Irish American representatives. The train was leaving the station and we needed to force through the amendment. We decided to vote against Simpson/Mazzoli."

And they would do so even though they essentially agreed with the bill's contents. However, it was what was absent from the bill that decided matters for Donnelly and his House floor allies.

"Tip (O'Neill) would be counting on us, we knew that. But we would save our votes until the last minute and hit the red lights together. That's what we did. The bill came crashing down. We killed it."

O'Neill had an idea Donnelly was behind this sudden disaster. Donnelly was summoned to the Speaker's bench. He unloaded his complaint quickly, before the gavel came down, figuratively, but not entirely short of literally, on his head.

"Mr. Speaker, they are refusing to include my amendment," Donnelly said.

O'Neill asked Donnelly how he could get him and his rebel group to vote for the bill.

"Include my amendment," came the reply.

Donnelly remembers the moment as pure O'Neill. "He said to

me, 'everyone thinks I'm now dressing you down Brian.' He winked at me and said 'I'm going to stare at you and look very stern. But don't worry, we'll look after the Irish.'"

Donnelly went back to his place, tail firmly between legs, tongue firmly between cheeks. O'Neill went off to discuss the unforeseen failure of the bill with the House Rules Committee. He came back the next day with a promise that a yes vote from Donnelly and his gang would be followed by the attachment of Donnelly's amendment. Thus the Donnelly visas, after something of a political breach birth, came into the world.

"This was one issue on which Irish American legislators were unanimous," Donnelly would say years later. "It was the first time in my generation that Irish Americans united on one issue. We could never get that with Northern Ireland."

That prevailing sense of unity was to carry over into the U.S. Senate to a degree. But the Senate was less sensitive to the groundswells of constituency opinion. A smaller political club—100 as opposed to 435 members—there was less chance that surprise votes could be pulled off at the last minute. The Senate was a chamber where political ambush was less the done thing than an apparently refined form of collegiate horse trading. Senate decision depended heavily on quid pro quo deals pulled out of the hat by virtue of personal relationships that often transcended the party divide. Favors were given and received. Historically, the Senate has tended to be cautious where perhaps the House of Representatives appeared, by comparison, a little rash and prone to populism. Senators did, however, pay heed to party colleagues in the House. Ted Kennedy was well attuned to the feelings and instincts of his House colleagues from Massachusetts. Brian Donnelly had Kennedy's ear and was briefing him about the growing problem for thousands of young Irish. Donnelly would later talk about Kennedy's "learning curve" on the issue. It would prove to be steep enough when it mattered.

Out on the streets, meanwhile, there were also lessons to be learned—harsh ones.

"John O'Donnell says the scars on his stomach are like an expensive map of Ireland—they cost him over 200,000 dollars." Thus the *Irish Press* reported, on April 11, 1988, the tale of a twenty-two-year-old man from Achill Island in Co. Mayo who discovered the hard way that being a hero was of little use if you didn't have a greencard to back up your heroics.

The previous November, O'Donnell had rushed to the aid of a friend who was being mugged on a Cleveland, Ohio, street. The two muggers took strong exception. Turning on the young Irishman, they stabbed him fifteen times with a kitchen knife.

For months, O'Donnell hovered on the line between life and death, at one point slipping into a coma. Had he known the cost of his daily hospital bill it might have finished him off altogether. Being oblivious had its virtues.

When he finally left hospital, almost five months after the attack, O'Donnell, a self-effacing individual who was rather less comfortable with the publicity given his bravery than his lack of status, felt that he was being mugged a second time over. He was drowning in hospital bills amounting to $225,000 and rising. On top of that, the publicity given his heroics in the Cleveland press had exposed his illegality, the reason for his lack of any medical coverage to meet the bills.

The *Press* report stated that what had happened to John O'Donnell was inevitable. "It was always going to happen to someone on a building site in New York, a bar in Boston, or a street in Cleveland. It will certainly happen again."

But by the time O'Donnell's story was making headlines, having one's cover blown in the matter of status was hardly news of itself. By the spring of 1988, it was fair to assume that most young Irishmen and women seen on the street of large U.S. cities were in fact undocumented—and this despite the new Donnelly visas. For by the time O'Donnell's plight became known, the Irish illegals story had gone on general release, by means of ABC *World News Tonight* and its anchorman Peter Jennings.

Don Martin represented the third cog in the IIRM's reform machine. Irish immigrants, new and established, could make an impression on politicians, Irish and U.S. But the U.S. politicians in particular would require an explanation of matters in roughly their own language. Martin, an attorney working for Capital Cities ABC would be that necessary interpreter.

Martin had vaguely heard about the new Irish and their problem with U.S. law. But it was a chance visit to a Queens bar that would put faces on rumors. In the late summer of 1987, Martin was taking a bus to his mother's in Maspeth. His mother was unwell. Martin decided to stop along the way for a drink. He chose a bar called "The Horse and Jockey." His wild ride to Washington was about to begin.

Martin walked into the place. He remembers a "huge mass of Irish faces." His arrival was akin to Clint Eastwood walking into a western saloon. "It was like somebody turned the radio off." Martin was carrying a briefcase and was wearing a raincoat. He looked like a fed. He picked up a copy of the *Irish Echo* from the bar. There was an ad in it headed "No Irish Need Apply." It had been placed by the Cork Association on behalf of the IIRM. The rumors he had heard were true after all. Martin decided then and there to get involved. He would use his connections to help these newcomers. As he pondered his coming involvement in the battle to legalize the Irish, some who would one day be helped by his interest were heading for the door. Martin became acutely conscious of his own presence. The bar was slowly but surely emptying. Wary Irish eyes glancing at the fed, the G-Man, INS agent or whatever he was in the raincoat with his head buried in the newspaper. The same appearance of corporate American respectability that would carry such cachet in Washington was scaring the bejazus out of the lads in the jeans. Within minutes, Martin found himself virtually alone. One or two Irish who had hastened from the bar would see him again a few months later in Gaelic Park in the Bronx at an IIRM mass rally. Still in his G-man clothes, Martin stood out from the crowd in purely visual terms. But by then he considered himself to be well and truly part of the Irish throng.

Martin would fairly describe himself as an emotional man and was certainly not afraid about stirring the pot over what he saw as a gross injustice. Martin worked from a simple principle. In his own words, he saw the problem of the undocumented Irish as being "a living, breathing indictment of American immigration policy."

He was prepared to put his money where his words were. In the March 12, 1988 issue of the *Irish Echo*, Martin had published an open letter to President Reagan. It was a blatant pitch to broad Irish American sentiment, which, up until now, had largely taken a back seat to the newly arrived upstart cousins.

The letter, which was signed, not by Martin himself, but by "The Irish Immigration Reform Movement," informed Reagan that the 1965 act had made Irish immigration to the U.S. "virtually impossible."

Martin had an idea that the Gipper could easily identify with heroes, real or mythical. And he was right. The ad included a "Roll of Honor" naming the 257 Irish-born immigrants who had won the nation's highest military award for bravery, the Congressional Medal of Honor.

Martin's concluding paragraph was almost Lincolnesque: "Mr. President, we do not think it requires any wild inference on our part to assert with confidence that these men would argue most forcefully and strenuously for their former countrymen, if they were able to do so. Indeed, we feel that in a very real sense they argue for us now, with a silent eloquence that will not go unheard."

Ted Kennedy was not going unheard either. With his ideological rival cum legislative ally, Alan Simpson, Kennedy had been busy cutting himself loose from his own handiwork in 1965. On March 15, 1988, two days before the annual green extravaganza that was St. Patrick's Day, Kennedy and Simpson engineered an 88–4 Senate majority in favor of a bill, their bill, that would widen the gap between contemporary law and the family reunification emphasis of 1965.

Included in the Kennedy/Simpson bill's provisions were 55,000 annual "independent immigrants" visas which would be awarded on a points basis. Points would be awarded English language skills, educational level, occupational demand and work experience. Kennedy commented that the bill would facilitate immigration from countries in western Europe which had fared badly since the sixties. Whatever about Capitol Hill and all its coded language, there were no prizes for guessing which particular corner of western Europe was looming largest back in Massachusetts.

The *Irish Echo*, in an editorial, welcomed passage of the bill and called it "wonderful news." The Senate, the paper opined, had said "yes" to "immigration reform" and a debt of gratitude was owed to Kennedy and Simpson. The latter contention was undoubtedly true, the former would have a harder time standing up under the eyeglass of history. But passage of the bill was certainly the first great legislative event of the IIRM era. The *Echo* was correct in suggesting that the House version of Kennedy/Simpson, being pushed primarily by Brian Donnelly and Brooklyn Democrat Charles Schumer, faced "tougher sledding." It would. One of the biggest ruts along the way was expected to be Rep. Peter Rodino, chairman of the House Judiciary Committee. He was planning to quit Congress after forty years. With the '88 elections looming, Rodino was the worst kind of politician to have blocking your path. He no longer had a constituency. Promises of election time support could no longer sway him.

"We hope that the gentleman from New Jersey, who has fought the good fight over the years, will make the immigration reform bill his last best fight," the *Irish Echo*'s editorial concluded. They were words more deeply rooted in hope than great expectation.

Still, hope and expectation were combining to fuel the IIRM's mounting campaign. Being an election year, 1988 was a potentially fertile one for those scattering political seed about the place. Members of Congress, mayors and legislators at every state and local level, even the odd presidential hopeful had, by quite early in the year, either been contacted by the IIRM or had seen fit to discover it in the A to Z list of Irish organizations with clout, real or perceived. Gary Hart, prior to his "Monkey Business" problems, had been one who had been added to the IIRM's contact list. The group itself, now likened to a kind of government in exile by the *Echo*'s Mike Devlin, was sprouting new branches all over the country. A grass roots organization of this kind, growing with such incredible rapidity, wrote Devlin, was "a politician's dream."

Not every politician. The Irish government was not beholding to any government in exile, especially when its members couldn't even vote. Frank Fahey, "Minister for Youth and Sport" in the Haughey government, had arrived early in the year to investigate conditions under which the illegal Irish were living. What he discovered was not, from his point of view, intolerable. "The vast majority" of the undocumented were "doing well and in reasonable employment," he decided. Most of the young Irish he met on his trip were, despite their obvious legal difficulties, "by and large happy with their lot."

He did not get that impression from IIRM leaders. Indeed, Fahey and the IIRM were to clash openly over the issue of funding of an IIRM office and the highly vocal style of the emigrant upstarts. An IIRM office, he claimed, would merely be a duplication of existing services, political code for a waste of taxpayer money. And while the organization was making a "significant contribution" to the immigration reform issue, the government in Dublin disagreed with "some of the mechanisms they want to use." Fahey was skeptical of the undocumented problem being highlighted amid all the St. Patrick's Day ballyhoo, or in the American national press. He preferred "quiet diplomatic lobbying around the country." Given the raucous origins of Fianna Fáil, Fahey's apparent devotion to form and political good manners appeared, to some, a tad ironic.

Fahey met with the IIRM twice in New York and the tension was more than apparent. The IIRM subsequently released a terse statement: "The IIRM made it quite clear that the success of Mr. Fahey's visit would depend on whether he had come to offer financial support to the Movement or not. This financial support was not forthcoming, thus Mr. Fahey's mission was a failure. Mr. Fahey's visit was a useless, cosmetic public relations exercise and a waste of the Irish taxpayer's money. At all meetings with the IIRM Mr. Fahey displayed a lack of knowledge of the American political system and a lack of awareness of the conditions and sentiments pertaining to the undocumented Irish community."

The new arrivals were getting stroppy. Clearly, Irish immigrant representatives were determined to relieve Fahey of his notion that the undocumented were, as he had put it himself, "happy with their lot." They clearly were not. And neither were they ready to roll over and play the role of the cherished departed ones. Fahey could not have been that surprised. His party had been well to the fore in trumpeting the arrival of Ireland's best and brightest generation. The fact that the same generation was now fighting against the prevailing circumstances of its own fate was only to be expected.

After the verbal lashing from the IIRM, Fahey found himself in the more congenial company of Mayor Ed Koch. Koch told Fahey that as far as he was concerned, the Irish could never be illegal in New York. Hizzoner then presented the Irish visitor with an official New York City necktie and told him that it had the power to protect the wearer from pestilence. Fahey might have been forgiven for thinking that the protection came a little after the fact.

A few weeks later, Charles Haughey paid a five-day visit to the U.S. In New York, Haughey met with Cardinal John O'Connor and made a point of thanking him for the work that both he personally and the church were doing for the illegal Irish. Haughey also discussed the immigrant situation with Ted Kennedy during a thirty-six-hour stopover at the Kennedy family compound in Hyannisport, Massachusetts. But while the illegals were clearly on his mind, "the boss" avoided an encounter with the rebellious IIRM.

Koch, meanwhile, was widely viewed in the Irish community as a strong ally, although as Mayor of New York he was assiduous in his efforts not to show favoritism to any one ethnic group. Still, it was felt that he had a soft spot for the Irish. Besides, his best known wardrobe item was the Aran sweater he pulled out every St.

Patrick's Day. Koch had gathered support around him in favor of extending the deadline that year, May 4, in the alien amnesty attached to the 1986 Immigration Reform and Control Act. The extension had been a prime topic of discussion at the 1988 Midwinter gathering of the United States Conference of Mayors. In general, the amnesty was turning out to be a bust and the Immigration and Naturalization Service was inclined to listen to pleas for an extension. It would not matter too much to the Irish however, given that most of the illegals from Ireland had arrived after the cutoff date, January 1 1982. And while the mayors pushed, the expiration date for the amnesty ultimately remained at May 4.

Koch was not the only "local" politician who was rushing to the aid of the beleaguered young Irish. The monthly meeting of the IIRM, in New York particularly, was fast becoming a must attend event. More than two hundred and fifty people turned out for the March, 1988 meeting. A variety of speakers took to the podium. One was State Assemblyman John Dearie, a prominent figure in New York Irish/Democratic party politics. Dearie told the assembled throng that because of the IIRM, "candidates for office can no longer not talk about Irish issues."

Politicians in office were indeed talking about Ireland. But when the subject matter was immigration, no Ireland was an island. Looking from a purely Irish perspective, it seemed that the main issue was visa numbers and who was championing the Irish cause. The same few heroes and villains appeared to be cropping up on a regular basis. But the ways of Congress could be confusing at times to the uninitiated. A bill that appeared to be a sure thing one day would seemingly vanish off the face of the earth the next. By the time that the amnesty provision passed into history, the Kennedy/Simpson bill was doing the rounds in the House of Representatives. At this stage it apparently held the promise of up to 10,000 visas a year for Ireland, greencards which would also be available to the illegal Irish already living in the U.S. As expected, Peter Rodino was proving to be a problem. He wanted the specified number of visas being proposed by Kennedy/Simpson to be spread between a larger number of countries than the bill proposed. That would mean fewer visas for Ireland. Still, some were encouraged that Rodino, who had been Simpson's main House ally in drawing up the 1986 act, was at least inclined towards passage of an immigration reform bill at all.

By early summer there were several such bills floating around the House chamber. The House Immigration Sub-Committee heard testimony at the end of June from several congressmen pushing their own proposals. Joe DioGuardi, a New York Republican, made clear his view that a bill he was sponsoring was good for the Irish and good for America. His bill would allow for a "new wave of Irish immigration that will again result in a better United States." Sub-Committee Chairman Roman Mazzoli, however, was cautious in his reaction to testimony. He said he was more in favor of immigration reform than against. It was hardly a ringing endorsement. A couple of weeks after the hearing, the *Irish Voice* reported in a front page headline that the "Immigration Bill Is in Trouble." Fears were being expressed that the summer was dragging on and with party conventions and congressional elections looming large, any efforts at reform would end up languishing in a "legislative limbo." "Mazzoli and Rodino," the *Voice* reported, had not "evinced any real enthusiasm" for the Kennedy/Simpson bill which was being seen as the real legislative groundbreaker.

The report was pessimistic but ended on an upbeat note when it stated that Ted Kennedy was considering "another strategy." Not for the first time it was becoming a case of "there's always Ted Kennedy."

Back in New York, the IIRM was taking encouragement from the news that it was to receive a $30,000 grant from New York City through the good offices of Queens Borough President Claire Shulman and Council Member Walter McCaffrey. Mayor Koch was adding words to money by urging illegal Irish to make use of city hospitals, schools and other facilities. "They're not illegal to me, they're undocumented," Koch said. New York, three thousand miles from Ireland, was doing its level best to be "home" for its new Irish residents.

Over the summer the temperatures soared. So did the estimates of the number of annual Irish visas that might fall from the tree if the latest batch of bills actually bore fruit. Eight to 10,000 became 14,500 to 15,000. By late July, Peter Rodino all of a sudden had his own bill on the floor in partnership with Roman Mazzoli. Rodino, earlier viewed as a potential enemy by the Irish, was now proposing an extension of the Donnelly Visa lottery. The Rodino/Mazzoli proposal was a near mirror image of Kennedy/Simpson but with even more visa potential for the Irish, combining as it did Kennedy/Simpson independent category visas and more Donnellys. Rodino's road to Damascus conversion was not entirely as a result of Irish lobbying although the IIRM's by now full-time lobbyist, Harris Miller, had been beating a lot of bushes in New Jersey.

The seventy-nine-year-old Rodino, who might have been thinking mostly of a quiet retirement at this stage, was also under severe pressure from groups representing Latino and Asian immigrants. As a result, Rodino's bill also proposed what the *Irish Voice* described as a "stunning" 800,000 visas for family reunification. And it took a little dig at its Senate cousin. There would be no points for speaking English. Still, the *Irish Echo* reported that the Rodino proposal emerged after the congressman had been paid several visits by Ted Kennedy. Jerry Tinker, Kennedy's senior aide attached to the House Sub-Committee, said at the time that Kennedy continued to press both Rodino and Mazzoli for a positive response. "He kept plugging ahead and was very determined. He spent a hell of a lot of time on it behind the scenes as well as publicly," Tinker said.

Kennedy's efforts eventually paid off. The Rodino/Mazzoli bill was now set to be discussed in hearings staged by Mazzoli's Immigration Sub-Committee on September 7. Time was short though. The one hundredth Congress was set to adjourn one month later, October 3. And between the hearings and adjournment there were only eighteen working days listed on Capitol Hill. The window of opportunity for the Irish appeared to be closing fast. But Rodino had some words of comfort, born out of many years of last minute wheeling and dealing. "It is expected that the Judiciary Committee and the Immigration Sub-Committee will review this proposal and proceed to mark-up in an expeditious fashion." Music to Irish ears indeed. And music that could just about be believed. The 1986 reform act almost died at the last moment but was saved by a filibuster on a defense issue that kept Congress detained in Washington longer than planned. Then again, defense was something of a sacred cow. Did anyone in Washington have the energy or commitment to launch a filibuster on behalf of one specific group of illegal aliens? It didn't look that way.

In an internal briefing memo drawn up in early September to coincide with another visit to New York by Tánaiste (deputy prime minister) and Minister for Foreign Affairs, Brian Lenihan, Irish officials stated that all advice received led to the conclusion that "a specific amnesty for the Irish would be impossible to achieve because of Congress's deep attachment to the principles of non-discrimination in the immigration area and the opposition of other ethnic groups."

Asian groups were singled out in the memo for having particular problems with the anticipated reduction in family reunification visas or the new emphasis on English language skills if Congress passed a bill similar to Kennedy/Simpson.

The memo concluded: "In view of these difficulties, both real and potential, the Embassy has been in close and continuous contact with Congressman Peter Rodino, a senior and influential Congressman from New Jersey, who is the Chairman of the House Judiciary Committee and is due to retire this Autumn. Congressman Rodino proved very sympathetic to our approach and promised to see what he could do to help. However, he warned that there was no chance of the Kennedy/Simpson bill getting through the house this Session. Following a meeting on July 27th between himself and Senators Kennedy and Simpson at which Senator Kennedy indicated he disagreed with Congressman Rodino's assessment, the latter has now introduced a Bill in co-sponsorship with Congressman Mazzoli who is Chairman of the House Immigration Sub-Committee. Before the measure was introduced, the Tánaiste's office rang the Congressman's office to make known the Tánaiste's appreciation for his efforts."

Such was the way things worked. The Irish Immigration Reform movement was also running up its phone bills in preparation for the Washington hearings. But as the Lenihan briefing memo made clear, there were no warm and fuzzy phone exchanges between Dublin and IIRM leaders in New York specifically. The memo stated: "On legal reform there is considerable interest among the Irish community in the present debate in Washington. Except for the IIRM, relations between the Consulate and the leading Irish American groups are excellent."

Some of those favored Irish American groups, and the out of favor IIRM (relations between consulates and IIRM branches in other cities were generally better) were by now heading to Capitol Hill for what turned out to be a memorable exercise in pumping up emotions and cranking up legislative machinery that was quickly winding down in anticipation of House elections.

The September hearings before the Immigration Sub-Committee were staged over two days, one week apart. The opening session on September 7 was staged in the full Judiciary Committee hearing room. This was Pat Hurley's Dublin Castle and Ted Kennedy's stage.

Chairman Roman Mazzoli proceeded cautiously, posing the question to his attentive audience as to whether or not the door to America was "open too narrowly, too widely or just right."

Kennedy went to work on familiar ground, telling the assembled House members that there was a "timeliness" about the proposed immigration legislation. Timing, as Kennedy well knew, had as much to do with an election as reform. He knew what buttons to press and where. He proceeded to the issue of fairness, pointing to the imbalances in immigration numbers which had inadvertently arisen in recent years. Nobody present was being blamed but they were being presented with an opportunity to be impartial and caring legislators.

Kennedy threw statistics at the committee: Only 1,852 Irish applicants qualifying for visas in 1986 even though the statutory ceiling for Ireland was 20,000. The Irish were simply missing out because they were not qualifying under family reunification rules. An "excessively restrictive force" had been in operation since 1965," Kennedy said. Few in the room knew that Kennedy was virtually speaking *ex cathedra* on the doings of '65.

Alan Simpson hammered away at the whole notion of basing U.S. immigration law on reuniting families. This was not in the national interest and was failing to meet the demands of the labor market. Kennedy and Simpson had rather different motives for testifying but their arguments were merging somewhere in the middle.

The politics and statistics had been thrown in the ring. The emotional fire was added by Tom Flatley, Mayo native and hugely successful Massachusetts-based businessman. Flatley had arrived in America in 1950, paying for his U.S. citizenship through service in the Korean War. He was a model success story, Irish and American, an older version of the kind of people he told the congressmen were now being almost entirely excluded because of the 1965 act. Apart from stating that the situation was "simply wrong," Flatley the businessman pointed to what many were saying was Ireland's best educated generation ever. All this talent was being potentially lost to Europe, Australia and other places. At this rate, he was telling them, there would be no more Tom Flatleys, ever.

The hearing gave the Irish side an opportunity to view the opposition. This was far from being a save the Irish benefit. Testimony was delivered by Asian and Hispanic representatives, labor leaders, government officials, on behalf of Jewish groups and the Catholic Church, which, while undoubtedly sympathetic to the mostly Catholic Irish and eager to see more NP-5 Donnellys visas made available, was also making it known that the idea of reuniting families could not be entirely sacrificed to the demands of the market. Significantly, the Commissioner of the Immigration and Naturalization Service, Alan Nelson signaled the Reagan Administration's wish to see some reform. Nelson expressed administration liking for the Kennedy/Simpson bill in particular. He felt that the issue of reform should be bipartisan. It was both a hint and a nudge.

The initial hearing presented the Irish with the first close up view of Congressman Howard Berman of California. California was the immigration cockpit of the day, as New York had been a hundred years before. Berman's concerns were fired up mostly by Asian and Hispanic lobbyists but he was aware that both coasts would have a say in any final determination. He announced a bill of his own with increased numbers of family reunification visas but also a 50,000 visa annual lottery for the young and single brigade, Irish and otherwise.

Berman seemed like a potential ally and outside the hearing room he was uttering reassuring words to Irish ears. But for the record, he sounded a warning: "I will strenuously oppose any backsliding to the days when the United States had a notion of which countries were the source of the most desirable immigrants."

Some groups, particularly the Asian Pacific American Legal Center and the National Council of La Raza, tried for a delay of game. They suggested pushing the issue on to the next Congress or establishing a panel of experts. Congressman Barney Frank, well aware of how things could be killed off by panels and committees, wondered aloud if these organizations were merely fearful of a bad result.

Outside in the corridor, Ted Kennedy was giving his "the key is to get into conference" pep talk. Kennedy's message clearly was that once in there would be a result, one way or another.

The Irish in America, not least in Massachusetts, had gained a reputation for working things out properly behind closed doors. Irish political voodoo depended heavily on eyeball to eyeball deal making, quid pro quo's laced with a whiff of tobacco, a sense that everybody should benefit but first and mostly us, ourselves, the Irish. Kennedy was an heir to much of that Honey Fitz and James Curley mystique. In one sense, the modern congress member was little different to the old style ward boss. Behind all the Beltway trappings there was more than a hint of a smokey room, street corner, political horse trader. In the end, it still all came down to the deal.

Edward Moore Kennedy represented different things to Irish Americans. He was at once hero and villain. Just being a Kennedy was reason enough for simultaneous worship and resentment. He was a hero to many liberals and arch villain to numerous conservatives. Not a few Irish American Catholics viewed him as a fallen angel who was still falling. But on that September day in a Washington corridor, Ted Kennedy was Santa Claus in a summer suit come early to the knot of needy Irish surrounding his portly frame. And this, at last, was surely Christmas Eve.

5

FAITH, HOPE AND POLITICAL CLOUT

*"The Irish are doing this all wrong. They are just getting
other immigrants' backs up."*

Rick Schwartz, National Immigration and Refuge Citizens Forum.

Sixteen months after it came into the world, the Irish Immigration Reform Movement had its own back up. And even if it was at pains to pay at least lip service to immigrants from other countries, a widespread perception of the group and its motives was a good deal less than flattering. For the very same reason that its name attracted the eye of Irish American legislators in Congress, the IIRM was prompting anxious commentary from non-Irish immigration advocates who took the view that the Irish undocumented problem came well down the ladder of priorities. The Washington immigration hearings, far from being an opportunity for establishing common ground, merely served to underscore fears that a purely Irish bill was being cooked up in Congress.

The Kennedy/Simpson bill in particular, which the Reagan Administration viewed most favorably, looked very green indeed. Yet, the Peter Rodino-inspired House equivalent was loaded with extra Donnelly Visas. Neither bill was being strongly welcomed by Asian and Hispanic lobbyists, although the House version had a clear edge because it retained a family reunification component. The Irish, meanwhile, were grasping at both. It was a case of any port in a storm.

Part two of the Immigration Sub-Committee hearing was on September 16. It was the IIRM's big moment and they were playing it safe. Don Martin, the group's Eliot Ness, by way of the Horse and Jockey pub, was pushed into the front line. It seemed like a smart move. Martin spoke with eloquence and barely restrained passion. He argued for greater numbers of legal immigrants from those countries blocked out by the 1965 act. This was the "reform" that the IIRM wanted. He also called for a compromise between the two bills before the Sub Committee, one that would keep family reunification laws intact even as an extended NP-5 program took care of the current generation of Irish.

But Martin didn't just stick to the nuts and bolts of immigration law. He went straight for the committee's heart, hoping all along that it had one.

"If all the men who have served in the uniform of the United States since 1861 were to parade before this Congress today it would constitute an army of millions," he said.

"Yet, in all that number just 3,439, or about a brigade, would wear a blue ribbon signifying the Congressional Medal of Honor. Of that brave number 257, or about a company and a half, were immigrants from Ireland. If those immigrants could speak to you now, we are certain that they would argue for fairness and for diversity. Indeed, we believe they argue for us now with a silent eloquence that will not go unheard."

It is probably true to say that some advocates for other national groups in the room, not to mention those from organizations that wanted all immigration curbed, were silently getting sick.

But Martin's blatant appeal to stars and stripes sentiment seemed to have some effect. "I'm glad to see that this generation of Irish Americans are as eloquent as those who went before them," said Chairman Mazzoli.

The Sub-Committee had heard the arguments. But despite the importance of the issue to all sides and the emotion of the moment, courtesy of the IIRM's Martin, it took no vote. And outside the hearing room there were still those who voiced caution. Jerry Tinker, Ted Kennedy's immigration point man, told Patricia James of the *Irish Echo* that even though the committee had absorbed all of the arguments it didn't really have to act at this juncture. Before anything would happen, he believed there would have to be a lot of activity behind the scenes. What lay ahead now, Tinker said, was "akin to pulling a legislative rabbit out of the hat."

But as the last words were being uttered before the committee, and the first words of reaction were beginning to flow, something else was stirring. The Irish full court press was on. Brian Lenihan was in town talking to all the relevant congressional players and anybody else who cared to listen, including Secretary of State George Schultz. It seemed as if something was coming down. But what?

The question was to be answered many times in the following couple of weeks, but never quite accurately. Rumors flew and hopes were raised time and again, only to be dashed. The politicians appeared to have their minds on only one thing—elections. As September began to fade, one report likened the pace of activity on immigration as being close to that of a trainee bomb disposal squad. There was talk of unofficial conferences involving Kennedy and Rodino; word that a stop-gap bill with NP-5 visas galore intended mainly for the Irish was now only days away. But a truly definitive headline remained elusive. "It is agonizing and nail biting but in the end we will have to be grateful for what we can get," said Irish diplomat James Farrell.

Whatever was taking shape, it wasn't looking like a comprehensive reform package although more Donnelly visas for the Irish were being spoken about with increasing frequency. Merely extending an existing visa program only required passage of amendments to existing legislation, not an entirely new act. Congress was now due to rise on October 15. It was coming down to the wire, as a headline in the *Irish Voice* suggested.

And then, on the day that September was poised to surrender to October, there was a huge breakthrough.

The phones began to ring, fast and furiously. It was Friday afternoon, only a few weeks to congressional elections. Members of Congress were planning weekend voter blitzes in far flung districts. But the numbers generating excitement in the ranks of Irish immigration campaigners had nothing to do with latest opinion polls. Rodino's Judiciary Committee had unanimously approved the House legislation that approved extension of the Donnelly program. As many as 30,000 greencards now appeared destined for eager hands, many of them Irish, over the coming two years. The first batch of 15,000 visas would be offered to applicants who had gone on a reserve list after already applying, but failing, to secure a Donnelly.

These first 15,000 visas would be applied immediately to that same number of applicants who constituted the "immediate reserve list." 9,866 of them were Irish. Another 15,000 would follow in fiscal year 1990, which actually started on October 1, 1989, exactly a year away. Again, these visas would be issued to people who had already tried, but failed, to secure a visa. Their names were resting in stacks of mail bags in Washington.

The Judiciary Committee-approved bill was a compromise. It was neither the Kennedy/Simpson nor the Rodino/Mazzoli version. It was a reduced and simplified measure tagged with Roman Mazzoli's name, although there were effectively many fingerprints on its covers. Charles Schumer's hand for one was clearly evident. Its official title was "Amendments in the Nature of a substitute for H.R. 5115" or more simply, "Immigration Amendments of 1988." It didn't sound very historic but few Irish cared. Also announced was a new 20,000 visa lottery for late 1990 and 1991 put together by Howard Berman. It was aimed at countries that had been securing fewer than 5,000 legal immigrants a year. Ireland qualified although it was quickly being suggested that a Donnelly windfall could push Ireland over the Berman limit. But no, the Berman proposal even contained a provision that would exclude Donnelly Visas being counted against the 5,000 limit. "Visa bonanza for Irish," was the front page headline in the Dublin-published *Irish Press* the following morning.

It was a clear victory, 50,000 visas in all. Yet it was not seen as enough. Adrian Flannelly, the New York Irish radio show host who had personally delivered thousands of Donnelly applications to Washington the previous year, was speaking for many: "While this legislation is a breakthrough, we must not rest on our laurels. There is a lot more work to be done for the illegals."

Flannelly wasn't alone in his caution. The legislators themselves, who were now committed to reviewing entirely immigration legislation the following year, were not running away with themselves. Mazzoli described his own handiwork as a "narrow effort." Rodino spoke with the experience born out of forty years in the Capitol Hill trenches: "I know immigration doesn't lend itself to quick fixes," he said. Brian Donnelly predicted a positive vote in the full House. Fuller reform of legal immigration would take longer. The bill, he said, was "the best result we can hope for at this stage."

The Irish government, not entirely adverse to even a quick fix, welcomed the bill. Brian Lenihan was awarded some of the credit for its success.

The IIRM also welcomed the visas but took the view that visa lotteries could not cover all the undocumented Irish. The campaign for comprehensive immigration reform would continue. But, in the meantime, there was a vote to be won. All 435 members of the House of Representatives were about to receive telegrams from the

IIRM advising them of the wisest course of action in the impending ballot.

It was left to Brian Donnelly to introduce formally the amendments bill on the House floor. It was approved unanimously on October 5 and passed on to the Senate. As was often the case, Congress went beyond its adjournment deadline. But it was to take two weeks before House endorsement was to be tested in the Senate chamber. The bill was introduced on Friday, October 21, by Democratic Leader Robert Byrd. It was passed late that evening, again in a unanimous vote and without a roll call. Vice-President Bush, gearing up for his White House bid, revealed the Reagan administration's thinking when he praised the new legislation for restoring fairness and balance to America's immigration system.

Said Bush without any hint or irony: "From Plymouth Rock to Ellis Island to our nation's many points of entry today, immigrants have always been the backbone of our dreams and accomplishments as a nation and we must continue to welcome all people seeking greater political and religious freedom and economic opportunity."

The IIRM didn't go quite so far, describing passage of the amendments as both a "minor" and "significant" legislative victory. Co-founder Sean Minihane said the amendments were "a step in the right direction." The effort to push through full-scale reform would continue in the next Congress. Ted Kennedy, standing for re-election himself on November 8, agreed, and so did Michael Dukakis, flag-bearer for the Democrats in the presidential race.

But as far as the amendments bill was concerned, all that was needed now was the current president's signature.

Ronald Reagan wore his Irish sentiments on his sleeve. But was he Irish up his sleeve too? The question was answered when reports emerged that Senator Jesse Helms had almost killed off the amendments bill in the Senate but was persuaded to look the other way at the last minute by Reagan. When it became known that Helms was going to be a problem, Irish diplomats called the White House. Reagan, in turn, phoned Helms and persuaded him to back down. It was a close call in every sense. The bill was approved by the Senate without a quorum. One dissenting voice would have killed it.

Reagan duly signed and virtually all the primary immigration players, with the exception of the retiring Rodino and a defeated New York Democrat, Rep. Joe DioGuardi, were returned to Congress in the elections. George Bush was now on his way to the Oval Office and his heart seemed to be in much the same place as Reagan's. Overall, matters seemed to be proceeding quite smoothly.

They were, until the Immigration and Naturalization Service reminded one and all that there was a long way to go yet. The election was still be analyzed and dissected when INS agents raided a nursing home in Boston. Five Irish nurses aides were arrested. A sixth almost qualified for the Olympics by jumping through an open ground floor window and sprinting across the grounds to safety. The five arrested had actually secured the jobs through an agency and possessed social security numbers. But there was a growing sense that the Irish were having things all their way in Washington. Arresting a few at least kept other immigrant groups from snapping at INS heels.

The ink on the Boston story was barely dry when the U.S. Secret Service—no less—busted a dozen Irish illegals in New Jersey in a phone home scam involving stolen credit card numbers. Stories such as this didn't quite fit in with the heroic imagery presented to members of Congress. But the hearings were over, the bill was signed and a few bad apples were not going to overturn the cart at this stage.

1988 gave up its ghost with word from the U.S. Ambassador to Ireland, Margaret Heckler, that interviews for Donnelly Visas would start in January. The *Irish Voice* reported that Ted Kennedy was planning to re-introduce his bill in the next session. In one sense the road ahead looked smooth. Of course, it wasn't to be quite that way.

Back in Ireland, the government was awarding itself merit badges. Brian Lenihan would later tell the Dáil that he had "lent his weight" to the compromise package which had emerged in Washington. But even amid the initial relief and euphoria, the Haughey government was coming under attack from the opposition for not securing a general amnesty for the illegal Irish, something which came within the remit of a U.S. president under the 1965 act.

In the pre-Christmas adjournment debate in the Irish Senate, the Seanad, the Fianna Fáil Minister of State at the Department of Foreign Affairs, Sean Calleary, Brian Lenihan's immediate subordinate, rejected suggestions from a couple of opposition senators that what had emerged from Congress was in fact rather disappointing. Calleary said that the recent amendments had resulted from the "tremendous amount of work of Senators and Congress-men." Calleary, perhaps drawing on his party's considerable stock of memories from the struggle for independence, rejected calls from Fine Gael senators for a government-funded advice center in the U.S. on the grounds that if all the out-of-status Irish people were to congregate in one place it might prove to be an easy target for a raid.

The official record of the debate had Calleary speaking thus: "The outcome of recent events to change US immigration law has been far from disappointing as far as Ireland is concerned. It represents a singular success for the Government and for their efforts. Since taking up office, we have given a very high priority to help to improve the situation of newly arrived immigrants in the US, and, not being political, a situation the previous Government did nothing about."

"Rubbish," replied Fine Gael Senator John Connor. And so ended the IIRM's second year.

But the idea of an executive amnesty had taken hold beyond the Irish capital. Back in New York, with the new year only days old, Mayor Ed Koch was urging president-elect George Bush to exercise such power on behalf of thousands of Irish immigrants who were suffering from "pain, anguish and inequalities" while "languishing in a troubling limbo." Bush agreed to consider Koch's request although few expected him to act. Koch's plea was at least partly prompted by reports of dozens of Irish being prevented from returning to the U.S. after spending Christmas in Ireland. Clearly, the intent of Congress still lagged well behind the application of laws at the U.S. frontier. Passing through U.S. immigration was already a nerve-wracking experience even for the legitimate. Writing in the *Irish Echo*, Debbie McGoldrick—who later moved to the *Irish Voice*—reported allegations of "undue pressure" being placed on Irish travelers heading back to the U.S. in the post-Christmas period. Stories of "aggressive questioning," baggage and even clothing searches by INS officers at the Shannon immigration "pre-clearance" facility began cropping up with increasing frequency. The INS denied harassment, stating that it was merely doing its job. But that job was now literally bringing tears to the eyes of young Irish people, by no means all of them illegitimate. Koch was right about the pain and anguish bit.

Margaret Curley, who was writing the weekly "Green Card"

immigrant column for the *Irish Voice* at the time, remembers receiving letters with tales of woe that were little short of incredible.

"Should I go home for my father's funeral was a question I was asked more than once. Some didn't go home for the funerals of parents because they had invested so much in their life in America.

"There was real fear," Curley later recalled. "I remember shortly after I began writing the column I was talking to this young girl who had come from Kerry. I told her I was going next to interview an INS official. She was panic stricken. She told me I was walking into the lion's den."

Curley's weekly mail stack threw up just about every kind of situation, critical, absurd even funny. She became aware of illegals using false social security numbers, the numbers of dead people or redundant J1 (summer student) numbers. "People would be absolutely terrified when they received, as many eventually did, notes in the mail from the Social Security Administration.

"I had a friend who was put in charge of vetting job applications in a company. It was after the 1986 law and she would have to ask applicants if they had a greencard. She didn't have one herself."

Curley also had to deal with many frantic inquiries on health issues. Many illegals would avoid hospitals or the doctor's office for fear of being reported to the INS. They would lie in their apartments and suffer through varied ailments or drag themselves to work because losing a job could be economically catastrophic.

By way of apparent contradiction, Curley would find her own work as a journalist made immeasurably easier by the open nature of the U.S. system and the relatively free flow of information, something largely denied the illegals themselves. Her column became a lifeline for countless undocumented, by no means all of them Irish.

The early months of 1989 witnessed rising hopes for Irish success in the Berman Visa program. The IIRM was, meanwhile, gearing up for a long haul campaign aimed at steering the congressional immigration debate as far in a pro-Irish direction as possible. But money was a bit of a problem. The American Ireland Fund was inviting funding applications from Irish American organizations in a position to aid immigrants. The IIRM was one of them. Problem was, there were over four hundred others on the AIF list for a share of $50,000. IIRM eyes were now looking to Dublin but Finance Minister Albert Reynolds ignored the U.S. even as he set aside half-a-million pounds in the budget for Irish immigrant welfare projects in Britain. The IIRM was both angry and puzzled. Taoiseach Charles Haughey had previously instructed the Friends of Fianna Fáil fundraising group in the U.S. to give $5,000 to the IIRM. So why was the group being snubbed now? No "specific proposals," came the reply from the Department of Foreign Affairs in Dublin. Relations between the IIRM and the Irish government were still in deep freeze—and at the worst time possible.

The Irish government's own estimates were now showing that emigration from Ireland was still rising and in fact had reached a new peak in 1988. The "net outflow" figure for the year was placed at 32,000, a rise of 5,000 over the '87 figure. The figures covered emigration to all countries but another round of mutually antagonistic number crunching between the government and the IIRM only added to the confusion. The government was working off a total net outflow figure to all other countries from 1981 to the end of '88 amounting to 131,000. The IIRM was arguing that this estimate might even be falling short of the number of Irish who had come to the U.S. alone. Not all of them were illegal. An estimated 15,000 had migrated legally to the U.S. in the same period; roughly 7,000 more were working in America on temporary visas while as many as 5,000 were preparing to arrive that coming summer on J1 student working visas.

St. Patrick's Day, 1989, saw just about all the undocumented—whatever their total number was—applying for Berman Visas, applications for which were being accepted by the U.S. authorities after March 1. The IIRM, again with a masterful eye for the emotional arm twist, had organized a "Mass of Hope" for March 16th in St. Patrick's Cathedral, New York. Despite financial worries there was no shortage of publicity. The IIRM had been excluded from the New York parade the year before because the parade committee really hadn't a clue who they were. But there were no such excuses now. The upstarts were in the parade—due to be led by the first ever woman grand marshal, Dorothy Hayden Cudahy. They were assigned very last place in the roughly five-hour human chain along Fifth Avenue. But they were refused permission by the parade committee to carry a banner. Still, this was progress of sorts. There was much joking about saving the best, if illicit, wine until last.

The *New York Times* ran another big story as did numerous other publications including *Time* magazine which splashed a story headed: "The Re-Greening of America." *Time* saw a better side to the undocumented story in the revitalizing of old rundown city neighborhoods but paid particular attention to the political clout which the young newcomers were bringing to bear.

"When the Irish get together," the story reported, "many U.S. politicians listen. Boston's Mayor Raymond Flynn last year announced that 'the welcome mat is out' for Irish aliens and has created an office to provide immigrants with legal aid. The administration of New York Mayor Ed Koch declared that the Irish aliens 'have nothing to fear in utilizing fully the services of the city.'" The story also credited the "Irish lobby" and Irish "political ties" with much of the shaking up of immigration legislation by Washington. The "new wave of Irish immigrants" was "showing its muscle."

The *New York Times* highlighted the IIRM's push for Berman Visa applications but stressed the clear difficulties: 20,000 visas, one application per person, 162 eligible countries and as many as eight million applications expected. It was clear that the Irish, who had swamped the multi-application Donnelly program, were facing a Mount Everest this time around.

But the Berman program, Pat Hurley told *Times* reporter Celestine Bohlen, was only part of the IIRM's long-term strategy. Hurley's name had been long out in the open. Now his face was revealed too, but only to those who knew him. The *Times* report carried a photo showing Hurley himself being photographed for a Berman application at an IIRM-sponsored application drive. The caption simply called him "an Irish immigrant." That he was.

Charles Haughey arrived in Washington for St. Patrick's Day. But plans for the annual presentation of a bowl of shamrock to President Bush were rather spoiled by the INS which, with uncanny timing, gave a number of illegal Irish a St. Patrick's Day greeting they were unlikely to forget. Hours before Haughey's arrival, six young Irish women working in a Boston bar were led out of the premises in handcuffs. Four men, meanwhile, were detained on a construction site in New Hampshire. They ended up in prison garb before being placed, again handcuffed, on a TWA flight to London out of Boston's Logan Airport. It was all highly embarrassing for Haughey. The shamrock diplomacy was looking rather withered as opposition politicians back in Ireland made hay with a vengeance.

Progressive Democrat TD Bobby Molloy, a onetime member of Haughey's Fianna Fáil, described Haughey's American visit as "a disgrace" in the light of the arrests.

The *Irish Press*, in a front page report, had Molloy pouring scorn on Haughey at a time when thousands of Irish were being forced to live as undocumented immigrants. "Mr. Haughey made cynical use of the passport in the last general election campaign implying that he was concerned at the plight of the Irish in America. Yet he continues to refuse any financial assistance to organizations like the Irish Immigration Reform Movement."

Molloy claimed that the IIRM was being forced to take second place to the professional fundraising of Noraid "which Mr. Haughey and Mr. Reynolds, the Finance Minister, apparently support." It was a low blow. Haughey was furious. To top things off, the IIRM was demanding that he put aside the shamrock and ask the American president to intervene directly on behalf of the detained illegals.

It was all something of a best and worst of times. Hopes were rising because of the extended Donnelly and new Berman programs. Yet, all too many illegal Irish were now really feeling the sharp economic and psychological pinch from years of living in the shadows.

"Sometimes we just want to give up and return to Ireland," a young couple in Philadelphia told Pamela Heneghan, the *Irish Echo*'s correspondent in the "City of Brotherly Love." Others were telling Heneghan about living in rat-infested housing, "some of the lads" getting so sick they had to go back to Ireland. Another couple with a young child and no medical coverage spoke of worrying every time the baby so much as coughed. It sounded like the nineteenth century.

The INS, meanwhile, was apparently increasing the pressure. There were unusual instances of Irish celebrities being prevented from entering the U.S. due to a new law which required visiting artists to meet the requirements of having an international reputation, being commercially successful and possessing "outstanding merit and ability." Subjective judgments all, but enough to stop well known (in Irish circles at least) Irish country singer Glen Curtin cold at Kennedy Airport. Up and coming Irish middle distance runner, Paul Donovan, a student at the University of Arkansas, was also prevented from returning to the U.S. when he was stopped in his tracks at St. Louis airport.

Stories such as these were nothing compared to an occurrence in early May when allegedly thirty-six armed immigration agents sealed off a Manhattan street and subway station in a dawn swoop on Irish employees arriving for work at a van hire company. What ensued was like a scene from a Keystone Cops movie with agents and workers running in all directions, the latter being described later by their lawyer as being "like chickens without heads." Six arrests were made. One man arrested was a very angry customer in search of a van hire, not a police cruiser. The other five were Irish, two legal and three illegals. The INS denied the figure of thirty-six agents and claimed only eight were involved in an "educational and informational visit" mounted as part of the service's task of enforcing the law. The IIRM erupted, describing the INS action as "outrageous." The *Irish Echo*, in an editorial, stated that the agents would be better employed chasing drug pushers.

The numbers of illegals arriving, meanwhile, continued to rise, even taking into account the wide disparity in the estimates of total numbers held by the INS and Irish government on one side, and the IIRM on the other. On top of this, early indications of what the Berman Visa lottery would bring were not good for the Irish. By the end of May over 3.2 million applications were stored in a warehouse outside Washington. The first three winners were from Pakistan, Iran and Kuwait. It sure didn't look promising from an Irish perspective. (Indeed, the Berman Visa scheme was a bust for the Irish. In all, only 205 visas were awarded to Irish applicants, in the course of the two-year program, out of the total of 20,000 visas on offer.)

Back in Ireland, meanwhile, Charles Haughey called an election for June 15. The IIRM resolved to make government financing of the reform cause in the U.S. an issue at the polls. Election-inspired lip service was no longer enough.

On the eve of the vote, the U.S. Senate Judiciary Committee approved a compromise immigration bill concocted by Kennedy, Simpson and Paul Simon of Illinois. The latter had mounted a successful assault on the English language provision in the points system visas held over from the 1988 Kennedy/Simpson bill. Oddly, in the vote on English, Kennedy did not vote against Simon's move. The only two negative votes in a 12-2 approval came from Simpson and Senator Strom Thurmond of South Carolina. The IIRM was disturbed and puzzled. A Kennedy spokesman explained that the English language provision had become a cumbersome obstacle to progress.

The bill offered 54,000 independent visas to be awarded in a points system based on age, education and special skills. Reform campaigners saw this as being a long way short of the Holy Grail. The Irish Consulate in New York was more sanguine. "The overall viability of the bill is considerably enhanced as a result of the compromise. The independent category remains untouched, and the bill provides a review of the immigration system," commented press officer Gerry Corr.

The bill was passed by the full Senate on July 13 by 81–17. The Irish American newspapers were not so taken by the turn of events. One report described passage of the bill as a "minor boost." However, the final version approved was slightly different to that passed by the Judiciary Committee. A number of amendments had been made, including one with a distinct Irish imprint on it.

By this time, the IIRM had an extensive network of nationwide branches with activists in virtually every major city. Chicago had a branch and it had made itself known to Senator Simon. Eugene Nestor, chairman of the Chicago branch, and the Rev. Dave Dillon buttonholed Simon at a fundraiser and persuaded him to meet them again to discuss the immigration bill. That meeting took place in Chicago in the rear seat of a chauffeured limousine. "We explained our situation to him and the ways in which his bill was hurting us. We told him that the twenty points in the independent category for English skills, which were deleted from Kennedy/Simpson as part of the compromise bill, raised the qualifying threshold way over our heads," Nestor later said.

Simon was sympathetic. He admitted to a false belief that the Irish had done well under the amnesty provisions of the 1986 act. Nestor and Dillon set his mind straight on that score. Simon didn't shower his Irish interlocutors with legislative candy but he did make a couple of post limo-ride changes. The Senate bill allowed for 10,000 of the annual 54,000 independent visas to be distributed over a three-year period to the thirty-six so-called disadvantaged countries. This at least gave some Irish a slightly better chance of securing one. Additionally, Simon's second amendment would offer fifteen points to applicants with guaranteed employment in the U.S., a move which gave undocumented Irish a possible edge over likely applicants still in Ireland itself, although there was now a diminishing number of those. Figures released in early September by the Irish government revealed that in the twelve-month period up to April 15, 1989, 46,000 people had quit the country. This was the highest annual emigration figure since the 1950s. It was enough to show up in the national demographics. Ireland's population was now falling. The government, however, expressed optimism that job creation plans in the pipeline would arrest the decline.

The House Immigration Sub-Committee, now chaired by Connecticut Democrat Bruce Morrison, met to consider testimony from various advocacy groups in early October. Morrison had first been elected to the House of Representatives in 1982. His interest in Ireland remained fairly dormant for his first couple of terms despite his Ulster Protestant roots. But he traveled to Ireland in 1987 with a congressional fact-finding delegation. The trip was sponsored by the Irish American Unity Conference, one of the more consistently active lobby groups on Northern Ireland. The North was the main focus of the visit but in meeting with U.S. diplomats at the embassy in Dublin, Morrison began to hear another story, one of an increasing flow of young, skilled Irish people who were heading to the U.S. and not coming back. They weren't all heading for Connecticut but Morrison's district was in the north east, in a state sandwiched between the next parishes of Boston and New York. He listened intently to the tale related by the diplomats.

By the time the fall hearings of 1988 took place before the House Immigration Sub-Committee, Morrison was a member by virtue of first having been elected to the full Judiciary Committee. He was rather in the background though, deferential to the more senior figures such as Roman Mazzoli.

But Don Martin and his lecture about all the Irish winners of the Congressional Medal of Honor brought the Connecticut representative bolt upright in his seat.

"I remember Martin testifying about the Medal of Honor winners," Morrison would later say. "That particular moment crystallized it for me. It was a very important moment for me." Morrison's Ulster Protestant blood was now well and truly up.

So it was fortuitous for the IIRM that, exactly one year later, the same Don Martin sat before the Sub-Committee now chaired by Morrison. Martin also had acquired a title: IIRM Political Action Coordinator.

On behalf of the IIRM, Martin proposed a "diversity" visa program which would last for at least a decade. Under the scheme, 60,000 visas would be allocated each year to the thirty-six countries hard done by in the 1965 act. An additional 20,000 visas a year would be set aside for countries deemed underrepresented, Ireland being included in this category, certainly at the outset. An additional 20,000 would be awarded to all the remaining countries. The diversity visas would be given out on the basis of a points system with points being awarded for age, education and, in a proposal clearly close to Martin's heart, on the basis of knowledge of U.S. government and history.

The IIRM wasn't finished yet. It proposed an annual allotment of 30,000 "replenishment" visas for the thirty-six countries which would not be tied to the points system. And in a statement of its all-Ireland yet pragmatic character, it proposed a special allocation of 7,000 visas annually for Northern Ireland. It was a series of proposals that were quite sweeping to say the least. If the Sub-Committee wanted to know what the Irish shopping list was, here it was in all its almost cheeky detail. By contrast, the various other groups testifying at the hearing pleaded largely for maintenance of the status quo especially with regard to family reunification. Martin went so far as to promise rebuttal testimony against this position. The IIRM was showing its teeth to potentially powerful friends or formidable enemies. It was a tactic not without risk.

"There appears to be a strong feeling in Congress that there's a need for reform to benefit independent immigrants," Martin said after the hearing. With regard to the Sub-Committee chairman at least, Martin wasn't far off the mark.

Martin's new title was reflective of an organization that had quickly shed its barricades image and was now operating simultaneously in various locations and at a number of levels. The IIRM now boasted a National Chairman in Sean Minihane. But if barricade polemics were required, Pat Hurley was always close at hand. A kind of minister without portfolio, Hurley shared Martin's emotional commitment to the idea of reform. The overall formula was seemingly working.

As Martin was testifying in Washington, two other IIRM "leaders"—the group was fairly loosely constructed in this regard—were heading for Dublin and a meeting with Bill Griffith, Head of Consular Affairs at the U.S. Embassy. Jim Larkin, Connecticut-based North East Regional Director and John Dillon, National Public

Relations Officer, discussed the immigration situation with Griffith during a meeting that lasted almost three hours. Dillon and Larkin were presenting Griffith with evidence they said backed up allegations that consular staff at the embassy were harassing Donnelly Visa applicants. Griffith vehemently denied this but did make the point that not a few interviewees arrived at the embassy with something of an "attitude." The meeting went well enough, not least because there were no Irish with attitudes in the room. All three men were American, a fact which was not going unnoticed. The IIRM had clearly been successful in building a bridge to Irish America. As such, it could not now be ignored when it came calling on either side of the Atlantic.

"Our meeting created a tone of cooperation with the embassy," Larkin, whose very name carried some cachet in Dublin, remarked afterwards.

Back in New York, IIRM contacts with various congressmen were bearing fall fruit. Representatives Eliot Engel and Charles "Chuck" Schumer, from the Bronx and Brooklyn respectively, indicated that they would be introducing bills containing independent visa categories. Schumer said he was distressed that the Berman scheme hadn't done more for the Irish and that he wanted to see more Irish come to the U.S. Significantly, Schumer expressed his thoughts after meeting with a delegation from the now ubiquitous IIRM. Brian Donnelly, meanwhile, was proposing to extend the NP-5 Donnelly program for an additional five years.

In Ireland, Foreign Minister Gerry Collins was telling the Dáil that November that the U.S. embassy had handed over 10,000 visas to Irish applicants that year. In New York, two young Irish women were sitting in a U.S. government car in handcuffs, being driven from the Bronx to INS offices in downtown Manhattan. One was in tears. She was a sensitive type and crying came easily. But she was now possessed by another emotion—anger. She was, as she would later say, feeling "madder and madder." It was a collective feeling now among the new Irish. They were, to borrow a phrase, sick and tired, mad as hell and weren't going to take it anymore.

But things would invariably get worse before they got better. Before the year was out, seven young Irish were detained by the INS as they appeared in a court in the Boston district of Brighton. The seven had been arrested following disturbances at a Halloween party. But the arrival of the INS prompted allegations that the feds had been tipped off by Brighton police. The complaint quickly found its way to Mayor Raymond Flynn's office where protecting the rights of the illegal Irish had the status of a solemn pledge. In San Francisco, three Irish illegals were detained at gunpoint by INS agents. There would be later denials by the INS regarding guns, but the agency was too slow off the mark. All INS statements now had to be cleared through Washington. The IIRM was much quicker to the trigger. The guns story took hold in the wider Irish American imagination despite the denial.

There was no Christmas package for the Irish that year from Congress. Indeed, House action on the various proposed bills had been put off until the New Year, in fact, as it was to be, the new decade. The paramount Irish story of the 1980s, one which had increasingly sidelined even Northern Ireland in the Irish American press, was about to spill over into the 1990s, the era of Mary Robinson, the diaspora, Bill Clinton and, in large measure, the time in which thousands of Irish would come to realize that they owed their life in America to a handful of well disposed politicians and a band of amateur lobbyists who had long since passed the point of ever taking no for an answer.

6

THE LONG LAST HURRAH

"We're the next parish all right—to every country with an airport."

Bruce Morrison.

The dawning of the 1990s ushered in what was to be a decade of dramatic change in Ireland, change in more than just appearances. The years ahead would unleash Mary Robinson, Bishop Casey, Jack Charlton, Veronica Guerin. There would be the uncovering of widespread criminal activity and corruption in Irish society, a cultural and economic revival and profound changes in the way southern Irish society viewed both itself and the world beyond its front door. North of the border there would be more of the same, a peace process and yet more of the same. Some historians might argue in the future that in the last ten years of the century, the island of Ireland was going through its very own version of the 1960s.

But for many of the young Irish in America, the passing of 1989 merely underlined the fact that they were entering a second decade locked outside the American Pale. Ironically, the cynicism many were now tempted to embrace would ultimately find aid and succor in more traditional forces—veteran politicians, established members of what was a still broadly conservative Irish and Irish American community, and, by no means least, the Catholic Church.

The church's role in Catholic Irish American society had been in many ways similar to that of the church back in Ireland itself. It was a communal bind, a bulwark against unfamiliar, and oft-perceived alien forces. In some respects, it held an even tighter grip on the faithful than the church in Ireland. It had to. America was both the land of greatest opportunity and the most formidable competition. It was also the land of near ultimate free speech, so there were critics in abundance, some of them especially vocal.

Adrian Flannelly, radio broadcaster and voice of record for the Irish community in New York since 1970, had been aware of the illegals problem since the beginning of the '80s. By the middle of the decade, Flannelly, whose rather droll and world-weary commentary provided listeners with relief from the endless pep and pop of mainstream radio, had found his whipping boy: the church. Flannelly told his listeners that the church was forgetting the Irish in favor of what were now more numerous Catholic ethnic immigrant groups.

Flannelly's criticism of the church's apparent failure to draw its crozier in defense of the arriving Irish could have been dismissed had he not put his sweat where his words were. When the first batch of Donnelly visa applications were being accepted in Washington, Flannelly drove south with his daughter Linda in a station wagon. In the back were 68,000 Donnelly applications from Irish hopefuls, mailed into the Adrian Flannelly Show at the Mayo-native's urging.

Flannelly was traveling as a journalist. The applications were being accepted from the stroke of midnight. When father and daughter arrived at the designated post office there was, as Flannelly puts it, "a line half-way around Washington D.C." Flannelly flashed his press ID and drove through the security cordon. Linda did the rest. The Irish applications were first into the mix. A number of lawyers were on hand and spotted Flannelly's caper. There was something of an uproar and for a moment Flannelly feared arrest. But they managed to bluff it out and escape into the night. It's impossible to assess accurately the exact effect of the midnight drive of Adrian Flannelly, but the Irish would ultimately look back on the Donnelly program with considerable satisfaction.

Flannelly's harping on the church continued on the air. At lunch one day in Tommy Makem's Irish Pavilion, a popular Manhattan Irish hostelry, Flannelly was approached by a man wearing a suit and a frown.

"I known who you are and Monsignor Murray is very annoyed with you," Flannelly recalls the man as saying. The man was James Hallisey, legal counsel for the Archdiocese of New York.

Murray, Executive Director of Catholic Charities, was well aware of Flannelly's criticism and was ready to meet his tormentor and talk business.

The church's position on immigration was something of an attempt to be all things to all men. Usually speaking through Archbishop Theodore McCarrick of Newark, the U.S. Catholic bishops had been urging an extension of the alien amnesty program, preservation of family reunification laws and separate legislation to deal with the undocumented, Irish included, who had entered the U.S. after the amnesty cutoff date. To the Irish faithful at least, the church hierarchy in America still sounded very green by name at least. But the cold fact was that most illegal aliens streaming into the U.S. during the 1980s were Catholic and most definitely not Irish. Mother Church had a large and diverse family to look after. The Irish would simply have to wait their turn at the table. But when Flannelly and Murray got together, that turn suddenly seemed a good deal closer.

The spring of 1987 saw Flannelly, the non-conformist, and Murray, the highly placed clerical trooper, meet to discuss what needed to be done. What emerged was the idea to bring over a number of priests from Ireland to work in specific parishes so that the new Irish might feel a little more at home. Beyond that, a new department would be set up in the archdiocese to act as a cushion for the Irish when they felt things slipping beneath them. Thus was born Project Irish Outreach. Cardinal John O'Connor, whose Irish roots were now being tugged at rather more than his Austrian ones, gave his nod of approval. O'Connor was well aware of the problem by now and had been in direct correspondence with Taoiseach Charles Haughey and President Reagan regarding the undocumented Irish and the obstacles they were facing.

In one letter to Reagan, O'Connor "invited" the gipper's attention "in a special way" to the undocumented Irish. O'Connor, whose generally conservative outlook was close to that of Reagan, wasn't shy about asking for favors. In the letter he requested an "Executive Order" granting amnesty to the illegal Irish.

Adrian Flannelly, meanwhile, was named first coordinator for PIO but felt he had other fish to fry. He managed to get a temporary replacement for what he describes as a nominal fee. Looking back, it now seems odd that a man with such an acid tongue when it came to the Catholic Church should have administered an arm of that same institution, if only for a few weeks. But that's just what Malachy McCourt, stage partner and brother of author Frank, did. Flannelly remembers memos from McCourt which were anything but holy in tone. But Project Irish Outreach was underway, even if there was a rogue at the helm.

Flannelly traveled to Ireland with Murray in September, 1987 in search of Irish chaplains and political comfort. Flannelly knew that both he and McCourt were not the kind of people that the distraught would want to meet with on a Monday morning in PIO's office. He suggested Patricia O'Callaghan, who had worked with Flannelly on his radio show, to Murray during the Irish visit. Flannelly called O'Callaghan in New York and told her to catch the earliest flight. She did. O'Callaghan was probably the only Irish person at the time who left the U.S. to be interviewed in Ireland for a U.S. job.

Flannelly and Murray's contacts with Irish political leaders also resulted in the setting up of the Immigration Working Committees in Irish consulates. And there was to be more. Flannelly, a founder member of the IIRM, didn't see the organization as having a lengthy shelf life and saw the need for a parallel group working alongside. The long-term outcome of such thinking was the Emerald Isle Immigration Center in New York, chaired by attorney Brian O'Dwyer, son of veteran civil rights lawyer and Democratic politician Paul O'Dwyer, and the Irish Apostolate of Brooklyn and Queens. The Emerald Isle Center was a prototype which now has equivalents in several cities. In addition to facilitating links with Irish politicians, Flannelly was a collarless door opener for Murray when it came to meeting those he describes as "political heavies" such as Ted Kennedy and Senator Alfonse D'Amato. In turn, Flannelly got to buttonhole Irish bishops and plead the case for direct assistance from the Irish hierarchy.

Flannelly, divorced and secular in outlook to put it mildly, was finding a new respect for the church or as he put it himself: "I had a newly regained respect for the collar. It was amazing to my mother."

Flannelly, to this day, believes that the IIRM would never have taken off without the support of the church. He takes the view that church backing also served to parry criticism of the upstarts from within the established Irish community and convert this to outright support. Even looking specifically at the IIRM, Flannelly's view is that the "real founder" of the group was Fr. Matt Fitzgerald.

By the end of the decade, the church's role, apparent and real, had turned 180 degrees. The church's new activities also began to generate considerable press coverage. The first immigration chaplain, Fr. Martin Keveny, arrived in early 1988. He was quickly followed by Frs. Michael Harrison, Joe Delaney and Sr. Lucia Brady. Irish kids who had grown up in Ireland hearing about exploits of Irish priests, brothers and nuns in remote corners of the earth were now, in an ironic twist, becoming the focus of a new wave of urban missionaries.

And there was work to be done in well-off, Christian America. Nobody was starving but there was anguish and loneliness aplenty. An example was the young Irish nanny who would call Project Irish Outreach several times a week as 1990 took root. Those calls, along with occasional trips to the supermarket, were the highlights of a life dominated by endless hours caring for the children of a career couple in prosperous Westchester County. She was paid a pittance and was required to start work at 7:26 a.m. every morning. As the anonymous nanny told Margaret Curley of the *Irish Voice*: "Not 7:25 a.m. or 7:28 a.m., it was 7:26 a.m." Back in Ireland, Mary Robinson was calling the women of Ireland to her banner. Some of those women, "Mná na hÉireann" as Robinson put it, would have been only too glad if they had a vote, could afford the airfare home or even a moment to contemplate politics, close by or far away. But for a diaper wielding army of young Irish women in the United States, it might as well have been 1890.

How big an army? Uncle Sam wanted to know. Officials from the U.S. Census Bureau had met with Irish immigrant advocates in the summer of 1989 in an effort to spur on Irish illegals to fill in the April 1990 census form, stressing that it was in strictest confidence. Such government concern over numbers was mirrored in the actions of the INS, although in a different way. The Irish had been detained at work and now it was to be at rest and play. In mid-January 1990, INS agents, acting on what they said was a tip off regarding an individual, raided an apartment in San Francisco where a group of young Irish men were sitting down to dinner. Three were arrested. "It's fierce bad to hear an informer turned in one of the boys. The government didn't ask the Irish their immigration status when they shipped them off to Korea and Vietnam," local Irish businessman Louis Roche told Marsha Smith of the *Irish Echo*. (What Roche may not have been aware of was that the U.S. government still expected male immigrants, even undocumented overstays, between the ages of eighteen and twenty-six to register under the Selective Services Act, which, in a time of crisis would revert to what it really was: the registration for the draft. Some illegal Irish did register and received a draft card which served as a potentially useful ID, especially when combined with a driving license.)

The IIRM's Jim Larkin was incensed over the San Francisco arrests. "I'm steamed," he said. "The Irish cannot afford to wait another twenty-five years for immigration reform."

Whatever about reform, there was at least money on the way from Dublin. After dodging the issue for the previous couple of years, Finance Minister Albert Reynolds set aside a little over $300,000 in his budget estimates for Irish immigrants in the U.S., including the IIRM. The IIRM, however, was wary. It had set itself up as a lobbying group in Washington and did not want to be seen in any way as an agent for what one IIRM spokesman described as a "foreign government." The air that spring was indeed heavy with irony.

Bruce Morrison, poised to introduce a bill of his own before the House of Representatives, was urging the IIRM to step up that very lobbying on behalf of Brian Donnelly's bill which, by mid-February, had picked up only twenty co-sponsors. Much of the IIRM's effort at this time was aimed at milking St. Patrick's Day to the very last drop. The group's public relations officer, John Dillon, was setting his sights anything but low with one month to go before the big day. "Our goal," he said, "is to get our message across to fifty million people through a combination of local and national media outlets." Dillon was aiming at the TV networks and editorial boards. Contact had been made over a period of months with roughly two hundred of the latter. The main effort was being concentrated on papers covering districts of key congressional legislators. The IIRM, in other words, had a hit list.

On February 21, Morrison's Immigration Sub-Committee met to hear submissions from mostly government witnesses including INS Commissioner Gene McNary. McNary was largely in favor of the Kennedy/Simpson Senate bill but that legislation was no longer alone in the world. Bills from Reps. Brian Donnelly, Lamar Smith, Hamilton Fish and Howard Berman were also in the mix. Charles Schumer and Eliot Engel were also promising bills while Bruce Morrison's proposal, the "Family Unity and Employment Opportunity Immigration Act of 1990," appeared imminent. Morrison, who had by now declared his candidacy for the governorship of Connecticut, wanted to see a unified bill marked up by the Sub-

Committee by March 14. Naturally, he wanted it to reflect his own bill which was offering something to everybody including 25,000 visas annually for fiscal years 1992-94 to those who entered before January 1, 1990. These visas would be distributed between the now well-known thirty-six disadvantaged countries.

"My proposal is a comprehensive package of immigration reforms which will unify families, identify labor needs and raise revenues to educate and train U.S. workers for the jobs of the future," Morrison told the *Irish Echo*'s Debbie McGoldrick.

Morrison's family roots endowed him with an immediate aura of sympathy for the Irish cause. "As soon as he was appointed chairman we knew we had to be close to him," Sean Minihane later recalled.

Morrison's good intentions towards the Irish were for real, but as he was now a leading power broker in the immigration debate with a gubernatorial campaign to run as well, Morrison was receiving support from and listening to, not just Irish advocates, but also Hispanic and Asian groups.

Morrison had early on spotted what he believed was a flaw in IIRM strategy, what he would describe as an "us and them attitude." Morrison remembers: "I talked about this with them over the years. By 1989 I was able to set the tone but at the beginning it was different. I told the IIRM that their presentation had a racial tone, that it was strategically flawed. There were enough anti-immigration advocates against everybody and the IIRM needed support from pro-immigration groups. I told them there were only two sides to the immigration debate, for it and against it. In the end, there was greater cooperation between the Irish and both Asian and Hispanic groups."

Sean Minihane would put it in more cautious words. It was, in his view, a case of to each his own. "Asians and Latinos were more interested in family preference. We couldn't object to that because we wanted to keep them away from what we wanted."

What the IIRM wanted was best said in a banner which, after a fair degree of wrangling with organizers, was about to be unfurled in the New York St. Patrick's Day Parade. It would read quite simply: "Immigration Reform Now." The IIRM's banner in the parade, which was duplicated and given to other marching contingents, and a second "Mass of Hope" the night before, constituted the highlights for March. In Washington, meanwhile, Bruce Morrison's bill, H.R. 4300, was getting tied up in procedural wrangling and undergoing a number of changes. It was finally reported out of the Sub-Committee in mid-April by a vote of six to four. The new version proposed 75,000 visas for fiscal 1991–93 to the thirty-six countries plus a diversity visa program—the brainchild of Brooklyn's Charles Schumer—to follow.

The next hurdle to cross was the House Judiciary Committee where opposition lurked in the form of Texan Lamar Smith among others. The *Irish Echo* came out with a rare front page editorial which stated that it was now "crunch time" for immigration reform.

"Roughly, between now and October, either a significant bill will pass or there may be a long, long wait for immigration reform," the editorial, written by editor John Thornton, stated. And perhaps sensing a change of mood in Washington, it continued: "Washington, like most centers of power, acts on public issues in a sort of cyclical fashion. Immigration has been to the fore as an issue for several years. Now there is a sense that the powers that be in the Capitol are tiring of the issue."

The IIRM wasn't tiring. In response to the favorable Sub-Committee report it was planning to step up a nationwide write-your-representative campaign. Lamar Smith was singled out for particular attention. There was a significant Irish American population in Texas but as was the case throughout much of the south and west, it was a little far removed in both space and time from immediate and contemporary Irish affairs. Still, there was more than enough Irish at the Alamo to pepper a Pat Hurley speech.

Morrison too was keeping his hand firmly on his legislative musket even while running for the State House in Hartford. "People have asked why should they want me to be governor of Connecticut when the (immigration) issue gets decided in Washington, but I say that I've now got one hell of a deadline to work with to get the job done," he told supporters at an Irish American fundraiser in support of his campaign held in New York in early May.

Morrison was urging even greater grassroots effort and went out of his way to congratulate the IIRM for having "recast this issue." The IIRM, he said, had "killed off the notion that giving an opportunity to the Irish or Poles is in any way contradictory with groups which favor family reunification." This was the candidate speaking and in retrospect it would appear fortuitous that Morrison was wearing two hats at the time. Other powerful immigration lobby groups were effectively feeding messages through him to the Irish. By hook or by crook, an alliance was forming with Morrison at the center. Morrison, at the fundraiser, concluded with fighting words: "Before I get to the governor's chair the buck stops at immigration reform, and I'm going to see that we get it and legalize the Irish."

Getting it would take a while. The summer dragged on. Congress went into recess, came out and went into recess again with no action before the Judiciary Committee. Lamar Smith was getting a lot of mail with Irish names in the return address space but he wasn't budging apparently. The Republican was becoming a prominent rallying point for the anti-immigration members, a counterpoint to Morrison. At the same time, twenty-six members of the house had now added their signatures to Morrison's bill. Joe Kennedy was the latest as Americans downed tools to celebrate Independence Day. July's main news was that the deep well of hope provided by the NP-5 Donnelly Visa scheme was about to dry up. Whatever happened now, just about anything would be good for the Irish.

In early August, just before Congress adjourned for a month, Morrison's bill finally came before the Judiciary Committee, chaired by a not entirely unsympathetic Jack Brooks, a Texas Democrat. His fellow Texan, Lamar Smith was not giving any clear ground despite the lobbying campaign directed by the IIRM and now also the Ancient Order of Hibernians. But even against the efforts of opponents, the bill passed by 23–12 and was now destined for the House floor in September.

The IIRM, meanwhile, was already looking ahead to a successful passage. But that would not be the end of the tale. President Bush had the power to say yes or deliver a veto and it was known that he favored the Kennedy/Simpson bill over the Morrison version. With that in mind, the IIRM had launched "Project One Million," an ambitious plan to cram the White House mail box with a million postcards urging the president to lend his weight to the reform effort and sign any bill passed by Congress. The *Irish Echo* included the postcards in its August 8-14 issue. On the front page, publisher Claire O'Gara Grimes urged readers to send in the cards. "The significance should not go unnoticed that this year the Ellis Island Immigrant Museum will open its doors for our reflection and gratitude. Today that immigration station does not hold the key to the future. H.R. 4300 does. I implore all our readers to mail the IIRM's postcard . . ."

Not only George Bush was feeling the heat. One member of Congress, yet another from Texas, had caused a storm during the Judiciary Committee debate. John Bryant, a Democrat, had let it rip even as the opposition's rampart was crumbling. "Why do we have Irish amnesty in this bill? Is that consistent with the notion of diversity? Do we need more Irish people that look just like me, look just like (Bruce) Morrison, look just like (Lamar) Smith to encourage ethnic diversity in this country? I do not think so." They were in fact pertinent questions. Bryant was, by his own description, Scots Irish by descent. But he was a law and order man first. He described the proposed visas in the Morrison bill for Ireland and the other thirty-five countries as effectively an "amnesty" for the Irish. "These folks," he said, had come to the country illegally. "They are working and because they have some friends in Congress they are going to get to stay here, and that is the only thing that is at stake, that is the only reason why that (the visa provision) is in this bill and that is not the way to make immigration policy."

"These folks" were now distinctly unhappy campers. "Texas has the fourth largest Irish population in the country and we will be publicizing the attitudes of Congressman Bryant when election time draws near," said the IIRM's Jim Larkin.

Against the flood of critical reaction, Bryant appeared to bend a little and conceded that he might not have all the facts at his fingertips. He said he would sit down with anyone who wanted to discuss the bill with him and was always willing to reassess his position if new facts warranted it. There were quite a few willing to sit with Rep. Bryant and bend his ear. Not just Irish lobbyists but also Italian, Polish, Slavic and others.

But that was one fight in Texas. The way things were shaping up in Washington it was starting to look like 1988 all over again. So much to do, so little time before Congress rushed home for elections.

September saw America's immigrant past celebrated in the reopening of a refurbished Ellis Island in New York harbor. Vice-President Dan Quayle turned up. Barbara Walters spoke proudly of her Russian roots and the entire affair was presided over by Lee Iacocca who had been given the task of turning a ruin into tourist hot spot. A number of immigrants who had passed through the Ellis Island station years before were honored that breezy, warm day. Among them was Johanna Flaherty, a sprightly eighty-four-year-old Irish woman who had first set eyes on America on a hot

August afternoon in 1923. Johanna's voyage across the Atlantic had been rough and the food on board varied from bad to downright lousy. But she was young, adventurous, hopeful. Most importantly, America wanted her and her Uncle Pat who made the voyage with her. But now, America wasn't quite so sure any more. Many undocumented Irish who read reports of the jamboree on the island that was once so symbolic of an open-armed America, couldn't avoid grasping at the new contradictions. There was more than a tinge of resentment. Why them and not us?

There was emotion in Ellis Island that day. In Washington, the prose was colder, the talk of quotas, visas, labor shortages, points systems. It didn't quite match the hype and the legacy swirling around in the harbor breezes.

Three thousand miles away, the Irish government was drawing up a study of the situation as it now stood. Again, the language was terse, academic. But the report's conclusion revealed some sense of urgency. "The Embassy at Washington," it stated, "will impress on our friends on the Hill our concerns regarding a relatively speedy passage of an agreed measure during this session of Congress." So there was a kind of link between past and present. It was the word "passage." In Johanna's time it referred to a voyage. In 1990, it translated into successful political action by the ship of state.

But success was still proving elusive. The 101st Congress was back in session after its high summer hiatus. As well as John Bryant, Lamar Smith was still cutting up rough over a number of Morrison bill proposals, particularly the 75,000 greencards which were now being dubbed "transition" visas. If Ellis Island was a world away from Ireland, Texas was another world away from Ellis Island in those early days of fall.

"While we accept as many immigrants as the rest of the world combined, we cannot accept everyone who wants to make a better life in the U.S.," a Smith spokesman said.

Bryant, still smarting from a torrent of criticism from his "look just like me" remarks, was holding fast to his opposing position. "The congressman sees no reason to change his position on the bill. It's a logical position because the immigration system which would exist under Morrison's bill is not in keeping with public policy," said his spokesman.

By this stage, mid-September, there were thirty-one co-sponsors of Morrison's bill and about as many days to go in the life of the

101st Congress. And there were other issues jumping the line in Washington. Saddam Hussein had made his move into Kuwait and the midnight oil, some of it Kuwaiti in origin, was burning in Washington. Saddam was lucky not to be the target of an IIRM smart letter blitz.

As was the case a couple of years previously, an Irish Foreign Minister, this time Gerry Collins, arrived at the eleventh hour to lend his weight to the argument. Collins, known for lengthy, impassioned speeches (he once rambled on at a New York Irish Consulate reception for an astonishing forty minutes), met with all the key legislators and came out sticking to that old standby, cautious optimism. "There is lots of goodwill going for us and lots of people who are committed to helping us as best they can," he said while attending the opening of the United Nations General Assembly in New York.

September turned into October and like the first gale of autumn, the immigration debate flared full force in the House of Representatives on Tuesday, October 2: "Why even waste our time on a bill that is going nowhere?" Rep. Gerald Solomon, a New York Republican, wasn't singing an Irish song when he delivered his view on H.R. 4300, known by now, more or less, as the Morrison Bill. Solomon's wisdom was to be disputed but he had blown away one prevailing view—that all the opponents of a bill favorable to the Irish came from south of the Mason-Dixon Line.

In a ninety-minute debate everyone's knuckles were showing. The bill was good for America, bad for America, good for some, lousy for others. Amendments were offered, accepted and thrown out. At one point Bruce Morrison paid tribute to Brian Donnelly and Donnelly returned the compliment. The Irish were ganging together for all to see. It was a red rag to the bill's opponents. Tuesday's business came to an end. The debate resumed the following day.

John Bryant pitched his flag, looked at Bruce Morrison and saw his Santa Anna. He offered his amendment which was simple and to the point. Scrub every last line of the bill except the part dealing with family reunification. Bryant criticized the bill for being a sop to Europe. It was nothing more than "a patchwork of special interest pleadings." There were more than enough House members with special interests close to their hearts to defeat Bryant's last throw of the dice.

In the end, as it always does, it came down to a vote. Morrison appeared confident. He knew the numbers. The bill was passed by 231-192 and went on to House Senate Conference for reconciliation with the Kennedy/Simpson measure. Heading for the conference table were transition visas, diversity visas, employment visas and a few more Donnelly Visas for some who lost out due to technicalities. It was pretty much all that the Irish had hoped for at that stage of the dying congressional year.

The following Sunday, the *New York Times* reported celebration in the heavily Irish district of Woodside in Queens. "For the Irish," *Times* reporter Marvine Howe wrote, "the most important part of the Morrison bill is the section that allows virtual amnesty to all the illegal Irish immigrants in the country, and to aliens from some other Western European countries." The idea of "all the illegal Irish" was perhaps stretching it a bit. But at least all of them now felt that they had a chance, assuming that the House and Senate could agree and President Bush signed the compromise that would emerge as a result. Conferees met on October 9 and 11. There was near total meltdown on several issues. Alan Simpson was proving to be difficult. Information was scant but editorials in both the *Wall Street Journal* and *Washington Post* suggested that Simpson was putting the brakes on the reform bandwagon. The *Journal*, a consistently pro-immigration voice, lashed out at Simpson, accusing him of backing off even his own reform proposals of the year before. The senator from Wyoming struck back, accusing the *Journal* of being goofy and stupid. All the while, the adjournment date for Congress was being pushed back, first to October 19 and then to the 23rd, much to the relief of Irish observers. It didn't have to go that far. A result emerged on Friday, October 19—a perfect result.

An agreed package came out which guaranteed at least 48,000 visas ending up in Irish hands, although only Irish hands from the Republic, over the coming three years. Northern Ireland applicants would have to fight it out with the other disadvantaged countries for 90,000 other visas over the three-year period beginning in fiscal 1992, which began October 1, 1991. These newly agreed visas were not being called "transition visas" any more, but few Irish cared. They were very quickly dubbed "Morrison Visas." All that remained now was formal ratification by the House/Senate Conference Committee followed by rubber stamp votes in the House and Senate. Alan Simpson had rowed in after all and his support removed the fears of some that President Bush might wield his veto pen. It looked like a grand slam home run. "Victory," the *Irish Voice* roared on page one in extra large type. "Irish Get Green Light," the *Echo* trumpeted. The big battle appeared to be over. But everybody had forgotten Murphy's Law.

Bruce Morrison takes up the story: "It was a touch and go conference. There were many moments when it seemed that Senator Simpson was going to get up and walk away. But (Senator Edward) Kennedy was always there. He was very supportive. The bill could have fallen down numerous times. John Bryant made an attack on one of the visa categories.

"In deference to Simpson we gave him a stupid little provision to do with driving licenses with biometric information. It was related to the idea of identity cards only in a remote way. It seemed harmless."

It seemed. The provision allowed for a pilot program in three states. Drivers' licenses would contain personal information including fingerprints that could be used to meet work authorization requirements. Nobody really asked Simpson how seriously he felt about this matter. And it wasn't Simpson who reacted when the bill came back to the House and Senate. It passed the Senate 89–8 on Friday October 26. The House was a different story.

Morrison again: "All of a sudden, out of nowhere comes Ed Roybal, a senior (Democratic) member from California. He launched an attack on the bill because of the drivers' licenses provision. Republicans had been voting no in the conference stages even though the White House was broadly behind the bill and their opposition was expected. But now we had liberal Democrats voting no because of Roybal's objection."

Roybal, a leading member of the Hispanic Caucus, was in fact pulling in sufficient Hispanic and African members behind his assault on the provision to ensure its collapse. The bill fell in the House amid near total confusion. Morrison was stunned. In one way it look eerily similar to the last minute rejection of the 1988 amendments, a coup engineered by Brian Donnelly. But the reason for failure then was a move in support of the Irish. This latest shocker had nothing to with them at all.

At this point the House/Senate immigration bill conference had been permanently dissolved. There was no procedural way back. Any new bill could have been killed by filibuster given that Congress was almost stampeding out the door to go to the hustings. There was one chance left. Morrison approached Joe Moakley, the Massachusetts Democrat who was chairman of the Rules Committee. Simpson, meanwhile, was flabbergasted by the sudden turn of events in the House.

According to Morrison, Simpson was more goal-oriented than ideological. "When he heard what had happened he almost chided us for putting this thing in and immediately agreed that it could be dropped."

What to do? It was in Moakley's hands. Irish luck then began to cancel out Murphy's Law. It wasn't that Moakley was badly disposed towards the bill, it was more a case of time running out. However, Moakley owed Morrison a favor. Moakley had all along been concerned about the plight of refugees from the civil war in El Salvador. Morrison had approached him well before the latest crisis and offered to help with the Salvadorean issue. The favor was now coming back from Moakley rather more quickly than Morrison had anticipated.

Moakley could resurrect H.R. 4300 from the grave by virtue of a Concurrent Resolution which presented the bill once more to both House and Senate, only without the former sop to Simpson. The resolution was approved in the early hours of Saturday morning by a reconvened House/Senate conference committee. That afternoon, both chambers approved the resolution. The effect of this was that the bill, minus the offending line, could now be voted upon again. The Senate proved to be no obstacle and after about an hour's debate the House approved it 265–118 with support now from even the likes of Lamar Smith. The "Immigration Act of 1990" had entered the world by virtue of a political c-section. Thousands of Irish who had made landfall in America in the 1980s were suddenly being offered a huge helping hand, assuming George Bush's hand provided the presidential signature.

Again, the main Irish papers were reaching for the big headline. "It's Finally Over," was the *Echo*'s, more with relief than any sense of triumph. "Signed and Sealed," the *Voice* told its readers. The bill was being immediately assessed as the most wide ranging change in U.S. immigration law in twenty-five years.

To many Irish, however, it would now seem almost as long again before President Bush signed the bill into law with that backwards left-handed scrawl that reminded so many Americans of grade school. Indeed, a few weeks did drag by. But Bush did sign, in the White House Roosevelt Room on November 29. The signing ceremony took all of ten minutes. It would change the face of Irish America.

The Morrison Visas would be offered only to applicants from the Republic in the first year but twelve months after they came into being, another bill opened them to Northern Ireland applicants in the second and third year of the scheme. The Irish border didn't matter to the Irish immigration lobby so it was made to vanish, if only for a while, for the greater cause.

During the height of the battle for visas there was enormous disagreement on the issue of numbers. How many illegal Irish were there in the U.S.? It certainly paid off for the IIRM to top load that figure in the early days because big numbers attracted media attention. As legislative action gathered pace, however, the IIRM felt it necessary to cool its jets a bit. Too few illegals and nobody would care, but too many would scare off legislators. Still, there was no arguing with the numbers of visas finally given out: 18,363 Donnellys and 51,714 Morrisons. Added to this the 205 Berman Visas, which made recipients into virtual human collectors items, and a couple of thousand Schumer diversity visas. The total for all by end of 1997 was in the region of 72,000. Despite this obvious success, there are still undocumented Irish living in the U.S. and they continue to come, although in nothing like the numbers of the early 1980s.

A huge number of people put their shoulders to the Golden Door in the battle for Irish visas. For the IIRM it was a triumph, but the strains were telling by the end of the campaign. The leading figures of the Movement would go their separate ways as it caved in at the top, compressed by personal fatigue and some open hostility between founding members. But the Movement had remained cohesive for as long as it really mattered. And it certainly had answered the early skeptics.

"At the end of the day, we made a lot of people happy. They might not know it but we did," would be Mae O'Driscoll's take on it all. Sean Minihane would return to Ireland in time with thoughts still fresh of much personal sacrifice by the IIRM's volunteers.

Minihane believes that while the 1990 act was a singular triumph, the IIRM had ultimately failed in its original objective, which was to secure reform favorable to the Irish in virtual perpetuity. But he knows when to call it quits. "The IIRM was a clear example of how a few dedicated people, a hard core of political operatives, can have a real effect in the relatively open American system."

Bruce Morrison credits the IIRM with an enormous grassroots energy level which, in the end, simply proved too fast and elusive for other groups who saw the Irish as competitors. The IIRM, he says, "benefited from being political lay people rather than professional lobbyists. They stood out as real human beings."

Of course, it was not just the IIRM. Other groups and individuals played their part. The Catholic Church, increasingly coming under critical fire even in "holy Ireland," demonstrated how positive a role it could play, if permitted, even in the temporal world. The Irish government, and especially its diplomats in the U.S., had answered many questions and soothed numerous concerns of legislators regarding the upstarts at the gates.

Chief among the upstarts, certainly one of the most passionate remained Pat Hurley. At the end of it all, Hurley owed his Morrison Visa less to Morrison himself than to Brian Donnelly. Pat, the illegal from Skibbereen, didn't qualify for a Morrison although he had applied in the belief that he could get one. Pat was both emigrant and immigrant twice over. His parents had moved to New Zealand for a time and Pat had actually been born in Wellington. The Hurleys returned to Co. Cork before Pat had turned five. He had an Irish passport but hadn't been born in the Republic. And unfortunately, New Zealand wasn't one of the fabled thirty-six countries.

This little twist in his life's story was imparted by Hurley to Brian Donnelly in a Washington D.C. hostelry on a summer's night in 1990, a couple of months before the Morrison bill was passed. Hurley was attending the AOH National Convention. He told Donnelly he had no visa at all and was afraid to return to Dublin in an effort to get one because he feared he would not be allowed back into the U.S. once it emerged that New Zealand was his birthplace. Donnelly, who was well aware of Hurley's prominent role by this stage, was taken aback, but instructed Hurley to send him all the details in writing to his office.

The result was a line in the 1990 bill inserted by Donnelly to the effect that any person who had applied for a Donnelly Visa, had been accepted for interview but had only then been found ineligible, would now be eligible. Jokes are made to this day about the "Hurley Act."

Hurley himself takes a serious view of the entire IIRM phenomenon. "It was a unique time in the history of the Irish American community. So many well educated Irish had arrived and found themselves economically stymied in the U.S., just as they had been back in Ireland. It was like a volcano waiting to explode. There was a feeling among us that this moment in time was demanding us to do something. The infighting at the end was regrettable. I regret that very much. I hope we made a difference."

With the passage of the 1990 Act the Irish who hummed to the songs of U2 were allowed to find what they were looking for, to make America their new, legitimate home. But they were to prove a restless lot. How different to previous generations they actually were, and how much the same, would unfold in the 1990s when the "New Irish," one hundred and fifty years after half their nation had vanished, would face America's boundless promise anew. In time they would find, to the surprise of some if not themselves, that not only were they settled and "doing well" in America, but that, together with their more deep rooted cousins, they were all of a sudden, in the words of the *New York Times*, in the ascendant again.

7

SAINTS AND SLUGGERS

"Use up the Irish. The dead cost nothing."
King Edward, "Longshanks," in the movie *Braveheart*.

You can't help but notice the size of the sky in Montana, that big sky. And in June it seems particularly enormous because so many days are cloudless. It is an inverted blue ocean. The sun beats down on the rolling prairie, the bluffs and hollows that dominate the eastern part of the state. Shade, where you can find it, is often provided by hardy cottonwood trees. It is just so at the place the Sioux call Greasy Grass. In the English language history books it is known as the Little Bighorn.

Standing on the long ridge overlooking the river's twisting course you notice the wind. It blows across the bluffs and through the tough prairie grass. It comes from one horizon and passes you, on to the other. This is an immense place, and, in the summer of 1876, a lonely place to die.

The battle that took place here, primarily on June 25th of that centennial year, was between two races and several cultures. The Native American force comprised an alliance of tribes and was led by more than one revered chief. Yes, there was Sitting Bull but also Crazy Horse, Gall and several others. George Armstrong Custer— "Boys, hold your horses, there are plenty of them down there for us all"—is the best remembered leader of the U.S. force. But the young men he was shouting at minutes before he charged to his and their doom also represented different white tribes. One of them was Irish.

In 1876, almost one third of the U.S. Army had been born outside the borders of the United States. The majority of immigrant soldiers in the ranks were Irish and German. President Woodrow Wilson would refer to both these European tribes at a later time, and in markedly different circumstances, as "hyphenated Americans." But on this day they were just scared young men who were quickly learning that the greatest adventure of their lives would likely be their last.

The total strength of Custer's regiment in that one hundredth birthday summer was in the region of 840 officers and men with 600 or so present for the battle. Not too many really. The post-Civil War Army was a seriously depleted one. The forces allocated to the western frontier were spread thin over hundreds of thousands of square miles of often empty territory—empty that is if you forget the frequently angry and frustrated native inhabitants. The popular idea of the only good "injun" being a dead one had been coined by General Phil Sheridan, "Little Phil," Civil War cavalry hero on the Union side who had been conceived in County Cavan and born either during his parents' ocean passage to America, or in Albany, New York; his mother could never quite remember.

Sheridan's thinking on "injuns" was doubtless familiar to the Irish who rode with Custer that day. By some estimates, as many as 250 of the regiment's officers and men were Irish born, Irish American or of Irish descent having been born in Britain. Some would die, rather horribly, thousands of miles from their native soil. Young men like Jeremiah Finley, Patrick Golden, Richard Farrell and Thomas Downing. Men like Robert Hughes, a sergeant and Dublin native. Hughes carried Custer's personal flag or guidon and perished on or close to Last Stand Hill, grasping perhaps for one last second a vision in his mind of the city by the bay he had left behind for whatever reason, or no good reason at all. Indeed, all the Irish-born who shed their blood for their adopted country at the Little Bighorn probably perished with at least some last thoughts devoted to their old one, the land that some of them could not wait to leave behind in a ship's wake. One or two might have dwelt for a fleeting second on the irony of their situation. They were, in effect, the armed agents of new world planters, the Sioux and Cheyenne playing the part of the trampled Irish. Over thirty Irish-born cavalrymen were destined to die in the Greasy Grass. Sergeant William Cashen from County Laois was one. He had managed to send a letter "home" before the expedition against Sitting Bull. In it he wrote: "If I will be lookey enough to get this thrue I will be a fearful warrior." He wasn't.

Captain Myles Keogh, the best known of Custer's Irish-born officers, might have contemplated the tall bending grass along Battle Ridge for a minute recalling the lush farmland of County Carlow, his birthplace. Keogh, veteran of the Papal army, Civil War hero and all round dashing cavalry officer, with a horse called Comanche under him, is believed to be the officer who, according to one Sioux warrior named Little Soldier, went down, gun blazing, shooting between the legs of his mount while clutching the reins. Other Sioux and Cheyenne witnesses later spoke of a particularly ferocious white soldier, widely reckoned to have been the gallant Keogh who, by now, had reached the second corner of his life's triangle, the final being his last resting place in upstate New York.

And of course it was Keogh. History would have it no other way. Standing alone and brave against the savages of an untamed wilderness was the young Irish officer, his adopted country's comic strip hero, drawing in his final moments on thousands of years of Celtic warriorhood. More Myles Keoghs and some decent repeating rifles at Little Bighorn and it might have all been very different. For here was yet another glowing example of a true, although fairly freshly minted American original: The fighting Irishman.

Life in the frontier army wasn't easy. It was lonely, poorly paid, often dull and repetitive, and the weather, particularly if your blood was of more temperate climes, could be especially brutal. The Seventh Cavalry was, theoretically at least, a dry regiment. But on a day such as this there was little time for formality. Custer's last stand took place at one end of a battlefield that stretched for several miles along the bluffs overlooking the river. At the opposite end to Last Stand Hill was a height which was defended by men under the command of Major Marcus Reno and Captain Frederick Benteen. This position above the cottonwoods and meandering stream was crawling with vengeful warriors as the 25th faded into the 26th. The water shortage for the troopers by dusk was critical, especially for the wounded. A party of volunteers ventured down to the river in search of water. One of them was Sergeant Mike Madden who was seriously wounded in his right leg for his troubles. Being the time and place it was the leg had to come off. Madden was given brandy to deal with the excruciating pain.

Losing his leg was one thing, but Madden clearly considered himself luckier than most. As legend has it, he enjoyed the brandy so much that he whispered to the surgeon: "Doctor, cut off me other leg." The surgeon demurred and Madden, along with his remaining limb, would leave the Little Bighorn alive. Unlike most

other members of the water party he did not, however, receive the
Medal of Honor. But he did go down in history; sort of anyway.
Here we had the jolly but hard fighting and always thirsty Irishman;
the very essence of the anti-hero frontier hard man; perverse flip
side to the pious, sober, God-fearing log cabin settler. We would
meet Mike Madden, in later years. He would be the sergeant in a
John Ford western or a war movie in which all those German comrades from the hills of Montana suddenly turned into an enemy in
spike-topped or coal scuttle helmets. Wherever America's enemy
was to be found, in real life or on the big screen, you didn't have to
look far to find the fighting Irishman, the rogue with a gleam in his
eye and hand always out for a wee drop. He was behind us, before
us, all around us. By Christ he was us. He threw himself at every
battle and every war, "fighting fiercely and dying bravely for this
country," as a 1996 Joint Resolution in the New Jersey State
Assembly would put it. Even after death, his ghost charged, medals
shimmering, at the members of Congress who considered what to
do with the illegal Irish of the 1980s. The Irish soldier would be
remembered in song and story and on battlefield monument. Or
on a commemorative plate: "Two continents, two countries, two
histories forever linked by the pursuit of freedom, justice and the
simple yearning for a better life." Words not to be found on some
columned pile in Washington D.C. but in a present day Blarney gift
catalog touting the virtues of a china plate depicting Irish Brigade
soldiers in the Union army at the battle of Gettysburg. Commercial endorsement is the ultimate seal of approval in the 1990s.
"Image is everything," said tennis player Andre Agassi in a TV
commercial. Well, nobody is going to sink good money into something if the image doesn't quite stand up. The fighting Irish are still
standing.

    "One of the traits of the very Irish is that the fight is paramount,"
was observed anonymously to New York magazine, profiling public
relations street brawler John Scanlon. Scanlon, clearly, was one of
the "very Irish." In America, the idea of being "very Irish" or sometimes "Irish Irish" draws the mind towards an individual who at
least was born Catholic, more often than not in a big eastern city,
but who might not be particularly religious in daily affairs. Being
"Irish" in this case comes before being Catholic just as with someone viewed as being "Catholic Irish" it is the other way around.
Irish Americans understand the code even if Irish-born arrivals

might take a little time to appreciate the nuance. To confuse the issue even more there are some, author of *The Boston Irish* Thomas H. O'Connor for one, who would have the Irish of Beantown in a unique category all by their lonesome. But even the idea of the singular Boston Irish leans more to "very" than "Catholic." It speaks more of politics than any higher calling.

The "very" or "Irish Irish" individual might be loosely understood to be someone who is not shy when it comes to lashing out, more often today with a sharp-tongued admonition or legal writ, as opposed to a fist. Such an individual, like a good whiskey, might be seen as one who has managed to avoid some of the diluting wrought by the great melting pot's sociological ice. Keogh, Madden, Scanlon, Celtic warriors all, originals of the species, spiritual kin if not immediate offspring of Daniel Patrick Moynihan's "wild Irish slums of the nineteenth century eastern seaboard."

For the Irish in America, in those days when the slums were truly wild, the image of the battered but noble fighter was at least an escape from being lampooned as squabbling apes. And besides, the role which the Irish were expected to play, at least superficially, seemed to fit into the wildness of America's expansionist years. The Irish were a good match for the young country, its landscape and restless people. The Irish had been denied the comforting certainty of self-definition for most of their island's recognizable history. Irish "civilization" was like a boxer on the ropes, arms held up in defensive posture, eyes half-closed, trapped in a small place with nowhere to run and damn little time to contemplate the glories of creation. Mostly, Irishness was defined as something opposite to a barbaric and alien Englishness. In post-famine America—a term which recognizes the Great Hunger as an American as well as an Irish story— prospects at least seemed a little better. The Irish found that they had social maneuverability, even in a society that had supposedly rid itself of old world class-based pomposity. And despite virulent anti-Catholicism, "No Irish need apply or "no Blacks, no Irish," the newcomers soon found others to look down upon, if they so desired, groups they could easily look in the eye and treat on roughly equal terms and yet others they could strive to emulate by wrapping themselves in the nearest yard of lace curtain. And all this within the boundaries of a society which, if you fought hard enough, with mind, body or whatever came closest to hand, would allow you to be just about anything that your heart desired. So it was said at any rate. It was an Irishman who coined the phrase "manifest destiny." By the time they arrived on America's shores in impressive numbers, the Irish were a coiled people, more than ready for a little favorable destiny, God-given or no.

A century later, Sinéad O'Connor, iconoclastic emblem of the new, hip, modern Ireland, would tear up a picture of Pope John Paul II on American television. The first word out of her mouth as she delivered this act of defiance was "fight." O'Connor followed "fight" with "the real enemy." The Irish were clearly still a little coiled.

The Irish in America remain trapped in a contradiction. O'Connor would likely recognize the hard drinking and fighting Irish stereotype. But along with much of her generation she would view it as having little or nothing to do with the contemporary image or interpretation of Irishness. Equally, many Irish Americans today react with energetic displays of sensitivity whenever they feel that the general Irish character is being unfairly treated. The old shibboleths regarding alleged Irish drinking or fighting habits continue to arise. The first instinct of the sensitive critic is to fight like hell for a retraction—in words or in writing. Then again, everything is judged by degrees. The Irish in America are not disinclined to wrap themselves in the fighting image under certain circumstances. "A Classic Boston Brawl Pits Mayor Against New Stadium," was a front page headline in the January 22nd, 1997 edition of the *New York Times*. The story was about local opposition in South Boston to plans for building a new stadium in the area for the New England Patriots football team. The headline most certainly prompted knowing smiles from Irish American *Times* readers. Certainly, there was no audible chorus of complaint. However, the reaction might have been more apparent had the headline read: "A Classic Boston Irish Brawl." The headline played it well. It conveyed a familiar concept with enough subtlety to avoid an outburst of opprobrium.

Not playing it so well, at least as far as one irate Irish American was concerned, was documentary film maker Ken Burns. After his mammoth treatment of the Civil War on public television—which brought forth the memorable words from historian Shelby Foote apropos the Battle of Fredericksburg: "Among the attackers was the Irish Brigade, shouting 'Erin Go Bragh!' and waving their green banners. They got within twenty-five paces of the stone wall. The men of the twenty-fourth Georgia who shot them down were Irish too"—Burns went on to make another blockbuster series on the history of baseball. The Irish were in the thick of the wheeling and dealing throughout the series and one or two disputes, on and off the mound, featured Irish American sluggers, businessmen and managers, one of them being John McGraw. The manner in which immediately recognizable Irish production devices were used to underline McGraw's Irishness was enough to infuriate Tom Culhane of Union, New Jersey who wrote in a letter to New York's *Village Voice*: "It's amazing that this series, financed by public television and hailed by many critics for showcasing the racist illtreatment that blacks faced featured the Irish in such a bigoted manner.

"Burns depicted drinking at games by Boston's Irish fans at the turn of the century, and it is stated that 'paddy wagons' were used to arrest unruly fans. When John McGraw is discussed, *Danny Boy* is played in the background—a tactic I haven't seen on television since the 1960s, when Hop Sing used to come on the kitchen on *Bonanza* and Asian music was played to let everyone know he was Chinese. And how many times was the point made about how much McGraw loved to fight? Ken Burns's discombobulated portrayal of the Irish as drunken brawling louts was a sorry waste of public funds."

The collective Irish character, if there be such a thing at all, has probably been paid greater attention in America than anywhere else on earth. Britain comes a close second. In Ireland itself, it was always more difficult to judge Irishness if for no other reason than there was no other ethnic or racial group with which to compare. By looking back from afar, the Irish in other lands, especially America and Canada, have better been able to take their own measure.

"They took pride in their physical endurance, reacted violently to challenge and could be both sweetnatured and aggressive. Yet even under the most adverse circumstances they retained a sense of humor." The Pulitzer Prize winning Irish-American historian John Toland wasn't writing about the Irish at all. He was referring to Koreans. But his next sentence closed the circle: "They were often called the Irish of the Orient."

The Irish of America emerged from the nineteenth century with considerable success under their belt, literally in some cases as the early records of world championship boxing clearly show. John L. Sullivan's was only the first of a string of Irish names to adorn the pugilistic hall of fame. The mention of Donnybrooks, faction fighting or draft rioting immediately conjured up images of Irishmen, and sometimes women, slugging it out with sundry opponents in the streets of cities including Boston—where, as related in O'Connor's *The Boston Irish*, the Irish, mostly "settled back in a spirit of sullen resentment against the Lincoln administration . . ."—or Philadelphia, a city which rested its reputation on the concept of brotherly love, but which witnessed some of the most ferocious anti-Catholic Irish rioting of the 1840s.

New York, meanwhile, became a virtual world capital of street fighting during the nineteenth century. Herbert Asbury's *The Gangs of New York* relates in considerable detail the wild battles of the heavily Irish gangs of the Bowery and Five Points districts of Manhattan up to and including the draft riots of 1863, the turbulent world of Peter Quinn's *Banished Children of Eve*. Gangs such as the Five Points, Bowery Boys, Dead Rabbits, O'Connell Guards and True Blue Americans would become the stuff of street legend.

The True Blue Americans were by no means the most violent but, wrote Asbury, were no less obvious by virtue of being relatively passive. "They wore stove-pipe hats and long black frock coats which reached flappingly to their ankles and buttoned close under the chin; their chief mission in life was to stand on street corners and denounce England, and gloomily predict the immediate destruction of the British Empire by fire and sword. Like most of the sons of Erin who have come to this country, they never became so thoroughly Americanized that Ireland did not remain their principal vocal interest.

Rather more than merely vocal were the Bowery Boys and Dead Rabbits. Asbury delivers a graphic description of what it was like to be a gang member when Irish America was still young: "Sometimes the battles raged for two or three days without cessation, while the streets of the gang area were barricaded with carts and paving stones, and the gangsters blazed away with musket and pistol, or engaged in close work with knives, brickbats, bludgeons, teeth and fists. On the outskirts of the struggling mob of thugs ranged the women, their arms filled with reserve ammunition, their keen eyes watching for a break in the enemy's defense, and always ready to lend a hand or a tooth in the fray."

New York's Five Points district in Lower Manhattan—an area in the "bloody ould Sixth Ward" bounded by Broadway, Canal Street, the Bowery and Park Row—would find resonance many years later in another fabled city. Irish rock singer Bob Geldof would sing of the "Five Lamps Boys coming on strong," Five Lamps being an area on the north side of inner-city Dublin. In both places, a bunch of fives or worse were for years an accepted way of settling disagreement.

Trouble often found the early American Irish outside the maniacal world of street gangs and it often came in the form of a raging anti-Catholicism.

Dr. Thomas Addis Emmet, grandson of Thomas Addis Emmet, attorney general of New York and brother of the hanged Irish revolutionary Robert, described in his 1911 autobiography, *Incidents of my Life*, a clash which bore early testimony to the hard times which Irish Catholics would have to endure before they eventually came to dominate the politics of New York City.

"On the 12th of July, 1824, a procession of Orangemen marched out of the city with banners flying and the band playing 'Croppies Lie down,' etc., to the little hamlet of Greenwich Village, then in the country between the present site of Jefferson Market and the North River. This village was settled at that time almost exclusively by Irish Catholics, who were chiefly laboring men. Mr. O'Conor stated that these people were obliged to live together to a great extent for their own protection, as a large portion of the New Yorkers were at that time very bitter and prejudiced against all those who differed with them in religious belief. The Orangemen marched deliberately to this village for the purposes of irritating the inhabitants, and succeeded so well that they received a most humiliating thrashing. As the fugitives were driven into the city, the worthy Sheriff proceeded to swear in a special posse, and on reaching Greenwich every man who could be found was arrested. On the following morning a hundred or more Irishmen were arraigned on the charge of rioting and disturbing the peace, with almost a certainty of conviction before them." Emmet, who defended the arrested Catholic Irish was himself Protestant Irish.

Another irony, though of more recent times: Irish gays and lesbians, many of them also resident in Greenwich Village, marching uptown with the purpose of irritating another group of Catholics, not least the members of the Ancient Order of Hibernians, which came into the world as a physical counterweight to the violent activities of Nativists and Know Nothings in the 1830s. This time however, the waters would be rather more muddied. Most members of the Irish Lesbian and Gay Organization were born Catholic in Ireland, as were the defenders of Greenwich Village in 1824. And unlike the nineteenth century, late twentieth century charges of alleged know nothingism took flight in all directions. 1824, for all its warts, was arguably a more simple, straightforward time in matters of colliding faith and conflicting morals.

The 1950s, many would have us believe, were also a simpler time. During the decade of "I Like Ike" tens of thousands of Irish packed suitcases and boarded ships and planes for America. They began arriving in the years following World War Two and during the conflict in a faraway Asian land populated by people of apparently Irish temperament. Long gone were the days of burning churches and faction fights. Irish America was by now deeply entrenched, the big city Irish political machines were at the peak of their power and John F. Kennedy was well on his way to standing atop the final unconquered summit. The big cities of the eastern seaboard, as well as their counterparts in the midwest, and west, were still a little wild at times, but newer immigrant groups were capturing the lion's share of popular imagination in the context of street-level dramatics. "West Side Story" with an all-Irish story-line and cast would probably not have been much of a hit.

Not that the Irish were suddenly passive. Sure, there was an established community already in place and neighborhoods that were well understood to be Irish, but big cities being what they were there was always just that little bit of friction, not quite enough room, one bunch of kids trespassing on the other gang's turf. Popular stories, not infrequently related by Jewish residents of Brooklyn in particular, have the little Jewish kid battling his way to school through a cordon of Irish bullyboys. And there was always that other "*cosae nostrae*," the Irish-Italian "thing."

Italian Americans still remember what they view as a pogrom against their people in New Orleans in 1891. The incident involved the hanging of a group of Italians in the city following the murder, in October, 1890, of police chief David Hennessy whose last words were reportedly "the Dagoes did it." There was a trial with both acquittals and convictions but local citizens took matters into their own hands, broke into the prison and lynched eleven Italian inmates. Not a few Irish hands are, to this day, seen to have been holding the ropes.

In turn of the century New York, the Irish and Italians could hardly avoid one another. And their meetings were often violent. One Italian New Yorker who came into early contact with his less than friendly Irish neighbors was Al Capone.

In his biography of the man who would later put Chicago on the world map in the most unflattering way, author Laurence Bergreen points out that the most widespread rivalry between youth gangs in the days when Capone was still a boy in Brooklyn was between the Irish and Italians. "The Catholicism shared by the two groups was, if anything, a divisive factor, for there was a constant rivalry over which group made better Catholics," Bergreen wrote in *Capone, The Man And His Era*. Bergreen describes one battle on Navy Street in which Capone and his pals beat back an attack by a local Irish gang. But it was a war without end, one which neither side could ever win. "In combat with their Italian counterparts," Bergreen wrote, "Irish gangs proved to be hardy, occasionally murderous, wielding sticks and stones in street combat."

Even though they won their fair share of brawls, the teenage Al Capone and his contemporaries had to acknowledge Irish hegemony to some degree. The Irish had simply reached America in large numbers first and had cornered the market in political posts and patronage jobs. As a result, the Irish were several rungs up the ladder of middle class respectability. Still, nothing remained the same for ever. As Capone was learning the ways of the street, the notorious Five Points gang across the East River had turned itself into a virtually all-Italian outfit headed by a former boxer named Paolo Antonini Vacarelli. But business was business and it was still better for a bit of Irish. The days of Rocky Marciano and Jake La-Motta were still a long way off. Vacarelli had fought under the name Paul Kelly. And the woman Al Capone would later marry was Irish. Her name was Mary Coughlin, or "Mae" to just about everyone who knew her. Immigrant or first generation Italian men might have had one very particular image of their Irish male counterparts, but they generally held an entirely different one of Irish women. Bergreen writes that by the standards of the day—the last days of World War One—the romance between Al Capone and Mae Coughlin was seen as being virtually interracial.

Years later, the Italian/Irish marriage phenomenon was still drawing on its illustrious and lusty past. By now, though, things had become a little more evenly mixed. Writer Pat Jordan, in the

August, 1988 issue of GQ magazine, passed on the words of his Italian mother: "When an Italian husband strikes his Irish wife, the first thing she does is call the police. And it's always an Irish cop who comes to the door. And what does he see? He sees this poor Irish girl holding a hand to her face and her Italian husband in the background. Now who do you think he's gonna hit with his night stick?"

A century or so after the great wave of Italian migration to the United States and one hundred and fifty years after the great Irish surge, both groups could still not quite shake each other's shadow. Even the aforementioned Sinéad O'Connor ended up in a spat with the most enduring symbol of Italian success in America, Frank Sinatra. It arose over her objections to the Star Spangled Banner being played before one of her concerts. Sinéad versus Sinatra might have been an even bigger "*cosa*" only for the fact that the Pope she picked as her real enemy was Polish.

Still, even if the "real enemy" had been Italian, her intervention would not have broken much new ground in a religious sense anyway. There had been a long history of rivalry for control of the Catholic Church in America involving Irish and Italian clerics. The Irish had made it to the high ground first and were more than a little disdainful of their Italian colleagues in Christ. As one nineteenth-century Irish Catholic priest put it to the Archbishop of New York: "They" (Italians) were "about the worst Catholics that ever came to this country." Italians, in turn, viewed Irish Catholics as being a bunch of stuffed-shirts. The Irish clergy were determined to keep outside influence at bay. Italians already had the Vatican and that was bad enough. The Irish attitudes towards other large Catholic groups, especially the Poles, was more tolerant. The Poles in particular matched the conservative nature of Irish Catholicism.

Nevertheless, there could be no avoiding contact, spiritual or physical. The Irish and Italians were destined to walk together in both truth and fiction in a social marriage that was most definitely for better and for worse. The Irish *consigliori* played by Robert Duvall in *The Godfather* was not a far-fetched character. When New York organized crime boss "Fat" Tony Salerno went to trial in 1987 one of his co-defendants was named Halloran. When the last of the "Westies" finally went down they did so in the declining shadow of Gambino crime family boss John Gotti, who had used the Manhattan West Side gang of Irish hoodlums for the kind of business that he didn't want to hear about at his own front door. Gotti's reputation as a man who could escape the clutches of the law was greatly enhanced when he was acquitted of hiring the Westies to shoot Irish-born carpenters union leader John O'Connor in May, 1986. The fact that O'Connor developed amnesia on the witness stand was not a complete surprise. Years later, it was revealed that Gotti's main enforcer and later mob turncoat, Sammy "The Bull" Gravano had relayed the message to O'Connor that a loss of memory on the witness stand was, all things considered, the wisest course of action. One thing that was particularly interesting about the trial was a daily newspaper reporter's description of the Westies—who were at least several generations removed by now from their Irish roots—as speaking in "brogues." For people back in Ireland reading accounts of O'Connor's near demise, the Athlone, Co. Westmeath-born union leader was the only Irish figure in a cast of highly dubious characters. All the rest were Americans, or perhaps New Yorkers. In New York itself it was more complex. Irish or Italian was still a very real distinction. To Gotti and his cohorts, O'Connor and the Westies were all a bunch of crazy Micks.

But if there were real differences, there were often strong, if arguably subtle, similarities. Any student of early and mid-twentieth century American gangland would have little trouble in matching every Italian name that crops up with an Irish one and vice versa. The Italians might talk about Cosa Nostra, "Our Thing," a lingual if not political equivalent of Sinn Féin, "Ourselves." But it never was quite like that. America always conspired to pull ethnic communities closer, often despite the best efforts of each single group. And with Irish and Italians, "close" was something of an understatement.

The pull and push effect of urban America's conflicting social forces can also be discerned in the uneasy relationship between the Irish, as represented in the main by Catholics, and American Jews.

Henry Feingold, editorial board chairman of the magazine Jewish Frontier, a left-leaning and pro-Zionist bimonthly out of New York, delivered his views on the relationship between the Irish and Jews in America in a 1996 essay headed "Irish Green Through a Jewish Lens Darkly." It all began with a tourist trip to Ireland itself, birthplace of one of Israel's presidents, the late Chaim Herzog, but not a land often visited by camera-wielding Jewish tourists from the United States. In casting judgment on Ireland and its condition,

social, religious, political and economic, Feingold drew comparison between the Irish in Ireland and the Irish in America with the
latter coming out ahead in terms of positive perception.

"My wife and I," wrote Feingold, "were blithely unaware of the
fact that the Irish were 'in' when we decided to visit that beautiful
green but troubled land this summer. Not until we returned did we
discover that we were on the lip of a new cultural wave. Advertise-
ments for Frank McCourt's *Angela's Ashes* were everywhere. We felt
a special attachment to McCourt since he was my daughter's English teacher at Stuyvesant High. On everyone's 'must' reading list
was Thomas Cahill's *How the Irish Saved Civilization*. The Riverdance troupe was packing them in at Radio City Music Hall and
Neil Jordan's film about the crusader for Irish independence,
Michael Collins, promised to become a box office hit."

Feingold travels to Ireland with less a sense of joy and anticipation than a sense that he was about to confront the origins of some
long held and deep-rooted fear.

"The lens through which I viewed the Irish was a Jewish one,
which is to say that it was a combination of fear and disdain. But as
a youth, other than my teachers, I rarely encountered Irish ethnics
in my daily life. Nor could I boast of the experience, mentioned so
proudly, in numerous Jewish memoirs, of having been beaten up by
neighboring Irish street gangs."

Feingold traced antagonism between Catholic Irish and Jew back
a century, to the time of the Mortara kidnapping, an 1859 incident
in Italy in which a child of mixed Catholic/Jewish birth, Edgar Mortara, was abducted by Catholic clergy. The negative image Jews had
of the Irish had been reinforced in Feingold's younger years, he
wrote, by "rumors that Father Coughlin's most enthusiastic listeners were the Irish of Boston, that Cardinal Spellman was anti-
semitic and that generally the priest-ridden Irish community was
the backbone of reaction in America. It was still strong when we
left for our trip. 'Why would anyone want to visit Ireland?' we were
asked. That was sometimes followed by the shared conventional
wisdom that the Irish in Ireland were 'nicer' than those in America. Few Jews of my generation were aware that the Irish were in
fact the most liberal of America's ethnics."

The "nicer" aspect of the Irish in Ireland was tempered somewhat by the reluctance of the Irish government during World War
Two, or "the Emergency" as it was officially known in Ireland itself,

to entertain the idea of opening the Irish Free State's door to any meaningful number of Jewish refugees fleeing Nazi persecution. The view in Dublin was essentially that large numbers of Jews would be socially unsettling. Jews did not mix well in Irish society and their presence to any considerable degree could have unsettling political repercussions.

Back in the U.S., the Irish and Jews were mixing it up. As Fintan O'Toole points out in his book, *The Ex-Isle of Erin*, no fewer than twenty-two movies were made in the 1920s dealing with Irish/Jewish relations in America.

"The depiction of romances between Irish girls and Jewish boys," wrote O'Toole, "was almost a stock-in-trade of popular drama. The vogue was inspired by Anne Nichols's 1922 comedy, *Abie's Irish Rose*, in which a Jewish boy and an Irish Catholic girl, afraid to tell their parents that they are in love, are married by a Methodist minister. It had 2,327 performances, one of the longest runs in the history of Broadway, and was also turned into a novel (1927), a radio serial (1942), and a movie (1946)."

The idea of the Irish/Jewish relationship being so dramatically different on opposite sides of the ocean finds support in Feingold's essay. The American Irish, he wrote, "are as different from the natives of Ireland as American Jews are from Israelis." Feingold also felt that the native Irish were "less exuberant" than their American cousins while in a larger geographic sense, both Irish and Jews were a people traumatized by history.

Such trauma, historical and contemporary, is at the root of a political imperative that survives to this day in most large U.S. cities, but particularly New York, that no matter what is the political flavor of the month, due attention must be accorded to those who consider themselves rooted in Ireland, Israel or Italy. The "three i's" might not be as dominant as they once were in urban politics, but no politician will thrive by ignoring them completely.

Occasionally the "i's" collide as they did during the one hundred and fiftieth anniversary of Ireland's Great Famine. Efforts by some Irish American campaigners to describe the Great Hunger as Ireland's holocaust ruffled more than a few Jewish feathers. "The Holocaust"—emphasis as much on the article as the noun—is a sacrosanct term to most American Jews and its overuse, they feel, distracts due attention from the twentieth century's greatest single crime against humanity.

But co-operation between Irish and Jewish interests in America is more the story of the 1990s. Not infrequently over the years, Irish Americans were prone to bemoaning the fact that Irish America wasn't doing as much for Ireland as Jewish America was doing for Israel. Even when Irish American anti-Semitism was being expressed, sometimes in coded language, there was more than a touch of discernible envy. That envy has been eroded to a considerable degree at one level due to the "Waldorf Factor." Irish charitable groups such as American Ireland Fund now raise hitherto undreamed of sums of money for Ireland. The group's activities are marked by lavish annual balls in a number of cities. The 1997 affair in New York raised money for, among other things, a Chair in Jewish Studies at Trinity College Dublin. New York University's Ireland House is "Glucksman Ireland House," a name derived from the marriage of American Ireland Fund National President, Loretta Brennan, to a leading Jewish Wall Street banker with Hungarian roots, Lewis Glucksman. The latter has been described by the *Sunday Business Post* newspaper in Dublin as "one of Ireland's greatest benefactors."

The "new" Irish/Jewish relationship is also represented by the likes of the Robert Briscoe Awards, presented annually by the Emerald Isle Immigration Center in New York to Jewish New Yorkers who have been of outstanding service to immigrants of any or all nationalities. Robert Briscoe was the first Jewish Lord Mayor of Leopold Bloom's hometown, Dublin. His son, Ben, is a pal of former New York Mayor Ed Koch, he of the chutzpah in an Aran sweater.

Irish American relations with Italians, Jews, African Americans, Native Americans, Asians and others have been part and parcel of the "Sinn Féin" story of the Irish in America. Inter-marriage has always been the cornerstone of the tale, although perhaps it has been less obvious at times than the noisy social collisions. That so many African Americans bear Irish names tells a tale in itself. Chinese Americans and Irish also have a history forged in both love and rivalry. The long-running 1970s TV cop show Hawaii Five-O not only made famous the character of Steve McGarrett, played by Irish American actor Jack Lord, but also that of Chin Ho, whose full name came out from time to time as "Chin Ho Kelly." The idea that everyone has a little Irish in them, or is at least Irish for one day a year, St. Patrick's Day, is one of the more easily accepted ethnicity-rooted clichés because it is usually offered as a compliment and received in the most positive light. The idea speaks of virtue today whereas, one hundred and fifty years ago, it might have been more than a little tinged with suggestions of vice and moral decay.

The Irish of those earlier generations in America were never fully defined without being immediately compared to other ethnic groups, usually unfavorably. In time, the formula derived from comparison between the Irish and others was merged with a growing chorus of Irish self-appraisal. After years of mixing, out popped the present day archetypal Irish American, in all his or her stereotypical glory. This popular image of the American Irish would find space in the pages of educational school textbooks which serve as fairly accurate barometers of general public perception, be they politically correct or otherwise at any given time.

Irish immigrants of the post-famine period were able to capitalize on their "good nature and warm-handedness," in the words of Thomas A. Bailey in *The American Pageant*. The countless American school students who read his work and others like it came away with a generalized view of a people who had fled famine and oppression in their own land, faced down discrimination in their new, adopted home, and eventually laid claim to all the treasures America could offer. The Irish, again in Bailey's words, "agreeable, generous, witty and lighthearted," if a little inclined to seek refuge from life's hardships "in the bottle, were the very epitome of the American spirit, a living symbol of a people's triumph over crushing adversity." Thus, Bailey's work and other twentieth century textbooks present the Irish in a far more positive light than the lampooning sheets of the nineteenth.

Textbooks, of course, have a finite off-the-shelf life and history is constantly being revised. Each generation of Irish arrivals in the United States has added or chipped away at the prevailing view of Irishness, the Irish and Ireland itself. Whether or not the Irish who came in the 1980s and '90s, the "New Irish" will profoundly change the textbook view of all three is yet to be decided. One thing, however, was quickly apparent: The new Irish had little trouble in making headlines. This really was no surprise. If they had departed a country which was still a little reluctant to embrace the idea of instant gratification, the exiled children of the new, modern Ireland, Mary Robinson's diaspora, would instantly recognize the opportunities which "the States" presented for virtually immediate economic rock, social roll and cultural revolution. Regardless of the pain that still came with separation from loved ones, the America that was so far away for past generations now seemed remarkably close and familiar, a ready made stage for a drama that was as much rooted in a changing Ireland as it was in the soon-to-be latest act in the Irish American pageant.

8

AN IRISH THING

"We urge you to stay and dance to your heart's content."
Bill Clinton to Mary Robinson.

The beer can arched through the air, landing with a frothy clatter. David Dinkins, all decked out in green, would later compare the moment to Alabama in the bad old days before and during the civil rights campaign. What had happened was that New York's first black mayor had found himself smack in the middle of a war, holy or unholy depending on individual perspective, between rival factions of the great Irish diaspora. The 1991 New York St. Patrick's Day Parade, the 230th consecutive, was by no means the first to be riven by internecine conflict. By the standard of some early parades, the beer-spattered fracas on Fifth Avenue was small potatoes. But there was no escaping the deep rift in attitude and belief between the beer thrower and his intended targets. St. Patrick, not for the first time, had been sent to a neutral corner while the Irish attempted to sort out their differences. "Beware the AIDS of March," roared one angry spectator's banner.

The parade had descended into the realm of discord and confrontation following the attempt by the Irish Lesbian and Gay Organization to secure a place in the parade line of marchers and walk up the avenue under its own banner. The parade organizing committee, staunchly Catholic members of the Ancient Order of Hibernians, had declined the request while stating that individual gay people could march with other parade units. ILGO, with a name guaranteed to attract media attention no less than the IIRM, had other ideas. Lines were thus drawn and a drama unfolded, the exact likes of which had never been seen before in Irish America. This was not merely a challenge to those who were currently in charge; it was a challenge to all that was in their charge, a near sacred annual homage to faith and fatherland stretching back to colonial times. David Dinkins, though he might not have considered it, was seen as a willing participant in a virtual *coup d'état* instigated and carried out by a group that would walk, not just on the asphalt of Manhattan's main thoroughfare, but on the graves of the countless Irish Catholic immigrants who had bound together the very fabric of Irish American society. The fact that most of the ILGO members were Catholic themselves didn't matter a whit. They were heretics, lucky to be showered with only booze. And yet, the confrontation on Fifth Avenue took place in a time when even heretical concepts such as "gay and Catholic" were finding succor in the highest realms of society back in the Ireland left behind by the ILGO protestors.

Several years before the beer battle of Fifth Avenue, an American visitor to Ireland was taking in the delights of Christ Church Cathedral in Dublin. It was Christmas Eve and after the carol service all in attendance adjourned to the crypt for tea and sandwiches. The American visitor was chatting with a friend when she took a step backwards only to collide with a man sipping from his cup. "Oh excuse me," the man said apologetically. The American excused herself in turn. Her companion smiled knowingly. "Do you know who that is?" he said. The American replied she had no idea. "That's the President of Ireland."

By Christmas, 1990, such a story would be unthinkable, even if the visitor had come from Mars.

Mary Robinson had been a fixture in Irish public life for a number of years before Irish voters allowed her a political apotheosis that would for ever change the style and, to a surprising degree, the very substance of Irish politics. It had not been too many years since the citizenry of the Republic had witnessed the lowest point in the history of the Irish presidency—supposedly a non-controversial constitutional post,—the 1976 resignation of Cearbhall O Dálaigh in the wake of his being characterized as a "thundering disgrace" by Minister for Defense Paddy Donegan. Donegan's outburst, at a dinner for army officers, was prompted by O Dálaigh referring new government emergency powers to the Supreme Court. It would not be entirely outlandish to suggest that the furor surrounding O Dálaigh's dramatic resignation awakened many Irish to the fact that Eamon de Valera was no longer rattling around in the president's official residence, Áras an Uachtaráin; indeed, that there had been another incumbent between Dev and O Dálaigh, namely

Erskine Childers. But all was soon to settle down again with the arrival of Patrick Hillery who served two seven year terms during which the collision under the flying buttresses of Christ Church amounted to something of an event in what was to be fourteen years of calm constitutional service between countless rounds of golf.

By the time Mary Robinson was all teed up and ready to go, following her out-of-the-blue election triumph in the early days of November, 1990, there was little doubt in anybody's mind that the entire Irish nation was about to be taken on a journey and that through Robinson's own eyes, all would be seeing the world as an entirely new kind of place, one where the idea of Ireland as a small, inward-looking island on the edge of Europe was out the window and the notion of "Irishness" was suddenly a globally marketed concept, no less international in scope or availability than free market economics or a can of Coke.

"The Ireland I will be representing is a new Ireland, open, tolerant, inclusive." The opening words of Robinson's inauguration speech, delivered on December 3, 1990, were well received by Irish the world over even if some didn't think that there was all that much wrong with the old Ireland, the one which had just been delivered a kick in the transom by Mary's well-heeled foot.

And there was more. Robinson was no rabble rouser, but she wasn't shy when it came to rousing sentiment or pricking conscience. Hers was a call to action, an Irish version of "ask not what you can do for your country." And the call went out far beyond Ireland itself.

"If it is time, as Joyce's Stephen Dedalus remarked, that the Irish began to forge in the smithy of our souls 'the uncreated conscience of our race'—might we not also take on the still 'uncreated conscience' of the wider international community? Is it not time that the small started believing again that it is beautiful, that the periphery can rise up and speak out on equal terms with the center, that the most outlying island community of the European Community really has something 'strange and precious' to contribute to the seachange presently sweeping through the entire continent of Europe? . . . I want this Presidency to promote the telling of stories—stories of celebration through the arts and stories of conscience and of social justice. As a woman, I want women who have felt themselves outside history to be written back into history . . . May God direct me so that my Presidency is one of justice, peace and love. May I have the fortune to preside over an Ireland at a time of exciting transformation when we enter a new Europe where old wounds can be healed, a time when, in the words of Seamus Heaney, 'hope and history rhyme.' May it be a presidency where I the President can sing to you, citizens of Ireland, the joyous refrain of the fourteenth-century Irish poet as recalled by W.B. Yeats: 'I am of Ireland, come dance with me in Ireland.'"

In time, Robinson would become the target of critical sniping for her oft tongue-tying speeches, delivered in what some would describe as "Robospeak." But for now it was all stirring stuff. No male politician anyone could think of would speak like this. Certainly, no male Irish politician would be inviting voters to dance. Like the Pope, Robinson had no divisions. But she apparently had a vision of a new and different Ireland, whatever that might be. It was off to see the wizard time. Over the seven years of her term, Robinson would stir up controversy at home and abroad. She would step on toes in Africa, Northern Ireland, the United Nations and on home soil.

In his account of the period he served as press secretary in the Albert Reynolds government, *One Spin on the Merry-go-round*, journalist Sean Duignan recounted a moment when Reynolds, always the savvy politician, took stock of the woman who was now defining the standards of Irish political popularity. Reynolds, wrote Duignan, "viewed the President with a mixture of mild awe and wariness." Duignan recorded a moment when Reynolds assessed his course of action in a situation where Robinson was a player. "No arguing with that," said Reynolds. "We walk around that. Let her off."

In her first Christmas message, only days after her inauguration, Robinson seemed to stare beyond Ireland's limited horizons to a distant glow of Irishness the world over. She sent "warmest greetings for Christmas to all Irish people at home and abroad . . . to our emigrants everywhere." Mary was suddenly up there with the Pope, delivering her version of *Urbi et Orbi*. She was matching Queen Elizabeth, who delivered an annual address to the British Commonwealth on Christmas Day. Ireland too, now had a commonwealth of sorts. Mary R, the elected uncrowned queen of Ireland, would, in time, call it the diaspora. ILGO and the Hibernians formed part of Mary's big inclusive family, a far flung clan bonded together by

Irishness, a new Irishness. How they behaved towards one another was quite another matter.

The more open, tolerant and inclusive Ireland of Robinson's mind's eye was, in fact, already taking shape before her elevation to head of state. Like an expert surfer she had merely caught the wave. Now, faraway shores beckoned.

In America, Robinson's triumph was quickly grasped by the press as an alternative to the flood of stories about the collapse of Communist eastern Europe and the growing Persian Gulf crisis. She was "Person of the Week" on ABC news and the print press was generous with its praise. Before being elected, Irish feminist writer Nell McCafferty predicted that Robinson, "this woman," as she called her, would "go where men have feared, or couldn't be bothered to tread." U.S. writers appeared to agree. To the *New York Times* she was a "spunky and principled campaigner." The *Boston Globe* decided that Robinson was a forward-thinking lawyer with a concern for civil rights causes in a conservative nation where the Roman Catholic Church wields overweening moral influence and men dominate politics.

"She has advocated such extreme minority views as legalizing divorce and contraception and decriminalizing homosexuality, often placing herself at odds with much of the country and the church," a *Globe* editorial opined.

But in line with much too, an ever growing much, some of it that was to find loud expression on the streets of New York a scant three months after her invitation to the world to come dance.

And it was fitting that the unfolding drama, the coming out of an expanded definition of Irishness, be played out in America, from where it would be relayed to a global audience. All manner of social reform was being advocated and embraced in Ireland by the time Robinson was elected, but the Irish stage had its limits, geographical and otherwise. New York, and to a lesser degree Boston, would provide the backdrop and St. Patrick's Day would be the catalyst. ILGO, never even heard of one minute, would end up blooming faster than the daffodils in those early days of spring.

The St. Patrick's Day Parade in New York has always been a flashpoint for dispute. The nineteenth century witnessed splits, battles with police and anti-Catholic *provocateurs*, feuding organizers and all manner of verbal rancor. St. Patrick himself had been the target of nativist spite in mid-century with one newspaper, the

True Sun, alleging that March 18th was devoted to the saint's wife. The struggle for Irish independence became a progressively stronger theme as the twentieth century advanced and by the 1950s the parade had been reinvigorated by a fresh influx of Irish immigrants and an even fresher supply of shamrock from Ireland which could be, by decade's end, flown across the Atlantic on Aer Lingus jets.

There were stills rows. In 1961, Brendan Behan was barred from taking part because the parade committee feared a one-man riot. Behan was invited to attend a party in Jersey City hosted by the mayor and had such a good time that he expressed gratitude to the New York parade committee for saving him from sore feet.

The renewed troubles in Northern Ireland were to spawn controversies of their own, not least the infamous closing of the doors of St. Patrick's Cathedral in 1983 as Grand Marshal Michael Flannery, head of the IRA support group, Irish Northern Aid, walked up the avenue. Flannery took it in his stride, not least because Cardinal Cooke had explained his position and likely response to Flannery in advance.

Despite the influx of a new generation of Irish in the 1980s, New York parade politics still rested in the hands of a comparatively small number of established Irish and Irish Americans, virtually all of them men. The New York parade stood out from all others because of its sheer size, quasi-military style, clearly evident Catholic ethos and the firm hand of successive parade committee chairmen, not least the legendary Judge James J. Comerford, a figure who inspired Calvin Trillin's opening line in a 1988 *New Yorker* magazine story: "Before there was democracy, there was Judge James J. Comerford."

The major change in the face of the parade in the 1980s had everything to with sex, albeit the straight variety. Trillin drew a rather sharp distinction between the St. Patrick's Day Parade and its Columbus Day counterpart, the only other parade allowed in the city on a business day. Sex and sensuality and the manner in which they were displayed were at the heart of the Irish/Italian divide—yet again.

In selecting their grand marshals, Trillin wrote that the Italians went for glory, no questions asked. St. Patrick's Day Parade grand marshals, on the other hand, were nearly always unknown outside the tight circle that voted for them.

Wrote Trillin: "In 1979, when the grand marshal for the St. Patrick's Day parade was John Sweeney, then the president of a local union that represented building cleaners, the grand marshal of the Columbus Day parade was Frank Sinatra. In 1980, the Irish had William Burke, a Transit Authority employee who had been executive secretary of the parade committee for many years; the Italians had Luciano Pavarotti . . . In 1983, the year Judge Comerford had planned to bestow the St. Patrick's Day honor on Al O'Hagan, of the Brooklyn Union Gas Company, the Italians selected Sophia Loren."

Six years after Sophia, Dorothy Hayden Cudahy became the first ever woman grand marshal of the St. Patrick's parade following a campaign on her behalf lasting several years, one that was born primarily in the press, not least the *Irish Echo*. Hayden Cudahy's ambition had been initially thwarted by Judge Comerford's successor, Frank Beirne, on the grounds that she was not a bona-fide member of the Ancient Order of Hibernians. All grand marshals were required to be AOH members in good standing. Hayden Cudahy was a member of the AOH Ladies Auxiliary, a branch of the organization which Beirne and the parade committee at the time did not recognize as being a fully integrated component of the Hibernian order. *Echo* editor John Thornton mounted a campaign which found support in the city's general press: "Just what is the Ladies Auxiliary part of—B'nai B'rith or the Daughters of Italy?" he wrote in a 1985 editorial. That same year, the Ladies Auxiliary became the Ladies AOH. It was now, quite simply, a female counterpart of the male AOH. Women would now be members of divisions, as were men, and they could also be nominated for the greatest honor Irish America could bestow.

Dorothy was a sixty-six-year-old grandmother and at first impression might have seemed to be fully in step with what many younger Irish viewed as an annual day out for an older generation lost in a fog of green sentiment. She wasn't. Indeed, some of her most fervent supporters came from the ranks of the newly arrived Irish, particularly the Irish Immigration Reform Movement.

The grand marshal's strongly nationalist views and allegations that she was overly sympathetic towards Noraid had raised doubts in the Irish government. The parade in New York, as well as several other major cities, was traditionally reviewed by Dublin's representatives, diplomats and visiting ministers. But there were sometimes problems, usually rooted in the Northern Ireland conflict. An Irish government boycott of the San Francisco parade was carried through in 1989 because grand marshal, Dan McCormick, was a member of Noraid.

In New York, the IIRM was rallying to Hayden Cudahy's side, scornful of any suggestion that she be snubbed by Irish officialdom. "At a time when thousands of Irish citizens are relying on the good-will intentions and support of great Irish-Americans like Dorothy Hayden Cudahy, the Irish government should show their gratitude for this support by completely supporting Dorothy and by partici-pating in the parade," the IIRM said in a statement. The kids were wagging the finger. In the end, the Irish government turned up to pay homage to Irish America's leading lady.

Two years after Dorothy's march into history, the Irish outdid even the Italians in the sexuality stakes. The rule book of the St. Patrick's Day Parade and Celebration Committee, drawn up in 1959, was particularly strict when it came to matters of decorum. It stated that "No marcher will be permitted to wear a garment which is of a burlesque or ridiculous nature or which violates the moral codes of public decency. Drum majorettes sparsely dressed, at the heads of bands, will not be permitted in the line of march."

But even this strict stipulation, not so strictly applied by 1991 it has to be said, paled into irrelevance once ILGO emerged from seemingly nowhere chanting: "We're here, we're queer, we're Irish."

ILGO was not, contrary to some belief, a tightly disciplined force of gay shock troops intent on turning Irish American mores and traditions on their head. Irish gays and lesbians who settled in U.S. cities during the 1980s and early '90s might have found them-selves in a country where the laws were more accommodating towards adult homosexual relationships than the Oscar Wilde-era legislation still pertaining in Ireland. Nevertheless, the personal strains involved in "coming out" were no less a factor in Greenwich Village than Dublin, Cork or Galway. Inevitably, Irish gays and les-bians found each other in their new big city homes, and just like their straight fellow Irish, contemporary and long dead, they formed an association.

Maire Crowe, a former *Irish Press* journalist who became part of the founding team at the *Irish Voice* newspaper, was the first to report the emergence of this hitherto unheard of and certainly unusual Irish organization.

"They weren't particularly organized at all. They seemed to be flying by the seats of their pants in the early days," Crowe later recalled.

At one point she and photographer James Higgins featured a group of ILGO founding members in a story published in the *Sunday Tribune* in Dublin. Higgins photographed the Irish gays and lesbians on the Promenade in Brooklyn Heights, the Manhattan skyline in the background.

Crowe remembers that the few in the story who formed the nucleus of ILGO were quite simply "thrilled silly" to be getting their names in the paper. It was early 1991. Within a few weeks, ILGO would be known the world over and, as a later book *Lesbian and Gay Visions of Ireland* contended, would force worldwide attention "on a redefinition of Irishness."

And force it did. Shortly before the 1991 parade, when ILGO and Mayor Dinkins became beer targets, the always just below the surface tensions in the Hibernians erupted full flow when one unit of the group, Manhattan Division 7, invited ILGO to march with its members after the parade committee, headed by Frank Beirne, turned down the gay group's request, filed in October, 1990, to march under its own banner. ILGO was consigned to a waiting list which virtually nobody beyond the parade committee knew even existed. Indeed, when word of the list emerged, parade committee chairman Beirne, a native of Co. Leitrim who died in 1996, admitted that he himself had never seen it. "I personally have not seen the list but there definitely is a written list. It's typed," Beirne told the *New York Post* a few days before the parade.

Thus, battle lines were drawn, not just between ILGO and the parade but within the Hibernians themselves, a more pluralistic group than many perceived, and between the parade committee and New York City which had strict laws on its books barring discrimination against gays and lesbians.

On the morning of the parade (which took place on Saturday March 16 because the parade is never held on a Sunday), the *New York Post*, which annually decks out its St. Patrick's edition front page in green trim, ran an old reliable as its front page splash headline: "Top O' The Mornin!" Overhead was a smaller headline: "Blue skies promised for the big parade." It was all to change rather dramatically in the next few hours. Indeed, the headline itself seemed to fly in the face of the sentiments that had been expressed in both written and spoken word in the days leading up to the parade. An example was a column in the *Post* itself on March 14 by Pete Hamill, one of a group of Irish American writers in New York occasionally referred to as the "Mick Clique:" "Here he comes again," wrote Hamill, "barely risen from the primeval bogs of Ireland, thick-headed, smug, invincibly stupid, wrapped in the flags of a bogus piety. Ladies and Gentlemen: the Terminal Donkey." Hamill was taking his poke at the parade committee. And he was by no means alone.

The headlines the morning after the parade were certainly an indication that a certain mule-like stubbornness was in the March air. Some commentators were even suggesting that the parade itself might be in terminal decline. "Erin Goes Boo, roared *New York Newsday.* "Parade's Over, But Fight's Just Begun," trumpeted the *Post.* Across the ocean in Ireland, the *Sunday Press* front page banner announced: "Green Gays make N.Y. Irish see red." The next day, the *Irish Press* reported the comparison drawn by Mayor Dinkins with Alabama. The principle Irish weeklies, *Echo* and *Voice*, were suddenly competing with the big papers on a story that had, on top of everything else, gone global. But they also had to report on the now smaller headline story—the parade itself. The *Echo* reported Cardinal O'Connor's plea for tolerance at a pre-parade Mass; the day out for huge numbers of people, marchers and spectators alike, which had little or nothing to do with the gay issue; and an analysis of the TV coverage. The conflict between ILGO and the parade organizers was carefully presented as being only one of several stories.

However, the *Echo*'s John O'Mahony described in a background report how, three days before the parade, there was stalemate while chairman Frank Beirne "had hunkered down behind his bunker walls of rules and regulations and even threatened to interfere with the gay pride march in June."

Legal action dominated the front page of the *Irish Voice* which ran a headline: "N.Y. City to File Discrimination Lawsuit Against Parade Committee." Both papers, with resources only amounting to a tiny fraction of those available to the big dailies, struggled to keep up with a complex situation that was changing by the minute, before and after the parade.

Voice editor Patrick Farrelly delivered "the Inside Story," or at least as much of it as could be crammed into a page. Amid the portrayal of Frank Beirne as a "tough and wily organizer" now "steeled" in his determination to keep ILGO out of the parade, and the further reporting that "the liberals in Division 7 see it as an issue to fight Beirne's leadership of the parade," Farrelly also included a line from ILGO's Anne Maguire, a line that almost sounded throwaway, but yet spoke volumes about ILGO's broader motivation: "What people didn't realize was that the Irish thing was equally important as the gay identity."

Writing later in the book *Lesbian and Gay Visions of Ireland*, published in 1995, Maguire mapped out the formation in 1990 of what was a self-help and support group, a human comfort blanket in an alien city, a means for young Irish gay and lesbian immigrants to face up to their sexuality together and the expected hostility that would invariably greet any collective coming out of the closet. Oddly enough, ILGO was shy about using the word "political" in its statement of purpose. The word suggested links to what was in many southern Irish social circles an almost taboo subject: Northern Ireland.

"The assumption that all Northerners were Provos and all Southerners were either apolitical or anti-Republican was rampant," wrote Maguire.

But it was on the matter of the parade that Maguire's thoughts in the book were to arouse a storm: "What is clear about ILGO and the St. Patrick's Day parade is that most people, particularly those of us who are most actively involved, have no inclination to be associated with, never mind march in, the parade. This, very simply, is where our 'coming out' took place in Irish America and where we were told that we did not belong, nor were we welcome."

Maguire's revelation, if such a word accurately describes it all, certainly raised some eyebrows but caused little uproar. That ILGO wasn't dead set on marching up Fifth Avenue in Arans and Tweeds was really no great surprise. One commentator compared Maguire's admission to a scene in the 1980s Irish film *Eat The Peach* in which a character played by Niall Toibin is lying in a hospital bed after being badly beaten up. His name is "Boots" because of the cowboy boots and ten gallon hat he habitually wears. He spins the yarn to all and sundry in the area that he lived for many years in America. Thinking that he might die, Boots pulls his visiting friend up close to him and in a gut-wrenching confession tells him that in fact he had never been to the States in his life. The reply: "Sure we all know that, Boots."

And just about everybody knew that ILGO had more than forty blocks of marching on its mind.

Still, the group had almost accidentally stumbled on something else. And Maguire, in her reference to the "Irish thing" was accurately reflecting a sense of change that was sweeping Ireland itself while, in the form of thousands of young emigrants, it was being swept across the ocean to Irish America. In both Ireland and America, the diaspora's seed and fruit, the sacred cows handed down by the generations were not looking so sacred any more. What was becoming more central to the emerging "new Irish" outlook was a sense that being "Irish," as with being "American" or "British," should not come with any preconceived strings attached. Being just Irish was enough. Anything else was largely your own business, even when it wasn't in line with outmoded legalities.

By 1993, the third year of ILGO's storming of the parade ramparts, it was no longer illegal for consenting adults to have homosexual relations in Ireland. Mary Robinson was inviting gays and lesbians to her official residence for tea and gay marching groups were being accepted in St. Patrick's Day parades in Irish cities with little or no fuss.

Back in America, Anne Maguire's "Irish thing" was a rough-hewn Irish version of *E Pluribus Unum*. Ironically, in a purely Irish context, the process seemed rather more advanced back in the old, supposedly puritanical, sod. In the years following the 1991 parade, ILGO would continue in its efforts to march under its own banner while in Boston a near mirror image struggle would erupt between the organizers of the Evacuation Day/St. Patrick's Day Parade and the Irish American Gay, Lesbian and Bisexual Group of Boston or GLIB. Beantown was in fact one-upping the Big Apple which seemed to be bereft of Irish bisexuals.

In 1992, ILGO was allowed to stage its own march before the main parade. In 1993, it would attempt to force entry onto the parade route. Dozens would be arrested and the pattern for the next several years would be set. "St. Patrick's Parade: It Gets Worse," stated the headline over a *New York Times* editorial at the time of the '93 march. In the following years, the parade organizers would continue to resist ILGO's tactics, on the streets and in the courts. The committee continued to enjoy widespread support. Many Irish Americans were less concerned about civil law as it applied to marching rights than a Catholic ethos that seemed threatened by a group which appeared dangerously hostile to the church. ILGO certainly harbored resentment towards what it saw as a homophobic church establishment, but it was to be other largely American gay groups that would inspire the harshest backlash. Groups such as ACT UP had battled the New York Archdiocese for years, their nemesis being the dominant and generally unflappable figure of Cardinal John O'Connor. The group's members regularly protested outside St. Patrick's Cathedral and at one point staged a loud and angry protest inside the greatest bastion of Irish American Catholicism—during Mass. The fury of many Irish Americans was only to be expected. The Ancient Order of Hibernians received the kind of call it hadn't heard in over one hundred years and rushed to the cathedral's defense. ILGO would be swept along in this backlash, a small fish in a much larger and very turbulent sea.

That sea would also toss around the Hibernians. There would be splits and schisms and disputes over the ultimate control of the parade; arguments over whether the national or state AOH could dictate events or whether the parade was entirely a matter for the New York County Hibernians and the parade committee which had always defended its turf against outsiders, even those from the State and National Hibernian ranks.

Frank Beirne would be expelled from the order only to be re-admitted on his death bed. The vast bulk of parade enthusiasts would continue to step out on St. Patrick's Day no matter what the weather or level of protest. The parade rolled on with the punches and ILGO, out of the closet, also stayed out of the line of march.

For Jack Irwin, a former AOH New York State President, the exclusion of the Irish gays was one of the few times he could recall near unanimous agreement between his brother Hibernians. "The Hibernians in New York and throughout the country were overwhelmingly against the gays being allowed in," the onetime child Broadway star would later recall. "And time proved that they did not have the right to be in the parade in the way they wanted to be."

In time, Anne Maguire was more than a little regretful that she had let the cat out of the bag by admitting that securing acceptance in the parade was not ILGO's true mission.

"In a political sense it's sometimes not smart to be honest. A lot of people were furious with me. In retrospect, it wasn't a smart thing to do." Still, I'm looking forward to the year two thousand, ILGO's tenth birthday."

But regardless of hidden motive, the spectacle of Irish gays versus the largest non-military marching event in the western world had been portrayed to a worldwide audience as a battle of the new against the old, on the streets and in the New York courts, where the Hibernians would eventually win out. Excluding that old reliable, Northern Ireland, the annual parade confrontation was now the second global Irish story of the decade, coming as it did hot on the heels of Mary Robinson's election. Number three was to be the Bishop Casey scandal and from there on the story of the new and changing Ireland just seemed to keep popping up in one form or another all over the place. It was added spice by a growing cast of meritorious and attention-grabbing characters, works of literature, art, scholars and stars—if precious few saints—from Robinson to the likes of U2 and Sinéad O'Connor, Seamus Heaney, Maeve Binchy, Jim Sheridan, Rosaleen Linehan ("the great" as *Time* described her), Brian Friel, Gerry Adams, Peter Sutherland, various sports stars, Dolores O'Riordan, Roddy Doyle, Frank McCourt, Michael Flatley and Jean Butler, Black '47, a veritable posse of new acting and talent, Oscars and Grammys, traditional musicians, Irish and Irish American, and an entire army of young, educated, confident Irishmen and women who now expected, nay demanded, that the broader world be their pearl-yielding oyster. And beyond even this galaxy there were the non-Irish-born Irish like the band Oasis, Jack Charlton and even Bill "I look Irish" Clinton. There seemed to be a line forming: "This way if you want to be Irish too!"

Somewhere along the line, Ireland became hot and more than a few sane individuals started talking about an Irish golden age. "Few countries have redefined themselves more than Ireland in the past two decades," U.S. News and World Report told its readers in a June, 1996 profile of Mary Robinson headed: "Irishness, she will tell you, is global."

In past times, it would have been a normal reaction to say that history would be sole judge of that. But the world no longer had the patience to wait for the historians to catch up. '90s Ireland was making history as it went along and it seemed immediately tangible, graspable, understood as history rather than just news. Certainly, one thing was plainly evident and that was the fact that the Irish were writing and talking about themselves at a hitherto unseen rate. Self-worship, self-criticism, self loathing, self-interest. All took a hold of Robinson's great diaspora. But above all, there was a terrible restlessness. The battles for U.S. visas having been won—even if the war for immigration reform had been lost—freedom to travel meant freedom to return "home." Ireland was also intruding into an America that was once the immigrant's great cocoon, the new home at the end of the one-way ticket. "Home," the one left behind, now came stopping by via satellite, telephone, e-mail and the internet. You could hear the folks back home on a computer, even see them. You could fall asleep in San Francisco listening to Irish radio on the worldwide web. Irish newspapers cropped up in big city news-stands. All was flux, and it was becoming increasingly difficult to forget what had been left behind.

Mary Robinson was restless too, surging through Africa or the corridors of the United Nations, chasing a career dream that would break her free from the restrictions of a job she had turned inside out. "Should This Woman Run The World?" The headline, in the June 15, 1996 issue of the *Nation* magazine was only suggesting what many were seriously asking. Mary Robinson was emerging as a possible new Secretary General of the United Nations, a sick political child in need of a good nurse. Robinson appeared to be the cure and she wasn't denying it too strongly as she crisscrossed the globe spitting fire at the evils of hunger and the trampling of human rights. And as she stirred the pot, the diaspora stirred with her. Just as Robinson's job was both springboard and restraint, mobility, and the new freedom to cross oceans and borders on a regular basis was now, for some of Mary's diasporites, almost a terrible curse. The age-old question asked by Irish parents: "Are you settled?" could now only evoke a shrug of the shoulder. There were no more one-way tickets.

Amid all the glory being heaped on all things Irish, the Irish, now some seventy million strong according to Robinson, managed to keep their teeth sharp and reserved for their very own. Irish journalism was also stirring, opinion and comment fast becoming master, hard news the servant. It was frequently self-indulgent but it could always turn the good phrase, the sharp backhand. Brendan O'Connor in the *Sunday Independent* newspaper: "Experts call it 'The Cranberry Syndrome.' It is more commonly known as PC MIC (Post-Colonial Massive Inferiority Complex). PC MIC refers to the incredulous delight with which we Irish greet anyone from abroad actually being interested in anything we produce. Imagine that! Someone noticed little ole us!"

Or Damien Kiberd in the *Sunday Business Post*, defending from critics the *Field Day Theatre Company Anthology of Irish Writing* and its editor, Derry-native Seamus Deane: "Confronted by scholarship of such excellence and motivated, largely, if not solely, by political bile, the pygmies had to search for an excuse to berate the anthology. One came readily to hand: There were not enough women writers represented in the three volume collection (the vast majority of the leading writers of the last one thousand years were, unfortunately, men) . . . Better still was to come, though, when Deane's book (*Reading in the Dark*) was short-listed for the Booker Prize some months ago (eventually finishing up a close second to the winner). Various Irish literary pygmies, authors of third and even fourth rate 'novels' some of which are openly anti-Irish, have been prostrating before the London literary establishment for years in an effort to win a Booker nomination.

"They have done everything except take off their trousers before their imperial masters (some may even have crossed that threshold of self-deprecation) in order to ensure the encomia of the British ruling elite."

Meanwhile, back in America, someone had the nerve to write about *How The Irish Saved Civilization*. The author's name was Cahill but he pronounced it the American way because he was American. Ireland, caught up in its sudden whirlwind of self-obsession, was not being permitted to exclusively redefine itself.

Cahill's book, a newly worked presentation of the role of early Irish Christians in saving Europe from its darker self, was subtitled "The Untold Story of Ireland's Heroic Role From the Fall of Rome to the Rise of Medieval Europe." That wasn't quite true. Every Irish kid had learned in school about the "Island of Saints and Scholars" and about how Irish monks and saints, male and female, had founded churches, monasteries and places of learning all over Europe at a time when the entire continent seemed to vanishing into a dark hole that consumed civilizations for supper. But the story was mostly unknown in mainstream America, and success or otherwise in America, the "New Rome," was now western civilization's primary measuring stick.

Cahill's timing couldn't have been better. Like Mary Robinson, he caught the wave. Writing in *Irish America* magazine after his cheekily titled tome had etched its way deep into the best-seller lists, Cahill expressed the sense of many: . . . "we have truly reached the Irish moment, a moment of unparalleled influence in America's (and perhaps the world's) imagination."

The irony of Cahill's success was that his thesis came at a time when Irish civilization—at least that part of it in the hands of those who had inherited the last vestiges of Ireland's medieval sanctity— seemed to be in need of some saving itself. The book, without really attempting to be such, came across to some as an exercise in nostalgia, a swan song for a glorious Ireland long dead, rather than a work in praise of a glorious, newly born and fully European nation.

Ireland in the 1990s certainly seemed to be thoroughly devoid of saints, while those who might be described as scholars spent their days arguing over the legacy of mostly twentieth century personalities who were either ikons or villains depending on the latest prevailing point of view.

Some reviewers lambasted *How The Irish Saved Civilization* for having the nerve even to stick to the subject matter heralded in its very title.

"Cahill," wrote one reviewer, Lawrence Osborne, "merrily tells us that we all owe Ireland an incalculable debt, for without her, we would be barbarians—the later defeats suffered by the land of monastic scholars and brilliant Latinists being just an ironic inversion of the older truth, namely that of the Gaels holding aloft the torch of civilization during the dark ages. That he has to downplay a puny little hamlet called Constantinople or a backwater like Muslim-Jewish-Christian Spain as repositories of this same western civilization is no matter. The important thing is to make the peripheral central and the reputedly 'backward' a progressive agency of civilization."

Cahill was in the process of getting around to some of the other historical powerhouses mentioned by Osborne—who might have done well to watch *Eat The Peach*—even as this review was being written. But in separate books in praise of Jews and others. At the same time, Mary Robinson was dwelling on the notion of the peripheral as being central for entirely different reasons. Osborne didn't quite seem to get the point of Cahill's exercise in the way that tens of thousands of book buyers were catching on to it. The fact was, Ireland's role in world history had long been consigned to dusty back shelves because the Irish had never much of an opportunity to have their own say, regardless of the popular view of the Irish being an exceptionally articulate and literary race.

Cahill's putting the case for an Irish global role, long before most human beings knew there was a globe, was simply something that nobody had succeeded with before. Ireland's role had long been historically ignored or understated while the glories of more powerful European nations and groups were old news. The book's central message simply rhymed with its time. Its title did the rest.

Cahill's work was in praise of a long past Ireland. Frank McCourt's *Angela's Ashes* was in praise of anyone's—his own included—ability to survive a more recent Ireland, or at least that part of it covered by the city of Limerick. Like Cahill, McCourt was writing from a later perspective provided by years of living in America. Had he remained in Limerick, it's unlikely that *Angela's Ashes* would ever have been written. Or if it had, it probably would have sold a few copies in Ireland itself before vanishing into the foggy Shannon air. Half the people in the Limerick of McCourt's youth probably could have had a go at writing a version of *Angela's Ashes*. But they didn't and McCourt did, an indication once again that you often have to step away from a place in order to see it.

McCourt may well turn out to be the greatest literary sensation of the 1990s, an "Irish-American raconteur," as Denis Donoghue's *New York Times* review described him, who has become everyone's favorite bedtime confessor. McCourt, despite his anti-clerical leanings, would have made a good priest, a local favorite in the confession box, dispenser of highly unusual penances.

McCourt and Cahill, both writing from the next parish, are towering parts of the new Irish story, even though they could be classified as Irish American, older Irish or both. When the *New York Times* wrote in October, 1996 that "The Irish Are Ascendant Again," the paper's writer, Dinitia Smith, described "this new Irish renaissance" as being "inseparable from the demographic weight of Irish immigration." She was right.

In subsequent stories in other papers: "Creative Spirits Soaring in Eire (*Daily News*, March 16, 1997), "Red hot and green" (*New York Post*, March 17, 1997), "'Riverdance' and the Eire Sensation, How America Got its Irish Up" (*Washington Post*, June 29, 1997), various writers touched on both the interplay and sometimes rivalry between Ireland and Irish America, a combination that had finally come together to produce a cultural combustion unseen before in the history of either nation.

Writing about the success of "Riverdance" and "Lord of the

Dance" in the *Washington Post*, Peter Finn placed both in the context of "a larger transatlantic phenomenon, previously unseen in the one hundred and fifty years of the Irish diaspora in the United States. In the 1990s, Irish and American culture have burst into full song—inventing fresh ideas of Irishness, cross-pollinating across the ocean, eliciting critical interest and, in the process, enjoying commercial success."

And it was important not to forget commercial success. In truth, the twin classifications, "Irish" and "Irish America," being veritable American fixtures and fittings, had a head start on most other old/new world combinations. How the Ottoman Turks saved civilization might have been an interesting try, but it's hard to see it catching on in Boston or Peoria. Equally, a story of growing up miserable in Calcutta probably would have flopped because what else would your average American reader expect?

McCourt's contention that there was nothing as miserable in the wide world as an Irish Catholic childhood surprised many. Even after reading his version of such an upbringing, many would still take issue with him. But that was after the book was bought.

Cahill and McCourt, like the Irish in general, long versed in the art of selling the line of triumph over misery, or misery amid triumph, were always on course for a collision with the new Irish ascendancy. The 1980s, and even more so the '90s, turned out to be the time when Irish triumph and Irish misery were in demand in equal measure.

The "new Irish"—immigrants, Irish residents and frequent flyer globe-trotting Irish—who populate the fawning newspaper and magazine stories are not so much new in the dictionary sense as they are simply the Irish who happened to be around when thorough change in Ireland couldn't be kept outside the half-door any longer. They have been made look new by circumstance.

The established Irish in America really have not changed all that much from the immigrants of yore. More of them are Republicans and a far greater proportion can claim to have visited Ireland or to have met a "real" Irish person. They face declining reasons to be misty-eyed about Ireland, because Ireland is becoming more and more like their own back yard.

Peter Finn, Irish-born himself, wrote of the Irish/Irish American cultural phenomenon of the late twentieth century as being previously unseen. True. But like an approaching comet it could be seen coming, possibly as long ago as the 1950s and most certainly by the 1980s when the newly arriving Irish immigrants were providing the faces and personalities that would become the near future's "new Irish" in America.

This sense of something new afoot was detected first in the Irish American press, which, like historian Felipe Fernandez-Armesto's description of the Irish themselves in his book *Millennium*, proved to be "peculiarly intractable," despite the continuous absorption of its lifeblood Irish immigrant readership into the greater American whole.

The 1980s would bring new voices to the fore and those voices would echo from one side of America to the other. The Irish, native-born or diasporite, have always enjoyed a good yarn. And even in the era of instant mass communication, where many display wonder at the technology of communication as much as what is communicated, there would be yarns aplenty to hold captive the new Irish mind, stories galore rooted in that elusive sprite, that "Irish thing."

9

A NEW IRISH JOURNALISM

*"The next great object of our undertaking is to give publicity
to the past and present wrongs of our native country, in such
indignant accents as will reverberate from one shore to the
other of civilized man."*

The *Emerald*, New York, Saturday, July 17, 1824.

Every week and every month of the year they roll off the presses.
Newspapers and magazines, newsletters and pamphlets. They are
the publications of the Irish American press, a tradition in type and
sometimes in hype, fueled for two centuries by the grievances of
eight. If war is the ultimate story, then Irish American journalism is
to be envied. There has been war enough to fill a million miles of
column inches. And in between, ample politics and backstabbing,
dances and romances, gossip and grudges, battles on the field of
sport and in the backstreets of Belfast. As pikes evolved into muskets and machine guns, the one constant implement in the battle for
Irish independence has been the newspaper, broadsheet and tabloid.
The *Emerald* had its day and countless other publications, prominent and obscure, followed in its wake, literally. And yet, when it
comes to the study of the history of the Irish in America, the newspapers are all too often given short shrift. Used for quotes and reference, yes. But rarely cast as separate and distinct forces; and when
mentioned in any detail at all, seemingly acting as mere props for
the ambitious and powerful figures who owned and published them.

But the writings and meanderings of countless individuals have,
for generations, pulled Irish America together, blending it into the
surprisingly tight weave it yet remains despite the powerful pull of
mainstream, strip-mall America. And now there are television,
radio, and web pages to add muscle to a great tug of war for an
audience that has less time in any day to consider Ireland or matters Irish, to consider much of anything at all.

The question invariably arises. Would there have been a discernible Irish American press if not for the troubled circumstances of Ireland's history? Certainly not in the form it has taken these past two hundred years. Yes, it would exist. But it would be missing much of the passion that has given Irish American journalism its own particular characteristics, especially in its formative years: Unambiguous protest arising from a deep sense of national injury; a traditional enemy and oft hate figure in England, a factor which gave cause to a frequent urge to be journalistically undisciplined, to take off the gloves and pour scorn regardless of circumstance or even fact.

Of course, the Irish in America didn't have always to look backwards to find injustice. There was plenty of it in the new homeland, particularly in the years preceding the rise of Irish political, economic and religious power.

Still, regardless of the very real injustices which provided a constant flow of grist for the Irish mill, much of what passes for journalism in Irish American history amounts to little more than endless diatribes dead aimed at the struggle for Ireland's destiny. It frequently had the appearance and tone of simple propaganda. Arguably of course, a propaganda for a noble cause, disseminated by and on behalf of a people long trampled down, indeed half erased from their native soil. There has not been a journalist born who doesn't at times feel the urge to rage when the situation calls for more than cold reportage. And Irish America's journalists had cause to rage down the years more than most.

If there is an initial defining age for Irish American journalism it is be found in the latter half of the nineteenth century, post-Famine and from about the time of the Fenian Rebellion. Papers like the *United Irishman*, the *Irish Citizen*, John Devoy's *Gaelic American*, the *Chicago Citizen* and Patrick Ford's *Irish World* battled it out, each more eager than the next to bash England on her crowned head, while saving the back of the hand for one another.

Recognizable Irish American journalism had emerged at the start of the century with the *Hibernian Chronicle*, which began publication in 1810. The *Emerald* came a few years later, as did the heavily Catholic influenced *Truth Teller* which rapidly became the growing Irish community's top seller in New York, just as the *Boston Pilot* did in its home town later in the century.

At the root of virtually all early Irish American journalism there are clearly discernible political, religious and financial motives. It rarely had much to do with high falutin' belief in the virtues of simple journalism as the end in itself, a concept that remains elusive even to this day. The early papers served as spring boards for the ambitious, the influential and the angry. They were often simply tools in the hands of those whose mission in life was to wage war against the old foe across the ocean, or new ones closer to fist.

Apart from the proprietors, the papers also served as a social ladder for those Irish immigrants eager to secure social advancement by means other than manual labor.

According to John Devoy biographer Terry Golway, journalism in the latter half of the nineteenth century, Irish and mainstream, became a stepping stone to the middle class for educated Irish-born and Irish American men, just as nursing served the same function for Irish women.

"Journalism became a chance to put on a tie. The *New York Herald* in the 1870s was loaded with Irish Americans and many of them were Fenians. Indeed, that paper was a hornet's nest of Fenians."

Injustice in Ireland was potent fuel for the Fenian pressmen. But a constant immersion in journalism inevitably exposes the journalist to the complications and contradictions inherent in even the most cut and dried political struggle. Along the written way, there would be inevitable compromise, a broadening of purpose and benefits for innumerable individuals who gave scant thought to the troubles they had left behind in Ireland. Somewhere along that way, the Irish American press grew up and began embracing something rather less noble and romantic than a perfect, mythical Ireland. It found its market, one that, despite a foundation in poverty, was still gifted with a relatively high rate of literacy thanks in good measure to the efforts of the Catholic Church.

But growing pains were unavoidable. The *Emerald*, for one, was long promised before it finally appeared on the mud and cobbled streets of early nineteenth century New York. The broadsheet's front page explanation of its tawdry time keeping was printed right at the top: "Want of punctuality, particularly in the conduct of public journalists, is at all times to be reprehended."

The paper then got down to what was always the primary business at hand in those post-Wolfe Tone times: "Our object, then is to expose the calumny, and punish the perfidy, of every wretch who dares asperse our country, and to remove from the minds of Americans those prejudices which would represent Irishmen as unworthy of their confidence and love . . . More than six centuries of carnage and bondage have done their worst: the most highly gifted portion of the human race has stood still in the path of regeneration; and our Isle, the most beautiful in the world, is weeping for the destitution of her children—the pity, yet the admiration of mankind . . . Our object shall be to elevate the Irish character to that degree which its merits deserve; to cultivate affectionate feelings between Irishmen and Americans; to aim with unwearied labour, at the instruction and amusement of our readers, and to proclaim to the world the past and present wrongs of our country."

One hundred and seventy-five years on, those final words could just as easily apply to the contemporary Irish American press.

The gap which the *Emerald* was attempting to bridge, and it named it, was that between "Irishmen" and Americans. The idea of there being such a thing as Irish Americans had yet to take a firm grip on the imagination of those who actually filled the category in 1824. It would begin to take stronger hold after the famine. Before the Great Hunger had run its course, in 1849, the *Irish-American* rolled off the presses. It was a weekly published by Patrick Meehan, Patrick Lynch and Edward Cole and it peaked in popularity in its first twenty years. Its position on the political situation in Ireland was mostly moderate and, as a result, it avoided the kind of fervent disapproval from the church that could mean the financial death knell for a paper purporting to serve the almost entirely Catholic Irish community. The *Irish-American* ceased publication in 1915.

Patrick Ford's *Irish World and Industrial Liberator* cranked up its presses in 1870 and in the following years became the dominant Irish newspaper in America, partly due to the fact that it paid close attention to matters of now Irish American concern as much as issues in Ireland itself, not least the cause of labor. Eventually becoming simply the *Irish World*, the paper bought the *Gaelic American* in 1950 and continued printing as the *Irish World* over the next two decades before succumbing to the effects of time and competition from the *Irish Echo*.

The *Irish Nation* was launched by Fenian John Devoy in 1881 and it took part of the name of an earlier radical nationalist publication, the *Nation*, which lived and died within the confines of 1848 just as another radical sheet, the *Citizen*, did in the twelve months of 1854. Devoy's paper was focused almost entirely on the situation in Ireland and went out of business after just four years. However, its agenda was revived by Devoy's *Gaelic American*, which was launched in 1903 and continued publishing until the *World*'s successful takeover bid.

Devoy's purpose did not mirror that of the earlier *Emerald*. Quite the contrary. He was more for blowing up bridges than building them, in every sense of the word. And his dedication to the supposedly loftier principles of journalism was never especially apparent.

Pandering, according to Terry Golway, had been an established tradition in Irish American journalism by the time Devoy arrived on the scene. Granted, the pandering was often directed at sentiment that was born of legitimate grievance. But Devoy was a master when it came to whipping up such sentiment and carrying it to even previously unscaled heights.

In the 1870s and 1880s, according to Golway, there were frequent crusades by Devoy against various evils, real and concocted. One campaign more justified than some was directed at offensive St. Patrick's Day cards—a battle that was still going on a century later.

According to Golway, Devoy was never a man to do things by halves. "The level of outrage often exceeded the offense. Devoy was clearly guilty many times of going over the top. He did not believe in assimilation. He wanted an Irish America that was solely devoted to freeing Ireland. He would pander to anything that would keep Irish America separate, distinct and in the ghetto."

The *Irish Advocate* wasn't too concerned about political ghettoes. It emerged in 1893 under the guidance of John C. O'Connor. The paper was largely apolitical, concentrated primarily on general news from Ireland itself but attracted a loyal and significant readership nevertheless. Before it went out of business, in 1989, the *Advocate*—it was normally referred to without the "Irish" prefix—actually found one particularly prized reader and became, for an instant, the envy of its competitors. Jackie Onassis was approached one evening by *Advocate* writer Fionnula Burke at a reception at the Pierpont Morgan Library in Manhattan. Jackie O was asked by Burke if she had ever read the *Advocate*. Onassis smiled graciously and replied that yes indeed she was a reader, at which point Burke presented her with the latest issue. Onassis left the reception still smiling, with the paper tucked under her arm. Jackie, discreet as always, did not do a Harry Truman with the paper and wave it about for all to see. So sadly, there was no conclusive photographic evidence of the *Advocate*'s rather neat little scoop, one that would turn out to be its last.

The *Advocate* was a victim of changing times. By 1989, the *Irish Echo* was facing the same dilemma. Two years before that, the *Irish Voice* had made its debut and for a while it looked as if the traditional pattern would repeat itself—that of a new upstart newspaper overlapping for a time with an older deep-rooted one before finally finishing the old-timer off. This had been the pattern in the past though it had often taken years to reach the inevitable climax. But the 1980s were not the 1880s. Life at every level was accelerated to the point that it seemed ludicrous even to try to compare the past with the present. Readers even lived longer. Still, the rumor was afoot: The *Voice* believed it could kill off the *Echo* before 1988 was out.

The *Voice*'s arrival at the end of 1987, and its rapid emergence into view the following year, came at a pivotal time for the Irish American community and its most prominent print voice, the *Echo*. The *Echo* was sixty years old in 1988, still a good deal younger than the *Advocate*, while it had yet to surpass either the extinct *Irish American* or *Irish World* in total lifespan. But it was clearly no longer a spring chicken at a time when the story of the Irish in America had reached a turning point by virtue of the large and rapid influx of young Irish immigrants.

Fortune had smiled on the *Echo* in the past. But there were no longer any guarantees. The paper had been founded by Monaghan native Charlie "Smash the Border" Connolly in 1928. The period was an exciting one for Irish American journalism. The Irish Free State had emerged from the ashes of civil war and partition. De Valera had recently formed Fianna Fáil. Immigrants, now from a partly free Ireland, were still landing in New York and Boston by ship. There was much to argue about, much to celebrate and even still, much to lament.

The link between the surging immigrant population of the time and the arrival of the *Echo* is underlined in the *Encyclopedia of New York*, edited by Kenneth T. Jackson, which states that the *Irish Echo* "created a demand for good musicians in Irish bars, restaurants, clubs, and ballrooms, as well as a new market for Irish records and radio broadcasts."

Indeed, the *Echo* had arrived at a time that was something of a golden age for Irish American radio in the greater New York area.

No fewer than twenty-two stations were broadcasting Irish shows in the years immediately following the *Echo*'s birth. The new weekly, by virtue of its immediate immigrant roots, was the *Irish Voice* of its day. But time would draw the paper deeper into its New York roots. The paper changed hands in the 1950s and was taken up by the Irish American and Bronx-based Grimes family, which, up until then, had concentrated its business efforts in the travel trade and, at one point, had been the lessee of Gaelic Park, a sporting battlefield trodden by waves of Gaelic footballers, hurlers and Camogie players.

The *Echo*, which in its earliest days was delivered by horse-drawn wagons from its Harlem offices, went from a broadsheet to a tabloid format under the control of Paddy Grimes and his son, John. It adapted itself to newer publishing technologies and, during the 1960s, steadily evolved into a paper covering both the immigrant Irish and Irish American community, not just in New York, but also in the surrounding states of the north east and even beyond. The paper was largely dictating its own course, focusing mostly on the Irish American community's inexorable progress towards middle class respectability. Then all hell broke loose in Northern Ireland.

There had been troubles before, of course. The *Echo* had given prominent coverage to the IRA border campaign of the 1950s, reporting for example, in its January 12, 1957 issue, an IRA attack on Derrylin police barracks in Co. Fermanagh, during which a young constable, John Scally—"a rookie in the constabulary"—and "three youths" were killed. The IRA men were described as "insurgents" and the paper reported that the raid was "the most daring" yet staged in the campaign. The *Echo* kept things reasonably balanced, reporting Irish Prime Minister John A. Costello's assertion that the country would never be united by IRA tactics. It also included a line from the London *Daily Mail* claiming that the Northern Ireland government in Stormont was "aware" that "the Russians" were backing the IRA border raids and were encouraging the IRA to prolong its campaign. This was no mean consideration in the "Commie"-spooked America of the 1950s and the inclusion of the *Daily Mail*'s line was only confirmation of the fact that the *Echo* was, by now, as much an American paper as it was Irish.

Still, the paper also allowed itself the latitude to vent forcefully on the issue of partition. The front page lead story on the raid concluded thus: "The sympathy of the mass of the people appears to be with the IRA and the Costello Government is finding itself in what seems to be a very unpopular condition in lending its aid to the Stormont Government to suppress the IRA in its efforts to force the British to abandon partition." This was hardly "smash the border" stuff. But it was a reminder that the *Echo* realized that its survival depended on far more than just the approval of governments and other powerful institutions, such as the church. Many readers openly supported the IRA while many more advocated rapid Irish unity by political means. But even what was now the paper's constitutional nationalist ethos would be severely tested by the outbreak of sustained violence in Northern Ireland in the late 1960s.

The troubles would draw the *Echo* into frequent condemnation of "the Brits" and would lead to the emergence of the *Irish People*, a far more radical weekly linked to the IRA support group, Irish Northern Aid. But inevitably, the mounting atrocities on both sides would mean that while the *Echo* might veer from one end of the spectrum of condemnation to the other—depending on who committed the latest outrage—it would ultimately find safest ground in the greenest part of the constitutional center, condemning violence but urging fundamental change as a means of tackling the roots of that violence; a dismantled border if not an entirely smashed one.

"The tradition of the paper put us on the republican side," John Thornton, *Echo* editor from 1963 to 1990, would later recall.

"But any time a heinous bombing took place we would have to explain the reason for it to the general public. That was very difficult to do. I remember, during the seventies in particular, it was a case of the Brits would do something, the IRA would do something, the loyalists would do something and it was, my God what's going to happen next. But we continued to support unity."

In doing so, the *Echo* reflected the position of the majority of its readers. But while it consistently advocated a removal of the border through negotiation, far more extreme solutions to the problems thrown up by partition would find weekly expression on the paper's letters pages. The reader pen would be repeatedly wielded in advancing the view that the power of the sword was greatest. Throughout the '70s and early '80s, the *Echo*'s letters-to-the-editor pages were an accurate weather vane for Irish American sentiment, much of it virulently anti-British in tone.

As the troubles rumbled on, there was still the business of finding new readers. In 1981, the *Echo* launched a separate edition, the

Boston Irish Echo. The move was a reaction to long endured complaints from Boston that the *Echo*, while the best paper going, was too much a New York oriented publication. The Irish American community was spread across all fifty states but rivalry between different communities in the major cities was a constant factor to be seriously considered by any paper. Irish America was just a larger version of Ireland itself in that respect.

The Boston Irish, not without reason, always saw themselves as unique, somehow the original Irish Americans. Besides, it was Beantown's own Tip O'Neill who had pronounced all news to be local. And New York wasn't local in Dorchester or "Southie." The complaint was consistent and caused much fretting in New York, although it was rarely appreciated by readers just how limited the resources of any individual Irish paper actually were.

Those resources would be stretched by the troubles and to new limits again as the 1980s wave of new immigrants gathered momentum. The *Echo*, while it had undergone several makeovers, in content and appearance, during the thirty years since the Grimes family had purchased it, was well settled by mid-decade into catering for its established readers. Being a small publication by comparison to the big dailies it fairly well knew its readership. And there had been little or no competition to contend with week in and week out, a fact of life often regretted by editor Thornton. All, however, was about to change. And utterly.

The premier issue of the *Irish Voice* went to press in the first week of December, 1987. Its birth had been rumored for some months and as the summer of 1987 passed into the fall, those rumors took firmer hold.

The *Echo* was outwardly secure but actually vulnerable to attack in the fast growing new market of incoming illegals. Added to this, the publisher, John Grimes, had died suddenly in late July. His widow, Claire O'Gara Grimes, was not only thrust into a job she had not contemplated, but also very quickly into a circulation war with a sharp and hungry new rival headed by Niall O'Dowd. The likes of this hadn't been seen since the *Echo* itself, once an upstart, had erupted on the scene in 1928.

At fifty-six pages, almost half of them taken by advertisers prominent in the Irish community, the first *Voice* and its "We'll Never Return—Young Illegals" lead headline nailed its colors to the mast from the outset. The story was flagged in red ink as an "exclusive." The first *Voice* would report on the newly arrived Irish in America, the North, and Ireland itself, roughly in that order of priority. The *Voice*'s top priority, the young Irish, was not, to that point at least, the *Echo*'s prime concern. Additionally, the *Voice* included gossip and columns designed specifically to attack long sacred cows like the New York GAA.

With an eye on Irish Americans, there was also a genealogy column in the first issue. The sense that the *Voice* was impatient to be up and at it was compounded by the fact that the first family name treated in this feature didn't begin with A. For some reason it was O'Callaghan. U2, meanwhile, dominated the premier issue's center spread.

The first editorial explained the paper's birth thus: "The pace of Irish American activities has made this new publication inevitable."

Compared to issues in the following few years, the first *Voice* was not a knockout. The paper would take a while to find its feet. Sure, there might well have been as many as 135,000 illegals out there—as the first editorial suggested—but who were they, where were they? The paper, based in midtown Manhattan, would have to seek them out, wherever they were. The first issue had no letters-to-the-editor page. Its birth had indeed been a well-kept secret.

No secret by issue two. "Gaelic Park Uproar—Ballot Cancelled" was the lead headline and the first line might have been a metaphor for a coming newspaper war: "Fights broke out, ballot papers were burned—and a fire engine arrived—as the New York Gaelic Athletic Association's election for a new president collapsed in chaos at Gaelic Park last Sunday."

By the new year, there was still no letters page. But a lack of correspondence could be borne when you could throw out a story such as "Slave Labor Girl Scandal." While many older Irish and Irish Americans, long used to the *Echo*'s mellow rhythms, had yet to become even conscious of the *Voice*'s existence, the same could not be said of the young Irish immigrants in Queens and the Bronx, desperate for news from home and stories closer to hand, all wrapped up in a colorful, brash, kick-butt tabloid which seemed to be talking about them—and to them.

Patrick Farrelly, former editor of the *Voice*, would later recall a time when *Irish America* magazine, Niall O'Dowd's first publishing venture in New York, had given a clue as to the possibilities for new Irish print ventures.

"Our feeling was that the *Echo* hadn't really caught on to the implications of the extraordinary wave of new immigration. Culturally, it wasn't able to react to it as fast as it should have. We saw a market the *Echo* just wasn't keyed into."

Farrelly had been working in San Francisco with O'Dowd on a monthly paper, the *Irishman*. But the immigrant wave was striking the east coast first and hardest. The two moved operations to New York where initial capital investment for the planned *Voice* was supplied by Ireland's largest company, the Smurfit Corporation, a multinational which, as Farrelly would later put it, "was playing with the idea of newspapers at the time."

The *Voice* would not be content to merely grab a slice of the *Echo*'s action. The suggestion was being widely aired that the new weekly expected to consign the *Echo* to the scrapheap. Some were even saying that the *Echo*, like some terminal cancer patient, had just six months. Patrick Farrelly was a little more cautious.

"In the back of our minds we felt there was room for only one paper in New York," he would recall, ten years into the *Voice* versus *Echo* era.

"We had a very specific agenda. We wanted to apply a vigorous journalistic analysis to the established Irish institutions of New York, the GAA, the Ancient Order of Hibernians, the church and the labor unions. We felt the *Echo* gave a who, what, where and when but it didn't analyze beyond that. We figured we could carve out a niche for ourselves and get noticed with a paper that was culturally tuned into a new wave of young Irish immigrants. They were young and brash and that's what we would be too."

Farrelly remembers the early *Voice* years as being hectic and journalistically productive. The *Voice* went after, as he put it, "everybody" and opened up a window on the politics of the Irish community. By focusing primarily on the new Irish, the paper had a considerable impact, not just on the lives of the new arrivals, but on the more established Irish and Irish American community for the simple reason that despite the apparent generation gap, the one never really existed in complete isolation from the other. But while the *Voice* was also persuading established Irish America to look anew at itself, it was, according to Farrelly, having a similar effect on the *Echo*.

"One of the biggest impacts the *Voice* had was that it improved the *Echo*. Rather than going under, the *Echo* slowly but surely revamped itself. It became a dramatically better newspaper. The *Voice* would never have got off the ground if the *Echo* had been that way in the beginning."

This is true to an extent. But apart from the very immediate consequence of new and hot competition, the *Echo* would likely have changed over time regardless of the *Voice*'s efforts, or even its very existence. The same wave of change that had stirred the rock pool enough to throw up the *Voice* was also causing changes at the *Echo*, a paper which had survived down the years largely due to its willingness to adapt to whatever the times demanded. And these were surely demanding times. The *Voice* did accelerate the pace of change at the *Echo*, but it was not the sole agent of such change.

Still, in its first years, the *Voice* was widely viewed as having the *Echo* at the very least on the defensive if not entirely on the run.

In her study of the new Irish, *Irish Illegals, Transients Between Two Societies*, Mary P. Corcoran testified as to the *Voice*'s strong appeal to the '80s new Irish.

"Good marketing is a hallmark of the *Irish Voice*. Strategies used to woo the young Irish audience include regular quizzes and competitions. The weekly green card column gives advice on a wide range of immigration matters, often in a question and answer format based on requests for information from readers."

Corcoran concluded that this effort to appeal to new Irish immigrants was not lost on readers. She included testimony from three.

"I prefer the *Irish Voice* to the *Irish Echo*. It has better news coverage. I think the *Voice* addresses itself to the young population. The *Echo*, in contrast, has played itself out."

"The *Voice* is a far better paper because it caters to young people. The *Echo* caters to people who have been in this country fifty years or more."

"I think the *Irish Voice* deals more with what is going on in Ireland, whereas the *Irish Echo* is more of an Irish-American newspaper."

Corcoran's book is a sociological study, written in the present tense. As such, it risked the appearance of being dated in an historical context if the *Echo* managed to turn things around, play itself back into the game, as opposed to out.

But for a while, it seemed as if the prediction of the first of the three *Voice* boosters was right on target.

"We managed to produce a lot of really good journalism," Patrick Farrelly would later recall.

"Northern Ireland week in and week out was a key story. But there was also tons of local stuff, for example the labor unions. At one point we were doing so much on local issues that I was turning sources down on the likes of the St. Patrick's Day Parade and the carpenters union."

Farrelly believes that the *Voice*'s journalism peaked in effectiveness during the period between 1989 and 1991, a span of time that witnessed triumph in the Morrison Visa campaign and ructions in the New York parade arising from ILGO's efforts to gain entry on its own terms.

Stories that made a deserved splash in this period included Farrelly's own exclusive regarding efforts by the FBI and the Northern Ireland police, the RUC, to turn a young undocumented Irish immigrant into an informer. "BLACKMAIL," the headline screamed across page one of the September 1, 1990 issue. It was a sure seller.

The follow up story one week later had Irish American lawyers, in the form of the Brehon Law Society, riding to the young Tyrone immigrant's rescue. The front page that week also had Irish rock singer and Band Aid founder Bob Geldof blasting Noraid-supporting Irish Americans for being ignorant about the troubles in Northern Ireland. Good Irish Americans and bad Irish Americans all on the same page. Another good sell. The latter story was written by Helena Mulkerns, an Irish-born writer whose natural journalistic outlet at the time could only have been the *Voice*. Within a few years, however, Mulkerns would be contributing to the *Echo*, her switching sides being part of what normally occurs when newspapers are engaged in head-to-head—and roughly equal—competition.

Immigration and immigrants were at the heart of the *Voice*'s strategy. The paper was neither expected nor really required to be objective on the matter. The paper was highly successful in adopting the cause of immigration reform and participating in the actual campaign to achieve it. By late 1991, the *Voice*'s commitment had clearly paid dividends. With applications pouring in for the Morrison Visa program, the paper hired a van, plastered a sign reading "*Irish Voice* Morrison Visa Express" on the side and drove sacks of applications to the collection address in Virginia. The October 15 issue featured the van, the mail sacks and a beaming trio of *Voice* staffers including immigration specialist and former *Echo* journalist Debbie McGoldrick, who had by then made the ten minute walk between the *Echo* and *Voice* offices in Manhattan. To this day, the Visa Express story represents for many, Patrick Farrelly included, the *Voice*'s finest hour.

Informing and entertaining those same Morrison winners would now be the *Voice*'s weekly task. In contrast to other earlier Irish American publications, the *Voice* was never shy when it came to sex or expressing its own views on supposedly risqué issues. "The Celtic Sex Connection? Hear Sexy 970-TARA Girls Talk" roared the front page on August 25, 1992. "Patriot Games, British Good Guys and Irish Psychos" the lead headline announced in the June 16 issue that same year. The story was a planned assault on the movie adaptation of a Tom Clancy novel which portrayed all its Irish characters as gun-toting psychopaths.

The *Voice* would continue to be quick off the mark when it came to tackling stereotyping, or what it felt was unfair treatment of the Irish by Hollywood, television or the mainstream print media. An attack dog stance was what readers had quickly come to expect from the paper and it seemed to make good marketing sense. An entire week would lapse between each issue. Wandering minds could be kept on track by promising more of the same in seven days.

Sometimes, the *Echo* was the target such as when the *Voice* didn't pass on the opportunity to link the closure of the *Boston Irish Echo* with the arrival of the new kid on the Beantown block—itself. "Since the arrival of the *Irish Voice* on the newsstands in Boston last December, the *Boston Irish Echo* has come under increasing pressure," the *Voice* stated in its August 27, 1988 front page story.

Sometimes the dig had less to do with the business of newspapers than with personalities and politics. *Voice* publisher Niall O'Dowd was not shy when it came to dispensing a tongue lashing in print, just as he did in March, 1989. The named target was *Echo* editor John Thornton. Thornton had taken a swipe at the *Voice* without naming the paper but it was fairly clear where the criticism was directed. O'Dowd retaliated, alleging along the way that a critical piece on President Ronald Reagan, penned by himself, had been censored a few years prior to that by *Echo* publisher John Grimes. Attacks like this had been absent from Irish American journalism for some time and the result of O'Dowd's attack was a lot of wagging tongues. The *Voice* was being noticed. That was part of the plan.

Taking aim at established newspaper journalists such as Mike McAlary of the *Daily News* also attracted attention to the new upstart. O'Dowd at one point took issue with a descriptive piece by McAlary of an Irish wake in which the columnist had made much of the smell in the room of stale whiskey. O'Dowd lashed out. McAlary lashed back. But O'Dowd was the mouse that roared and his paper was named in the *Daily News*. Game, set and mouth.

Another direct swipe at the *Echo* stemmed from an op-ed written for the *Echo* by Sinn Féin President Gerry Adams in 1989. It was in response to an opinion piece published in the *Echo* by SDLP leader John Hume. The Adams reply didn't immediately appear in the *Echo* and this prompted a *Voice* front page story headlined "Sinn Féin Alleges *Irish Echo* Censorship." The story was written by Patrick Farrelly. Unfortunately for the *Voice*, the Adams piece ran in the *Echo* that very same day. There were subsequent suggestions that publication had been vigorously opposed by *Echo* publisher Claire Grimes. Grimes was certainly wary of Sinn Féin and Gerry Adams, but her approach to running the editorial side of the *Echo*'s business was almost entirely hands off. The Adams piece was always going to run because the ultimate decision to use or not use it was in the hands of the editor and the paper's journalists.

Inevitably, these spats would attract wider attention. There are few stories more appealing to a paper or a magazine than the story of a good old circulation war, a battle to the death in ink. One of the first upstart *Voice* versus tired old *Echo* stories appeared in the glossy magazine *Manhattan Inc.*, in December, 1989. As was the case in virtually all these stories, the writer went for fuel to the upstart first.

Under a photo of a determined looking Niall O'Dowd standing beside a printing press, the *Inc.* story, written by Everett Potter, set the stage. O'Dowd lit his fuse and fired away: "There's a flood of young Irish coming in, and as far as I'm concerned, the *Echo*'s outdated."

O'Dowd was, at the time, convinced that there was only room for one paper. "If they (the *Echo*) were going to put us out of business they should have done it in the first six months."

Echo publisher Claire Grimes was, according to Potter, charming, upbeat, and forthright about the war. Then he wrote: "There isn't one," she snaps. There were other wars though. *Manhattan Inc.* itself soon snapped the dust. The *Echo* and the *Voice* soldiered on.

In those early days, the *Echo* sought refuge on what it felt was the safer ground provided by the turned cheek. It would have been impossible anyway to knock the *Voice* off in six months, a year or even two. As Jimmy Breslin pointed out at the time, Niall O'Dowd was no genius for surviving the often fatal first year of publication. "He just can count," Breslin told Dick Cavett in a TV interview with O'Dowd sitting a couple of feet away.

The upstart versus the old stager story popped up a number of times in the following years. Both papers became quite practiced at the art of exchanging barbs via an intermediary. The last such story of the first half dozen years of "the war" appeared in the *Chicago Tribune* in May, 1993. Again, it was the *Voice* that was first sought out and again it was the *Echo* that had to defend itself against a reporter who had been well primed by the time he arrived at the *Echo*'s Fifth Avenue offices.

But by now, there had been changes at the *Echo*, quite dramatic ones, and the *Tribune* writer, Mike Dorning, was quick to add to his report that the *Voice* had "galvanized its rival."

Still, the *Voice* was, as the *Tribune* put it, the "liberal upstart *Voice*," flashy and irreverent, while the *Echo* was the "sober" and conservative older relative. The liberal versus conservative tag was often mistakenly applied by readers and commentators alike. The pure political definitions don't really sit that well with publications. The *Voice* could be extremely "liberal" towards those groups, individuals and causes it favored. It could be quite illiberal when it came to those it disliked or disagreed with. The *Echo* had its own likes and dislikes too, but continued to lean towards the middle ground during the first half of the 1990s. Hence the "sober" tag. This might have been less exciting for some readers, but any other course might have given the appearance of panic and self doubt. The *Echo* kept its nerve and settled for its more "conservative" image.

By January 1997, the headline atop the "war" story had hardly changed. "Ancient Hibernian and an Upstart Serve the Irish of 'the Next Parish,'" announced the *New York Times*. But the playing field was more even now, and evidently so to *Times* writer, Mary Jo Murphy.

"The *Irish Echo* and the *Irish Voice* scooped each other in last week's issues" . . . "Perhaps the *Voice* shows off its green knickers a bit more than the staid *Echo*" . . . the *Echo* "has at last found the pulse of the new immigrants, whose special needs the *Voice* was founded to address."

It had been almost ten years. The *Voice* had triumphed by surviving not just the first twelve months, but a lengthy lifetime in the here today, gone tomorrow business of newspaper publishing. The *Echo*, in turn, had survived its greatest challenge in almost seventy years. And it had turned several corners, sometimes by its own volition, sometimes as a result of the activities of groups such as the IIRM or ILGO and sometimes because of the *Irish Voice*. Along the way it had launched a magazine supplement, *IE*, and had gathered a new and young editor in Tom Connelly, a veteran of the *Concord Monitor*, *New York Post* and *Daily News*. A platoon of young writers and production staff were beginning to throw out *Voice*-like headlines such as "Immaculate Deception"—which appeared during the Bishop Casey affair and annoyed some of the paper's more religious readers—and "Library Looted?" after an investigation by columnist Jack Holland into the sorry state of the American Irish Historical Society archives in New York.

The *Echo*'s investigative skills and ability to entertain had also been honed through the work of Eileen Murphy, Harry Keaney and Kevin McHugh, whose reporting on the shooting dead of Derry native Hessy Phelan, and the involvement in Phelan's last moments of an off duty New York City police officer, left the city's big dailies trailing in the dust. Kevin McHugh died all too soon, aged twenty-seven, in September, 1997.

By then, despite years of trauma, drama and competition, the *Echo* was facing its seventieth birthday feeling fairly satisfied with itself but at the same time aware that its survival for seven decades had much to do with its willingness to change with the times.

By contrast, the *Voice*'s teeth had been worn down a bit by years of chomping. Patrick Farrelly, although he still occasionally contributed, was gone, although writer Brian Rohan retained some of Farrelly's hard edge. Niall O'Dowd's interest had turned more to the peace process in Northern Ireland, although in a typically singular manner. O'Dowd had become a player himself in the early peace process and his paper had acted as a willing platform for Sinn Féin to explain itself and its new approach to Irish Americans. Such close relationships between a party and a paper were nothing new. In some respects, the *Voice*/Sinn Féin relationship was similar to that between Fianna Fáil and the *Irish Press* which, sadly and ironically, ceased publication in 1995 just as U.S. involvement in the peace process was reaching unprecedented levels. Such relationships bring both benefits and risks. Publishers, and a surprising number of journalists, often favor them. But ultimately, the verdict on such an experiment is in the hands of readers.

Still, the *Voice* was not being inconsistent in its new pursuit. It had clearly demonstrated over the ten years that there was a real desire for journalistic change and innovation in Irish America. And it had satisfied much of this demand. The *Echo* had been swept along by these new forces too and was widely viewed as a far better paper as a result of the "war" with the *Voice* which, by late 1997, was more cold than hot.

However, regardless of which paper had emerged with market advantage, what had clearly happened since 1987 was the emergence of a new kind of Irish journalism in America. It was more critical, direct, aggressive and self-confident. It was not afraid either to challenge the old and traditional or to fight in order to preserve it. And it certainly wasn't afraid to give the major media outlets a bloody nose if one was deserved.

As a result, there indeed appeared to be room for two Irish American weeklies with ambitions stretching to all corners of America. But it was no longer a matter of just the upstart and the old Hibernian. There were other papers abroad, ready to patch into local markets while taking advantage of the lower overheads made possible by new technology. They were mostly monthlies, but they were filling in where the New York weeklies left off. The *Irish Edition* in Philadelphia, the *Boston Irish Reporter*, the *Irish Herald* in San Francisco, the *Irish American Post* in Chicago and the *Desert Shamrock* in Arizona, were all claiming a slice of the heritage handed down by the *Truth Teller, Emerald, Gaelic American* and all the rest. On top of these, there were the glossies: *Irish America* magazine, now a dozen years on the go with six issues per annum and the drawing power to attract a president of the United States to its annual awards dinner; and a newer arrival, the *World of Hibernia*, with four issues a year replete with stories of the global Irish, past and present, and tales of the contemporary good life, Irish style. Both were aimed heavily at an Irish American market which, by now, was well settled at the top of the socio-economic tree.

In addition to all these, there remained the stalwart that was Irish radio, and the new upstarts, television and the worldwide web which could bring Irish radio and even television into American homes. American-based TV shows such as *Irish Eyes* and *Erin Focus* had given way in the latter part of the '90s to the Stateside series, shown both in Ireland and on the PBS network across the U.S. The dominant weekly show aimed at both an Irish and Irish American audience was by now *Out of Ireland*, presented by Irish-born Patricia O'Reilly and relayed coast to coast, again on the PBS network.

O'Reilly had been one of the first of the newly arrived Irish journalists to collide with the old way of doing things. She had covered a St. Patrick's Day Parade row over the manner in which the grand marshal was elected—or anointed as some had it. O'Reilly was asked to appear before the parade committee to clarify matters regarding her story. One of the first questions she was asked at the meeting, which was held behind closed doors, was whether she had her lawyer present. O'Reilly had no lawyer, but she had a notebook, an attitude and a new way of reporting that was to shake up profoundly the prevailing view of the established order.

Still, even as the new Irish, journalists included, ascended to hitherto unscaled heights in late 1990s America, there were troubling signs on the horizon. The immigrant flow, so vital for Irish American journalism, had all but dried up. Where there had been many thousands only ten years before, there were now only hundreds arriving each year. Additionally, many of the 1980s Irish were heading back to try their luck in post Mary Robinson Ireland, now the land of the Celtic Tiger.

All things seemed to point to uncertain times ahead although there were promising signs of a new market for Irish American journalism to foster—that of young Irish Americans, increasing numbers of whom had made the cultural link with Ireland in the context of music, literature and politics.

For Patrick Farrelly, this new twist to the story was the wave of the foreseeable future: "The level of knowledge and interest in Ireland is," according to Farrelly, "nothing short of phenomenal."

So uncertainty yes, but also a new potential. With the closing years of another century of Irish American journalism there still remained, as the *Emerald* would have had it, great undertakings for those with an appetite for good stories, stirring headlines and a little print war on the side.

10

A SO-CALLED IRISH VIEW

"There's no such thing as British aggression."
FDR to Irish foreign minister Frank Aiken, March, 1941.

The March wind whipped in from the Hudson River, along Forty-third Street and right past the door of the *New York Times*. It was a raw, bitter wind and it was appropriate. This was a rather raw and bitter occasion. Outside the door of arguably the world's most important newspaper, a small group of men and women huddled close together atop an open trailer. They clutched pieces of paper and took turns at a microphone denouncing the powers that remained warm and seemingly oblivious in the building that housed the "Old Gray Lady of Forty-third Street."

This was no offbeat bunch of radicals damning the establishment. Rather, it was an assembly made up of some of the city's political elite. There was a future mayor in the group, David Dinkins; a future Brooklyn District Attorney, Charles "Joe" Hynes; a destined-to-be Congressman in Peter King, and a living legend in the city's political life, Paul O'Dwyer. There were lawyers too, members of the Brehon Law Society, an Irish American group made up of attorneys with a keen and critical eye for the singular style of jurisprudence as it pertained in the Northern Ireland of the 1980s. Chief among them was attorney Richard Harvey, British in origin, and with a touch of Shakespearean drama about his person.

Harvey had just returned from Belfast and the funeral of lawyer Pat Finucane, a man who had specialized in defending Irish Republican defendants, mostly members of the IRA. Finucane had been gunned down in his home in front of his family by masked loyalist gunmen. Only a short while before the shooting, a British government minister, Douglas Hogg, had denounced lawyers that he believed were too close to the IRA in a speech on the floor of the

House of Commons. Hogg didn't mention Finucane by name. He didn't have to.

The widespread feeling was that loyalists had taken encouragement from Hogg's speech and that Finucane had been marked for death as a result. Had such an event occurred in New York, or indeed anywhere in the United States, there would have been no question of the *New York Times* covering what was an assault on the very workings of justice.

Harvey told the crowd that he had returned from Belfast and had asked his wife to see the newspaper cuttings regarding the murder of Finucane, particularly the *Times* cuttings. He was a *Times* reader. All of them on the trailer were *Times* readers.

"There were none," said Harvey. "I could not believe it. The first amendment belongs to the people, not to the *New York Times*. It is the peoples' right to know. The British Government will rue the day it encouraged the murder of Pat Finucane and the *New York Times* the day it chose to ignore it."

There was no report of the demonstration in the *Times* next day. The paper did eventually get around to reporting Finucane's murder. It was mentioned in another story about a month after the shooting. It was left for Jimmy Breslin, then with *New York Newsday*, to draw the comparison between the Ayatollah Khomeini fingering author Salman Rushdie for death and a member of the government that was Washington's closest ally calling for lawyers representing IRA members to be "dealt with." Breslin pointed out that the only difference between the two was that Rushdie was still alive.

It was a time of discontent. As was often the case, Irish Americans who felt passionately about the troubles in Northern Ireland were left angry when the mainstream American press failed to cover the North in a manner they believed to be fair and unbiased. For those running the major papers, the *New York Times, Los Angeles Times, Washington Post, Boston Globe*, Northern Ireland was a problem that would flare up and vanish just as quickly from the radar screen. There had been periods when it was hot news. The early civil rights marches, the first couple of years of the troubles, Bloody Sunday, the hunger strikes. But mostly, Northern Ireland was a far flung corner of even the United Kingdom, never mind the world. The London bureau would look after it if somebody went nuts and started shooting.

How does a centuries-old life and death story become non-news? Invariably, time erodes even the sharpest of story angles and by 1989, the year of Pat Finucane's death, Northern Ireland, an endless tale of woe, was very long in the tooth indeed. And it was really just a security problem, and Mrs. Thatcher had it under control and the situation was improving for Catholics and the entire Communist world seemed to be tottering on the brink, the money wasn't available for another bureau and so on and so forth.

Seventy three years before the huddled, angry chorus on the trailer, the affairs of Ireland were front page news in the *New York Times* and just about every other newspaper in America. In the middle of Britain's direst hour, as the Kaiser's troops threatened to overwhelm Europe, the Irish had stabbed England in the back. The *New York Times*, for one, was having none of it.

In its edition of Wednesday, April 26, 1916, the *Times* reported in its headline: "Troops crush revolt in Dublin; Take Post Office Seized by Rioters."

The story was written in London, and from that vantage point the men and women volunteers of the newborn Irish Republic were indeed little more than treacherous rioters.

The *Times* editorial in the aftermath of the Easter Week Rising was written in New York, but it might as well have been penned in London. Still, because it was a New York written editorial, Pearse, Connolly, Clarke and the rest who would die by firing squad were at least now accorded the title of rebels although they remained, in the paper's view, "like forward children, causing untold annoyance to others, but themselves suffering the heavier penalties of misbehavior."

To Irish Americans, this wasn't a paper standing for the legacy of Bunker Hill or Valley Forge. But Irish America had been forewarned by John Devoy who, in his opposition to the Clan na Gael dynamite campaign in England during the 1880s, had deduced how quickly terror could be turned by its victim into far reaching and fruitful propaganda. "England," Devoy wrote, "having the ear of the world and control of all the agencies of news supply, would see to it that the world was duly shocked."

This was no less so in December, 1921 when the *Times* splashed across its front page the agreement between the Lloyd George government in London and the Irish negotiators from Sinn Féin led by Michael Collins and Arthur Griffith. In eight columns across the top of page one, it was announced that Ireland was to be a "Free State Within the British Empire." The deal had been worked out in London so perhaps it was fitting that the story be datelined London, as it was. But even the "Dublin Rejoices" off-lead story was penned in Belfast. London was still, and would remain for decades, the prime source of *Times* and other U.S. reporting on a divided Ireland. Not until the troubles would journalists be drawn closer to the Irish flame. But even then, the problems of Ireland would be reported, or spiked, on the desks of various London bureaus. Devoy's warning was to be true for an entire century.

Still, the fact that U.S. reportage on Ireland was somewhat Anglo-Centric was not entirely the result of British perfidy and American obsequiousness. The Free State and later the Irish Republic's attitude to world affairs would stir the pot of resentment quite briskly in places where U.S. public opinion was first concocted. Irish neutrality in World War Two might have spared de Valera's crossroads Ireland the physical wrath of the Third Reich, but there had to be unwelcome consequences. And there have been, right up to the present day.

Winston Churchill's attitude to Irish neutrality was almost totally hostile. His attitude to Ireland itself was more complex. His physician, Lord Moran, would record that Churchill looked on independent Ireland as an anxious father would view a "wandering daughter." Long before Mary Robinson's candle in the window, Britain's great war leader had lit one for Ireland, hopeful that the lost child would someday return, attracted by the enduring light of a superior British civilization.

De Valera and neutrality was another matter. In his victory Europe speech on May 13, 1945, Churchill patted himself on the back for being so restrained towards the reluctant Irish state, if not the "thousands of southern Irishmen, who hastened to the battle front to prove their ancient valor." Despite such individual sacrifice, Churchill still let rip: "This was indeed a deadly moment in our life, and if it had not been for the loyalty and friendship of Northern Ireland, we should have been forced to come to close quarters with Mr. de Valera, or perish for ever from the Earth." De Valera did not quite rise to the bait, but in his distinctly measured response, did make the point that "it is indeed hard for the strong to be just to the weak."

More than fifty years later, the complex relationship between neutral Ireland and battling Britain would prompt another round of argument on the letters page of the *New York Times*. "The denial of southern Irish ports to allied ships was surely responsible for untold losses of allied personnel and *matériel*. The important role of Northern Ireland was recognized by Ge. Dwight D. Eisenhower, but everything that happened there was known to the Germans in the Republic," wrote reader Peter Garlick in a letter published February 2, 1997. "No wonder Harry S. Truman had little use for the Irish Prime Minister Eamon de Valera," he concluded.

Another reader, Jim McManus, rose to Ireland's defense arguing that Ireland's nonbelligerency had favored the Allies. Downed fliers were returned to the Allies and more than 80,000 Irish citizens had joined up with the British forces during the war. The tension between de Valera and Churchill, McManus further argued, had more to do with 1916 than with the war.

One way or the other, northern solidarity and southern neutrality would be factors in Anglo-Irish relations for many years after de Valera and Churchill drew their respective lines in the sand. Margaret Thatcher was still holding to the Churchill doctrine in the 1980s as illustrated in Chris Ogden's biography *Maggie*. Dublin's hostile reaction to the sinking of the Argentinean warship *General Belgrano* during the Falklands/Malvinas War, according to Ogden, sent Thatcher into a rage. "Dublin's reaction reinforced her natural antipathy toward the Irish, whom she considers, in large part, shiftless, sniveling, and, because of their World War Two neutrality, spineless."

In Thatcher's own account of her years as British Prime Minister, she left no one in any doubt as to her feeling about Dublin's errant behavior during the conflict in the South Atlantic. To "no great surprise the Irish caused us some concern," Thatcher wrote. "Later it became clear they were not to be relied upon."

Such criticism of an independent Ireland acting independently has, over the years, consistently found safe haven at the highest levels of U.S. government. And the suspicion directed at Dublin could just as easily be directed at Irish America. Sean Cronin, in his *Washington's Irish Policy 1916–1986*, points to the U.S. Consul General in Belfast during World War Two who saw Irish America as an agent for fomenting tension between GIs based in Northern Ireland and British soldiers. In one report, the diplomat summed the situation up thus: "One cannot but notice the anti-British sentiments of Irish-American soldiers. One is impressed by the fact they for the most part express an Irish Nationalist point of view in the so-called Irish question. In talking with the senior Catholic chaplain in the American forces a few days ago, he expressed the opinion openly that the British should get out of Northern Ireland. In other words, there is a disposition on the part of those who have religious and kinship ties with the Catholic population of Ireland to espouse the so-called Irish point of view."

The U.S. Minister in Dublin during the war, David Gray, was of like mind. For Gray, the so-called Irish point of view found an outlet in the "subversive American press" which would be "fed from Eire with a formidable anti-partition, anti-British propaganda as the war ends." The "subversive American press" in this context was, according to Gray, "certain Irish-American newspapers."

The end of the war brought little change in this sidelining of Irish feelings. Indeed, with the advent of the Cold War, neutral Ireland found that it had even less influence in Washington. British influence, on the other hand, was very much in the ascendant. According to Sean Cronin, the birth of NATO resulted in virtually any U.S. policy on Ireland having to be cleared first by London. This was particularly so whenever the subject of U.S. arms sales to the Republic arose.

"The State Department," according to Cronin, "treated Ireland as a British possession, or at least as an appendage of Britain."

And what applied at the highest government levels also applied in the press. In the years following the war, the Irish government's view was, for a time, disseminated through an organization called the Irish News Agency. The *New York Times* at one point told the INA to stop sending its releases to Forty-third Street.

Acceptance of Ireland's view would receive more sympathetic treatment from President Kennedy, although Kennedy walked around the issue of partition, at least in public, during his 1963 Irish visit. This avoidance of the island's most glaring sore was mutually agreed in advance by JFK and the Irish government. Nevertheless, partition did enter into Kennedy's decision to decline an invitation from Northern Ireland's Prime Minister, Captain Terence O'Neill, to include the North in his Irish sojourn. This was seen as wise. A North visit would have caused uproar in Irish America only a year and a bit before the 1964 presidential election.

Historian Timothy Sarbaugh, writing years later in the *Recorder*, the journal of the American Irish Historical Society, pointed to considerable but not openly expressed Irish frustration with Kennedy. The young president, in the Irish view, was very pro-British, something of an anglophile and inclined to view partition as an internal Irish affair rather than an issue largely in the hands of the British. The June 1963, visit, according to Sarbaugh, was replete with references and rhetoric tied to the Cold War and Ireland's symbolic presence in the world as a small, democratic nation standing defiantly against Communist tyranny. For Kennedy, the Berlin Wall was the prime issue, not the border that snaked through the Irish countryside.

Richard Nixon was the next president with Irish roots but it was to mean little. At one point, in the early days of the Northern Ireland troubles, Nixon's Secretary of State, William Rogers, described as "outrageous" a suggestion by Senator Edward Kennedy that the U.S. could act as a mediator in Northern Ireland. For the head of the U.S. government's diplomatic arm to describe a proposal of diplomacy as a means of ending a violent conflict in such a manner said much of the prevailing attitude in Washington at that time.

The Irish view on the North was still being dismissed as unhelpful but by the 1970s Irish neutrality was no longer a thorn in Washington's side. Henry Kissinger accompanied Nixon on his roots-finding trip to Ireland in October, 1970. In his memoir, *White House Years*, Kissinger wrote that the Irish stop had "no great international significance, except that Ireland has not been totally passive in world affairs. It has served, and can in the future, as a constructive and reliable neutral." Words of praise it seemed, but the key word in Kissinger's assessment was "served." Overall, Kissinger saw the presidential visit as a means for Nixon "to bring his claim to Irish ancestry to the attention of Irish-American voters and to pay off an obligation to a wealthy American contributor at whose extravagant castle we stayed." A few nukes in the castle's dungeon and Kissinger would have doubtless written more.

As a candidate for the presidency, Jimmy Carter uttered words that were a clear sign of a possible new view. But it would not be Carter himself who would give effect to those words. On October 26, 1976, in Pittsburgh, Carter responded to representations from the Ancient Order of Hibernians and Fr. Sean McManus of the Irish National Caucus: "it is a mistake for our country's government to stand quiet on the struggle of the Irish for peace, for the respect of human rights, and for unifying Ireland." Not surprisingly, this statement caused uproar. Carter the president would be more cautious in his language than Carter the candidate.

Carter's successor, Ronald Reagan, had Irish roots rather more obvious than Nixon's. But his commitment to the special relationship with Britain overwhelmed any emotional attachment to the old sod and his special relationship with Margaret Thatcher precluded any significant independent U.S. action on Ireland. Reagan was supportive of closer co-operation between Dublin and London but when it came to the North he was content to keep his distance. Even before his election, when a few green words might have done him no harm with Irish American voters, Reagan had made his personal neutrality on Irish partition quite clear: "I have no views on Irish unity," he told the *Irish Times* in October, 1979. With such a lack of view as his starting point, Reagan could have written editorials on the subject for the vast majority of U.S. daily or weekly publications in the early 1980s, none of which—with the exception of the *Christian Science Monitor* for a time—had an Irish bureau or correspondent.

Ironically, it was Reagan's political soulmate, Thatcher, who threw the first spanner in the works. Her refusal to concede to the demands of the 1981 hunger strikers had stirred fury in Irish America and distinct unease in even U.S. bastions of anglophile thinking. Her infamous "out, out, out" dismissal of the proposals drawn up by the New Ireland Forum in 1984 raised hackles in even such viscerally sympathetic papers as the *Washington Post* and *New York Times*.

But overall, the pattern of U.S. media thinking would hold to its tried and tested course through the early 1980s.

Journalist and author, Jack Holland, learned at first hand how difficult it was to pry open the door that was largely closed to an Irish perspective on Ireland.

"After I first arrived in the United States in 1977, I tried to have my work on Northern Ireland published in a wide number of publications. But just about everywhere I went, I was faced with disinterest. Virtually the only exceptions were the *Nation* and the *Village Voice*."

Holland was to make his own study of U.S. press attitudes in his 1987 book, *The American Connection*. In the chapter devoted to U.S. media coverage of Northern Ireland, Holland wrote that three things emerged from a review of Northern Ireland coverage, which, by the 1980s, impressed Holland as being "often extensive."

Holland cited the first as being a general consensus on North-ern Ireland among major newspapers and magazines. Secondly, that consensus was essentially the same as that of the British gov-ernment, while thirdly, this consensus was remarkably consistent until about 1979.

Up to that time, Holland concluded, U.S. writers were apt to settle into the cozy armchair of stereotyping. He illustrated this with a segment of a report by Gloria Emerson of the *New York Times*, written in the early days of the troubles: "In London there was a sense of something dark, inexplicable and strange in the Irish soul that foreigners cannot explain—or quite ignore."

Holland backed up his assessment thus: "In early 1972, *Newsweek* lamented the prospect of England being dragged into the 'deadly Irish quagmire' by 'two fanatical religious armies' i.e. the Catholics and the Protestants. The image of the unreasoning, fanatical Irish suggested something primitive. *Time* wrote that the crisis was due to the 'truculent tribalism' of the Northern Irish. Thus the magazine could imply that the Irish needed the British."

There were other American writers at work during the early troubles who took a rather different view. Irish Americans such as Pete Hamill and Jimmy Breslin were more inclined to travel to Northern Ireland and meet face to face with the truculent natives. What followed were up-close and personal accounts of life in a soci-ety largely controlled by the military. This was better, Holland felt, but, in his view, the product of such street reporting could often lean a bit too much towards the sentimental. Still, sentimentality was a journalistic venial sin compared to the torrent of brief and spin reportage that was the norm.

There was nothing sentimental about the hunger strikes, but the hunger protests of 1980 and 1981, and what Holland described as the "growing access" for the Irish diplomatic service to editorial board rooms in the U.S., began to exert change on established American attitudes in the early 1980s.

"By 1985, the *New York Times* had published a rare investigative piece on the alleged shoot-to-kill policy of the Northern Ireland police by its reporter Jo Thomas," Holland wrote in *The American Connection*.

The story by Thomas was indeed something of a milestone. But it was to pale into the background when overtaken by the story of Jo Thomas herself and her discovery that "All the News That's Fit to Print" wasn't always actually printed for the benefit of *Times* readers.

Thomas was first sent to Northern Ireland, via London of course, in 1984. She had joined the *Times* in 1977, had worked in the Miami and Washington D.C. bureaus. She had amassed eighteen years experience in the news business and knew her way around a story.

The shoot-to-kill story involved three dead men in Co. Armagh. It would eventually turn into the "Stalker Affair" and destroy the career of John Stalker, Deputy Chief Constable of the Manchester police. It would also have a profound effect on the career of Jo Thomas.

But unlike the worldwide headlines surrounding Stalker, what would happen to Thomas would receive little or no coverage. As she put it herself later in the Columbia Journalism Review and subsequently in the 1991 book, *The Media and Northern Ireland*: "What happened to me was quieter."

Thomas's habit of digging below the official line put her quickly offside with British officials. She was denied access to material normally available to the press. In time, the word to Thomas from the *Times* office back in New York was to stay out of Northern Ireland. In February, 1986, Thomas was "abruptly" ordered back to the United States.

"In light of constant complaints that I had been paying too much attention to Northern Ireland, I suspected this was the cause, and one senior editor confirmed that this was so. The foreign and other senior *Times* editors, however, said that while my work was good it was not distinguished and they wanted to replace me with one of the finest writers on the paper."

It was clearly not just a matter of writing style. A *Times* report passes through multiple layers of editing before seeing the light of print. Thomas was a good writer to begin with. The *Times* was in the habit of hiring only those it considered top drawer. What had happened was that Thomas had crossed the British lion by ignoring the British line on Northern Ireland—worse, ignoring it in Northern Ireland.

"It is the misfortune of Northern Ireland," she subsequently wrote, "to be covered from London, that most beguiling of cities. Like many Americans, I was an enthusiastic anglophile when I went there, and I loved the place. Publisher A.O. Sulzberger invited me to lunch at the Savoy the day I arrived. It was easy to feel important. It was easy to feel well-informed. American journalists get a weekly confidential briefing at No. 10 Downing Street and another at the Foreign Office. They are also invited to dinner at the best places and to lovely parties. British officials are careful to make close friendships with members of important American news organizations."

Thomas was finding out that one of the most powerful weapons in the arsenal of any modern media-savvy government is nothing more than a good lunch, in the right place and at the right time. This was also the case in Washington, Dublin or Belfast. But in London, Thomas had landed in the journalistic lunching capital of the world.

In time, Thomas would come to the conclusion that all the fuss and hospitality was aimed at a single purpose and that was defining the parameters and terms under which the overall Northern Ireland story would be treated and discussed.

In February, 1989, a few days before the windswept demonstration outside the Manhattan headquarters of the *Times*, Thomas was one of a number of journalists and political figures to speak at a forum organized by the Kennedy School of Government at Harvard University. It was the first time her experiences as a reporter in Northern Ireland were laid bare before a predominantly Irish American audience.

Thomas told those gathered that evening that normal reporting practice did not apply in the North.

"And there's a good reason for it," she said. "A real reporter, one member of the British government once told me, would be considered the most dangerous person there. What would be more dangerous than a bomb? The most dangerous thing in a corrupt or unjust society is the truth."

Thomas left the *Times* in 1987 and taught journalism at the University of Illinois for seven years. But the times were clearly changing at the *Times*. The paper lured her back in 1994. There was no debate over past differences, no explanations or apologies. "We agreed to disagree," Thomas would later say from Denver where she was assigned to cover, somewhat ironically, the Oklahoma City bombing trials.

Another speaker at the Harvard forum did not appear particularly dangerous, at least on the surface. Kevin Cullen of the *Boston*

Globe was one of the few U.S. journalists who had amassed enough experience as a reporter in Northern Ireland to be considered an expert on the story. Jim Mulvaney of *New York Newsday* was another as was Thomas. But when it came to American journalists who could command the same plaudit, most of the rest of the fingers on anyone's hands would be left idle at this point.

Cullen told the Harvard gathering that the U.S. press had been "falling down on the job in Northern Ireland." The prevailing attitude in most of the American press was that Northern Ireland's woes would go on for ever. There was no story beyond the body count.

By 1997, Cullen was sent to Dublin to run the *Globe*'s new Irish operation. He would be the first American journalist to head up a full time Irish bureau. The *New York Times* had previously assigned one of its retiring foreign editors, James Clarity, as a part-time correspondent in Dublin. Almost thirty years into the troubles, with over 3,000 dead, close to 40,000 injured and incalculable economic loss, Ireland had finally become a story worthy of individual attention. And not just Northern Ireland. The profound changes sweeping through southern Irish society were as much if not more of a draw at this point than the waning troubles and the emerging peace process. That process was icing on the cake for Cullen and Clarity whose bureaus, in the political vernacular of the time, ended up being a pair of cross border bodies. Ireland, though far from being united, was at least now a single beat. This was the case at least for Cullen. Clarity's access to Northern Ireland stories was not yet total. The *Times* London bureau still had its own claim on Belfast.

"It doesn't take a brain surgeon to tell you that covering Ireland from London doesn't make any sense," Cullen would say several weeks into his Irish posting. But he is inclined to reserve judgment on the significance of his pioneering role: "It will either be a blip or a benchmark."

As Cullen was settling into his new Irish task, Jim Mulvaney was working at the *Daily News* in New York as Assistant Managing Editor. It's the kind of job that comes with a short leash attached to a city room desk. But Mulvaney had already done his share of exotic reporting from far flung places. He was in Beijing in 1989 when Chinese rulers began taking lethal exception to some of China's ruled. Five years before that, however, Mulvaney had been based in Ireland for a year. He was there as both journalist and academic. It became, in the end, impossible to separate both.

Mulvaney was attached at the time to the Long Island paper, *Newsday*. In the summer of 1984 he obtained a fellowship from St. John's University that required his spending time in Ireland, south and north, writing stories for St. John's as if they were being written for *Newsday*. The academic twist was an exercise in comparative journalism. Mulvaney would be writing his stories as an Irish-based correspondent would. His work was to be compared with stories written by London-based journalists covering Ireland for major papers, particularly the *New York Times*, *Boston Globe*, *Baltimore Sun*, *Washington Post*, *Chicago Tribune* and *Los Angeles Times*. The idea was to monitor those papers for signs of bias or British briefing-inspired language.

Mulvaney would later recall: "If you came through London you would get the Foreign Office briefing and arrive in Northern Ireland scared stiff. The people who were not based in Ireland were writing pro-British stories and when in Northern Ireland they would only ever talk to the established unionist and nationalist leaders."

Mulvaney took to the streets of Belfast, not all of them main. He began frequenting both republican and loyalist hang outs, including one notorious loyalist drinking club on the Shankill Road.

"It was a dirty, dangerous place but I had my mates there, guys with names like Twister and Spinner. We would watch American Football on the TV and drink pints."

Mulvaney brought his father, visiting from New York, for lunch one day with Andy Tyrie and the late John McMichael who would later pluck Mulvaney "like a baby" from a very dangerous confrontation during a loyalist riot in Portadown, one where journalists were being openly attacked.

"*Newsday* had started using my stories by now and they couldn't get enough once the appetite was whetted."

The paper's readers, many of them Irish American, were now reading about loyalists as well as the likes of Gerry Adams and Danny Morrison with whom Mulvaney also supped in places such as the republican-run Felons Club on the Andersonstown Road.

Mulvaney's tales of another side of Belfast largely unfamiliar to Irish Americans lured an ambitious young politician from Long Island into what would be for him a lion's den.

Mulvaney once took Peter King to meet his pals Tyrie and McMichael. Pints were off the menu. Tea was the order of that par-

ticular day as it always was in Ulster Defense Association headquarters on the Newtownards Road.

Mulvaney well remembers the encounter: "There was this old
crone who made the tea and the ritual was that you always had to
say this was the best tea in Belfast. We talked. After a while it was
noticed that King wasn't drinking his tea. Tyrie grabbed the cup
and I remember him saying 'for God's sake Peter if we wanted to
kill you we would shoot you in the head, not poison your tea.'"

Mulvaney still thinks highly of King for his willingness to step
across the divide and meet with loyalists, an action not without
some personal risk. (King wasn't actually the first U.S. politician to
do so. Congressman Mario Biaggi had met with loyalist leaders in
1979, albeit in the more neutral confines of Belfast's Europa
Hotel.) Mulvaney also remembers the tea as being pretty stewed
and awful and figures King was right not to touch it, whatever
about what Tyrie was thinking.

Mulvaney's time in Ireland—he had a room in Dublin as well as
Belfast—coincided in part with that of Jo Thomas, a reporter he
remembers as being able to recognize the subtleties of the place.
Kevin Cullen would follow soon after. All three employed similar
work methods and stand out as reporters who stood more than
ankle deep in the Irish story.

Oddly enough, Mulvaney's verdict on the economic feasibility of
an Irish bureau for *Newsday* was a negative one.

"*Newsday* had one correspondent per continent and Ireland
wasn't important enough at the time, although Ireland was in
many ways a more important story for us than, say, France. But
the *New York Times* had five correspondents in London and one
of those could have been in Dublin. And it certainly makes sense
for the *Boston Globe* to have someone in Ireland considering its
market."

The later emergence of Dublin as a base for U.S. journalists—
the *Tampa Tribune* announced in 1997 that its European bureau
would be located in the Irish capital—would go some small way
towards trimming London's dominant influence. But the British
capital would remain the focal point for most journalists whose job
description carried a footnote about occasionally having to cross
the Irish Sea.

During his visit to New York in September, 1997, Sinn Féin
leader Gerry Adams would point to this in a press conference at the

Waldorf Astoria Hotel. While he found the media in the U.S. "very open," Adams was moved to qualify his praise: "Unfortunately, much of the news comes from London." The words might have been those of John Devoy.

The British government spends millions of dollars in the United States each year getting its views across, on a variety of issues, to the American press and public. By London's own estimates, roughly five million has been spent on combating the MacBride Principles campaign alone. Many believe that the total since the fair employment campaign for Northern Ireland began in 1984 is far higher than that. At one point, $13 million was a widely mentioned sum.

In addition to the British government, the combined forces of the British press enjoy influence, access and ownership in both Ireland and North America. In the Republic of Ireland, at least as many people obtain news from British electronic and print media outlets as the Irish equivalent. In his contribution to the 1997 book, *Media in Ireland: The Search for Diversity*, Dr. Brian Feeney expressed the view that it was more likely a majority of Irish people who were obtaining news coverage from British outlets.

"Ireland's position must be unique in this respect in that the television viewers are exposed to the attempts at primary definition by another country's government," Feeney wrote.

Sometimes, the David versus Goliath image has been used to advantage by those Irish who would be inclined to view the British press with particular caution. Gerry Adams fired a slingshot in March, 1994, at the opening of the Sinn Féin office in Washington D.C. when he told *Newsweek*: "The British have six hundred employees in America working for their embassy. We'll have one Irish woman. I think the British are at a disadvantage."

The British view is, of course, entirely legitimate from a British point of view and is frequently so from a U.S. or even Irish perspective. The arguments against MacBride have a valid basis and it would have been highly surprising if the British government had not risen to challenge a campaign aimed at putting into rapid reverse a situation in Northern Ireland in which, at the outset, Catholics were more than two-and-a-half times more likely to be unemployed than Protestants. The British agree with the need for greater equality, but want to realize it on their own terms. The MacBride Principles are Irish America's terms.

What was often surprising to MacBride backers was the willingness of U.S. editorial boards to swallow the British take on Northern Ireland employment, hook, line and sinker.

This was illustrated in a December, 1991 story in the *Irish Echo* which highlighted the treatment of a California MacBride bill in three leading dailies prior to the measure being vetoed by Governor Pete Wilson.

According to the *Echo*, the *San Francisco Chronicle*, *San Diego Union* and *Los Angeles Times* "all considered the MacBride bill worthy of editorial comment, and in all cases condemnation. Not one treated the issue with the importance underlined by news or feature page coverage."

The *Echo* continued: "Added to this lopsided approach was an apparent willingness to accept a particular side of the MacBride argument to such an extent that editorials in all three papers bore a strong resemblance in tone and language."

What had happened was that editorial page offices in the three papers had been briefed in advance by a British representative. The result was a chorus of editorial parrots. But this was no great surprise because even by late 1991, with the Anglo-Irish Agreement well established and the Irish and British governments soon heading for even closer cooperation by virtue of the Framework Documents and Downing Street Declaration, there was still no discernible Irish point of view doing the rounds of editorial board rooms. Not that MacBride would have been a first priority for Dublin, which had its own reservations over the years about what the British were apt to describe, with little evidence or justification, as an IRA "Trojan Horse."

For most of the 1970s, and several years into the 1980s, one of Dublin's main diplomatic objectives had been to blunt the IRA and Sinn Féin's influence in America. Both were considered a threat to the security of the Irish Republic. The level of emphasis varied somewhat depending on which parties were in government, and the attitudes of the various diplomats charged with conveying Dublin's message in Washington. But by the late '80s, the perception of Irish republican America as a potential threat had faded while co-operation with London had reached new heights. At odds with this warming Anglo/Irish trend was the growing sense in Dublin that the time had arrived to take a more forceful leading role in the U.S., to knock on editorial doors and bend appropriate ears to something novel and formerly unseen—a slowly emerging but clearly distinct Irish view which, it was felt, could be made more readily understandable to Americans by virtue of what could be viewed as, somewhat ironically, the Trojan Horse of closer Anglo/Irish co-operation.

There was no big bang that gave birth to this revised expression of Irish independence. At times, it almost seem to occur by default. In one mid-1990s interview on the PBS Lehrer Newshour, Irish Ambassador Dermot Gallagher and his British counterpart, Robin Renwick, were jointly interviewed on developments in the North. For almost the entire interview it seemed like a collision of Tweedledum and Tweedledee, which is to say no collision at all. But in the final moments of the interview, Gallagher, who was known for holding strong nationalist views, suddenly hoisted his tricolor flag. He seemed to realize that he and Renwick had come across like nodding donkeys. Gallagher reminded Renwick that there were two majorities on the island of Ireland, the clear implication being that the day would come when the majority, in the all-Ireland sense of the word, would have to have its say.

What might have been said first was said last. But it was said, and it was a momentary hint of what was actually going on in the hidden world of diplomacy between friends who, while not in direct competition for the last great power's favors, were not entirely of one mind as to how matters should proceed on the most pressing issue of mutual concern. Irish government policy was not, at this point, the same as British government policy. Friendship apart, the sometimes subtle differences would have to be explained to Americans—and all against the tide of pre-briefed reportage flowing daily in huge quantity from London.

From the early '90s on, Irish diplomacy in the United States adopted a new tactic. The news story was untouchable, but as one Irish diplomat put it: "We can get at the opinion maker, the editorial writer and the columnist and any American journalist who is being sent to Ireland to do a particular story."

Borrowing from the media itself, Irish diplomats charged with courting the American press, while numbering only a fraction of their British counterparts, developed the idea of a "target audience" made up of print, television and radio journalists. Top of the target list were editorial writers.

The idea behind this was that while the percentage of Americans who actually read newspaper editorials was relatively small, those that did were often policy makers and the kind of people who themselves changed minds on issues such as Ireland. In this gameplan, the *New York Times* was seen as the pinnacle.

Dermot Brangan, who spent six years as press officer at the Irish consulate in New York, was quickly made aware of how influential the *Times* was, not just in New York, but right across the country.

"The one paper that editorial writers would refer to, that tended to drive them towards writing an editorial or would influence them in future editorials was the *New York Times*. The only other paper that comes close to that is the *Washington Post.*"

One of the reasons that places the *Times* ahead of the others is that it tends to be opinionated in its editorials. After presenting various arguments, it usually delivers its view very clearly. The *Washington Post* and the *Boston Globe*, both important opinion formers from an Irish diplomatic perspective, tend to write editorials in more of an "on the one hand and on the other" hand style. The viewpoint, at the end of this process, tends to be somewhat blunted as a result.

Most U.S. editorials over the years of the troubles tended to be in reaction to violence, particularly that of the IRA. The position of successive Irish governments was absolute condemnation of violence, so for years it found itself having little to add to what U.S. journalists were already saying. Irish diplomats were like Protestant missionaries in the Vatican. They would be listened to politely and then effectively shown the door. The 1985 Anglo/Irish Agreement began to change that because it acknowledged a separate Irish role in Northern Ireland. U.S. editorial boards began to learn about the subtle differences between Dublin and London, differences which had always been there, but hidden by an overwhelming consensus on violence which had smothered the other strands in the story.

The difference would be rather more than subtle when it came to a visa for Gerry Adams. In the cold days of January, 1994, Irish diplomacy in the United States was pushing with all its limited might on behalf of a man who, only a short while before, had been seen as a mortal enemy of the Irish State. Taoiseach Albert Reynolds was behind the push, but Irish diplomats, used to considerable latitude and independence of action in their daily work, were careful not to push too obviously. They let it be known that if the Irish view was sought, it would be promptly delivered on the side of a visa, and that such a visa would, in Dublin's view, assist Adams in his efforts to secure an IRA cease-fire.

The British, meanwhile, were arguing against the visa with both the Clinton administration and the same editorial writers, not least the *New York Times* editorial writer with responsibility for matters Anglo/Irish, Karl Meyer. Despite invocation of the long standing special relationship between Washington and London, the Irish view, to the surprise of many, won out.

The *New York Times* was not the first major U.S. daily to support an Adams visa. Almost a year prior to the last verbal battle over a visa for the Sinn Féin President, the *Plain Dealer* in Cleveland was one paper which supported a lifting of the visa ban if for no other reason than that Adams would be exposed to the full rigor of American press scrutiny. This editorial, of April 27, 1993, was a signpost along the road. Before that year was over, the word was out that the British government had been secretly negotiating with the IRA. As was often the case, it was British journalists—this time from the Sunday paper, the *Observer*—who had uncovered a big Northern Ireland story. The initial denial of such contact by Prime Minister John Major had prompted a severely critical editorial in the *New York Times* headlined "Tell the Truth About the IRA." The editorial accused Major of having "blundered gratuitously." From this point on, the British argument against an Adams visa would be starting from an unfamiliar position of disadvantage.

Winning over the *Times* to the Irish view was not a sure thing, however. A number of Irish diplomats recall that editorial writers would frequently play devil's advocate, employing both Washington and London inspired arguments against any radical change in editorial tack. It was easier for them to stick to tried and tested positions.

Nevertheless, days before Adams was due to appear at a conference in New York organized by the National Committee on American Foreign Policy, the *Times* nailed its new colors to the mast. "Grant Gerry Adams a Visa," the headline commanded on January 28. The editorial presented arguments pro and con and portrayed the Clinton administration as "squirming" over the visa issue.

But the bottom line stood out: "A broad spectrum of Irish-Americans now see an opportunity for engaging Mr. Adams in serious discussion of joining a promising peace initiative. Mr. Clinton would honor wider principles of free speech by admitting Adams."

While the central premise of the editorial was ground-breaking, it was also wryly observed by some that the *New York Times* had also discovered something new in a "broad spectrum of Irish Ameri-cans." The habit of many American publications over the years had been to lump Irish America into one narrowly defined category, a gallery to be played to by those troublesome Irish elements who might conspire to disturb the tranquillity of America's closest ally, in pursuit of the unobtainable in a remote corner of that ally's land.

The *Times* editorial was an indication of profound change and was cause for some celebration in Irish diplomatic outposts. There was now an Irish line, successfully pushed by a New York and Washington-based Irish diplomatic team of just four individuals dealing with press relations. Together, they had successfully matched the British line promulgated by almost thirty individuals based in New York alone. Indeed, to put things in a finer perspec-tive, the day that the *Times* Adams visa editorial hit the streets, the British Embassy staff in Washington outnumbered the entire Irish Department of Foreign Affairs staff, based in Ireland and around the world combined. The mouse had roared and won. Within days, the victory would turn into something of a rout, helped by loud expressions of British diplomatic and public anger directed at both the *Times* and White House.

Said one source subsequently who witnessed the fallout at first hand: "The British raked the Americans over the coals on the Adams visa to the point of questioning collective U.S. sanity on this issue. The Americans became extremely annoyed."

And this was again reflected in a *Times* editorial. British hubris and little else was responsible for the most eye-opening *Times* edi-torial headline of them all: "The Lion Whines About Mr. Adams."

That editorial, published on February 5, 1994, went down as the *coup de grâce* after all that had gone before. Finally faded were the Irish rioters of 1916, now replaced by the British whiners of 1994.

The editorial read: "When President Clinton granted a two-day visa to Gerry Adams the wise course would have been to cut its losses and dismiss the matter as an internal U.S. affair—as the British initially seemed to be doing. Then early this week, Prime Minister John Major and his Foreign Secretary, Douglas Hurd, inexplicably threw a fit. The U.S. Ambassador to Britain was sum-moned to Downing Street for a harsh lecture, and the British pub-lic was treated to the peculiar TV spectacle of a Larry King interview on CNN with Mr. Adams, in which an actor spoke the Sinn Féin leader's responses.

"Under British law Mr. Adams can be seen but not heard on television, and instead of challenging this bizarre censorship, CNN cravenly chose to comply. A similar ban in the Irish Republic was allowed to lapse on Jan. 19, and Mr. Adams's voice can now be heard by many Britons with access to Irish radio and TV. If Mr. Major is indeed serious about his government's new peace initiative on Northern Ireland, he should also be ending censorship and encouraging debate. The British media, however, lack our safeguards for free speech, making them much more vulnerable to politicians' whims. In this case, it seems appropriate to ask just what the old lion is afraid of.

"Mr. Adams made the most of British mistakes without expressing a single new thought. For millions of Americans, the novelty was seeing a live Irishman expressing such views. In seven TV interviews and five press conferences, his equivocations about the Irish Republican Army's indiscriminate killings fully justified Washington's barring his entry on eight previous occasions.

"When he applied last week, however, there were new circumstances. Britain and the Irish Republic had jointly appealed to Sinn Féin in December to renounce violence and take part in a new peace initiative, the first break in the ice. Meanwhile, Mr. Major, his hand forced by leaks, confirmed that his Government was already engaging in secret discussions with Mr. Adams—a development that makes hypocritical the British outburst against Mr. Adam's visit. Apparently Mr. Major considers it appropriate to talk to Mr. Adams in secret, but inappropriate for the United States to allow him to talk to its people in public.

"Senators Edward Kennedy and Daniel Patrick Moynihan joined thirty-eight other members of Congress in urging Mr. Clinton to allow Mr. Adams to take part in a New York conference attended by other Northern Irish leaders, notably John Hume, who speaks for the province's nonviolent nationalist majority. And so the President, for principled as well as political reasons, let Mr. Adams in.

"Americans are rightly appalled by violence in Northern Ireland, carried out by Protestant paramilitary groups as well as IRA gangs, some with criminal sidelines. Yet censorship and visa blackmail are not the answer. Mr. Clinton was right to let Americans hear and question Gerry Adams."

While the editorial got its digs in all around, it was the extreme criticism aimed at the Major government in particular that so quickly revealed it to be a dagger in the heart of the habit, stretching back decades at the *Times*, of giving the British the benefit of the doubt. Some viewed it as appropriate, others inappropriate and yet others saw it as ironic that the "live Irishman" who now had such an unprecedented chance to deliver the Irish view to a mass audience was one whom most Irish people were content, until a few days before, to see muzzled.

But while Adams was the public voice, the views expressed behind the scenes by a small number of Irish politicians and diplomats, John Hume included, had ensured acceptance of this new Irish view, one that was even broad enough to include Gerry Adams and his equivocations.

To a lesser extent, the new Irish view clashed with the British over the question of fundraising in the U.S. for Sinn Féin. But the other sharp divergence, one that was on a par with the Adams Visa imbroglio, followed in the wake of the effective rejection by the Major government, in early 1996, of the Mitchell Report. It was now the Irish side's turn to be angry and the message was relayed to editorial writers from New York to San Francisco. The result, was that the British, as one diplomat put it, were "universally vilified" for taking what was seen as an entirely negative and unhelpful stance against a report compiled by the main symbol of U.S. efforts to secure a realistic settlement in Northern Ireland.

As one longtime observer put it: "The report was a means for the British to get off the hook but they chose to stick to their guns and insist on weapons decommissioning. It was a mistake and they got whacked for it."

Throughout the following few years the newly accepted and still evolving Irish view would be relayed to a growing number of people in the United States by an expanding number of diplomats, journalists and visiting politicians, unionist and loyalist as well as nationalist and republican. There was already a foundation for this laid by a relative handful of American journalists who had employed sound reporting instincts and yes, occasionally a smidgen of sentiment, to better inform Irish Americans and Americans in general about a story that was not going to fade away by being simply ignored.

In time, the new Irish view would find itself welcome in the White House; and while the British would continue to enjoy enormous influence with, and access to, the centers of opinion formation in the U.S., things were definitely no longer what they once were. What lay tantalizingly ahead would be a new basis for debate on the future of Ireland, one in which Ireland was no longer some distant, incomprehensible problem—a "pet boutique" project as Thomas Friedman referred to it in the *New York Times*—but a priority in U.S. foreign policy, an article of faith in the home of the president, and, perhaps of most far-reaching significance, a story which refused to be condemned to the sidelines as a curious, but sad wee tale, thrown together after lunch in one city and at the end of a day trip to another.

11

THE NEW PATRIOT GAME

"I have learned all my life cruel England to blame. And so now I am part of the patriot game."

Line from the rebel song, *The Patriot Game.*

The meeting had degenerated into a heated exchange. And neither man was giving ground. In subsequent years, even members of the United States Senate sitting on powerful investigating committees in Washington would suffer the biting edge of this man's lawyerly tongue. Harold Ickes was having none of it. Governor Clinton was far too busy to devote precious time to a bunch of Irish Americans hung up on an obscure issue such as Northern Ireland. The other man in the office, which was serving as the headquarters of the increasingly troubled Bill Clinton primary campaign in New York, this spring day in 1992, was John Dearie. Dearie was an attorney too, and a New York State Assemblyman serving the Bronx. He was attempting to convince Ickes that Clinton's attendance at an Irish American forum he had planned would be to the candidate's electoral advantage. It might even put him over the top in a state where former California governor Jerry Brown, who had recently carried neighboring Connecticut, was running strong. Apart from that, the crowd at the forum would only want to hear about Clinton's loftier ideas on Northern Ireland. They wouldn't care a hoot about Gennifer Flowers.

Dearie stood six feet six inches in his stocking feet so at least nobody was going to throw him physically out of the room. And he was being stubborn. The outcome of this argument would play a crucial role in determining much of the course of Irish history for years to come. It would undoubtedly save lives. But nobody was thinking about such niceties at this moment. It was all about time, schedules, votes, Bill Clinton's ambition and his fast sagging energy reserves. The phrase "running for president" is one that can be taken literally. Dearie's final encounter with Ickes had followed a formal refusal by the Clinton campaign to include the Irish forum in the running schedule. This had prompted an angry response from Dearie. It was being suggested by his office that the Clinton people had strung the Irish along for weeks and were now, at the crucial moment, dismissing as unimportant the sentiments of Irish Americans, not just in New York, but right across the country.

It was turning into an ugly Democratic Party family feud. The forum itself had never been intended as just a Democratic event, even though the organizers were from that party. George Bush and Patrick Buchanan had both been asked to attend. Both had declined, prompting the retort from Dearie that the positions of both men were clear anyway because they were "practicing anglophiles," a jibe which Bush probably took in his stride although it was guaranteed to annoy the Catholic Irish American, Buchanan. The failure of any GOP candidates to see a long-term opportunity from turning up at the Irish forum only underlined the paucity of the party's thinking on Ireland at the time. Many who would take an interest in the forum were so-called "Reagan Democrats." Clinton's people were by now actively courting this segment of the voting population. But someone in the Clinton camp had forgotten that a lot of them were also Irish Americans.

Only a few weeks before the Dearie-Ickes encounter, Sinn Féin had produced a document entitled *Towards a Lasting Peace in Ireland*. It was the culmination of years of debate within the republican movement that began with the early 1980s hunger strikes and the declared tactic of advancing the republican cause with a ballot box in one hand and an Armalite rifle in the other. *Towards a Lasting Peace* had been carefully crafted by Sinn Féin's political tacticians. The first line in the document's introduction did not refer to Irish unity. Instead, it pushed forward the notion of peace. "The heart-felt aspiration of most people in Ireland is for peace," it stated. A few lines down there was a reference to something few had heard about as the troubles entered their fourth decade: "A peace process."

But while the document referred to the Irish and British governments, the "international community," the "European dimension" and, most prominently, the United Nations and the role it could play in achieving a settlement, it almost completely left out the United States. There was a passing reference to "Washington" and that was about it. Sinn Féin was perhaps taking its own name, which places emphasis on "ourselves," a little too closely to heart. Yes, Irish America had always been a factor, but America itself, the institution, the power, was quite something else. It seemed distant, peripheral and often pro-British when viewed from West Belfast, the border counties or Sinn Féin headquarters in Dublin. Irish America, by contrast, was a resource, a comfort and a refuge. But more in the context of a war. It wasn't really a winning political player. The British and American political establishments had seen to that.

The ink had barely dried on the blue-covered Sinn Féin manifesto when John Dearie walked into the Clinton office for the final time. Dearie was the latest in a long line of Irish Americans who had devoted much of his political life in an effort to insert the United States squarely into the Irish/British conflict. He wasn't particularly confident of success. And he was certainly unaware at that moment just how close he was to Irish America's political Holy Grail.

Dearie's interest in a U.S. role, which he saw as taking shape in the form of a peace envoy, had been sparked twelve years before. It was the 1980 presidential campaign and Republican hopeful, Senator Howard Baker, had arrived in Albany to make his pitch to New York legislators, both Republican and Democrat. Baker's meeting with the Democrats was going quite well when Assemblyman Sean Walsh from the Bronx stopped him cold.

Dearie remembers: "Sean asked Baker what was his position on Northern Ireland. Baker replied by saying that in his twenty-four years in Congress he had never been asked that question. He was very frank and honest about it, but it led me to think that there was a need to educate candidates and make it clear to them that Ireland was something more than a fourth rate policy consideration for the State Department."

Three years later, Dearie put his thoughts to paper in a *New York Times* op-ed. A resolution supporting an envoy was passed by both houses in the New York State Legislature and in October, 1983, Senator Daniel Patrick Moynihan introduced a resolution in the U.S. Senate calling for the same initiative. Co-sponsors included Senators Ted Kennedy and Chris Dodd. A similar resolution was proposed in the House of Representatives. These resolutions were carefully crafted to avoid any suggestion that a U.S. envoy would have to deal with Sinn Féin or the IRA. They were, as such, moderate, constitutional proposals from members of the Friends of Ireland Group in Congress, a group trusted by the Irish government.

Congressman Mario Biaggi put together his own version which allowed for contacts between an envoy and Sinn Féin. Meanwhile, the Irish Embassy in Washington released a statement on October 24, 1983 welcoming the Friends' version. The statement lauded the action of the Friends in promoting interest in the Northern Ireland problem. "The resolution of Senators Moynihan and Kennedy is seen as a helpful, responsible and imaginative initiative," the statement concluded.

The resolutions were to appear again in 1985. Irish government support for the Friends initiative remained, but it was not enough to impress the State Department which all but ignored Dublin's position in a letter to the chairman of the Senate Foreign Relations Committee: "We consider that the naming at this time of a special envoy to Northern Ireland would serve no useful purpose. Neither the Irish nor the British governments believe that such a diplomatic approach at this time would help in any way to promote reconciliation between the communities and an end to the violence."

Apart from the fact that the statement about Irish government opposition was quite simply untrue, the letter was another remarkable example of the U.S. government's diplomatic headquarters pouring scorn all over the very idea of diplomacy. It also clearly illustrated the entrenched and powerful obstacles which the likes of John Dearie would have to circumvent in order to break the White House mold.

In 1984, with the Democrats gearing up to take on President Reagan, Dearie had introduced the New York St. Patrick's Day Parade to something that would adorn many lapels in years to come: An Irish peace ribbon. It was a small but highly visible step.

Dearie then set out to organize an Irish American Political Forum that would be open to all candidates in the run up to the November election. It was a task that he would initially find "impossibly difficult." But with help from political friends and allies, he managed to lure former Vice-President Walter Mondale to a forum in June. It was attended by a handful of local political activists in the Bronx. Mondale endorsed the idea of an envoy, pinned on a ribbon, and lost the November election. Still, it was a start.

Four year later, Michael Dukakis and Al Gore turned up at forum number two held in a Manhattan hotel and said things that were again music to Irish American ears. Jesse Jackson had promised to show up but had fallen sick. Dearie and his pals later met with Jackson privately to talk about Ireland. The Republicans were still keeping their distance, but questions were also put to George Bush that year by the *Irish Echo* and there was a response to the queries from the Bush campaign. Bush wasn't about to break the long established habit of keeping the U.S. at arm's length from Northern Ireland. But even answers, via fax, were considered an advance.

By 1992, the forum had established itself to the point where many expected it to happen as a matter of course. But it wasn't that easy. Such was the manic pace of a candidate's progress from state to state, that it was the way of things that little or nothing could be deemed as finalized until it was virtually taking place. Dearie had made half-a-dozen visits to the Clinton New York headquarters without much luck. Finally, he stood before Ickes and played his last card. A fifth ace.

"We argued and argued. Ickes eventually asked if anybody else was turning up to the forum and I said sure, Jerry Brown will be there."

It was a Friday. The forum, already rescheduled, was finally supposed to happen on Sunday evening. Nobody had spoken to Jerry Brown at all. Dearie was winging it but he had finally secured the ear of Clinton's top man in the Empire State. And Ickes was now clearly concerned by Brown's apparent intention to reach out to Irish Americans. With his man stumbling in the polls, every vote suddenly counted.

The problem for Dearie was actually to get hold of "Governor Moonbeam." That task was performed by John Connorton, a friend of the Assemblyman and one of the Democratic Party's most influential backroom figures in the city. Connorton turned up at a Brown rally in Manhattan next day. The two men knew each other and Brown trusted Connorton's judgment. He agreed to turn up the next night at the Sheraton Hotel, which, as luck and Dearie both conspired to have it, was Clinton's operational base in the city. The forum had been first set for the College of Mount Saint Vincent in the Riverdale section of the Bronx on Saturday night. But with Clinton such an important prize, the last minute switch was made. The cards, fifth ace and all, were now on the table. If Clinton was going to be snagged anywhere it was in New York City. The exact borough didn't really matter now.

The 1992 forum was the first of the three to date to actually look the part. There was a packed room, a line of TV cameras, including one from C-SPAN, two candidate speakers and a panel which itself was a sign of the times. It included two Irish Americans, Mayor Raymond Flynn of Boston and Noraid leader Martin Galvin; Patrick Farrelly of the *Irish Voice* and the author, immigrants both, made up the interrogative foursome. Clinton and Brown had a sold out Sunday schedule. Both attended a National Organization for Women rally in Washington D.C. Clinton headed back to New York City later that afternoon and Brown flew upstate to Buffalo.

By that Sunday evening, April 5, most Irish Americans were putting their money on Brown. His views on Ireland and his Irish American roots were already widely known. Clinton, the man and his beliefs, remained largely a mystery. Only days before, the *Irish Voice* had come out with an editorial endorsing Brown and ridiculing the man from Arkansas.

"The Clinton candidacy," the editorial declared, "has been favored by the establishment in the Democratic Party and its friends in the media since Michael Dukakis lost to George Bush in 1988. Clinton is the most conventional of candidates and his policies—what can be gleaned of them—would make for business as usual."

Whatever about his policies, Clinton was punctual. He turned up on time, at about 8 p.m. and said just about everything the partisan audience wanted to hear. Brown was delayed upstate and didn't arrive until midnight. He stole the show but lost the primary two days later. By Wednesday morning, many were buying copies of the Irish American papers to see what the guy who was now calling himself the "Comeback Kid" had actually said. It wasn't particularly astonishing. Other candidates in the past, and Jerry Brown too, had endorsed an envoy, expressed support for the MacBride Principles and had damned the treatment of IRA man Joe Doherty. But Clinton had said it and now, all of a sudden, he looked like being the Democratic nominee. Better again, some were suggesting that he even had a fighting chance against an incumbent who had won a war. Who the hell was this guy Clinton? Even in a purely Irish context, Clinton himself could barely answer the question. As he had departed the forum room he was buttonholed by Conor O'Clery of the *Irish Times* who asked him if he knew of Martin Galvin's Noraid role. "Come on, give me a break, I'm doing my best," Clinton replied. Hope's big hope for presidential glory didn't realize it, but his best was yet to come.

Bill Clinton's stunning election win the following November seemed to paralyze Irish America for a moment. Had he really said all those things back in April? Had he actually promised an American envoy? Clinton's win was front page news in the Irish American papers. The promises from the past spring were being dusted off. Some were easy to pull off the page. Clinton had replied quite simply "yes" the night at the forum when asked if he would appoint a U.S. peace envoy.

For good measure he had then added: "I think sometimes we have been a little too reluctant to engage ourselves in a positive way in pursuit of our clearly stated interests and values because of our longstanding special relationship with Great Britain and also because it (Northern Ireland) seemed such a thorny problem."

All those months ago, Clinton had further spoken of a role for the United Nations, Amnesty International and the Irish government. He had also referred to the positive impact of Mary Robinson's presidency on both sides of the Irish border and he had supported the view that Sinn Féin's Gerry Adams be allowed into the U.S.

Clinton had, at the time, placed particular emphasis on Adams's stature as an elected member of the British parliament, a job Adams had lost in the British general election just days after the Sheraton gathering.

In the last days before the U.S. presidential election, Clinton had reiterated his envoy pledge in a wide-ranging statement aimed at Irish American voters. It was disseminated via Bruce Morrison, now chairman of the Irish Americans for Clinton/Gore campaign group. The statement avoided the tricky matter of an Adams visa, but at that point the envoy plan was the bigger story.

"I believe the appointment of a U.S. special envoy to Northern Ireland could be a catalyst in the efforts to secure a lasting peace," Clinton said in the pre-election statement. Crucially, the envoy idea was also being backed by Al Gore, who was widely perceived as being the foreign policy half of the Clinton ticket.

But nobody else really mattered by the November morning after the election. The "we," whom Clinton had characterized as being once reluctant, was now led by himself, the forty-second President.

The British formally congratulated the new man in the White House but were uncomfortable and unsure about the election outcome. The response to the envoy idea had, rather unwisely, been made clear before the actual election itself. And it had been distinctly frosty. "We do not need a peace envoy, thank you very much," Northern Ireland Secretary, Sir Patrick Mayhew, was quoted as saying in the British daily, the *Independent*.

Mayhew's dismissive tone was to be the first of repeated British blunders that, in a very critical way, would contribute to Clinton's following up on pre-election Irish pledges as much as sustained pressure from now excited Irish Americans.

The British government suddenly had another twist to the Irish problem on its plate. And for the first time in the twentieth century, that problem was the President of the United States. Unlike Irish America, much of which could be easily caricatured, ignored or contained, the White House was not something that could be openly treated as a problem at all. One hundred and seventy-eight years previously, it had been just such, and the solution was to burn it. But that was no longer an option.

The British establishment's attitude to Irish America and Irish Americans had never been particularly favorable. At the very least, Irish Americans were naive and misguided when it came to the "Irish question." At worst, they were a dangerous threat. The British press had its stock Irish American characters always waiting in the wings. The image of the drunken Irish American throwing dollars into the passing IRA hat in some down-at-heel bar in Boston or New York was an old standard. The Kennedys were always good for copy too. Fleet Street had never forgotten, nor forgiven, old Joe Kennedy's support for American neutrality in World War Two. In British eyes, the sins of the father were the sins of the sons, and grandchildren.

An inkling of these attitudes was never hard to detect. They were clearly illustrated by top newspaper columnist Bernard Levin in his 1989 book, *A Walk Up Fifth Avenue*. Levin, chief columnist at the time for *The Times* of London, was touted in the sleeve notes of his book as "the greatest journalist of his generation."

The book, which formed the basis for a television documentary, described a tour of the famed New York street. Of course it was impossible to avoid several references to Irish Americana, including the St. Patrick's Day Parade, which, according to the greatest journalist of his generation, was populated by marchers "who seriously claim Irish descent" but "have no more right to it than is given by their descent to the floor in a Third Avenue bar after drinking too many doubles of Jameson's whiskey."

Levin typified a certain British view of Irish Americans. One that cropped up almost daily at some point or other in portions of the British press. Remarking on "the eagerness and satisfaction with which people thousands of miles away from the scene contemplate murder," Levin knew of no more extreme form of this "vicarious advocacy" than "the American-Irish thirst for English blood."

Levin's views of the Irish in Ireland were not entirely sanguine either. Ireland, he wrote, should be classified as part of the Third World because the Irish "limp tragically behind most of the world in terms of initiative, energy, enterprise and success."

As for the Irish contribution to the United States, Levin, at some point along Fifth Avenue, found it to be "strikingly meagre." The Irish had "given the country, or at least the eastern part of it, many politicians and policemen, and a few crooked but successful nineteenth-century industrialists; but a comparison with the success of the Jews and the blacks and for that matter the Poles, and now the Chinese, leaves the Irish far behind."

Three years after Levin's ramble, the potential for Irish American mischief had suddenly arisen again. For a group of people who had contributed so meagerly to the great American story, the American Irish had proven, if nothing else, that they had a talent for influencing the influential and commanding more space than they presumably deserved in the tomes of supreme British journalists. Bill Clinton's Irish views hadn't grown on a tree. Some Irish Americans, crooked or otherwise, had clearly been hiding just a little initiative, energy and enterprise. Success now threatened to follow.

The tendency of not a few British politicians and journalists to belittle Irish America had also formed like a cloud over Bill Clinton's head. That now famous photo of a teenage Clinton shaking the hand of President Kennedy was causing knees to jerk from Wapping to Westminster. Well before the election there was reason to believe that the Clinton family tree was not all rooted in the "Mother Country." Worse, it had branches in the "Auld Sod."

Clinton, of course, had attended Oxford. But at a bad time. The young Clinton, bearded amid the cloisters, had devoted his energies to opposing the Vietnam War as much as enhancing his love of the higher glories of British upper class civilization.

Years later, there would be many theories as to why Clinton was so primed for a complete reversal of U.S. non-policy towards Ireland. Jimmy Carter had made the first move towards such reversal with his brief statement on Ireland issued from the White House in 1977. But the statement, with its promise of U.S. aid and investment in the event of a settlement in Northern Ireland, was not strong enough to rock too many boats. Besides, as former Irish Ambassador to the U.S. Sean Donlon later pointed out—in an *Irish Times* article—British diplomats in Washington had succeeded in delaying the Carter statement for months, despite its overall good intentions and rather innocuous expression of support.

When Bill Clinton began making pledges on Ireland in the months preceding the '92 election, the British had held fire because it was felt that George Bush was unbeatable. When Bush began to look vulnerable, all hell broke loose and the lines began to tighten between the Republicans in Washington and Conservatives in London, a relationship described by Sidney Blumenthal in the *New Yorker* magazine as "the blue international."

Bush's troubles resulted in the direct intervention of Conservative party strategists who flew to Washington in a last ditch effort to save the Bush presidency. There followed the infamous "good hunting" telegram on election morning from British Foreign Secretary Douglas Hurd to former Secretary of State James Baker who by then was in charge of the floundering Bush campaign. Hurd's telegram all but willed a Bush victory.

Later there was to be the passport files story in the *Washington Post*, one which had British and U.S. State Department officials combing files in an effort to find out if Clinton had ever applied for British citizenship as a means of avoiding Vietnam. When the day of his inauguration finally arrived, Bill Clinton could rightly say to himself that whatever fealty he owed the special alliance with Britain, his obligation to the then sitting British government was a big fat zero. As had been the case on other occasions in history, Britain's plight became Ireland's opportunity.

In later years, some would suggest that simmering inside Clinton's mind was a deep-rooted resentment over being treated as something of a country bumpkin at Oxford, not just by some of his British hosts, but also by resident Americans with blood ties to the aforementioned blue international. Also, while at Oxford, Clinton would have been aware of the first rumblings of troubles in Northern Ireland reflected in the civil rights protests. The marches were modeled on the civil rights campaign in the southern U.S. states. Coming from Arkansas, it would have all looked very familiar to student Clinton.

As one Irish diplomat later put it: "When Clinton arrived at the White House he brought very few WASPS with him. And to Washington he was an outsider. He had never supped at the British Embassy table. Even then it was apparent that his character and wit were very Irish, and this came out more and more over time."

White Anglo Saxon Protestants would play their part in the administration, as in all before, but Clinton's first term crew was decidedly eclectic and it included the "Massachusetts Mafia," a group with ties to that state and, in some case that state's most enduring political force, the Kennedys. Nancy Soderberg, Susan Brophy and Mark Gearan were all Capos in this wheel within wheels. George Stephanopoulos, who had Clinton's ear on just about everything, was quickly picked out by Irish diplomats as being positively anti-British when the mood took him. And there was plenty of opportunity to take a swipe at the British in those first days of the forty-second presidency.

Even House Speaker Tom Foley, widely viewed as being an anglophile, took umbrage at British actions, telling Conor O'Clery—for his book *Daring Diplomacy*—that "British meddling was outrageous and I think it went very deep with Clinton."

There would be those who would later play down suggestions of such ill feeling. Nancy Soderberg, who would become a central figure in the Clinton Irish policy as a staff member in the first-term National Security Council, would take the view that Clinton didn't really hold a grudge, at least not against John Major.

"Clinton did have a lot of respect for Major. The passport business didn't faze him for long and besides, once the British realized we weren't going to go nuts, they settled down."

In time, and as recounted in detail in O'Clery's book, veteran activists on Irish issues made sure that the new Clinton White House, while not going nuts, would neither be allowed settle on its pre-election laurels. The crucial thing for Irish America in the wake of Clinton's election was to continue to present a determined and cohesive message. This was largely accomplished, primarily by the Americans for a New Irish Agenda group, which was simply Irish

202 THE NEW IRISH AMERICANS

Americans for Clinton/Gore in a new suit. In January, 1993, representatives of the group flew to Clinton's home base in Little Rock to meet with Chris Hyland, charged during the campaign with reaching out to ethnic groups such as the Irish. The agenda might have been new, but its emissaries were old hands: The O'Dwyers, Paul and Brian, Ray Flynn, John Dearie, Joe Jamison of the Irish American Labor Coalition, *Irish Voice* publisher Niall O'Dowd, Bob Linnon of the Irish American Unity Conference, billionaire businessman Chuck Feeney and Mike Quinlin, an adviser on matters Irish to Flynn and a contributing writer for the *Irish Echo*. Bruce Morrison, delayed by snow, hooked up by telephone. The man who entered the Irish American arena because of Northern Ireland, only to veer up the avenue of immigration reform, was now returning to his starting point.

Meanwhile, the wheels were churning in Congress where Joe Kennedy had introduced a Joint House Resolution calling on the new president to appoint a new U.S. peace envoy to Northern Ireland, sooner rather than later.

The hackneyed image of the beer-soaked Irish American Patriot Game, was, by Clinton's inauguration day, becoming ragged and redundant. The New Patriot Game, while not yet there for all to see, was finally getting its chance to play in the open. "Finally" because it wasn't really that new at all. Sure, Irish America had never shied away from the gun and bullet option in Ireland; but neither had it ever neglected politics. Sinn Féin were not the first to twin the ballot box and public sentiment with the raised rifle. Irish American activists, even when they had disagreed fundamentally on the searing question of liberation through violence, had for years seen the necessity of underpinning any future U.S. role in Ireland with a thick layer of politics and economic clout. They had worked, often thanklessly, on building an Irish American platform propped up by these twin fundamentals. The platform merely required a sympathetic president. Now, presto, one was at hand.

Back in the 1970s, as the Northern Ireland troubles reached new levels of unspeakable horror, the headlines in the mainstream press were more often than not generated by atrocities, especially those committed by the IRA. For most Irish Americans, the waters were becoming muddier by the minute. It was ever more difficult to see the nobility in the cause of a united Ireland as the bloodshed grew worse by the day.

A minority of Irish Americans continued to view the troubles as a war, the casualties being regrettable but inevitable. Through the lens of the *Irish People* newspaper in particular, the grim battle for control of Northern Ireland's streets was relayed from across the Atlantic every week. The Dublin and Monaghan bombings of May, 1974 would result in years of speculation and accusation concerning alleged British involvement. For the *Irish People*, there was no question about it: "Britain Again Bombs Dublin," the headline in the May 25th issue screamed. Week by week, readers were brought face to face with British perfidy, Special Air Service death squads, brave IRA volunteers, murdered Catholics and "Free State" collaboration. There were hardly enough pages to get it all in, although even sports had its place in the middle of the struggle. "Ireland Beat England In Rugby," was always going to dominate the paper's sports coverage in the February 23, 1974 issue, only a few weeks before the most lethal single bombing attack of the entire troubles.

Still, despite even sports, and headlines such as "IRA Destroys British Economy" and "IRA Determined To End British Rule Now," the *People*'s ability to broaden its readership base and secure wider support for its controlling patron, Irish Northern Aid— Noraid—would always be limited by the overwhelming public revulsion towards violence. What the paper, Noraid and American Irish Republicans in general needed, in order to draw even a few drops of sympathy from the revolted, were issues that came without an ultimate moral price tag.

Martin Galvin, who would emerge in the 1980s as Noraid's most prominent voice and end up questioning the future president, was assigned the task in 1979 of presenting Americans with issues they would not immediately run away from. It was no easy task.

"There was no publicity department at the time and there was a critical situation developing in the H-Blocks," Galvin would later recall.

"We knew by then that public awareness in the United States would be vital if we were to be in any way effective. Up to then, the British had been defining the terms of the conflict in Ireland for Americans. So we set up a publicity and lobbying department and began bringing over former prisoners to the U.S."

In some cases "bringing" entailed smuggling. But live bodies in America did go some way towards countering the chill effect brought about by dead bodies in Ireland. Real people telling first person stories served to counter the kind of knee-jerk reactions fostered by more abstract reports of faceless terrorists going about their dastardly business. Galvin, for one, noticed immediate results.

"We found that people were more inclined to be involved and this in turn led to politicians becoming interested. These new issues began to receive greater prominence after the 1981 hunger strikes and it led to the considerable dispelling of the myth fostered by the British that we were all just misguided Americans."

The new issues were related to Northern Ireland but were not totally immersed in the daily bloody fare of the troubles. They were more political and economic, easier to grasp and retain. They carried no moral price tag. Indeed, they were a bargain basement treasure trove to those who realized that, in a conflict such as Northern Ireland's, the winning of the argument might be the only victory at the end of it all. The new issues included the MacBride Principles, a visa for Gerry Adams and Joe Doherty.

Journalist Pete Hamill remembers the years after World War Two as a time when a sense of Irishness in America was defined as much as anything else by what you were against. "I'm not a big fan of identity politics, but in those days there was no freshness. Instead there was a contracting of that sense of Irishness."

The troubles in Northern Ireland, in Hamill's view, were to change everything for Irish Americans. "Across the water, people were fighting and dying for what they believed was a basic right to a national identity which had become blurred by assimilation in America and partition in Ireland itself."

If economic difficulties in the 1980s launched so many young Irish people on a voyage to the United States, the troubles in Northern Ireland had also spawned its own generation of exiles. Some were running from employment or housing discrimination. Some were running out of fear of random violence. And some were on the run. Joe Doherty, Belfast IRA volunteer numbered among the latter. His would be quite a story.

On any given day in New York, from June 18, 1983 to the late months of 1991, when he was transferred to a federal prison in Pennsylvania, Joe Doherty could be found within the cramped confines of the Metropolitan Correctional Center in Downtown Manhattan. And many, politicians, lawyers, high-ranking religious leaders, went out of their way to find him.

Doherty had been captured in Belfast in early May, 1980 after a wild shootout on the Antrim Road involving his IRA unit and a team of Special Air Service men led by Captain Herbert Westmacott. The British officer was killed in the exchange of fire before Doherty and his fellow IRA men surrendered. Doherty would later escape from Crumlin Road prison in Belfast and flee to the U.S. He would be arrested by the FBI on that June day in 1983 while tending bar in Clancy's, an imbibing emporium on Third Avenue where conversation often drifted into talk of the troubles, the Brits and the "'RA."

Joe Doherty lost his battle, first against extradition and then deportation. But in the almost nine years he spent imprisoned, many would come to believe that he had largely demolished the view that all IRA members were somehow faceless, mindless, psychopathic thugs hell-bent on murder. The hunger strikers in 1981 had done much the same thing in Ireland. But proximity always heightened the effect. Here was a "terrorist" who would draw Cardinals of the Catholic Church to his cell, mayors of New York, Senators and Congress members of the United States, lawyers and human rights activists. He would have a week in New York proclaimed in his honor while a slice of street outside the forbidding mass of the MCC building, at the junction of Park Row and Pearl Street, would bear the name "Joseph Doherty Corner."

It was to Doherty's distinct advantage that he was intelligent, articulate and telegenic. To some, he would be never anything more than a murderous Provo. Yet he spent hours of his "free" time turning down marriage proposals, or offers of adoption from American women who hoped he was motherless.

Successive administrations, that of Presidents Reagan and Bush, would move legal mountains to prevent him from securing bail and to see the back of him. In February, 1992, this effort would finally succeed. Joe Doherty was sent back to Belfast where he would become just another republican prisoner, one of the lads. Behind him, in the United States, there would be a legal uproar, accusations of unconstitutional behavior on the part of successive attorneys general and claims that the judiciary's independence had become subordinate to the political and foreign considerations of the day.

There had been no supreme propagandist running the legal and political circus that would propel the name Joseph Patrick Doherty all the way through the doors of the United States Supreme Court, one hundred and thirty-two names of Congress members close behind, bound within the covers of an amicus brief the envy of political prisoners all over the planet. But if there had been one, he or she would have concluded at the end that the Joe Doherty case was a peculiar triumph. It had generated enormous media coverage, much of it, although by no means all of it, sympathetic. The case, pushed relentlessly by Doherty's lawyers Mary Pike and Steve Somerstein, had cast sometimes embarrassing light on the actions and motivations of governments, and it had enormously broadened the base of support for various Irish American causes across the entire country.

Doherty himself was meat in the sandwich, and his prison life would drag on for years in Northern Ireland. His case had spanned a period when the U.S. press, despite all the "Free Joe Doherty" cries from such a varied slice of American life, was still disinclined to look too far behind the IRA mask. The 5–3 Supreme Court decision against Doherty's plea for a political asylum hearing was broadly welcomed by editorial writers who viewed Doherty as being little more than a terrorist killer, notwithstanding the fact that exactly who fatally wounded Captain Westmacott in the Antrim Road shootout was never finally determined.

The *New York Times* decided that while the case had been "marked by rough justice," the outcome was "roughly just."

The *Daily News* in New York decided that whatever people thought of the situation in Ireland "harboring convicted killers in America will not make matters any better."

The *Boston Herald* proclaimed that Doherty wasn't a patriot, freedom fighter, political prisoner "or any of the other exalted titles bestowed on him by his misguided American admirers. He's a convicted killer."

Within a few years, there would be other Joe Dohertys, loyalist and republican. But they would be supping in the White House. They would enjoy the exalted title of peacemakers, bestowed by new, hitherto elusive, admirers, not a few of them writers of newspaper editorials.

At the same time, there would be other arrivals from Northern Ireland still carrying some of the old baggage: Deportees, escapees and extraditees, individuals with families and reason enough to quit Ireland for ever. Some would fight to stay and succeed, while others would follow the Doherty path back. America, despite its generosity and expansive freedoms, could never be taken for granted by those once considered behind the mask and beyond the pale.

Those very American freedoms, so attractive to those who would seek to use them as a means to escape their Irish past, had also fostered an array of purely political and economic based campaigns directed at Northern Ireland by groups such as the Irish National Caucus, Irish American Unity Conference and American Irish Political Education Committee. By far the most far-reaching campaign was that in support of the MacBride Principles.

The nine fair employment guidelines for Northern Ireland, named after the Irish statesman and Nobel Peace Prize winner Sean MacBride—who had been an early but largely frustrated advocate of a more direct U.S. role in the partition issue—were to draw support from a far wider spectrum of Irish America than just about any other single issue in the 1980s and '90s. The simple reason for this was that the principles were simple to understand and embrace. They advocated peaceful economic change, not violence. And while they would be primarily aimed at redressing an imbalance which saw Catholics in Northern Ireland more than two-and-a-half times more likely to be unemployed than Protestants, the principles also carried an egalitarian sting in their tail. They applied equally to parts of the North where Protestants felt their job prospects were diminished by local demographics that favored Catholics.

On the surface, the MacBride campaign seemed just the kind of non-violent movement that would siphon potential Irish American support from more violent tactics. But for the first ten years of the campaign, which began in late 1984, the MacBride Principles would prompt the most steadfast and entrenched opposition from the British government. Millions of dollars would be spent, editorial writing ears would be bent and municipalities would be threatened with economic retribution by British diplomats charged with conveying London's utmost annoyance.

As Andrew Wilson put it in his book, *Irish America and the Ulster Conflict 1968–1995*: "The Thatcher administration . . . launched a concerted effort to destroy the MacBride campaign. The British Information Service in New York and consuls nationwide worked against proposed state and municipal legislation."

British action was well expressed in a late 1993 letter from the British Consul General in New York, Alistair Hunter, to Philadelphia Mayor Ed Rendell, whose City Council was at the time considering a MacBride bill.

The letter, a late twentieth century equivalent to a gunboat on the Delaware, did not attempt to veil what was clearly a threat: "As you know," Hunter wrote, "Britain is the largest overseas investor in Pennsylvania. More than a third of all foreign-owned companies in the Delaware Valley are British owned." Hunter went on to remind Rendell of the mayor's efforts to lure more British investment and to strengthen other mutually beneficial business relationships, including the British Airway–U.S. air alliance.

"Passage of this ordinance would harm your efforts," Hunter bluntly stated. He further warned Rendell that existing contracts between Philadelphia companies and British concerns, including one linking a Philadelphia food service provider with the British Ministry of Defense, would be placed in jeopardy. The Hunter letter, and similar missives sent to other state and city authorities by British diplomats were examples of what the British themselves might describe as "putting a bit of stick about."

Sometimes, the U.S. State Department would aid this effort, as was the case during the Bush administration when John Wilson, then chairman of the Council of the District of Columbia, received a letter from the State Department concerning a D.C. MacBride initiative that read in part: "Although the Department of State fully supports the non-discrimination and full-employment objectives of the MacBride Principles, we are concerned that incorporating them into legislation could inhibit job-creating investment." The letter went on to back up this concern by referring to the views of John Hume, the most prominent nationalist opponent of the MacBride Principles being applied in Northern Ireland. The letter cited Hume's opposition as the reason why the Bush administration had "consistently opposed federal, state and local legislation which would require American and other firms in Northern Ireland to adhere to the MacBride Principles."

Whatever about the White House nodding at John Hume's feeling on the issue, the British attitude towards MacBride required no outside prop. While accusations were often made that the campaign was a smokescreen for Sinn Féin and the IRA, which it was not, the heart of the matter was the issue of control. London genuinely wanted to tackle employment discrimination in Northern Ireland, but on its own terms and in its own time. The British would introduce the Fair Employment Act for Northern Ireland in 1989, which Andrew Wilson has described as a move which London hoped would "effectively cripple the fair employment issue in America." MacBride supporters were unimpressed and damned the new legislation as being toothless.

More than ever, the British government now viewed the MacBride Principles as an external threat promoted by ever growing numbers of misguided Irish Americans, and some rather dubious Irish expatriates, not least Fr. Sean McManus, head of the Washington D.C.-based Irish National Caucus.

There was legitimate concern in London that the demands made by MacBride backers would discourage potential U.S. investment in Northern Ireland. That there were far more discouraging aspects of Northern Ireland society likely to discourage an entrepreneur was beside the point. At the end of the day, though, significant British acquiescence to Irish American demands for MacBride's implementation, whatever about heartfelt American sensibilities on the overall fair employment question, would have been as shocking as they would have been unnatural under heaven. It all boiled down to a question of sovereignty, over issues as much as territory.

MacBride, simply put, was an unwelcome intruder, an economic whip to beat the Brits with. "The campaign," as one "Restricted" British government document put it in June, 1992, "still provides a useful tool for those who wish to discredit HMG's policies in Northern Ireland and the threat which it poses to investment must remain major cause for concern."

The threatening aspect came in several forms as far as London was concerned. McManus and the Caucus, consistently the most obvious group in the lobbying and publicity campaign across the U.S., would be a formidable and exceedingly annoying foe in the race to get first to the hands-on potential MacBride legislation. McManus would early on display a keen sense of what the American press wanted in a story that, at best, might start out as a peripheral issue connected to a remote place. The very fact that McManus, a member of the Redemptorist order from County Fermanagh, wore a clerical collar, was an angle in itself. In time, McManus would become known to some journalists as "Fr. Fax" because of his ability to react so speedily to new twists in the MacBride campaign, sometimes, because of his own active role, even before they occurred.

But press-pleasing statements and lobbying alone does not a successful campaign make. At the root of the MacBride campaign's longevity has been economic muscle and money. Mayor Raymond Flynn was the first to wield the really big stick in 1990 with a Boston bill allowing the city to pull pension fund dollars from non-MacBride complying U.S. companies doing business in Northern Ireland and reinvesting the money with companies that were in compliance. New York City and State would also pass so-called contract compliance bills and by the mid 1990s, fifteen states and over thirty municipalities would have MacBride legislation of some form or another on the books.

New York City's Comptroller's office in particular had become a nerve center for MacBride activity under successive Comptrollers Harrison "Jay" Goldin, Elizabeth Holtzman and Alan Hevesi. The constant hand on the tiller through these three administrations was Pat Doherty. Doherty, the office's Investment Responsibility Director, would opt for a more subtle approach than the various lobbying groups, but the Comptroller's office could always afford the quieter approach given that it was sitting on a pension fund worth in excess of $50 billion.

All that money would find its way into numerous financial ventures around the globe where connections to Northern Ireland, while obscure at first glance, were in fact quite tangible. Sometimes, New York dollars would end up right in the middle of Northern Ireland's troubled employment story, as illustrated by an *Irish Echo* report in May, 1992: "In an ironic twist to the extensive privatization policies extolled by former British Prime Minister Margaret Thatcher, the infamous Ballylumford power station outside Belfast is now having to deal with the requirements of MacBride Principles legislation passed by New York City.

"The Ballylumford plant, which passed into the private hands of British Gas on April 1, is now part-owned by the city. New York pension fund investment in British Gas equity amounts to just over 8.5 million shares, valued at over $40 million."

Ballylumford had been a symbol of loyalist economic and political power, in every sense of the word, back in 1974 during the loyalist workers strike, an action which brought about the collapse of the Sunningdale power sharing agreement. Now, those in charge of running it would have to answer questions about the MacBride meetings at shareholder meetings.

Investment dollars, and subsequent unqualified support from the likes of future president Bill Clinton and Irish Foreign Minister David Andrews, in September 1992, solidified the MacBride campaign's role in shaping the future of the employment picture in Northern Ireland, long considered an essential issue by nationalists determined to see an end to forced Catholic economic migration.

There would be spats and hiccups, vetoes and congressional approval and, by 1997, an apparent calm in what had formerly been an especially contentious area of debate. But the essential problem of an imbalance of employment opportunity in Northern Ireland remained. How long that would be the case was difficult to predict, but a "Confidential" British government document, compiled the same month that David Andrews gave Dublin's nod to the MacBride campaign, presented this somewhat less than sanguine view of the future: "An analysis of the key area of employment suggests that the unemployment differential is unlikely to alter significantly over the next decade, in spite of the strengthened fair employment legislation."

The MacBride campaign, once described in an *Irish Voice* story as the "greatest grassroots Irish American phenomenon of recent times" seemingly faced a task unfinished by the late 1990s, despite all it had accomplished. Still, Fr. Sean McManus would credit the campaign with "changing the very nature of discrimination in Northern Ireland for all time."

With its second decade of existence well advanced, the grassroots aspect of the MacBride Principles campaign had actually ceded ground somewhat to the loftier heights of congressional debate. What was especially noticeable by the late 1990s, however, was the bipartisan nature of support for the principles on Capitol Hill. Republicans and Democrats alike were lending support and sponsoring legislation. This had always been the case to a degree, but there appeared little doubt that Bill Clinton's embracing of the fair employment guidelines spurred things on considerably. This was the essence of the New Patriot Game, American style: Issues that were once taboo or condemned to partisan limbo were now seen as legitimate fare for the big political bear hug.

The IRA cease-fires were undoubtedly also making it easier for hitherto reluctant politicians, while the new opportunities for Gerry Adams and Sinn Féin to reach out directly to Irish Americans on American soil, coupled with the growing consensus among various

212 THE NEW IRISH AMERICANS

hues of Irish nationalists had clearly calmed many mainstream American concerns.

Then there was the arrival of Tony Blair at 10 Downing Street, an event which future writers concerned with Ireland or Irish America will either deck out in lights or portray as a false dawn. Equally, there has been the new willingness of unionists and loyalist leaders to travel to the United States and engage in debate with Irish America. The symbolism of President Mary Robinson shaking hands with loyalist leaders—in New York—was not lost on any side. Clearly, and despite Ulster Unionist Party leader David Trimble's contention that America is not a broker in Northern Ireland, much of the inevitable brokering on behalf of the people of Northern Ireland is going to be hammered out, either on American soil, or with Americans in the room.

Above all these factors sits the two-term presidency of Bill Clinton, in strictly Irish American historical terms, a most monumental event. The long-term implications of Clinton's interest and involvement in Ireland might not be clear for some years. The only certainty would appear to be that Clinton will keep his presidential toe in the Irish door until he hands over to his successor in January, 2001. Certainly, for Clinton, there is no going back before then.

As Nancy Soderberg put it: "President Clinton always had a gut sense about Ireland and he was not hard to convince, although he had to make the tough decisions. He realizes it's a long-term commitment."

Soderberg's view, and others share it, is that no matter who is in the White House in the foreseeable future, Democrat or Republican, Ireland will remain a U.S. foreign policy issue. But there remains the question: to what degree?

Daring Diplomacy author Conor O'Clery has concluded that U.S. interest will remain beyond the Clinton years, but its intensity will depend on external factors.

"It depends a lot on who the president is and on the situation of the day in Northern Ireland. Bill Clinton was personally and emotionally interested in Ireland and his presidency coincided with a historic moment when the United States could make a difference, when it had indirect leverage with the IRA through the granting of visas, fundraising and access, and when the so-called special relationship (with Britain) was at a low ebb.

"Clinton's biggest contribution was probably to send George Mitchell to chair the talks process. Future presidents will have their own international priorities and will probably make judgments about getting involved in Ireland based on the perceived achievements of the Clinton administration. That is, if it is perceived as helping to bring about a settlement, the onus will be on future presidents to stay engaged to nurture a successful U.S. foreign policy, but if not, it will be more tempting to back off.

"But this doesn't take into account a new level of political sophistication in the Irish American community which so successfully used its leverage on Irish policy and will have learned lessons for the future. The new element in American politics is a heightened feeling of responsibility for the legitimate concerns of forty million people of Irish descent about the conflict in Ireland. U.S. involvement in the mid 1990s was expressed on two levels: It could influence the paramilitary parties by what was in its giving, and bring its prestige to bear on the peace process by simply being interested. These both could easily be withdrawn by a future president, especially if the IRA returns to its campaign."

The prospects for Irish policy in the event of a return to power of a Republican president are less certain by virtue of the scant GOP track record at presidential level. At the same time, one of the most important developments in Irish American politics during the 1990s has been the emergence of interested and active GOP legislators in Congress, not least House members Peter King, Ben Gilman, James Walsh and Chris Smith.

King's connection to both sides in Northern Ireland goes back even beyond his tasteless tea ceremony with Andy Tyrie and John McMichael. From the time when the British ambassador in Washington accused him of having blood in his hands—prompted by King's sponsorship of a visit to Washington of Sinn Féin's Caoimhghín O Caoláin the day after the 1993 IRA bombing of a fish shop on Belfast's Shankill Road—King has emerged as one of the most influential figures on Capitol Hill dealing with Ireland. He believes that no matter who sits in the White House, Ireland will, in the years to come, enjoy equal status with the likes of Israel or South Africa.

Said King in the fall of 1997: "I argued with Irish Republicans for a cease-fire so that U.S. policy would be locked into place by the time the next president is in the White House."

Clearly, the personal inclination of upcoming presidents is key. The issue of Ireland's future and Anglo/Irish relations is complex and frequently frustrating. It runs far beyond merely pointing an angry finger at "cruel England." At the very least, should the presidency pass from Bill Clinton to Al Gore, there is a widespread belief in place that the policy of U.S. engagement will largely continue. John Dearie saw to it, before the 1996 presidential election, that Gore would lay it on the line, which the Vice-President did to Irish American applause at a forum in a Manhattan hotel atop the site of the hospital that witnessed the first cries in the world of Eamon de Valera.

That forum, John Dearie's grand slam, was number four in a series now heading for its second century and another shot in the arm for the new, but still evolving, Irish American Patriot Game.

Pat Hurley goes to war in his gansey (sweater).

Photo by Martin Sheerin

Sean Minihane gets the message out—in style.
Irish Voice photo

Sean Minihane, Brian Donnelly, Mae O'Driscoll and Brian O'Dwyer.
Irish Echo photo by Tom Matthews

Brian Donnelly and an Irish immigrant named Maureen O'Hara.

Irish Voice photo

By 1989 the IIRM had a platform, even if the banner was looking a little limp. New York St. Patrick's Day Parade Committee Chairman Frank Beirne is at left; Pat Hurley is looking to his left; Jack Irwin is about to make a speech correction; and Congressman Tom Manton is speaking.

Irish Echo photo

Dorothy Hayden Cudahy takes a moment on her black asphalt road to be congratulated by Cardinal John O'Connor during the 1989 New York St. Patrick's Day Parade.

John Dearie (left) gets his man, Walter Mondale, thus setting in motion a process that would eventually lead to Bill Clinton's door.

The MacBride Principles on fair employment are discussed by the man who made them a hot political issue, Fr. Sean McManus, and the man who gave them a name, the late Sean MacBride.

Irish Echo photo

*Joe Doherty can certainly count on the support of
Congressman Gary Ackerman, but even political friends could not
stop his eventual deportation.*

Politics and seltzer water. Pete King (right) meets John Hume in Derry.

Irish Foreign Minister Dick Spring got on well with Bill Clinton.
Golf in Co. Kerry was always a good way to warm the conversation up.

White House photo

The priest and the future Prez. Fr. Sean McManus and then Governor Bill Clinton pictured at the 1992 Irish American Political Forum in Manhattan.

Bruce Morrison.

Pete Hamill.
Eamonn Farrell, Photocall

The torch passes. Bruce Morrison and Congressman Charles "Chuck" Schumer who became a champion of Irish immigrant rights in the 1990s.

Transatlantic pillars of Irish Republicanism Caoimghín O Caoláin of Sinn Féin (left) and Martin Galvin.

The First Breakfast. Irish Republicans meet American Republicans. On the left, Martin McGuinness and Gerry Adams; on the right, Newt Gingrich, to his left Ben Gilman, and Peter King to his right.

New York's first black mayor David Dinkins was highly visible in Irish affairs including the ILGO/parade controversy and the Gerry Adams visa issue.

Nobel Laureate Seamus Heaney.

Irish film's leading man, Jim Sheridan.

A new Irish Voice: Bono.
Photocall

Three Irish Democrats: Ray Flynn, Bill Clinton and Paul O'Dwyer.

Immigrant helping hand: the Irish Immigration working committee meets at the Irish Consulate in New York. Irish Foreign Minister Ray Burke is seated directly in front of the cameraman while Adrian Flannelly (hand to face) is to Burke's left.

*James Baker, who annoyed Irish Americans with his comments
at the 1996 GOP convention, with Irish Foreign Minister Gerry Collins.*

Photo by deKun, Washington D.C.

*New York City Comptroller Harrison "Jay" Goldin with two giants
of Irish twentieth-century political life on both sides of the Atlantic:
Sean MacBride (center) and Paul O'Dwyer (right).*

Irish Echo photo

A couple of blackguards who talked big and made it big. The McCourts, Malachy (left) and Frank.

THE NEW IRISH AMERICANS

"In a perfect world, after an alien is arrested, the alien is detained and deported."

Immigration and Naturalization Service "Year End Summary" statement to the press.

The car came to a sudden halt. Two men jumped out. They were dressed in casual but not country working clothes. One wore an army style coat, the other a leather jacket, something dangling over his shoulder. The men were in a hurry. They slid down the side of the road, hopped a narrow stream and began trudging up the hillside. The air was raw with the taste of an early west of Ireland winter. Snow had fallen on the upper reaches of Maumtrasna, one of the Partry Mountains in County Mayo.

The men were searching for sheep. More precisely, they were looking for sheep with sheepish grins, wooly beasts destined for a newspaper photograph. The two paused. One cursed loudly as water from rain and melting snow seeped into his running shoes. The mountain was like one enormous sponge. On top of it all (in every sense) there were no sheep in sight. After a few more minutes of wet-footed slogging, the men stopped. The one with the camera fiddled with the machine and placed it on a rock. The two walked ahead of the camera, bent almost double into the slope. The camera's automatic timer reached the crucial moment and the lens shutter clicked. The men came back, grabbed the camera and began what was a messy, almost sliding descent. A few days later a photograph appeared in the Dublin-published *Evening Press* newspaper. It took up most of a broadsheet page. It was filled by two rear ends, a vista of snow and a large swathe of sky. The caption informed readers that the rear ends belonged to a pair of shepherds searching for lost sheep in the Partry Mountains following winter's first snowfall. There were no shepherds of course. Indeed, there were few people at all in the area, prone as it always was to emigration. The shepherds were long gone, as likely as not plying a new trade in America. It was the mid 1980s. A time for Irish sheep to fend for themselves.

A decade later, early May, 1995. Ireland was strutting its stuff. This was not the old Ireland of small farms, sheep-dotted mountains and small country towns near devoid of young men and women. The scene was unfolding under a broad tent on the South Lawn of the White House. It was the culmination of a three-day trade and investment conference in the U.S. capital, a showcase for the new, emerging Ireland. The Ireland of Mary Robinson, the peace process, computer factories, fast-food restaurants, motorways and countless golf courses.

As always at an Irish gathering, there was at least some talk devoted to the weather. It was hot and sticky and an early summer thunderstorm was brewing just to the west of the Potomac. As the sky darkened, the throng of visitors—politicians, diplomats, business people, Irish-American activists, journalists and well-known faces such as Ethel Kennedy and her son-in-law, Guildford Four member Paul Hill—exchanged banter and views on the conference, a much-hyped event that had largely lived up to the pre-billing. President Clinton had just announced his intention to visit Ireland later in the year. Gerry Adams had shaken hands with Northern Ireland Secretary, Sir Patrick Mayhew, albeit behind closed hotel doors.

The handshake had occurred at the Sheraton, a chain that the Irish seemed to reserve for groundbreaking political events. For the three days of the conference, the hotel had witnessed a coming together of northern and southern Irish political and economic life the likes of which had never before taken place anywhere. Perhaps coming together was putting it a little strong. The conflicting forces in Irish politics had shared the same roof for a few days, even the same bars. But between the divergent ends of the political spectrum, the republicans and loyalists, the shared roof was as far as it went. They bought their own drinks, and in the corridors and conference rooms where great plans for a possible future Ireland were being drawn up, the old enemies made sure that appropriate distance was maintained.

Back on the South Lawn, the storm was gathering strength, rumbling and flashing over the Washington Monument. As it reached its peak, a military band marched to the rear of the now rain soaked canopy. Its members, red-uniformed and gold-braided, struck up "Hail to the Chief" and, as if on cue, an ear-splitting crack of thunder exploded immediately overhead. Down came the gods from Olympus, Bill and Hillary Clinton. The people in the tent cheered and applauded, as relieved to have survived nature's momentary fury as much as they were delighted to hail the new chief, the man who would save Ireland from itself.

Three thousand miles away, that very hour, the *Irish Press* newspaper (founded by Eamon de Valera, "the Chief") was closing for good amid the bitterness and rancor of yet another in a succession of confrontations between employees and management. The *Press* had for years symbolized de Valera's ideal of an inward-looking Ireland full of hard-working, God-fearing folk somehow impervious to foreign, alien ways. Since the mid-1930s it had served as a shepherd-in-print for de Valera's loyal flock. The paper had worked hard to shed its old image in the years immediately preceding 1995. But not quite hard enough. Ironically, at this most triumphant hour for Irish national self-esteem, Ireland was losing its most nationalist journalistic voice. It was a contradiction that would trouble more than a few. There would be much chest beating, often by people who never bought any of the *Press* group's three titles. The reaction was akin to city dwellers in the developed world lamenting the death of distant rainforests. But soon it was on to the next story, the next tent. Ireland was a modern market economy and sentiment didn't sell papers. Besides, there were other publications to report on the new, very hip and rapidly changing Ireland.

The 1990s, globally one of the more stable decades of the century, stand out in an Irish and Irish-American context for an American president making peace in Ireland a stated personal priority; IRA and loyalist cease-fires and broken cease-fires; Irish American peace delegations; Gerry Adams on *Larry King Live*; Sinn Féin collecting unprecedented sums of money across America; President Clinton and Hillary visiting Ireland; Clinton shaking hands with Gerry Adams on the Falls Road; Hillary Clinton returning to Ireland; Albert Reynolds tripping up at his moment of triumph; successive Irish governments reaching out to sections of Irish America once considered beyond Dublin's political pale; enormous social and economic change in the Republic and profound political shifts in the North; Mary Robinson being here, there and seemingly everywhere; Mary McAleese emerging from Belfast to be President of Ireland, and in the eyes of many, Ireland in the fullest geographical sense.

Arguably, the first seven years of the decade eclipse any other this century has seen from an Irish perspective, perhaps only with the exception of the period 1916–1923. And yet, by 1997, the new ascendancy of all things Irish in America seemed suddenly threatened, not just by the fact that emigration to the U.S. had dropped to a trickle, but that the U.S. Congress seemed intent on keeping it that way.

There appeared to be no immediate crisis, because emigration from Ireland had trailed off due to better economic circumstances on the island. Ireland's economy was in far better shape than at any time in its history. But a late entry to the economic boom and bust cycle was no lasting hedge against future emigration. Even as the "Celtic Tiger" roared, there were those who could see trouble coming down the pike.

1997 would mark the tenth anniversary of the founding of the Irish Immigration Reform Movement. But those who would look back on the heady days when "Legalize the Irish" was a loud and common cry would do so with mixed feelings. Much had been achieved by the IIRM's brash campaigning, but the "reform" in the movement's title clearly remained elusive.

The IIRM remained in legal existence but, as the tenth anniversary rolled by, it was something of a dormant volcano, silent as Congress rolled on, churning out punitive new immigration and welfare regulations for generations of immigrants and would-be immigrants as yet unseen. The sense was that the American welcome mat was being slowly but inexorably pulled back, for the Irish and everyone else.

"There should have been a guaranteed number of visas for Ireland each year in perpetuity, but that didn't happen." IIRM cofounder Sean Minihane was offering his assessment to the *Irish Echo*, which marked the tenth anniversary with a story headed "Unfinished Business." Pat Hurley was of similar mind: "The work of the IIRM remains unfinished. We did the best we could considering we were only part-timers. But the overall objective was not met. The law was not changed to facilitate permanently immigration from Ireland."

Hurley saw the Schumer diversity visa program, which provided a potential two or three thousand Irish visas per year, as a lifeboat for some Irish, but he expressed disappointment that other Irish saw green cards as mere travel documents, insurance policies for those who had no intention of actually living in the U.S. "There are many people here," said Hurley, "who didn't get green cards and who really deserved them."

Hurley was touching on a sensitive subject. Present-day Irish immigrants, children of the global consumer society where personal choice is sacred, do come in multiple varieties. While many are still one-way migrants, content with the ease that modern air travel allows for visits to family back in Ireland, many others are return-ticket migrants, more inclined to work in America, make money and then return to settle in Ireland. More hold green cards but choose to stay in Ireland, the plastic symbol of U.S. permanent residence being a parachute, set aside for the evil day when Ireland, for whatever reason, becomes an economic dead end once again. And, there are the undocumented and the adventurous. No matter what the circumstances in Ireland, there will always be those Irish who are drawn to America.

In the 1990s, yet another variation of the Irish migrant has emerged: the mid-Atlantic dual citizen maintaining business interests in both the U.S. and Ireland. In some cases, movement depends less on a consideration of country of residence than it does on prospects within multi-national corporations, industries or technologies. Arguably, a form of third country is emerging, populated by an Irish diaspora pulled together by airline schedules, fiber-optic lines and web pages. Overall, the current circumstances are unprecedented in the annals of Irish emigration to the United States and Canada. Many Irish now look to America with less of a "save us" attitude than with a starting point of "you need us" and "how can this relationship be mutually beneficial." By contrast, U.S. legislative attitudes appear to be returning to a view of new immigrants as a potential social burden or unwelcome moral obligation.

Commentators on both sides of the Atlantic have attempted to pin down the consequences of a situation that is in flux, clearly replete with both positive and negative aspects.

The negative was reflected in a June, 1995, story by Feargal Keane in the Dublin-based *Sunday Tribune* newspaper. Keane's story spoke of a "Lost generation scattered to the four winds." Keane was playing up an Irish government-sponsored advertising campaign from 1985 aimed at a worldwide audience and designed to lure foreign investors to the country. The campaign focused on twenty university graduates. The slogan beneath the photograph of these smiling freshmen members of Ireland's educational elite was: "The Irish: Hire Them Before They Hire You." Keane had found that while the selected twenty were all alive, healthy and doing well ten years on, seven of them were thriving in other countries and an additional five had only just returned to Ireland having spent most of the intervening ten years working abroad.

The positive, however, gradually became the dominant tone in the next few years as the pace of emigrants returning "home" gathered momentum. It was evident in a column penned by Tom McGurk in the Dublin-published *Sunday Business Post*, just after Christmas, 1996.

Headlined, "The Irish Family is Together Again," McGurk's story pointed to the phenomenon of Irish transients now in apparent constant transit. "Since the beginning of the eighteenth century," he wrote, "emigration from Ireland has been the Irish escape route in the face of economic dispossession. Like the Jews, the Irish tribe began wandering the world. Exiles became emigrants, and fortunately in this generation they have largely become commuters. Today as part of the new age in Ireland, we have a whole generation of young people for whom the Irish Sea and the Atlantic pose no terrors. They commute to Europe and America with an ease that belies the terrors those journeys once held for their grandparents' generation."

The phenomenon of the returning emigrant had also caught the attention of Garret FitzGerald, who had presided over the government of Ireland at a time when so many young people were packing their bags and fleeing. Perhaps with some sense of justification and relief, he wrote in the *Irish Times* in August, 1997: "The truth is that emigration today is totally different in character from that which we knew in the past. It seems that the majority of those leaving in recent years to work elsewhere did so with the intention of returning home. And a large proportion do in fact come back . . ."

The new twist to an old story was enough to catch the eye of U.S. publications including the *Wall Street Journal*, which came out with a story that burned out the photocopiers in Irish government diplomatic outposts around the globe. The story was headlined "The New Sod: Ireland Takes Off as Emigrés Return." From an official Irish standpoint, the story was a public relations windfall offered up by a newspaper with a worldwide "quality" readership.

To add to all this, the new Ireland was even sweeping away all the hackneyed Hollywood images, according to *USA Today*, which, in another story out of the "image is everything" file, described the new Irish as a "self-confident tribe of computer experts, pharmaceutical executives and European business executives" who were replacing "the Ireland of farmers in tweed caps."

The *New York Times* came out with its own version of the changing Ireland story that was, by 1997, all but taken as gospel. "Irish Eyes Turning Homeward As a Country's Moment Comes," was the heading in a March, 1997, front page *Times* story by London-based Warren Hoge. "Now quite suddenly and dramatically," Hoge wrote, "they are no longer leaving, and thousands who had fled are coming back. Ireland, the country that once stood accused by James Joyce, its most famous writer, of conferring honor only on those who went into exile, and that as recently as 1991 was still losing 26,000 people a year, is in the unaccustomed role of no longer being an emigrant nation. The end of this dominant feature of Irish life is emblematic of the profound changes that have come over this society."

But was it the end? The pattern of Irish emigration throughout the twentieth century has been quite distinct. In rough terms, there has been a new wave of Irish arriving on America's shores every thirty years. If that pattern holds, the next wave will arrive any time after 2010. That's certainly how Niall O'Dowd, whose publishing enterprises were based on the '80s immigrant tide, is inclined to view the future.

"It is the striking thing about Irish emigration this century. Every thirty years you have another wave. In the '20s you had the Civil War emigrants to America. In the '50s there was economic emigration from Ireland, mainly composed of the sons and daughters of small farmers in the west. In the '80s there was the entirely new issue of emigration by young and well educated Irish who arrived in America and became the illegals."

Regardless of what tack U.S. immigration law might take in the near future, O'Dowd sees no reason for the thirty-year pattern, or something resembling it, not carrying over into the new millennium.

He also traces a line between the Troubles in Northern Ireland and the immigrant wave of the 1980s. The combination, he has concluded, changed Irish America profoundly and in a manner not initially anticipated.

"I think the plight of the illegals forced a great rethink on the part of the entire community, both Irish-born and Irish American. This issue in particular created a consensus in the community. With Northern Ireland there had always been battles between Irish Americans and Irish governments. On emigration, after being initially shy in talking about it, the Irish government did get behind the great groundswell of action in Irish America. I think that this joint position on the plight of the illegals essentially led to the groundswell on Northern Ireland, the Irish government and Irish America working together.

"In parallel with this was the emergence of a much more unified Irish community in America and the extraordinary changes in Ireland itself. Together, this has led to the new Irish dominance in world literature, music and other areas. So you end up with the best of both worlds, the reinvention of the Irish-American identity, which today is so evident to everybody, but which has really been in the works since the 1980s."

Certainly, the visible change in attitude on the part of Irish governments to the Irish in the United States, Irish-born or of whatever generation Irish American, has been one of the more singular developments of the 1990s. Gone are the days when the Irish government sought assistance from trusted friends such as Tip O'Neill, Ted Kennedy, Hugh Carey and Daniel Moynihan—the "Four Horsemen"—to jam a finger in the dike in an effort to stem the tide of Irish-American passion and support for the likes of Sinn Féin and the IRA, and even groups posing far less a threat to Dublin's authority, real or imagined. During the 1970s and early '80s, Irish governments could easily wag the finger at Irish Americans who rarely traveled to Ireland, or Irish emigrants who had departed well before Northern Ireland had gone up in flames. With the '80s generation, better educated, familiar with the nuances of the Troubles and generally more questioning on matters political, it was more difficult for Dublin governments to marginalize hitherto unwelcome Irish opinion, freed up as it was in America from the political and intellectual chill that repeatedly paralyzed real debate on the troubled island itself. Besides, many of the new Irish were from the North, often of a strongly nationalist persuasion, and had scant regard for Dublin's sentiments one way or the other.

At the same time, the '80s Irish had other new issues to work with, not just the North itself, or even immigration reform, but others born of a new and vigorous sense of entitlement. One such was the demand of many Irish-born immigrants in the U.S., and other countries, for continued full voting rights in Ireland—a hook that successive Dublin administrations had managed to slip despite repeated pre-election hints, outright promises and the clear sympathy of some politicians; Labor Party minister Michael D. Higgins for example, who, in a lecture delivered at the launch of the *New Hibernia Review* in February, 1997, spoke of emigrants learning "what it means to be Irish, for nobody ever knows what his country is like until he has been out of it, experiencing the life of another for the purpose of contrast and comparison."

Higgins, not for the first time in his career, set himself against the grain by continuing: "Given that no people can ever fully define itself from within, exile is indeed the cradle of nationality."

Yet, despite such prominent admiration for the departed and now apparently newly enlightened, the promise of voting rights flared and faded with various elections. One Irish government minister was honest enough to reveal the real state of mid-1990s Irish government thinking during a visit to New York. "It's all bullshit," the minister said. Whatever it was, the manifesto that was to propel Fianna Fáil's Bertie Ahern to the Taoiseach's desk in 1997 once again promised to extend the franchise to the oft-praised, but largely muzzled diaspora.

The reluctant attitude of successive Irish governments towards the demand of emigrants for Irish votes has not been entirely confined to those governments. Most people in Ireland, those that vote, have inclined to agree with slogans such as "no representation without taxation." Irony, so, was heavy in the air when Mary McAleese, born and resident in part of the United Kingdom, and who paid taxes to the British government, was elected head of a state that denied votes to her and her fellow Northerners, even those with Irish passports.

Voting frustrations aside, the new Irish in America are no different from their forebears in reserving much of their energy and time for politics. Air travel and information age technology have combined to reduce dramatically the width of the Atlantic. Politically inclined Irish emigrants have little difficulty in keeping up with events in Ireland, while Irish Americans travel to Ireland in ever growing numbers. And no day passes without some seats on a trans-Atlantic flight being occupied by activists and campaigners, politicians and pundits, from Ireland, north and south. Throughout the 1970s and '80s, when Ireland and Britain often resembled a political frozen tundra due to the Troubles, America had served as a sanctuary for all opinion. James Prior, a Northern Ireland Secretary under Margaret Thatcher, signed his name to a banning order aimed at Noraid's Martin Galvin only to find himself later, in 1985, face to face with Galvin on ABC's *Nightline* show. And just as a future British ambassador would accuse an American congressman of having blood on his hands for entertaining a Sinn Féin visitor, Galvin would accuse the British visitor of having blood on his hands because of British military actions in the North. The encounter between the two, or between Prior and any Sinn Féin representative, would not have been possible at the time on either Irish or British television because of security-rooted censorship laws.

America as neutral ground, a place where controversial opinion could be unleashed with relative abandon, had been recognized by all parties to the Irish/British conflict for years. But it has been the broader umbrella of the peace process and President Clinton's direct intervention that has thrust the U.S. into the efforts to resolve the conflict. The result has been greater opportunity for all sides to express views, directly or indirectly, to each other; an obligation on the part of all parties to listen to the advice, praise and criticism of a powerful neutral observer (both its government and media); and, on occasion, opportunities for head-on collisions between opposing forces, such as the *Larry King Live* appearance involving the Ulster Unionist Party's Ken Maginnis and Gerry Adams.

The question of a visa for Gerry Adams, which became bogged down in the U.S. courts during the 1980s, took political flight in the '90s once it became known that John Hume, a political saint in Washington's eyes, had been negotiating a joint approach to the Northern Ireland impasse with the Sinn Féin leader. Revelations of secret talks between Adams' party and the British government, the on-target political instincts of Taoiseach Albert Reynolds, the Downing Street Declaration, the active support of a growing number of Congress members, not least Senator Edward Kennedy, combined with the emergence of a relatively unencumbered Bill Clinton, all combined to set the stage for a series of visits that some, although not all, would see as being more far-reaching than the Eamon de Valera tour of the United States in 1919–1920.

The fuse that would ultimately lead to the blowing away of the last vestiges of a twenty-year ban on Sinn Féin leadership access to the U.S. would be lit by the Irish-American peace delegation to Northern Ireland in September, 1992. The group, led by Bruce Morrison, and also including in its first incarnation Niall O'Dowd, businessman Chuck Feeney and Bill Flynn, Chairman and CEO of the Mutual of America insurance company, traveled to Belfast and tackled the question of when, rather than if, Adams would be permitted to make his American debut.

Irish-American corporate money, Flynn's in particular, would push the Adams visa denial issue right before the eyes of the American public as it tacitly did in December, 1993, with a full-page ad in the *New York Times* signed by one hundred and fifty Irish-American business, labor and cultural leaders. The ad lavished praise on all parties involved in the search for Irish peace while urging even bolder steps. It did not, however, directly demand an Adams visa.

That demand became more apparent a few weeks later in another full-page ad, in both the *Times* and *Washington Post,* announcing an invitation to an Irish peace conference in New York hosted by the National Committee on American Foreign Policy, of which Flynn was chairman. The five pictured Northern Ireland leaders invited to the conference included Adams. Adams was ultimately granted his visa and, his party's isolation ended, the Sinn Féin leader would begin a series of U.S. tours—interrupted for a time by an end to the first IRA cease-fire—that would considerably broaden the width and depth of the debate in the United States concerning the problems of a small island not much larger than Maine.

The visits by Adams and other Sinn Féin leaders would, in turn, increasingly lure unionists across the water, often to a more sympathetic welcome than some might have expected from "misguided" Irish Americans. There would be criticism too. Ulster Unionist Party leader David Trimble would be labeled the David Duke of Ireland by the Irish American Unity Conference in a *New York Times* op-ed page ad.

That same page would have columnist William Safire complaining, during the second Adams U.S. visit in late 1994, that most Americans simply didn't get the picture about Northern Ireland.

Unionists, too, would use American soil to get back at adversaries from back home. Trimble's party established its own Washington area office in response to Sinn Féin's creation of a Friends of Sinn Féin outpost on Capitol Hill.

When Adams arrived in the U.S. with Martin McGuinness and Caoimghín O Caoláin in the late summer of 1997, the Ulster Unionist Party—North America blazed away thus: "When Gerry Adams comes to the United States, he likes to pose as the representative of a democratic political party, Sinn Féin, seeking fairness in Northern Ireland and a talks process to end the violence—but his message is tailored for a U.S. audience. There is much that is left out. In the U.S., Gerry Adams seeks the mantle of peacemaker. In Northern Ireland it's a different story: he and his colleagues in Sinn Féin/IRA are unwilling to give up the leverage they get from their campaign of murder and intimidation."

The U.S. press would reflect both this and the counter view. During the same three-man Sinn Féin tour, Stephen Rosenfeld of the *Washington Post* emerged as one of a growing number of U.S. journalists willing to give Sinn Féin a fair hearing, but for fair exchange. Wrote Rosenfeld after sharing a dinner table with Adams: "He (Adams) preferred to talk about two other things, related. The first is the British history in Ireland that, by his telling, is not only long but irredeemably violent and anti-democratic. The second is the uphill battle he is waging against what he sees as British brainwashing of the American press, a matter of special concern at a moment when all-party negotiations are drawing near.

"Somebody else's duplicity and America's own innocence: These are the familiar contents of many a brief that foreigners seeking understanding and support for their cause regularly bring to these shores. There is always some degree of substance to those appeals, too. In this instance, Britain's ties to America have unquestionably won London the benefit of many unexamined doubts on the Irish issue."

Rosenfeld went on to state that Sinn Féin "conceals its hand behind slogans and vagueness. It does not define the 'compromise' it pledges. It puts off the hard decisions by citing the parallel conversions that must be undertaken by political fronts of the Protestant paramilitaries in Northern Ireland."

It had always been argued that one factor in favor of granting Adams a U.S. visa was that he would be exposed to the scrutiny of the world's most free and vigorous press. Here was a case in point. Rosenfeld had shared a table with Adams, was clearly ready to give him a sympathetic hearing, but just as equally prepared to direct what was widely viewed as being justified criticism. Still, all would benefit from the new, broader debate underway. If Gerry Adams had lessons to impart to Americans, he had lessons to learn as well. All the northern political leaders had. And so too did the American and Irish-American press, perhaps for too long comfortable leaning one way a little more than the other.

The press, a human creation, is not perfect. And there are times when it seemingly goes out of its way to be grossly imperfect. Deliberately appealing or lazily pandering to the prejudices of readers is a habit of old. And it was never more evident, during the peak years of the northern Troubles when formula often took precedence over deeper investigation. There were, and are, American journalists more inclined than most to swim against the prevailing current. And at times they have startled mainstream American thinking, if only for a moment, with writing such as this: "Orlando Bosch is a Cuban, convicted felon, a man once charged with masterminding the bombing of a civilian airliner in which seventy-three people died. On July 17 he was paroled in Miami and is now, somewhat relatively speaking, a free man." The "viewpoint" story in the *Wall Street Journal*, July 26, 1990, was by Alexander Cockburn. Bosch, Cockburn acknowledged, did face restrictions imposed by an electronic ankle trace bracelet and a tapped phone, but the point of the story was to contrast judicial treatment of an anti-Castro suspected mass-murderer with Joe Doherty, "an Irishman, neither charged with nor convicted of any offense against U.S. criminal law" who had by then started "his eighth year in a tiny cell in the Metropolitan Correctional Center in Manhattan" where he was "the longest-held prisoner in the history of that institution."

There were always journalists who would challenge the status quo, as it was both accepted and ignored. But other factors, governments and politicians, would serve to raise the profile of Ireland in the American consciousness as the peace process took root. The overriding desire to hold the IRA, Sinn Féin, and various unionist and loyalist groups within the boundaries of the process would be illustrated in the aftermath of the February, 1996, Canary Wharf bombing and the collapse of the first IRA cessation of violence. There followed the expected and by now almost ritual condemna-

tion of the IRA. But editorial writers also looked beyond the imme-
diate carnage. The bombing prompted an editorial in the *Boston
Herald*, the headline above which did not immediately attack the
IRA, but rather denounced "John Major's bad faith."

A few days later "Keep Adams in the loop," would be the headline in the same paper despite widespread denunciation of both the
IRA and Sinn Féin. The *Boston Globe*, not often seen as being especially "green" in its editorial approach, also absorbed the bombing
while urging that the "peace process must continue," a statement that
at least implied that the bombing did not warrant immediate excom-
munication of Sinn Féin from the now very battered process itself.

The old journalistic limits of tolerance were being pushed out
and the same was true for politics. The Democrats, traditionally a
political haven for generations of immigrant Irish, were discovering
that ancient loyalties were being increasingly tested as the 1990s
advanced.

Not that all Republicans were suddenly wrapping themselves in
Irish flags; far from it. But social and economic shifts in Irish America were throwing the Irish-American vote into sharper relief for the
GOP. Some Republicans were quick to latch on to the changes and
even take a swipe at old friends.

It was widely noted how unusual it was for a British ambassador
to Washington to end up in a public row with a prominent Republican governor. But that was the case in late 1996 when Sir John
Kerr and New York Governor George Pataki sparred on the mine-
field that was the lingering debate over alleged British culpability
for the mass death during the Great Famine in Ireland, one hundred and fifty years previously. But the Pataki–Kerr exchange of letters, with allegations of cold-blooded British perfidy and neglect
being charged and denied, was merely one example of the old giving way to something entirely new.

The old way, the special relationship between blue-blooded
America and the "mother country," still had its say, as was the case
when former GOP Secretary of State, James Baker, condemned the
visa for Gerry Adams before his party's 1996 National Convention
in San Diego. "We have," said Baker, "also seen a representative of
the IRA hosted in the White House just prior to its resumption of
terrorist bombings in London. The result has been the worst relationship with our closest ally, Britain, since the Boston Tea Party."
The old blue line was fighting still, but Baker's words, interpreted

by some irate Irish Americans as a virtual apology for American independence, prompted immediate criticism from both main political parties, Republicans as well as Democrats.

The Democrats, though clearly now facing competition from Republicans for the votes of those Irish Americans who would consider Ireland an election issue, could at least be assured that similar sentiments would likely not be expressed at a Democratic convention. Apart from that, the Democrats had Bill Clinton, who, despite his undoubted respect for his predecessor, Franklin Delano Roosevelt, would be the last politician on American soil to come out with a line suggesting there was "no such thing as British aggression." Clinton apart, there were now not a few from both sides of the American political aisle who, by the resumption of the IRA cease-fire, were well aware that the problems in Ireland were not solely the work of any one side, and that the British government, be it led by John Major or Tony Blair, was not an institution that had deserved the unquestioning loyalty and acquiescence of Washington on matters relating to the Maine-sized chunk of the "old country."

The Blair government, which had enjoyed the advantage in opposition of seeing what tactics worked and fizzled during the first phase of the peace process, was quick to seize the peace process initiative, which for a time had rested more heavily on the South Lawn than on the sward at the rear of Number 10 Downing Street (which had once served as an IRA mortar target). And Irish Americans, even those who had a right to be a little jaundiced by virtue of years in the political trenches, were quick to give the new British administration a sporting chance. There was such a thing after all, it seemed, as bad Brits and good Brits. "Major's Britain Didn't Want Peace," stated the main headline in the monthly newsletter of the American Irish Political Education Committee, a group that had been a longtime watchdog and prescient analyst on behalf of the more politicized Irish American community. "New Labour—New Opportunity" was a later newsletter banner that referred positively to the arrival of Tony Blair. Irish America, while always quick to condemn Britain if need be, was also prepared to respond favorably if the British appeared to be acting in good faith, relative or absolute.

Still, the battle for public opinion would not fade with mere change of government in London. Those who paid close attention to such details would notice, as 1997 gave way to 1998, that the oft-repeated British article of faith—that the Republic of Ireland could not bear the economic burden of unity with the north, a sorry place that was Britain's burden alone—had reinvented itself to meet new times and challenges. The new line, being uttered by British politicians and journalists alike, bestowed great praise on the Republic of Ireland for shedding all its old social and nationalistic burdens and transforming itself into the Celtic Tiger. On the other hand, however, the new line also suggested that it would be an enormous shame if such spectacular economic gain was lost for the sake of Northern Ireland, that historical ball and chain that, of course, Britain was still prepared nobly to drag along and subsidize. A message such as this, simple but to the point, did not have to be uttered too loudly to have an effect in the Republic. More republican-leaning Irish politicians had often over the years touted the economic benefits for the south of unification with the north. But that was when the Republic had relatively little to lose. In the era of the peace process, an increasing proportion of discussion devoted to the matter of a settlement, and its likely implicit acceptance of partition versus unity, centered on jobs, investment, peace and stability through economic prosperity as much as political agreement. By now, the Republic of Ireland appeared as if it had in fact something to lose, at least in the event of a union with the north forced against the wishes of hostile unionists.

Irish America, itself increasingly prosperous, could readily appreciate the emergence of economic arguments, largely devoid as they were of dark tales of past injustices and battles three centuries gone by. But being declared a reemerging ascendant culture by so many authoritative voices in America also carried new burdens and responsibilities. Many would recognize the growth of a more varied Irish American cultural outlook, less rooted in the politics of a divided Ireland, spawned by a fusion of new Irish immigrants, the children and grandchildren of earlier immigrants, and a healthy appetite for culture-rooted commercial success, often evident in the tendency of the new, and ascendant, Irish American culture's habit of debunking what would be frequently depicted as a more primitive antecedent across the water.

How close, or how different, was this new Irish America to an Ireland that was also breaking free from the strictures of its own past? Not close enough, certainly, for the newly widowed mother in the movie, *The Brothers McMullen,* who fled back to Ireland as soon as her dead Irish American husband was safe in the ground. Two cultures going through a renaissance simultaneously might provide untold opportunities for fusion, but it can also lead to tensions and misunderstandings. They can seem so much alike, but also never quite the same. Still, one does not escape the other's shadow. If Ireland has played its part in spawning a vibrant new Irish America, this giving has always been reciprocated. As the late Irish-American social historian, Dennis Clarke, wrote in the journal, *History Ireland*: "The history of the Irish in the United States is a subject without which modern Irish history itself simply cannot be made intelligible."

The flip side of this is that Irish America had always needed periodic waves of fresh-faced Irish immigrants in order to reinvigorate its heart and soul. Much of what has replenished Irish American culture in the 1990s has been injected by Irish-born immigrants, those who stayed regardless of tragedy, homesickness or economic disadvantage, or by first and second generation Irish Americans, those with relatively close family and cultural ties to Ireland. An Irish America solely dependent for its cultural base, its sense of unique self, on third, fourth and fifth generations is an Irish America as yet unseen.

The Irish who landed in America in the 1980s, while initially hindered by the novel problems posed by illegality, did win through to a point where they could set out on the path to economic security and social acceptance beaten down by earlier immigrants. The same can't be said with certainty for the young men and women of any future immigrant wave. The experiences of even the recent past are already an unsteady barometer as the new century approaches. Immigration from Ireland in the twenty-first century might quite simply cease in a historically recognizable sense. Leo Mohan, writing in the *Philadelphia Irish Edition*, sees the new immigration laws emerging from Washington, ten years after the IIRM's birth, as setting the clock back as much as that same number of years in terms of achieving legal status for many recent and future Irish arrivals.

"What is now clear," Mohan wrote in May, 1997, "is that Irish persons have little or no hope of securing legal status in the U.S. under the terms of the new law. The current mechanisms for doing so do not suit the traditional patterns of the Irish."

Still, regardless of whether or not Irish immigration retains its traditional form—cyclical influxes of mostly single individuals unable to benefit from the family reunification emphasis in U.S. immigration law—there remain favorable forces that have always played a role on behalf of the arriving Irish. And these forces will likely survive, no matter what legislative curve balls lie ahead. Certainly, there should be no underestimating the power of well disposed Irish American sentiment, a phenomenon that has long impressed even the most cynical Irish, and from which succeeding generations of Irish immigrants have been able to draw comfort. It was just that way with Congressman Bruce Morrison, drumming his fingers through a routine congressional hearing, until one speaker started talking about dead Irishmen.

The power of sentiment was again illustrated on an October day in 1997 when a large crowd, mostly Irish American, gathered at the site of the 1862 Civil War battle of Antietam in western Maryland. They came to dedicate a memorial to the fallen of the Union Army Irish Brigade, a formation composed of mostly off-the-boat Irish immigrants. The effort to see the monument placed on the battlefield had taken eleven years. The National Park Service had decided that no more such memorials would be allowed at the place that had witnessed the bloodiest single day in American history. But the Park Service failed to reckon with the stubborn determination of a bunch of Irish Americans, who, with the backing of Ted Kennedy, managed to sway the bureaucratic mind to the point where a memorial was ultimately allowed. The Irish Americans had given years of their lives, for no financial reward (indeed quite the contrary), to an idea that would serve as a physical tribute to Irish-born men who had perished, in a battle for America, before they had even time to earn the hyphenated appellation: Irish-American.

The monument dreamers didn't have to do it. Nobody would have been critical of a surrender in the face of outright government decree. Yet they persevered, spurred on by a determination rooted in a sense of kinship, common cause and admiration for long dead Irishmen who had cleared the way for their generation's right to proclaim themselves as being fully fledged Americans or fully fledged Irish Americans; whatever suited the moment.

It would be unduly pessimistic to suggest that the twenty tons of Wicklow granite now planted atop the Maryland soil stands as a marker to a glorious moment in Irish America that is past, destined not to repeat itself in any shape or form. The circumstances of Irish America's future will be formed by many events, individuals, trends and movements. One of the more immediately discernible is a falling birth rate in Ireland, a trend that can't but play heavily on the level of Irish emigration to America in the coming years.

Acceptance of future Irish immigration, whatever its numerical level, might not any longer depend upon volume of blood shed or numbers of medals secured for a newly adopted country. But it remains certain that those Irish who envision their destiny in America will continue to need Irish America's outstretched helping hand, not so much if times are good, certainly in abundance if times turn bad. As 1998 dawned, times appeared to be turning just that way. With immigration in general in its sights, Congress had thrown up barriers of exclusion aimed at the undocumented of all nationalities. Illegality now brought with it the risk of long periods of exclusion from the U.S. – three years if an individual stayed six months beyond a holiday visa, ten years if the overstay period exceeded a year. Another decision of Congress to kill off an obscure immigration provision called Section 245 (i), would mean that illegals could no longer adjust their status on U.S. soil. Returning to the individual's particular country of origin would result in the exclusion periods kicking in. The undocumented, Irish included, were being squeezed in a legislative vice. At the same time, pressure was also being placed on the Schumer diversity visa scheme, an Irish immigration lifeline. It was trimmed by five thousand visas a year by Congress before the end of its 1997 term. These changes took place against the backdrop of relatively little immigration from Ireland, so those voices raising early cries of alarm found it difficult to induce the sense of urgency in Irish America so evident in the 1980s. At the same time, the emerging situation appeared far more grave than the decade before when being illegal and Irish could be tolerated so long as the individual could stay out of the physical clutches of the INS while visas were being fought for in Washington. In the late 1990s, the Washington visa machine was all but clapped out.

Irish America has always been a combination of established Irish Americans and new Irish arrivals. The analogy of a pool at the tide's edge being periodically replenished with new water seems to fit. What has never been seen in the history of Irish America and Irish migration to the U.S.—a story of success and triumph born out of initial failure and tragedy—is an Irish America denied that replenishment over a sustained period. It might have happened anyway due to long-term economic prosperity in Ireland. That would have been an acceptable way for a tradition to die. But having the door slammed shut in Washington is not the way the story was supposed to end. The irony hangs heavy. The level of daily contact and travel between the U.S. and Ireland has never been greater. Even the St. Patrick's Day Parade organizers reached across the ocean—not to everyone's delight—to declare Albert Reynolds grand marshal of the 1998 New York Parade, for over two hundred and thirty years the preserve of Irish already planted on American soil.

But if the future of Irish immigration seems uncertain, even doubtful, there is yet a chance that it will remain an option for the future. As best as can be determined, the Irish of an early twenty-first century will still be in a position, if circumstances require, to turn to a newly energized Irish America, forged by a blend of twentieth-century American Irish and Irish immigrants, not least the one-time illegals of the 1980s who unfurled a banner demanding "Legalize the Irish" and proclaimed the right, as countless others did before them, to be called the new Irish-Americans.

BIBLIOGRAPHY

Armesto, Felipe Fernández. *Millennium, A History of the Last Thousand Years*. New York: Scribner, 1995.

Asbury, Herbert. *The Gangs of New York*. New York: Alfred Knopf, 1927.

Bailey, Thomas A. *The American Pageant, A History of the Republic*. Boston: D.C. Heath & Co., 1967.

Bergreen, Laurence. *Capone, The Man and the Era*. New York: Simon & Schuster, 1994.

Brinkley, Alan, Richard N. Current, Frank Freidel, and T. Harry Williams. *American History, A Survey*. New York: McGraw Hill, 1991.

Cahill, Thomas. *How The Irish Saved Civilization, the Untold Story of Ireland's Heroic Role from the Fall of Rome to the Rise of Medieval Europe*. London: Hodder & Stoughton, 1995.

Coffey, Michael, and Terry Golway. *The Irish in America*. New York: Hyperion, 1997.

Cronin, Seán. *Washington's Irish Policy 1916–1986*. Dublin: Anvil Books, 1987.

Duignan, Seán. *One Spin on the Merry-go-round*. Dublin: Blackwater Press, 1995.

English, T.J. *The Westies, Inside the Hell's Kitchen Irish Mob*. New York: G.P. Putnam & Sons, 1990.

Holland, Jack. *The American Connection*. New York: Viking, 1987.

Keatinge, Patrick. *The Formulation of Irish Foreign Policy*. Dublin: Institute of Public Administration, 1973.

Kiberd, Declan. *Inventing Ireland, the Literature of the Modern Nation*. Cambridge, MA: Harvard University Press, 1995.

Levin, Bernard. *A Walk Up 5th Avenue*. London: Sceptre, 1989.

McManus, Fr. Sean. *The MacBride Principles, Genesis and History*. Washington D.C.: Irish National Caucus, 1993.

Miller, Kerby A. *Emigrants and Exiles, Ireland and the Irish Exodus to North America*. New York: Oxford University Press, 1985.

O'Clery, Conor. *Daring Diplomacy, Clinton's Secret Search for Peace in Ireland*. Boulder: Roberts Rinehart, 1997.

O'Connor, Thomas H. *The Boston Irish, A Political History*. Boston: Back Bay Books, 1995.

O'Toole, Fintan. *Black Hole, Green Card. The Disappearance of Ireland*. Dublin: New Island Books, 1994.

O'Toole, Fintan. *The Ex-Isle of Erin, Images of a Global Ireland*. Dublin: New Island Books, 1996.

Quinn, Peter. *Banished Children of Eve*. New York: Penguin, 1997.

Ralston, Bill. *The Media and Northern Ireland, Covering the Troubles*. London: Macmillan, 1991.

Wilson, Andrew J. *Irish America and the Ulster Conflict 1968–1995*. Washington D.C.: Catholic University of America Press, 1995.

INDEX

*f*P

For thus says the Lord—Who created the heavens—God Himself—Who formed the earth and made it, Who established it and did not create it to be a worthless waste: He formed it to be inhabited—I am the Lord and there is no one else.

Isaiah 45:18

NATURE'S DESTINY

How the Laws of Biology Reveal Purpose in the Universe

MICHAEL J. DENTON

THE FREE PRESS

New York   London   Toronto   Singapore   Sydney

The Free Press
A Division of Simon & Schuster
1230 Avenue of the Americas
New York, NY 10020

The Free Press and colophon are trademarks
of Simon & Schuster Inc.

Designed by Carla Bolte

Manufactured in the United States of America
10 9 8 7 6 5 4 3 2 1

Library of Congress Cataloging-In-Publication Data

Denton, Michael.
        Nature's destiny : how the laws of biology reveal purpose in the
universe / Michael J. Denton. p. cm.
        Includes bibliographical references and index.
        1. Technology.   2. Cosmology.   3. Philosophical anthropology.
1. Title.
BD541.D46   1998
124—dc21   98-3295   CIP

ISBN: 0-7432-3762-5

For information regarding special discounts for bulk purchases, please contact
Simon & Schuster Special Sales at 1-800-456-6798 or business@simonandschuster.com

A c k n o w l e d g m e n t s

I would like first to thank my editor Bruce Nichols at the Free Press for applying his considerable skills in changing what was initially a heavy indigestible manuscript into a far more readable and accessible text. I would also like to thank David Berlinski who initially suggested the Free Press as a possible publisher. It was through David that the manuscript eventually got to Bruce Nichols's desk. I became acquainted with David through a mutual friend of ours, Professor M. P. Schutzenberger, a leading French mathematician, anti-Darwinist, and member of the French Academy. Professor Schutzenberger was known to both David and myself and to his very many academic colleagues affectionately as "Marco." It was through one of many conversations with Marco in his flat near the Bois de Boulogne in Paris, in 1989, that I first learned of Lawrence Henderson's great book *The Fitness of the Environment* and of the concept of the unique fitness of the cosmos for carbon-based life. Had Marco not brought *The Fitness* to my attention, then certainly this book would never have been written. I also owe a debt to the works of the physicists Paul Davies and John Barrow and others in the anthropic camp which stimulated and encouraged me to consider examining the fitness in the biological realm.

During the four-year gestation period when the manuscript was going through many revisions and drafts, many academic friends and colleagues provided useful criticisms and suggestions. I am particularly grateful to colleagues at the University of Otago, in particular to Dr. Mike Legge and Dr. Craig Marshall in the Biochemistry Department, and to Dr. Dorothy Oorschot in the School of Medical Sciences, who read early drafts and offered many helpful criticisms. I am also grateful to Jim Kern, a well-known nature photographer in the United States and close friend, who also read early drafts and whose support and enthusiasm for the book never wavered. While the book was in preparation, I had many interesting discussions with him regarding its content and philosophical implications while staying at his home near St. Augustine, Florida. I am also grateful to my London agent Christopher Shepheard-Walwyn for his efforts in editing an early and very unpolished version of the book and for his support for the project from the beginning.

I would like to take this opportunity to thank the following for granting permission to reprint previously published material:

Professor N. J. Berril's daughter, Lyn, for the use of several figures from her father's book *Biology in Action*. Vance Tartar's daughter, Wanda, for allowing me to use a drawing from her father's book *The Biology of Stentor*. Professor A. E. Needham's widow, Nita, for her kind permission to cite several sections from *The Uniqueness of Biological Materials*. Professor J. T. Edsall for his permission to use quotes and a figure from his book *Biophysical Chemistry*. Professor Robert Goldberg for granting me permission to use several long quotes from *Molecular Insights into Living Processes*. Professor Victor W. Rodwell for the use of several figures from *Harper's Biochemistry*. Professor Harold Morowitz for the use of a quote from *Cosmic Joy and Local Pain*, published by Ox Bow Press. Dr. Jearl Walker for permission to quote from her article in the "Amateur Scientist" section of *Scientific American*. Professor Leslie Orgel for the reproduction of a figure from *The Origins of Life on Earth*. The MIT Press for permission to reproduce Robert Fludd's *Ultriusque Cosmi Historia Oppenheim* from Bernal's *Science in History*. The Anglo-Australian Observatory for permission to reproduce the photograph of the Messier Galaxy by David Malin. Appleton & Lange for permission to reproduce figures from Milton Toporek's *Basic Chemistry of Life*. Williams & Wilkins Company for permission to copy the figure of the bronchial tree from Best and Taylor's *Physiological Basis of Medical Practice*. Garland Publishing for the use of the figure of cytochrome oxidase from *The Molecular Biology of the Cell*. Professor S. J. Singer for permission to reproduce his drawing of the cell membrane in *Science*. Professor M. L. Land for permission to use two figures of the eye of the scallop from the *Journal of Physiology*. David Scharf for allowing me to reproduce his photograph of the eye of the lobster. *Scientific American* for allowing me to redraw their illustration of the optical system of a reflecting eye. Wiley & Sons for permission to use material from I. H. Segal's *Biochemical Calculations.* Cambridge University Press for permission to quote from Paul Davies's *The Accidental Universe* and from Knut Schmidt-Nielsen's *Scaling.* W. W. Norton & Company for the use of excerpts from *Wonderful Life: The Burgess Shale and the Nature of History* by Stephen Jay Gould. Copyright © by Stephen Jay Gould, reprinted with permission of W. W. Norton & Company. W. H. Freeman & Company for the use of the quote by J. S. Lewis from *Earth* by Press and Siever, copyright © 1986 by W. H. Freeman & Company, used with permission. Random House for permission to quote from Loren Eiseley's *The Immense Journey* (1947) and from Carl Sagan's *Cosmos* (1980), copyright © 1980 by Carl Sagan Publications, Inc. International Thomson Publishing Services for the use of several sections from A. J. Gurevich's *Medieval Culture.* The Peters Fraser & Dunlop Group Ltd., for permission to quote from Julian Huxley's *Uniqueness of Man* and from Arthur Koestler's *The Ghost in the Machine.* Columbia University Press for permission to quote from *Evolution Above the Species* by Bernard Rensch. Copyright © 1959 by Columbia University Press. Reprinted by permission of the publisher.

Contents

N o t e   t o   t h e   R e a d e r

> Time out of mind it has been by the way of the "final cause," by the
> teleological concept of end, of purpose or of "design," in one of its
> many forms . . . that men have been chiefly wont to explain the
> phenomena of the living world: and it will be so while men have eyes to
> see and ears to hear withal. With Galen as with Aristotle, it was the
> physician's way; with John Ray as with Aristotle it was the naturalist's
> way; with Kant as with Aristotle it was the philosopher's way. . . . It is a
> common way, and a great way; for it brings with it a glimpse of a great
> vision, and it lies deep as the love of nature in the hearts of men.
>
> —D'Arcy Wentworth Thompson, *On Growth and Form,* 1942

The aim of this book is, first, to present the scientific evidence for believing
that the cosmos is uniquely fit for life as it exists on earth and for organisms
of design and biology very similar to our own species, *Homo sapiens,* and
second, to argue that this "unique fitness" of the laws of nature for life is entirely consistent with the older teleological religious concept of the cosmos
as a specially designed whole, with life and mankind as its primary goal and
purpose.

Although this is obviously a book with many theological implications,
my initial intention was not specifically to develop an argument for design;
however, as I researched more deeply into the topic and as the manuscript
went through successive drafts, it became increasingly clear that the laws of
nature were fine-tuned for life on earth to a remarkable degree and that the
emerging picture provided powerful and self-evident support for the tradi-

tional anthropocentric teleological view of the cosmos. Thus, by the time the final draft was finished, the book had become in effect an essay in natural theology in the spirit and tradition of William Paley's *Natural Theology* or the Bridgewater Treatises.

The basic thesis of the book, that the cosmos is uniquely fit for human existence, is of course not novel. For centuries before the birth of modern science, this thesis was one of the foundational axioms of medieval Christianity. More recently, it has begun to reemerge in various fields of science, most notably in physics and cosmology. Readers familiar with the views of physicists such as Freeman Dyson, Fred Hoyle, and Paul Davies will be aware that over the past few decades many physicists have pointed out that the existence of life in the cosmos is critically dependent on the laws and constants of physics having the precise values they do. The values are so critical that several well-known authors have argued that the cosmos gives every appearance of having been very finely adjusted or "prefabricated" for our existence.[1] As Paul Davies points out in his *Accidental Universe:* "If nature had opted for a slightly different set of numbers, the world would be a very different place. Probably we would not be here to see it." In his words: "The impression of design is overwhelming."[2] Because of the perceived support for the traditional teleological worldview of the major religious traditions, the views of Davies and others have received wide publicity.

There is, however, a fundamental problem with any attempt to argue for the biocentricity or anthropocentricity of nature based on evidence drawn only from physics. While such evidence may be sufficient to argue that the cosmos is arranged for "complex chemistry," solar systems, or even intelligence, it is necessarily insufficient to argue that the cosmos is in some sense uniquely fit for the specific type of *biological life as it exists on earth,* that is, for organisms constructed out of carbon compounds based in water and utilizing DNA and proteins for self-replication. And it is completely incapable of providing any support for the notion that our own species, *Homo sapiens,* has any special place in the cosmos.

Davies is careful to distance himself from any claim that humanity is central in the cosmic scheme: "Where do human beings fit into this great cosmic scheme? Can we gaze out into the cosmos, as did our remote ancestors, and declare God made it all for us? I think not."[3] And in his latest book he states explicitly that "I am not saying that we *Homo sapiens* are written into the laws of physics in a basic way."[4] And continues: "We should not expect extraterrestrial life to resemble our own in its basic chemistry. . . . There is no need, for example, to demand liquid water or even carbon. We could anticipate exotic life forms, such as creatures that float in the dense atmosphere of Jupiter or swim in the liquid nitrogen seas of Titan."[5]

Contrary to Davies and others, I believe the evidence strongly suggests that the cosmos is uniquely fit for only one type of biology—that which exists on earth—and that the phenomenon of life cannot be instantiated in any other exotic chemistry or class of material forms. Even more radically, I believe that there is a considerable amount of evidence for believing that the cosmos is uniquely fit for only one type of advanced intelligent life—beings of design and biology very similar to our own species, *Homo sapiens.* I do not agree with Davies when he claims, "The physical species *Homo sapiens* may count for nothing."[6]

To defend the postulate that the cosmos is specifically fit for biological life *as it exists on earth* necessarily involves consideration of a vast number of natural laws, phenomena, and processes which are quite outside of the areas of physics and cosmology and pertain uniquely to the biological realm, phenomena such as the thermal properties of water, the characteristics of the carbon atom, the solubility of carbon dioxide, the self-assembling properties of proteins, the nature of the cell, and so forth. Although from the evidence of physics we may be able to infer that the cosmos is uniquely fit for chemistry, stars and planets, or even intelligent beings, we cannot infer that it is specifically fit for large, air-breathing terrestrial mammals. Only through biology can our unique type of carbon-based life and especially advanced forms like ourselves lay claim to a central place in the cosmic scheme.

———

This book is divided into two major parts. In Part 1, evidence is presented that the laws of nature are uniquely fit for the being or existence of the type of carbon-based life that exists on earth. The chapters in this section deal with evidence drawn from many areas of the biological sciences, from molecular biology to mammalian physiology. The physical and chemical properties of the fundamental constituents of the cell, such as water, carbon dioxide, the bicarbonate buffer, oxygen, DNA, proteins, the transitional metals, the cell membrane, etc., are systematically reviewed to show that the existence of carbon- and water-based cellular life depends critically on a number of remarkable adaptations in the properties of many of life's basic constituents. What is particularly striking is that, in almost every case, each constituent appears to be the only available or unique candidate for its particular biological role and, further, gives every appearance of being ideally fit not in one or two but in all its physical and chemical characteristics. Also reviewed is evidence drawn from other areas of science that attests to the fitness of the earth's hydrosphere, the fitness of the electromagnetic radiation of the sun, and the fitness of the periodic table for the carbon-based type of life as it exists on earth. As the book also shows, the existence of some higher forms of life, such as large warm-blooded, air-breathing terrestrial vertebrates, are critically dependent on the properties of some of the basic constituents of life, such as water, carbon dioxide, and oxygen; in other words, not only are the laws of nature fit for the cell and for simple microbial life, but also for advanced complex organisms very like ourselves.

The argument developed in Part 1, that the cosmos is uniquely fit for *life's being*, leads naturally to the second argument, developed in Part 2, that the cosmos is fit also for the origin and evolutionary development of life—*life's becoming*. It is hard to escape the logic of this connection, for if the first argument is accepted, that the existence of the life forms on earth, both microscopic and macroscopic, depends on a remarkable set of mutual chemical and physical adaptations in the nature of things, the second argument, that the evolutionary development of this same set of life forms was also written into the cosmic script and directed from the beginning, is hard to refuse. Or, put another way: if the laws of nature are so finely tuned to facilitate *life's being* in the form of a unique set of carbon-based organisms, both simple and complex, on the surface of a terraqueous planet like the earth, then it seems conceivable that *their becoming* through the process of evolution might have been determined also by natural law.

At present, the evidence that the cosmos is uniquely fit for *life's being* is certainly far more convincing than the evidence that it is also fit for *life's becoming*. Nonetheless, even though direct evidence for believing that life's becoming is "built in" is lacking, there are many features of the cosmos that make sense if the becoming of life is in some way programmed into the laws of nature. Facts such as the synthesis in stars throughout the cosmos, of carbon and the more complex atoms essential for life, by intricate processes; that interstellar space contains vast quantities of organic carbon compounds[7] and some meteors such as the Murchison meteor contain considerable quantities of amino acids,[8] the building blocks of life; that planets like the earth which are probably capable of sustaining carbon-based life would appear to be very common if not almost ubiquitous throughout the cosmos[9]—all these make eminent sense if life is a natural phenomenon programmed into nature from the beginning, and fated inevitably to arise and evolve on any suitable planetary environment.

The claim that the constituents of life are uniquely designed for the roles they serve cannot be defended convincingly without detailed discussion of the relevant scientific facts. This is true of any similar type of teleological argument. If we are to argue, for example, that the components of a watch are all specially designed to function together to tell the time, the argument can only be convincing if we have some understanding of the structure and workings of the watch. We have to open up the watch, to observe the mechanisms within, particularly the reciprocal fit of the various cogs to one another and have some comprehension of the way the mechanism works overall. And we need to understand clearly, as William Paley emphasized in his famous discourse on the watch, "that if the parts had been differently shaped from what they are," the watch could never function.[10] The same is true in arguing that the constituents of the cosmos are uniquely fit for life. The argument only works if we have some knowledge of "the machinery of the cell" and some understanding of the many reciprocal adaptations in the nature of its constituents that make life possible. Consequently, the presentation of the argument in a book of this sort is quite challenging, because the nature of these mutual adaptations can only be fully appreciated by a relatively in-depth and detailed presentation of the relevant scientific facts.

However, despite the technical nature of many sections of the book, I believe that most areas covered can be easily grasped by anyone with a high-school knowledge of biology and chemistry. And even a committed reader with no scientific training should be able to grasp the essence of the argument in most of the chapters, even if this necessitates skipping some of the more highly technical sections. There are several chapters which require very little scientific background. And most chapters include at the beginning an introductory section requiring very little specialized knowledge, in which I have attempted to explain the main theme of the chapter.

I have also tried to organize the presentation of the evidence so that many of the chapters represent a fairly independent module which can be read and understood without reference to other chapters or arguments in other sections of the book. I hope this makes the book easier for a nonspecialist to handle. Finally, as mentioned above, each chapter begins with an italicized précis that may allow nontechnical readers to skip ahead.

Further, as with any such argument because the argument is essentially accumulative, deriving its power from the sheer number of the adaptations observed, it is essential that as many as possible of these are presented and discussed. The conclusion is convincing primarily because so many independent arguments, each drawn from a great number of different areas of science, all appear to point in the same direction. This inevitably involves a degree of repetition that will be a problem for some readers. However, a degree of repetition is the very essence of the whole line of attack.

Because the validity of the argument depends on so many independent lines of evidence, the conclusion is not materially threatened because the whole picture is not yet complete or because this or that phenomenon such as the origin of life or the mechanism of evolution is not understood. Just as the meaning of a jigsaw puzzle may be obvious long before all the pieces are perfectly placed, so too my argument does not necessitate that everything be explained. Nevertheless, critics of the argument will have certain clear avenues of attack. They can argue (correctly) that I have been selective in my topics. The burden of disproof will, however, rest on them to show that an area I ignored somehow opens up the possibility of either nonearthlike life in the cosmos or a superior alternative to one of the constituents of life—for example, water, carbon dioxide, etc. Or they may argue that my position merely reflects a lack of imagination and that I have not discussed possible alternatives in depth. But again, the burden of proof will be on them to offer specific alternatives. I do not see how I can be accused of omitting discussion of alternative forms of life, based in silicon or liquid ammonia or within the field of nanotechnology, when no detailed blueprints for such hypothetical life forms have ever been developed.

Although there has been little debate or interest in the question of the fitness of the cosmos for life in mainstream biology since the Darwinian revolution, and indeed the idea has been very unfashionable in many circles in the English-speaking world, interest in the question has never been completely extinguished. Throughout the twentieth century, a number of first-rate biologists have kept the tradition alive. These have included Lawrence Henderson, professor of biological chemistry at Harvard University during the first quarter of the century and author of the great classic *The Fitness of the Environment* (1913);[11] D'Arcy Wentworth Thompson, author of another great classic, *On Growth and Form* (1942);[12] George Wald, professor of biology at Harvard in the fifties and sixties, discoverer of the role of vitamin A in vision, who was one of the leading authorities on the chemistry of photoreception;[13] A. E. Needham, Oxford zoologist and author of an excellent and comprehensive review, *The Uniqueness of Biological Materials* (1965);[14] and Carl Pantin, professor of zoology at Cambridge during the sixties and author of the widely acclaimed *The Relations Between the Sciences,* published in 1968.[15]

My chapters on the properties of water, carbon, oxygen, and carbon dioxide borrow heavily from Henderson's *Fitness* and can be considered to a large degree an update of that great classic in the light of modern knowledge. Another major source cited in several chapters is Needham's *The Uniqueness of Biological Materials.*

One recent book that invites some comparison is Stuart Kauffman's *At Home in the Universe,* in which he argues that much of the course of evolution has been determined and driven by self-organizing and emergent properties of complex systems.[16] There is certainly more than a whiff of teleology about Kauffman's arguments, and his overall conclusion is consistent with my own when he claims, for example: "We will have to see that we are all natural expressions of a deeper order. Ultimately, we will discover in our creation myth that we are expected after all."[17] And further: "We may be at home in the universe in ways we have hardly begun to comprehend."[18]

Another book that also invites comparison is *Vital Dust* by the biologist and Nobel laureate Christian de Duve. De Duve has also "opted in favour of a meaningful universe"[19] and argues that the cosmos is fit for the origin and evolution of life and that the progress of evolution from simple to complex life forms was largely inevitable. However, de Duve's position falls a long way short of defending the traditional anthropocentric view of the cosmos. The unique fitness of the laws of nature for the biology of higher, air-breathing life forms such as ourselves is not discussed in any depth and nowhere does de Duve argue that the pattern of evolution was directed specifically toward the human race. Regarding man's place in the cosmos, de Duve concludes in his final chapter, "The human mind may be only a *side link* in an evolutionary saga far from completed."[20] (My emphasis.)

Because this book presents a teleological interpretation of the cosmos which has obvious theological implications, it is important to emphasize at the outset that the argument presented here is entirely consistent with the basic naturalistic assumption of modern science—that the cosmos is a *seamless unity which can be comprehended ultimately in its entirety by human reason and in which all phenomena, including life and evolution and the origin of man, are ultimately explicable in terms of natural processes.* This is an assumption which is entirely opposed to that of the so-called "special creationist school." According to special creationism, living organisms are not natural forms, whose origin and design were built into the laws of nature from the beginning, but rather contingent forms analogous in essence to human artifacts, the result of a series of supernatural acts, involving God's direct intervention in the course of nature, each of which involved the suspension of natural law. Contrary to the creationist position, the whole argument presented here is critically dependent on the presumption of the unbroken continuity of the organic world—that is, on the reality of organic evolution and on the presumption that all living organisms on earth are natural forms in the profoundest sense of the word, no less natural than salt crystals, atoms, waterfalls, or galaxies.

In large measure, therefore, the teleological argument presented here and the special creationist worldview are mutually exclusive accounts of the world. In the last analysis, evidence for one is evidence against the other. Put simply, the more convincing is the evidence for believing that the world is prefabricated to the end of life, that the design is built into the laws of nature, the less credible becomes the special creationist worldview.

Ironically, both the Darwinian and the creationist worldviews are based on the same fundamental axiom—that life is an unnecessary and fundamentally contingent phenomenon. Where the creationist sees organisms as the artifacts of God the supreme engineer, the Divine watchmaker, Darwinists see them as the artifactual products of chance and selection. That both should view life as contingent is not so surprising considering that both doctrines developed in the early nineteenth century, the heyday of the machine age, when organisms were widely seen to be analogous in some way to machines. Clearly, if life's design is indeed embedded in the laws of nature and the major paths of evolution are largely determined from the beginning, then neither creationism nor Darwinism can possibly be valid models of nature.

My argument may be unpalatable for completely different reasons to certain liberal theologians. Academic theology in the twentieth century has largely abandoned traditional natural theology. Many have held the view "that theological propositions and scientific propositions somehow occupy different epistemological realms. Hence the neo-orthodox wall between religion and science."[21] Some liberal theologians have recently explored the relationship between science and theology,[22] showing how, in Arthur Peacocke's words, "God creates in the world through what we call 'chance' operating within the created order."[23] Yet nowhere do they attempt to present a natural theology (they may even object to the term) along traditional lines. The aim of their work is to show how it is *possible to believe in God* while at the same time accepting the findings of science. It is not to argue that the *facts of science provide evidence* that the laws of nature are uniquely prefabricated for life as it exists on earth, including complex forms such as our own species.

Another final point that perhaps should be clarified here at the outset is that I am using the term "anthropocentric" throughout the text in the generic sense. The cosmic "telos" I have in mind is advanced carbon-based humanlike or humanoid life. It is not specifically our own unique species *Homo sapiens*. At present, there is insufficient evidence to argue that the laws of nature are uniquely fit for *every detail* of human biology exactly as found in our own species today. However, I believe that the current evidence points strongly in this direction and that future scientific advances will confirm the absolute centrality of mankind in the cosmic scheme.

In the last analysis, the teleological perspective presented and defended here is good for science, because it renders scientific knowledge relevant to human existence. In the doctrine of final causation, science unites man and cosmos. The pursuit of scientific knowledge becomes no longer of merely practical value but also vital and central to the spiritual and intellectual life of man.

—Michael J. Denton
Dunedin, November 1996

Microcosmos.

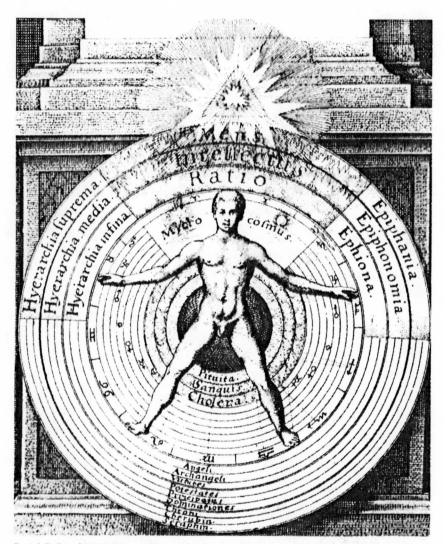

From J. D. Bernal (1969) *Science in History,* vol. 1 (London, MIT Press) p. 274. Original in Robert Fludd's *Utriusque Cosmi . . . Historia Oppenheim,* 1617–1619.

Prologue

> The ancient opinion that man was microcosmos, an abstract or model
> of the world, hath been fantastically strained by the alchemists, as if
> there were to be found in man's body certain correspondences and
> parallels which should have respect to all variety of things, as stars,
> planets, minerals, which are extant in the great world.
>
> —Francis Bacon, *The Advancement of Learning,* 1605

Living as we do in the late twentieth century, in a culture that has rejected the traditional teleological view of man as the center and purpose of the cosmos, which views our human existence as in essence a matter of profound contingency, it is fascinating to recall just how different was the medieval worldview in the late fifteenth century, shortly before the birth of modern science.

For both Christian and Islamic philosophers and theologians of the Middle Ages, the cosmos was a unique whole specially designed by God with man as its central focus and purpose. All facets of reality found their explanation in this central fact. Man was the inner microcosm. Every aspect of his being reflected the outer macrocosm, the universe in its entirety and all it contained.

For Christian scholars, the biblical revelation, and particularly the Incarnation, sanctioned the profoundly anthropocentric character of their medieval worldview. The extraordinary anthropocentricity of the culture of the Christian Middle Ages was wonderfully conveyed by Aron Gurevich in his classic work *Categories of Medieval Culture:*

The effort to grasp the world as a single unified whole runs through all the medieval summae, the encyclopaedias and the etymologies. . . . The philosophers of the twelfth century speak of the necessity of studying nature; for in the cognition of nature in all her depths, man finds himself . . . underlying these arguments and images is a confident belief in the unity and beauty of the world, and also the conviction that the central place in the world which God has created belongs to man.

The unity of man with the universe is revealed in the harmony interpenetrating them. Both man and the world are governed by the cosmic music which expresses the harmony of the whole with its parts and which permeates all from the heavenly spheres to man. *Musica humana* is in perfect concord with *musica mundana*. Everything that is measured by time is bound up with music. Music is subordinate to number. Therefore both macrocosm and manmade microcosm are ruled by numbers which define their structure and determine their motion. . . . It is in numbers that the secret of the beauty of the world lies; for the medieval mind the concepts "beauty," "orderliness," "harmony," "proportion," "comeliness," and "propriety" were very close to each other if not identical.[1]

So intensely anthropocentric was their conception of nature that, as Gurevich points out:

Each part of the human body corresponded to a part of the universe: the head to the skies, the breath to the air, the stomach to the sea, the feet to the earth; the bones corresponded to the rocks, the veins to the branches of the trees.[2]

The presumption that the entire cosmos was man-centered, that every facet of reality and all the laws of nature reflected this central reality, was the overriding axiom upon which the whole civilization of medieval Europe was built. Not even the slightest deviation from such an all-embracing man-centered teleology was compatible with the Christian revelation. For the Bible implied that the great drama of human history was central to the purpose of God in creation. The earth was the unique and divinely chosen stage for the drama, and God himself had taken on the form of a man to bear the sins of creation.

Even after the medieval period, for many early modern thinkers such as Francis Bacon, whose scientific philosophy, with its emphasis on experiment, had an empirical tendency that was quite similar to that of modern science, mankind's teleological centrality in the natural order was presumed without question. The following section from Bacon's *De sapientia veterum* illustrates Bacon's commitment to an intensely anthropocentric framework:

> Man . . . may be regarded as the centre of the world . . . if man were taken away from the world, the rest would seem to be all astray, without aim or purpose . . . leading to nothing. . . . the whole world works together in the services of man . . . in so much that all things seem to be going about man's business and not their own.[3]

The anthropocentric perspective was not, of course, restricted to the West. It was highly developed in the Islamic world in the ninth and tenth centuries. And Judaism, Hinduism, and Buddhism also view mankind as significant in the cosmic scheme. In ancient Indian thought, for example, the general ethos was "one of an integrated man-spirit-cosmos view, a wide and comprehensive view of nature in which the *Homo sapiens,* or man, the thinker, occupied a distinct place."[4] According to the eleventh-century neo-Confucianist philosopher Shao Yung, "Man is central in the universe, and the mind is central in man. . . . Man occupies the most honoured position in the scheme of things because he combines in him the principles of all species. . . . The nature of all things is complete in the human species."[5]

The idea is practically universal, being expressed in all human cultures, as John Barrow and Frank Tipler summarize:

> the idea that humanity is important to the cosmos and indeed the idea that the material world was created for man both seem to be present in many cultural traditions; they may even be universal . . . a cursory search of the anthropological literature shows teleological notions defended in Mayan, Zuñi (New Mexican Indian) . . . Sumerian, Bantu, ancient Egyptian, Islamic-Persian, and Chinese.[6]

It is remarkable to think that only five centuries separates the current skeptical ethos in the West from this profoundly teleological view of reality.

The anthropocentric vision of medieval Christianity is one of the most extraordinary—perhaps the most extraordinary—of all the presumptions of humankind. It is the ultimate theory and in a very real sense, the ultimate conceit. No other theory or concept ever imagined by man can equal in boldness and audacity this great claim—that everything revolves around human existence—that all the starry heavens, that every species of life, that every characteristic of reality exists for mankind and for mankind alone. It is simply the most daring idea ever proposed. But most remarkably, given its audacity, it is a claim which is very far from a discredited prescientific myth. In fact, no observation has ever laid the presumption to rest. And today, four centuries after the scientific revolution, the doctrine is again reemerging. In these last decades of the twentieth century, its credibility is being enhanced by discoveries in several branches of fundamental science.

Part 1

LIFE

Chapter   1

The   Harmony   of
the   Spheres

*In which evidence from physics and cosmology suggesting that
the laws of physics are fine-tuned for carbon-based life, is briefly
summarized. The fitness of the universe for life depends on a
number of factors, including: the relative strength of the four
fundamental forces (gravity, electromagnetism, and the strong
and weak nuclear forces), the speed of expansion of the universe,
the spacing and frequency of supernovae, the nuclear energy
levels of certain atoms, etc. If these were not precisely what they
are, then carbon-based life would certainly not exist. Many
previous authors have covered this ground, but it bears repeating
and is introductory to the theme of the book.*

The spiral galaxy Messier 83, NGC 5236.

It has been shown in the preceding chapters that a great number of qualities and laws appear to have been selected in the construction of the universe; and that by the adjustment to each other of the magnitudes and laws thus selected, the constitution of the world is what we find it, and is fitted for the support of vegetables and animals in a manner in which it could not have been, if the properties of the elements had been different from what they are.

—William Whewell, Bridgewater Treatises, 1833

This now tells us how precise the Creator's aim must have been, namely to an accuracy of one part in $10^{10^{123}}$. This is an extraordinary figure. One could not possibly even write the number down in full in the ordinary denary notation: it would be 1 followed by 10^{123} successive 0's. Even if we were to write a 0 on each separate proton and on each separate neutron in the entire universe—and we could throw in all the other particles for good measure—we should fall far short of writing down the figure needed.

—Roger Penrose, *The Emperor's New Mind,* 1989

On July 4 in the year 1054 A.D., Chinese astronomers observed a spectacular event in the sky. In the constellation of Taurus, the Bull, a brilliant new star suddenly appeared. So brilliant was this new star that it was easily visible in daylight and its light at night like that of the full moon. Carl Sagan relates how on the other side of the world the ancestors of the Hopi Indians also recorded this remarkable event:

> Halfway around the world in the American Southwest, there was then a high culture, rich in astronomical tradition, that also witnessed this brilliant new star. From carbon 14 dating of the remains of a charcoal fire, we know that in the middle eleventh century . . . the antecedents of the Hopi were living under an overhanging ledge in what is today New Mexico. One of them seems to have drawn on the cliff overhang, protected from the weather, a picture of a new star. Its position relative to the crescent moon would have been just as was depicted.[1]

What the Hopi Indians and the Chinese astronomers had observed was a supernova. Supernovae are among the most dramatic of all astronomical phenomena. An entire star self-destructs in a colossal explosion, scattering all its constituent matter and energy in a gigantic wave through adjacent regions of space.

As a result of advances in astronomy and physics over the past half century, we now know that the dying of stars in these immense self-destructive explosions is intimately related to our own existence as living organisms on earth. All the elements necessary for life—carbon (C), nitrogen (N), oxygen (O) and iron (Fe), etc.—are manufactured in the nuclear furnaces in the interiors of the stars. If these elements are to accumulate in rocky planets such as earth, they must be released from the stellar interiors and dispersed widely throughout the cosmos. The crucial release and dispersal of these key building blocks of life is one of the results of a supernova explosion. It is in the dying of stars that life has its birth.

Biocentric Fine-Tuning

Over the past three decades, facts such as these drawn from astrophysics and cosmology have led many physicists to argue that the cosmos appears to be finely tuned for life. The evidence and argument has been presented many times;[2] consequently, I will not discuss it in great detail here. Nonetheless, it is the foundation upon which the argument from biology rests, so a brief review is in order.

Supernovae play another role which is critical to the existence of life. The shock waves they generate are probably important in initiating the condensation of interstellar gas and dust into planetary systems such as our own solar system. Those ancient stargazers in China and America would surely have been amazed to know that without such strange new stars, like that which so dramatically lit up the sky on that far-off July night, there would be no astronomers, no stargazers, no earth, perhaps no life of any sort.

The fateful connection between those ancient astronomers and the new star they had witnessed involves more than the mere fact that such explosions spill the atoms of life into the cosmos and set in motion the turbulence that causes the birth of planets. If that supernova had been closer to the earth, then it might have bathed the earth in a lethal radiation, obliterating life. If it had been very close, the earth might have been engulfed in a fireball and vaporized. The frequency and distribution of exploding stars are therefore also critical parameters. Supernovae are essential for life—without them none of the chemical building blocks of life will ever accumulate on the surface of a planet like earth—but they are also immensely destructive phenomena, eliminating all life on any nearby solar systems.

The distances between supernovae and indeed between all stars is critical for other reasons. The distance between stars in our galaxy is about 30 million miles. If this distance was much less, planetary orbits would be destabilized. If it was much more, then the debris thrown out by a supernova would be so diffusely distributed that planetary systems like our own would in all probability never form.[3] If the cosmos is to be a home for life, then the flickering of the supernovae must occur at a very precise rate and the average distance between them, and indeed between all stars, must be very close to the actual observed figure.

In addition, it turns out that the production of the key elements for carbon-based life not only requires the enormous energy levels within the interiors of stars but is also critically dependent on what appears to be another set of very precise conditions in the nuclear structure of certain atoms, more specifically, the nuclear energy levels of the atoms ^{8}beryllium, ^{12}carbon, and ^{16}oxygen. These energy levels affect the manufacture and abundance of carbon, oxygen, and other heavier elements essential for life. If they had been slightly different, no life-giving carbon or oxygen would have been manufactured.

That the manufacture of the key elements of life should depend on a set of such highly specific conditions is commented on by Paul Davies in his book *The Accidental Universe*.[4] Fred Hoyle considers the carbon-oxygen synthesis coincidence so remarkable that it seems like a "put-up job." Regarding the delicate positioning of the nuclear resonances, he comments:

> If you wanted to produce carbon and oxygen in roughly equal quantities by stellar nucleosynthesis, these are the two levels you would have to fix, and your fixing would have to be just about where these levels are actually found to be. . . . A commonsense interpretation of the facts suggests that a super intellect has monkeyed with physics, as well as chemistry and biology, and that there are no blind forces worth speaking about in nature.[5]

The picture that has emerged from modern physics and astronomy suggests that the formation of the chemical elements for life, and planetary systems capable of sustaining life and evolution over millions of years, are only possible if the overall structure of the universe and all the laws of nature are almost precisely as they are.

Physicists recognize four fundamental forces. These largely determine the way in which one bit of matter or radiation can interact with another. In effect, these four forces determine the main characteristics of the universe.[6] They are the gravitational force, the electromagnetic force, the strong or nuclear force, and the weak force.

An extraordinary feature of these four fundamental forces is that their strength varies enormously over many orders of magnitude. In the table below they are given in international standard units:[7]

The forces of nature.

Gravitational force	=	$5.90 \cdot 10^{-39}$
Nuclear or Strong force	=	15
Electromagnetic force	=	$3.05 \cdot 10^{-12}$
Weak force	=	$7.03 \cdot 10^{-3}$

The fact that the gravitational force is fantastically weaker than the strong nuclear force by an unimaginable thirty-eight orders of magnitude is critical to the whole cosmic scheme and particularly to the existence of stable stars and planetary systems.[8] If, for example, the gravitational force was a trillion times stronger, then the universe would be far smaller and its life history far shorter. An average star would have a mass a trillion times less than the sun and a life span of about one year—far too short a time for complex life to develop and flourish. On the other hand, if gravity had been less powerful, no stars or galaxies would ever have formed. As Hawking points out, the growth of the universe—so close to the border of collapse and external expansion that man has not been able to measure it—has been at just the proper rate to allow galaxies and stars to form.[9]

The other relationships and values are no less critical. If the strong force had been just slightly weaker, the only element that would be stable would be hydrogen. No other atoms could exist. If it had been slightly stronger in relation to electromagnetism, then an atomic nucleus consisting of only two protons would be a stable feature of the universe—which would mean there would be no hydrogen, and if any stars or galaxies evolved, they would be very different from the way they are.[10]

Clearly, if these various forces and constants did not have precisely the values they do, there would be no stars, no supernovae, no planets, no atoms, no life. As Paul Davies summarizes:

> The numerical values that nature has assigned to the fundamental constants, such as the charge on the electron, the mass of the proton, and the Newtonian gravitational constant, may be mysterious, but they are crucially relevant to the structure of the universe that we perceive. As more and more physical systems, from nuclei to galaxies, have become better understood, scientists have begun to realise that many characteristics of these systems are remarkably sensitive to the precise values of the fundamental constants. Had nature opted for a slightly different set of numbers, the world would be a very different place. Probably we would not be here to see it.
>
> More intriguing still, certain crucial structures, such as solar-type stars, depend for their characteristic features on wildly improbable numerical accidents that combine together fundamental constants from distinct branches of physics. And when one goes on to study cosmology—the overall structure and evolution of the universe—incredulity mounts. Recent discoveries about the primeval cosmos oblige us to accept that the expanding universe has been set up in its motion with a cooperation of astonishing precision.[11]

In short, the laws of physics are supremely fit for life and the cosmos gives every appearance of having been specifically and optimally tailored to that end: to ensure the generation of stable stars and planetary systems, to ensure that these will be far enough apart to avoid gravitational interactions which would destabilize planetary orbits; to ensure that a nuclear furnace is generated in the interior of stars in which hydrogen will be converted into the heavier elements essential for life; to ensure that a proportion of stars will undergo supernovae explosions to release the key elements into interstellar space; to ensure that galaxies last several times longer than the lifetime of an average star, for only then will there be time for the atoms scattered by an earlier generation of supernovae within any one galaxy to be gathered into second-generation solar systems; to ensure that the distribution and frequency of supernovae will not be so frequent that planetary surfaces would be repeatedly bathed in lethal radiation but not so infrequent that there would be no heavier atoms manufactured and gathered onto the surface of newly formed planets; to ensure in the cosmos's vastness and in the trillions of its suns and their accompanying planetary systems a stage immense enough and a time long enough to make certain that the great evolutionary drama of life's becoming will inevitably be manifest sometime, somewhere on an earthlike planet.

And so we are led toward life and our own existence via a vast and ever-lengthening chain of apparently biocentric adaptations in the design of the cosmos in which each adaptation seems adjusted with almost infinite precision toward the goal of life.

That there is indeed a deep teleological connection between the Chinese stargazers and the new star which exploded into that July night in 1054 A.D. has now been established beyond any reasonable doubt. There is simply no tolerance possible in the design of the celestial machine. For us to be here, it must be precisely as it is.

The new picture that has emerged in twentieth-century astronomy presents a dramatic challenge to the presumption which has been prevalent within scientific circles during most of the past four centuries: that life is a peripheral and purely contingent phenomenon in the cosmic scheme. These advances in astronomy and physics have established what for Newton and generations of natural theologians was only an affirmation of belief: that there is indeed a deep and necessary connection between virtually every characteristic of the cosmic stage and the drama of life. It is ironic that those very features of the cosmos that were so troubling to the astronomers of the early seventeenth century—its vast size and the apparently infinite number of stars stretched out across its immensity—which inclined Kepler to wonder, "How can all things be for man's sake?"[12] and which seemed to render the earth an irrelevant mote of dust in the cosmic scheme, have turned out to be absolutely critical and essential for our existence.

The evidence provided by modern cosmology and physics is exactly the kind of evidence that the natural theologians were looking for in the seventeenth century but failed to find in the science of their day. This can be seen in this short passage from Richard Bentley's famous "A Confutation of Atheism from the Origin and Frame of the World," published in 1692. It was prepared under the guidance of Newton and may well represent a position close to Newton's own.

> Let us now turn our thoughts and imagination to the frame of our system, if there we may trace any visible foot steps of the Divine Wisdom and Beneficence. . . . What we have always seen to be done in one constant and uniform manner; we are apt to imagine there was but that one way of doing it, and that it could not be otherwise. This is a great error and impediment in a disquisition of this nature: to remedy which, *we ought to consider every thing as not yet in Being;* and then diligently examine if it *must needs have been at all, or what other ways it might have been as possibly as the present;* and if we find a greater Good and Utility in the present constitution, than would have accrued either from the total Privation of It, or from other frames and structures that as possibly have been as It: *we may then reasonably conclude, that the present constitution proceeded neither from the necessity of material Causes nor the blind shuffles of an imaginary Chance,* but from an Intelligent and Good Being, that formed it that particular way out of choice and design. And especially if this Usefulness *be conspicuous not in one or a few only, but in a long train and series of things,* this will give us a firm and infallible assurance, that we have not passed a wrong judgement.[13] [My emphasis.]

If the existence of life had been compatible with a greater range of values for the fundamental constants, or, in other words, if the design of the celestial machine could have been different at least to some degree and yet still have sustained life, then the teleological conclusion would be far weaker. It is the necessity that it be exactly as it is—adjusted to what is in effect near infinite precision *in a long train and series of things* that makes the teleological conclusion so compelling.

As Davies comments in the last paragraph of *The Cosmic Blueprint,* "The impression of Design is overwhelming."[14] And Paul Davies is not alone.

Several well-known physicists and astronomers, among them Brandon Carter, Freeman Dyson, John Wheeler, John Barrow, Frank Tipler, and Sir Fred Hoyle, to cite only a few, have all made the point in recent publications— that our type of carbon-based life could only exist in a very special sort of universe and that if the laws of physics had been very slightly different we could not have existed. With the evidence as it now stands, it is not surprising that there now exists a significant body of opinion within the scientific community prepared to defend the idea that the universe is in some way profoundly biocentric and gives every appearance of having been specially designed for life. As a result of these discoveries, there is now a teleological intellectual current within modern physics, cosmology, and astronomy which is remarkably concordant with the older anthropocentric view and strikingly out of keeping with the antiteleological tendencies that have come to be universally associated with advances in scientific knowledge for most of the recent past.

As mentioned above, this is not the place to give a comprehensive review of the anthropic principle or to enumerate the many life-giving coincidences in the structure of the cosmos as revealed by twentieth-century astronomy and physics. The topic has been covered in a number of recent scholarly books. This brief discussion of the anthropic principle has been introduced here primarily to illustrate that the apparently triumphant antiteleological tide of skepticism which has gripped the western mind with elemental force for nearly four centuries has now decisively turned in at least one major area of science, and also because it forms a natural introduction to a book that deals with evidence for design in biology and which is in many ways an extension of the anthropic position into the biological sciences.

From Physics to Biology

Why has twentieth-century biology lagged behind physics in the rediscovery of teleology? Curiously, biology, which was so influenced by the nonbiocentric physics of the nineteenth century, has remained immune to the new biocentric-teleological physics of the late twentieth century. The prevailing view within the biological sciences is still that life and man are fundamentally contingent phenomena. This is a natural deduction from the Darwinian idea of evolution by natural selection. As Stephen Jay Gould puts it:

Homo sapiens I fear is . . . in a vast universe a wildly improbable evolutionary event.[15] . . . biology's most profound insight into human nature status and potential lies in the simple phrase, the embodiment of contingency: *Homo sapiens* is an entity not a tendency.[16] . . . If you wish to ask the question of the ages, Why do humans exist? . . . We are the offspring of history, and must establish our own paths in this most diverse and interesting of conceivable universes— one indifferent to our suffering.[17]

The new anthropic vision of the physicist and the Darwinian contingent paradigm which dominates modern biology are diametrically opposed worldviews. Yet, where physics led in the seventeenth century, biology eventually followed, and it is doubtful whether modern biology can for long resist the new teleological current now flowing within cosmology and the physical sciences.

This new teleological current would be challenging enough to the *contingent biology* even if the life-giving coincidences were restricted to the realm of physics and astronomy. But the coincidences do not stop at the distribution of supernovae or with the resonances of the energy levels of the carbon and oxygen atoms. They extend on into chemistry, into biochemistry and molecular biology, into the very fabric of life itself. Advances in chemistry, biochemistry, physiology, and molecular biology, commencing at the beginning of the last century, but mainly over the past fifty years, have revealed an additional set of mutual adaptations or coincidences in the chemical and physical properties of water and in many other of the key constituents of life—of precisely the kind that one might expect to find if the cosmos is indeed the biocentric whole that astronomy suggests.

Chapter 2

The Vital Fluid

*In which it is argued that water gives every appearance of being
uniquely fit for the type of carbon-based life that exists on earth.
Every one of its chemical and physical properties seems maximally
fit not only for microscopic life but also for large warm-blooded
organisms such as mammals, as well as for the generation and
maintenance of a stable chemical and physical environment on the
surface of the earth. Some of the properties of water reviewed
include its thermal properties, its surface tension, its capacity to
dissolve a vast number of different substances, and its low viscosity,
which allows small molecules to enter and leave cells by diffusion
and which also makes possible a circulatory system. If the properties
of water were not almost precisely what they are, carbon-based life
would in all probability be impossible. Even the viscosity of ice is fit.
If it were any greater, then all the water on earth might be trapped
in vast immobile ice sheets at the poles. If the thermal properties of
water were even slightly different, the maintenance of stable body
temperatures in warm-blooded organisms would be problematical.
No other fluid comes close to water as the ideal medium for carbon-
based life. Indeed, the properties of water in themselves provide
perhaps as much evidence as physics and cosmology in support
of the proposition that the laws of nature are specifically arranged
for carbon-based life.*

The earth from space.

Courtesy NASA.

For is not the whole substance of all vegetables mere modified water?
and consequently of all animals too; all of which either feed upon
Vegetables or prey upon one another? is not an immense quantity of
it continually exhaled by the Sun, to fill the atmosphere with Vapours
and Clouds, and feed the Plants of the Earth with the balm of
Dews . . . . It seems incredible at first hearing, that all the Blood in our
Bodies should circulate in a trice, in a very few minutes: but I believe it
would be more surprising, if we knew the short and swift periods of the
great Circulation of Water, that vital Blood of the Earth which
composeth and nourisheth all things.

—Richard Bentley, "A Confutation of Atheism from the
Origin and Frame of the World," 1692

Although water is one of the most familiar of all substances, its remarkable nature never fails to impress. As a liquid, it accumulates on the earth's surface in bodies varying in size from the great oceans to small lakes to tiny puddles. In motion it may swirl violently down a great cataract, or flow serenely as a mature river meandering across a plain. On the surface of large bodies of water, the wind pushes up waves both great and small. Tiny droplets of the substance form the matrix of the clouds. Slightly larger drops fall through the atmosphere from the clouds to the ground as rain. As a solid, it falls as snow blanketing the earth in white, it forms the great ice sheets of the polar regions and the valley glaciers in the mountains, and it forms the frosted pattern on a windowpane in winter. In the higher latitudes water forms the entire scenery of the earth, the ice caps at the fringes of the polar continents, the icebergs floating in the restless gray and ice-cold sea, the spray carried from wave tops by the wind and frozen instantly into tiny pellets of ice in the subzero temperature and splattered like shrapnel onto the nearby ice shelves. Even the sounds associated with water are no less diverse: there is the rhythmic pounding of the surf, the deafening roar of a great waterfall, the babbling of a mountain brook, the gentle patter of summer rain, the clatter of hail against an iron roof, the grinding booms and sharp reports of an advancing glacier, and the thunder of an avalanche.

These diverse manifestations of water are remarkable indeed. But as we shall see, they are not nearly as extraordinary or amazing as the various ways in which water is so ideally and uniquely adapted to serve its biological role as the medium or matrix for life on earth.

Water has long been seen to have some special significance. That it is essential to life has been evident since the earliest of times, and many cultures have invested it with magical life-giving qualities. It is fitting that Thales, the first of the Greek philosophers, should have based his science on the assertion that water is the origin of all things, and that Bentley should describe it as "the vital blood of the Earth."[1]

Water forms the fluid matrix in which occur all the vital chemical and physical activities upon which life on earth depends. Without water, life that exists on earth would be impossible. If the vital activities of the cell are the movements of pieces on a chess board, then water would be the board. Chess is impossible without the board; life is impossible without water. Water also forms most of the bulk of most living things. Most organisms are made up of more than 50 percent water; in the case of man, water makes up more than 70 percent of the weight of the body.

The Necessity of Liquid

That life is based in a liquid medium is certainly no accident. For it is difficult to imagine how any sort of complex chemical system capable of assembling and replicating itself, of manipulating its atomic and molecular components and drawing its vital nutrients and constituents from its environment—that is, anything that displays the characteristics we attribute to life—could exist except in a liquid medium.

As A. E. Needham points out in *The Uniqueness of Biological Materials,* the other two states of matter, the solid and the gaseous, would seem to be excluded on fundamental grounds. In the case of both a crystalline solid, where the atoms are held in regular crystalline arrays and a glassy solid, where the atoms are irregularly packed, the atoms are in rigid contact with one another and there is very little scope for the occurrence of the dynamic molecular processes associated with life to occur. In gases, on the other hand, the constituent atoms are freely mobile, and consequently gases are far too volatile and labile to be considered seriously as candidates for the chemical matrix of life.[2] We are all familiar with clouds which are nebulous masses of tiny liquid droplets—or in more scientific terms, "segregations of liquid-in-gas colloids." Clouds are a rare exception to the rule that segregating subsystems are unusual in a gas. However, the very transience of cloud patterns graphically illustrates the unsuitability of gas as a medium for the support of stable, segregating subsystems.

If the laws of physics sanctioned matter to exist in our universe only in the solid or gaseous state and outlawed liquids, then life, defined above as a *complex chemical system capable of assembling and replicating itself, of manipulating its components and drawing its vital nutrients and constituents from its environment,* would almost certainly not exist. Interestingly, John von Neumann, one of the fathers of the computer, in his *Theory of Self-Reproducing Automata,* envisaged his mechanical replicators floating on an infinite lake, the surface of which was covered with all the basic constituents they required to construct themselves. In other words, the medium in which the replicators "lived" was a fluid.[3]

Because the full impact of the argument for the fitness of water is accumulative and depends on a relatively exhaustive consideration of all the individual adaptations which seem to fit water so ideally for its biological role, it is important that no adaptation is omitted, even if it is very well known, so that all the evidence is laid out as comprehensively as possible and in some detail.

Water's Unique Thermal Properties

Curiously, even as recently as the late eighteenth century, shortly after Antoine Lavoisier had first determined the chemical structure of water and shown that it was made up of two hydrogen atoms combined with one oxygen atom, its chemical and physical properties were insufficiently understood to argue that it was specially adapted for life. Just how little was known of the properties of water around 1800 is obvious from this section in Paley's *Evidences*, where he concedes that "when we come to the elements . . . we come to those things of the organisation of which, if they be organised, we are confessedly ignorant," and continues by quoting an earlier writer as observing "that we know water sufficiently to boil, . . . to freeze, . . . to evaporate . . . without knowing what water is." And as Paley notes, even after Lavoisier's discovery, "The constituent parts of water appear in some measure to have been lately discovered, yet it does not, I think, appear, that we can make any better use of water since the discovery than we did before it."[4]

The first significant consideration of water's fitness came only thirty years after the publication of Paley's *Evidences* when William Whewell, master of Trinity College, Cambridge, examined the topic in his Bridgewater Treatise entitled *Astronomy and General Physics Considered with Reference to Natural Theology*, published in 1832.[5] During those thirty years scientific knowledge had rapidly increased and Whewell was able to present the first systematic argument for the fitness of water.

Although Whewell's discussion of the properties of water is somewhat vague and nonquantitative from a modern perspective, and although he restricts his discussion to the thermal properties of water and their apparent adaptation to climatic amelioration, it nevertheless represents the first significant systematic consideration of the unique fitness of water and represents an enormous advance on Paley's *Evidences*. Beginning with its thermal properties, he points out:

Water expands by heat and contracts by cold [but if this contraction were continued all the way to the freezing point] . . . the lower parts of water would have been first frozen and being once frozen hardly any heat applied at the surface could have melted them. . . . This is so far the case that in a vessel containing ice at the bottom and water at the top, Rumford made the upper fluid boil without thawing the congealed cake below.

Now a law of water with respect to heat operating in this manner would have been very inconvenient if it had prevailed in our lakes and seas. . . . They would all have had a bed of ice, increasing with every occasion, till the whole was frozen. We would have no bodies of water, except such pools on the surfaces of these icy reservoirs as the summer sun could thaw to be again frozen to the bottom with the first frosty night. How is this inconvenience obviated?

[This situation] is obviated by a modification of the law which takes place when the temperature approaches this limit. Water contracts by the increase of cold till we come near the freezing temperature; but then . . . expands till the point at which it becomes ice. Hence the water [at 4°C] will lie at the bottom with cooler water . . . above it. . . . In approaching the freezing point the coldest water will rise to the surface where congealment will take place. [But this is only part of the story.] . . . Another peculiarity in the laws which regulate the action of cold on water is, that in the very act of freezing sudden and considerable expansion takes place. . . . [Consequently, ice floats.][6]

Thus, because of these two anomalous properties, water is not bound up in vast beds of submarine ice. We now know that these two properties of water are practically unique, a fact not known in 1832, as Whewell admits: "We do not know how far these laws of expansion are connected with or depend on, more remote and general properties of this fluid or of all fluids."[7] Note that what we have here are two different characteristics of water, *both of which are mutually adapted toward the end of preserving bodies of liquid water on a planetary surface.*

One of Whewell's most interesting insights comes in a passage in which he points out that some of the thermal properties which endow water with its peculiar fitness, such as the decrease in the density of water below 4°C, and the fact that the density of ice is less than that of water, seem to be due to an apparently contrived violation of what would appear to be a natural law:

This gradual progress of freezing and thawing, of evaporation and condensing, is produced, so far as we can discover, by a particular contrivance. Like the freezing of water from the top, or the floating of ice, the moderation of the rate of these changes seems to be the result of a *violation* of a law: that is, the simple rule regarding the effects of change of temperature which at first sight appears to be the law and which from its simplicity would seem to us the most obvious law for these as well as for other cases is modified at certain critical points *so as* to produce these advantageous effects.[8]

In recapitulating his argument, Whewell concludes that the various thermal properties of water, including the anomalous expansion below 4°C and its expansion on freezing, which together contribute to its remarkable fitness for the preservation of water in the liquid state, appear to be mutually independent properties. Moreover, he continues, as far as we can tell, these properties could have been different. And in a key section of his treatise, he concludes that where we see a number of natural phenomena, all of which might have been different and which also seem to be providentially arranged for the "welfare of things," this is very suggestive of design. In his own words from this classic of natural theology, he lays down the basic logic of his argument:

> All natural philosophers will, probably, agree, that there must be . . . a great number of things entirely without any mutual dependence. . . . Laws are unlike one another . . . steam . . . expands at a different rate to air . . . water expands in freezing, but mercury contracts . . . heat travels in a manner quite different through solids and fluids. We have . . . fifty substances in the world; each of which is invested with properties . . . altogether different from those of any other substance.
>
> There are, therefore, it appears, a number of things which might have been otherwise . . . substances, which might have existed any how exist exactly in such a manner . . . as they should to secure the welfare of other things . . . that the laws are tempered and fitted together in the only way in which the world could have gone on.[9]

Following Whewell, by far the most important discussion of the unique fitness of water and still the most significant to date was that of Lawrence Henderson, then professor of biological chemistry at Harvard University, in his great classic *The Fitness of the Environment,* published in 1913.[10] Henderson is remembered by every student of biochemistry and medicine as the Henderson of the Henderson-Hasselbach equation. *The Fitness of the Environment* must rate as one of the most important and influential books in the biological sciences in the first decades of the century. This is acknowledged by Joseph Needham in his *Sceptical Biologist,* published in 1929. It made, according to Needham, "unquestionably, the most important contribution to the philosophy of biology"[11] in the first quarter of the century, and this view was recently seconded by Harold Morowitz, professor of biophysics at Yale, in his *Cosmic Joy and Local Pain* of 1987.[12]

The Fitness of the Environment differs from Whewell's *Astronomy and General Physics* in two important respects. It is quantitative and comparative. Moreover, the chain of adaptations enumerated by Henderson is greater, and because something of the chemical nature of life was understood by 1900, Henderson is able to show water to be ideally fit, not only for the maintenance of global climatic stability but also to function as the matrix of living matter.

The Fitness of the Environment deals with the peculiar fitness not only of water but with other important chemical components of living things, including carbon dioxide, carbonic acid, and carbon compounds in general. The book was published in 1913. Since then and particularly over the past forty years, a vast amount of new knowledge of chemistry and molecular biology has accumulated, but this has not only entirely confirmed Henderson's position but extended it to a degree that would have seemed unimaginable in 1913.

Henderson's aim was not to present an argument for design (although his arguments could be used for that purpose) but merely to argue for an undeniable yet mysterious biocentricity in the order of things and to establish that the key components of life, including water, carbon dioxide, and bicarbonate, exhibit together a unique mutual fitness which could hardly exist in any other equivalent set of chemicals. To show, in other words, that

> in fundamental characteristics the environment [that is, the various chemicals and physico-chemical processes which constitute living things and the chemical and physical character of the hydrosphere] is the fittest possible abode for life.

He continues by admitting that

> This is not a novel hypothesis. In rudimentary form it has already a long history behind it, and it was a familiar doctrine in the early nineteenth century. It presents itself anew as a result of the science of physical chemistry.[13]

In presenting his argument for the unique fitness of water, Henderson alludes to the following thermal properties:

1. The anomalous facts (already referred to above) that water contracts as it cools until just before freezing, after which it expands until it becomes ice, and that it expands on freezing. These properties are practically unique.

2. When ice melts or water evaporates, heat is absorbed from the environment. Heat is released when the reverse happens. This is the phenomenon known as latent heat. The latent heat of freezing of water is again one of the highest of all known fluids. In the ambient temperature range only ammonia has a higher latent heat of freezing. Water's latent heat of evaporation is the highest of any known fluid in the ambient temperature range.[14]

3. That the thermal capacity or specific heat of water, which is the amount of heat required to raise the temperature of water one degree centigrade, is higher than most other liquids.

4. That the thermal conductivity of water, which is its capacity to conduct heat, is four times greater than any other common liquid.[15]

5. That the thermal conductivities of ice and snow are low.

If it were not for the properties given in point 1, most of the water on earth would be permanently frozen into vast beds of ice at the bottom of the oceans. Lakes would freeze completely from the bottom up each winter in the higher latitudes. Without those properties in point 2, the climate would be subject to far more rapid temperature changes. Small lakes and rivers would vanish and reappear constantly. Without 3, the difference between winter and summer would be more extreme and weather patterns would be less stable,[16] and the great ocean currents such as the Gulf Stream, which currently transfer vast quantities of heat from the tropics to the poles, would be far less capable of moderating the temperature differences between high and low latitudes. Without 2, again, warm-blooded animals would have a far harder time ridding their bodies of heat. Henderson was particularly struck by the adaptive significance of the cooling effect of the latent heat of evaporation in the case of warm-blooded animals. Because, as Henderson points out, "in an animal like man . . . heat is a most prominent excretory product, which has to be constantly eliminated in great amounts, and to this end only three important means are available—conduction, radiation, and evaporation."[17] But at body temperature, as Henderson continues, "very little heat can be lost by conduction or radiation and evaporative cooling is therefore the only significant means of temperature reduction." And he concludes: "To sum up, this property appears to possess a threefold importance. First, it operates powerfully to equalise and to moderate the temperature of the earth; secondly, it makes possible very effective regulation of the temperature of the living organism; and thirdly it favours the meteorological cycle. All of these effects are true maxima, for no other substance can in this respect compare with water."[18] Conversely, as the temperature falls, condensation occurs and this releases heat which tends to counteract the rate of temperature fall. Moreover, as Henderson points out, there is another aspect of the fitness of the latent heat of evaporation—the fact that as the temperature rises so does the rate of evaporation and so consequently does the cooling effect of evaporation. So the *cooling effect of evaporation increases when the usefulness of the property is most needed.* Without 4, it would be harder for cells which cannot use convection currents to distribute heat evenly throughout the cell.[19] Without 5, the protective insulation of snow and ice, essential to the survival of many forms of life in the higher latitudes, would be lost. Also, water would cool more rapidly and small lakes would be more likely to freeze completely.

And so, as Henderson argues, it turns out that not one or two, not most, but *all* the thermal properties of water are mutually adaptive not only for the maintenance of thermal stability on a planetary scale but also for the buffering of individual macroscopic life forms against sudden temperature changes. Even the low conductivity of ice is adaptive, protecting life from frost and the water below the ice from excessive cooling. Amazement mounts at the wonderful elegance and parsimony in the way the various thermal adaptations of water conspire together to achieve so many different life-sustaining ends. For example, the preservation of large bodies of liquid water on the earth's surface is ensured almost entirely by the thermal properties of water itself and of its solid form, ice. This is a particularly critical suit of adaptations because liquid water is essential to all life on earth, not only because water is the matrix in which life's chemistry occurs, but also because without bodies of liquid water no aquatic life would be possible and the evolution of complex life forms would almost certainly have been impossible. Further, the preservation of large bodies of liquid water in the oceans ensures temperature stability worldwide, which in itself ensures climatic stability on which the existence of large complex life forms depend. Moreover, complex macroscopic life forms astonishingly utilize *these same thermal properties* to buffer themselves against thermal change, which is the inevitable outcome of their metabolic processes. And so via a series of deeply interconnected and wondrously teleological thermal adaptive properties, water bestows its vital magic on earth and its living inhabitants.

The parsimony and elegance in this design is self-evident. As far as its thermal properties are concerned, water would appear to be uniquely, and in many different ways ideally, adapted for life on earth. In thermal terms, water is the unique and ideal candidate for its biological role.

Surface Tension

Of course, the thermal properties of water are by no means the only physical characteristics which make this remarkable fluid so supremely fit for its biological role. Yet another is its very high surface tension. This has many biological implications.[20] It is the high surface tension of water which draws water up through the soil within reach of the roots of plants and assists its rise from the roots to branches in tall trees. Large terrestrial plants would probably be a physiological impossibility if the surface tension of water was similar to that of most liquids. Recently, A. E. Needham commented on the utility of the high surface tension of water:

> Water has a uniquely high surface tension exceeded by few substances other than liquid selenium and this at a very much higher temperature. Water, therefore, is ideal for the formation of discrete living bodies, with stable limiting membranes. Air-water interfaces are less important, perhaps, than those between water and lipids, which likewise have high values. Other biologically useful consequences of the high tension are that materials which can lower the tension, surface active materials, tend to accumulate at the surface, and also to orientate there. Most of the biologically important carbon compounds have this property, which promotes their aggregation and concentration, as well as the formation of organised membranes.[21]

Remarkably, the very high surface tension, because it tends to draw water into the narrow cracks and fissures in the rocks, assists in the process of weathering and washing chemicals from the rocks. Also, when it freezes, the rocks are fragmented, which in turn also assists the weathering process and the formation of soils.[22] Here is another instance where a physical property of water is adapted for a role in fashioning the planetary environment for life while at the same time being adapted for a number of specific biological functions.

The Alcahest

All the various physical properties of water which endow it with such a remarkable biological fitness would of course be of no utility if its chemical properties were not similarly fit. Water could have no biological role if it was not a good solvent. The capacity to dissolve a great number of different chemical substances is presumably a criterion that must be satisfied by any fluid if it is to function as a matrix for any kind of chemical "life" remotely similar to our own.

It turns out that, as a solvent, water is indeed ideally fit, so much so that water approaches far nearer than any other liquid to the alcahest, the universal mythical solvent of the alchemists.[23] This is a property of critical importance to water's biological role. Felix Franks recently commented on the solvent action of water:

> Other remarkable properties include the almost universal solvent action of liquid water, making its rigorous purification extremely difficult. Nearly all known chemicals dissolve in water to a slight, but detectable extent.[24]

Water's power as a universal solvent is also geologically significant, as the distribution of vital minerals through the hydrosphere would be far less equitable if its solvation powers were less marked.[25]

The solvation power of water and the distribution of diverse chemical species in large amounts throughout the hydrosphere is illustrated by the vast amount of dissolved materials carried to the sea by all the rivers of the earth in one year. This quantity has been estimated to be some 5 billion tons. Henderson lists thirty-three different elements which can be found in the sea, and probably many more are present in trace amounts. To illustrate the utility of its solvation power in biological systems, he cites over fifty different compounds which are found dissolved in human urine.[26] Today one could cite many hundreds.

As one might expect from such a universal solvent, water is also a surprisingly reactive chemical. It catalyzes almost all known reactions.[27] But although quite reactive, water is far less reactive than many other liquids. Many well-known acids and alkalies are far more chemically reactive, and will dissolve substances almost insoluble in water in a matter of seconds. Yet these liquids react with the chemicals dissolved in them, exhausting themselves and consuming the solutes.[28]

Water could not fulfill its biological role if it was a highly reactive fluid, like sulfuric acid, or if it was an entirely unreactive fluid like liquid argon. It seems that, like its other properties, the reactivity of water is ideally fit for *both its biological and its geological role.*

We should note in passing that in his discussion of water Henderson omits two characteristics of water which might have been construed at the time as "defects" in its fitness for life. First, many compounds containing long hydrocarbon chains such as the lipids are virtually insoluble in it. Second, many synthetic reactions in organic chemistry can only be carried out in the absence of water. We now know, as we shall see in the following chapters, that the first of these two apparent defects, the insolubility of hydrocarbons, plays a vital role in the design of the cell system, while the other defect is circumvented by carrying out many of these synthetic reactions in special water-excluding reaction chambers in the center of proteins.

Viscosity and Diffusion

One physical property of water that was not discussed in Henderson's *Fitness* is its viscosity. The viscosity of liquids varies considerably. The viscosity of tar, glycerol, olive oil, and sulfuric acid are respectively, 10 billion times, one thousand times, about one hundred times, and twenty-five times that of water. Compared with many liquids, water has a low viscosity. Although the viscosity of water is close to the minimum known for any fluid, a few other liquids have viscosities less than water. The viscosity of ether is four times less, liquid hydrogen a hundred times less. However, as a rule, only gases have viscosities markedly less than water.[29]

The fitness of water would in all probability be less if its viscosity were much lower. The structures of living systems would be subject to far more violent movements under shearing forces if the viscosity were as low as liquid hydrogen. Shearing forces are set up in a structure when a force applied to it tends to distort its shape. A structure composed of pitch, which has a high viscosity, will tend to resist such shearing forces far more effectively than a structure composed of treacle.

If the viscosity of water was much lower, delicate structures would be easily disrupted by shearing forces and water would be incapable of supporting any permanent intricate microscopic structures. The delicate molecular architecture of the cell would probably not survive.

On the other hand, if the viscosity was much higher than it is, no fish or anything we would call a fish would be possible. One can well imagine the difficulty of attempting to sail or swim through treacle! Nor would any microorganism or cell be able to move. If the viscosity of water was higher, the controlled movement of large macromolecules and particularly structures such as mitochondria and small organelles would be impossible, as would processes like cell division. All the vital activities of the cell would be effectively frozen, and cellular life of any sort remotely resembling that with which we are familiar would be impossible. The development of higher organisms, which is critically dependent on the ability of cells to move and crawl around during embryogenesis, would certainly be impossible if the viscosity of water was even slightly greater than it is.

Viscosity also has a very important influence on the vital process of diffusion, and this has enormous bearing on the existence of our type of cellular life. It is difficult to see how else but by diffusion the necessary flow of matter into and out of any conceivable chemical self-replicating system based in a fluid medium could be maintained.

Diffusion rates in water are very rapid over short distances. Oxygen, for example, will diffuse across the average body cell in approximately one-hundredth of a second.[30] The very great rapidity of diffusion of small molecules in water over short distances explains why small microorganisms, bacteria and protozoa, and even very small multicellular organisms are able to obtain their nutrients and get rid of their waste products simply by diffusion, without the need for a circulatory system.

The rate of diffusion of a molecule in a fluid varies inversely with its viscosity. If the viscosity goes up, the rate of diffusion goes down.

If the viscosity of water had been, say, ten times greater and diffusion rates ten times less, it would be far more difficult for organisms to derive their vital nutrients by diffusion to sustain their metabolic activities. This is because the volume of a sphere is the cube of its diameter; consequently, to maintain the same level of metabolic activity, cells would have to be a thousand times smaller. In which case only the very simplest of microbial cells would be possible. If diffusion rates were a hundred times less, cells would have to be a million times smaller to maintain their metabolic activities—a volume equivalent to a sphere containing a few protein molecules.

The low viscosity of water is fit in another way because in a liquid of low viscosity the rate of diffusion of different molecules does not vary greatly from molecule to molecule.[31] Measurement of the actual diffusion rates of a variety of compounds in water shows that the diffusion rate varies inversely as the cube root of the molecular weight. This is a fascinating and important law, which is probably of critical significance. As Herbert Stern and D. L. Nanney explain in their *Biology of Cells,* "it means that the rate of diffusion is much the same for most molecules."[32] Even in the case of a molecule like a protein, of molecular weight a thousand times that of glucose, its rate of diffusion is only ten times slower. As the range of molecular weights of the great majority of key metabolites used by the cell, such as the sugars and amino acids, is no more than tenfold, the resultant variation in diffusion rates is very small.

To serve its biological role, diffusion must not be only very rapid over short distances, but its rate must be approximately the same for most of the key metabolites used by the cell. Both these criteria are satisfied by the diffusion of small metabolites in water.

The diffusion of molecules in any fluid, whatever its viscosity, including water, has an important characteristic in that it is *very rapid over short distances but very slow if there is far to go.* In fact, the diffusion time increases with the square of the diffusion distance. Thus, if the diffusion distance is increased ten times, the time taken will be increased a hundred times. The physiologist Knut Schmidt-Nielsen calculated that in the case of oxygen diffusing into the tissues, it will attain an average diffusion distance of 1 micron (one-thousandth of a millimeter) in one ten-thousandth of a second, 10 microns in one-hundredth of a second, 100 microns in one second, 1 millimeter in one hundred seconds, 10 millimeters in three hours, and *1 meter in three years.*[33]

Viscosity and the Circulatory System

Because of the increasing inefficiency of diffusion as a transport mechanism over distances greater than a fraction of a millimeter, no highly active organism more than a few millimeters thick can acquire and dispose of its metabolites by diffusion. Hence, to be viable all large organisms must have some additional means of acquiring and disposing of metabolites. In practice, this means some sort of circulatory or perfusion system.[34] In mammals billions of tiny capillaries permeate all the tissues of the body, transporting the necessary nutrients, including oxygen and glucose, to within diffusional reach of all cells where metabolic activities are occurring. Because diffusion is so ineffective over large distances, no active cell can survive in a mammal unless it is within about 50 microns from a capillary. In the active muscles of a guinea pig, there may be 3,000 open capillaries per square millimeter of muscle. This is a great number, occupying approximately 15 percent of the volume of the muscle, equivalent to 10,000 tiny parallel tubes running down a pencil lead.[35]

However, a capillary system will work only if the fluid being pumped through its constituent tubes has a very low viscosity. A low viscosity is essential because flow is inversely proportional to the viscosity. A twofold increase in viscosity causes the flow to halve. From this it is easy to see that if the viscosity of water had a value only a few times greater than it is, pumping blood through a capillary bed would require enormous pressure and almost any sort of circulatory system would be unworkable. One can readily appreciate the problem by trying to envisage pumping treacle through a narrow glass tube.

But there is a further, very striking relationship between the diameter of the tubes and the resistance to flow, one which imposes enormous design constraints on any sort of circulatory system. The resistance to flow is inversely proportional to the *fourth power* of the diameter of the tube. Which means that halving the diameter of a tube causes a sixteenfold increase in resistance to the flow of fluid through the tube.

Very little decrease in the size of capillaries could be achieved even if the viscosity of water was an order of magnitude lower. To achieve the same rate of blood flow through a capillary half the size of those which exist in the mammalian body with the same blood pressure would require either a lowering of viscosity of sixteen times, or a sixteenfold increase in pressure. In fact, no liquid at body temperature is known which has a viscosity this low. The bioengineering problems associated with redesigning a muscular pumping system like the heart to generate a perfusion pressure sixteen times as great would appear insurmountable. The smallest capillaries are about 3 to 5 microns in diameter. Given the viscosity of water, the laws which govern the flow of fluids through small tubes, and the design constraints on muscular pumping systems, the figure of 3 to 5 microns is equivalent to a physical constant—there is no way in which it could be decreased!

It is fortunate that capillaries can function down to such a small size. Because diffusion in a liquid is only effective over very small distances, the existence of higher organisms is only possible because of the existence of a myriad of tiny capillaries permeating their tissues. If the viscosity of water had been slightly greater and the smallest functional capillaries had been 10 microns in diameter instead of 3, then the capillaries would have had to occupy virtually all of the muscle tissue to provide an effective supply of oxygen and glucose. Obviously, the design of macroscopic life forms would be impossible, or enormously constrained.

The tiny diameter of the capillary also has another essential bearing on its primary function as a carrier of nutrients to the tissues. This is because the tension in the wall of a tube equals the product of the pressure within the tube and the diameter of the tube.[36] This implies that for a given pressure the tension in the wall increases in direct proportion to the radius of the tube. For this reason, as Schmidt-Nielsen points out, a large artery must have a thicker wall than a small artery. However, in the case of capillaries, "because of their very small radius a wall consisting of a single layer of cells has sufficient strength. Thus the smallness of the capillary has the important consequence that its walls can be thin enough to permit rapid diffusional exchange of material between the blood and the tissues."[37]

It seems, then, the viscosity of water must be very close to what it is if water is to be a fit medium for life. It is sufficiently high to provide some protective buffering against shearing forces for the delicate structures of the cell and sufficiently low to ensure diffusion rates fast enough to allow for material exchange between the cell and its environment. In the case of higher organisms it must be low enough to permit perfusion of the tissues via a system of capillaries down to 3 to 5 microns in diameter, which are sufficiently small to bring within diffusional distance all the tissue cells of the body without their occupying a large proportion of the volume of the tissues. If it was much higher, diffusion would be prohibitively slow, and while very simple cell systems might be possible, large, complex, metabolically active organisms would not. No conceivable set of compensatory changes—increasing the number or diameter of the capillaries, increasing the flow rate or decreasing average cell size, etc.—could be engineered to make mammalian life possible.

Non-Newtonian Fluids

There is a final and fascinating aspect of the phenomenon of viscosity related to the viscous properties of nonhomogeneous fluids which has an important bearing on the function and design of the circulatory system. Ordinary homogeneous fluids have a constant viscosity. Their flow is directly related to the pressure applied. However, as Marcus Reiner points out in his *Scientific American* article "The Flow of Matter," when a nonhomogeneous fluid, containing a suspension of particles like blood, is forced to flow through a tube, it exhibits a curious behavior: when the pressure is doubled, the rate of flow may triple. Remarkably, its viscosity becomes less as the pressure is increased. Liquids that behave in this way are called non-Newtonian.[38]

Now this apparently esoteric aspect of the phenomenon of viscosity is no triviality but rather a crucial adaptive property of blood. It means that when the blood supply to a tissue must be increased severalfold, because blood behaves as a nonhomogeneous fluid consisting of red cells suspended in a watery fluid, then as the perfusion pressure increases, *the viscosity conveniently declines.* This effect greatly facilitates the increased delivery of blood to an organ when its metabolic activity is increased. The twenty-fold increase in the perfusion of mammalian muscles as strenuous activity commences is only possible because of this characteristic of a non-Newtonian fluid.

What is particularly remarkable about this adaptive property is that the packaging of the hemoglobin (the oxygen carrying molecules in the red blood cell) in small particles, i.e., the red cells, rather than having them free in solution in the plasma, is itself adaptive, but for reasons completely unrelated to fluid flow or viscosity. These include the linking of the association and dissociation of oxygen and hemoglobin to a variety of sophisticated metabolic controls, which among other things assist in the buffering of the body against changes in its acidity and assist in the transport of carbon dioxide to the lungs. If the oxygen carrying molecules were free in solution, many of these adaptations associated with the reversible oxygenation of hemoglobin would have been in all likelihood impossible, and at the same time the advantage of the anomalous drop in viscosity when a suspension of particles is subjected to increased perfusion pressure would not accrue.

The Viscosity of Ice

Remarkably, the viscosity of ice, the solid form of water, is also adaptive for life on earth. Just as the viscosity of liquids varies greatly, the viscosity of solids also varies over many orders of magnitude. Pitch, one of the least viscous of solids, has a viscosity about 10^{12} (1 trillion) times greater than that of water, while ice, which is a crystalline solid, has a viscosity 10^{16} times that of water. The rocks which make up the crust of the earth have viscosities ranging between 10^{25} and 10^{28} times that of water. So the range of viscosities of solids is 10^{16}.[39] If the viscosity of ice had been several times lower than it is, then glacial activity would have been much less effective in grinding down the mountains and releasing vital minerals into the hydrosphere. If ice had the viscosity of pitch, then glaciers would only have been a few feet thick and would have run gently down mountainsides, making little impression on the much harder rocks that make up the earth's crust.

On the other hand, it is fortunate that the viscosity of ice is not much higher than it is. If it were anything approaching that of granite, then all the water on earth would be immobilized at the poles and on the high mountain ranges. The earth's higher latitudes would have been covered in vast sheets of granite-solid ice caps and the earth would have been sterile. There would be no liquid water on earth and no life. Today about 10 percent of the earth's water is locked up as ice in the Antarctic and Greenland ice caps. It is possible that even if the viscosity of ice had been only 100 times greater, there would have been far less liquid water on earth and the climate would have been subject to rapid fluctuations from extreme heat to extreme cold, and it is very doubtful whether life as rich as it now exists on earth would have evolved. The actual value of the viscosity of ice would appear to be yet another adaptation of "water" that ensures that large bodies of liquid water can exist on a planetary surface such as the earth's.

The Density of Water

Unlike viscosity, which varies over many orders of magnitude, the density of substances on earth varies much less. Tar, which has the same density as water, is billions of times more viscous. The density of water is 1 gram per cubic centimeter. The density of air at atmospheric pressure is about one-thousandth that of water; the density of tar and glycerol is about the same as water. The density of petrol is about 0.65 and that of many hydrocarbons ranges from between about 0.7 and 0.9 gram per cubic centimeter. Apart from the lipids and fats, many organic compounds which form the basic fabric of the cell have densities very close to that of water. Other well-known substances are more dense than water. Many common minerals have densities between three and seven times that of water. The density of two of the heaviest substances, mercury and gold, are 13.6 and 19 respectively.[40]

It is clear that as living organisms are made up largely of water, then the density of water largely determines their weight. In the case of large terrestrial organisms on a planet the size of the earth, if water were several times as dense, then the maximum size that could be attained would be only a fraction of that actually attained by existing organisms. An upright bipedal humanoid species of design similar to *Homo sapiens* would not be feasible, for the weight of the body might well prevent its being lifted off the ground and maintained in an upright position. Nor could the limbs be moved unless the proportion of muscle was greatly increased. This is because—for reasons that will be discussed in chapter 11—the power exerted by muscles per unit volume of muscle tissue cannot be much increased. If our limbs were four times their current weight, the muscles would have to be four times the volume to achieve the same level of mobility.

One set of adaptations that would theoretically be facilitated if water were less dense and organisms consequently less heavy per unit volume are those associated with flight. However, as far as aquatic life is concerned, the consequences of water having a density much less than 1 gram per cubic centimeter would be severe. In such a hypothetical world, all other things being equal, carbon-based life forms (composed of 30 percent nonaqueous materials, mainly organic carbon compounds) would tend to sink like lead balloons to the ocean floor. On the other hand, if water was just a fraction heavier than it is, all carbon-based aquatic life would be restricted to floating on the surface. It is doubtful that many life forms, particularly microorganisms, could survive the intense ultraviolet radiation that they would be subjected to if they were restricted permanently to the upper few millimeters of the sea.

Recent Discoveries

Over the last few decades additional properties of water have come to light which further confirm its remarkable fitness. Morowitz points out:

> The past few years have witnessed the developing study of a newly understood property of water [i.e., proton conductance] that appears to be almost unique to that substance, is a key element in biological-energy transfer, and was almost certainly of importance to the origin of life. The more we learn the more impressed some of us become with nature's fitness in a very precise sense. . . . Proton conductance has become a subject of central interest in biochemistry because of its role in photosynthesis and oxidative phosphorylation.[41]

As Morowitz explains, both these key processes use proton conductance and hydrated ions which are major features of water:

> Once again the fitness enters in, in the detailed way in which the molecular properties of water are matched to the molecular mechanisms of bioenergetics. A property never imagined in Henderson's time turns out to be a significant part of the fitness of the environment.[42]

Coincidence upon Coincidence

This very brief review of some of the properties of water is by no means exhaustive. There are in fact several other ways in which the properties of water are mutually fit for various biological processes, but these are more appropriately considered as they arise in consideration of the fitness of the other components of life in the following chapters. What is so very remarkable about the various physical properties of water cited above is not that each is so fit in itself, but the astonishing way in which, in many instances, several independent properties are adapted to serve cooperatively the same biological end.

Take, for example, the weathering of rocks and its end result, the distribution of the vital minerals upon which life depends via the rivers to the oceans and ultimately throughout the hydrosphere. It is the high surface tension of water which draws it into the crevices of the rock; it is its highly anomalous expansion on freezing which cracks the rock, producing additional crevices for further weathering and increasing the surface area available for the solvation action of water in leaching out the elements. On top of all this, ice possesses the appropriate viscosity and strength to form hard, grinding rivers or glaciers which reduce the rocks broken and fractured by repeated cycles of freezing and thawing to tiny particles of glacial silt. The low viscosity of water confers on it the ability to flow rapidly in rivers and mountain streams and to carry at high speed those tiny particles of rock and glacial silt which contribute further to the weathering process and the breaking down of the mountains. The chemical reactivity of water and its great solvation power also contribute to the weathering process, dissolving out the minerals and elements from the rocks and eventually distributing them throughout the hydrosphere.

The properties of water which enhance weathering.

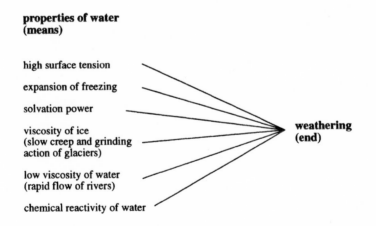

Consider also the way the various thermal properties of water cooperate to preserve large bodies of water on the surface of the earth. First, when water is cooled, its high heat capacity retards its rate of cooling. As it cools below 4°C, the coolest water rises to the surface, forming an insulating blanket on the surface which prevents further heat loss. Eventually, the surface layer freezes—a process which because of the high latent heat of fusion gives out a considerable amount of heat, thus retarding further the temperature fall. After ice has formed, because it is lighter than water, it remains on the surface, preventing, because of its poor conductivity, further cooling of the water below. Further freezing now occurs at the interface between the ice and the water so that the latent heat given out will be trapped, because of the poor conductivity of ice, *below the surface of the ice,* thereby warming the water below and thus retarding further cooling. Eventually, no matter how cold the air above the sea, the layer of ice will not increase beyond a few meters thick. Moreover, if large quantities of ice are formed in some situations because of the relatively low viscosity of ice, eventually it flows downhill or outward toward warmer temperatures or toward the sea, where it inevitably melts, generating liquid water again.

The properties of water which together tend to preserve it in the liquid state.

**properties of water
(means)**

high thermal capacity

conductivity of water

expansion of water on freezing

expansion of water below 4°C ————————→ **preservation of liquid water
(end)**

low heat conductivity of ice

high latent heat of freezing

relatively high viscosity of ice

Keeping Cool

As a final example, consider the way that the large heat capacity, high latent heat of evaporation, heat conductivity, and low viscosity conspire together to serve the end of temperature regulation in a large organism like a man.

All activity, including the work of machines, requires the expenditure of energy, and this necessarily involves the generation of heat. During a one-hour run over a distance of ten miles, an average man will generate a considerable amount of heat. Yet at the end of the run his body temperature will only be raised a few degrees. We are so familiar with this fact that it never occurs to us that there might be something unusual about it. But in fact it is a remarkable phenomenon.

Altogether, the work expended when a 100-kilogram man runs 10 miles in one hour will generate approximately 1,000 kilocalories of heat. If none of this heat were lost from the body during the run, it would raise the temperature of the body by 10°C. Such a temperature rise would almost certainly be fatal. If the body was constructed mainly out of, say, iron, salt, lead, or alcohol, rather than water, the temperature would be raised by 100°C, 50°C, 300°C, and 20°C respectively. The reason for the relatively modest rise in body temperature of only 10°C is that the heat capacity of water is greater than most other substances and greater than all known liquids except ammonia within the temperature range commonly encountered on the earth's surface.

But water has another unique advantage for temperature regulation. As we saw above, the latent heat of vaporization of water is the highest of any liquid in the ambient temperature range. Thus, in addition to buffering the rise in temperature, because of its very great heat capacity, the very great cooling effect when it evaporates from the skin further attenuates the rise in temperature. The evaporation of one liter of sweat from a 100-kilogram man removes about 600 kilocalories of heat from the body, lowering the body temperature by 6°C. If water was substituted for, say, alcohol or ammonia, then the cooling on evaporation would only be 2.2°C and 3.6°C respectively. Moreover, at body temperature, radiation and conduction are insufficient to rid the body of heat, so the whole burden is thrown on evaporation.

But there is much more to the story than this. Even these two nearly unique thermal properties of water would not in themselves be sufficient to maintain temperature stability unless the heat generated in the core of the body could be transported to the surface of the body. There are only two ways by which this could be done: conduction or convection.

The range of thermal conductivities among common substances is considerable. Silver and copper, for example, two of the most efficient heat conductors, have thermal conductivities more than ten thousand times greater than some of the poorest conductors, like silica gel and wood, and some thousand times greater than that of water. Liquids are poor conductors compared with metals, but of all liquids, again water is at a unique maximum, having a thermal conductivity several times as great as the vast majority of liquids at ambient temperatures.[43]

Although the thermal conductivity of water is high compared with most other liquids, it is still too low to transport heat from the center of the body to the periphery at the rate required to rid animals of the heat generated by metabolism. Only if conduction is assisted by some sort of convection mechanism is it possible to transfer heat from the core of the body to the skin. There is indeed such a convection mechanism: the circulatory system, which conveys in the average adult man nearly 6 liters of blood throughout the body, through every organ, via the capillaries, every minute carrying with it any heat generated in the body's core to the periphery. But the circulatory system, as we have seen, in turn depends on another important physical property of water, its viscosity, having almost precisely the very low value it does.

If the conductivity of water had been several times less, like that of absorbent cotton or wood, then even with the circulatory system conductivity would almost certainly have been too low to transfer heat to the surface of the body, and its elimination from the body, especially in situations of strenuous exercise, would pose insurmountable problems. The body would seize up like an overheated car engine. On the other hand, if the thermal conductivity of water was many times more, like that of copper, then the temperature of living things would equilibrate very rapidly with their environment, so that temperature regulation would be far more difficult to achieve. Changes in the environmental temperature would be rapidly conducted (as is the case with a piece of metal) throughout the body of the organism, which consequently would suffer continual swings of temperature. Small warm-blooded animals would probably be impossible, and even a large organism would experience difficulties in drinking a large quantity of cold water. To be fit for macroscopic life the thermal conductivity of water must be close to what it is.

We see, then, that the very modest rise in body temperature after strenuous exercise is no ordinary phenomenon. It turns out to be dependent on the unique fitness of water as a buffer against changes in temperature. This fitness is dependent on four quite different physical properties of water that all exhibit a coincidental mutual fitness and which together perfectly fit water for this biological role.

No other liquid is known which can even remotely approach the fitness of water for temperature regulation of a large terrestrial carbon-based form of life at the ambient temperature range of 0°C to 50°C. And, moreover, although some liquids such as ammonia and liquid sodium exhibit some of the thermal properties of water, none possess quite the same set of mutually adaptive properties. At certain temperatures liquid sodium, for example, exhibits a higher latent heat of evaporation than water but its thermal conductivity is very many times more than water, too high to permit any theoretical organism based in that medium to maintain a steady temperature in the face of environmental challenges.

Heat loss in our marathon runner involves the following adaptations:

The properties of water involved in temperature regulation.

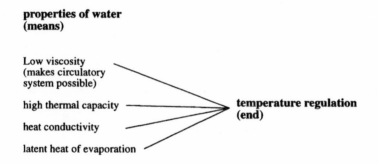

Conclusion

The evidence reviewed in this chapter indicates that water is uniquely and ideally adapted to serve as the fluid medium for life on earth in not just one, or many, but in *every single one* of its known physical and chemical characteristics.

The unique and ideal fitness of water can be illustrated in graphic form by plotting all known fluids against their utility for carbon-based life as shown on page 46.

As Henderson concluded,

> If doubts remain, let a search be made for any other substance which, however slightly, can claim to rival water as the milieu of simple organisms, as the milieu intérieur of all living things or in any of the countless physiological functions which it performs.[44]

The unique fitness of water.

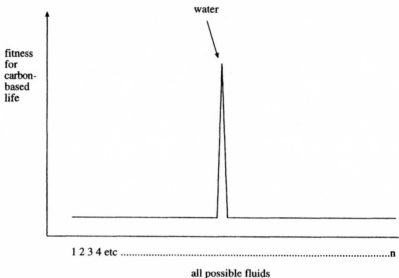

all possible fluids

There is indeed no other candidate fluid which is remotely competitive with water as the medium for carbon-based life. If water did not exist, it would have to be invented. Without the long chain of vital coincidences in the physical and chemical properties of water, carbon-based life could not exist in any form remotely comparable with that which exists on earth. And we, as intelligent carbon-based life forms, would almost certainly not be here to wonder at the life-giving properties of this vital fluid. And if there is life like our own anywhere in the cosmos on some other earth, there will also be water and in all probability there will be seas and rivers and clouds and rain. There will be storms and waterfalls and icebergs, and surf will break on the beaches of that distant world.

In the many mutually adaptive properties of this most remarkable of all fluids, we are brought dramatically face-to-face with an extraordinary body of evidence of precisely the sort we would expect on the hypothesis that the laws of nature are uniquely fit for our own type of carbon-based life as it exists on earth.

Chapter 3

The Fitness of
the Light

*In which it is shown that the electromagnetic radiation reaching
the surface of the earth is uniquely fit for carbon-based life. The
sun's radiation is mainly in the visual range—from the near
ultraviolet to the near infrared. Not only is most of the
electromagnetic radiation outside this tiny range harmful to life,
but the energy levels within the visual spectrum are precisely fit
for photochemistry. Remarkably, the atmospheric gases,
including water vapor and liquid water, absorb virtually all the
harmful radiation outside the visual range and transmit only
this tiny band of biologically useful radiation. These
coincidences provide convincing evidence of nature's fitness for
carbon-based life. On top of its utility for photochemistry the
wavelength and energy levels of visual light are fit for biological
vision with a camera-type eye of the sort utilized in higher
vertebrates, including man. Like water, the light of the sun
appears to be of optimal biological utility.*

The electromagnetic spectrum.

The range of electromagnetic wavelengths is 10^{25}. As shown in the figure, the shortest gamma rays have wavelengths of 10^{-16} microns and the longest radio waves have wavelengths of about a kilometer or 10^9 microns (one micron is one-millionth of a meter or one thousandth of a millimeter).

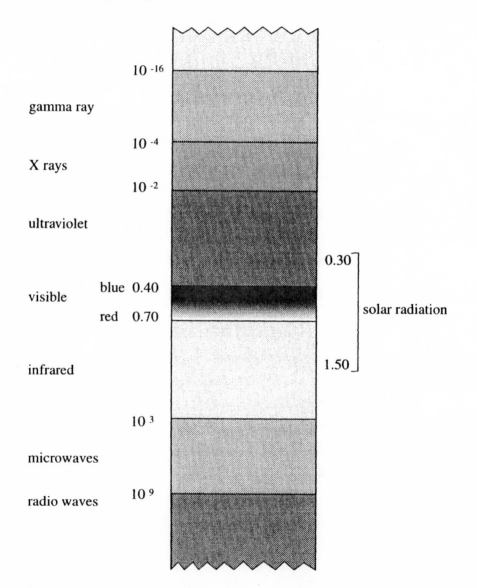

Think of the Sun's heat on your upturned face on a cloudless summer's day; think how dangerous it is to gaze at the Sun directly. From 150 million kilometers away, we recognize its power. What would we feel on its seething self-luminous surface, or immersed in its heart of nuclear fire? The Sun warms us and feeds us and permits us to see. It fecundated the Earth. It is powerful beyond human experience. Birds greet the sunrise with an audible ecstasy. Even some one-celled organisms know to swim to the light. Our ancestors worshipped the Sun and they were far from foolish.

—Carl Sagan, *Cosmos,* 1980

It may form an interesting intellectual exercise to imagine ways in which life might arise and having arisen might maintain itself, on a dark planet; but I doubt very much that this has ever happened, or that it can happen.

—George Wald, *Scientific American* magazine, 1959

As Sagan so rightly comments, ancient man was right to worship the sun as the giver and sustainer of life.[1] The sun provides heat and light, both of which are essential to life.

It is the heat provided by solar radiation in the infrared region of the spectrum which warms the earth, keeping the mean temperature of the earth above the freezing point of water and within the temperature range where the chemical reactions upon which life depends can occur. It is the sun's heat which energizes the great water cycle, drawing water by evaporation from the oceans into the atmosphere which then, via the precipitation of rain and snow, forms rivers and glaciers which carry the evaporated water back again to the ocean. And it is the energy provided by solar radiation within the visual region of the spectrum which drives the process of photosynthesis through which light energy is utilized to synthesize the fuels of life, the sugars and fats, which power the activities of virtually all complex forms of life on earth.

The sun's radiation is essential in two ways: it provides the heat energy which keeps the earth's temperature within the appropriate range for life and it provides the light energy necessary for photosynthesis.

The Electromagnetic Spectrum

Both heat and light are forms of radiant energy known as electromagnetic radiation. All the various different types of electromagnetic radiation, including heat and light, flow through space in the form of energy waves analogous to ripples on the surface of a pond. And just as the waves on the surface of a pond may have different wavelengths—small ripples may be only a few centimeters from crest to crest, while large waves might be more than a meter—so similarly the wavelength of the various types of electromagnetic radiation also varies, but over a vastly greater range.

The longest electromagnetic waves are radio waves, which measure several kilometers across (10^9 microns), while the smallest are the gamma rays, which measure less than a trillionth of a centimeter (10^{-16} microns) across. The wavelength of microwaves is around 1 centimeter (10^4 microns). The wavelength of visible light ranges from about one ten-thousandth of a centimeter (0.70 microns) at the long, or red, end of the spectrum to about one twenty-five-thousandth of a centimeter (0.40 microns) at the short, or blue, end of the spectrum. The wavelength of infrared, or heat, radiation ranges from one ten-thousandth of a centimeter (1 micron) to one-tenth of a centimeter (10^3 microns).

Note that the wavelength of the longest type of electromagnetic radiation is unimaginably longer than the shortest by a factor of 10^{25}, or 10,000,000,000,000,000,000,000,000. Some idea of the immensity this figure represents can be grasped by the fact that the number of seconds since the formation of the earth 4 billion years ago, is *only* about 10^{17}. To count 10^{25} seconds we would have to keep counting every day and night through a period of time equal to *100 million times the age of the earth!* If we were to build a pile of 10^{25} playing cards, we would end up with a stack stretching halfway across the observable universe.

Remarkably, although the wavelength of electromagnetic radiation in the cosmos varies over such a colossal range, 70 percent of the electromagnetic radiation emitted from the surface of the sun is concentrated in an exceedingly narrow radiation band extending from the near ultraviolet (0.3 microns) through the visible light range into the near infrared (1.50 microns). This minute band represents the unimaginably small fraction of approximately one part in 10^{25} of the entire electromagnetic spectrum—equivalent to one playing card in a stack of cards stretching halfway across the cosmos, or one second in 100 quadrillion (100,000,000,000,000,000) years.

There is nothing exceptional about this amazing compaction of the sun's radiant energy into such a small radiation band. The spectrum of radiation emitted by a star is determined by its surface temperature. The temperature of the sun's surface is close to 6,000°C. Because the sun is an "ordinary, even mediocre, star,"[2] being about in the middle of the range of stellar temperatures and sizes, many stars have surface temperatures close to this value and emit nearly all their radiation in this same very small band.

Solar Radiation

When electromagnetic radiation interacts with matter, energy is imparted. If the radiation is highly energetic in the X-ray or gamma-ray regions, this can tear atoms and molecules apart. On the other hand, radiation in the radio region imparts so little energy that it passes through matter with hardly any detectable effect. Only radiation in this tiny band—in the visual and infrared region—interacts gently enough with matter to be of utility to life. Consequently, the fact that the sun's radiation (and that of many main sequence stars) is compressed into this tiny region of the spectrum is of enormous biological significance.

Atoms and molecules only react together when they possess energies equal to or greater than a particular threshold value, which is known as their energy of activation. For the great majority of chemical reactions which occur in living things, the activation energy of the reactions (the amount of energy needed to cause a chemical reaction between two molecules) generally lies between 15 and 65 kilocalories per mole. The common way of expressing these energy levels is in terms of quantity of heat—i.e., calories—per quantity of matter (moles). These energy levels are provided by electromagnetic radiation between 0.80 microns and 0.32 microns, more or less exactly that provided by visible light.[3] Radiation at wavelengths slightly longer than 0.70 microns is too weak to raise molecules into energy states which can activate chemical reactions. But on the other hand, radiation in the ultraviolet (shorter than 0.30 microns) is too energetic and causes disruption of life's delicate molecular structures.

The correspondence between the "energy needs" of biological chemistry and the "energy levels" of solar radiation was discussed by George Wald in a well-known *Scientific American* article entitled "Life and Light." As Wald comments, "the radiation that is useful in promoting orderly chemical reactions comprises the great bulk of that of our sun. The commonly stated limit of human vision—400–700 millimicrons—already includes 41% of the sun's radiant energy."[4] The diagram below illustrates the intensity of solar radiation between 0.20 microns and 1.50 microns.[5]

Infrared radiation is also essential to life but for a different reason. When radiation in the infrared region of the spectrum interacts with matter, energy is imparted, which causes the random movement and vibration of atoms and molecules to increase. This we register as heat. As already mentioned, it is the heat imparted to the earth by radiation in the infrared region of the spectrum that keeps the earth's hydrosphere warm, keeps water a liquid, and drives the climatic systems and the water cycle.

Moreover, heat energy is important in another way. At least some heat is necessary for chemical reactions, because to interact chemically with one another, atoms and molecules must come into contact and this can only occur if they are in motion and may collide. Note, however, that heat energy is only of utility to the orderly chemical processes of life in a narrow temperature range—approximately that in which water is a liquid, a point discussed again in chapter 5. The heat imparted to the earth's hydrosphere by infrared

The solar spectrum, showing the intensity of the sun's radiation between 0.1 and 1.50 microns.

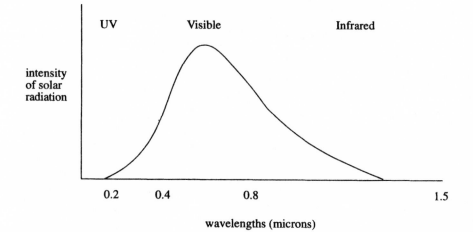

wavelengths (microns)

radiation from the sun would, if unchecked, eventually raise the temperature of the earth by many hundreds of degrees. At such temperatures the velocity of atomic and molecular collisions becomes such that the orderly chemistry of life is impossible. The earth escapes this fate because—via a variety of feedback systems (see next chapter) and other not fully understood controls—over time heat loss exactly balances heat gain.

That the radiation from the sun (and from many main sequence stars) should be concentrated into a minuscule band of the electromagnetic spectrum which provides precisely the radiation required to maintain life on earth is a very remarkable coincidence described as "staggering" by Ian Campbell in *Energy and the Atmosphere.*[6] Note that the compaction of solar radiation into the visible and near infrared is determined by a completely different set of physical laws to those that dictate which wavelengths are suitable for photobiology.

Our amazement grows further when we note that not only is the radiant energy in this tiny region the *only radiation of utility to life* but that radiant energy in most other regions of the spectrum is *either lethal or profoundly damaging.* Electromagnetic radiation from gamma rays through X rays to ultraviolet rays is all harmful to life. Similarly, radiation in the far infrared and microwave regions is also damaging to life. Just about the only region of the electromagnetic spectrum which is harmless to life apart from the visible and the near infrared is the region of very long wavelength radiation—the radio waves. So the sun not only puts out all its radiant energy in the tiny band of utility to life but virtually *none, in those regions of the spectrum which are harmful to life.* This coincidence is expressed in graphic form in the two diagrams below.

The electromagnetic spectrum and radiant energy output of the sun.

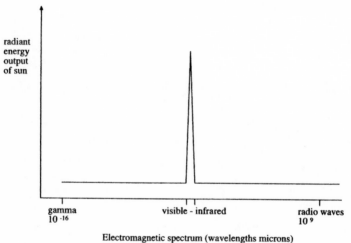

Electromagnetic spectrum (wavelengths microns)

The region of the electromagnetic spectrum of utility for photochemistry.

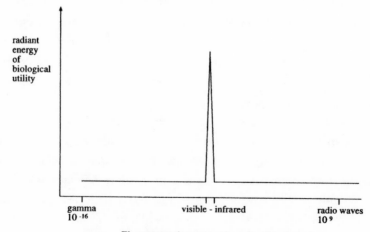

Electromagnetic spectrum (wavelengths microns)

The Absorption of the Atmosphere

Now this is a remarkable enough coincidence in itself. But there are further coincidences to consider. To be of any utility to life, the radiation of the sun has to reach the surface of the earth. To do so it must pass through the atmosphere. Necessarily, any atmosphere surrounding a terraqueous planet containing carbon-based life is bound to contain some carbon dioxide gas, water vapor, at least some nitrogen, and for advanced highly active life forms considerable concentrations of oxygen. It is difficult to see how the actual concentrations of these gases could be very different from what they are in any atmosphere supporting a carbon-based biosphere (see discussion in chapter 6). At the temperature range that exists at the earth's surface, there is bound to be water vapor in considerable amounts in the atmosphere.

The fact that the atmospheric gases oxygen, nitrogen, carbon dioxide, and water vapor transmit 80 percent of the sun's radiation in the visible and near infrared and allow it to reach the earth's surface is another coincidence of enormous significance. The great majority of all atoms and molecular substances are completely opaque to visible light and radiation in the near-infrared region of the spectrum. Window glass, an example of a transparent solid which transmits light in the visible region, is exceptional. If the atmosphere had contained gases or other substances which absorbed strongly visible light, then no life-giving light would have reached the surface of the earth. In the case of nearly all solid substances, layers only a fraction of a millimeter thick are sufficient to prevent the penetration of light. Even the atmospheric gases themselves absorb electromagnetic radiation very strongly in those regions of the spectrum immediately on either side of the visible and near infrared. The diagram below indicates the spectral regions absorbed by the atmosphere.[7] Note that the only region of the spectrum allowed to pass through the atmosphere over the entire range of electromagnetic radiation from radio to gamma rays is the exceedingly narrow band including the visible and near infrared. Virtually no gamma, X, ultraviolet, far-infrared, and microwave radiation reaches the surface of the earth.

Despite these three remarkable coincidences, life would still not be possible without a fourth coincidence—the fact that liquid water is highly transparent to visible light.

The regions of the electromagnetic spectrum absorbed by the atmosphere.

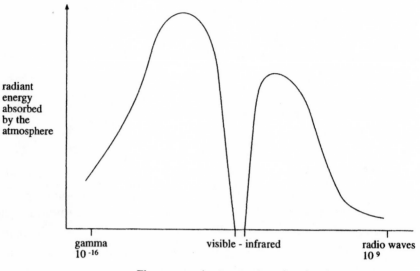

Electromagnetic spectrum (wavelengths microns)

The Absorption of Water

The significance of the transparency of water to light cannot be exaggerated. All biological chemistry occurs in liquid water. If the energy of sunlight is to sustain life in the ocean then it must be capable of penetrating some distance below the surface of the sea. Even on land if light energy is to reach the chemical machinery of the cell it must invariably penetrate a thin layer of water.

Nearly all electromagnetic wavelengths are strongly absorbed by water, except radio waves and light within the visible spectrum.[8] Even far ultraviolet and infrared radiation, the two bands immediately adjacent to the visible band, are absorbed readily by water and only penetrate a fraction of a millimeter below the surface. The absorption of visible light by water varies markedly across the visible spectrum. No red light can be observed below 18 meters. Yellow light only penetrates to 100 meters. By 240 meters most of the green and blue light has been absorbed. The absorbency spectrum of liquid water is shown in the diagram below.[9]

The very remarkable fact that the only region of the spectrum allowed through the atmosphere and allowed to penetrate liquid water is the tiny range of the spectrum useful for life is commented on in the latest edition

The regions of the electromagnetic spectrum absorbed by water.

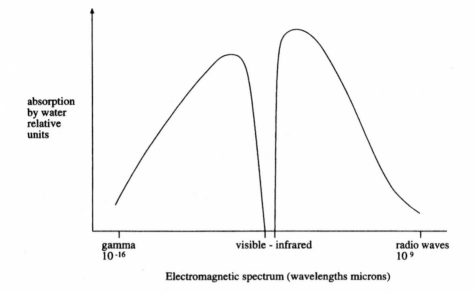

Electromagnetic spectrum (wavelengths microns)

(15th) of the *Encyclopaedia Britannica:* "Considering the importance of visible sunlight for all aspects of terrestrial life, one cannot help being *awed* by the dramatically narrow window in the atmospheric absorption . . . and in the absorption spectrum of water."[10] (My emphasis.)

The fact that light at the blue end of the spectrum penetrates further into water than light at the red end may explain why chlorophyll so strongly absorbs light in the blue region. The question as to why in a biocentric world chlorophyll should absorb light in a region of the solar spectrum where the incident radiation is not maximum is raised in chapter 9. We have here in the differential penetration of light a possible answer to the conundrum. Photosynthesis in water, especially several meters below the surface, is only possible if chlorophyll absorbs light in the blue end of the spectrum.

The fact that water absorbs light in the far ultraviolet is of obvious biological significance, as it acts as another device to shield life from the damaging influence of ultraviolet radiation. Note that there are three independent mechanisms attenuating the UV flux reaching biological systems:

1. The radiant output of the sun falls dramatically from 0.40 microns to 0.30 microns so that very little ultraviolet radiation leaves the sun in the first place.

2. Ozone in the upper atmosphere absorbs UV light strongly below 0.30 microns.

3. Water (liquid and vapor) absorbs strongly below 0.20 microns.

These factors together create a discontinuity at about 0.30 microns (see diagram below).

The fact that water absorbs damaging UV radiation while allowing visual light to penetrate to considerable depths has a very important consequence; it means that photosynthesis can occur in water even in the absence of the protective ozone layer. This apparently esoteric fact was of crucial significance to the evolution of life on earth because it allowed primitive microscopic plant life to thrive in the primeval oceans before the advent of oxygen and the protection of ozone. It was through their activities that the original anoxic atmosphere was eventually converted to the oxygen-containing atmosphere of today. *If damaging UV radiation had penetrated as deeply as visual light, then photosynthesis could never have been exploited to generate the current oxygen-containing atmosphere.* And as we shall see in chapter 6, without oxygen in the atmosphere, actively metabolizing complex multicellular life forms would not have been possible, and lacking the protection of ozone, terrestrial plant and animal life would have been enormously constrained if not impossible. In a very real sense, the existence of all complex life on earth is dependent on the relative absorbance of UV and visual light in water being very close to what it is.

The very small amount of ultraviolet radiation that does reach the earth's

Mechanisms attenuating the ultraviolet flux reaching the earth's surface.

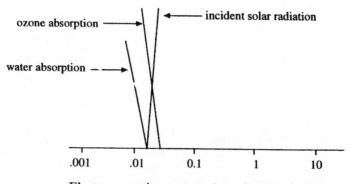

Electromagnetic spectrum (wavelength microns)

surface has clearly not hindered the evolution and development of life on earth. The spectacular success and persistence of life over the past 4 billion years indicates that life can thrive when subjected to at least some ultraviolet radiation and that the ultraviolet reaching the earth's surface must have had little, if any, deleterious effect on life in general. In fact, very small amounts of ultraviolet may have played a significant role in evolution by raising slightly the average mutation rate. Without mutations, there can be no evolutionary change, and it is possible that the raised levels of mutation caused by the ultraviolet flux could have played a critical role in the evolutionary history of life.

In man and other vertebrates ultraviolet radiation (between 0.29 and 0.32 microns) is essential for the synthesis of vitamin D. This occurs in the skin when it is irradiated by ultraviolet light. As vitamin D is vital for the maintenance and control of calcium levels in the body and for the formation of bone in all vertebrates, and as the only means of its synthesis is via ultraviolet light in the skin, then as far as humans are concerned, ultraviolet light is essential to life. The fact that a vital vitamin is produced in this way raises the question as to whether low levels of ultraviolet radiation may have other important biological influences.[11] Another important role of near UV light may be the photochemical release of nitrogen from aquatic dissolved organic matter. This plays an important role in the recycling of nitrogen in marine and freshwater ecosystems.[12]

As well as strongly absorbing ultraviolet light, liquid water also strongly absorbs radiant energy in the infrared region. Very little radiation in the infrared region penetrates more than a few millimeters into water, which means that all the heat reaching the surface of the sea is absorbed and retained in the surface layers.[13] As was mentioned in chapter 2, water, like all other fluids, is a poor conductor of heat. This helps retain the heat in the surface layers of the ocean. Consequently, in most parts of the sea there is a relatively thin surface layer about 20 meters thick of warm, less dense water. Below 100 meters the temperature of the sea in all parts of the globe falls rapidly till it reaches about 4°C at 1,000 meters below the surface. The retention of heat in the thin surface layer facilitates the transference of heat to the air and winds and by surface currents to colder regions of the ocean, thereby assisting in the maintenance of global temperature equilibration. In the higher latitudes this retention of the heat at the surface of the ocean tends to slow down the rate of freezing.

So both the transparency of water to visible light and its opacity to infrared radiation contribute to the fitness of the earth's hydrosphere for life. The radiation needed for photobiology, radiation in the visible region of the spectrum, penetrates to depths of 100 meters, while the infrared needed to warm the hydrosphere and drive the climate and the water cycle is retained in the surface layers where its utility is greatest. And in addition, all highly destructive ultraviolet radiation below 0.20 microns is almost entirely absorbed in the first few millimeters.

Another fascinating aspect of the fitness of the electromagnetic spectrum for life is the fact that both types of useful radiation, the visible and the infrared, are adjacent in the spectrum. What we have in effect are two adjacent playing cards back-to-back in a deck which extends across the cosmos. Just as the transparency of water to visible light and the fitness of the solar radiation for photochemistry are of necessity, so the close proximity of these two vital types of radiant energy gives every appearance of also being of necessity. If these two vital types of radiation were far apart in the spectrum, the possibility of prearranging nature so that they could both reach the surface of a watery planet in appropriate quantities from one unique source, such as the sun, would in all probability have been impossible.

We should indeed be *awed* and *staggered* by this series of coincidences: that the electromagnetic radiation of the sun should be restricted to a tiny region of the total electromagnetic spectrum, equivalent to one specific playing card in a deck of 10^{25} cards stretching across the universe; that the very same infinitely minute region should be precisely that required for life; that the atmospheric gases should be opaque to all regions of the spectrum except this same tiny region; that water should likewise be opaque to all regions of the spectrum save this same infinitesimally tiny region, etc. It is as if a cardplayer had drawn precisely the same card on four occasions from a deck of 10^{25}.

Even with all these coincidences, unless the sun's radiation reaching the earth's surface had remained virtually constant throughout the past 4 billion years, life could never have survived and evolved as it has. The sun is fit as an energy source for carbon-based life forms not only in providing radiant energy with precisely the levels necessary for life, but also because it has provided that vital and necessary energy at an almost perfectly constant intensity for unimaginable eons of time. Even the slightest change in the output of radiant energy from the sun at any stage during the history of life would have had disastrous consequences.

Alternatives to Light

Life does not depend on light. There is a vast diversity of microbial species which can survive in total darkness and which derive energy from the oxidation of substances such as hydrogen, hydrogen sulfide, and ferrous iron that are generated by geochemical processes in the earth's crust. It is even possible that a considerable proportion of the earth's biomass may consist of bacteria in the crustal rocks. Near the deep-sea hydrothermal vents a quite complex community of multicellular species is sustained by nutrients synthesized by bacteria which derive their energy from the oxidation of sulfides released from the vents. Geothermal springs are another site where a complex biota of microorganisms derive energy from the oxidation of hydrogen sulfide.[14] However, it is difficult to imagine how these other potential sources of energy could sustain complex aquatic or terrestrial ecosystems on the surface of a planet like the earth. And it is difficult to envisage the evolution of advanced and complex life forms in such restricted environments as microscopic fissures in the crustal rocks, thermal springs, or deep-sea hydrothermal vents.

In the last analysis, there is no alternative to stellar radiation to sustain a rich and diverse biosphere over billions of years on a planetary surface like the earth's. If the radiant energy of stars was not fit for photochemistry and to provide the heat to energize a hydrosphere like that which exists on earth, then the cosmos would in all probability be only capable of sustaining carbon-based biospheres far less complex than our own.

Fitness for Vision

The light of the sun is uniquely fit in yet another way for life on earth—the energy levels and wavelength of electromagnetic radiation in the visual spectrum are both uniquely fit for high-resolution vision.

One reason that visual light is fit for biological vision is that if an eye is to "see" it must be able to detect the type of radiation forming the image. Light radiation is the only type of electromagnetic radiation that has the appropriate energy level for detection by biological systems. UV, X ray, and gamma rays are too energetic and are highly destructive, while infrared and radio waves are too weak to be detected because they impart so little in energy interacting with matter. Moreover, most electromagnetic radiation outside the visual region is strongly absorbed by water and other biological materials, so it is difficult to imagine what biological substances could be utilized for the construction of a lens sufficiently transparent to transmit and focus the radiation. Our ability to discriminate between different wavelengths in the visual spectrum—i.e., to see colors—is also dependent on the perfect correspondence between the energy levels of electromagnetic radiation in the visual region and those required for photochemical detection by biological systems.

Not only are the *energy levels* and absorbance characteristics of light waves fit for detection by biological systems, but the *actual length of the waves* in the visual region of the spectrum is perfectly fit for the high-resolution camera-type eye of the precise design and dimension as that found in all higher vertebrate species, including man.

Instrumental Constraints

The wavelength of light imposes constraints on the design and dimension of the eye mainly because of the phenomenon of diffraction, which is an inevitable consequence of the wave nature of light itself. Like the ocean swell entering a small harbor, when light waves pass through a small aperture, they suffer dispersion or diffraction. As a consequence, when light from a point source in the visual field (A or B, in the diagram below) passes through the pupil and is focused on the retina, instead of being focused to a point, it spreads out into a tiny disc surrounded by concentric rings (a, b). The disc is known as the Airy disc.(See opposite.)

And again just like an ocean swell entering a harbor, where the degree of diffraction is determined by the size of the swell, in the case of light, the larger the wavelength, the larger the diffractional effect, the larger the Airy disc, and the poorer the resolution. At any wavelength the phenomenon of diffraction and its consequence, the Airy disc, imposes a limit on the resolving power of any sort of optical instrument, camera, or eye.

In addition to wavelength, the other factor which influences diffraction is aperture. And again in terms of the ocean swell–harbor analogy, just as the greater the opening of the harbor the less the swell is diffracted, so the greater the aperture the less the diffraction in the case of an optical instrument.

In short, the size of the Airy disc is determined by two primary factors— the *wavelength of the radiation* itself and the *size of the aperture* of the instrument.

The Airy disc.

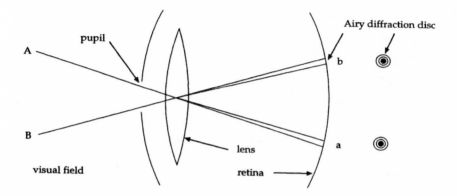

To achieve optimal resolving power the effect of diffraction must be minimized. One way this may be achieved is by increasing the size of the aperture. The resolving power of the Mount Palomar telescope is a thousand times greater than that of the human eye, mainly because its aperture (the mirror) is approximately a thousand times wider than the pupil of the human eye.

Unfortunately, in the case of the eye, which focuses an image by refraction through a lens, because chromatic and spherical aberration also increase as the aperture is increased, increasing the size of the aperture can only bring limited improvement in resolution. Therefore, minimizing the effect of diffraction involves the satisfaction of several conflicting criteria: if the aperture of an eye or a camera is increased, then the diffraction may be decreased and resolution improved but spherical aberration is also increased, thereby minimizing any improvement that might have been gained; if the pupil or aperture is decreased, then although spherical and chromatic aberration is decreased, diffraction effects increase and the resolution is decreased while at the same time the illumination of the retina (or photographic plate in the case of a camera) is decreased, and so on.[15]

Although large telescopes have very much greater resolving power (aperture) than the vertebrate eye, their field of view is far smaller and only distant objects can be brought into focus. In the case of an eye, any advantage that might be gained in resolution would be more than offset in the case of an organism by the decrease in the field of view and the inability to bring objects close at hand into focus.

Consideration of the many conflicting criteria which must be satisfied in attempting to optimize the resolution of a camera-type eye utilizing light of a wavelength of about 0.5 microns, including minimizing diffraction, maximizing illumination, maximizing field of view, minimizing spherical and chromatic aberration, etc., suggests that all high-resolution optical devices will necessarily be of the same design and dimensions. Each will consist of a small lightproof hollow rounded structure between 1 and 6 centimeters in diameter, containing at the front an aperture or "pupil" through which the light can enter, capable of varying from about 1 to 8 millimeters in diameter, and a lens through which the light can be focused onto a light-sensitive plate. In fact, all high-resolution vertebrate eyes and high-quality modern cameras approximate to this design.

In such an eye, the minimum-sized Airy disc formed on the retina from a point source of light will be about *2 microns* in diameter, which is the size of the Airy disc in many vertebrates, including man. This cannot be reduced and represents the optimum resolving power of the vertebrate eye. As one of the foremost authorities in this area, Horace Barlow comments:[16] "It is easy to verify that the highest resolving power achieved by man is quite close to the limiting resolution set by the diameter of the pupil and the wavelength of light."

Note that although many factors influence the resolving power of the vertebrate eye, it is the *actual wavelength of light* itself, or more specifically the degree of diffraction that inevitably occurs when radiation of that specific wavelength passes through an aperture, which more than any other factor determines the actual dimensions of the high-resolution vertebrate camera eye. For example, if the wavelength of light had been ten times less (0.05 microns), then an eye with the resolving power of the human eye would need to be only a few millimeters in diameter. Conversely, if the wavelength of light had been ten times greater (5 microns), then an eye with the same resolving power would need to be 25 centimeters in diameter—larger than the human head.

Note that the optimized vertebrate camera eye is quite a large object on the scale of all biological structures on earth, which range from about ten-thousandths of a micron, the size of small subcellular structures, to 100 meters (1 billion microns) in the case of a California redwood. Clearly, if the minimum possible size of the camera-type eye constructed out of biological materials had been only ten or twenty times more, then no large organism would have possessed high-acuity vision. To begin with, its shape must be held in an approximately globular conformation. This is partly achieved in the case of many vertebrates by placing the eye in a round bony socket (which also preserves the eye's delicate structure from damage). Another adaptation which helps maintain the spherical shape of the eye is the maintenance of a relatively high hydrostatic pressure in the interior of the eye.[17] But even with these adaptations, the globe of the human eye still suffers some degree of distortion.[18] In the case of some whales, which have the largest eyes of any mammal, more than half the mass within the globe is made up of an immensely thickened tough fibrous coat. So thick is this coating that it may make up three-quarters of the length of the anteroposterior axis of the eyeball. This is considered by some to be an adaptation to maintain the approximately spherical shape of the eye against distortion when the whale dives to great depths.[19] The size of the lens, which is made up of living tissue and which must obtain its nutrients by diffusion, must also place an upper limit on the size of the vertebrate camera-type eye. From these and many other considerations it seems likely that the size of the vertebrate camera eye approximates closely to the maximum possible size of a camera-type eye constructed out of biological materials.

But although the high-resolution camera eye is quite a large structure, it is still small enough for function and anatomical placement in a very wide variety of large terrestrial organisms, including the human species.

Thus, various factors, including the wavelength of light, diffraction, the size of aperture, and chromatic and spherical aberration, together impose what we might term, after Horace Barlow, an *instrumental* limit on the resolution of the camera-type eye. However, this *instrumental* limit is not the only limit to the resolving power of the eye.

Micro-optical Constraints

Clearly, no eye can resolve images smaller than the diameter of its individual photoreceptor units, and because of the inevitable constraints on cell design it is difficult to envisage photoreceptors much smaller than a few microns in diameter. (Most cells in higher organisms are between 10 and 50 microns in diameter.) This suggests that the cellular limit cannot be far removed from the *instrumental* limit of 2 microns imposed by the various factors alluded to above. Interestingly, the smallest photoreceptors in the vertebrate retina are in fact about 2 microns across.[20]

Moreover, recent work in the field of fiber optics suggests that even if photoreceptors could be theoretically reduced in size below 2 microns in diameter, no improvement in resolving power would be gained because there are other constraints arising from the wavelength of light which impose a minimum size on photoreceptor cells.[21] As one authority comments: "Optical cross talk between receptors would occur if they were smaller and packed more closely together than about 2 microns. . . . On this view, limiting retinal resolution, expressed in linear units, is the same in all eyes and results from the properties of light passing through a set of waveguides. As expected on this view, cones smaller than 2 microns across have never been found."[22]

This is another remarkable coincidence. The two optical limits to the resolving power of the eye—the one set by the waveguide optics of the photoreceptor, which we might refer to as the *micro-optical* limit; the other set by the laws of classical optics relating to the resolving power of a camera-type eye, the *instrumental* limit—*have the same value: 2 microns.* Moreover, both these limits imposed on the resolving power of the eye, the micro-optical and the instrumental limit, one imposed by the laws of fiber optics, and the other by the laws of classical optics, correspond very closely with a third—the *cellular* limit—imposed by purely biological constraints which limit the minimum size of any sort of feasible cellular receptor system. Our high-resolution vision is only possible because these three limits precisely coincide.

There is almost certainly yet another factor which imposes a limit on the minimum possible size of the photoreceptor cell—the need of the cell to respond to exceedingly small quantities of light energy. The amount of light falling on the retina from a distant star is 1 trillion times (10^{12}) less than that from a brightly lit snowfield.[23] The extreme sensitivity of the eye to very small quantities of light makes vision possible at night and in other situations of low light intensity.

The eye is able to detect extremely small quantities of light because each photoreceptor is able to respond to a single photon of light—the smallest possible quantity of light energy.[24] A photon of light is detected in the photoreceptor cell when it interacts with a single light-sensitive molecule, called rhodopsin. The photoreceptor cell is able to interact with a single photon only because it is packed with many millions of rhodopsin molecules, which maximizes the probability that an individual photon will be absorbed.[25] The need for many millions of rhodopsin molecules in an individual photoreceptor cell, if the cell is to detect a single photon, is another factor imposing a lower limit on the size of the photodetector cell. Only relatively large photoreceptor cells could detect individual photons and make night vision possible. The energy change resulting from the interaction of a single rhodopsin molecule with a single photon of light is extremely tiny, and the cell is only able to detect it after it has been massively amplified via a complex chain of enzymic reactions, which ultimately change the electrochemical state of the cell.[26] Because of the complexity of the molecular system needed to amplify the tiny initial signal, it is hard to believe that any photoreceptor cell capable of responding to a single photon of light, and of therefore "seeing" in the dark, could be much smaller than the photoreceptor cells in the vertebrate retina.

The energy levels and the wavelength of light are of course only two aspects of the natural order that must possess precisely the properties and values they do for high-resolution vision to be possible. There are other features as well: there is the transparency of water to light; there is the low refractive index of water; there is the diffusion rates of small organic compounds in water to nourish the lens, which is a living tissue; there is the necessity for a large nervous system to analyze the visual data; and so on.

Seeing Outside the Visual Spectrum

Finally, let us consider some of the hypothetical problems that would be met in attempting to construct a biological high-resolution camera-type eye to "see" in wavelengths outside the visual region of the spectrum.

For example, to obtain, with infrared or radio waves, the same degree of resolution as that which can be achieved with the human eye and many other optimized vertebrate camera eyes would require eyes of vastly increased size, even if a biological detector device could be constructed. To obtain the same resolving power as that of the human eye with, say, radio waves with a wavelength of 100 centimeters would require a reflector disc 10 kilometers in diameter. Even far-shorter-frequency radio waves, or microwaves of 1 millimeter wavelength, would require a lens or disc with a diameter of 10 meters to equal the resolving power of the human eye. So in addition to the profound difficulty that would be encountered in designing biological detector devices capable of measuring the low energy levels of infrared and radio waves, there would also be the tremendous engineering challenge of having to construct immense telescopes of planetary dimensions. Evidently, the infrared and radio regions of the spectrum are totally unfit for biological vision.

Curiously, not only is light far fitter for biological seeing and particularly for high-resolution vision than infrared or radio waves, it would also seem to be fitter for nonbiological eyes such as the radio and infrared telescopes used by astronomers. Even though a vast diversity of materials can be recruited for constructional purposes, no telescope has been built with a resolving power remotely equal to the human eye using wavelengths longer than those in the visual spectrum. A cursory comparison of the many photographs taken of galaxies and other astronomical objects through light, infrared, and radio telescopes shows clearly the far greater resolving power of optical devices in the visual region of the spectrum.[27]

UV, X ray, and gamma rays are also unfit for biological vision. One reason already alluded to is that the energy of the radiation at these shorter wavelengths is so high that it would be bound to destroy any biological materials used in the construction of a hypothetical eye designed specifically to see in these regions of the spectrum. And again (as in the infrared and radio regions of the spectrum), the design of imaging devices to function in the UV, X-ray, and gamma-ray regions poses severe engineering problems even outside of biology! In the UV region, for example, a lens must be made of special materials that are transparent to UV light. Substances such as quartz and metal fluorides are commonly used. Unfortunately, because nearly all substances absorb in the far UV, focusing an image requires reflection optics in a vacuum chamber.[28] The use of X rays is also problematical. Because X rays are only reflected if they hit a metal surface at a very shallow angle, the design of X-ray telescopes is necessarily complex, involving a series of highly polished nickel-coated surfaces of first a paraboloid and then a hyperboloid surface.[29] Similarly, gamma rays cannot be focused through a lens because all substances absorb them. Even reflection cannot be used because gamma rays are far smaller than the atoms making up any mirror. To detect the radiation in this region of the spectrum, a variety of electronic systems are used, including scintillation counters, proportional counters, and microchannel plates.[30] Despite the progress made by astronomers over the past thirty years to construct telescopes which utilize the various short-wavelength regions of the spectrum, to date their resolving power is still far less than conventional light telescopes.

Assuming, for the sake of argument, that we could get around the detection problem and find some biological material capable of focusing UV and X rays, the theoretical resolving power in the far UV, where wavelengths are a hundred times less than in the visible band, would be a hundred times better. For X rays ten thousand times less, the resolving power would be theoretically ten thousand times better. However, no improvement in visual acuity could be gained by having such eyes, because the smallest possible biological photodetector cell would be many orders of magnitude larger than the tiny UV or X-ray images that could theoretically be focused on such a hypothetical "retina."

Compared with the visual spectrum, the other regions of the electromagnetic spectrum are not only totally unfit for biological vision, they would also appear to be far less fit for nonbiological vision. Even today, despite the development of radio and X-ray telescopes, much of our knowledge of astronomy has come from observations made through light telescopes. The following diagram summarizes some of the conclusions discussed above.

And so it would appear that for several different reasons the visual region of the electromagnetic spectrum *is the one region supremely fit for biological vision* and particularly for the *high-resolution vertebrate camera eye of a design and dimension very close to that of the human eye.*

The fitness of the visual spectrum for vision.

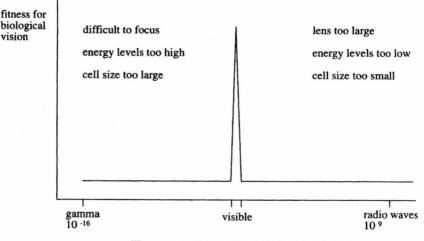

Electromagnetic spectrum (wavelength microns)

Conclusion

While high-quality vision may not be essential to all life on earth, human existence would be inconceivable without it. While other species may be as reliant on seeing as humans are for survival, our uniquely human desire for knowledge could only have been satisfied, as Aristotle rightly points out in the opening paragraph of his *Metaphysics,* by the gift of sight. Virtually all our knowledge of the world, and particularly scientific knowledge, acquired over the past four centuries has been largely dependent on our possession of eyes of very high resolving power, or visual acuity, and capable therefore of bringing us a very detailed and information-rich image of our surroundings.

We saw in the previous chapter that water, in many fascinating and highly intriguing ways, is uniquely and ideally fit for the type of carbon-based life that exists on earth, not just for simple unicellular microbial life but also for large terrestrial organisms. The evidence presented in this chapter shows that the light of the stars is also, no less than water, supremely fit for life, again in a multitude of different ways. Moreover, again, as in the case of water, this fitness is not merely for simple microbial life, but for large complex organisms such as ourselves. It is fit to provide the warmth upon which all life on the earth's surface depends. It is fit for photosynthesis, which generates the reduced carbon fuels, whose oxidation provides energy for all complex life on earth, and it is fit for vision, the key adaptation through which our own species gained knowledge of the world.

Chapter 4

The Fitness of the Elements and the Earth

In which the biological significance of various elements of the periodic table is examined. The fitness of the cosmos for carbon-based life is highlighted by the fact that the cosmic abundance of the elements corresponds to their abundance in living organisms and that the space between the stars is filled with immense quantities of organic compounds. Further representatives of every class of atoms in the periodic table are necessary for life. Even uranium atom 92 is essential for life, providing the heat and energy required for tectonic activity and the turnover of the earth's crustal rocks, which in conjunction with the water cycle ensures the chemical constancy of the earth's surficial layers. The properties of some of the minerals which play such a vital role in the maintenance of this chemical constancy are examined. The fact that recent astronomical studies suggest that solar systems not too dissimilar to our own, containing rocky planets somewhat like the earth, may be relatively common can be taken as further evidence of nature's fitness for carbon-based life. It is concluded that habitats like the earth which are so fit for a rich complex carbon-based biosphere are not freakish events but rather the inevitable end of natural law.

The periodic table of the elements.

The first atom in the periodic table is hydrogen (H), atom 1, the next is helium (He), atom 2, and the third is lithium (Li), atom 3, and so on. Sodium (Na) is atom 11, potassium (K) is atom 19, and cesium (Cs) is atom 55. The last atom is uranium (U), which is atom 92. The atoms from scandium (Sc) to zinc (Zn) are known as the transition metals. The atoms from lanthanum (La) to ytterbium (Yb) are known as the rare earth metals and are chemically very similar. The atoms can be classified into groups numbered 1 to 18 (see the diagram). All the members of each family are quite similar chemically. For example, all the members of group 1—lithium (Li), sodium (Na), potassium (K), rubidium (Rb), cesium (Cs), and francium (Fr)—are all metals and are highly reactive. On the other hand, all the members of group 18—helium (He), neon (Ne), argon (Ar), krypton (Kr), xenon (Xe), and radon (Rn)—are all inert gases. Most of the elements are metals. Metals tend to give up electrons in chemical combination while nonmetals tend to accept them. The nonmetals occupy the upper right-hand side of the table. Familiar nonmetals are the gas nitrogen (N), which makes up 80 percent of the atmosphere, silicon (Si), one of the major components of the granite rocks, carbon (C), sulphur (S), and chlorine (Cl), which is one of the atoms in common salt (Na Cl). Iron (Fe) is one of the commonly used metals and also forms the molten core at the center of the earth.

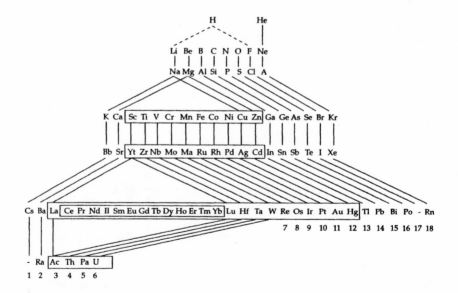

This, as most other of the Atheists' Arguments, proceeds from a deep Ignorance of Natural Philosophy; for if there were but half the sea that now is, there would be also but half the Quantity of Vapours, and consequently we could have but half as many Rivers as now there are to supply all the dry land we have at present, and half as much more; for the quantity of Vapours which are raised, bears a proportion to the Surface whence they are raised, as well as to the heat which raised them. The Wise Creator therefore did so prudently order it, that the seas should be large enough to supply Vapours sufficient for all the land.

—John Ray, *The Wisdom of God Manifested in the Words of Creation*, 1701

The earth, "with its atmosphere and oceans, its complex biosphere, its crust of relatively oxidised, silica rich, sedimentary, igneous, and metamorphic rocks overlying [a magnesium silicate mantle and core] of metallic iron, with its ice caps, deserts, forests, tundra, jungles, grasslands, fresh-water lakes, coal beds, oil deposits, volcanoes, fumaroles, factories, automobiles, plants, animals, magnetic field, ionosphere, mid-ocean ridges, convicting mantle . . . is a system of stunning complexity."

—J. S. Lewis, in F. Press and R. Siever, *Earth*, 1986

The entire cosmos and all the vast diversity of objects which it contains—
the stars, the earth, elephants, clouds, supernovae, volcanoes, waterfalls,
mountains, and automobiles—is ultimately made up of 92 atoms (see the
periodic table of the elements on page 72). These 92 atoms are the basic elemental units or building blocks which, by combining with each other according to the laws of chemistry, form all the vast diversity of substances and
materials with which we are so familiar—granite, wood, plastic, agate, salt,
proteins, hair, gasoline, penicillin, and so on.

The Structure and Classes of Atoms

Chemists usually refer to atoms by an abbreviated symbol consisting most
often of one or two letters. Thus, sodium is Na, oxygen is O, carbon is C,
chlorine is Cl. Each atom consists of a nucleus containing one or more
subatomic particles known as protons, which carry a positive charge, and
neutrons, which carry no charge, and a series of 7 concentric electron orbits,
or shells, each at a different radius from the center of the atom (electrons
carry a negative charge). Each orbit or shell may contain only a certain maximum number of electrons. The first shell may contain a maximum of 2
electrons, the second 8, the third 18, the fourth 32, the fifth 50, and so on.
   The simplest atom is that of hydrogen, which contains only one proton
in its nucleus and one electron in the first electron shell. Carbon contains 6
electrons in its electron shells, and 6 protons and 6 neutrons in its nucleus.
The inner or first shell is complete, containing the maximum of 2 electrons.
The second shell is incomplete, containing only 4 electrons out of the maximal permitted number of 8. Uranium (U), which is the largest of atoms
that occurs naturally, contains a total of 92 electrons and 92 protons and
more than 100 neutrons in its nucleus.
   Hydrogen (H) and helium (He), which make up the main substance of
the stars, are by far the most abundant atoms in the universe. The least
abundant elements are 10^{12}, or a trillion, times less abundant than hydrogen. Of the 24 most abundant elements, all are either essential for life or are
utilized by some organism for some vital process. The only exceptions to
this are the 3 inert gases argon (Ar), neon (Ne), and helium (He). The 5
most abundant elements are hydrogen (H), helium (He), oxygen (O), carbon (C), and nitrogen (N), and these, with the exception of helium, form
the bulk of all the macromolecules utilized in living organisms.

As discussed in chapter 1, all the elements, including those key atoms of life such as carbon and oxygen, are synthesized in the interior of the stars. The process starts with hydrogen, and through a process of fusion whereby atoms combine with each other in various ways, gradually all the atoms of the periodic table are built up. The fact that only a select number of atoms are manufactured results from a set of generative rules, which restrict stable combinations of protons, neutrons, and electrons to a few unique permissible patterns. These patterns represent the 92 naturally occurring atoms of the periodic table. Interestingly, the atoms are only stable up to atom 83, bismuth (Bi). Beyond this element the atoms are unstable and are continually breaking down into smaller elements. Thus, uranium (U), element 92, decays via the short-lived radioactive elements thorium (Th), protoactinium (Pa), radium (Ra), radon (Rn), polonium (Po), astatine (At) into bismuth (Bi) and finally lead (Pb). During the process a variety of different types of highly energetic particles are given off. If the 7 short-lived radioactive atoms are discounted, this leaves only 85 stable elements. The biological significance of the radioactive atoms will be discussed below.

Because of their structure and particularly because of the characteristics of their surrounding electronic shells, atoms can be grouped into classes which exhibit unique chemical and physical properties. For example, there are metals and nonmetals. The nonmetals occupy the upper right-hand side of the periodic table and the nonmetals the rest of the table. Within the metals, group 1, including sodium (Na), potassium (K), and cesium (Cs) are known as the alkali metals and all have many properties in common. Then there are the alkaline earth metals in group 2, which include calcium (Ca) and magnesium (Mg) and which also have many properties in common. They are all highly reactive, with low melting points. Likewise, the so-called halogens in group 17, including fluorine (F), chlorine (Cl), bromine (Br), and iodine (I), are all reactive nonmetals and also closely resemble each other in many of their chemical properties. It was the fact that the elements could be grouped into distinct families which led the Russian chemist Dmitri Mendeleev to his discovery of the periodic table of the elements in 1869.

As we shall see in the following chapters, many different atoms are used in living things, and in many cases life is critically dependent on these atoms having precisely the properties they possess. Of the 92 naturally occurring atoms, 25 are presently considered essential for life. Of these 25, 11 are present in all living things and in approximately the same proportions. These are hydrogen (H), carbon (C), oxygen (O), nitrogen (N), sodium (Na), magnesium (Mg), phosphorus (P), sulfur (S), chlorine (Cl), potassium (K), and calcium (Ca). Together these atoms make up 99.9 percent of the human body. Another 14 atoms are present in very small amounts in most living organisms, but often in varying amounts, and are known as trace elements. These are vanadium (V), chromium (Cr), manganese (Mn), iron (Fe), cobalt (Co), nickel (Ni), copper (Cu), zinc (Zn), molybdenum (Mo), boron (B), silicon (Si), selenium (Se), fluorine (F), and iodine (I). Another 3 atoms, arsenic (As), tin (Sn), and tungsten (W), are known to be essential in many organisms, but in many cases their biological role is obscure.[1]

Yet another 3 atoms, bromine (Br), strontium (Sr), and barium (Ba), are found in many species, although their role and whether or not they are essential is not yet clear. There are even organisms which accumulate unusual quantities of aluminum and lithium, atoms which are generally considered toxic to most life forms.

Thus, life processes utilize atoms from nearly all the groups in the table. As J. J. R. Fraústo da Silva and R. J. P. Williams comment:

> The biological elements seem to have been selected from practically all groups and subgroups of the periodic table (the only exceptions are groups III A and IV B, besides that of the inert gases) and this means that practically all kinds of chemical properties are associated with life processes within the limits imposed by environmental constraints.[2]

Cosmic and Biological Abundance of the Elements

Most of the atoms actually utilized in living organisms occur in the first half of the periodic table from hydrogen (H), atom 1, to molybdenum (Mo), atom 42. After molybdenum only selenium (Se), iodine (I), and tungsten (W) play any role in living things, and even these atoms are not essential in most organisms. The fact that the atoms in the first half of the table are also the most abundant fits well with the notion that the atom-building system is designed specifically to generate the elements of life. Note that the atoms from carbon (C) to iron (Fe), which are the most important atoms utilized by living things, are all relatively abundant.

The chart below shows the approximate relative cosmic abundance of all the naturally occurring elements from atom 1, hydrogen (H), to atom 92, uranium (U).[3]

The cosmic abundance of the elements.

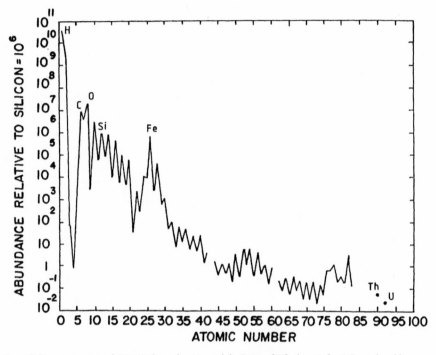

From C. Ponnamperuma, ed. (1983) *Cosmochemistry and the Origin of Life*, chap. 1, fig. 6. Reproduced by permission of Kluwer Academic Publishers, Holland.

Some of the common and important atoms are indicated in the chart using their conventional chemical symbols. The gaps in the chart are due to atoms 43, technetium (Tc); 63, promethium (Pm); 84, polonium (Po); 85, astatine (At); 86, radon (Rn); 87, francium (Fr); 88, radium (Ra); and 91, protoactinium (Pa), which are short-lived radioactive elements and only occur in nature in vanishingly small amounts. The two dots at the right end of the chart are the two long-lived radioactive elements: atom 90, thorium (Th), and atom 92, uranium (U).

As the chart below indicates, there is a very striking correlation between the abundance of the elements and their utility for life.[4]

Relative abundance of the first thirty-one elements in the cosmos and in living organisms on the earth's surface.

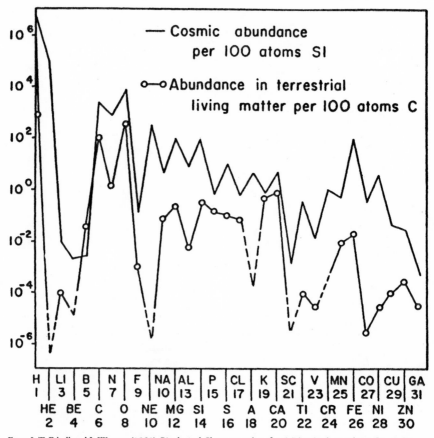

From J. T. Edsall and J. Wyman (1958) *Biophysical Chemistry,* vol. 1, fig. 6 (New York: Academic Press). Reproduced by permission of the publisher.

And in addition to this striking correlation, recent studies have revealed that interstellar space is filled with vast quantities of water, methane, ammonia, carbon monoxide, and many other organic compounds. The quantities are immense—up to 200 million solar masses in our own galaxy. The cosmos is literally overflowing with the basic constituents of carbon-based life.

The Biological Significance of Radioactivity

Nearly all the atoms in the second half of the table which are nonessential to life are also very rare. As can be seen in the chart above, the abundance of the atoms from atom 44, ruthenium (Ru), to atom 92, uranium (U), are all very close to 10^{10} times less common than hydrogen and about a million times less common than most of the essential atoms, such as carbon (C), oxygen (O), nitrogen (N), sulfur (S), and iron (Fe). However, although very rare, the fascinating question arises; why, if the cosmos is specifically fit for life, are there many atoms apparently not utilized in carbon-based life? What possible relevance do the atoms of the second half of the table have to the phenomenon of life?

This question cannot be dodged in any argument for the biocentricity of nature. If the atom-building rules have indeed been arranged to construct a set of atoms with a peculiar utility for the carbon-based life forms that exist on earth, then surely all the atoms, right up to uranium, must be in some way "adapted" for life. Although the number of atoms essential for life is continually rising as research proceeds, it is very doubtful if any biological role will ever be found for the majority of the atoms in the second half of the table. A striking feature of the periodic table is that a great many of the nonessential atoms in the second half of the table have very similar chemical properties. For example, the so-called rare earth metals, atoms 58 to 70 in the periodic table—cerium (Ce) to ytterbium (Yb)—can hardly be distinguished from one another; their chemical and physical properties are virtually identical.[5] This in itself suggests that the utility for life of most of this series of thirteen elements could only be minimal. It is doubtful that biochemical systems could be designed to distinguish between them on chemical grounds.

There are some immediate, at least partial, answers to these questions. We can readily explain the existence of the six inert gases—helium (He), neon (Ne), argon (Ar), krypton (Kr), xenon (Xe) and radon (Rn)—as the inevitable result of the rules which govern the assembly of atoms from the three basic subatomic particles: the proton, the electron, and the neutron. These rules include, for example, a number of stringent restrictions on the configuration of the electron shells. The existence of these rules necessarily means that some atoms will have complete electron shells and will be unable to undergo chemical interactions with other atoms.

The existence of these noble gases which play no role in biology is therefore of necessity. Given the atom-building rules as they are, then inevitably some atoms will be inert and will not enter into chemical combination with other elements. Similarly, the existence of a vast number of possibly lifeless planetary systems unsuitable for carbon-based life is an inevitable consequence of the general laws of nature which generate planetary systems. Even in our own solar system there are a total of sixty-two planets and moons, although more than half the moons are very small objects, being in many cases only 10 to 100 kilometers in diameter. Although Mars and other planets may have allowed primitive life to flourish briefly in the past and some of the moons of the giant outer planets may even contain primitive life at present, only the earth is fit for a biosphere containing a rich and complex variety of carbon-based life forms.

Given the laws of chemistry, which are in fact basically a set of rules that govern the way atoms may combine, an almost unlimited number of compounds and minerals will be formed of necessity. The fact, for example, that carbon adopts a crystalline form—a diamond, if compressed under pressures at which no living thing could survive—has no direct relevance to life but is an inevitable result of the properties of carbon when subjected to the natural conditions which exist within the earth's interior. The properties of steam at very high temperatures and pressures are irrelevant to life but inevitable given the basic chemical and physical properties of water. Again, the fact that carbon dioxide forms a solid at temperatures slightly lower than any found on earth is of no direct relevance to life. All such phenomena are the result of the operation of the general laws of nature and the inherent nature of matter in conditions of temperature and pressure far outside that compatible with life. If there are to be any laws of chemistry and physics, then inevitably there are bound to be a vast number of chemical and physical phenomena of no direct utility to life. Even in the field of artificial life, where experimental worlds sometimes called "toy universes" are generated in computers from sets of rules, many phenomena are inevitably generated which are not of any direct relevance to the major focus of interest, which is the creation and behavior of the artificial life forms.[6]

It is impossible to speculate as to what sorts of alternative atom-building systems might have been used to avoid the existence of chemically unreactive atoms. But on very general principles it is hard to see how any such generative system derived from the application of a simple set of building rules or laws of nature could avoid at least some degree of redundancy and unwanted atoms. This sort of redundancy is inherent in all combinatorial mechanisms for generating complexity. We see it in the vast diversity of sentences permitted by the rules of grammar and in the vast diversity of chemical compounds generated by the rules of chemistry. We see it in the vast number of carbon compounds which chemistry permits and in the vast number of gene sequences that can be derived by combining the four bases in the DNA.

While it is possible to rationalize the existence of the six inert gases as "of necessity," given the atom-building rules actually utilized by nature, the question still remains, why does the atom-building process continue right up to and through the long list of near-identical, rare earth elements, and on to the radioactive elements from atom 84 to atom 92, the last naturally occurring atom, uranium (U)? One answer to this riddle may lie in the critical role that uranium (U) and the other radioactive elements have played in the geophysical evolution of the planet and in those processes which have created on its surface a unique physical and chemical aqueous environment known as the "hydrosphere," which is supremely fit to support carbon-based life over vast periods of time.

The role played by the heavier unstable elements in fashioning the surface of the earth into a stable home has only become apparent as a result of advances in the earth sciences over the past three decades. We now know that uranium and the other radioactive elements have played a critical role in the evolution of the earth because of the heat provided by their radioactive decay. As Frank Press and Raymond Siever point out in their well-known textbook *Earth:* "The heavy elements uranium and thorium . . . are not very plentiful on earth. Their occurrence is measured in a few parts per million. . . . Yet these elements had a profound effect on the evolution of the earth because of their *radioactivity*."[7] As Press and Siever calculate, the amount of heat produced in one year by radioactive decay in the granite which forms the major component of the earth's crust "is equal to 1,000 times the energy released each year by earthquakes and about 250,000 times the energy of a 1-megaton nuclear explosion."[8] Interestingly, the heating of the earth was assisted by the poor thermal conductivity of rock. If rock had not been such a good insulator, the earth may never have warmed.

It was this radioactive heat which was responsible for warming the interior of the earth shortly after the formation of the planet.[9] As the warming continued, eventually the temperature reached the melting point of iron, when drops of iron began to form and began falling to the center of the earth, releasing huge amounts of gravitational energy that was eventually converted to heat, which raised the temperature further to about 2,000°C and caused a large fraction of the earth to melt.[10] This crucial event marked the beginning of the process referred to as differentiation, which converted the earth from a largely homogeneous body, with roughly the same kind of material at all depths, to a zoned or layered structure with a dense iron core, a crust composed of lighter material with lower melting points, and between them, the mantle.[11] Without differentiation, no life; without radioactivity, no differentiation.

An important aspect of differentiation was the process of chemical zonation, which led to the current distribution of the elements and their compounds from the core to the crust. This process did not lead to a vertical arrangement of the elements based entirely on their relative weights. The reason is that the elements combined into a variety of compounds, and it was the physical and chemical properties of these compounds—properties such as melting points, chemical affinities, and densities—that governed the distribution of elements, rather than the properties of the elements themselves. For example, it is because of the properties of the silicates rather than their constituent atoms—silicon (Si), oxygen (O), calcium (Ca), magnesium (Mg) and aluminum (Al)—that the crustal rocks are largely composed of these five atoms. The silicates melt at relatively low temperatures and when molten are relatively light. Necessarily, they rose during zonation and accumulated in the crust. While the silicates rose, other elements fell. Gold (Au) and platinum (Pt), which have little chemical affinity for silicon (Si) or oxygen (O) and are heavy, are very rare in the crustal rocks.[12]

Although many of the heavy elements such as gold (Au), platinum (Pt), silver (Ag), and mercury (Hg) have little affinity for oxygen and are rare in the crust, uranium (U) and thorium (Th), on the other hand, readily form oxides and silicates and are far more common than gold in the earth's crust.[13] The fact that the majority of the uranium and thorium rose to the surface layers during differentiation is fortunate and may be of great significance. Rock is not a good conductor, and it is possible that unless a major fraction of these radioactive elements had floated to the surface, the heat generated by radioactivity may not have been so easily lost by conduction from the crustal layers. Being trapped in the earth's interior may have caused a very large increase in temperature over time, and with no conductive escape this might have led to a far more violent level of volcanism and turbulence in the earth's center. This may well have repeatedly destabilized the crustal layers and the hydrosphere in violent and explosive episodes of volcanism, rendering the earth's surface far less fit as a habitat for life.

The actual cosmic abundance of the radioactive elements has also been critical to their geophysical role in heating the earth. If too abundant, the earth-sized planets would be molten for eons of time; if too rare, no heating would ever have occurred.

Plate Tectonics

The heat provided by radioactive decay was not only responsible for triggering the initial differentiation and chemical zoning of the planet, the outgassing of water, and the formation of the hydrosphere, it has also been responsible for the massive convection currents deep in the Earth's mantle which have been continuously moving the great crustal plates over the surface of the Earth for the past 4 billion years.[14] The development of the theory of plate tectonics was perhaps the major revolution in the earth sciences in the twentieth century. As Hazel Rymer points out in *Nature,* before the 1960s "the Earth was seen as a sphere with a thick, inert, rocky mantle encasing a central molten core. The complex pattern of land and sea masses was believed to be essentially static. By the end of the [plate tectonic] revolution, only the core remained. The mantle had become a solid yet flowing region, convecting heat from within the Earth through a thin, strong and brittle shell that was broken into a few large plates moving laterally on and with the mantle."[15]

A detailed description of plate tectonics is beyond the scope of this chapter. But briefly, when two tectonic plates collide, one plate, "the overriding plate," is crumpled and uplifted into great mountain chains, while the other, "the underlying plate," is forced down into the Earth's interior. This remarkable process results in the continual recycling of the Earth's crustal material, including the many elements essential for life.

In itself the tectonic cycle would be insufficient to maintain an environment fit for life. It is only through the integration of the tectonic cycle with another great geophysical cycle, the hydrologic cycle, that the physical and chemical constancy of the environment is ensured. The water cycle is so familiar that it needs little further comment here except to say that it is almost entirely due to the weathering by water that the elements in the uplifted crustal rocks are returned again to the sea. The extraordinary mutual fitness of these two cycles for the maintenance of the constancy of the environment is self-evident (see below). Like two gigantic cogwheels engineered to fit perfectly together, these two great cycles have turned together in perfect unison for billions of years, ensuring the continual turnover and essential cycling of the vital elements of life.

Thus, the chemical and physical stability of the Earth's surficial environment is the result of the two great interacting geological recycling systems: the "cold system," or the water cycle, operating on the surface of the planet and energized by the sun, via which the mountains are continually worn and washed into the sea and deposited ultimately as sediments on the ocean floor; and the hot system, the "tectonic cycle," energized by the heat produced by radioactive decay, via which the materials deposited in these oceanic sediments are thrust up and returned to the surface again through volcanism or through the uplift generated by colliding plates.[16]

There is nothing contingent about the existence of these two remarkable and mutually fit interacting cycles. The existence of both systems is probably inevitable in any planet of the same size, elemental composition, dis-

The tectonic and water cycles.

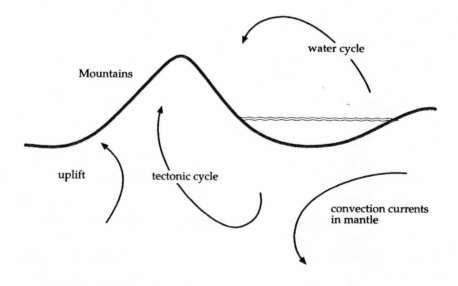

tance from its sun, and history as the Earth. The water cycle is inherent in the properties of water, while the vast quantities of water which make up the oceans, rivers, etc., on earth and which make the cycle possible are themselves the inevitable result of the outgassing of the volatiles from the Earth's interior as it heated up shortly after its initial formation. Likewise, the existence of the great tectonic plates made up mainly of lighter silicate material, and the great convection currents deep in the Earth's mantle which drive the crustal plates across the Earth and empower the whole tectonic cycle of crustal renewal, are no-less-inevitable characteristics of a planet like the Earth. It is now known that similar geophysical processes have played a role in shaping the surfaces of the moon, Mars, and Venus. And in the case of Mars, there is clear evidence, in the existence of sinuous, long dried-out riverbeds and great canyons like the Valley of the Mariners, that the ancient Martian surface suffered erosion by water in ways strikingly similar to that which is still occurring on earth.

The water cycle has long been a source of wonderment and a popular topic of natural theology. Yi-Fu Tuan in his *Hydrologic Cycle and the Wisdom of God* points out that the concept of the hydrological cycle was from 1700 to 1850 the "handmaiden of natural theology as much as it was a child of natural philosophy."[17] And, as he continues:

> Of the three classes of evidence—astronomical, terrestrial and biological—terrestrial evidence proved in some ways to be the most difficult to draw upon in support of the notion of a wise and providential God. Until the concept of the hydrologic cycle was introduced and elaborated, it was difficult to argue convincingly for a rationality in the pattern of land and sea, in the existence of mountains, in the occurrence of floods etc.
>
> The hydrologic cycle served as an ordering principle, and when combined with the geologic cycle, it assumed a grandeur of inclusiveness that makes some of our modern efforts to describe the earth look like a medley of disjointed facts and ideas.[18]

The Magnetic Shield

The earth has a magnetic field which shields it from ionizing radiation from the sun and cosmic radiation originating from the depths of space. The way in which the field is generated has not yet been fully worked out, yet it seems likely that the movement of molten iron in the center of the planet, driven by convection currents, plays a critical role.[19] About 1 billion amperes of current is needed to produce the earth's magnetic field. This is nearly as much electric current as the total amount generated by man throughout history.

We now know that the magnetic field deflects away from the earth, the solar wind, cosmic radiation, and the intense ionizing radiation which periodically bursts from the surface of the sun, preventing all but about 0.1 percent from reaching the earth. The biological significance of this protective shield is controversial. Even without the shield, the atmosphere would absorb most of this radiation before it reached the earth's surface. Moreover, during periods when the earth's magnetic field reversed, the earth was temporarily left without any protection, perhaps for a duration of several years, and such reversals have occurred repeatedly.

Another possible "biological role" of the magnetic field may be to protect the ozone layer, which prevents most of the damaging ultraviolet radiation from reaching the earth's surface. Ionizing radiation, which reaches the upper atmosphere, is known to be a major cause of nitrous oxide (NO) production, which in turn causes the destruction of ozone. Without the magnetic field, it is doubtful if more than a fraction of the current ozone levels could be maintained.[20]

Silicates and Clay

Another feature of the earth which is ultimately the result of the heat generated by radioactivity is the fact that the surface rocks of the earth are largely *silicates*. This apparently esoteric fact is of great biological significance because the end product of silicate weathering by water and carbon dioxide is clay, which forms a major component of soil and plays a vital biological role by absorbing and retaining water and the key elements for plant life.

This water- and ion-absorbing characteristic of clay resides in its unique layered structure—like the pages of a book—in which each page consists basically of a layer of silicon and oxygen atoms. These atoms carry charges which attract other charged atoms (ions) and water so that the whole structure acts as a great reservoir holding ions in the soil and preventing their being leached out by water as it percolates through the soil. The total internal surface area of clays vastly exceeds the area of their external surfaces.[21] As two leading soil scientists point out: "*Next to photosynthesis and respiration, probably no process in nature is as vital* to plant life as the exchange of ions between soil particles and growing plant roots. These cation and anion exchanges take place mostly on the surfaces of the finer or colloidal fractions of both the inorganic matter—clays and humus."[22] "*Cation exchange joins photosynthesis as a fundamental life-supporting process.* Without this property of soils terrestrial ecosystems would not be able to retain sufficient nutrients to support natural or introduced vegetation."[23] (My emphasis.)

There seems little doubt that were it not for the almost universal occurrence of clay minerals in soil, there would be no large terrestrial plants on earth and consequently no large terrestrial mammals.[24] In a very real sense our existence depends on the fact that the most common crustal rocks weather to what would appear to be an ideal material for the growth of plant life, absorbing both water and the essential nutrients needed for growth.

It is surely a "coincidence" of great significance that the very rocks which by virtue of their viscosity and density will inevitably form the crustal rocks on a planet like the earth are weathered by the two substances water and carbon dioxide, the key ingredients of any carbon-based biosphere, into a substance that forms an ideal substratum for the growth of plants.

It is clear from this brief excursion into the fields of geophysics and geochemistry that uranium is in a very real sense, *no less than carbon, essential for life.* Moreover, to get to uranium from hydrogen, obeying the atom-building rules which nature has decreed means that inevitably a considerable number of "intermediate atoms" such as the "rare earths" will necessarily be created, albeit in very small amounts. So we can at least tentatively conclude that the whole periodic table is in essence biocentric, from alpha to omega, from hydrogen to uranium, the last naturally occurring element. Moreover, although many of the elements in the second half of the table seem, at present, of no direct relevance to life, we should recall that the origin of life is still mysterious, and it is certainly conceivable that the properties of many of the elements considered nonessential today may eventually prove to have some exotic but perhaps critical biological role in the process.

The Properties of Minerals

It is obvious that a great many of the physical and chemical properties of the minerals that make up the earth's crust and mantle must be very close to the observed values or the whole crustal recycling system would be untenable; indeed, the earth would be, in all probability, unrecognizable and quite incapable of supporting carbon-based life.

Consider viscosity—not of water, but of rock. The fact that rock subjected to the high temperatures and pressures found in the earth's mantle has a relatively low viscosity is clearly critical to the whole design of the tectonic system. All substances, even the most solid, are viscous to some degree. The viscosities of various familiar substances range over twenty-eight orders of magnitude, from water to granite. The viscosity of the crustal rocks is so great that such rocks flow only very slowly. But they do flow. They erode more quickly than they flow, but they flow.[25]

If the crustal rocks were less viscous, say, like pitch, the mountains would have melted into vast flat plains and nothing we would call a mountain chain would exist on the surface of the earth. If the viscosity of the rocks of the mantle had been substantially less, the convective turbulence would have been immense and the surface of the earth subject to daily movements and volcanism. If the viscosity of the mantle had been much greater than it is, on the other hand, the convection currents would have ceased and the tectonic system would have ground to a halt.

And it is not only the viscosity of the minerals which must be very close to the observed values. If the elements essential for life are to be effectively recycled through the crustal rocks and hydrosphere, the solubility of the various compounds in which the key elements occur in the crustal rocks must also be close to the observed values. For example, the solubility of silicate minerals (which contain the element silica) is thousands of times lower than the solubility of the carbonate minerals (which contain carbon) such as calcite and dolomite, which make up limestone. If the carbonates had been less soluble, then all the carbon on earth would have been locked up in the limestone sediments and there would have been insufficient carbon in the hydrosphere to support life. On the other hand, if the silicates had been as soluble as the carbonates, then the hydrosphere would have been overwhelmed with vast quantities of potassium, aluminum, silica dioxide, calcium, chloride, and other elements converting the sea into a supersaturated viscous sludge.

Every one of the cycles essential to life on earth—the carbon cycle, the oxygen cycle, the nitrogen cycle, the phosphorus cycle, the sulfur cycle, the calcium cycle, the sodium cycle, and so on—involves a host of different chemical compounds and processes which carry the essential elements from the rocks to the sea, where they are deposited in the oceanic sediments, incorporated into the crustal rocks, and then via tectonic uplift and volcanism carried again to the surface, where the weathering cycle can recommence.[26]

Given the vast diversity of chemical compounds and the vast range of chemical and physical properties they exhibit, it is remarkable that so many of the elements can be so efficiently cycled. It is very easy to imagine changing the properties of only one key compound in any one of the critical cycles to see that carbon-based life would be impossible. We saw in chapter 2 that if the latent heat of evaporation and condensation of water had been much less than they are, then small pools of water would completely evaporate after even a small rise in temperature and small lakes would only exist as ephemeral phenomena. Similarly, if for example, limestone had been as insoluble as quartz, then almost certainly carbon would not have been available in the waters of a planet like the earth.

Moreover, although each element is recycled via a unique set of processes and reactions, these cycles are also interdependent. The iron cycle is intimately influenced by the cycles of other metals, and of phosphorus, sulfur, dioxygen, and carbon. Even the intensity of light reaching the surface of the earth influences the flux of iron throughout the hydrosphere.[27] And in the case of the carbon cycle, the level of carbon in the sea is dependent on the level of calcium, which itself is influenced by the level of phosphate ions and so on. Given the complexity of the geochemistry of the earth's crust and hydrosphere, the constancy of so many variables—the mean temperature of the sea, the carbon dioxide concentration in the air, the salinity of the sea, the annual rate of deposition in the sea of about twenty-five or so different elements for nearly 4 billion years—is surely as extraordinary as any topic discussed in this book.

The maintenance of the approximately constant levels of each of the twenty-five or so elements essential to life in the hydrosphere over the past 4 billion years via a set of interlocking cycles—the water, carbon, iron, magnesium, tectonic cycle, and so on—conjures up the image of a vast terrestrial clock with the size and configuration of all its component cogs superbly tailored to fit perfectly together to ensure that the whole turns harmoniously and fine tuned to ensure that the individual cycles turn at the appropriate rate to maintain the required level of each of the elements, essential to life, in the hydrosphere.

Gaia

The constancy of the chemical and physical characteristics of the hydrosphere, maintained as it is by a complex and exquisitely integrated set of interlocking geochemical cycles, has led a number of authors to regard the earth as a homeostatic system analogous to a living organism. As Siever comments in a *Scientific American* article entitled "The Dynamic Earth": "In spite of all the changes that are observed at many different scales of space and time, the Earth as a whole stays remarkably constant. . . . it has become apparent . . . that the core, the mantle, the crust, the oceans and the atmosphere can be . . . viewed as a complex, interacting system in which there is a cyclic flow of materials from one reservoir to another. . . . The Earth as a vast recycling system has its counterpart in the physiological model of dynamic equilibrium known as homeostasis."[28]

Consider two of the earth's feedback systems. One well-known example regulates the temperature of the earth. When the temperature rises, more clouds are formed. These clouds reflect back more of the sun's radiation into space, which has the effect of lowering the temperature—an example of negative feedback control.

Another so-called negative feedback system is the control of the levels of CO_2 in the atmosphere via the weathering of silicate rocks. As the CO_2 level goes up, the temperature increases due to the greenhouse effect. However, the rate of uptake of CO_2 by the weathering of silicate rocks also increases, removing CO_2 from the atmosphere, which tends to cause the temperature to fall. This is widely considered to be one of the principle long-term feedback controls on atmospheric CO_2.[29]

A particularly fascinating aspect of the role of silicate in CO_2 is the necessity for tectonic uplift if the silicate is to be exposed in any quantity to the atmosphere. Without uplift and the formation of mountain chains, the silicates would remain buried and inaccessible to weathering except for a thin superficial layer.[30]

The way in which these various factors—tectonic uplift, the crustal silicates, etc.—work together to ensure temperature stability and constant carbon dioxide levels over millions of years is very striking. The fact that (1) the silicates are the major crustal rocks, that (2) their weathering by the two major components of a carbon-based biosphere, water and carbon dioxide, produces a substance—clay—which is an ideal substratum for the growth of plants, and that (3) at the same time, the very same weathering process controls, via a negative feedback loop, both global temperature and carbon dioxide levels (which must be stringently controlled if plant life or any form of life is to thrive on earth) is further striking evidence of the fitness of the cosmos for carbon-based life.

Some of the feedback systems involve the integration of physical and biological phenomena. For example, when the amount of carbon dioxide in the atmosphere rises, this has a warming effect. However, the warming influence stimulates plant growth which extracts some of the increased carbon dioxide from the air. And in the sea the microscopic organisms that make up the plankton increase in concentration and carry increased amounts of carbonate in their minute shells to the bottom of the ocean, thus lowering the overall carbon dioxide levels in the hydrosphere.

Many other instances in which the constancy of some aspect of the earth's environment is maintained by the integration of biology and chemistry are described by James Lovelock in his book *Gaia.* In this work he develops the concept of the earth as a living organism "with the capacity to keep our planet healthy by controlling the chemical and physical environment."[31] If the Gaia hypothesis is correct, then Gaia would be, as Lovelock points out, "the largest living creature on Earth"[32] and we and all other living things would be parts and partners of a vast being who in her entirety has the power to maintain our planet as a fit and comfortable habitat for life.

Although the position taken here differs from Lovelock's Gaia hypothesis, there are some obvious parallels and the two viewpoints are not, of course, mutually exclusive. From the teleological position advocated here, when biology interacts with chemistry to maintain the constancy of the environment, this is the result of a *preexisting* mutual fitness of carbon-based life and the earth's hydrosphere. Thus, the constancy of the environment does not arise because the earth is itself a "living, self-regulating entity" but rather because the laws of nature are fit to that end.

However, Gaia is a hypothesis which cannot be so easily dismissed. Are the cells of our body aware of the organism they serve? Does an ant know it is part of a greater whole? Do most humans consider themselves components of a global ecological system? Recent work has shown that trees communicate with each other via chemical messages, or pheromones, which are carried from one tree to another in the air. When the trees on the edge of a forest suffer some injury, which might be from insects or microorganisms, they send messages across the forest warning the other trees of the impending attack. Forewarned of the danger, the trees preempt the attack by secreting chemicals that are harmful to the invading insects or microorganisms. In the case of the African Acacia, the pheromone is ethylene gas.[33] It is possible to think of all the individual members of a particular bacterial species as being members of a superorganism spread out all over the earth.[34] This is not so far-fetched as it seems, because all the members of a bacterial species are in continuous genetic communication by the exchange of genetic material via the plasmid system. If one individual bacteria acquires resistance to an antibiotic, it is this genetic communication system which spreads resistance very rapidly throughout the world to all the other bacterial members of the same species.

The Earth's Fitness

This excursion into the earth's sciences has shown that the criteria that must be satisfied by a planet if it is to possess a stable hydrosphere fit for carbon-based life are quite stringent. Press and Siever comment:[35] "Life as we know it is possible over a very narrow temperature interval . . . this interval is perhaps 1 or 2% of the range between the temperature of absolute zero and the surface temperature of the sun." And they note that this range of temperatures is only found on a planet at approximately the distance that the earth is from the sun. Continuing, they comment on the size of the Earth:[36]

> Earth's size is just about right—not too small that its gravity was too weak to hold the atmosphere and not so large that its atmosphere would hold too much atmosphere including harmful gases. . . . the Earth's interior is a delicately balanced heat engine fuelled by radioactivity. . . . were it running too slowly . . . the continents might not have evolved to their present form. . . . Iron may never have melted and sunk to the liquid core, and the magnetic field would never have developed. . . . If there had been more radioactive fuel, and therefore a faster running engine, volcanic dust would have blotted out the Sun, the atmosphere would have been oppressively dense, and the surface would have been racked by daily earthquakes and volcanic explosions.[37]

At present, astronomers know of only one planet, Earth, which satisfies all the necessary criteria and is fit for a rich diverse biosphere of carbon-based life. Mars and some of the moons of the outer planets, such as Europa, may harbor life at present or may have harbored it in the past. Mars may have been once far warmer and wetter than it is today. But at present in our own solar system, none of the other eight planets, including Mars, nor any of their fifty-four moons which surround them, are remotely as fit for complex carbon-based life as is Earth. None have provided anything resembling the wondrously stable watery and terrestrial environment for the thousands of millions of years during which life has existed and evolved on earth.

However, from everything that we now know of planetary evolution, there are no grounds for concluding that the peculiar fitness of the earth is a matter of contingency. On the contrary, the general character of the earth, its division into core, mantle, and crust, its hydrosphere, the plate tectonic system and the recycling of the crust, its chemical composition and particularly the characteristic distribution of the elements in the various layers—all these features are, as far as we can tell, the inevitable result of the interaction of a number of natural processes and phenomena including gravity, the unique physical and chemical properties of the atoms themselves, and the actual cosmic abundance of the elements in the starting material that coalesced together as the planet formed.

The proportions, for example, of the various atoms making up the various layers—core, mantle, etc.—were largely determined by their original abundance in the dust ball from which the earth formed and by their physical and chemical properties. The fact that iron, silicon, and oxygen are among the most common of the elements in the cosmos and form many nonvolatile compounds explains why together they form 80 percent of the mass of the earth. The heaviness of iron and the relative lightness of silicates (composed mainly of oxygen and silicon) explains why the earth's core is nearly 100 percent iron and why only about 6 percent of the crust is composed of iron and why the two atoms silicon and oxygen make up nearly 70 percent of the crust. The relative rarity of hydrogen, carbon, and nitrogen on earth, despite their cosmic abundance, is also explained by the fact that many of their compounds are either light or form volatile compounds which were presumably lost to space during the early history of the planet.

The size and mass of the earth has also been a critical determinant in its evolution. The fact that large planets such as Jupiter and Saturn are largely hydrogen and helium is probably the result of their larger gravitational fields, which were sufficiently strong to hold the lightest elements. Their composition reflects the cosmic abundance of the elements in the dust and gas cloud from which they initially formed. It seems likely that only planets with a relatively small mass and a weak gravitational field can lose their hydrogen and helium and other lighter volatile atoms and compounds. On the other hand, planets with a mass considerably less than that of Earth are probably too small to maintain a hydrosphere such as we have on Earth. From this it seems probable that the range of mass and hence strength of gravitational field, compatible with the formation of a solid rocky planet with a hydrosphere like Earth's, is quite small and very close to that of Earth itself.

The impression gained from these considerations is that there is nothing unusual about Earth and that, given the cosmic abundance of the elements, the laws of nature will generate a planet with chemical and physical characteristics very similar to those of Earth, with a hydrosphere supremely fit for life. The fact that the other rocky planets, Mars, Mercury, and Venus, and the Moon appear to have undergone analogous changes serves to support the conclusion. Recent studies of the voluminous data brought back by the various space missions to Mars since the 1970s, reviewed by Jeffrey Kargel and Robert Strom in *Scientific American,* suggest that in the past Mars may have been a world remarkably similar to Earth: "with flowing rivers, thawing seas, melting glaciers and perhaps abundant life."[38] The evidence suggests that Mars has experienced a complex climatic history punctuated with many relatively warm episodes. The evidence for glaciation on Mars consists of geological features which closely resemble those on Earth: "bouldery ridges of sediment left by melting glaciers at their margins and meandering lines of sand and gravel deposited beneath glaciers by streams running under the ice . . . and apron-shaped lobes of rocky debris seen on the flank of some Martian mountains [which are probably] 'rock glaciers' like the ones that form within the Alaska Range."[39] And even the recent pictures beamed back to earth by NASA, from the Mars Rover, are reminiscent of a typical desert scene on Earth today.

We still have insufficient knowledge of planetary evolution to be able to provide a really convincing explanation of why the evolution of the atmospheres on Mars, Venus, and Earth turned out so differently. Why, for instance, did Mars cool down and lose its seas? Why is Venus so hot? But reasonably plausible explanations can be provided. In answer to the question "How did the three planets—especially Earth—get to their present-day states?"[40] Ann Henderson-Sellers suggests: "The most important parameter, by a long way, is the mean global surface temperature at the time when an atmosphere began to form. This determines where the water goes to, and that in turn determines the evolution of the planetary system from then on. . . . Crucially the temperature of Venus then was high enough for water to be kept in its vapour state trapping infrared radiation, eventually producing a runaway greenhouse effect. . . . The intermediate position of our planet resulted in temperatures that ensured condensation of water vapour released into the atmosphere, forming large oceans, permitting carbon dioxide solution and leading to the formation of sedimentary rocks. . . . With carbon dioxide removed from the atmosphere the path of future temperature evolution was determined."[41]

Although the criteria which must be satisfied to form a planetary surface fit for life may indeed be stringent, nature gives every appearance of having been specifically arranged to that end. From what we now know of the history of the solar system and of the various geophysical and geochemical processes that molded the planets since they first formed out of a mass of cosmic dust some 4 billion years ago, the characteristics of Earth and in particular the maintenance of the hydrosphere and its relatively constant chemical composition—i.e., an environment fit for life—is not a matter of chance. Indeed, given a rocky planet with the mass of Earth, formed out of the matter of the cosmos about the same distance from its sun, it seems inescapable that it will turn out to be very similar to Earth. Given gravity, the cosmic abundance and properties of the atoms, the properties of the minerals formed by the combining of atoms, the phenomenon of radioactivity, the viscosity of silicate rocks, etc., then an earthlike planet with a stable hydrosphere, with oceans and rivers and rain, with mountains and volcanoes, with clay soils, with calcite rock, with a silicate crust, with plate tectonics, may be an almost inevitable end of geophysical evolution. The fact that two adjacent planets in our own solar system, Mars and Earth, are so strikingly similar, provides strong evidence in support of the notion that life-supporting planets are the inevitable end of natural law.

Whose natural law?

Other Solar Systems

If the cosmos is indeed uniquely fit for life as it exists on earth, then the existence of planetary systems capable of harboring life should be relatively common. Over the past few years techniques capable of detecting large planets the size of Jupiter and Saturn have for the first time provided convincing evidence that other planetary systems do in fact exist and may also be quite common.[42] If the views of Israeli astrophysicist Noam Soker are correct, and "stars like the sun, with several gas giant planets are the rule rather than the exception," then perhaps a significant proportion of planetary systems will resemble very closely our own—having large gaseous planets in the outer regions and small rocky planets in the inner regions.[43] As Sagan comments: "For a range of plausible initial conditions, planetary systems—about ten planets, terrestrials close to the star, Jovians on the exterior—recognizably like ours are generated."[44] Just what proportion of planetary systems will closely resemble our own is, however, controversial.[45] But even if only one in a hundred or one in a thousand solar systems resembles our own, this would still mean that there might be unimaginable numbers of planets very similar to the earth throughout the cosmos, all capable of sustaining carbon-based life very similar to that which exists on Earth. Indeed, as the authors of a recent *Nature* article comment: "Our inference . . . suggests that planetary systems are abundant in the Galaxy. We speculate that if life arises readily on terrestrial planets, then life, too, may be abundant. The recent announcement that rocks from Mars may contain evidence of life would, if confirmed, support this speculation. Our nearest neighbours may be very near indeed."[46] There may even be life in the oceans of Europa, perhaps drawing energy from geothermal sources like the hydrothermal fauna on the ocean floor of our own planet.

And there is another final and intriguing twist to the story. The fact that a significant proportion of all planetary systems may contain large Jupiter-sized gaseous planets in the same approximate position they occupy in our solar system has further teleological significance: first, because recent theoretical modeling of the dynamics of solar systems suggest that a large gaseous planet occupying the same position as Jupiter does in our own solar system confers dynamical stability to the whole planetary system, ensuring that the orbits of the other smaller planets are stable over billions of years and, second, because as planetary scientist George Wetherill points out, "without a large planet positioned precisely where Jupiter is, the earth would have been struck a thousand times more frequently in the past by comets and meteors and other interplanetary debris."[47] Wetherill continues that if it were not for Jupiter "we wouldn't be around to study the origin of the solar system."[48]

The evidence increasingly suggests that not only are there planetary systems surrounding nearly every sun, but many may resemble our own—containing rocky planets of just the right size and at just the right distance from their sun to sustain a carbon-based biosphere like that of Earth over billions of years. Moreover, many may also often contain Jupiter-sized planets of just the right size and in just the right position to confer long-term dynamical stability to the system and to protect the rocky life-bearing planets from the destructive effect of meteor bombardment. The emerging picture is entirely in keeping with the teleological preassumption that nature is ordered to generate terraqueous planets closely resembling Earth—uniquely fit for the origin, and evolution, of carbon-based life.

As we did with water and carbon, we can represent again the unique fitness of the earth for our kind of carbon-based life in the form of a graph plotting all known planetary environments against their utility or fitness for carbon-based life. What we get is a unique optimum indicated by the uniqueness and sharpness of the peak. This is perfectly consistent with the hypothesis: that there is one environment determined by the laws of nature (the hydrosphere of a planet of the same size and distance from its sun as Earth) that is uniquely and ideally fit for carbon-based life. If there had been

The unique fitness of the earth's hydrosphere for carbon-based life forms.

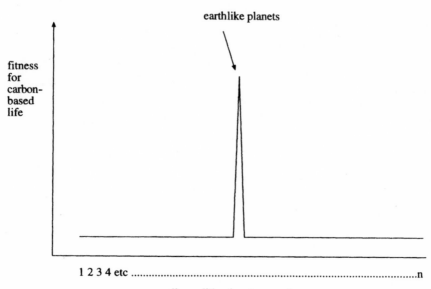

earthlike planets

fitness
for
carbon-
based
life

1 2 3 4 etc ....n

all possible planetary environments

several other types of environment having some fitness for carbon-based life, so that the plot resembled the pattern seen in the graph below, the design hypothesis would have been effectively disproved.

The comparative fitness of the earth's hydrosphere in a nonbiocentric cosmos.

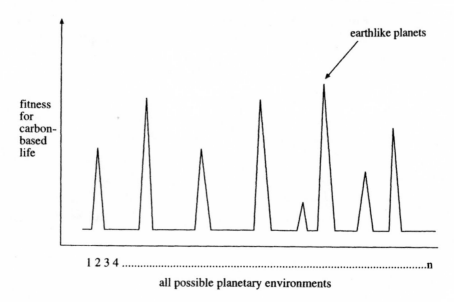

fitness for carbon-based life

earthlike planets

1 2 3 4 ....n

all possible planetary environments

Conclusion

We have learned several lessons from this excursion into the earth sciences: first, that atom building must continue to uranium if there is to be life; second, that the existence of a stable hydrosphere uniquely fit for life on the surface of a planet like the earth is not a matter of chance but the determined end of natural law; and third, that the existence of carbon-based life in this unique and marvelously stable hydrosphere depends on a vast panoply of geophysical and geochemical conditions and processes as well as the physical and chemical properties of a very great number of chemical compounds, minerals, and gases.

And we also learn that what appears to be the ideal and unique physical and chemical environment for life, the earth's hydrosphere, depends on a series of genuine and profound coincidences in the nature of things. There is the coincidence that main sequence stars like the sun provide a uniquely constant and ideal source of radiant energy to energize the water cycle on which life itself depends while at the same time emitting visible light of just the required energy levels for photobiology. Then there is, first, the coincidence that planets the size of the earth have just the proper mass to heat up sufficiently to cause, by outgassing, the formation of a hydrosphere shortly after their formation; second, that this mass provides sufficient gravitational force to retain the atmosphere and hydrosphere after the initial formation; and, third, a planet of a mass equal to the earth's has the required geophysical properties to drive the crustal tectonic cycle, which itself is so perfectly fit to function in unison with the water cycle.

It is hard to escape the feeling that planets fit for our type of life will not only have seas and booming surfs and gentle rain, they will also have volcanoes and great mountain chains on which glaciers will form and from which rivers will emerge and carry the vital nutrients of weathering into the seas and throughout the hydrosphere. There will be continental drift and plate tectonics. It is a familiar picture, and not in the least contingent, but rather the inevitable and determined outcome of natural law.

Chapter 5

The Fitness of Carbon

In which evidence is presented for believing that the chemical properties of the carbon atom are uniquely fit to form the complex molecules required for life. Silicon, which is carbon's sister atom in the periodic table, falls far short of carbon in the diversity and complexity of its compounds. The fitness of carbon compounds for life is maximal in the same temperature range that water is a fluid. Both the strong covalent and the weak bonds are of maximal utility in this same temperature range. Such coincidences are precisely what one might expect to see in a cosmos specially adapted for carbon-based life.

The compounds of carbon.

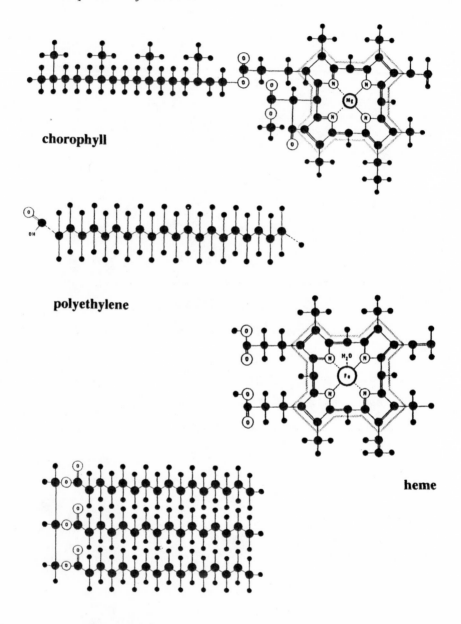

chorophyll

polyethylene

heme

triglyceride

From N. J. Berrill (1966) *Biology in Action* (New York: Dodd, Mead), fig. 3.8 and fig. 3.16. Reproduced by permission of N. J. Berrill.

Nature has been kinder to us than we had any right to expect. As we look out into the universe and identify the many accidents of physics and astronomy that have worked together for our benefit, it almost seems as if the universe in some sense must have known that we were coming.

—Freeman Dyson, *Scientific American* magazine, 1971

I should consider that I know nothing about physics if I were able to explain only how things *might* be, and were unable to demonstrate that they *could not be otherwise.*

—René Descartes, letter to Mersenne, 1640

We saw in chapter 2 that water is wonderfully fit for its biological role, giving every appearance of being ideally and uniquely "prefabricated" in all its chemical and physical properties to serve as the matrix of carbon-based life as it exists on earth. And we have also seen, in the previous two chapters, that both the light of the sun and the earth's crustal rocks and hydrosphere are also remarkably fit for life in many different ways. Together they create a unique, chemically and thermally stable environment which has been bathed in a limitless and constant source of radiant energy for 4 billion years.

However, the hypothesis that the cosmos is uniquely and ideally fit for life cannot be secured by showing that one or two, or even several, of the conditions necessary for life appear to be ideally adapted to the ends they serve. If the hypothesis is true, then we should expect to find that all the basic conditions for life and all of the components of living organisms are ideally and uniquely adapted to the particular biological ends they serve, "as if the Creator has given us a kit of prefabricated parts ready made for the work in hand," in the words of Robert E. D. Clark.[1] We shall see in this chapter, and the following chapters, that this does indeed appear to be the case.

Organic Compounds

A house is built up from wood, brick, stone, and metal components. A car engine is built up mainly from metal components. Many household goods are constructed out of plastic components. Computers are composed of various components made up of plastics, metals, and silicon chips. In the case of living organisms, the basic chemical building blocks utilized in their construction are organic compounds—molecules composed of the atom carbon (C), in combination with a handful of other atoms which include hydrogen (H), oxygen (O), and nitrogen (N).

The world of life is very much the product of the compounds of carbon. All the machinery of the cell, and all the vital structures of living organisms from the molecular to the morphological level, are constructed from the compounds of carbon. Structures as diverse as the cell membrane, the horns of an elk, the trunk of a redwood, the lens of the eye, the venom of a spider, the petals of a flower, the DNA helix, and the blood pigment hemoglobin, are all composed almost entirely of compounds made up of combinations of the carbon atom with hydrogen, oxygen, and nitrogen.

The possibility that living things might be some sort of carbon-based chemical machine had already been raised in the late eighteenth century when Antoine Lavoisier and Pierre Laplace established that water and carbon dioxide are the products of animal and human respiration and that the oxidation of carbon and hydrogen was the source of animal heat and an essential process of life.[2] However, the critical role of carbon and its compounds in the design of life was only fully appreciated in the second half of the nineteenth century. A major distraction in the early nineteenth century in the way of a true appreciation of the marvels of carbon chemistry was the vitalistic doctrine prevalent at the time. According to vitalism, living substances were in some essential way different from nonliving, and their synthesis in living things was the result of some mysterious vital force. Chemistry was therefore divided into two divisions: inorganic, which dealt with the substances and compounds of the inorganic world and which were amenable to scientific analysis, and organic, dealing with the substances of life. The nature and formation of organic substances was imagined to be beyond scientific analysis.

Vitalism remained unchallenged throughout the period between 1780 to 1828, when chemistry was being established as a science and chemical knowledge rapidly increased. By 1820, forty different elements were known, and the great Swedish chemist Berzelius had himself described the preparation, purification, and exact quantitative analysis of two thousand different compounds. It was also well established by then that the element carbon was a key constituent of life.[3] It was only after the synthesis of urea by Friedrich Wöhler in 1828, and shortly afterward of many other undoubted constituents of animals and plants, that the way was open to bring the study of biochemicals fully into the scope of science.

Shortly after Wöhler and the collapse of the vitalistic doctrine, the English chemist William Prout suggested for the first time in his 1834 Bridgewater Treatise entitled *Chemistry, Meteorology, and the Function of Digestion* that the carbon atom may be uniquely fit for life because of its potential to form vast numbers of diverse compounds.[4] After 1840 the development of organic chemistry as a unique branch of chemistry gathered momentum. And as Henderson points out, by the turn of the nineteenth century it was clear that, in the number and diversity of its compounds, carbon is without peer among the other 92 elements. At least 100,000 different compounds were known.[5]

The Carbon Atom

The reason for the unique diversity and number of carbon compounds lies in certain unique characteristics of the carbon atom, atom 8 in the periodic table.[6] As the British chemist Nevil Sidgwick explains in his classic textbook *Chemical Elements and Their Compounds:*

> Carbon is unique among the elements in the number and variety of the compounds which it can form. Over a quarter of a million have already been isolated and described, but this gives a very imperfect idea of its powers, since it is the basis of all forms of living matter. Moreover it is the only element which could occupy such a position. We know enough now to be sure that the idea of a world in which silicon should take the place of carbon as the basis of life is impossible. . . . [7]

Two of the reasons for the great diversity of carbon compounds compared with silicon given by Sidgwick are, first, that "silicon compounds have not the stability of those of carbon, and in particular it is not possible to form stable compounds with long chains of silicon atoms," and, second, because "the affinity of carbon for the most diverse elements and especially for itself, for hydrogen, nitrogen, oxygen and the halogens, does not differ very greatly: so that even the most diverse derivatives need not vary very much in energy content, that is thermodynamic stability."[8] Yet another characteristic of carbon is its capacity, by sharing two or more of its electrons with another atom, to form what are known as multiple bonds. Silicon does not share this capacity, and its chemistry is consequently much less rich and diverse.[9]

Covalent Bonds

When carbon combines with other atoms to form organic compounds, the bonds between the atoms are known as covalent bonds or "ordinary chemical bonds." In all the molecular structures shown in figure 5.1, the atoms are all linked together by covalent bonds. Covalent bonds are formed when atoms share electrons in their outer electron shell in an attempt to complete the shell. We saw in the previous chapter that each shell can contain up to a certain maximum number of electrons. The innermost shell can contain up to 2 electrons, the next shell can contain up to 8 and the next, up to 18.

In the diagram below, which shows the atomic structure of water (H_2O), note that by sharing electrons the outer shells of both the oxygen and the two hydrogen atoms are complete. Oxygen has only 6 electrons in its outer shell and requires 2 additional electrons to fill this shell with its maximum permitted number.

The structure of water.

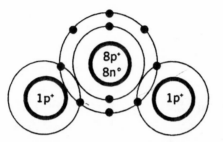

From fig. 3 in M. Toporek, *The Basic Chemistry of Life;* © 1968 by Appleton & Lange, Stamford, Conn. Reproduced by permission of the publisher.

In the compound methane (CH_4), shown below, by sharing electrons each of the hydrogens is able to make its outer shell up to 2 electrons (the maximum permitted for the inner shell) while the carbon atom is able to make its outer shell up to 8 electrons, which is again the maximum permitted.

The structure of methane.

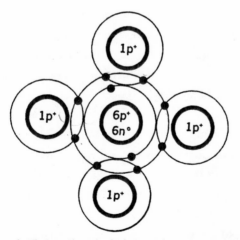

From fig. 3 in M. Toporek, *The Basic Chemistry of Life;* © 1968 by Appleton & Lange, Stamford, Conn. Reproduced by permission of the publisher.

The Diversity of Carbon Compounds

Carbon, linked with the first atom in the periodic table, hydrogen, forms the vast family of hydrocarbons, which is divided into several subdivisions. Even within this small subgroup of organic compounds, the diversity of chemical and physical properties is great. Within this group are found natural gas, liquid petroleum, gasoline, kerosene, lubricating oils, greases, and waxes. The hydrocarbons ethylene and propylene form the basis of the petrochemical industry and are used to form the plastics polyethylene and polypropylene. Other hydrocarbons form solvents such as benzene, toluene, and turpentine. Naphthalene, a solid hydrocarbon, is the insecticide in mothballs. Hydrocarbons combined with chlorine or fluorine form anesthetics, various solvents, fire extinguishers, and the Freons used in refrigeration. Some hydrocarbons are long chainlike molecules such as pentane and butene. Others contain cyclic or ringlike formations such as benzene.

C_2H_5OH

In conjunction with both hydrogen (H) and oxygen (O) another vast set of carbon compounds is derived. These include the alcohols, such as ethanol and propanol, the aldehydes, the ketones, and the fatty acids. Fatty acids are composed of a long hydrocarbon chain which is attached to a carboxylic acid group at one end. Another group of compounds composed of carbon, hydrogen, and oxygen are the sugars, including glucose and fructose. Cellulose (the hard substance of wood), beeswax, vinegar, and formic acid all belong to this group of carbon compounds.

Carbon combined with hydrogen, oxygen, and nitrogen leads to a further multiplicity of compounds, including the building blocks of proteins—the amino acids. Also within this group are a set of cyclic compounds known as the nitrogenous bases, some of which are important building blocks of DNA. The stimulant caffeine, which occurs in coffee and tea, is also a nitrogenous base.

The total number and diversity of possible chemical structures that may be constructed out of carbon, oxygen, hydrogen, and nitrogen is virtually unlimited. Almost any imaginable chemical shape and chemical property can be derived. Together these elements form what is in effect a universal chemical constructor kit, which is ideally suited for the construction of complex chemical machines containing a great variety of chemical devices and calling for a vast number of different chemical components of different chemical and physical properties.

THE FITNESS OF CARBON · 109

A striking aspect of this great molecular plenitude is that the atoms which comprise it—carbon, hydrogen, oxygen, and nitrogen—are among the first few atoms manufactured in the stars and also among the most abundant overall in the cosmos. And remarkably, two of these atoms, hydrogen and oxygen, form water, the matrix of carbon-based life. It is as if from the very moment of creation the biochemistry of life was already preordained in the atom-building process, as if Nature were biased to this end from the beginning.

The Mildness and Metastability of Carbon Compounds

The diversity of carbon compounds is only one of many factors which make carbon chemistry so fit for the intricate and complex metabolic processes of life. Another factor is the mildness of the chemical properties of most organic compounds. No organic acids are as violently reactive as sulfuric or nitric acid, no bases as corrosive as caustic soda. This curious mildness arises in part from the relative inertness of the carbon atom.[10] In addition to their mildness, organic compounds tend to exhibit what the great biologist J. B. S. Haldane called a characteristic "metastability," a word he defined in a symposium some time ago:

> A metastable molecule means one that can liberate free energy by a transformation, but is stable enough to last a long time unless it is activated by heat, radiation, or union with a catalyst. For example trinitrotoluene is highly metastable; a kilogram of it liberates a lot of energy. Glucose is mildly metastable, but will liberate some energy if turned into ethanol and carbon dioxide. . . . most organic molecules are metastable.[11]

This term very nicely captures an essential characteristic of organic compounds and one which makes them of great utility to living chemistry. This metastability arises because, although relatively stable, most are also quite reactive and readily undergo covalent chemical reactions with other carbon compounds under relatively mild conditions. In other words, they do not require much energy to be activated for covalent chemical reactions at ambient temperatures and conditions.

A. E. Needham commented in his *Uniqueness of Biological Materials* on the characteristic metastability which allows their manipulation without prohibitively high-energy expenditure or release: "Carbon compounds are notable for lability as much as their stability. Few remain unchanged when heated above 300°C. . . . As in so many respects carbon seems to have the best of both worlds, combining stability with lability, momentum with inertia. . . . [12] The heat of formation of carbon compounds from their immediate precursors is rarely very great, so that, once the initial steps of carbon dioxide reduction have been effected, a large variety of compounds form relatively spontaneously."[13] Henderson was also struck by the same point.[14]

However, this "metastability" which is so crucial to the utility of organic compounds is only manifest in a very narrow temperature range. As the temperature rises above 100°C, organic compounds become increasingly reactive and chemically unstable. We are all familiar with this phenomenon. Cooking nicely illustrates it. Even the gentle heating of meats or other foodstuffs, for some time, at temperatures of only about 90°C, called simmering, can cause dramatic changes in their chemical and physical characteristics. The softening of meat occurs because the collagen fibers which make up the tendons and fibrous sheets are converted into soft gelatin, which offers no resistance to a knife.[15] When sugars are heated above 100°C, they are rapidly degraded, undergoing complex chemical reactions with themselves and other biomolecules in the food. These changes are referred to as caramelization and browning in the kitchen. Many vitamins, including vitamin C, folic acid, and some of the other B vitamins—B1 and B6, for example— are rapidly broken down above 100°C.[16] Recent studies of the stability of organic compounds at 250°C, including one report in the journal *Nature,* showed that the half-life of many of the key organic compounds used by living things, including such important compounds as amino acids, used in the construction of proteins, the bases used in the construction of DNA, and the energy-rich phosphate compound known as adenosine triphosphate, or ATP (see Appendix) which plays a vital role in the energy metabolism of all living cells on earth, decompose at rates too fast to measure, or have half-lives lasting minutes or seconds at 250°C.[17]

The instability of most organic compounds, especially as temperatures rise above 100°C, was discussed by Miller and Orgel in their book *The Origins of Life on the Earth.*[18] In the case of the amino acid alanine, for example, its half-life is 20 billion years at 0°C, 3 billion years at 25°C, but only ten years at 150°C, a decrease of more than a billionfold.

While foodstuffs, made up of organic carbon compounds, undergo considerable physical and chemical changes during cooking, the metal or glass containers remain unchanged. Put a piece of glass, a piece of metal, a piece of rock, etc., in a cooker, and while foodstuffs will char, burn, or decom-

THE FITNESS OF CARBON · 111

pose at 150°C, the inorganic materials will remain unchanged. And at temperatures much above 100°C to 150°C, the reactivity and instability of organic compounds increases prohibitively and their utility for biochemistry rapidly diminishes. At low temperatures other problems emerge. Below 0°C, reaction rates are so enormously slowed that anything we would recognize as a "biochemistry" utilizing the compounds of carbon becomes impossible.

The effect of temperature on the rates of chemical reaction is quite dramatic: for each 10°C fall in temperature the rate of reaction declines by a factor of two.[19] It follows from this relationship that a fall in temperature of 100°C will slow chemical reactions nearly a thousand times! Even a temperature change of far less than 100°C causes a quite dramatic slowing of reaction times. Reactions occurring in the human body at 38°C would take place sixteen times slower at 0°C and sixty-four times slower at −20°C. As Robert E. D. Clark points out, at temperatures below −100°C all chemical reactions become vanishingly slow and at the temperature of liquid air, "only a very few reactions take place at all and these involve the exceedingly active element fluorine in its free state."[20] Even though some organic chemistry would be possible at temperatures as low as −40°C, as Wald points out, "the process that led to the origin of life within a period of perhaps a billion years upon this planet might take some 64 billion years at −40°C."[21]

The vast and unique plenitude of organic compounds can only be exploited by living systems within a temperature range of approximately −20°C to 120°C. It is only within this range that the majority of carbon compounds have their characteristic metastability, which permits the intricate and sophisticated manipulation of their constituent atoms by the chemical machinery of life.

The Temperature Range of Organic Chemistry

Now although the temperature difference between −20°C and 120°C, i.e., 140°C, appears from our ordinary perspective to be considerable, it represents in fact an unimaginably tiny fraction of the total range of all possible temperatures. Temperatures in the cosmos range from 10^{32}°C, (10 followed by 31 zeros), which was the temperature of the universe shortly after the big bang, to very close to absolute zero, which is −273.15°C.[22] The temperature inside some of the hottest stars is several billion degrees,[23] and even inside our own sun, which is not particularly hot for a star, the temperature is tens of millions of degrees and its surface temperature is 6,000°C.

The diagram below indicates the temperature range in which carbon compounds exhibit the necessary metastability to make them of utility to life. It is surely a highly suggestive coincidence that the chemical reactivity of the one great class of compounds, uniquely fit in so many other ways to serve as the building blocks of life, is of *optimal utility for the complex atomic and molecular manipulations associated with life in precisely that temperature range—0°C to 100°C—in which water, the one fluid supremely fit to serve as the matrix for carbon-based life forms, exists as a liquid at sea level on the earth.*

It is interesting to note in passing that liquid water would not exist on earth if the atmospheric pressure was less than half what it is. Which implies (since the density and pressure of a planet's atmosphere is largely determined by its size) that it is unlikely that planets much smaller than the earth would contain large quantities of liquid water for any long period of time. At pressures much higher than atmospheric, liquid water can exist at temperatures of up to several hundred degrees. Much of the water in the earth's crust is in fact much hotter than 100°C. However, water at such temperatures is of little utility for carbon-based life.

Most of the matter in the cosmos is either vastly hotter (the interior of stars) or much colder (interstellar space) than the surface of the earth. And it seems likely that one of the few environments in the cosmos where liquid water in quantity between 0°C and 100°C can exist—i.e., in the temperature range in which organic compounds are metastable and the chemical bonds which link their constituent atoms can be manipulated with "ease"— is on the surface of a planet like the earth. This reinforces the conclusion

The temperature range within which organic chemicals are metastable and of utility for biochemistry.

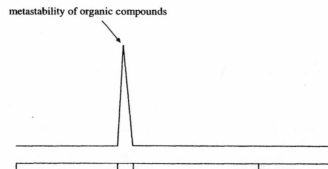

metastability of organic compounds

-297 °C	0 °C - 100 °C	2000 billion °C	10 ³² °C
(absolute zero)		(centre of hottest star)	(big bang)

reached in the previous chapter that the surface of rocky planets like the earth provide an environment uniquely and ideally fit for carbon-based life, in not one but in several different ways.

The Weak Bonds

The covalent chemical bonds which link the atoms together in organic compounds are not the only type of chemical bond utilized in living systems. There is another class of bonds, known as weak, or noncovalent, bonds. There are several different types of weak bonds.[24]

These bonds are about twenty times weaker than covalent bonds, and they play a vital role in holding together the different parts of large organic molecules, such as proteins in complex, unique three-dimensional forms (this topic is touched on again in chapter 8). In the diagram below, the atoms (shown as black dots) of an organic molecule are linked by covalent bonds shown as continuous lines joining the individual circles.

An organic compound showing its constituent atoms (black dots) linked together by covalent bonds (black lines).

The complex, three-dimensional, functional form of large biomolecules, such as proteins and DNA, is maintained by weak bonds which hold the atoms together in different parts of the molecule. This is shown in the diagram below, where the weak bonds are represented by broken lines.

An organic compound held in a unique 3-D form by weak noncovalent bonds (dotted lines).

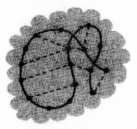

If we think of a string of beads or plastic balls held together in a three-dimensional cluster by pieces of tape, we have an analogy which conveys something of the difference between covalent and weak bonds. The string represents the strong covalent bonds, and the pieces of tape, the weak bonds. Nearly all the biological activities of virtually all the large molecules in the cell are critically dependent on their possessing very precise 3-D shapes. Nature has provided no other glue to hold together the molecular superstructure of the cell. While we cannot have carbon-based life in the cosmos without covalent bonds, as there would be no molecules, just as certainly, we cannot have carbon-based life without these weak noncovalent bonds—because the molecules would not have stable, complex 3-D shapes.

We have seen above that the covalent chemistry of carbon is of maximal utility for life in a very narrow temperature range which corresponds approximately with the range in which water is a liquid. Remarkably, these weak bonds are also of utility in approximately the same small temperature range. In fact, weak bonds are even more temperature-sensitive than covalent bonds. Most weak bonds in existing biomolecules such as proteins are disrupted by increases in temperature which leave covalent bonds intact.

The disruption of weak bonds occurs in two very familiar processes in the kitchen—in the heating and beating of egg white, both of which cause the egg white to whiten and coagulate. In a fascinating discussion in *Scientific American* in 1981, Jearl Walker described the role of the weak bonds in the making of a lemon meringue pie:

> When a cook forces a whisk through egg whites, shearing the fluid, some of the weaker bonds are ruptured and parts of the 3D structure of the proteins [present in the egg white] are destroyed. The cook does not totally disrupt the proteins because the forces [the covalent bonds] holding them in their primary structures are comparatively strong. . . . Any such altering of the structure of a protein is called denaturing.
>
> Once the proteins are partially unravelled [denatured] they begin to attach themselves to one another to form a three-dimensional mesh or gel. This interaction between the proteins is unlikely before denaturation because the proteins are relatively globular and relatively few of their sites for possible [weak] bonds are exposed.
>
> When the mixture is heated . . . the heat further denatures the proteins, un-

ravelling them further and thus enabling the mesh to stretch . . . coagulating the whites into a firm structure.[25]

Because covalent bonds are far more robust, neither beating nor heating has any significant effect and most remain intact. In effect weak bonds are even more "metastable" than covalent bonds.

The extreme sensitivity of the weak bonds to increases in temperature limits their utility in maintaining the three-dimensional form of complex biomolecules to temperatures not far above 100°C. It seems likely that no protein could be designed to function at temperatures much above 120°C.[26] There is little experimental evidence as to the utility of weak interactions below 0°C. But it seems likely that the thermal energy at temperatures much below 0°C and certainly below −20°C would be insufficient to allow the formation and breakdown of weak bonds at speeds remotely compatible with any sort of functional biochemistry.

We can conclude that the weak bonds are only of utility for holding organic compounds into complex 3-D forms, within the temperature range of approximately 0°C to 100°C (see diagram below).

What we have, then, is another coincidence of critical significance—that the weak bonds, which are of a completely different nature from the strong covalent bonds, are also of utility in a temperature range which very nearly corresponds with that in which water exists as a liquid.

Out of the enormous range of temperatures in the cosmos, there is only one tiny temperature band in which we have (1) liquid water, (2) a great

The temperature range within which weak bonds are of utility to biological systems.

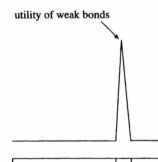

utility of weak bonds

-273.15 ºC
(absolute zero)   0 ºC - 100 ºC   2000 billion ºC
(center of hottest star)   10 ³² ºC
(big bang)

plenitude of metastable organic compounds, and (3) weak bonds for stabilizing the 3-D forms of complex molecules.

Conclusion

In short, then, the covalent compounds of carbon, and especially those containing oxygen, hydrogen, and nitrogen, the substances of life, possess just those characteristics of complexity, diversity, and metastability essential if any sort of complex chemical system is to *manipulate its atomic and molecular components in complex and intricate ways.* Moreover, this plenitude is of maximum utility in the same temperature range that water, the ideal matrix for life based on carbon chemistry, is a liquid, and where the weak bonds can be utilized to maintain the delicate three-dimensional molecular conformations upon which the functions of the cell's molecular machinery depend.

Carbon is so uniquely fit for its biological role, its various compounds so vital to the existence of life, that we may repeat the aphorism, "If carbon did not exist, it would have to be invented." The unique fitness of the carbon atom can be represented graphically as shown below.

The utility of atoms for the construction of complex chemical systems.

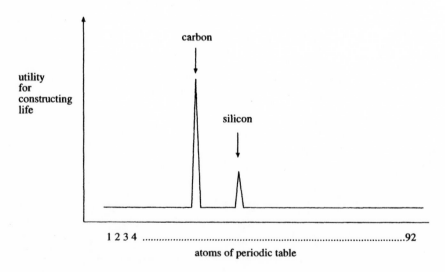

Chapter 6

The Vital Gases

In which the various adaptations which permit the use of oxidation by living systems to generate energy are examined. Oxygen is a very reactive atom and it can only be utilized by biochemical systems because of a number of adaptations, including: the attenuation of its reactivity below about 50°C; its low solubility; the fact that the transitional atoms such as iron and copper have just the right chemical characteristics to manipulate the oxygen atom; that the end product of the oxidation of carbon is carbon dioxide, an innocuous gas. Moreover, the reaction of carbon dioxide with water provides living things with a buffer—the bicarbonate buffer which has just the right characteristics to buffer organisms, especially air-breathing organisms, against increases in acidity. The chain of coincidences in the nature of things which permit higher forms of life to utilize oxygen provides further evidence of the unique fitness of nature for carbon-based life. Many of these adaptations are of special utility for large air-breathing organisms, including the fact that both oxygen and carbon dioxide are gases at ambient temperatures. Another fascinating coincidence is that only atmospheres with between 10 and 20 percent oxygen can support oxidative metabolism in a higher organism, and it is only within this range that fire—and hence metallurgy and technology—is possible.

The human lung, showing the bronchial tree.

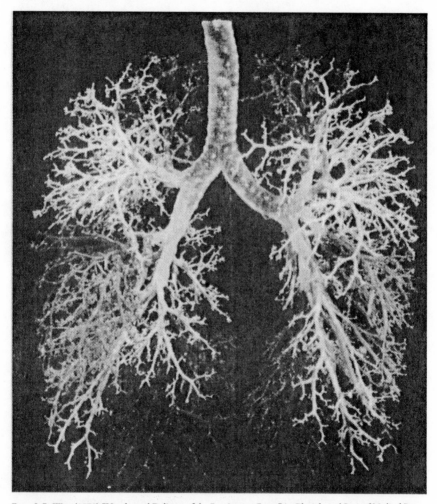

From J. B. West (1979) "Uptake and Delivery of the Respiratory Gases," in *Physiological Basis of Medical Practice*, 10th ed., J. B. Brobeck, ed. © 1979 Williams and Wilkins, Baltimore, fig 6.3. Reproduced by permission of the publisher.

And the Lord God formed man of the dust of the ground, and breathed
into his nostrils the breath of life, and man became a living soul.

—Genesis 2:7

In many science-fiction novels distant life-supporting planets resemble earth in many key respects. They often have water (if not quite as much as on earth) and complex plants and animals similar to those on earth. But the first thing humans must do on landing on an alien world is test the air to see if it is breathable. Apparently, sci-fi novelists assume that the one element of the earth's biosphere that can most easily vary is its atmosphere. Are they correct? Actually, no. As we shall see, only an atmosphere with very specific characteristics can support the life of complex, active air-breathing organisms such as mammals. And it is no accident that it also contains oxygen.

Oxidation

A major requirement for life is energy, and chemical reactions are an obvious source. Living things do, in fact, exploit a vast variety of chemical reactions to supply their energy needs.[1]

However, the great majority of the chemical reactions utilized are classed as oxidations. Oxidation is a very familiar type of chemical reaction. Two examples are burning wood and rusting iron. Life on earth utilizes a great diversity of oxidations. The bacteria at the base of the hydrothermal food chain oxidize hydrogen sulfide to sulfate and water. Other bacteria oxidize ferrous iron and hydrogen to ferric iron and water respectively. To a nonchemist it may seem curious, but not all oxidations require free atmospheric oxygen. Many can occur in an anaerobic environment, because in the absence of oxygen other compounds such as sulfates or nitrates which contain oxygen are used in place of oxygen itself.[2]

All higher organisms obtain their energy supply from one of the most important chemical reactions on earth—the complete oxidation of reduced hydrocarbons to carbon dioxide and water:

reduced carbon compounds + oxygen = water + carbon dioxide

As the oxidant in this reaction is oxygen itself, the process can only occur in an aerobic environment. This key reaction provides *many times more energy than any of the multitude of alternative energy-generating reactions.* Without it, higher active forms of life would not be possible.[3] The energy generated is used to manufacture the energy-rich molecules of ATP (adenosine triphosphate) in the mitochondria—a process called oxidative phosphorylation. (See chapter 9 and Appendix, section 3, for further details.)

Oxidation has many advantages. First, oxygen far surpasses any other chemical element except fluorine in the amount of energy liberated in the process of combining with other elements. Fluorine is, however, dangerously reactive at ambient temperatures. Also, while the chemical combination of hydrogen and oxygen results in the formation of water, when fluorine reacts with hydrogen, the product hydrofluoric acid is one of the most dangerously reactive of all acids. Moreover, fluorine has a great affinity for carbon and consequently the bonds between fluorine and carbon are very strong and can only be broken with considerable difficulty.[4]

Second, the compounds of carbon and hydrogen, which are the two most common atoms in organic compounds, are especially well qualified to be reservoirs of chemical energy liberated by oxidation, because hydrogen far exceeds any other element in the amount of energy that it yields upon oxidation and carbon is surpassed only by hydrogen and one other element, boron. Although there is less energy in compounds of hydrogen and carbon that also contain oxygen, such as sugars, proteins, and fats, a sufficient amount remains to make them highly efficient energy stores, holding far more energy than most other elements and far greater reservoirs of energy than the compounds of any other elements. Henderson was struck by the coincidence that oxygen is very nearly the most reactive atom, releasing great amounts of energy when reacting with other atoms, and that of all oxidations, those of reduced carbon compounds yield the most energy: "The very chemical changes, which for so many other reasons seem to be best fitted to become the processes of physiology, turn out to be the very ones which can divert the greatest flood of energy into the stream of life."[5]

The Reactivity of Oxygen

Could our atmosphere contain more oxygen and still support life? No! Oxygen is a very reactive element. Even the current percentage of oxygen in the atmosphere, 21 percent (partial pressure 150 mm Hg), is close to the upper limit of safety for life at ambient temperatures. The probability of a forest fire being ignited by lightning increases by as much as 70 percent for every 1 percent increase in the percentage of oxygen in the atmosphere.[6] As James Lovelock puts it in *Gaia:* "Above 25% very little of our present land vegetation could survive the raging conflagrations which would destroy tropical rain forests and arctic tundra alike. . . . The present oxygen level is at a point where risk and benefit nicely balance."[7]

A forest fire is ample witness both to the enormous energy released by the combustion or oxidation of organic compounds and testimony to the great increase in the reactivity of oxygen as the temperature rises. The greatly increased reactivity of oxygen and the consequent danger of runaway combustion as the temperature rises above about 50°C imposes an upper temperature limit on a carbon-based biosphere possessing an atmosphere like that of the earth.

Some authorities in the field of oxygen chemistry have wondered humorously why humans don't spontaneously combust, since our bodies contain so many atoms of carbon and hydrogen.[8] We do not combust because of the curious relative chemical inertness of the molecular species dioxygen (O_2), which is the molecular form of oxygen at ambient temperatures. The reason for this relative inertness lies in certain unique features of the oxygen atom. These were discussed by M. J. Green and A. O. Hill in a recent article.[9]

Curiously, the inertness of O_2, although essential if carbon-based life is to coexist with oxygen, is sufficient to pose a significant obstacle to its use in biological systems. This was already perceived to be a problem as early as the mid nineteenth century.[10] Advances over the past seventy years have revealed that the utilization of oxygen by living things is due to the catalytic action of a number of enzymes. These enzymes in turn utilize the properties of the transition metal atoms such as iron and copper, which have exactly the right atomic characteristics to carry out the activation of the O_2 molecule (see chapter 9). Activated by metal catalysts, oxygen becomes potent and highly reactive.[11]

The vigor of the reaction between carbon and oxygen is further attenuated by what Sidgwick referred to as the "characteristic inertness of carbon."[12] We have all experienced the relative unreactivity of carbon at ambient temperatures—when trying to start a coal or wood fire, particularly on a cold evening, i.e., to initiate the chemical combination between oxygen and carbon. And we have also all experienced the enormous energy released when the carbon in the coal or wood is finally coaxed to react with the oxygen and the fire starts to burn. The character of a simple wood or coal fire teaches important lessons in the chemistry of carbon and oxygen. A fire is difficult to start but, once started, releases great quantities of heat and energy and is difficult to stop. This curious unreactivity of the carbon and oxygen atoms at ambient temperatures, combined with the enormous energies inherent in their combination once achieved, is of great adaptive significance to life on earth. It is this curious combination that not only makes

THE VITAL GASES · 123

available to advanced life forms the vast energies of oxidation in a controlled and orderly manner but has also made possible the controlled use of fire by mankind and allowed the harnessing of the massive energies of combustion for the development of technology.

To summarize, oxygen is fit (1) because of the great amount of energy released when it combines with hydrogen and carbon, and (2) because its chemical reactivity is attenuated at ambient temperatures (below about 50°C), allowing living systems to utilize this awesome energy source in a controlled and efficient manner.

The Solubility of Oxygen

The chemical fitness of oxygen to living systems can only be exploited if additional conditions are satisfied. The solubility and rate at which oxygen diffuses in water is obviously critical. Since water is the matrix of life, if oxygen was either insoluble in water or chemically unstable in an aqueous solution, it would be incapable of playing any biological role.

The amount of a gas dissolved in a fluid depends on two factors: the partial pressure of the gas in the atmosphere, or air phase, in contact with the fluid, and the solubility of the gas in that particular fluid, which is a physical constant. For example, in the case of oxygen, the amount of oxygen that dissolves in a body of water is dependent on the solubility constant of oxygen and the partial pressure of the oxygen in the air above the water.

The earth's atmosphere contains about 21 percent oxygen, and consequently the partial pressure of oxygen is 150 mm Hg (21 percent of atmospheric pressure at sea level). Each 100 milliliters of water in contact with the air contains about 0.45 milliliters of oxygen gas at sea level.

It turns out that the solubility of oxygen is just sufficient to allow organisms, especially those with a high metabolic rate, to utilize oxidation as a means of energy generation. If it was any lower, organisms would not be able to extract oxygen from an aqueous solution at a sufficient rate to satisfy their metabolic needs. Even as it is, all actively metabolizing organisms depend on complex physiological adaptations to extract and transport sufficient quantities of oxygen to satisfy their energy needs. The delivery of sufficient oxygen to supply the metabolic requirements of the human body is critically dependent on the integrated activity of the circulatory and respiratory system and the special oxygen-carrying blood pigment hemoglobin.

The design constraints are such that it is hard to see how the oxygen-carrying capacity of the blood could be much increased.

But even if the blood's oxygen-carrying capacity could be increased several times by the use of, say, some imaginary superhemoglobin, the oxygen atoms would still have to diffuse across an aqueous layer to be "taken up by the carrier" in the lungs and diffuse across another aqueous layer when "leaving their carrier" in the tissues. As the rate of diffusion of oxygen in water is directly related to its solubility, the solubility of oxygen poses an absolute limit on the rate at which any hypothetical carrier could be loaded or unloaded with oxygen and consequently an absolute limit on the rate of delivery of oxygen to the tissues. In effect, no matter how good the capacity of the carrier system, the amount of oxygen the tissue fluids can hold is limited by the solubility constant of oxygen. If a gas is insoluble in water, then no matter how efficient a carrier molecule, the gas can never diffuse through an aqueous medium.

Clearly, if the solubility of oxygen or its rate of diffusion in water had been significantly less, then no conceivable type of circulatory or respiratory system would have been capable of delivering sufficient oxygen to support the metabolic activities of highly active, warm-blooded, air-breathing organisms in an atmosphere with a partial pressure of oxygen of 150 mm Hg.

The solubility of oxygen and hence the amount of the gas that a particular volume of water can contain falls rapidly as the temperature of water rises. The solubility at 0°C is twice that at 30°C and nearly four times that at 100°C.[13] The fact that the metabolic demand for oxygen doubles with every ten-degree increase in temperature[14] is also bound to impose an additional burden as the temperature rises above body temperature. At 58°C the demand for oxygen would theoretically be four times greater than at 38°C (the normal body temperature of many mammals), but this is just when the solubility and availability of oxygen is rapidly diminishing. *It would seem that while primitive unicellular forms of life can exist at all temperatures at which water is a liquid, higher complex multicellular life—which depends on the energy released from the complete oxidation of reduced carbon by free oxygen—is restricted to a temperature range between 0°C and 50°C.*

In passing, it is interesting to note that the specific heat of water is at its lowest between 35°C and 40°C, not far below 50°C. It is within this small temperature range, where water is most easily warmed and organisms can most easily activate their chemical machinery,[15] that most active organisms, including our own species, maintain their body temperature. It is conceivable that this same temperature range may be the optimum for the functioning of proteins and for the replication of nucleic acids and many other biochemical and physiological processes.

Because the problem of runaway combustion imposes an upper limit on the level of oxygen in the atmosphere which is close to the current partial pressure of oxygen in the earth's atmosphere of 150 mm Hg, if the solubility constant of oxygen had been significantly lower, then oxygen would be of little utility to life on earth, especially to organisms with high metabolic rates, such as mammals. It is doubtful indeed if any complex active organisms would have been possible, as no other chemical means of energy generation remotely as efficient as oxidation is available to carbon-based life forms.

On the other hand, had oxygen been more soluble than it is, this would have also produced very serious problems and would have greatly detracted from its fitness. As discussed above, oxygen is basically a very dangerous reactive substance and is highly toxic to life at levels above those normally encountered in nature. Oxygen toxicity is caused because a small proportion of oxygen atoms are continually interacting with water, producing highly reactive damaging radicals.[16] If for any reason this process increases beyond the normally low levels that occur naturally, it can be fatal. As Irwin Fridovich comments: "All respiring organisms are caught in a cruel trap. The very oxygen which supports their lives is toxic to them and they survive precariously, only by virtue of elaborate defence mechanisms."[17]

Many body cells die if directly exposed to the oxygen in the atmosphere,[18] and in fact the partial pressure of oxygen in most of the tissues is only about 50 mm Hg, which is about one third of that in the atmosphere.[19] In medicine, for example, great care must be taken in various medical procedures where oxygen is being used for therapeutic purposes. A raised partial pressure of oxygen may cause serious oxygen toxicity in a relatively short time.[20] Even slight increases in the level of oxygen dissolved in the blood can cause oxidative damage in the lungs and retina and other tissues. In fact, all organisms which utilize oxygen possess a number of enzymes specifically designed to eliminate reactive oxygen radicals. These enzymes utilize the properties of certain metal atoms, particularly the transitional metals that possess properties which are perfectly fit to handle and tame these reactive radicals. The problem of oxygen toxicity clearly imposes a limit on the maximum allowable level of oxygen in the atmosphere. Intriguingly, this is about the same value as that imposed by the problem of runaway combustion. Here we have a genuine coincidence—a case where two unrelated phenomena impose the same limit on a particular value.

It is evident, then, that oxygen's solubility (and diffusion rate) in an aqueous fluid must be very close to what it is. This is all the more remarkable considering the fact that the solubility of substances in water varies over many orders of magnitude. The solubility of many common gases varies over a range of nearly 1 million. The solubility of carbon dioxide, another gas of vital importance to life, is about twenty times greater than that of oxygen.[21]

Three authorities recently summed up the fitness of oxygen thus: "Oxygen is . . . the only element in the most appropriate physical state, with a satisfactory solubility in water and with desirable combinations of kinetic and thermodynamic properties."[22] The utilization of oxidation by living organisms is dependent on the possession by oxygen of a precise set of chemical and physical properties which are perfectly fit for its biological role in the temperature range at which complex life functions on earth. Between 0°C and 50°C in an atmosphere containing about 21 percent oxygen, sufficient oxygen dissolves in water to support oxidative metabolism. At temperatures much above 50°C the reactivity of atmospheric oxygen becomes too great, while in water the amount dissolved falls to levels which are probably increasingly insufficient to sustain active oxidative metabolism.

In summary, oxidation is fit because (1) of the enormous energies released when oxygen combines with other atoms, (2) the activity of oxygen is attenuated at ambient temperatures, and (3) oxygen has the appropriate solubility in water. Further, as we shall see in chapter 9 the utility of oxygen for life can only be exploited because the transitional metals have just the correct electronic properties to transport and handle it in an aqueous solution. These same metals also play a key role in the mitochondria in the generation of the energy-rich molecules of ATP.

Large complex, metabolically active life forms such as ourselves are entirely dependent on the energy released from the complete oxidation of reduced carbon:

$$\text{reduced carbon} + \text{oxygen} = \text{water} + \text{carbon dioxide}$$

And this reaction can only be exploited because oxygen has the precise properties it has. Two scholars recently noted: "For those who find it a meaning-

E.T.'d ?

THE VITAL GASES · **127**

ful pastime to speculate on the existence of intelligent life elsewhere in the universe, they might heed the caveat that the evolution of large complex forms of life on Earth was only possible due to the advent of atmospheric oxygen and the subsequent evolution of oxidative phosphorylation. This requirement significantly reduces the probability of the evolution of complex life forms on some remote planet."[23]

Curiously, the very many simple microbial species that utilize reactions which do not require the presence of free oxygen in the atmosphere are probably essential to aerobic life in a number of ways. For example, many may be involved in the cycling of the elements through the hydrosphere, and it may be that the origin of life occurred in an anoxic environment; and save for the capacity of some primitive unicellular organisms to thrive without oxygen, it may never have occurred.

Atmospheric Pressure

It is not only the chemical and physical properties of oxygen that must be precisely as they are if oxidation is to be exploited by carbon-based life forms on a planet like the earth; the overall composition and general character of the atmosphere—its density, viscosity, and pressure, etc.—must be very similar to what it is particularly for air-breathing organisms.

In addition to the 21 percent oxygen, the earth's atmosphere also contains about 78 percent nitrogen and has a pressure of 760 mm Hg and a density at sea level of about 1 gram per liter. Its viscosity at sea level is about one-fiftieth that of water. Current research suggests that the atmospheric pressure of the earth's atmosphere has been between about 500 mm and 1,000 mm Hg throughout most of the history of the earth.[24]

The total pressure of the earth's atmosphere is critical to life, particularly to highly active aerobic organisms like mammals, which depend on a complex respiratory system to deliver the oxygen in the air to the blood in the lungs. Recall first that respiration in vertebrates involves drawing air into the lungs (inspiration) via a system of branching tubes into tiny air sacs, or alveoli, where the oxygen in the air is absorbed by the blood, and then its expulsion (expiration) via the same set of tubes. Again, it is hard to imagine how the respiratory system in higher vertebrates could be much improved. In the adult human, gaseous exchange occurs across a special respiratory membrane lining the lungs which consists of 300 million alveoli. The total surface area available for oxygen absorption is 50 to 100 square meters, about the area of a tennis court. The process of drawing air into and expelling it from the lungs is critically dependent on the fact that both the viscosity and the density of the air which contains the vital oxygen are very low—about one-fiftieth and one-thousandth respectively of that of water. Even with these low values the total work of breathing is considerable. Although at rest this takes up only a small fraction of the total consumption of oxygen, during voluntary hyperventilation up to 30 percent of the oxygen consumption of the body is devoted to the work of breathing.[25] The very low viscosity and density are particularly critical because a significant proportion of the work of breathing is involved in overcoming what is termed "airway resistance," and this is determined directly by the density and viscosity of the air.[26]

However, as the atmospheric pressure is raised, the density also increases. Breathing becomes much more difficult. At about three times atmospheric pressure, extended periods of strenuous work become impossible because the effort involved in moving the air takes up a prohibitive proportion of the total energy available. When the pressure is increased to several times atmospheric pressure, this resistance becomes prohibitive.[27] It is clear that if either the viscosity or the density of air were much greater, the airway resistance would be prohibitive and no conceivable redesign of the respiratory system would be capable of delivering sufficient oxygen to a metabolically active air-breathing organism. If the atmospheric pressure were ten times greater, the work of respiration would be prohibitive. If it were about ten times less, the body fluids would vaporize at 38°C.[28]

By plotting (as shown opposite) all possible atmospheric pressures against all possible oxygen contents, it becomes clear that there is only one unique tiny area, A, where all the various conditions for life are satisfied.

It is surely a coincidence of enormous significance that several essential conditions are satisfied in this one tiny region in the space of all possible atmospheres. Fire is possible, but runaway combustion is avoided, oxygen toxicity is relatively low, the solubility of oxygen is sufficient to support oxidative metabolism, and the density is sufficiently low so that the work of breathing during strenuous exercise is not prohibitive.

And what is perhaps even more remarkable is that long-term atmospheric stability on a planet the size of the earth may only be possible in this same unique region of the atmospheric space. James Lovelock has recently specu-

The region of atmospheric space fit for life.

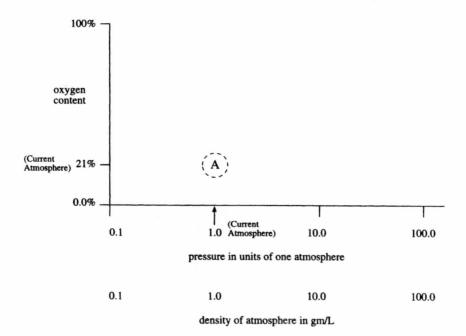

pressure in units of one atmosphere

lated along these lines.[29] Of course, because climatic modeling is still in its infancy, it is impossible to know to what extent this may be true. However, it would seem relatively likely that if the atmospheric pressure was, say, only one-fifth as great as it is, the seas might eventually vaporize and the increased water vapor in the atmosphere might cause a massive and runaway greenhouse effect. On the other hand, if the atmosphere was several times more dense, this might reduce the amount of water vapor in the atmosphere and the continents might be converted to arid wastelands.

The current atmosphere of the earth is the natural result of planetary evolution resulting from a complex set of feedback controls involving complex interactions between the hydrosphere, the biosphere, and the material making up the crust of the earth. That such a process should have generated an atmosphere with just the appropriate amount of oxygen and of the appropriate pressure to support active aerobic metabolism and maintained it for perhaps half a billion years is again perfectly in keeping with the biocentric hypothesis. It may be that all planets of the size and composition of the earth the same distance from their sun—i.e., those capable of sustaining a biosphere like our own—will inevitably, after billions of years of planetary and crustal evolution, end up with a stable atmosphere of composition somewhat like that of Earth—in region A.

Oxygen makes another contribution to life in providing the ozone layer in the upper atmosphere which performs the vital function of protecting life from what would otherwise be lethal levels of ultraviolet radiation. The ozone shield effectively absorbs all the damaging UV radiation below 0.30 microns. Although a small amount filters through—between 0.30 and 0.40 microns, as we saw in chapter 3—only a small amount of the total radiant energy of the sun reaches the earth's surface in this near-ultraviolet region of the spectrum. Curiously, ultraviolet radiation is a particularly potent activator of oxygen in the near ultraviolet and it is via the activation of oxygen that ultraviolet radiation exerts many of its mutagenic effects.[30] In effect, oxygen, by providing ozone in the upper atmosphere, protects life not only from ultraviolet radiation but also from its own reactivity, which is dangerously enhanced by ultraviolet light.

The major source of oxygen in the earth's atmosphere is the process of photosynthesis, which involves the building up of sugars from water and carbon dioxide, using energy provided by sunlight. It is fortunate that the oxygen thus formed creates the ozone shield to prevent lethal UV from reaching the earth's surface, because photosynthesis itself obviously necessitates direct exposure to the sun's radiation, which, in the case of many terrestrial plants, would be impossible without the protection of the ozone layer. Thus, oxygen, via a strange sort of self-referential loop, provides the crucial protecting shield for the delicate machinery that generates it in the first place, attenuating both the flow of UV as well as its own photo activation by UV light.

We are so familiar with the act of breathing that it mostly goes unnoticed. But it is far, very far, from ordinary. Our ability to breathe and to utilize the vital properties of the oxygen atom depends on a long and deep chain of coincidences in the nature of things. There is in the end nothing contingent about the choice of oxidation as the major source of energy for life on earth. Without the energy inherent in the chemistry of oxidation, life would have remained frozen forever at the primitive unicellular stage it reached on earth long before the Cambrian explosion and the development of complex multicellular life. It is not that life adapted to oxygen or to the atmospheric conditions on the earth, but rather that long ago, long before the first organisms, long before the formation of the earth, the design of oxidative metabolism and the general character of the atmosphere of our planet was already built into the order of the cosmos.

Carbon Dioxide

Despite all the energy that oxidation supplies to life, unless the end products of oxidative metabolism were innocuous and harmless and easy to dispose of, oxidative energy would not be available to life. In fact, the final two products of the oxidative breakdown of organic compounds are water and carbon dioxide.

reduced carbon + oxygen = water + carbon dioxide

Water is not only harmless to life, it is the very matrix of life. And we have already seen just how wonderfully and in so many ways water is adapted to life. Organisms have at their disposal a great number of means by which to rid themselves of excess water produced in the course of metabolism: via kidneys, via evaporation, via contractile vacuoles, and so forth.

The other end product of oxidative breakdown of organic compounds, carbon dioxide (CO_2), possesses a number of physical and chemical properties which are critical to life on earth. If carbon dioxide had been a toxic substance, if it had been a liquid insoluble in water, if it had been a solid, if it had dissolved in water forming a strong acid, the complete oxidation of carbon to carbon dioxide would have been impossible and complex carbon-based life would in all probability never have evolved. However, carbon dioxide is none of these things.

Excretion

In fact, carbon dioxide is a relatively unreactive compound and a gas at ambient temperatures. That it is a gas should, as Needham points out, "be emphasised since it is one of the very few gaseous oxides at ordinary temperatures (water vaporises more than most others)."[31] Moreover, that carbon dioxide is an innocuous soluble gas which can be readily excreted from the body of terrestrial organisms via respiration is of enormous utility. As Henderson says:

In the course of a day a man of average size produces as a result of his active metabolism, nearly two pounds of carbon dioxide. All this must be rapidly removed from the body. It is difficult to imagine by what elaborate chemical and physical devices the body could rid itself of such enormous quantities of material were it not for the fact that . . . in the lungs . . . [carbon dioxide] can escape into air which is charged with little of the gas. Were carbon dioxide not gaseous, its excretion would be the greatest of physiological tasks; were it not freely soluble, a host of the most universal physiological processes would be impossible.[32]

The Regulation of Acidity

The gaseous nature of carbon dioxide is not only of great utility for excretion in the case of terrestrial organisms. It is also of great utility for the regulation of the level of acidity in the body.

Most of the carbon dioxide transported from the site of its production in the tissues to the lungs is not merely a simple solution of the gas. As every medical student learns, from estimates of the total amount of carbon dioxide dissolved in the blood and from estimates of the difference in the amount of dissolved carbon dioxide in arterial and venous blood, it can be shown that most of the 200 milliliters of carbon dioxide produced per minute in an average adult human cannot be transported in simple physical solution to the lungs. When carbon dioxide is dissolved in water, it gradually interacts with water molecules to form carbonic acid (H_2CO_3), which then ionizes to produce hydrogen ions (H^+) and the base bicarbonate (HCO_3^-):

$$\text{carbon dioxide} + \text{water} = \text{hydrogen ions} + \text{bicarbonate base}$$

Now the fact that the gas CO_2 reacts reversibly with water to produce the base bicarbonate has physiological consequences of very great significance because it provides the organism with a wonderfully elegant means of protecting or buffering itself against fluctuation in the level of acidity of the body.

As can be seen from the above equation, when acid (hydrogen ions, H^+) accumulates in the body, the hydrogen ions combine with bicarbonate (HCO_3^-) to produce water and carbon dioxide (CO_2), which can be excreted readily from the body via the lungs. In effect, the excess acid (hydrogen ions) is simply breathed out of the body.

Hence, an organism's defense against the accumulation of acid, which is an inevitable consequence of the oxidative metabolism of organic compounds, is provided by one of the major end products of this same metabolic process, carbon dioxide and its hydration product bicarbonate. The other major product is water, itself the ideal medium for life. Amazingly, it is water, the other final product of oxidative metabolism, which dissolves the CO_2 and carries it to the lungs, and it is water which reacts with carbon dioxide to generate bicarbonate, "the perfect buffer."

Many authors have commented on the fitness of the CO_2– bicarbonate buffering system for the maintenance of acid-base balance. Henderson comments: "there is I believe, except in celestial mechanics, *no other case of such accuracy in a natural regulation of the environment.* Moreover the chemist has discovered no means of rivalling the efficiency and delicacy of adjustment of the process."[33] Like Henderson, the protein chemist John Edsall was also struck by the remarkable nature of the system: "The combination of the acidity and buffering power of H_2CO_3 with the volatility of CO_2 provides a mechanism of unrivalled efficiency for maintaining constancy of pH in systems which are constantly being supplied as living organisms are with acidic products of metabolism."[34]

The bicarbonate–carbon dioxide buffer system is a paragon of elegance and efficiency which solves two basic and very different physiological problems—the ridding of the body of the end product of oxidative metabolism, and the maintenance of acid-base homeostasis in the same basic equation:

$$\text{carbon dioxide} + \text{water} = \text{hydrogen ions}^+ + \text{bicarbonate}^-$$

Moreover, this remarkable system is particularly fit for air-breathing terrestrial organisms like ourselves. And there are additional subtle aspects of the CO_2– bicarbonate buffering system which contribute further to its fitness for acid-base homeostasis. (For a more detailed description of the nature of buffers and of the bicarbonate buffer system, see Appendix, sections 6 and 7.)

It turns out, then, that both the maintenance of acid-base balance in the body and the excretion of the end product of oxidative metabolism, CO_2, depend crucially on the chemical and physical properties of CO_2 itself and its hydration product, bicarbonate. *Thus both the problem of excretion of the end product of carbon metabolism and the problem of acid-base balance are both elegantly solved in the properties of the same remarkable compound—carbon dioxide. It is a solution of breathtaking elegance and parsimony based on another set of mutual adaptations in life's constituents.*

The diagram below summarizes the basic interactions which occur during oxidative metabolism.

Oxidative metabolism.

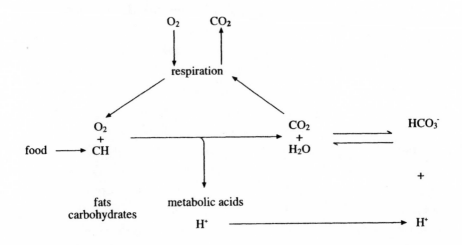

Although the above scheme is well known, it remains a paragon of elegance and parsimony. The elegance of the fact that both O_2 and CO_2 enter and leave the body via the same route, which depends on their both being gases at ambient temperatures. The fact that CO_2 is both the major excretory product of oxidation and at the same time, by reacting with water, the source of bicarbonate, which mops up excess acid produced inevitably during periods of relative oxygen lack. The fact that both CO_2 and bicarbonate are innocuous compounds, that both are soluble in water. The fact that oxygen is soluble in water and its reactivity is attenuated at ambient temperatures. The fact that oxidation is the most efficient means of energy generation and so on. The mutual fitness of the chemical actors for their respective roles in this the central metabolic drama of life is simply astounding. If these compounds did not possess precisely the chemical and physical properties they do, the drama would be impossible, and it is exceedingly difficult to envisage an alternative.

Curiously, despite the fact that these key components have precisely the properties required for their biological roles, which together make the execution of oxidative metabolism a marvel of parsimony and efficiency, we are seldom struck by the immensity of the teleology which underlies it all. Failing to see the wood for the trees, we take the entire system and all the coincidences for granted, assuming erroneously that things could not have been otherwise. This same point was made by Richard Bentley in his "Confutation of Atheism," which is one of the classics of seventeenth-century natural theology and was cited in chapter 1. It is worth repeating:[35]

> What we have always seen to be done in one constant and uniform manner; we are apt to imagine there was but that one way of doing it, and that it could not be otherwise. This is a great error and impediment in a disquisition of this nature: to remedy which, we ought to consider every thing as not yet in Being; and then diligently examine if it must needs have been at all, or what other ways it might have been as possibly as the present.

For Bentley's point is well taken. Things could have been otherwise as far as we can tell. For example, if O_2 and CO_2 were not gases, the design of large terrestrial carbon-based organisms obtaining energy by oxidative metabolism would in all probability be impossible. Carbon-based life forms such as mammals are critically dependent not only on the fact that O_2 and CO_2 are gases but also on the low viscosity of water which makes possible (as we saw in the previous chapter) a circulatory system which is itself essential if the gaseous properties of O_2 and CO_2 are to be exploited. Water is not only a key chemical player in the metabolic scheme of oxidative metabolism, but also through its low viscosity it provides the physical means, i.e., the circulatory system, by which the various chemical and physical properties of the other players, particularly the gases O_2 and CO_2, may be utilized in the case of large terrestrial life forms.

Every detail of the chemistry of carbon dioxide we examine seems to reveal additional aspects to its fitness. For example, take the actual process of hydration itself. Because of certain molecular characteristics of the carbon dioxide molecule, the process of hydration occurs relatively slowly. Now this apparently esoteric point, the slowness of the hydration of CO_2, happens to be of great physiological importance. If hydration was instantaneous, this would mean that whenever the metabolism of carbon was increased, the increased quantities of CO_2 generated would immediately hydrate, producing carbonic acid which would then dissociate, releasing H ions and subjecting the cell to sudden violent fluctuations in acidity that might well be lethal in higher organisms. Undoubtedly, the slowness of the hydration of CO_2 contributes further to the biological fitness of carbon dioxide. In the body the speed of hydration is increased by the presence of the enzyme carbonic anhydrase, which catalyzes the hydration reaction in the red blood cell and in the lining of the lungs.[36]

The unique utility of the bicarbonate buffer system for carbon-based life forms can be represented again in graphic form as shown below.

It should be noted that the CO_2-bicarbonate system is not just the main buffering mechanism responsible for the maintenance of the neutrality of the body fluids; it also plays the same role on a global scale, preserving the neutrality of the oceans and all bodies of water on the earth's surface. Weak solutions of carbonic acid also play a role, probably quite vital, in the process of weathering by greatly increasing the rate at which minerals are washed out of the rock. As Henderson comments, "it is the united action of water and carbonic acid . . . which sets free the inorganic constituents of the earth's crust and turns them into the stream of metabolism."[37]

The fact that CO_2 is very soluble in water means that wherever there is water on the planet, CO_2 will be also present to provide a ready source of carbon atoms for the synthesis of biological materials.

Another feature related to its solubility, which ensures the universal distribution of CO_2 throughout the hydrosphere, is the fact that its absorption coefficient in water is close to one. This means that whenever water is in

The fitness of buffers for pH homeostasis.

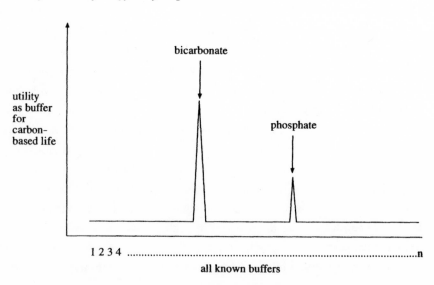

contact with air, and equilibrium has been established, the amount of CO_2 per liter of water will be equal to the amount per liter in air. Thus, as Henderson remarks, "the waters can never wash [CO_2] out of the air, nor keep it from the waters. It is the one substance which thus, in considerable quantities relative to its total amount, everywhere accompanies water."[38] Not only does the gaseous nature of carbon dioxide greatly facilitate the excretion of the carbon from the body of large organisms; this same gaseous nature and its solubility and absorption properties provide what would seem to be the perfect means of distributing the carbon atom to every part of the hydrosphere in the atmosphere and in the rivers, lakes, and seas.

Photosynthesis

Photosynthesis is almost the exact reverse of oxidation. During oxidation, reduced carbon compounds such as sugars and fats are converted to carbon dioxide and water. In photosynthesis light energy is used to convert water and carbon dioxide to oxygen and reduced carbon compounds. The essence of the process can be represented by the reaction:

$$\text{water} + \text{carbon dioxide} = \text{oxygen} + \text{reduced carbon}$$

Photosynthesis is another absolutely vital biological process. Nearly all complex plant and animal life on earth depends upon it. It generates all the fuel—the reduced carbon compounds such as the sugars and fats, etc.— which energize complex life on earth. Like respiration, it is so familiar that its remarkable nature fails to strike us. And like respiration, it is very hard to imagine any other process which could replace it to sustain complex life. Simple forms of life can obtain energy from sources other than sunlight, but for a rich, complex world on the surface of a planet there is no alternative to photosynthesis. And just like respiration, photosynthesis is possible only because each of the key players in the process—water, carbon dioxide, and oxygen—have precisely those properties they have. The fact that both CO_2 and O_2 are gases which can be readily taken up or excreted by the plant cells is crucial; also important are the facts that carbon dioxide is distributed universally throughout the hydrosphere, that water is ubiquitous, and that the solubilities of carbon dioxide and oxygen are as they are. Moreover, we have already seen that in addition to all this, the sun's light is perfectly fit for photochemistry, and the transparency of the atmosphere and liquid water are perfectly fit for sunlight's penetration to the surface of the earth. Photosynthesis also depends on the unique light-absorbing characteristics of the magnesium atom in chlorophyll, which is touched on again in chapter 9.

Conclusion

The three basic chemical reactions upon which all higher life depends are:
   1. Oxidation.

> reduced carbon + oxygen = water + carbon dioxide

   2. The regulation of acidity.

> carbon dioxide + water = hydrogen ions + bicarbonate base

   3. Photosynthesis.

> water + carbon dioxide = oxygen + reduced carbon

They can only be exploited by living organisms because of a unique fitness in the nature of things. It is solely because of this unique fitness that higher organisms can obtain, via photosynthesis, an almost unlimited supply of food in the form of reduced carbons, can carry out the oxidation of reduced carbon compounds to provide energy, can rid themselves of the end products of oxidative metabolism, and can maintain acid-base homeostasis. The treatment here is by no means exhaustive. Many other important compounds involved in oxidative metabolism such as the sugars, the sugar-storing molecule, glycogen, and the phosphates also appear uniquely fit for the key roles they play in the process. (See Appendix, sections 1 and 3.)

And so the coincidences lengthen further. In case after case, the constituents of life—water, the carbon atom, the oxygen atom, carbon dioxide gas, the bicarbonate base—turn out to be uniquely and ideally fit in so many diverse and complex ways for their respective biological roles.

Henderson's conclusion in *The Fitness of the Environment* has certainly stood the test of time:

> Accordingly, we may finally conclude that the fitness of water, carbonic acid, and the three elements make up a unique ensemble of fitness for the organic mechanism. . . . There is nothing about these substances which is . . . inferior to the same thing in any other substance . . . not a single disability of the primary constituents . . . has come to light.[39]

The fitness . . . [of these compounds constitutes] a series of maxima—unique or nearly unique properties of water, carbon dioxide, the compounds of carbon, hydrogen and oxygen and the ocean—so numerous, so varied, so complete among all things which are concerned in the problem that together they form certainly the greatest possible fitness.[40]

Conclusion

From the evidence presented so far, we are now in a position to play the "life game" advocated by Robert Clark in chapter 8 of his book *The Universe: Plan or Accident?* (cited at the beginning of chapter 5) where he suggests we imagine ourselves in the position of Plato's Demiurge, setting out to create life from scratch, being free to choose at every stage of the process the most ideal materials and components available and being constrained only by the laws of physics. Playing the game is instructive, for it highlights one of the main arguments of the book, namely that the laws of nature are fit for only one specific type of life—that which exists on earth. To start the game we must choose an atom out of which to create life. And, in Clark's words, "we soon find that carbon is the most promising . . . as we continue we find, with increasing astonishment, that it is not a case of carbon will do, but that carbon atoms have all the properties we could desire."

Having decided to use carbon, we face our next problem: we must find a medium in which to base our carbon-based life. We examine several liquids and soon find one—water—which seems to have some of the properties we need. Again, our astonishment grows as we find that water has not only one or two useful properties but seems mutually fit for carbon-based life in almost all of its characteristics. Next we face the problem—how shall we ensure that the carbon atom is always readily available? "One possible solution," Clark suggests, "might be to place the carbon in the air, since air is the only material disseminated over the whole earth. For this a gaseous compound would be necessary."

However, as Clark points out, such a "compound would also have to fulfil rather exacting conditions." To begin with, it would be preferable if it were a highly oxidized compound if we are planning to utilize the energy of oxidation to drive our chemical machine, for only a highly oxidized substance can coexist with atmospheric oxygen. The best possible solution would be an oxide containing the maximum amount of oxygen. Moreover, as Clark continues, our carbon-containing oxide must be soluble in water but not so soluble that it is washed out of the atmosphere. "Carbon dioxide might be the compound we require. If this will not do, it seems that nothing can take its place. It is the oxide of carbon richest in oxygen and so stable in an oxygen-containing environment." But does it have, asks Clark, all those properties we desire? "We find with delight, that the gas dissolves in about an equal volume of water—just what we want."

However, oxides are often troublesome compounds. In water they usually produce powerful acids or bases. "What we need is a very weak acid, . . . one that will not interfere with the valuable properties of water. . . . The strengths of acids vary by factors of billions. We consult our tables of these strengths—hardly two are close together and none are close to that of water. Anxiously we measure the strength of the acid formed when our gas dissolves in water. . . . The incredible happens again! It comes out right!"

And continuing our life game, next we must find a means of obtaining energy. Clearly, the oxidation of reduced carbon compounds is an ideal candidate. When reduced carbon compounds are oxidized, we find that the process generates water, our chosen matrix for life, and carbon dioxide, our chosen means of universally distributing the carbon atom over the earth. So oxidation will do wonderfully. But what about the solubility of oxygen and its reactivity? Amazingly, its solubility is right and its reactivity attenuated to just the right extent.

For life we need the carbon atom and water, and for complex life we need oxygen, we need carbon dioxide, we need bicarbonate, we need the transitional metals, we need an atmosphere like that on earth, and we need all their chemical and physical properties precisely as they are. And for life anywhere in the cosmos it will be the same. For there is no alternative. So if there is in some distant galaxy another carbon-based biosphere as rich as our own, containing large active terrestrial organisms, they will, like us, inhale oxygen and exhale carbon dioxide and use the bicarbonate buffer system. No matter how many times we play the Demiurge, we will always be led via the same chain of mutual adaptations to the same unique solutions.

Chapter 7

The Double Helix

In which evidence is presented which supports the notion that DNA and RNA may be uniquely fit for their respective biological roles—DNA as the genetic data bank and RNA as the temporary information carrier—in complex carbon-based life forms. DNA is fit for its biological role in a number of ways: it is chemically stable in an aqueous medium, its structure allows for highly accurate and rapid duplication, it possesses conformational plasticity which enhances its informational capacity and facilitates DNA-protein interactions, and it has an enormous capacity for compaction because of its supercoiling ability.

Three representations of the double helix of DNA.

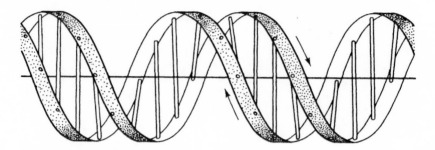

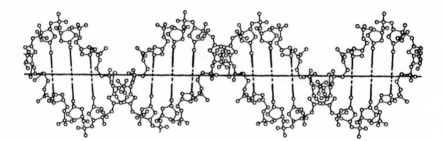

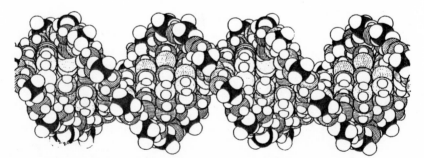

From S. Miller and L. Orgel (1974) *The Origins of Life on the Earth* (Englewood Cliffs, N.J.: Prentice-Hall), fig. 6.8. Reproduced by permission of Leslie Orgel.

That morning Watson and Crick knew . . . the entire structure: it had emerged from the shadow of billions of years, absolutely pure and simple, and there was seen and understood for the first time.

—H. F. Judson, *The Eighth Day of Creation,* 1979

I would rather stress that the structure made Watson and Crick. After all, I was totally unknown at the time and Watson was regarded as too bright to be really sound. But what I think is overlooked in such arguments is the intrinsic beauty of the DNA helix. It is a molecule which has style, quite as much as the scientists.

—Francis Crick, *Nature* magazine, 1974

Much of our current knowledge of the biochemical basis of life has resulted from a succession of discoveries from the late 1940s to the early 1960s which completely transformed the biological sciences. These discoveries, collectively known as the molecular biological revolution, revealed for the first time the molecular structure and biological function of some of the most important macromolecular constituents of the cell, including DNA, RNA, and proteins, and revealed for the first time the mechanism by which living things achieve the miracle of self-replication. It has turned out to be one of the most remarkable stories in twentieth-century science.

Curiously, over the same period of time, while biology was being transformed, dramatic developments were also occurring in the fields of information theory, cybernetics, and artificial intelligence, developments which subsequently led to the information revolution and the computer age of today. These parallel developments led to a rather strange historical coincidence. While biologists were busy working out the actual basis of biological replication, information theorists were working on the theoretical possibilities of constructing artificial systems capable of self-replication, machines that could make themselves, or, in other words, "artificial life."

One of the greatest of these figures was the mathematician John von Neumann, who developed his model of a self-replicating machine in the early 1950s before the actual self-replicating machinery of the cell had been worked out.[1] Von Neumann, as was mentioned in chapter 3, visualized the surface of a vast body of fluid covered with infinitely many copies of each kind of element required for the construction of the automaton, distributed in random fashion over the surface of the lake. The automaton, like an animated erector set, floats on the surface of the hypothetical lake and, by picking up elements from the fluid and assembling them together, eventually constructs a copy of itself. The automaton consists of two components: an information bank and a mechanical assembly unit capable of manipulative robotic activities—what von Neumann called the "constructor." The information bank provided all the information and instructions necessary to direct the constructor to assemble a copy of itself. When the constructor had finished constructing a copy of itself, it then made a copy of the information bank and inserted this new copy into the newly assembled offspring constructor. Thus, the automaton makes a complete copy of itself.

Artificial Life

The subject of artificial life has recently become a scientific discipline in its own right. Recently, a symposium entitled "Artificial Life" and subtitled "The Proceedings of an Interdisciplinary Workshop on the Synthesis and Simulation of Living Systems," devoted entirely to the subject, was held at the Santa Fe Institute in New Mexico. The organizer of the symposium, Christopher Langton, explained:

> Artificial Life is the study of man-made systems that exhibit life-like behaviour characteristic of natural living systems. . . . By extending the empirical foundations upon which biology is based beyond the carbon-chain life that has evolved on earth, Artificial Life can contribute to theoretical biology by locating *life as we know it* within the larger picture of *life as it could be*.[2] [My emphasis.]

The idea that self-replicating machines will eventually be built that will equal or even surpass life in sophistication and complexity in the not too distant future has become almost a defining characteristic of late-twentieth-century science fiction. Indeed, much of the literature in this field is concerned with the increasing difficulty of distinguishing between life and machinery. And there is no doubt that technology today has advanced to levels that were undreamt of, simply unimaginable, even as recently as fifty years ago. At an ever-accelerating rate one technological advance has followed another. We have built machines in which we have flown like a bird and others in which we have traveled to the bottom of the ocean. With radio telescopes we have listened to the murmurs of the most distant galaxies. We have trod in moon dust and we have sniffed the air of Mars. We have machines that can calculate a billion times faster than a man.

The gap between living things and machines seems to have narrowed with every advance in technology. This trend has become particularly obvious over the past few decades. Today there seems hardly any feature of living systems that does not have some machine analogue. Machines use artificial languages and memory banks for information storage and retrieval. Advanced machinery utilizes elegant control systems regulating the assembly of parts and components. Fail-safe devices and proofreading systems are utilized for quality control; assembly processes utilize the principle of prefabrication. All these phenomena have their parallel in living systems. In fact, so deep and so persuasive is the analogy that much of the terminology we use to describe the fascinating world of the cell is borrowed from the world of late-twentieth-century technology.

And the achievements to date may be vastly exceeded if the development of a new field of microminiaturized technology—nanotechnology—is successful. Conrad Schneiker recently reviewed the history of this fascinating field. He relates that it was the science-fiction author Robert Heinlein who first envisaged the possibilities of nanomachines: "the extensive use of teleoperator hands . . . complete with sensory feedback for full remote-controlled telepresence . . . for building and operating a series of ever smaller sets of such mechanical hands . . . the smallest of which were hardly an eighth of an inch across, used to manipulate living nerve tissue."[3] But it was physicist Richard Feynman who authored the definitive source paper on the subject:

> [Consider] the final question as to whether, ultimately . . . *we can arrange the atoms the way we want, the very atoms all the way down!* . . . [when] we have some control of the arrangement of things on a small scale we will get an enormously greater range of possible properties that substances can have, and different things that we can do. . . . if we go down far enough, all our devices can be mass produced so that they are absolutely perfect copies of one another.[4]

More recently, various workers in the field of nanotechnology have expanded in more detail the revolutionary concept of machinery in the nanometer range, envisaging gears, bearings, and motors scaled down to the atomic level, and even the construction of a nanocomputer, much smaller than a bacterial cell, based on logic operations mediated entirely by molecular rods made of carbine, sliding into ON or OFF positions in a complex maze of channels embedded in a three-dimensional matrix composed of atoms near carbon in the periodic table. One of the gurus in the field, Eric Drexler, has envisaged tiny factories, smaller than a grain of sand, containing molecular assemblers, tiny atomic machines that could assemble, atom by atom, bearings, rods, rollers, etc.[5] He has envisaged rows of these miniature assemblers programmed to assemble all manner of specific machines. Drexler has even envisaged a microminiaturized submarine smaller than a red blood cell which could be programmed to hunt out and destroy invading bacteria or cancer cells even in the smallest capillaries. According to an article in a recent issue of the *Scientific American:*

> Such products, depending on design and purpose, might roam through the human body, invading cancerous cells and rearranging their DNA. Other ma-

chines might swarm as a barely visible metallic sheen over an outdoor construction site. In a few days an elegant building would take shape. . . . Every hour entire factories no larger than a grain of sand might generate billions of machines that would look like a mass of dust streaming steadily from the factory doors—or like a cloudy solution suspended in water.[6]

The sheer genius of modern technology and its achievements encourages the belief that, however complex life's design, it must eventually be equaled in a machine. Possessing a technology so sophisticated that we can contemplate the design and construction of a submarine as small as a red blood cell, a computer smaller than a bacterium, objects which are every bit as complex in terms of number of components per unit volume as living systems, encourages the belief that machines will one day be built which are capable of self-replication, and that artificial life based on a completely different design to that on earth will finally be achieved.

The Magic of Self-Replication

Yet despite the dreams of artificial life and the gurus of nanotechnology, the undeniable fact remains that many characteristics of living organisms are still without any significant analogue in any machine which has yet been constructed. Every living system replicates itself, yet no machine yet possesses this capacity even to the slightest degree. Nearly half a century after von Neumann, Claude Shannon, Norbert Wiener, and their circle dreamed of self-replicating machines, the dream is nowhere near realization. Nor does there exist even a well-developed, detailed blueprint in the most advanced area of nanotechnology for a machine that could carry out such a stupendous act. In the case of von Neumann's model, for example, no serious consideration was given to the fuel and energy supply problem. Von Neumann assumed conveniently that his automata would have unlimited energy!

The challenge is enormous. A self-replicating machine requires a data storage system which must be accessible or comprehensible to the constructor device. It requires that the constructor be assembled from a very small number of readily available substances. It requires a means of energy generation, storage, and distribution to its working components and so forth. None of these problems has been solved. Yet every second, countless trillions of living systems from bacterial cells to elephants replicate themselves on the surface of our planet. And since life's origin, as the earth has circled thousands of millions of times around the sun, endless life forms have effortlessly copied themselves on unimaginable numbers of occasions.

And it is not just the act of self-replication which has not been copied in our technology. Even the far less ambitious end of component self-assembly which is utilized by every living cell on earth, exhibited in processes as diverse as the assembly of viral capsules to the assembly of cell organelles such as the ribosome, a process whereby tens or hundreds of unique and complex elements combine together, directed entirely by their own intrinsic properties without any external intelligent guidance or control, is an achievement without any analogue in modern technology.

The well-known self-reorganizing, self-regenerating capacities of living things have been a source of wonderment since classical times—phenomena such as the growth of a complete tree from a small twig, the regeneration of the limb of a newt, the growth of a complete polyp, or a complex protozoan from tiny fragments of the intact animal. These are all phenomena without analogue in the realm of the mechanical. Imagine a space ship, a computer, or indeed any machine ever conceived, from the fantastic star ships of science fiction to the equally fantastic speculations of nanotechnology, being chopped up randomly into small fragments. Imagine every one of the fragments so produced (no two fragments will ever be the same) assembling itself into a perfect but miniaturized copy of the machine from which it originated. Nature does this constantly. It is an achievement of transcending brilliance which goes beyond the wildest dreams of even the most ardent proponents of artificial life. I doubt there is anyone who has witnessed the regeneration of a protozoan through a microscope who has not been struck with an almost metaphysical awe at the wonder of the process.[7]

The contrast between the apparent ease with which life forms assemble and replicate themselves and the absolute failure to simulate this effortless activity in any sort of nonliving artificial system is very striking. While engineers have been dreaming about the possibilities of artificial self-replicating automata over the past fifty years, advances in biology since the early fifties have gradually revealed how the miracle of self-replication is actually realized in living things.

The Structure of DNA

One of the crucial requirements for self-replication is a means of storing information in some sort of data bank. In the case of living organisms this critical function, that of the information bearer, is of course carried out by the molecule now referred to universally by the three-letter acronym DNA, for dioxyribonucleic acid. The blueprint for every organism on earth—for humans, redwoods, flies, and mushrooms—is encoded in a linear script in this remarkable polymer.

Every human body cell contains a one-meter-long string of DNA coiled into a tiny ball about 5 microns (five-thousandths of a millimeter) in diameter in the cell nucleus. The DNA polymer itself is made up of four subunits called nucleotides (see below). Each nucleotide consists of a phosphate (P), a ribose sugar (the pentagon), and one of four bases: guanine (G), cytosine (C), thymine (T), or adenine (A).

The DNA in the cell is composed of two strands—i.e., is double stranded

A short section of DNA.

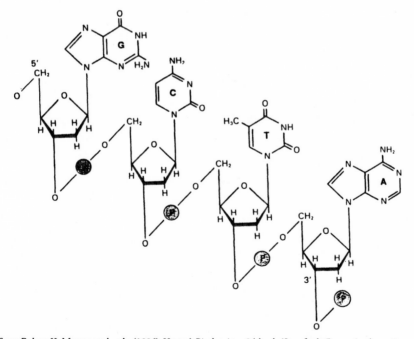

From Robert K. Murray et al., eds. (1996) *Harper's Biochemistry,* 24th ed. (Stamford, Conn.: Appleton & Lange), fig. 37-1. Reproduced by permission of V. W. Rodwell.

(see figure on page 142), and the two strands are twisted around one another to form the celebrated double helix. The genetic messages are encoded in the sequence of the bases in the molecule in exactly the same way a sequence of letters forms a word in a human language. From the initial fertilization of the egg cell every single one of the unimaginable infinity of biochemical and developmental events which shapes the growing mass of embryonic cells into a human form is under the control of the DNA master tape. It is this remarkable information bearer that has carried the human blueprint down through time, through all the generations since the birth of the human race. And it is the DNA that will carry the human blueprint forward into the distant future.

Now on any design hypothesis one would expect to find such a key component to be ideally fashioned for the biological end it serves, and in this regard DNA certainly does not disappoint.

The elucidation of the double helical structure of DNA in 1953 was undoubtedly the single most important advance in biological knowledge in the twentieth century. "Double helix" soon became a household term, as did the names of its codiscoverers, Watson and Crick. It was on Saturday morning, February 28, 1953, that the structure of the double helix finally dawned on them. That morning in their lab at Cambridge they assembled out of crude cardboard cutouts the first molecular model of the helix. The beauty of the solution to the problem of heredity manifested in the double helix is self-evident. Pull the two complementary strands of the double helix apart and each single strand forms a template which elegantly directs by the chemical rules of base pairing the synthesis of two daughter helices, each chemically identical with the original helix (see opposite).

The beauty and elegance of the solution caused a sensation at the time. Horace Judson captures the drama of the Saturday morning in the Cambridge lab when the solution finally dawned:

> Twenty angstrom units in diameter, seventy billionths of an inch. Two chains twining coaxially . . . one up, the other down, a complete turn of the screw in 34 angstroms. The bases flat in their pairs in the middle, 3.4 angstroms and a tenth of a revolution separating a pair from the one above or below. The chains held by the pairing closer to each other, by an eighth of a turn, one groove up the outside narrow, the other wide. A melody for the eye of the intellect, with not a note wasted.[8]

The replication of DNA.

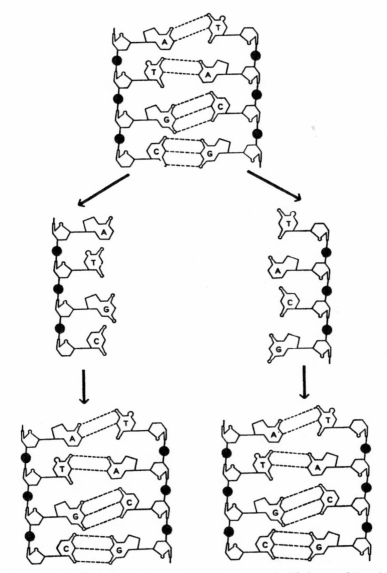

From Jacques Monod, *Chance and Necessity*, trans. A. Wainhouse; © 1972 by Alfred A. Knopf. Reproduced by permission of the publisher.

The structure of DNA was "flawlessly beautiful" according to Judson in *The Eighth Day of Creation.*[9] It had style and intrinsic beauty, according to Crick.[10]

The geometric perfection of the molecule is particularly evident in the fact that the strength of each of the five hydrogen bonds—the two between adenine and thymine and the three between guanine and cytosine—is optimal because each of the hydrogen atoms points directly at its acceptor atom and the bond lengths are all at the energy maximum for hydrogen bonds. This is most remarkable, for it confers great stability on the molecule and makes for highly accurate base pairing during replication.

Hydrogen bonds between complementary bases in the DNA.

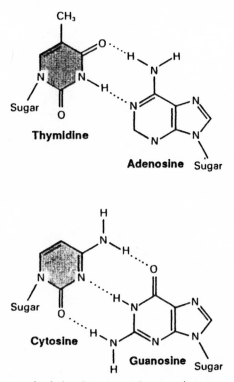

From Robert K. Murray et al., eds. (1996) *Harper's Biochemistry,* 24th ed. (Stamford, Conn.: Appleton & Lange), fig. 37-3. Reproduced by permission of V. W. Rodwell.

Metastability

Since 1953 a great deal has been learned of this remarkable molecule, and it has become increasingly apparent that it possesses additional properties, not suspected in 1953, which contribute further to its fitness for its biological role. To begin with, as befits the information bearer, DNA has turned out to be a remarkably stable molecule. Most researchers in molecular biology are familiar with the stability of DNA; it is more stable than the great majority of laboratory biochemicals. Unlike many biochemicals, it remains relatively stable in a solution, even at room temperature for months. The stability of DNA in an aqueous solution is due in part to the negatively charged phosphate groups on the backbone, which tend to retard hydrolytic breakdown of the molecule. The negatively charged phosphate groups are also necessary to maintain the solubility of DNA, which is essential for function in an aqueous environment. Recently, DNA has been extracted from the bones of Neanderthals, and some workers have claimed to have extracted it from fossil insects and leaves up to 100 million years old. The movie *Jurassic Park* may have been science fiction, but the very great stability of DNA is well established.

Although the two strands of the helix bind strongly, their affinity is not so great that they cannot be pulled apart and manipulated by the biochemical machinery of the cell. Rapid dissociation of the two strands is essential during replication. The flexibility of DNA and its ability to adopt a variety of different conformations also plays an essential role in gene expression (see below). The negatively charged phosphate groups in the backbone may again play a role here, causing a degree of repulsion between the two backbones which weakens the overall affinity of the two strands. Obviously, there is a conflict between the need for stability—essential for the genetic repository—and the need for flexibility and conformational variety—essential for gene expression and replication. It is likely that the strength of binding of the two strands in the DNA helix must be very close to what it is for biological function. If it were any stronger, both strands would be frozen into an immobile, lifeless embrace. But if it were weaker, the molecule would fall apart. The biological function of DNA is therefore dependent on the molecule possessing a certain metastability—a term, which, as we saw earlier, was used by Haldane to describe the basic character of all organic molecules.

Compaction

Another feature of DNA which contributes to its fitness is its remarkable compacting capacity. The amount of information carried in the chromosomes of higher organisms like man is very great, and it requires an enormous length of DNA to encode it. In man, for example, this requires a length of DNA 1 meter long. Yet, as mentioned above, this 1-meter-long molecule is compacted into a tiny ball less than 5-thousandths of a millimeter in diameter.[11] How is this achieved? Anyone who has worked with DNA will be aware that DNA solutions of approximately 1 milligram of DNA per milliliter of solution are very viscous and difficult to manipulate. Yet in the cell nucleus the concentration of DNA is about a thousand times greater. This super packing capacity is possible because one of the hidden talents of DNA helices is their capacity to twist and bend into superhelices, and these superhelices can be bent into higher-order helices, and so on, thereby permitting the highly dense packaging that is actually observed in the cell nucleus.

Recently, the structure of one of the fundamental compacting units in the nucleus—the nucleosome—was worked out.[12] It consists of a coil of DNA wrapped around a cluster of proteins known as histones. Interestingly, the negatively charged phosphate backbone and the small groove of the helix are both critically involved in binding the helix to the histone core. So it seems that the negative charge on the phosphates has other roles in addition to protecting the DNA from hydrolysis and lowering the binding affinities of the two strands to a level commensurate with biological function.

The ability of DNA to store information is so efficient that all the information needed to specify an organism as complex as a man weighs less than a few trillionths of a gram. The information necessary to specify the design of all the organisms which have ever existed on the planet, a number, according to G. G. Simpson,[13] of approximately 1 billion, could be easily compacted into an object the size of a grain of salt!

The compacting ability of DNA is critical to its biological role. Many processes in which DNA is involved, such as meiosis and mitosis, would be impractical if the DNA molecule could not be tightly compacted. If DNA did not have the compacting capacity it does, the cell system would have to be radically redesigned. The cell, for example, might have to be much larger to accommodate a vast tangle of disordered DNA fibers. However, there are diffusional constraints on cell size. Cells cannot be much larger, as they are dependent on diffusion for their supply of oxygen and nutrients. As we have seen in chapter 2, diffusion is only efficient over distances not much greater than the average diameter of the cell. The diffusional constraint on cell size suggests that the compactness of DNA makes a vital contribution to its biological fitness.

In addition to its transmission from one generation to another, the information in any molecule playing the genetic role would also have to be retrievable or accessible.

How Information Is Retrieved

In the case of DNA, this means that components of the cell must be able to recognize specific regions of the helix. These components are of course the proteins. Over the last decade it has become clear that specific proteins recognize particular sections of the helix by feeling for the unique electrostatic shape of target sequences within the major and minor grooves of the helix. Just how proteins recognize sections of DNA is a fascinating story in itself, which, as we will see in the next chapter, depends on a set of coadaptations between proteins and DNA.

When the problem of protein-DNA recognition was first considered in the early 1960s, it was a matter of some speculation as to how it worked. The trouble was that the helix was believed to be so regular that it was hard to see how one part would differ sufficiently from another to allow recognition to occur. We now know that because of its basic metastability (discussed above) different regions of the helix exhibit a vast number of unique variations in structure and conformation.

To begin with, there is a considerable degree of electrostatic variability in the major groove which proteins can "feel" when searching for particular base sequences. Moreover, all along the helix there are minor structural variations caused by differences in the actual base sequence itself. Groove width, local twist, displacement of average base pair from the helical axis—all vary in different sections of the molecule. Moreover, DNA, because of its metastability, is also more flexible than was originally assumed and can adopt a number of different conformations. These various departures from "helical perfection" confer unique stereochemical properties to different sections of the DNA helix which can be recognized by proteins, thus providing an additional crucial element to the fitness of DNA for its biological role—making the information stored in its base sequence more readily decipherable.[14]

So DNA is not only fit for self-replication and for the transmission of information, but it also lends itself to information retrieval because of the many subtle minor distortions which it can undergo and which can be recognized by proteins that interact with specific sections of the DNA.

It is evident, then, that DNA has not one, but many properties which are wonderfully fit for its role as the genetic molecule: (1) the essential double helical structure, which is fit for self-replication and for the transmission of genetic information, (2) great chemical stability in water, (3) a metastable character consequent on the relatively low binding affinity of the two strands, which assists the machinery of the cell in pulling apart the helix— for example during replication—and which confers flexibility on the molecule permitting it to adopt a variety of alternative shapes which are critical to gene expression, (4) the tiny distortions along the length of the helix—another consequence of its metastability—which greatly facilitates information re- trieval by proteins, (5) the ability to be superfolded and -compressed into highly compact structures, which allows the storage of massive amounts of information in very tiny volumes (an essential requirement if it is to per- form the genetic role in complex multicellular forms of life).

RNA

RNA is also a nucleic acid polymer that is very closely related chemically to DNA. In the cell, RNA carries the genetic message from the DNA in the nucleus to the cytoplasm, where the message is translated.

A short section of RNA.

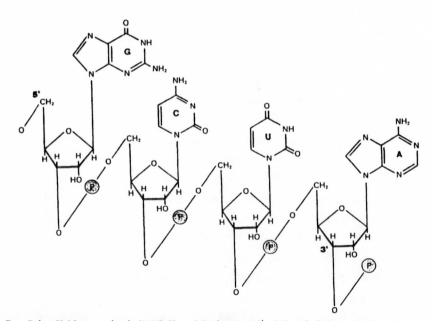

From Robert K. Murray et al., eds. (1996) *Harper's Biochemistry,* 24th ed. (Stamford, Conn.: Appleton & Lange), fig. 37-6. Reproduced by permission of V. W. Rodwell.

The flow of information from DNA via RNA to protein.

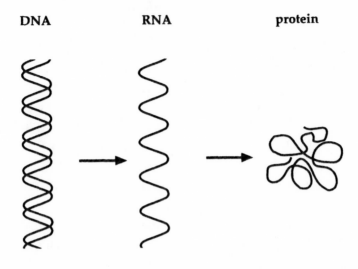

DNA **RNA** **protein**

Although the chemical differences between DNA and RNA are very small, they have a significant influence on their chemical properties. Double-stranded RNA polymers exhibit fewer of the minor structural distortions which make the DNA helix so ideal for protein recognition.[15] Also, the double-stranded RNA helix has a very deep major groove, which is less accessible to proteins than in the case of DNA.[16] This means that the base sequence in a section of double-stranded RNA cannot be recognized as easily by proteins as it can in DNA. Consequently, information encoded in sequences of double-stranded RNA is less accessible or decipherable than in DNA. And as the double-stranded structure is the most chemically stable form of either DNA or RNA, then on this count DNA is clearly fitter than RNA to serve as the ultimate repository of genetic information, which must be both stable and accessible.

However, protein recognition of particular RNA molecules, or sections of particular RNA molecules, is vital if RNA is to fulfill its biological role in the cell. It is proteins which handle and process the RNA and assist in the transport of RNA molecules from nucleus to cytoplasm. But where RNA is less fit than DNA for protein recognition in the superstable double helical conformation, in the cell much of the *RNA is single-stranded* and proteins therefore do not have to recognize sections of RNA molecules in the hard to recognize, double-helical form. Single stranded RNA folds into complex 3-D conformations and it is mainly these shapes which are recognized by proteins. The RNA molecule is not only a "tape" but a "tape" which folds into a "shape." In this combination of information and conformation RNA is perfectly adapted for its biological role.

Moreover, RNA, by virtue of its additional hydroxyl group, is more reactive than DNA and therefore less stable and again less fit than DNA to serve as the ultimate repository of genetic information. Anyone who has had any experience in preparing DNA and RNA in a laboratory will attest to the relative instability of RNA compared to DNA. Because of the ability of single-stranded molecules to adopt complex 3-D conformations, RNA is capable of catalytic activities which cannot be performed by the stiff double-stranded DNA helix. Remarkably, these catalytic abilities enable RNA molecules to change their chemical structure, allowing them to convert themselves, during processing in the cell nucleus, from the large initial copy of the DNA sequence to the far smaller messenger RNA sequence, which is translated by the ribosome into the amino acid sequence of a protein (see below).

As more is learned of these two molecules, it is becoming increasingly apparent how their many subtle structural differences are adapted for their respective biological roles—DNA as the permanent accessible stable information store of the cell and RNA as the transitory carrier of the genetic information from the DNA to the translational machinery.[17]

The formation of mRNA from the larger initial transcript of the DNA.

DNA   **Initial RNA transcript**   **mRNA**   **protein**

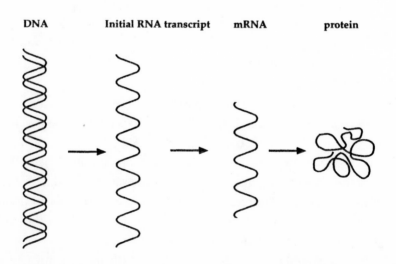

Possible Alternatives

Although it is clear that both DNA and RNA are wonderfully fit for their respective biological roles, the question remains, are they uniquely fit? Or might there be other candidate information carriers even fitter than either DNA or RNA? Is every chemical detail of the two molecules essential for biological function? Could different bases be used? Could different sugars be used? Could the phosphate be replaced by some other joining molecule? None of these questions can be answered definitely, but the evidence suggests that any change would be detrimental and no other polymers are known which possess precisely the chemical and physical properties of DNA and RNA.

DNA and RNA are two members of a vast class of closely related nucleic acid polymers, some of which have been recently synthesized. Some have hexoses (a six-carbon sugar) instead of riboses (a five-carbon sugar) in the backbone, others such as the peptide nucleic acids (PNA) have a peptide backbone linked together by amide bonds.[18] The study of these "alternatives" is preliminary. However, they have already provided evidence that the fidelity of base pairing in DNA and RNA is probably dependent on the sugar being a ribose rather than a hexose. And in the case of one recently synthesized "alternative RNA" in which a slightly different ribose is incorporated, the strands are less flexible than in the case of natural RNA, and this may reduce its fitness for biological function.[19] In the PNAs the binding affinities of the two strands may be too strong for biological function. As mentioned above, it is likely that the precise binding strength and flexibility of the strands in DNA and RNA are critical for biological function, conferring on the molecules a crucial "metastability" which is not possessed by any of the alternative closely related nucleic acid polymers.

One fascinating aspect of this work is the possibility that some of the various alternative helical replicators, such as the PNAs, may have been used by very primitive life before the current DNA-RNA system evolved. They may even have played a crucial role in the origin of life. If indeed some alternative DNA-like replicators were utilized by early life on earth, then on purely selectionist grounds it is hard to see how they could have been superior and yet selected against and thus have lost out in the evolutionary race.

Different Bases

Some years ago one of the world authorities on DNA structure pointed out: "It is sufficient to note that there are *very few* additional complementary pairs which can fit into the DNA."[20] Recently, chemists have incorporated some of these additional base pairs into DNA. However, although the evidence is not conclusive, it seems unlikely that DNA constructed out of any of the unnatural base pairs would be as biologically fit. Studies of alternative base-pairing schemes involving various unnatural bases in DNA helices are very preliminary but tend to support the view that DNA constructed out of these unnatural bases would probably not be as chemically stable nor as faithfully copied as DNA constructed out of the 4 natural bases.[21] In the view of Wolfram Saenger, one of the world's leading authorities on nucleic acid chemistry, the 4 natural bases are superior in many critical ways compared with the various unnatural alternatives.[22] Theoretical consideration of the chemical characteristics of the natural and alternative unnatural bases in Saenger's words makes it "clear why nature has selected the four natural bases as primary tools."[23] That there may be only these 4 bases available has important implications related to the encoding of information for the specification of proteins and for the retrieval of genetic information by proteins from DNA.

Although the current evidence is insufficient to establish absolutely the unique fitness of DNA and RNA for their respective biological roles, all the available evidence is at least consistent with this position. According to Wolfram Saenger, the available evidence strongly suggests that the natural nucleic acids are optimally fit for their respective biological roles and any chemical change to the phosphate radical, the riboses, or to any of the 4 bases used would certainly decrease greatly their biological fitness and may even abolish it. (See endnote for Saenger's summary of the fitness of the natural nucleic acids.)[24]

The Fitness of the Code

Every high-school student knows that the linear nucleotide sequence of a gene contains a message specifying the amino acid sequence of a protein, and that this message is decoded via a system of rules, the genetic code, which relate particular DNA sequences 3 bases long, known as codons, to one of the 20 amino acids used in the construction of proteins (the structure and functioning of proteins is dealt with in the next chapter).

Is the genetic code uniquely and ideally adapted for its biological role? Is it, in other words, the best possible coding system we can envisage? Or might an alternative coding system have been possible using more or less than the 4 bases in DNA or using a different set of amino acids? This is a problematical area and no clear answer can be given at present. However, some of the possible alternative arrangements would appear to be less fit.

The genetic code.

UUU	Phenylalanine	UCU	Serine	UAU	Tyrosine	UGU	Cysteine
UUC		UCC		UAC		UGC	
UUA		UCA		UAA	Stop	UGA	Stop
UUG		UCG		UAG		UGG	Tryptophan
CUU	Leucine	CCU	Proline	CAU	Histidine	CGU	Arginine
CUC		CCC		CAC		CGC	
CUA		CCA		CAA	Glutamine	CGA	
CUG		CCG		CAG		CGG	
AUU	Isoleucine	ACU	Threonine	AAU	Asparagine	AGU	Serine
AUC		ACC		AAC		AGC	
AUA		ACA		AAA	Lysine	AGA	Arginine
AUG	Methionine or start	ACG		AAG		AGG	
GUU	Valine	GCU	Alanine	GAU	Aspartic acid	GGU	Glycine
GUC		GCC		GAC		GGC	
GUA	Valine or start	GCA		GAA	Glutamic acid	GGA	
GUG		GCG		GAG		GGG	

Note that because of its primary base-paired structure DNA can only be constructed with pairs of complementary bases. Therefore, the number of bases used in its construction has to be an even number. The consequences of using only 2 bases (i.e., 1 base pair) rather than the 4 actually used in natural DNA was raised briefly by Alexander Rich: "We may ask why nucleic acids have four units in them at the present time. . . . In order to contain information, it is obvious that two bases would be enough; for example, simply adenine and thymine. A primitive organism whose nucleic acid contained only two complementary bases could still develop a similar type of biochemical system for information transfer."[25]

Consider a DNA molecule made up of only 2 bases, adenine and thymine. It would be formed of (A-T) base pairs as shown below:

DNA constructed out of two bases: A and T.

A--T
A--T
T--A
A--T
T--A
T--A
T--A
A--T
A--T

The table below shows the number of codons available, either 2, 3, 4, 5, or 6 nucleotides long, in a coding system using only 2 bases:

Genetic coding systems utilizing two bases.

Coding system using 2 nucleotide bases					
Number of nucleotides in codon	2	3	4	5	6
Number of codons	4	8	16	32	64

From the above table we can see that to code for 20 amino acids the codons would have to be at least 5 bases long. A potential problem would be that with only 32 different codons such a system would not provide many alternative codons for the same amino acid. Most amino acids would be specified by only one codon. The actual 4-base coding system involves a relatively high level of redundancy, so that most of the amino acids are specified by more than 1 codon.

The redundancy of the code was a considerable puzzle in the early 1960s when the details of the genetic code were first worked out. Since then, as knowledge of gene expression has increased, it has become increasingly clear that without the flexibility the redundancy confers, the embedding of additional information in protein coding sequences related to sophisticated types of gene regulation would be impossible.

To achieve the same level of redundancy with a 2-base system, we would have to increase the length of the codons to 6 bases long. This would provide the same level of redundancy as in the existing code. However, the genes and messenger RNA molecules in such a system would be twice as long and energy required for protein synthesis would be doubled. The transfer RNA molecules (the molecules which recognize particular codons and transfer the appropriate amino acid to the growing polypeptide chain) would in all probability have to be larger, as might the entire protein synthetic apparatus. The process of protein synthesis would in all probability be slowed down considerably. In short, such a system would be more complicated than the existing system, cost twice as much in terms of materials and energy, and provide no obvious advantage.

What would the consequences be of using a coding system utilizing more than 4 bases—6, 8, or 10, perhaps? A hypothetical double-stranded DNA molecule constructed out of 3 different base pairs, including the 2 base pairs A-T and G-C used in natural DNA and a third hypothetical base pair X-Y, is shown below:

DNA constructed out of six bases: A, T, G, C, X, and Y.

C--G
T--A
X--Y
G--C
C--G
T--A
Y--X
T--A
C--G

Although it is possible to imagine a coding system using 6 bases, it is difficult to see how it would be advantageous compared with the existing 4-base system. The table below shows the number of codons available, either 2, 3, or 4 nucleotides long, in a coding system using 6 bases:

Genetic coding system utilizing six bases.

Coding system using 6 nucleotide bases			
Number of nucleotides in codon	2	3	4
Number of codons	36	216	1296

The use of 6 bases would clearly involve certain problems. If the codons in a 6-base system were 2 bases long, this would provide 36 different codons sufficient to specify 20 amino acids. However, 32 codons may not provide the necessary element of redundancy. Moreover, the fidelity of a theoretical decoding mechanism based on matching only 2 base pairs would probably be lower than the existing system.

On the other hand, if three nucleotides were used in a 6-base system, this would mean that 216 codons would be available for specifying amino acids. If all these 216 codons were to be used, the complexity of the transitional system would be considerably increased, involving four times the number of transfer RNA molecules. But if a proportion of codons were not used to specify amino acids and were in other words nonsense codons, this would vastly increase the chance of a mutation destroying the meaning of the genetic message. The use of 6 different nucleotides would also involve additional metabolic pathways for their synthesis, as well as complicating the mechanism of DNA synthesis.

An imaginary 6-base system is in any case only hypothetical because, as was mentioned above, on the evidence available, nature has not provided an extra base pair capable of quite the same perfect base pairing as that which occurs between the A-T and G-C base pairs in natural DNA.

We could continue the game by considering other possible coding systems. However, given our current understanding of protein chemistry, it is increasingly hard to escape the conclusion that we need no more than 20 amino acids to specify for proteins with a diverse range of functional properties. To specify for 20 amino acids in a DNA sequence, the current system based on 4 nucleotides, consisting of 64 codons made up of 3 nucleotides each, with a considerable degree of redundancy, is just about the most elegant solution possible.

It is fortunate, then, that nature provides 2 unique base pairs for the construction of the DNA helix. If there was only 1 base pair available, then the utility of DNA for encoding information for the specification of proteins made out of 20 amino acids would be greatly diminished. That there are in all probability no additional base pairs available with the same ideal qualities as the 2 actually utilized in the structure of DNA is no drawback. Because unless more than 20 amino acids were required for some reason—and it is difficult to imagine what this might be, given the fantastic functional diversity of natural proteins—no obvious advantage would accrue by increasing the coding potential of DNA by incorporating additional base pairs.

If the coding system can be flawed in any way, it is in the curious variation in the number of codons specifying different amino acids. The amino acid serine, for example, has 6 codons, while methionine and tryptophan have only one. Yet serine is not used six times more frequently in proteins than tryptophan or methionine. Most other amino acids are specified by 2 or 4 codons. But again, there does not seem to be any exact relationship between number of codons and frequency of occurrence of an amino acid in proteins. Does this mean that the code is less than ideal, or is it possible in this case that there may be a number of equally "ideal" alternatives so that no particular system is preferable? A graph plotting all possible coding arrangements against their utility would contain multiple peaks.

However, from the evidence currently available we cannot be sure that the codon assignments are not in fact optimized for a variety of functional reasons which have not yet been clearly defined. The apparently excessive number of codons for serine and threonine may be related to the fact that these amino acids are favored for phosphorylation, which involves the addition of a phosphate group to a protein. Phosphorylation changes the activity of a protein and is used widely by cells as a regulatory device. The fact that proline has 4 codons may relate to its helix-breaking properties (a probable reason for its original choice as one of the 20 amino acids in the first place—see the discussion in the next chapter). Before concluding that the code is not maximally fit, we should remember also that the origin of the coding system and its early evolution are still mysterious. It may be that there is a reason for these apparent anomalies rooted in as yet undiscovered necessities associated with the evolution of the code.

The fitness of various possible coding systems.

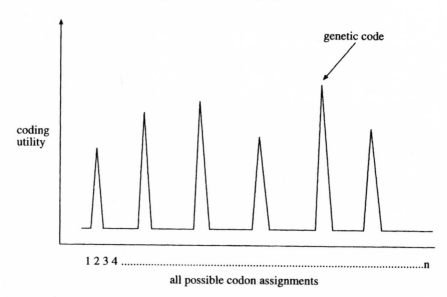

all possible codon assignments

Conclusion

If life is the result of design, then every component must be perfectly fit for the end it serves. There can be no exceptions. If the genetic code is indeed less than optimum, then the entire teleological worldview collapses. Fortunately, in the case of the code we still have insufficient knowledge of protein structure and function to judge the code as clearly "nonoptimal." Our knowledge of evolution is also incomplete. In the case of DNA and RNA, we are on safer ground; nearly everything we have learned since 1953 is at least consistent with the possibility that DNA and RNA are both ideally and uniquely fit.

And DNA may be fit for its biological role in other ways of which at present we have only the haziest notion. For example, DNA can form many other conformations in addition to the double helix. It can also form what are called cruciform structures and the so-called triple helices. Triplex DNA is particularly intriguing, as there are a number of possible biological processes in which it could function, such as in recombination and in regulating gene expression.[26] Then there is the equally intriguing possibility raised recently by a paper in *Science* that DNA may provide the basis for a subcellular computing system.[27]

Although as we have seen in this chapter, DNA molecules are wonderfully fit to perform the function of information carrier, such long, relatively stiff polymers are not fit to manipulate individual atoms or molecules by making and breaking specific chemical bonds. DNA cannot in itself carry out all the various sophisticated manipulative and structural functions which must inevitably be performed in any self-replicating system in the process of copying itself. It cannot in itself perform the task of "constructor device."

This essential need for automated constructor devices or robots to carry out the instructions encoded in the memory bank is one of the major unsolved problems in the design of artificial self-replicating machines. It is certainly very difficult to imagine how any sort of self-replicating machine would be feasible and function unless its component "constructor or manipulator devices" (capable of reading and decoding the message in the data bank and carrying out its instructions) were self-assembling to a very large degree. Clearly, the subproblem of designing self-assembling devices will have to be solved before anything approaching genuine artificial self-replication can be attempted. The daunting nature of this subproblem was nicely captured by Ted Kaeler, a contributor to a recent symposium on nanotechnology, when he described the current predicament as an "impasse or wall": "I view the problem of developing a proto assembler as a *wall.* We are on one side of the wall and on the other side of the wall there is an assembler that can make other assemblers."[28]

The biological solution to the "constructor device problem," the way through the wall, is of course to be found in the characteristics and properties of a remarkable class of self-assembling biopolymers—the proteins. As I shall try to explain in the following chapter, as the universal nanoconstructors in a self-replicating automaton, they have no peer. They represent a solution of surpassing brilliance to von Neumann's problem of the universal constructor.

Chapter 8

The   Nanomanipulators

In which it is argued that no other class of polymers are known
which are as fit as proteins for the central biological role they
play in living systems. The functional and structural properties
of proteins are astoundingly diverse, and in addition, proteins
are capable of self-assembly. Because of their ability to adopt
alternative shapes, the biological activities of proteins can be
finely regulated—a phenomenon known as allostery. The
mutual adaptations of proteins and DNA are also examined,
including the fit of the α helix into the large groove of the DNA
and the fact that the a *helix can "feel" about 4 bases in*
the DNA. It is concluded that the evidence is consistent with
the possibility that the DNA-protein partnership is uniquely
fit for its biochemical role.

The atomic structure of the protein cytochrome

Showing all the atoms in the protein except for hydrogen. The protein is made up of a long chain of 104 building blocks known as amino acids. Embedded in the center of the protein is one heme molecule, which is a planar cyclic compound made up of nitrogen and carbon atoms and containing at the center of the ring one iron atom (Fe). Altogether, the protein contains about 1,000 atoms and the complexity of their spatial arrangement is apparent. In the cell, cytochrome *c* is found in the mitochondrion and forms part of what is known as the respiratory assembly—a set of proteins involved in generating energy from oxidative metabolism. Its major function is to shuttle electrons across the membrane surrounding the mitochondrion. The protein measures about 5 nanometers, or five-millionths of a millimeter, across.

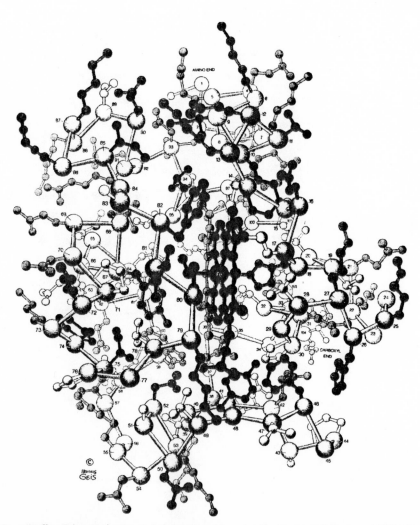

From Geoffrey, Zubay, *Biochemistry*, 2nd ed. © 1989, p. 59; reprinted by Prentice-Hall, Englewood Cliffs, N.J., p. 59. Reproduced by permission of the publisher.

We would like to think ourselves necessary, inevitable, ordained from all eternity. All religions, nearly all philosophies, and even a part of science testify to the unwearying, heroic effort of mankind desperately denying its own contingency.

—Jacques Monod, *Chance and Necessity,* 1972

It struck me recently that one should really consider the sequence of a protein molecule, about to fold into a precise geometric form, as a line of melody written in canon form and so designed by Nature to fold back upon itself, creating harmonic chords of interaction consistent with biological function: One might carry the analogy further by suggesting that the kinds of chords formed in a protein (incorrectly folded) . . . are dissonant, but that, by giving an opportunity for rearrangement . . . they modulate to give the pleasing harmonics of the native molecule. Whether or not some conclusion can be drawn about the greater thermodynamic stability of Mozart's over Schoenberg's music is something I will leave to the philosophers of the audience.

—Christian Anfinsen, *New Perspectives in Biology,* 1964

Where DNA is the data bank of life, the ultimate repository of all biological information, the proteins are life's animated actors, the universal constructor devices, the nanomanipulators which translate the one-dimensional DNA dream into the vital three-dimensional reality of the cell. By reading and following the instructions in the DNA, the proteins manipulate the atoms and molecules of life into the trillions of unique and specific conformations upon which the miracle of self-replication and self-assembly depends.

As the constructor devices of the cell, they represent what is in effect the realization of von Neumann's dream. As much as DNA, they are the secret of life. Without what Jacques Monod called their "demoniacal functions,"[1] we would certainly not be here to marvel at the sheer brilliance of the solution they represent.

For over 4 billion years, these tiny nanoconstructors have been reading DNA scripts. Building atom by atom, they assembled over eons of time every living structure that ever existed on earth. They built the first cell; they built the human brain; they erected the dinosaurs and all past life on earth. All the vital chemical functions of every cell on earth are all dependent on the activities of these tiny nanomachines. The living kingdom, in a very real sense, has its being and origin in the infinitely rich, ever-changing patterns woven from the interactions of these tiny fragile collections of dancing atoms, a billion times smaller than the tiniest visible speck of dust.

It we think of the cell as being analogous to a factory, then the proteins can be thought of as analogous to the machines on the factory floor that carry out individually or in groups all the essential activities on which the life of the cell depends, apart from the transmission of genetic information, which as we have seen is the role of the DNA. Proteins are also the basic structural building blocks of the cell, for it is largely by the association of different proteins that all the forms and structures of living things are generated. In terms of the factory, proteins form not only the machines but the walls, roof, floor, stairwell, and doors as well.

Protein Diversity and Versatility

The diversity of the structural and functional properties of proteins is astounding. Some proteins form the hard Teflon-like materials which make up hair, nails, and feathers. Others form tough nylonlike materials which make up the tendons that attach muscles to bone and the fibrous sheaths which encase the various compartments and organs in the body. Some form the rubberlike elastic materials that surround the major arteries in the body, while others maintain the smooth elasticity of skin. Still others make up the transparent materials which form the lens of the eye.

In addition to their structural roles, proteins play an infinite variety of functional roles in the cell. They can act as catalysts speeding up the rates of chemical reactions billions of times. Working closely together in teams, proteins can build up all the chemical components of the cell, including complex lipids and carbohydrates. As well as building things up, proteins can utilize their catalytic powers to break down the cells' macromolecular constituents back into simple organic compounds. It is through the catalytic activity of proteins that cells derive their energy. It is through these same catalytic powers that the energy of the sun, trapped by the chloroplasts, is converted into reduced carbon fuels, the basic energy source of life.

It is proteins that form the essential components of the contractile assemblies in the muscles, providing organisms with the capability of movement. It is proteins which comprise the basic building blocks of the tubule system of the cell, providing the scaffold which determines the shape of the cell. These same tubules also provide the cell with a system of interconnecting conduits for the movement of the cells' constituents in an orderly fashion around the cell. In addition to forming the structural basis of the cells' transport system, it is proteins which also perform the role of transporters, selectively binding to certain chemicals at particular stations in the cell and then releasing them at other sites. Proteins also play the role of chemical messengers, being manufactured in one location and then traveling to another site where they bind to some other molecule to cause some appropriate chemical response. It is proteins which are also the receptors of chemical messages, selectively binding to "messenger molecules" (which are often other proteins) and responding to the arrival of the "message" by bringing about, generally via specific interactions with other proteins, changes to the functional state of the cell. Proteins also form the gates and pumps that control the passage of innumerable different types of chemicals through the cell membrane, either by opening and closing chemical channels or by actively pumping chemicals from one side to another. The list of structural and functional properties of proteins is virtually endless.

Although some of the properties of proteins are equaled by particular types of polymers or other classes of compounds. For example, in its elasticity and strength, collagen resembles nylon; the toughness of keratin, the protein which makes up nails and hair, is rivaled by the carbohydrate polymer chitin; the transparency of the crystallines of the eye is like that of the plastic Perspex; and so forth. However, no other individual class of molecules is known which possesses even remotely such a diversity of properties. Moreover, their catalytic properties are effectively unparalleled by any other type of molecule. So are their powers of molecular discrimination whereby one particular protein molecule is able to interact with unerring specificity with another specific molecule in the cell.

The very great structural and functional diversity of proteins is one of the key characteristics of these remarkable molecules which contributes to their unique fitness as the molecular constructor devices of the cell. To appreciate more fully some of the other characteristics of proteins that tailor them so superbly for their biological role as the working components of life, it is necessary to digress here and review some basic aspects of their chemical design for those readers unfamiliar with this area of biochemistry.

Protein Structure

It is immediately obvious even to someone without any previous experience in molecular biology that the arrangement of the atoms in a protein (see figure 8.1) is unlike any ordinary machine built or conceived by man, or indeed unlike any object of common experience with which we are familiar. On superficial observation one is immediately struck by the apparent illogic of the design and the lack of any obvious modularity or regularity. The sheer chaos of the arrangement of the atoms conveys an almost eerie, otherworldly impression.

A similar feeling of the strangeness and chaos of the arrangement of atoms in a protein struck the researchers at Cambridge University after the molecular structure of the first protein, myoglobin, had been determined in 1957. As one researcher put it at the time:

> Perhaps the most remarkable features of the molecule are its complexity and its lack of symmetry. The arrangement seems to be almost totally lacking in the kind of regularities which one instinctively anticipates, and it is more complicated than had been predicted by any theory of protein structure.[2]

Ten years later another member of the original Cambridge team confessed that the diversity and complexity of the 3-D atomic configuration of proteins is "so baffling that it stops protein crystallographers remembering the conformation of any protein but their own."[3]

Despite the complexity of proteins, their basic chemical structure is relatively simple. All are polymers built up from twenty different small organic molecules called amino acids. The figure below shows the chemical structures of four amino acids. Each amino acid contains an amino group (NH_2) and a carboxyl acid group (COOH) linked by a carbon atom (the α carbon atom), as well as a unique side chain.

Because of their different side chains each amino acid has different chemical properties. Some amino acids, like alanine in the diagram below, have uncharged side chains so are relatively insoluble in water. These are the hydrophobic, or water-avoiding, amino acids. Other amino acids have charged side chains and are soluble and hydrophilic. In a protein the amino acids are

Symbolic diagrams of four amino acids.

Note that the molecular skeleton enclosed within the dotted frame is the same in all. The attached groups, or radicals, outside the chain give each amino acid its unique chemical characteristics. Glycine, the simplest amino acid, has one hydrogen atom outside the frame. In alanine, the hydrogen atom is replaced by a CH_3 group. In cysteine, a sulfur atom has been incorporated with the CH_3 group. In tyrosine, a benzene ring has been incorporated.

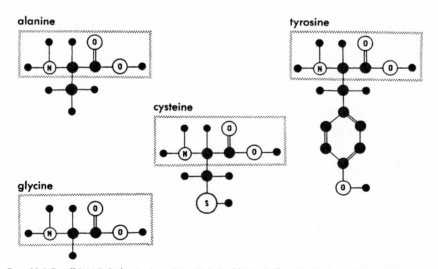

From N. J. Berrill (1996) *Biology in Action* (New York: Dodd, Mead), fig. 3.10. Reproduced by permission of N. J. Berrill.

linked by their amino and carboxyl acid groups to form a long linear polymer which is known as the primary structure of the protein. The figure
below shows a short section of a polypeptide chain.

*A short section of the amino acid backbone of a protein. Showing the linked carbon (large filled
circles) and nitrogen atoms (N) forming the backbone or chain and the attached hydrogen (small
filled circles) oxygen (O) and amino acid radicals (R).*

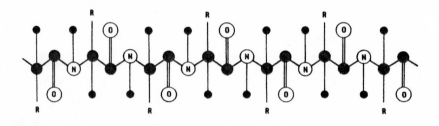

From N. J. Berrill (1996) *Biology in Action* (New York: Dodd, Mead), fig. 3.11. Reproduced by permission of
N. J. Berrill.

The backbone, which is formed by linkage of the amino acid and carboxylic acid groups, is identical throughout the molecule. It is the unique
side groups that jut out from the backbone which confer different chemical
properties to different regions of the amino acid chain. The linear sequence
of amino acids in a protein can be thought of as a sentence made up from a
long combination of the 20 amino acid letters. Just as different sentences are
made up of different sequences of letters, so different proteins are made up
of different sequences of amino acids. In most proteins the amino acid chain
is between 100 and 500 amino acids long. Proteins are therefore like DNA—
in that they are basically polymeric molecules—but much shorter than
DNA, which is generally many millions of units long. Each different protein has a unique amino acid sequence, and this is known as its primary
structure.

The primary structure of a protein may also be thought of as analogous
to a series of plastic table-tennis balls strung together like beads on a string.
The figure below shows the primary structure of the small protein ribonu-
clease. The amino acids are numbered from 1 to 124. The usual three-letter
abbreviation is used to indicate each amino acid in the chain. For example,
Lys stands for lysine; Ser, for serine, etc.

The primary structure of the protein ribonuclease.

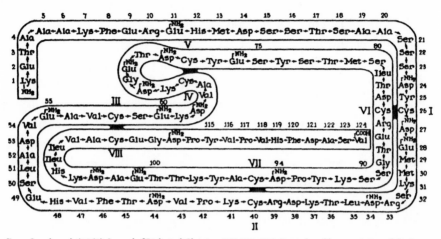

From Smyth et al. (1963) *Journal of Biological Chemistry* 238:227–234. Reproduced by permission of the American Society for Biochemistry and Molecular Biology.

Could Nature Have Chosen Other Amino Acids?

At this point, let us stop to consider an obvious question. Over two hundred amino acids occur in nature. The number of amino acids which are theoretically possible is enormous. Even in the human body many amino acids that do not occur in proteins are utilized for a variety of metabolic functions. If the laws of nature are programmed for life as we know it, there should be something special about the choice of these particular twenty amino acids. As discussed in the previous chapter, in the case of DNA it is relatively easy to rationalize the choice of the four bases on grounds of their superior fitness. However, in the case of the twenty amino acids, it is very difficult to judge whether the structure or function of proteins would have been better if a different selection of amino acids had been chosen for their construction.

From our current understanding of the structure and function of proteins, it is possible to list at least some of the criteria that must be satisfied in the choice of amino acids used if an amino acid sequence is to fold into a stable form. There is clearly a requirement that a proportion of the amino acids possess hydrophobic side chains and that these chains be not too large or they would be impossible to pack neatly together into the protein interior. There is a requirement that a fraction of the amino acids have side chains which specifically favor what are known as α helix and β sheet formations, two very common 3-D conformations adopted by sections of the polypeptide chain in most proteins that play a crucial role in stabilizing the final and intermediate 3-D form of the protein. The α helix is a conformation in which a section of the amino acid chain is twisted into a helical conformation. The β sheet formation occurs when adjacent sections of the amino acid chain are stacked on top of one another in a series of layers. There is the requirement that some of the hydrophilic side chains be positively and others negatively charged. Finally, there is the requirement that all side chains, whether hydrophobic or hydrophilic, must not be too disruptive of either α helix or β sheet conformations.

Examination of the twenty amino acids used in proteins shows that several have hydrophobic side chains, half are good α helix formers, and half are β sheet formers. The choice of side chains looks to be just about right. It is less easy to rationalize the choice of individual amino acids. However, the inclusion of the smallest and simplest amino acid, glycine, may be necessary because of its essential role in one of the most important of all proteins— collagen—which forms the fibrous matrix that binds and holds together all the cells and tissues of multicellular organisms. Every third amino acid in the coiled polypeptide chains of collagen is glycine, and its small size plays an essential role in the design of the collagen molecule because it allows the coiled chains to wrap tightly together, conferring on the collagen fibers far greater tensile strength than would be possible if glycine were replaced by any other amino acid with a longer side chain. Without glycine, collagen fibers might not possess the requisite strength to glue together the cells of multicellular life forms. The sulfur-containing amino acid cysteine may also be essential because of the transitory role played by disulfide bonds in stabilizing transient intermediate conformations via which many proteins fold into their final native form.[4] The choice of serine, threonine, and tyrosine may have been dictated because their hydroxyl groups lend themselves to phosphorylation, one of the key mechanisms whereby the cell regulates the activities of protein. Proline may be included because it is a helix breaker. Moreover proline is also used in the construction of collagen in which it may play, like glycine, an essential role.

Finally, in this context it is interesting to note that the amino acids in proteins are often modified chemically in a variety of ways after the amino acid chain has folded into its native form. In effect, because of these chemical modifications, nature has available far more amino acids than the twenty actually used as the basic building blocks of proteins.

Protein Folding

The chemical bonds which link the successive carbon atoms in the backbone of the protein are known as covalent bonds. As discussed in chapter 5, covalent bonds are formed when atoms share electrons to complete electron shells. And as explained, nearly all the atoms in the organic compounds utilized in living organisms—sugars, amino acids, fats, the nucleotide bases in DNA, etc.—are linked together by covalent bonds. There are, however, as also mentioned in chapter 5, another class of chemical bonds which do not involve sharing electrons but arise out of weaker electrostatic forces between adjacent atoms, and these are known as noncovalent bonds, or weak chemical bonds. The linear chain of amino acids folds automatically under the influence of these weak electrochemical forces into the complex three-dimensional aggregate of atoms.

In terms of the "string of plastic balls" analogy, we can think of the folded three-dimensional conformation of a protein as being analogous to the string of balls tightly folded together to form a globular mass of balls in which each ball is stuck loosely to one or several of its neighbors with lengths of tape. The tape represents the weak chemical bonds that hold together the various parts of the protein structure.

Folding occurs in such a way so as to bring about the maximum number of favorable atomic interactions between the various constituent amino acids. During the folding, which takes a fraction of a second, negatively charged groups tend to associate with positively charged groups, and hydrophobic side chains tend to stack at the center of the molecule while hydrophilic side chains tend to arrange themselves on the surface in contact with water. The final three-dimensional arrangement of the atoms is dictated directly by the primary amino acid sequence. The figure below shows the folded chains of a protein in its native conformation.

Because the unfolded amino acid chain is capable of folding into its native form in vitro without assistance from any other component of the cell in which it is synthesized, this must mean that the information or direction for the folding process is contained in the amino acid sequence. This is somewhat analogous to the situation in origami, where all the instructions

*The weak chemical bonds which hold a protein in its native
3-D conformation.*

The hydrophobic core, shaded, consists mainly of hydrophobic amino acids.

hydrogen bonds between
adjacent stretches of
amino acid chain

hydrophilic amino acids
on the outside of molecule

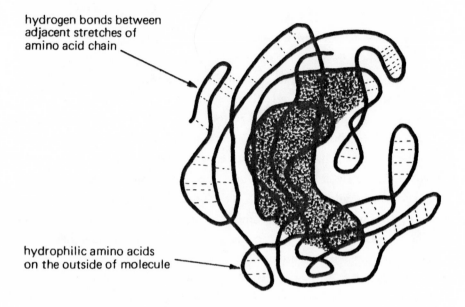

necessary to reach the final folded 3-D form are contained in a series of lines
drawn on the initial 2-D piece of flat paper.

The mechanism by which proteins achieve the extraordinary end of self-
assembly is a subject of intense research. Already it is clear that the folding
process is complex and depends on global cooperative interactions, which
involve a high proportion of all the amino acids scattered all along the sequence of the chain. Recent evidence suggests that the folding may occur
(again, as in origami) through highly specific or even unique pathways involving partially folded intermediates which exhibit (as in origami) nonnative conformations, i.e., conformations which are not present in the
final native folded form. This must mean that in many biological proteins
the amino acid sequence not only specifies the native conformation but
also specifies a folding pathway which includes in some proteins the specification of partially folded nonnative intermediate conformations; and
these, like stepping-stones, lead the folding process along an energetically
favorable route to a magic disclosure, the exquisite beauty of the three-
dimensional native form of the protein.

The ability of proteins to assemble themselves automatically is a key capability which is essential to their biological role as the atomic manipulators or constructor devices of the cell. No sort of self-replicating machine could function unless its component machinery was self-assembling. The inability to specify completely feasible self-assembling robots able to assemble themselves *without assistance from any external agent* lies at the heart of the failure to achieve self-replication in artificial systems.

Proteins are not the only polymers which can fold themselves into specific three-dimensional forms. Such a capacity is inherent in many complex organic molecules. Recently, organic chemists have created a variety of polymers, known as "foldamers," which can mimic proteins in folding themselves into specific 3-D forms. Moreover, it seems likely that artificial enzymes and foldamers mimicking some of the structural roles of proteins may be created in the next ten years. But even if artificial proteinlike foldamers are achieved, it seems likely that they will be very heterogeneous in terms of subunits and chemical design. The study of these alternative polymers is still in its infancy, but there are no grounds for believing that any one single generic class of foldamers will exhibit the complexity, the range of chemical and structural abilities, and the precise degree of metastability essential for allostery (a subject discussed below) of natural proteins. It seems likely that, as in the case of the study of alternative DNA polymers, study of these foldamers will merely underline the unique fitness of proteins for their biological role.

Within the context of current scientific knowledge proteins are, as far as we know, the only available molecular constructor devices possessing, first, the capacity to carry out a vast diversity of structural and functional chemical roles, involving every imaginable type of specific atomic and molecular manipulations and, second, the capacity to assemble themselves automatically without the help of an external agent.

There is a fascinating aspect to the story of protein folding. The hydrophobic force not only folds the protein into its native conformation, but by packing together the hydrocarbon side chains of the hydrophobic amino acids, it creates a nonaqueous microenvironment in the center of the protein. This nonaqueous core has enormous functional significance. It provides a chamber where various chemical reactions may be carried out which would be impossible or very difficult in an aqueous medium (including the syntheses of the hydrophobic amino acids and lipids). In effect, those amino acids that are only sparingly soluble in water are forced by water into a tight water-avoiding ball. This ball provides the environment in which synthetic reactions, particularly condensation reactions that involve the removal of a molecule of water and which are almost impossible to carry out in an aqueous medium, can be easily performed. The two defects of water mentioned in chapter 2—that it is unable to dissolve lipids and compounds containing hydrocarbon chains and that it is a poor medium for carrying out organic syntheses—are both overcome in the center of a protein. One defect—the insolubility of hydrocarbons—is, as it were, utilized to overcome the other!

The Relative Strength of Weak and Strong Bonds

As the constructor devices of the cell, it is the proteins that carry out all the atomic manipulations upon which life depends. To carry out these nanomanipulations proteins must necessarily associate intimately with other molecules in the cell. The molecule that a protein associates with, whether it is a small molecule like an amino acid, or a large molecule like another protein, is termed a "ligand."

Nearly all these associations between a protein and its ligand are formed by the weak chemical bonds. As we have seen (in chapter 5 and in the discussion above), it is these bonds which hold biomolecules, including proteins, in their characteristic or native three-dimensional form. Because of the weakness of these bonds a stable interaction between a protein and a ligand can only occur if this involves multiple weak interactions.

The strength of the weak bonds is obviously critical to the ability of the proteins to interact selectively with other ligands in the cell. If the weak

The ligand binding site of a protein.

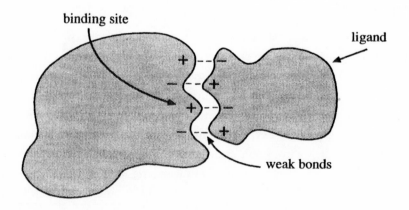

bonds were weaker, then no protein would be able to bind specifically to any other molecule in the cell.

If on the other hand these bonds were stronger, then proteins and their ligands would be bound so strongly that, once in place, they could never be removed. Consequently, the rapid association and dissociation of the protein and ligand on which so many protein functions, such as enzymic functions, depend would be impossible. In effect, proteins and all the constituents of the cell would be frozen into rigid immobile structures. The low diffusion rates would be incompatible with cellular existence. As Watson points out in *Molecular Biology of the Gene,* the low energy levels of these bonds are precisely what is required for enzymic function:

> Enzyme-substrate complexes can be both made and broken apart rapidly as a result of random thermal movement. This fact explains why enzymes can function so quickly, sometimes as often as 10^6 times per second. If enzymes were bound to their substrates by more powerful bonds they would act more slowly.[5]

Just as the strong and weak atomic forces must be exactly as they are, so both the absolute and the relative strength of the weak and strong chemical bonds must be very close to what they are or biochemistry would be impossible. In fact, the weak bonds are about twenty times weaker than the strong. This 20-to-1 ratio is vital because it means that for the majority of substrates the combined energy of binding to the catalytic site is close to that of an individual covalent bond. Which means that enzyme-substrate interactions have sufficient energy to strain and break individual covalent bonds within the substrate, thus making it possible for enzymes to carry out the various specific atomic manipulations upon which the life of the cell depends.

If we imagine a world in which the ratio between the strength of covalent and weak bonds was, say, 2 to 1 rather than 20 to 1, then the weak interactions would tend to rip the strong bonds apart. Pulling off and reattaching our tape would break the very string holding our plastic balls together.

On the other hand, if the ratio between the strength of covalent and weak bonds was increased to 200 to 1, combinations of weak bonds would be incapable of achieving the necessary energy levels to strain, break, and form specific covalent bonds within the substrate. The atomic manipulation of matter by proteins would be impossible.

The Miracle of Self-Regulation: Allostery

It is because the energy levels of the weak bonds, which hold protein molecules together in their characteristic three-dimensional form, are so low that proteins exhibit their characteristic "metastability," which is manifest in their fragility and instability in the face of very minor physical or chemical challenges. Increase their temperature a few degrees, and they unfold. Change the chemical character of the medium they are in ever so slightly, and they, again, unravel. Attach another molecule to their surface, and they change shape. Proteins are stable, but only just. They are delicately balanced, on the threshold of chaos.

Precisely because of their metastability and the weakness of the interactions that hold them on the edge of chaos, the conformation of a protein can easily be altered if it binds to another molecule. Any such interaction will cause molecular distortions which will be transmitted throughout the molecule. These discrete conformational changes effect the functioning of the protein. In the case of an enzyme, they often result in significant changes in its activity.

These reversible conformational changes which are transmitted through a protein when it binds to another molecule are the basis of allostery. Via such changes, the function of a protein may be modulated by association or dissociation with other molecules in the cell. An important aspect of this phenomenon is that the interactions are between the protein and each ligand separately and not between the ligands themselves. Consequently, the protein is able to integrate information from several different chemical inputs, each being determined by the concentration in the cell of a particular chemical. Thus allostery confers on proteins a remarkable dual ability—to carry out unique chemical reactions while at the same time integrating information about the concentration of various chemicals in the cell, and to respond intelligently to this information by turning up or down their own enzymic activity. In this, allosteric enzymes function like electronic relays.

Jacques Monod, who discovered the phenomenon, was not exaggerating when he called it "the second secret of life." For it is hard to exaggerate the significance of the *dual functionality* this phenomenon confers on these remarkable microminiaturized machines. Proteins are not only capable of carrying out a specific chemical reaction but are also able to integrate and intelligently respond to changes in their chemical environment. In other words, the functional units that carry out the basic chemical processes are also regulatory units. It is this dual functionality which is crucial to the coherent functioning of the cell, allowing it to avoid the chemical chaos that would ensue were enzymic activity not precisely tuned to the ever-changing requirements of the cell.

In this remarkable dual ability, to combine the role of microprocessor and functional machine in the same object, proteins are far in advance of any artificial device. Invariably, in artificial machines even the most advanced modules which regulate and integrate the function of the machine are separate from the working parts. In an oven there is a thermostat (regulator) and a heating device (functional unit). In a protein they are one and the same.

By sensing the concentration of molecules one or several chemical steps removed from the reaction catalyzed by the protein itself, and then responding to this information intelligently by increasing or decreasing its own activity, allosteric proteins are able to control the flow of metabolites along a metabolic pathway. It is a vast integrated network of such proteins in the cell that in Jacques Monod's words "guarantees the functional coherence of the intracellular chemical machinery."[6]

If it were not for this remarkable phenomenon, the control and regulation of the cell's metabolic activities would seem to present almost insuperable problems. It would appear that the self-regulatory capacity of proteins is not a gratuitous characteristic but rather a necessity. For at present it is impossible to envisage any alternative regulatory system which could maintain the homeostatic state of cellular metabolism at such a peak of efficiency and coherence. If proteins were incapable of self-regulation, we would have to envisage a vast, almost infinite regress of molecular control devices external to and separate from the individual enzymes which carry out the actual chemical work of the cell. Even if one were to postulate such a cybernetic system, it is hard to see how the actual activity of individual enzymes could be modulated other than by the conformational transitions actually utilized in allosteric enzymes to turn up or down their catalytic activities.

Could There Be Other Proteins

On any design hypothesis the specific proteins utilized by living organisms should be the fittest available candidates for their specific biological roles. Hemoglobin, for example, should be the fittest oxygen-transporting protein. Collagen should be the fittest structural protein for binding together the cells and tissues of multicellular organisms. While there could perhaps be "alternative" proteins of very different amino acid sequence and perhaps even basic design which are functionally equivalent to hemoglobin or collagen, if the teleological position is correct, then no "alternatives" should be fitter than the natural products. Unfortunately, protein chemistry is not sufficiently advanced to provide any clear answers. Consequently, the teleological position cannot be subjected to a vigorous test.

Recent advances in protein chemistry have revealed that the millions of different functional proteins appear to fall into about a thousand major families which share basic structural characteristics. But it is still uncertain whether these families represent a major fraction of all possible structural forms or just a small subset. Again, our knowledge is too limited.

RNA

During the 1980s the unexpected finding was made by Thomas Cech that RNA molecules could act like enzymes and catalyze chemical reactions. Since then a considerable number of RNA-catalyzed reactions have been documented.[7] However, despite their many catalytic capabilities, it seems very unlikely that RNA molecules could carry out the vast diversity of biological functions carried out by proteins. For example, many synthetic reactions catalyzed by proteins are carried out in hydrophobic niches where water is excluded and RNA molecules are unable to form large nonpolar niches. The chemical properties of RNA molecules are also less diverse, being constructed out of only four bases, while proteins are made up of twenty different amino acids. Also, as the authors of a recent review point out, RNA is far less fit for allosteric regulation than proteins.[8] RNA strands are also far less amenable to being folded into complex, compact molecular structures. Although we cannot completely exclude the possibility, it seems extremely unlikely RNA could substitute for proteins in the great majority of diverse devices and materials used in living systems.

Although RNA molecules cannot compete with modern proteins, RNA, because it can both carry information and function as an enzyme, may have served the function of both DNA and proteins in the most primitive cells shortly after the origin of life. It is an intriguing fact that RNA molecules are particularly suited for carrying out manipulations of RNA molecules— self-manipulations—and in a world where the cell was largely a collection of RNA molecules, this may have been an ability of critical significance.

Could Nanotechnology Provide an Alternative to Proteins

The uniqueness of proteins as atom-manipulating assemblers was also high-lighted in a recent *Scientific American* review of the latest state of nanotech-nology and the immense technical difficulties that will have to be overcome before any artificial device remotely as capable of manipulating atoms and molecules could be constructed.[9] The review showed just how far nanotech-nology is at present from creating artificial nanoassemblers capable of carry-ing out the sorts of atomic or molecular manipulating tasks carried out with such effortless efficiency by biological proteins. According to George M. Whitesides, an authority on molecular self-assembly who was cited in the article, the nanoists' dream of self-replication is "at the moment . . . pretty much science fiction. . . . Even after a fair amount of thought, there is no way that one could see of connecting this idea to what we know [now] or can even project into the foreseeable future."[10] The article also cites the chemist David E. H. Jones, best known perhaps as the author of the "Daedalus" column in *Nature* who has "provided a pointed critique of the idea that individual atoms could serve as constructor elements in the ulti-mate erector set."[11] Jones points out just how challenging are the many dif-ficulties that need to be overcome before an artificial nanoerector could be built: "Single atoms of the more structurally useful elements at or near room temperature are amazingly mobile and reactive . . . they will combine instantly with ambient air, water, each other, the fluid supporting the as-semblers or the assemblers themselves."[12] Jones believes the advocates of nanotechnology fail to take into account many critical questions, such as: How would the assemblers obtain information about which atom is where in order to manipulate it? How would the assemblers know where they are in order to navigate from the atom supply point to the correct position in which to place the atom? As Jones concludes: "Until these questions are properly formulated and answered, nanotechnology need not be taken seri-ously."[13] As the author of the article concludes, in the face of so many seem-ingly intractable problems, the nanotechnology dream of constructing an artificial self-assembling atom-manipulating device currently resembles a form of postmodern alchemy: "just another latter day cargo cult."[14]

Peerless Molecular Machines

From this very brief review of the properties of these remarkable nanoma-nipulators, we can conclude that, as candidates for the basic constructor role in a self-replicating nanomachine, proteins are fit, first, because of their functional and structural diversity (a remarkable enough characteristic given that all proteins are short polymers composed of a string of a hundred or so amino acids), second, because of their ability to assemble themselves, and, third, because they can perform the additional miracle, through the phe-nomenon of allostery, of regulating their own activities as well as integrating their individual activities with other proteins and enzymes to create a cyber-netic control network of unparalleled elegance and efficiency.

In the entire realm of science no class of molecule is currently known which can remotely compete with proteins. *It seems increasingly unlikely that the abilities of proteins could be realized to the same degree in any other material form.* Proteins are not only unique, but give every impression of being ideally adapted for their role as the universal constructor devices of the cell. Again, we have an example in which the only feasible candidate for a particular bio-logical role gives every impression of being supremely fit for that role.

And there is yet another, final aspect to the remarkable fitness of proteins.

The Fitness of Proteins for DNA Recognition

While proteins are wonderfully fit for the role of the constructor devices, performing all the various structural and functional activities which must be performed during the replicative cycle of the cell, they are not suited to per-forming the genetic role. It is only because, first, the information necessary to specify a protein can be encoded in the DNA sequence, and second, the information stored in the DNA can be readily retrieved and decoded by proteins, that the replication of living systems can proceed. Neither of these tasks could be achieved were it not for the fact that both molecules exhibit a set of remarkable adaptations which marvelously tailor them to function to-gether.

To begin with, DNA and proteins are both linear polymers made up of a limited number of subunits, which means that the sequence in one can be readily translated into the sequence of the other. If proteins had been more complex structures, say, branched polymers like polysaccharides, they could not have been readily encoded in the DNA or in any other linear type of molecule. No matter how fit as atomic manipulators, they would not be fit for encoding in DNA.

From first principles, proteins, because of their limitless variety, functional diversity and inherent flexibility, and their ability to undergo allosteric transitions, etc., are obvious candidates for the crucial function of recognizing and binding to a particular section of a DNA molecule. But on top of their general properties, which tailor them so superbly for almost any conceivable biochemical task, there is a fascinating and highly specific aspect of protein structure that appears to fit them precisely for DNA recognition: the fact that the α helix of a protein, one of the most common conformations found in proteins, fits almost perfectly into the major groove of the DNA helix.[15]

As mentioned above, the α helix conformation is a region of the amino acid chain of a protein which is twisted into a helical conformation. There are about 3.6 amino acids per turn of the helix—about 18 amino acids in five turns. The figure below shows a short stretch of an α helix, showing the carbon and nitrogen atoms of the amino acid backbone. The carbon atoms

The α *helix.*

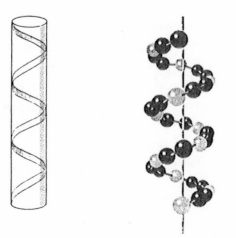

From figure 2.38 in W. T. Keeton (1976) *Biological Science,* 3rd ed. (New York: Norton). Reproduced by permission of the publisher.

are shown in black. Note the atoms of the backbone follow a helical path. The side groups of the amino acids (not shown in the figure) project outward from the central backbone.

The fact that one of the most fundamental protein conformations fits very neatly into the large groove of the DNA obviously greatly facilitates protein DNA recognition because it allows the protein to have intimate access to the DNA sequence. Of course, there are many other conditions which must be met in addition to this coincidence if proteins are to be able to recognize particular sequences in the DNA.

To begin with, if a protein is "to read" a particular base sequence in a particular region of the DNA, the protein must be able to distinguish between the different base pairs along the helix. Of course, the protein cannot actually "see" but must feel the sequence of the DNA like a blind person reading braille until it finds (feels) the sequence it is looking for. It turns out, and this is surely another coincidence of great significance, that of the two grooves in the DNA, the major and the minor, *it is the major groove*—the one into which the α helix happens to fit so perfectly—that provides hydrogen bond patterns which are distinctive for each of the four base pairs and can therefore be felt by the α helix. (The minor-groove hydrogen bond patterns are not so distinctive.) So the actual base sequence of the DNA can be "felt" most readily by a protein feeling the sequence in the major groove. In effect, the major groove is fit for protein recognition not only because its dimensions match that of the α helix but also because in the large groove each base pair presents a unique electrostatic pattern which greatly facilitates sequence recognition—quite literally the "feeling" by the α helix of the base sequence of the DNA. The large groove therefore exhibits two independent adaptations for its role in protein-DNA recognition—its electrostatic variability and its dimensions, which match closely that of the α helix.

The mutual fitness of the large groove and the α helix for DNA-protein recognition must be considered a coincidence of very great significance, as recent work in this area has revealed that a great many DNA-recognizing proteins insert a protruding α helix into the major groove of the DNA helix when binding to the DNA.

But this is only the beginning of the story of the mutual fitness of proteins and DNA. As was mentioned in chapter 7, it seems that nature has provided only 4 bases capable of forming geometrically perfect base pairs and possessing the required chemical stability to function in the genetic tape. Another coincidence is that an α helix can "feel" no more than about 4 contiguous bases in the large groove of the DNA.[16]

Recent work has confirmed that in the case of most DNA recognition proteins there are generally 4 or less contiguous bases which are critical in DNA recognition by an α helix, except for one important set of DNA-recognizing proteins that use a special type of helix, known as a zinc finger. Zinc fingers are used very widely as DNA-recognizing motifs by proteins in higher organisms. As two authorities comment in *Science*: "The helix of each zinc finger fits directly into the major groove of the DNA, and the side chains from the amino-terminal portion of the helix contact the edges of the base pairs. . . . Each finger makes its primary contacts along a section of the large groove three base pairs long."[17] From detailed study of DNA-protein interactions over the past ten years, it appears, as a rule, that either three or four contiguous base pairs are involved in direct binding of α helices to their DNA target sequences.

The four bases in the DNA can be arranged in 4^4, or 256, different base sequences 4 bases long (quadruplets)—i.e., ATAT, GTAT, TGCT, TCTT, etc. This raises the interesting possibility that perhaps each different DNA sequence 4 bases long, or quadruplets, might be recognized by a specific α helix—in other words, that there might be a code relating each unique quadruplet of bases in the DNA to a particular α helix. However recent work suggest this is unlikely to be the case.[18]

The fact that DNA is made up of 4 bases has further implications. From simple combinatorial considerations it is easy to show that using 4 bases, unique recognition sequences in the genomes of higher organisms must be about 15 bases long. Remarkably, as Mark Ptashne shows in his book *A Genetic Switch,* specific reversible binding of a protein to a particular DNA sequence requires about 10 to 18 weak interactions, and it turns out that this is just about the number of weak bonds that occur when alpha helices of a recognition protein associate with a DNA sequence about 15 bases in length. Using 2 bases, recognition sequences would have to be 20 to 30 bases long and the number of bonds involved would be approximately doubled. This would mean that, given the strength of the bonds, the binding by proteins to such extra-long recognition sites would be so strong that it would be in effect irreversible. Using 6 bases, if nature had provided them, simple calculation shows that it would be possible, in higher organisms, to have unique recognition sequences only 8 bases long. This gains no advantage, however, because a sequence 8 bases long is too short to provide the requisite number of weak interactions to tie a recognition protein to a specific sequence in the DNA.[19]

From this brief review of protein-DNA interactions and the discussion of the code in the previous chapter, we are led to an intriguing conclusion— that the use of 4 bases for the construction of the DNA double helix is fit for two completely independent biological functions: First, for a coding system (the genetic code) to specify proteins composed of twenty amino acids, and second, for DNA-protein recognition, involving the recognition by proteins (using mainly α helices) of unique target sequences in the genome.

The protein-DNA recognition system contains a particularly intriguing play on the number four. In the largest genomes unique combinations of 4 bases are about 15 bases long. As we have seen above, given the existing energy levels of the weak chemical bonds involved in protein-DNA binding, protein recognition complexes can bind reversibly to DNA sequences up to this length but not to lengths much greater. We have also seen that because of the natural twist in the DNA double helix, protein recognition motifs such as the α helix can only feel along about 4 bases in the DNA double helix. It has often been said that God is a mathematician; on the evidence of molecular biology we might add that He is keen on the number *four*.

Conclusion

Everything that has been learned about the chemical and physical properties of DNA and protein since the early 1950s increasingly confirms the wonderful fitness of these two remarkable molecules for their respective biological roles in the replicative cycle. The number and complexity of their mutual adaptations is growing continually as biological knowledge advances. But already the picture is impressive enough: the mutual fit of the α helix into the large groove of the DNA; the fact that both DNA and proteins are linear polymers so that the information in a DNA sequence can be translated via a coding system into the amino acid sequence of a protein; the fact that the four bases confer geometric perfection and great chemical stability on the DNA helix; the fact that four bases seems to be the ideal number for two different coding systems—the well-known genetic code specifying for the 20 amino acids in proteins and the DNA-protein recognition system whereby proteins are able to recognize unique DNA sequences long enough to function as unique target sequences in the genome; the fantastic diversity of proteins and their ability to regulate their own activities; the fact that the energy levels of the weak interactions are at precisely the level needed to confer on proteins their metastable character and to bind reversibly to unique DNA sequences and thereby to retrieve the information in the genes.

We have seen that, in the case of water, the carbon atom, the process of oxidation, the light of main sequence stars, the earth's hydrosphere, etc., the evidence suggests strongly that each is uniquely and optimally fit for its particular biological role. If the teleological position is correct, the DNA-protein system should also be uniquely and maximally fit for the advanced type of cellular life that exists on earth today. Note that the teleological position does not imply that *all* self-replicating chemical systems will necessarily utilize or depend on this particular partnership, that self-replication can only be achieved using DNA and protein. The early evolution of life, for example, may have proceeded via a series of simpler replicating systems— which contained neither DNA nor proteins—including some based entirely on RNA or RNA analogues. Teleology only implies that the partnership should be uniquely fit for the self-replication of a biochemical system as sophisticated and complex as the current cell system. And the evidence is certainly consistent with such a conclusion. Considering the bewildering suite of mutual adaptations—discussed above and in the previous chapter—it seems hardly conceivable that there could be any other two molecules as mutually fit, or more perfectly adapted to play the fundamental roles of "information bearer" and "constructor device" in a self-replicating automaton as complex and intricate as the cell.

Chapter 9

The Fitness of the Metals

In which the unique chemical properties of the metals are examined. In keeping with the concept that the cosmos is uniquely fit for carbon-based life, living things utilize the properties of metals from each of the main subgroups of the periodic table, and even particular metals, such as iron, calcium, copper, molybdenum, and magnesium, appear to be adapted for specific biological processes of a critical significance without which no world of life remotely as rich as ours would be possible. Iron and copper are essential for the manipulation of oxygen, molybdenum for nitrogen fixation, etc. It is concluded that there could be no biology or biosphere without metals.

The Hot Springs of the Waikato in New Zealand

From Oliver Goldsmith (1876) *A History of the Earth and Animated Nature.* Hot springs, geysers, and volcanoes provide dramatic evidence of the heat and turbulence within the crustal rocks of the earth. The heat in the earth's core and crustal rocks is derived primarily from two sources—from the continual radioactive decay of uranium and from energy liberated shortly after the earth's formation as iron was drawn by gravity to the center of the earth to form its molten core. Without the two metals, uranium and iron, the earth would be cold and dead and there would be no tectonic turnover of the earth's crust to ensure the vital chemical constancy of the earth's surficial layers.

Chlorophyll, for example, contains magnesium and it is thought that the process of reduction in the leaf may depend upon the characteristic of this element. . . . In like manner, haemoglobin contains iron and the capacity of haemoglobin to unite with oxygen and as oxyhaemoglobin to carry it from the lungs to the tissues is unquestionably due to the chemical behaviour of that metal.

—Lawrence Henderson, *The Fitness of the Environment,* 1913

Why grass is greene, or why blood is red. Are mysteries which none have reach'd unto. In this low forme, poore soule, what wilt thou doe?

—John Donne, *Of the Progresse of the Soule,* 1633

Of all the metals there is none more essential to life than iron. It is the accumulation of iron in the center of a star which triggers a supernova explosion and the subsequent scattering of the vital atoms of life throughout the cosmos. It was the drawing by gravity of iron atoms to the center of the primeval earth that generated the heat which caused the initial chemical differentiation of the earth, the outgassing of the early atmosphere, and ultimately the formation of the hydrosphere. It is molten iron in the center of the earth which, acting like a gigantic dynamo, generates the earth's magnetic field, which in turn creates the Van Allen radiation belts that shield the earth's surface from destructive high-energy-penetrating cosmic radiation and preserve the crucial ozone layer from cosmic ray destruction. And it is iron which by its delicate association with oxygen in the hemoglobin in human blood is able to convey in subdued form this most ferociously reactive of atoms, the precious giver of energy, to the respiratory machinery of the cell, where oxygen's energies are utilized to fuel the activities of life.

Without the iron atom, there would be no carbon-based life in the cosmos; no supernovae, no heating of the primitive earth, no atmosphere or hydrosphere. There would be no protective magnetic field, no Van Allen radiation belts, no ozone layer, no metal to make hemoglobin, no metal to tame the reactivity of oxygen, and no oxidative metabolism.

The intriguing and intimate relationship between life and iron, between the red color of blood and the dying of some distant star, not only indicates the relevance of metals to biology but also the biocentricity of the cosmos and why we are indeed, as Sagan so succinctly expressed it, "in the most profound sense children of the Cosmos."[1]

Our understanding of the important role of metals in biology was virtually nonexistent in Henderson's day. Even as recently as a few decades back, knowledge in this field was so limited that Sir Hans Krebs was able to comment "that for all he and I knew most metal ions found in biology could be damaging impurities and therefore had been sequestered or rejected."[2] We now know that Krebs was quite wrong and that metals play so vital a role in living systems that one of the experts in this field, Professor Robert J. P. Williams of Oxford University, in a fascinating review entitled "The Symbiosis of Metals and Protein Function," which summarized current knowledge in this area, concludes:

> In this essay I have not wanted just to repeat the message that metal ions are incorporated and used in biology in a particular way. Rather I wish to assert that

biology without metal ions does not exist any more than biology exists without DNA or proteins. Metal ions are . . . an essential part of energy and dynamics. . . . No matter what we know about DNA and RNA and even of sugars the nature of the machinery of life rests with these two components, metal ions and proteins. . . . The all pervading influence of metal ions in biological systems is such that I now declare that in my mind there is *no biology without metal ions*.[3] [My emphasis.]

More than half of the most abundant atoms in the cosmos are metals, including sodium (Na), potassium (K), calcium (Ca), magnesium, (Mg), iron (Fe), and Copper (Cu) (see chapter 4). Iron, for example, is nearly as common as carbon. Given their abundance, in any biocentric view, one would expect that the metals would be of considerable utility for life. And it has turned out that many of the metals do indeed play a vital role in some of the most fundamental biological processes and the evidence increasingly suggests that many of these processes are dependent on the precise chemical and physical properties of particular metal atoms. Close to one-third of all enzymes involve a metal ion as an essential participant.[4] An excellent review of this topic is given by Fraústo da Silva and Williams in their *Biological Chemistry of the Elements*.[5]

Electron Conductors

One key role plays by metals in the cell is the formation of electronic circuits, and one area where these play a vital role is in energy metabolism. Moreover, it is only the transitional metal atoms, particularly iron and copper, which possess precisely the properties required to form an electronic circuit. No other atoms will do. Only the transitional metals, having far more complex electron shells with many more energy states than the simpler atoms such as sodium (Na), calcium (Ca), carbon (C), nitrogen (N), etc., possess the appropriate electrochemical characteristics to trap and channel electronic energy. The unique electric conducting properties of the transitional metals are also utilized in human technology to make wire conductors. As Fraústo da Silva and Williams comment, "man makes his wires from metals such as copper; biology makes hop conductors from metal ions embedded in protein."[6]

It is only by utilizing the conducting properties of the transitional metals that the cell is able to channel the electron flow through discrete energy steps and utilize each energy drop to perform useful chemical work. No organic compounds can substitute for the transitional metals in this regard. It is fortuitous indeed that the transitional metals possess precisely those unique chemical characteristics essential for stepwise electron transport in the respiratory assembly and in the photosynthetic apparatus. If no atoms in the periodic table were specifically fit for this highly specialized role, then the controlled and efficient utilization of the energy of oxidation could not be achieved. Advanced life forms would in all probability be impossible. If we are to have electronic circuits in living organisms, these will be made of transitional metal wires. But the transitional metal atoms not only provide the electronic circuits of the cell upon which the efficient exploitation of oxidative energy is critically dependent, they also possess precisely the required complement of chemical and physical properties which permit organisms to manipulate the oxygen atom, without which oxidative metabolism would be impossible.

Oxygen Transport

The capacity of the transitional metal atoms to handle oxygen is illustrated by the oxygen-carrying molecule, hemoglobin, which transports oxygen in the blood of higher vertebrates, including humans. Hemoglobin is made up of the protein globin, the small planar cyclic compound heme, and the iron atom which is chelated with the heme. The figure below shows the structure of heme.

The structure of a heme.

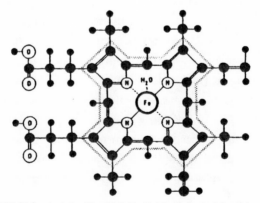

From N. J. Berrill (1966) *Biology in Action* (New York: Dodd, Mead), fig 3.16. Reproduced by permission of N. J. Berrill.

The oxygen-carrying capacity of mammalian blood is about 25 milliliters of oxygen per 100 milliliters of blood. This is fifty times the amount that can be dissolved in ordinary solution! However, an efficient respiratory pigment must satisfy additional criteria beyond the mere ability to carry large quantities of oxygen. As Ernest Baldwin points out in his *Introduction to Comparative Biochemistry*: "It must take up oxygen where the partial pressure is high and give it up again equally readily to the tissues in which the pressure is low. . . . in other words, the compound of the . . . respiratory pigment with oxygen must be such that it readily dissociates."[7]

The reversible binding between iron and oxygen in hemoglobin depends on three critical properties: on the hydrophobic nature of the interior of proteins, on the unique characteristics of the iron atom complexed with the heme moiety in the globin, and on the unique characteristics of the dioxygen molecule that are complementary to those of the iron atom and allow association and dissociation at precisely the range of oxygen concentrations that permit uptake in the lungs and release in the tissues.

Consideration of the detailed events which occur during reversible binding suggests that no other metal atom could exactly mimic the properties of iron in heme.[8] None of the other transitional metal atoms closely related to iron will substitute for iron in hemoglobin, because none are of precisely the same size, nor do any possess precisely the same chemical characteristics allowing them to undergo the same subtle changes on associating with oxygen.

As the efficient transport of oxygen is essential to the viability of any large active organism with a high metabolic rate, a molecule with the properties of hemoglobin would seem to be essential. Might there be any alternatives to hemoglobin? None of the many other oxygen-carrying molecules which occur in the blood of invertebrates, such as the copper-containing proteins of the molluscs, come close to the efficiency of hemoglobin in transporting oxygen in blood. As Ernest Baldwin commented, "Mammalian haemoglobin is far and away the most successful of the respiratory pigments from this point of view," and Joseph Barcroft has written of it that "but for its existence, man might never have achieved any activity which the lobster does not possess."[9]

The question arises as to whether a respiratory pigment designed on radically different principles to hemoglobin might be possible. The question was raised by Earl Frieden when he asked, "Why has no other essential metal . . . or other type of respiratory protein developed to satisfy this important function?" Because, he continues, such a pigment "needs to be able to form a stable dissociable complex with the highly reactive molecule, O_2, and, as he points out: "Transition metals excel in this capacity; few other chemical groups can do this. In fact all efforts to devise other physiologically compatible, model oxygen carriers have failed to date. . . . The compounds that come closest to emulating the oxygen-binding properties of haemoglobin . . . *contain transitional metal ions.*"[10] (My emphasis.)

It would seem that in designing an oxygen-transporting molecule from first principles we are led inevitably to a molecule very like hemoglobin and to the choice of iron or at least one of the transitional metals to carry out the key oxygen-binding role. Water would also almost certainly have to be excluded from the binding site, and this would lead inevitably to something like the hydrophobic heme cleft in hemoglobin. The evidence is consistent with the possibility that hemoglobin is the ideal and unique respiratory pigment for metabolically active air-breathing organisms such as ourselves, and that its unique abilities depend in turn not only on the unique properties of the transitional metal atoms but on the specific properties of one of these atoms—iron.

The elegance of the way the hemoglobin system functions is simply astounding, and a source of wonder to everyone who is familiar with its intricate ingenuity. And as with the elegance of so much of the biochemical machinery of life, this elegance is only possible, as in so many other instances, because of the provision by nature of atoms and molecular structures perfectly fit for particular vital biological functions.

The fitness of the iron atom for reversible binding to oxygen is of course only one of many mutual adaptations in the nature of things which make possible the delivery of oxygen to the metabolically active tissues in a large organism like a mammal. There is also the fact that oxygen is soluble in water; that the viscosity of water is sufficiently low to make the design of a circulatory system possible; that the viscosity of a non-Newtonian fluid—i.e., one containing a suspension of particles—decreases as the pressure increases, a phenomenon which greatly facilitates the propulsion of the blood through the tissues in times of high metabolic activity; that carbon dioxide is a gas, and so on.

Manipulating Oxygen

The unique oxygen-manipulating capabilities of the transitional metals are also utilized in a variety of enzymes that defend the cell from the destructive effects of oxygen. One such "protector" enzyme, which occurs in all aerobic organisms and which utilizes the properties of the transitional metal copper, is known as superoxide dismutase. The reaction it catalyzes furnishes a means of disposing of a highly reactive (and highly destructive) oxygen radical, the superoxide ion O_2^-.[11] And as Frieden points out, the protection offered by the activities of this enzyme "is a *prerequisite for the adaptation of all living cells to the utilisation of oxygen.*"[12] (My emphasis.)

One of the most important of all enzymes that utilize the oxygen-handling capabilities of the transitional metals is cytochrome *c* oxidase, which is the terminal member of the respiratory assembly and performs the critical final reaction of oxidative metabolism. This involves uniting the electrons flowing through the respiratory assembly to atoms of oxygen and hydrogen. It sits astride one of the bilayer lipid membranes in the mitochondrion (the organelle concerned with energy generation).

On its significance, Frieden comments: "If a biochemist is asked to identify the one enzyme which is most vital to all forms of life, he would proba-

Cytochrome oxidase.

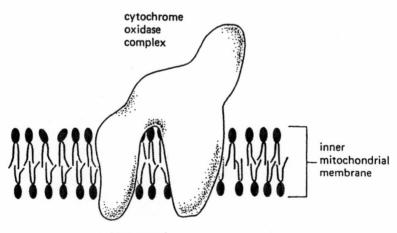

From B. Alberts et al. (1983) *The Molecular Biology of the Cell* (New York: Garland Publishing) fig. 9. 31. Reproduced by permission of the publisher.

bly name cytochrome *c* oxidase. This is the enzyme, found in all aerobic cells, which introduces oxygen into the oxidative machinery that produces the energy we need for physical activity and biochemical synthesis. . . . This enzyme may be regarded as the ultimate in the integration of the function of iron with copper in biological systems. Here in a single molecule, we combine the talents of iron and copper ions to bind oxygen, reduce it with electrons from the other cytochromes in the hydrogen electron transport chain and, finally, to convert the reduced oxygen to water."[13] The diagram below, redrawn from a recent *Science* article,[14] shows the electrons flowing within the molecule, through a "transitional metal wire" composed of a succession of iron and copper atoms which conducts them to the final catalytic center where they cause the reduction of oxygen to form water.

Cytochrome c *oxidase.*

Showing the electron flow and chemical reactions.

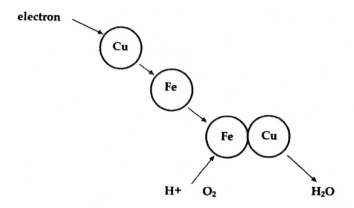

Remarkably, cytochrome *c* oxidase also contains two other metal atoms—zinc (Zn) and magnesium (Mg)—although their function is mainly structural. All in all, the activity of this remarkable nanomachine depends on the unique properties of four metal atoms—iron (Fe), copper (Cu), zinc (Zn) and magnesium (Mg) and as well as these metal atoms, like any other protein, its basic structure is built up of hydrogen (H), carbon (C), nitrogen (N), oxygen (O), and sulfur (S). In other words, here is one atomic machine which is composed of and exploits the unique chemical and physical properties of nine of the ninety-two naturally occurring elements.

Molybdenum

Another transitional metal atom which appears to possess unique properties essential to life is molybdenum (Mo). Molybdenum is an essential component in the two enzymes involved in nitrogen fixation: nitrogenase, which catalyzes the reduction of nitrogen to ammonia and nitrate reductase, which catalyzes the reduction of nitrate to nitrite. These two activities are absolutely critical to life on earth. All the nitrogen utilized by living things is initially captured via these two reactions. As two authorities point out: "The molybdenum atom possesses a number of unique characteristics which can account for its role in these two critical reactions. No other atom, with the possible exception of vanadium (V), could possibly substitute for molybdenum."[15] And they raise the fascinating question "Is the requirement for molybdenum an absolute necessity or could the chemistry have been done in some other way and is what we observe an accident?"[16]

It is hard to believe that the choice of molybdenum is accidental. While molybdenum is one of the commonest metals in seawater, its availability on land is patchy. Because the ability to fix atmospheric nitrogen and utilize it for organic syntheses is obviously of great selective advantage, if there was any alternative to molybdenum, particularly in those environments where molybdenum is rare or unavailable, then surely some microorganism would have discovered it at some stage during the 4 billion years of evolution. The absence of any alternative suggests strongly that the vital processes by which nitrogen enters the biosphere are absolutely dependent on the special characteristics of the molybdenum atom. Again, we have what appears to be another case in which life on earth is critically dependent on the specific chemical properties of a unique constituent.

Rapid Information Transmission

Being far smaller than even the simplest organic compounds such as sugars and nucleotides, the metal ions of sodium, potassium, magnesium, and calcium diffuse far more quickly in aqueous solutions and are therefore ideal for rapid information transmission.

The capacity for rapid movement, however, is not the only criteria which must be satisfied by a chemical messenger. A chemical messenger must not only be able to move quickly but also to associate reversibly with a specific target in the cell. The necessity for specific high-affinity binding largely excludes the monovalent metal ions sodium and potassium, which are too "simple" to be conveniently utilized in this role. Of the two divalent ions calcium and magnesium, the binding of calcium to most sites is a thousand times tighter and hence the most fit for this role.

In biological systems, it is calcium which is preeminently used where chemical information must be transmitted at great speed, as in the triggering of muscle contraction, transmission of nerve impulses across the synapse, triggering hormone release, the changes following fertilization, etc. As Williams points out in his review, "Amongst the metal ions available to biology *only calcium* can be high in concentration, can diffuse rapidly, can bind and dissociate strongly."[17] (My emphasis.)

Of particular relevance to its role as the "mercury of the cell" is the fact that the chemical characteristics of the calcium ion are perfectly fit for specific association with proteins—the key functional biomolecules in the cell and as such the most likely components of all the cell's nanomachinery to be receivers and transducers of chemical information. And for protein binding, calcium is far superior to magnesium. This is because, first, magnesium requires a more regular geometrical binding site than calcium and such sites are difficult to arrange in a protein because of the basic irregularity of its structure and, second, because of the particular affinity of calcium ions for oxygen atoms, which are readily provided by the amino acids of proteins. Proteins in their molecular irregularity and in their possession of readily accessible oxygen atoms provide an ideal molecular matrix for the design of calcium binding sites.

Another fascinating aspect of the calcium-protein relationship is the capacity of the α helix, which as we have seen is one of the basic structural subunits used in the building of proteins, to react with great rapidity to the stimulus of calcium binding. As one author, commenting on the suitability of the helical structures in proteins to respond rapidly to the stimulus of calcium, remarks: "The proteins which are in the muscle or the internal filamentous units of cells must have activity matching that of calcium. . . . These proteins are largely based on helices. In a general sense a helical rod is useful in that its movement economically connects activities at either end through rotational-transitional movements like that of a screw or worm gear. It is fast since helix-helix movements need not break hydrogen bonds. We see in the helix the potential for matching the dynamics of the calcium ion."[18]

Magnesium

Magnesium is calcium's sister atom in the periodic table and is similar in many of its properties to calcium, but it binds to proteins less quickly and less tightly than calcium. It is certainly less fit for the role of chemical messenger than calcium, but its gentler affinity for proteins is utilized by the cell in the more subtle molecular rearrangements which accompany enzymic activities. In present day life forms its involvement is vital to many crucial enzymic processes.

Of particular interest is the role of magnesium in photosynthesis. The chlorophyll molecule, the green pigment of plants, which is the key component in the photosynthetic apparatus, contains one centrally positioned magnesium atom. Although the magnesium can be replaced by copper, nickel, cobalt, iron, and zinc, none of these metals can mimic the light-absorbing capacity of magnesium. Compared to iron, for example, the light absorption of magnesium is several thousand times greater. Precisely what it is about the magnesium atom that confers on chlorophyll its magic light-absorbing capacity is not known. But there must be, as Melvin Calvin comments, "something very special about the electronic structure of the magnesium"[19] and about the way the chlorophyll molecules are packed together in the chloroplast. Whatever the basis for the unique properties magnesium confers on the chlorophyll, it is clear that the capture of light energy is remarkably efficient.

An intriguing aspect of the light-absorbing properties of chlorophyll, which seems to be an exception to the general rule that the constituents of life seem maximally adapted to their biological roles, is the curious point that the light-absorption properties of chlorophyll are maximum in the violet and near ultraviolet and in the red and infrared regions of the spectrum. These regions do not coincide with the regions of the spectrum which contain most of the sun's radiant energy at the earth's surface, which is in the blue-green range. George Wald, who elucidated the biochemistry of vision, raised this question in 1959 in a *Scientific American* article entitled "Life and Light": "What properties do the chlorophylls have that are so profoundly advantageous for photosynthesis as to override their disadvantageous absorption spectra."[20] Chlorophyll would appear on the face of it to be less than maximally fit for its biological role; maximal fitness would appear to demand that it absorb light in the blue-green range of the spectrum.

However, in the case of other apparent "defects" in the fitness of the basic ingredients of life, such as water's inability to dissolve hydrocarbons and oxygen's low solubility in water, it often turns out that, with increasing knowledge, such anomalies are revealed to be highly beneficial in some respect that was overlooked at the time. Another example may be the apparently anomalously high absorption by chlorophyll of light in the violet and near-ultraviolet regions of the spectrum. As mentioned in chapter 6, this region of the spectrum is damaging to life largely through the production of free radicals of oxygen. It is possible that the anomalous absorption of radiant energy in the violet and near-ultraviolet region of the spectrum may confer on chlorophyll an element of biological fitness previously unsuspected, that of attenuating the flux of ultraviolet radiation. Sunburn is less severe on grass than on sand.

There are several other metal atoms—vanadium (V), chromium (Cr), manganese (Mn), cobalt (Co), nickel (Ni), copper (Cu), and zinc (Zn)—which are also essential to life and where the unique property of the individual atom appears to be exploited in some vital biological process. An excellent summary of the biological role of these metals is given in *Biological Chemistry of the Elements,* cited earlier.

Conclusion

The emerging picture of the role of metals in biology is increasingly one in which it appears that all the metals in each of the main subgroups of the periodic table possess unique properties that are fit for particular vital and essential biological roles. Without them life remotely as rich and complex as it exists on earth would be impossible. The transitional metals, for example, give every impression of having been tailored to form the electronic circuits of the cell and to manipulate in various ways the oxygen atom. Moreover, it increasingly appears that even individual metal atoms such as calcium, iron, copper, magnesium, and molybdenum may be uniquely fit for some of the biological roles they serve. Iron may be uniquely tailored for the sort of reversible binding to oxygen which occurs in hemoglobin, and magnesium for the absorption of light in chlorophyll. Trying to envisage life without metals is every bit as difficult as imagining human technology without them, for, as Robert Williams concludes: "There is no biology without metals.[21] . . . metal elements in some organisation are of the essence of life as much as this is true of amino acids and nucleotides."[22]

T h e   F i t n e s s   o f
t h e   C e l l

In which it is argued that the cell is uniquely and ideally fit to function as the basic unit of carbon-based life. Cells are capable of carrying out any instruction, adopting any shape, creating the vast diversity of multicellular organisms and ultimately the whole world of life. Evidence is examined which suggests that the cell membrane is uniquely and ideally fit for its role of bounding the cell's contents and conferring on the cells of higher organisms the ability to move and adhere selectively to one another. These critical properties are also dependent on the size of the average cell being approximately what it is and on the viscosity of cytoplasm being close to what it is. The membrane is also fit, in that its selective impermeability to charged particles confers additional electrical properties, which form the basis of nerve conduction. A variety of coincidences underlying the ability of cells to selectively adhere and move are discussed. The known properties of cells are remarkable enough, but there is still much to learn. The possibility that cells may possess powerful computing abilities and may even be able to behave intelligently is considered.

The protozoan Stentor.

This protozoan organism consists of a single cell about one-fifth of a millimeter long. Small fragments of the cell, less than one-hundredth of its volume, are capable of regenerating a tiny but exact replica of the whole cell.

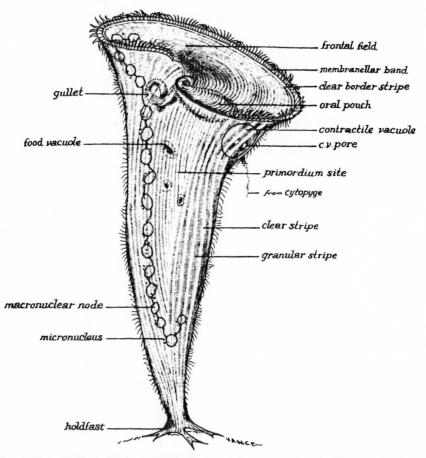

From V. Tartar, (1961) *The Biology of Stentor,* p. 8 (London: Pergamon Press). Reproduced by permission of Wanda Tartar.

Its talents are legion, but its size is minuscule. *E. Coli* is a cylindrical organism less than 1 nm in diameter and 2 nm long—20 would fit end to end in a single rod cell of the human retina. . . . Yet it is adept at counting molecules of specific sugars, amino acids, or dipeptides; at integration of similar or dissimilar sensory inputs over space and time; at comparing counts taken over the recent past; at triggering an all or nothing response; at swimming in a viscous medium . . . even pattern formation.

—H. C. Berg, *Cold Spring Harbor Symposium on Quantitative Biology,* 1990

212 · NATURE'S DESTINY

Cells amaze. Even to a nonbiologist cells convey the impression of being very special, unique objects with extraordinary capabilities.

Considering their accomplishments, it is hard to believe that there could exist any other sort of organized material form, some other type of nano-erector device remotely equal to the cell. It is these remarkable specks of organized matter that have constructed every multicellular organism that ever existed on earth. It is cells that assemble the human brain, putting down a million connections a minute for nine months during gestation. It is cells that build blue whales, butterflies, birds, and grass. It is cells that built the dinosaurs and all past life on earth. Through the activities of some of the simplest of their kind, over the past 4 billion years they gradually ter-raformed the earth, generating oxygen via photosynthesis and thereby releasing its energizing powers for all the higher life forms.

The cell betrays every evidence of being uniquely and wonderfully adapted for its assigned task. The diversity of cell form is every bit as bewildering as the diversity of carbon compounds or proteins. Cells exhibit not only a vast diversity of form but also a diversity of functional and behavioral capacities of bewildering richness. They are miracles of nanotechnology. Some can move by the rowing action of cilia or by the propellerlike action of the bacterial flagellum. Others can creep and crawl. They can estimate the concentration of compounds in their immediate environment. They can change their form and chemical composition. They can put out pseudopodia and grasp small objects in their immediate vicinity. They possess internal clocks and can measure the passage of time. They can sense electrical and magnetic fields. They can synchronize their activities and can combine forces and crowd together to make a multicellular organism. Cells can communicate via chemical and electrical signals. They can encase themselves in various armorlike skins. They can replicate themselves with what seems to be surpassing ease and, as mentioned in chapter 7, even reconstruct themselves completely from tiny fractions of their mass.[1]

Cells can survive desiccation for hundreds of years, and so on and on. In short, they can *do anything, adopt almost any shape, obey any order,* and seem in every sense perfectly adapted to their assigned task of creating a biosphere replete with multicellular organisms like ourselves. The astounding nature of the nanotechnological miracle the cell represents is self-evident.

From the knowledge we now have of the molecular machinery that underlies some of their extraordinary abilities, it is clear that cells are immensely complex entities. On any count the average cell must utilize close to a million unique adaptive structures and processes—more than the number in a jumbo jet. In this the cell seems to represent the ultimate expression in material form of compacted adaptive complexity—the complexity of a jumbo jet packed into a speck of dust invisible to the human eye. It is hardly conceivable that anything more complex could be compacted into such a small volume. Moreover, it is a speck-sized jumbo jet which can duplicate itself quite effortlessly.

The fitness of the cell for its biological role in the assembly and functioning of multicellular life gives every indication, as with so many of life's constituents, of being unique. In the case of many of their key properties and abilities, it is very difficult to imagine how these properties and abilities could be actualized except in a material form with the precise characteristics of the living cell. In other words, if we were to design from first principles a tiny nanoerector about 30 microns in diameter with the capabilities of the cell—with the ability to measure the chemical concentration of substances in its surrounding medium; with the ability to measure time, to move, to feel its way around in a complex molecular environment, to change its form; with the ability to communicate with fellow nanoerectors using electrical and chemical messages and to act together in vast companies to create macroscopic structures—we would end up redesigning the cell.

Lipids

An important class of biomolecules that play a critical role in many aspects of the life of the cell are the lipids, which include the fats and the fatty acids. Lipids are found in all living things. They have many different functions. They are a major source of cellular energy. They function as electrical insulators and as detergents. They form the waxes which coat the feathers of birds. Some function in the gaseous state as pheromones, substances which attract other organisms of the same species.[2]

All types of lipids contain long hydrophobic chains of carbon and hydrogen atoms which are insoluble or only sparingly soluble in water. The structure of the fatty acid stearic acid is shown below.

The chemical structure of stearic acid.

The fact that many types of lipids are insoluble in water is of great biological significance. Without insoluble components, the compartmentalization of the cell and the persistence of cellular structures would not be possible. Lipids are also the major component of the bounding bilayer membrane which surrounds every living cell. (See page 216.) If there were no carbon compounds insoluble in water, such as the lipids, organic chemistry would not be fit for life. Correspondingly, if water was truly a universal solvent, the alkahest of the alchemists, it would not be a fit medium for life because no compartments or stable structures would be possible and all the cells constituents would merely dissolve away.

The hydrocarbon chain length of most of the lipids which occur in the cell is generally between 16 and 18 carbon atoms long. This chain length is fit for a number of reasons. Chain lengths of more than 18 carbons long are too insoluble to be of biological utility—they cannot be mobilized at all in water—but less than 16, they are too soluble.[3] Fortuitously, lipids containing chains of this length are also fluid or near fluid over the temperature range in which most metabolic processes occur in living things. If lipids of these chain lengths had been solid at ambient temperatures, no structure constructed out of them would possess the necessary plasticity to function in the cell. Moreover, because they are also more viscous than water when fluid, they act to buffer the organs of higher organisms against shearing forces.[4] The lightness of lipids compared to water also has significant biological consequences. It gives aquatic life buoyancy. The subcutaneous lipid of warm-blooded animals also acts as a heat insulator, preventing heat loss. The extreme example of this is the cetacea with a layer of blubber up to 15 inches thick, which allows them to thrive in the polar seas.[5] (See Appendix, section 2, for more details on the fitness of lipids.)

In addition to providing the cell with stable structures, boundaries, and compartments, the nonpolar hydrophobic nature of lipids is also of great utility because lipid aggregates provide the cell with tiny nonaqueous microenvironments. Such hydrophobic microenvironments are vital to the life of the cell, because many of the synthetic and enzymic processes upon which the life of the cell depends can only occur in a microenvironment where water has been excluded. So their insolubility plays two roles in the cell, creating the stable insoluble boundaries between compartments and the vital hydrophobic microenvironments in which so much of the cell's synthetic chemistry takes place. Without the hydrophobic properties of the lipids, carbon-based life would not be possible.

The Cell Membrane

One of the most important structures in the cell, which is largely composed of lipids, is the cell membrane. It is difficult to see how a cell could survive without some sort of bounding membrane which was relatively impermeable to the cell's constituents, especially to small metabolites such as sugars and amino acids, to prevent its contents from diffusing away into the surrounding fluid. Such a membrane would also have to be relatively plastic and able to maintain a continuous barrier between the cell and its environment in the face of the ever-changing shape of the cell. As one leading biologist points out, it is essential that the cell membrane should behave like a "two-dimensional liquid" and be able to flow in all directions over the surface of the cytoplasm to maintain a continuous barrier between the cell and its surroundings in the face of "of the ever changing protrusive activities of the cell surface."[6]

The lipid bilayer satisfies these criteria admirably. Being hydrophobic, it satisfies the criterion that it must be impermeable to the majority of the cell's constituents, such as sugars, amino acids, and other organic acids which are soluble in water. Moreover, the lipid bilayer also has precisely that fluid character needed to preserve a continuous barrier surrounding the ever-turbulent and motile mass of cytoplasm. It is in fact highly fluid and has a level of viscosity like that of olive oil.

The structure of the lipid bilayer is shown below. Note the lipids making up the membrane are phospholipids, which are lipids containing a charged phosphate group at one end. The phosphate end is hydrophilic—water loving—while the fatty end is hydrophobic—water hating. When the structure assembles itself, the hydrophilic phosphate groups orient themselves facing the water, while the hydrophobic hydrocarbon chains orient themselves away from the water.

Another factor which contributes to the fitness of this remarkable structure is that it forms *automatically* around the outer surface of the cell, like the spreading of a monomolecular film of immiscible substance (typically a lipid) on the surface of water. As cell biologist John Trinkaus comments:

> Because water is itself a strongly polar molecule, the polar phosphate of the membrane lipids will inevitably be attracted to the surfaces of the membrane, both external and cytoplasmic. And just as inevitably their nonpolar fatty acid parts will tend to be squeezed into a nonpolar phase in the interior of the membrane. . . . The beauty of it is that everything arranges itself. . . . Simply

The structure of the cell membrane.

external aqueous phase

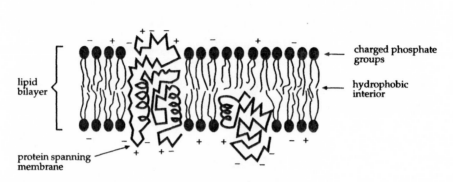

charged phosphate groups

hydrophobic interior

lipid bilayer

protein spanning membrane

internal aqueous phase

Redrawn from S. J. Singer and G. L. Nicholson (1972) "The fluid mosaic model of the structure of cell membranes," *Science* 175:720–731, by permission of Professor S. J. Singer.

because of their intrinsic chemical nature phospholipids *naturally* and *spontaneously* self-assemble to form a bilayer in a watery solution. . . . It is, as it were, "the nature of the beast" for them to do so.[7]

There is not the slightest element of contingency in the fact that a lipid bilayer forms the boundary layer surrounding the cell. No other material is known which could substitute for this particular structure. The properties of impermeability, fluidity, and spontaneous assembly would seem to be essential characteristics in any membrane system surrounding the cell. Yet this unique combination of characteristics is only found in the lipid bilayer— another case where a key biological function is carried out by an adaptation which appears to be both *unique and ideal* for its assigned role. The existence of the cell is in effect absolutely dependent on the lipid bilayer possessing the precise suite of biochemical and biophysical characteristics that it does.

The lipid bilayer has another property inherent in its hydrophobic nature—that of an electrical insulator.[8] Because it is impermeable to charged particles such as the ions of sodium (Na^+) and potassium (K^+) and hence capable of restricting their movement across the membrane to specially designed ion gates, the cell is able to generate an electrical potential between the inside and the outside of the cell, the so-called membrane potential, by pumping charged particles through the ion gates in the membrane. If the lipid bilayer was not an insulator, cells would not be able to maintain the membrane potential, and many biological phenomena such as the transmission of nerve impulses, which depend on the membrane potential, would not be possible. In addition to its insulating characteristics, the lipid bilayer is fit for the generation of membrane potential in another way—it provides an ideal environment in which the membrane proteins which pump the ions in and out of the cell can reside and function.[9]

That one of the properties of this remarkable structure, its insulating character and the membrane potential it automatically generates, should provide precisely the electrical characteristics required for the transmission of electrical impulses between cells and ultimately for the construction of the nervous system is surely a fact and coincidence of very great significance. No less than its insulating, electrical properties and its ability to self-assemble, the nervous system itself is also, in a very real sense, in "the nature of the lipid bilayer beast."

The electrical properties of cells depend on many other factors in addition to the insulating properties of lipid membranes. The propagation, for example, of the nervous impulse depends on the rapid transmission of a wave of depolarization along the nerve fiber. The speed of depolarization is itself due to the speed of diffusion of sodium and potassium cations through special gates in the membrane of the nerve cell. This process is again greatly enhanced by the low viscosity of water and by the unique properties of the cations themselves.

Cell Adhesion

The ability of cells to selectively adhere to one another is one of their most important characteristics. According to one authority, "the adhesions that cells make with one another lie at the very basis of multicellularity. The form and functioning of all creatures that consist of more than one cell depend on their cells adhering firmly to one another and to the extracellular materials that intervene."[10]

The surface of a typical cell is not smooth but rather rugged, and many cells make initial contact with each other via microprotrusions on their surface. These are often .1 micron across the tip and have an area in the range of one-hundredth of a square micron. It is by using these microprotrusions, like a cat its whiskers or a man his hands, that a cell explores its microenvironment and is able to "taste" and "feel" the surface of the other cells in its immediate environment.

The actual process of adhering to another cell occurs via special adhesion molecules which are positioned on the microprotrusion as is shown in the diagram below. Pairs of adhesion molecules bind to each other via complementary matching surfaces using the same principle of lock-and-key matching recognition used by proteins to recognize their substrates. The bonds between two adhesion molecules are referred to as affinity bonds. Each affinity bond consists of a number of weak, or noncovalent, bonds. The strength of each affinity bond between two cells is made up of the sum of the various weak chemical bonds which bind the two adhesion molecules together. The diagram below illustrates two cells linked via an affinity bond at the end of a microprotrusion.

An affinity bond linking two cells.

Note one nanometer (nm) is one-millionth of a millimeter. A typical body cell, such as a lymphocyte, has a cell surface area of 200 square microns (a micron is one-thousandth of a millimeter). The number of adhesion molecules per cell is about 100,000, that is, 500 per square micron. Most cells contain a great many different types of adhesion molecules.

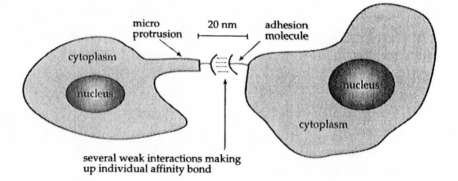

The fact that cells make initial contact via microprotrusions, often called filopods, is not accidental. The outer surface of cells is negatively charged, so cells tend to repel one another electrostatically. However, these repulsive forces become smaller as the contact area decreases in size down to the protrusion surface area of about .01 square micron, and the energy required to bring the tiny area of the tip of a microprotrusion into intimate contact with an adjacent cell membrane in order to make affinity bonds is no longer prohibitive.

Cell adhesion via microprotrusions also plays an important role in cell navigation. One of the most important mechanisms by which cells find their way as they migrate through the developing embryo is by successively adhering to a series of target cells or structures that lead them through the embryo to their assigned place. This inevitably involves their pushing and thrusting their way past other cells. To search for their next target they put out filopods in many directions until the correct contact is made. A cell unable to send out projections of this sort would be unable to feel any directional clue that was not in its immediate vicinity. Such a restriction would make direction finding by cells well nigh impossible, analogous to trying to find one's way through a dark room without using one's hands.

Consideration of the size of individual adhesion molecules (many are approximately 10 nanometers across) and the small area of a filopod tip suggests that packaging constraints will limit the number of adhesion molecules that can be fitted onto one tip.[11] Moreover, even when a filopod probe is very close to another cell surface, only a proportion of the adhesion molecules on the filopod tip will be able to make affinity bonds with the target cell surface. To make the affinity bond, the two complementary matching surfaces of the adhesion molecules must come into almost perfect alignment at distances of less than a nanometer. This is a very stringent requirement and suggests that initial binding can only invoke a small fraction of the available adhesion molecules on the tip of the filopod. Unless individual affinity bonds were relatively strong, sufficient to bind the protrusion to its target cell securely in the face of the various shearing forces usually met with in biological systems, no protrusion would ever bind to a target cell. The phenomenon of selective cell adhesion would be severely constrained and the use of tiny protrusions for pathfinding by embryonic cells would in all probability be impossible.

Recent studies have measured the strength of individual affinity bonds. Remarkably, these turn out to be on average equivalent to the force needed to lift 40 nanograms (there are 1 billion nanograms in one gram), which is enough to tie a filopod to a specific contact point. These studies have shown that only between one and ten affinity bonds are sufficient to hold two cells together against most of the common forces met with in biological systems. As few as thirteen affinity bonds will hold a lymphocyte to another cell in a fluid with the viscosity of water flowing at 1 centimeter per second. An individual filopod by which, as we have seen, many cells make contact with their environment and other cells, may be stabilized by as little as two affinity bonds. Individual affinity bonds, in short, are of sufficient strength to tether a filopod to its target cell.[12]

The contact of a particular filopod to its target is stabilized by the rapid migration and accumulation of additional specific adhesion molecules to the filopod tip. It is interesting to note that the two-dimensional mobility of proteins embedded in the membrane is only possible because of the unique fluidity of the cell membrane, a characteristic touched on above.

At any one time, most cells in developing embryos must be able to "feel" and make contact with a considerable diversity of cells and extracellular features in their immediate environment. It is hard to imagine how cells could do this any way except by using filopods.

Note also that the strength of the affinity bonds upon which the whole filopod adhesion system is based is ultimately determined by the strength of the weak chemical bonds. We have already seen that proteins would not be stable, nor enzymes bind their substrates, if these interactions were several-fold weaker. Here we have another instance in which an important biological process is also critically dependent on the absolute strength of these same weak interactions. Any weaker, and specific cell-cell binding via adhesion molecules on the surface of cells would be impossible. Any stronger, and, once formed, it would be very difficult for cells to detach themselves from one another.

The phenomenon of selective adhesion via filopods is only possible because, first, the cytoplasm is highly deformable and of low viscosity, and lends itself to being drawn into a long fingerlike extension; second, the repulsive negative electrostatic forces between the small area on the tip of a filopod and the target cell is relatively low; third, more than one specific adhesion molecule can be placed strategically on the end of a filopod tip, and fourth, the relative strength of affinity bonds is sufficient to bind cells against the various shearing forces tending to pull them apart.

Crawling

Yet another vital characteristic of cells is their ability to crawl, which is no less important and critical than their adhesive properties. Selective adhesion would be of little utility if cells could not move toward particular targets. Indeed, higher forms of life would not exist if cells could not crawl, and we would certainly not be here to ponder the phenomenon.[13] In crawling, a cell puts out fan-shaped extensions called lamellae, the leading edge of which make transient attachments with the underlying surface, and as they glide forward, they pull along the cell body passively behind them. The process is somewhat similar to the crawling of a snail, in which the snail's foot is analogous to the lamellae and the shell analogous to the cell body.

The process involves continual restructuring of the cell's substance and continual changes to its shape and form.[14] These necessitate that the cytoplasm be readily deformable—in other words, must have the quality of a relatively viscous colloidal material so that the interior of the cell can be drawn into the advancing protrusion. Yet the cell's interior must also contain stable structural elements making a mechanically rigid scaffold so that traction forces can be exerted between the adhesion points on the undersurface of the lamellae and the mechanically rigid scaffold.

It is clear that the ability to crawl requires the satisfaction of exacting criteria. The cytoplasm must be of the appropriate viscosity so that it can be deformed and drawn into the leading edge. If too viscous, the cell's contents would be immobilized. The cell must be able to reversibly adhere to the substratum, and, as we have seen, the phenomenon of adhesion depends critically on the strength of weak chemical bonds. The cell must be capable of generating sufficient traction forces to pull the mechanically rigid scaffold and the cytoplasmic contents enmeshed within it toward the leading edge. These same traction forces must also be sufficiently powerful to pull apart the affinity bonds as the cell moves away from a region to which it was previously tied. Discussion of just how finely balanced these various forces must be is a subject of many recent papers in cell biology.[15] If the value of the viscosity of water which forms the matrix of the cell, the energy levels of weak chemical bonds which determine the strength of affinity bonds, and the power of the traction forces of the cell's myosin motors were all slightly different from what they are, crawling would in all probability be impossible. And as crawling itself plays such an essential role in all developmental processes it is difficult to see how higher organisms could be assembled if these values had been even slightly different from what they are.

Interestingly, both crawling and adhesion are also dependent on cells being approximately the size they are. If diffusion had limited cells to a size range of ten to a hundred times smaller than they are, then crawling would be impossible, as the required molecular machinery and its regulatory mechanisms could hardly be packaged into a volume a thousand to a million times smaller than the average animal cell. As the surface area of such a cell would be a hundred to a thousand times less, the total number and diversity of cell surface adhesion molecules would also be drastically reduced. So too would be the utility of selective cell adhesion as a mechanism for organizing the arrangement of cells during development. Such tiny cells would hardly be able to put out complex arrays of protrusions to feel their way through a developing embryo. Indeed, the surface of such tiny cells might have to be entirely devoted to devices involved in transporting materials across the bounding cell membrane and leave little room for adhesion molecules. Lacking the ability of selective cell adhesion, even if such small cells could crawl, it is doubtful if this ability could be utilized to generate the complex patterns of cell movement and association which underlies much of the morphogenesis of higher organisms.

Again, one is struck with the central importance the low viscosity of water plays in so many aspects of biology. The relatively rapid diffusion rates of small molecules in water permits the relatively large size of animal cells: between 10 and 50 microns across, containing more than a trillion atoms, and large enough to contain the necessary molecular machinery for crawling. It also ensures that the cytoplasmic mass of such cells has a low viscosity and can be mobilized relatively easily by the molecular motors in the cell. Cells are also large enough to deploy a large number and diverse set of adhesion molecules on their surface so that their crawling can be specifically directed by selective cell adhesiveness during embryogenesis. If the various interactions and metabolic transformations on which the life and replicative abilities of the cell depends had only been possible at higher molecular concentrations of these key constituents, the cell's interior would have been too viscous to move. But if the cell's interior had been less viscous, then dragging its contents forward on a mesh of mechanically rigid components would have been problematical, as the cytoplasm would keep flowing back through the mesh.

What is particularly striking is that many of the unique abilities of cells, such as their ability to selectively adhere to objects in their environment and to crawl, are critically dependent on the unique global properties of the cell's cytoplasmic mass and on the cell membrane having almost precisely the properties it does.

The plastic, metastable character of cytoplasm, which is so fit for crawling and selective adhesion, has not been created by natural selection. On the contrary, it is an inherent property of an aqueous solution of the constituents of the cell. Start with those key constituents of life—DNA, protein, sugars, lipids, etc., which are uniquely and ideally adapted for their various roles in the living process, including self-replication—dissolve them in water at the precise concentrations necessary for cell function and self-replication, and as if by magic, a colloidal substance is formed—cytoplasm—possessing just those qualities required to permit cells to crawl and to selectively adhere to each other and hence to assemble higher organisms and ultimately to make a world of life. It is surely highly suggestive of design that a soup of these basic vital ingredients at precisely the concentration required to carry out the miracle of self-replication surrounded by the lipid bilayer should have, coincidentally, precisely that suite of biophysical properties of viscosity, density, excitability, etc., ideally and uniquely suited for the cell to carry out its designated task of building a biosphere of multicellular life.

It is hard to escape the conclusion that the ability of cells to selectively adhere and to crawl, twin abilities upon which the assembly of multicellular organisms during development is critically dependent, could only find instantiation in an entity of the size and with the global biophysical and biochemical properties of the average animal cell.

Osmosis

Another physical phenomenon which has a critical bearing on the design of the cell, and particularly on the design of the cell membrane and hence the ability of cells to crawl and adhere, is the phenomenon of osmosis and its consequence, osmotic pressure. Osmosis is an inevitable consequence of the process of diffusion. It occurs wherever two solutions, one dilute and one concentrated, are separated by a membrane that is permeable to water but not to the solutes. In such a situation water moves from the dilute to the concentrated solution—in other words, the solution containing the most dissolved particles. The influx of water can only be prevented by applying hydrostatic pressure to the concentrated solution. This reverses the influx and forces the water back across the semipermeable membrane into the dilute solution.

Cells, in the human body and in nearly all other complex organisms, tend to contain a greater concentration of dissolved particles than does the extracellular fluid which surrounds the cell. There are two causes for this. The first is the so-called Gibbs-Donnan effect,[16] which arises because the surface of the proteins in the cell contains many positively and negatively charged groups and these attract a large number of counterions, including small organic molecules. The net effect is an increase in the concentration of particles inside the cell compared with that in the extracellular fluid. The second is that the cell necessarily contains a large number of small organic compounds which result from the cell's own metabolic activities. As the cell membrane is permeable to water (but not to proteins and many of the ions and small organic compounds in the cytoplasm), and as water moves by osmosis from a dilute to a more concentrated solution, every cell in the body of man and all other animals would suffer a persistent influx of water which, if the cell took no action to reverse, would ultimately have disastrous effects. The pressure inside the cell would increase, causing swelling of the cell until eventually the fragile cell membrane would rupture.

There are only two strategies available to avoid this consequence. One is to surround the cell in a very strong, rigid wall. This is the strategy adopted by plant cells, which are encased in a firm cellulose lining that is strong enough to resist the pressure that develops inside the cell by the osmotically driven influx of water. Bacterial cells have also adopted a similar strategy.

The other strategy—the one universally used by animal cells—is to continually pump ions such as sodium out of the cell and thereby maintain "unnaturally" lower concentrations of small inorganic ions in the cytoplasm than in the extracellular fluid outside the cell, which in turn draws water out of the cell.[17] By this ingenious strategy animal cells can avoid rigid cell walls. The pliable, nonrigid, and relatively fragile cell membrane suffices to hold the cell's contents together. The sufficiency of the typical animal cell membrane is of great significance, for as we have seen, many of the critical properties of cells such as crawling and adhesion depend on the pliability and deformability of the membrane.

This continual pumping strategy requires enormous amounts of energy, up to one-third of the total energy supply of many cells (two-thirds in the case of nerve cells).[18] This is why poisons which interfere with the cell's ability to generate or utilize energy cause immediate swelling of the cell. There is yet another element of fortuity in the fact that this massive pumping activity is commensurate with the energy-generating capacity of cells. Had the Gibbs-Donnan effect been just very slightly more intense, the basic design of the cell as a concentrated soup of proteins bounded by a pliable semipermeable membrane would not have been feasible. Cells would have had to devote all their energies merely to avoid the inrush of water, cell swelling, and death.

It is also fortunate that the absolute pressures generated by osmosis are not any greater than they are. Surprisingly, even quite dilute solutions can exert enormous osmotic pressures. A solution of 7 grams of salt dissolved in 100 milliliters of water develops an osmotic pressure of about 60 atmospheres, equivalent to the pressure 2,000 feet below the sea.[19] To prevent the water moving from the distilled water into the salt solution, a hydrostatic pressure of 60 atmospheres would have to be exerted on the salt solution—this would be equivalent to a column of water 2,000 feet high. Clearly, if the absolute value of the pressures generated by osmosis had been much higher, then no feasible cell could be designed to survive contact with very dilute aqueous solutions. The cell walls in the roots of plants would have had to be many times stronger and thicker to resist the increased pressures. And even in the cells of animals where the solute concentration in the intracellular and extracellular fluids are almost exactly balanced, minor fluctuations in their relative concentrations could well prove disastrous. If osmotic forces had been, say, ten times greater, the minor but relatively sudden dilution of the body fluids which occurs on drinking water might create osmotic imbalances of catastrophic consequence. Only if the cell walls of animal cells were far more rigid (like plant cells) would they have been capable of existence in a world where the pressures generated by osmosis had been ten times greater. But then the cell membrane would not possess those many critical characteristics upon which the world-building abilities of cells depend.

Energy Balance

Cells require energy not only to defend themselves against osmotic pressures by continuously pumping ions out across the cell membrane. They are also faced with the uphill task of continuously replacing all their molecular constituents, and this also requires energy. The half-life of many proteins in the cell varies from a few minutes to several days. Even those proteins which have relatively long half-lives, such as the hemoglobins, the proteins forming the contractile apparatus in the muscles and collagen, the major component of tendons, all turn over eventually and have to be replaced.

One reason for the relatively short half-life of many proteins is the highly reactive oxygen radicals which are ever present in the cell. These cause deleterious chemical changes that render them nonfunctional. If unchallenged, the accumulation of abnormal nonfunctional proteins would eventually clog up the cell's machinery and bring the life of the cell to a halt. Not only must the cell continuously replace these damaged proteins, but an additional energy burden is imposed by the need for their selective degradation. In fact, cells contain a whole set of enzymes whose only purpose is to selectively remove damaged proteins.

In an adult human about 15 percent of the energy expended is devoted to protein synthesis alone.[20] Clearly, if the stability of proteins in the face of oxidative and other types of chemical degradation was even slightly less, then the energy burden imposed on cells would be insurmountable and the cell system would not be possible in any recognizable form.

Are Cells Intelligent?

Crawling and selective adhesion, etc., are just some of the remarkable properties packed into these tiny particles of matter. Cells possess many other properties in addition to these. Even the smallest, simplest cells dazzle us with their abilities. The abilities of the tiny bacterium *E. coli,* which is far smaller than an animal body cell, are simply amazing. It can, for example, estimate the concentration of many of the common and important molecules it comes in contact with, and from the result of such calculations change the direction in which it is swimming toward the richest source of nutrient.[21]

But some of the behavioral repertoires of unicellular organisms such as amoebas many million times the size of a bacterial cell are even more amazing and truly astonishing, for a colloidal mass of protoplasm, although far bigger than a bacterium, is still only the size of a speck of dust. The dramas played out in a drop of water are almost as rich and diverse as those played out on the plains of Africa. In 1910, one famous scholar gave a very graphic description of an amoeba hunting prey. It is worth citing at length:

> Amoeba frequently prey upon one another. Sometimes the prey is contracted and does not move; then there is no difficulty in ingesting it. . . . But the victim does not always conduct itself so passively as in this case, and sometimes finally escapes from its pursuer. This may be illustrated by a case observed by the present writer. . . . I had attempted to cut an amoeba in two with a tip of a fine glass rod. The posterior third of the animal, in the form of a wrinkled ball, remained attached to the rest of the body by a slender cord. The Amoebae may

One amoeba hunting another.

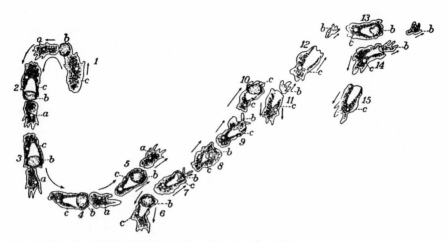

From H. S. Jennings (1905), *The Behavior of Lower Organisms,* figure 21.

be called Amoeba *a* while the ball will be designated *b* [see fig. 10.5, above]. A larger amoeba (*c*) approached, moving at right angles to the path of the first specimen. Its path accidentally brought it in contact with the ball *b*, which was dragging past its front. Amoeba *c* thereupon turned, followed Amoeba *a*, and began to engulf the ball. A cavity was formed in the anterior part of Amoeba *a* . . . [sufficient to engulf the ball]. Amoeba *a* now turned into a new path; Amoeba *c* followed. . . . After the pursuit had lasted for some time, the ball *b* had become completely engulfed by Amoeba *c*. The cord connecting the ball with Amoeba *a* broke and the latter went on its way. . . . Now the anterior opening of the cavity in Amoeba *c* became partly closed, leaving only a slender canal. . . . There was no adhesion between the protoplasm of the ball and Amoeba *c*. . . . Now the large Amoeba *c* . . . began to move in a different direction . . . carrying with it its meal. But the meal—ball *b* now began to show signs of life, sent out pseudopodia, and became very active; we shall henceforth refer to the ball as Amoeba *b*. It began to creep out through the still open canal, sending forth its pseudopodia to the outside. Thereupon Amoeba *c* sent forth its pseudopodia in the same direction, and after creeping in that direction several times its own length, again engulfs *b*. The latter again partially escaped, and was again engulfed completely. Amoeba *c* now started again in the opposite direction, whereupon Amoeba *b*, by a few rapid movements, escaped from the posterior end of Amoeba *c*, and was free—being completely separated from *c.* Thereupon Amoeba *c* reversed its course again, overtook *b,* engulfed it completely again. . . . Amoeba *b* then contracted into a ball and remained quiet for some time. Apparently the drama was over. Amoeba *c* went on its way for about five minutes without any sign of life in Amoeba *b.* In the movements of *c, b* became gradually transferred to its posterior end, until there was only a thin layer of protoplasm between *c* and the outer water. Now *b* began to move again, sent pseudopodia through the thin wall to the outside, and then passed bodily out into the water. This time Amoeba *c* did not reverse direction and attempt to recapture Amoeba *b.* The two Amoebae moved in opposite directions and became completely separated.[22]

The amoeba, although the size of a small speck of dust, exhibits behavioral strategies which seem objectively indistinguishable from those of animals far higher up the scale. If an amoeba were the size of a cat, we would probably impute to it the same level of intelligence as we do to a mammal. Just how do such minute organisms integrate all the information necessary to make such apparently calculated intelligent decisions? While the processes underlying the selective stickiness of cells, their crawling ability, and even the molecular counting ability of *E. coli* referred to above have been worked out at least to some degree, accounting for the amoeba's behavior, the way it integrates all the information necessary to pursue its prey, its decision to change direction, its persistence in the pursuit when its prey escapes, the sudden breakout of the smaller amoeba from its imprisonment in the interior of its captor at the moment when the wall of protoplasm was at its thinnest—all this remains to be fully explained in molecular terms.

The behavior exhibited by both the pursued and the pursuer must involve an extraordinary level of sophisticated information processing. It is not at all clear how this is done; despite all the advances in computer technology, building completely autonomous robots to mimic the behavior of an amoeba is quite beyond our capacities at present. The behavior of the amoeba in pursuing its prey and our inability to give a coherent account of this in molecular terms shows that there is still a vast amount of complexity in the cell still remaining to be uncovered, highlighting again how much we still have to learn.

The possibility that there could be radical new levels of complexity in the cell is raised by some recent ideas proposed by Stuart Hameroff of the University of Arizona. According to Hameroff, the traditional estimates of the brain's computing power based on a neural net assumption that each "neuron-neuron synaptic connection is a fundamental binary switch led to clas-sical estimates of the brain's information processing capacity of $4 \cdot 10^{12}$ bits per second (40 billion neurons changing their state 100 times per sec-ond)."[23] However, Hameroff suggests that there might be another comput-ing system within each cell based on the "microtubules" which make up the cytoskeleton of the neurons. The microtubules are tiny tubes made up of protein subunits that form an important component of the cytoarchitecture in virtually all the cells of higher organisms. Such a subcellular system would vastly add to the power of the brain's computing capacity, for it would mean that within each neuron there was a minicomputer with computing power equivalent to that of an IBM desktop computer![24]

Hameroff's ideas cannot be ruled out of court, although there is no direct evidence for his claims at present. But as he notes, "single-celled organisms like amoeba and paramecium perform complex tasks without benefit of synapse, brain or nervous system."[25] And as he points out, such subcellular minicomputers could regulate and organize processes like transport, cell growth, cellular movement, as well as the guidance and movement of single-celled organisms. Perhaps the amoeba is far more intelligent than our cur-rent knowledge of the cell suggests. Maybe its hunting strategies are aided by a subcellular computer of immense power. Even in the case of insects, it has always been something of a puzzle just how their complex behavior could be packed inside brains which, by vertebrate standards, are extremely small. The abilities of insects puzzled Darwin: "It is certain that there may be extraordinary mental activity within an extremely small absolute mass of nervous matter; thus the wonderful diversified instincts, mental powers, and affections of ants are notorious, yet their cerebral ganglia are not so large as the quarter of a small pin's head. Under this point of view, the brain of an ant is one of the most marvellous atoms of matter in the world, perhaps more so than the brain of man."[26] Although considerable progress has been made since Darwin's day in explaining insect behavior in terms of a few stereotyped routines, the possibility that subcellular computing devices may play some role in their behavior cannot be entirely ruled out.

The concept of subcellular computing devices using the microtubules was discussed by the British physicist Roger Penrose in his latest book, *Shadows of the Mind.*[27] If there is any truth in Hameroff's suggestion, then the human brain itself may be vastly more complex than currently sup-posed.[28]

There may be other types of subcellular computational devices in addition to the microtubules. Many protein networks in the cell may serve this function.[29] In short, there is much that remains to be discovered. Cells may possess many additional abilities, vastly more complex and sophisticated than any we know of at present. But as it is, from the scientific knowledge we have already acquired, there is no doubt the cell represents an exceptional and unique material form. And one which, as in so many other instances, seems ideally and uniquely fit for its biological role in creating the world of multicellular life. Is it conceivable that there could exist some other tiny material form which could compact, into so small a volume, so many extraordinary abilities as a living cell?

Conclusion

We are now in a position to consider playing again the game we borrowed from Robert Clark and started in chapter 6, when we imagined ourselves as Plato's *Demiurge* creating a world of life from scratch. As we saw starting the game with the carbon atom, two primary requirements would be a medium in which our carbon-based life could function and a vehicle to distribute the carbon atom to all parts of our imaginary biosphere. When we searched through the vast number of known fluids and the vast number of carbon compounds, we found only two—water, and the gas carbon dioxide—that would do. We found that they would not only do, but were amazingly fit for their respective functions, and in many ways. We found oxidation to be the obvious choice for energy generation and it too was amazingly fit for carbon-based life in many ways. As the game continued, for every new constituent we required, there was a ready-made solution that seemed ideally and uniquely prefabricated, as if by design, for the biological end it serves.

Having now reviewed, in the past few chapters, the mutual adaptations of DNA and proteins and the utility of the various metals for carbon-based life, we can continue our game toward the creation of a complex self-replicating system and again everything continues to fall into place with ridiculous ease. We would need molecular machines to manipulate atoms and we would find that proteins are ideal for this role. We would then find that they are also wonderfully fit to function in conjunction with the nucleic acids which we discover are themselves ideal as information bearers. We would want to control and manipulate oxygen, and we would find yet again ideal oxygen manipulators in the transitional metals. Finally, we would want to wrap up our constituents into a small packet or cell, and we would find to our astonishment that there exists a very simple means of bounding the cells—a lipid bilayer which has a suite of properties that are, again, just what we need. Even more remarkable we find that when we have packed all our constituents into our "cell," the viscosity of the resulting material and the size and properties of the membrane are all just about right for crawling and selective adhesion, properties we need to build multicellular organisms and a vast complex world of life. We would find an ideal source of energy in the radiant light of main sequence stars, and ideal habitats for our carbon-based life on the trillions of earthlike rocky planets which abound throughout the cosmos. At every step in the game we would find the same ready-made solution for each particular biological end we sought. And this would be repeated in case after case, leading down through a long, seemingly endless chain of coincidences from the carbon atom to the cell and eventually to a world of life very similar to that which exists on earth.

In short, the cell system as revealed by molecular biology has turned out to be a unique and peerless whole in which every component is uniquely fashioned by the laws of nature for its designated role, a three-dimensional jigsaw in which all the pieces fit together as perfectly and harmoniously as the cogs in a watch. As we have seen, every constituent—water, the carbon atom, dioxygen, carbon dioxide, bicarbonate, the lipids, the lipid bilayer membrane, the double helix, the proteins, the genetic code, the iron atom, the molybdenum atom, calcium, magnesium, sodium and potassium ions, and so on—appears unique and ideally adapted for its respective biological role. There are many other constituents, not reviewed here, which also give the appearance of being specially fit for their biological roles. These include the sugars and the storage form of sugar, the compound glycogen.[30] The phosphate radical which occurs in the energy-carrying molecule ATP and is also used as the joining radical between adjacent bases in the DNA is also uniquely fit for its many biological roles. And again, as in so many instances, there is no alternative—no other compound will substitute for the phosphate radical in the many functions it performs in the cell.[31] (See Appendix, section 3.)

Future work may well reveal that many other of the cell's constituents are also uniquely fit for the biological roles they play. This was hinted at by George Wald when he raised the possibility that chlorophylls, the heme pigments, the carotenoids, and vitamin A (involved in photoreception) may all possess properties that fit them uniquely to perform their specific functions, so much so that all carbon-based life forms anywhere in the cosmos would of necessity be forced to use these very same compounds in attempting to achieve the same ends for which they are now utilized on earth.[32] The fact that vitamin A is used in every known visual system throughout the animal kingdom is highly suggestive.[33] Is it possible that without vitamin A there might be no vision? The universal occurrence of the compound acetylcholine in organisms as diverse as plants, protozoans, and mammals, and its use as a neural transmitter in organisms belonging to virtually every animal phylum, struck Carl Pantin as suggestive that it might possess properties for neurotransmission that are not available in any other molecule.[34]

Even above the level of the individual molecule, many of the structural materials used by living things, materials such as bone, skin, tendon, calcareous shells, chitin, and wood, which are what a structural engineer would class as composites, are also remarkable for their apparently ideal biomechanical characteristics.[35]

A final and very remarkable aspect of the fitness of the constituents of life is that most of the key organic building blocks—sugars, amino acids, nucleotides, etc.—can be manufactured in a relatively small number of chemical steps from a small number of readily available simple molecules. It is a remarkable fact that the great majority of the atoms used in their synthesis are derived from only three very simple molecules that are available freely and in great abundance on the surface of the earth: water, carbon dioxide, and nitrogen. Not only are the key components of life wonderfully fit for their biological roles, they are all only a very small chemical distance away from such universally available starting materials. Indeed, there are not many steps from hydrogen itself—the starting point of atom creation in the stars—to the ingredients of life.

But not only is this remarkable set of key building blocks readily synthesized from available materials, they can all be readily interconverted via a small number of chemical steps. It is fortuitous, indeed, that so many of the key molecules of life, which possess so many unique chemical and physical properties, all exist within easy chemical reach of each other. The astonishing chemical proximity of all life's constituents is surely a fact of very great and crucial significance. The fitness of the individual ingredients, such as lipids, proteins, and DNA, although remarkable enough, is insufficient in itself; it is only because all the components of life can be derived easily from simple starting materials and interconverted readily that the miracle of the cell and self-replication is possible.

Contrast this with artificial systems, even fantastically simple ones quite incapable of replication, such as a motor car or a computer or a typewriter. In the case of such artificial machines, each individual component, such as a metal rod, a silicon chip, or a plastic disc, can only be manufactured by long circuitous routes involving complex industrial processes that may involve temperatures of 1,000°C and all manner of diverse chemical processes.

The emerging picture is obviously consistent with the teleological view of nature. That each constituent utilized by the cell for a particular biological role, each cog in the watch, turns out to be the only and at the same time the ideal candidate for its role is particularly suggestive of design. That the whole, the end to which all this teleological wizardry leads—the living cell—should be also ideally suited for the task of constructing the world of multicellular life reinforces the conclusion of purposeful design. The prefabrication of parts to a unique end is the very hallmark of design. Moreover, there is simply no way that such prefabrication could be the result of natural selection. Design in the very components which make an organism possible cannot be, as Carl Pantin pointed out some time ago, *the result of natural selection.*[36] The many vital mutual adaptations in the constituents of life were given by physics long before any living thing existed and long before natural selection could have begun to operate.

In the current molecular biological picture of life, we have found a "watch" more complicated and more harmonious than any conceived by William Paley, exhibiting in its design precisely what Richard Bentley was looking for, a *"usefulness conspicuous not in one or a few only, but in a long train and series of things."* (My emphasis.)

Chapter 11

Homo   Sapiens :
Fire   Maker

*In which it is argued that our species may be uniquely fit to explore
and understand the cosmos and that the laws of nature appear also
to be uniquely fit for large organic forms of our size and dimension.
The evidence is not conclusive, but highly suggestive. Our species
exhibits a set of adaptations which are collectively unique among
carbon-based life forms on earth. These include high intelligence,
linguistic ability, the hand, high-acuity vision, the upright stance,
sociability. Moreover, the design and dimensions of the human body
are fit for the handling of fire—a crucial ability, because it was only
through the conquest of fire that humans discovered metals, developed
technology and science, and ultimately came to comprehend the
laws of nature and grasp the overall structure of the cosmos. Many
coincidences appear to underlie our fitness for handling fire and our
fitness for understanding the cosmos. For example, the earth's size
and atmosphere are fit both for beings of our size and dimension
and also for fire. The strength of muscles is commensurate with
mobility in a being of our size on a planet the size of the earth. The
laws of nature conform to mathematical patterns which the human
mind seems curiously adapted to grasp. In conclusion, the cosmos
appears to be fit for our being and our understanding.*

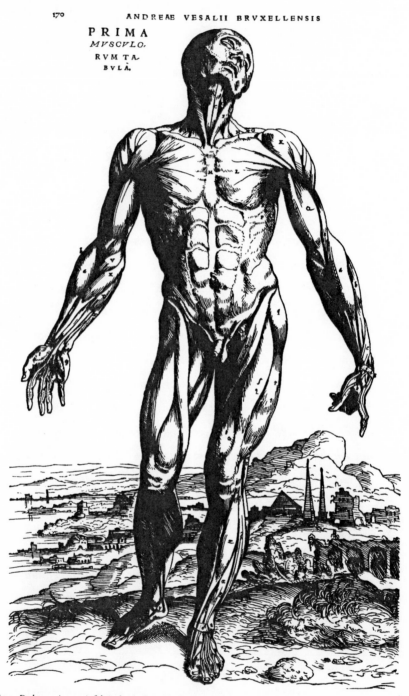

ANDREAE VESALII BRVXELLENSIS

170

PRIMA
MVSCVLO,
RVM TA
BVLA.

From *De humani corporis fabrica* by Andreas Vesalius.

How noble in reason, how infinite in faculties, in form and moving, how express and admirable in action, how like an angel in apprehension, how like a God! the beauty of the world; the paragon of animals.

—William Shakespeare, *Hamlet*

"For what purpose," asks Cicero, "was the great fabric of the universe constructed? Was it merely for the purpose of perpetrating the various species of trees and herbs which are not endued even with sensation?— the supposition is absurd. Or was it for the exclusive use of the inferior animals? . . . which, although endued with sensation, possess neither speech nor intelligence. For whom then was the world produced?— doutbless for those beings who are alone endued with reason."

—John Kidd, Bridgewater Treatise, *The Physical Condition of Man*, 1852

The ancient Greeks, who had an answer to most things, believed that Prometheus brought down fire from heaven—and got himself into much trouble with Zeus for doing so. "From bright fire," says Aeschylus in *Prometheus Vinctus*, "they will learn many arts."

—A. J. Wilson, *The Living Rock*, 1994

Of all the many varied life forms on earth, only our own species, *Homo sapiens,* is capable of any genuine understanding of the world. By any standards our success in comprehending and manipulating nature has been astounding. In the space of only four centuries since the scientific revolution, we have measured the diameter of galaxies, we have probed into the heart of the atom, we have peered back to the very beginning of time, and in the past few decades we have even contemplated traveling to the stars.

Our intellectual endowment is certainly remarkable, but are we unique, as the anthropocentric thesis predicts? Could such genius and abilities be instantiated in some other material form? Could some other thinking being radically different in design to *Homo sapiens* have been equally successful at unraveling the secrets of nature? Could there even be, as modern science fiction implies, a veritable phantasm of other beings utterly alien and exotic but just as "noble in reason and infinite in faculties" as ourselves?

From the evidence presented in the previous chapters, such a phantasm of alien beings—designed along entirely different principles and instantiated in an exotic chemistry—looks increasingly implausible. For as we have seen, it would appear that there are few if any alternative ways of putting together the atoms of the world into a complex self-replicating system as sophisticated as the living cell. If we start from the carbon atom, our route is highly constrained. Having chosen carbon, we must next choose water, then proteins, DNA, oxygen, and so on until we arrive eventually at the design of the living cell as manifest in all living things on earth.

But even if life based on the carbon atom is the only form allowed by physics, it is obvious from the variety of life on earth that the possible number of complex carbon-based multicellular life forms is immense and that our own species, *Homo sapiens,* is but one within a universe of possibilities. Could it be that within this plenitude the only type of organism capable of manipulating and exploring and eventually understanding the world is an upright bipedal primate of biology and design very close to that of *Homo sapiens*? I believe the evidence strongly suggests that the answer is yes.

Key Adaptations

Six adaptations have been widely cited as being crucial to the unique success of our species: (1) high intelligence, (2) linguistic communication, (3) highly developed visual ability, (4) possession of a superb manipulative tool—the hand, (5) our upright stance, and (6) our being a highly social species. In addition to these six adaptations, our technological success has depended on a crucial ability—the ability to handle and control fire, which led in turn to the development of metallurgy and ultimately, through the use of metals, to scientific and technological knowledge. Although the evidence currently available is insufficient to prove the case, it is hard to imagine these adaptations plus the additional ability to handle and manipulate fire (which poses its own rather specific design constraints on an organism) being possessed by any organism markedly different to a modern human.

As far as our cognitive capacities are concerned, it is true that other species—dolphins, parrots, seals, and apes—possess intelligence, but none, as far as we can tell, comes close to the intelligence of man. At present, the basis of our unique cognitive capacity is quite mysterious. (See discussion below.) It may be rooted in some curious wiring feature of the primate brain or may be in some way connected with the evolutionary path which led to modern man. Whatever it is about the architecture of the human brain that confers such a high level of intelligence, and whatever evolutionary processes led to such a prodigious development, as far as life on earth is concerned, our intelligence far surpasses that of any other known form of life.

Language

Language is another unique distinguishing characteristic of man. No other species possesses a communication system remotely as competent for the transmission of new information or abstract concepts as human language.[1]

Of course, in themselves neither intelligence nor the capacity for language are sufficient to provide an organism with the ability to understand the world. The body must also be fit for the task. The brain and its capacity for abstract symbolic manipulation must be conjoined with body and organ systems through which the brain can interact with the outside world. It is only because our brain can sense and experience the world and translate our thoughts into actions that we are able to explore, manipulate, and ultimately understand the world. A computer, no matter how "intelligent," is unable to communicate with the outside world via a "body," and is thus incapable of such exploration.

Further, capacity for speech would be of little utility without the appropriate equipment to produce it. Human speech depends not only on our special cognitive abilities but also on our possessing the appropriate organs to generate complex sound patterns. In fact, modern man's speech-producing apparatus is quite different from the comparable systems of living nonhuman primates. Nonhuman primates have supralaryngeal vocal tracts in which the larynx exits directly into the oral cavity. In the adult human the larynx exits directly into the pharynx. This confers on man the capacity to generate a far richer phonetic repertoire than that available to a chimpanzee.[2] Many vowels and consonants used in human language could not be reproduced by a chimp. A chimp with a human brain could formulate sophisticated thoughts but would lack the ability to communicate verbally as efficiently as a human.[3] Our vocal apparatus is in all probability at least as important as our bipedalism as a prerequisite to our becoming fully human.

Language also presumes a gregarious social animal. Man in common with all the other primates is highly social. No solitary species would develop a language. Sociality in general was probably an essential element in man's biological and intellectual evolution.

Vision

Our visual ability is hardly less significant than our ability to communicate by speech. Possessing intelligence and speech but lacking good eyesight, it is difficult to imagine how humans could have acquired extensive knowledge of the world. Aristotle, in this famous section from the beginning of his *Metaphysics,* acknowledges the importance of vision to our ability to comprehend the world:

> All men by reason desire to know. An indication of this is the delight we take in the senses . . . and above all in the sense of sight. . . . The reason is that this, most of all the senses, makes us know and brings many differences to light.[4]

We saw in chapter 3 that the resolving power of the human eye is close to the optimum for a camera type of eye using biological cells as photodetectors. Its visual acuity cannot be improved to any significant degree by making changes in its absolute size or the relative size of its components. For this reason nearly all the eyes of those higher organisms which possess high-acuity vision are approximately the same design and dimension, roughly between 2 and 6 centimeters in diameter. As we saw, compared with most other biological structures, the size of the high-acuity vertebrate camera eye is quite large. Although it is only about one-thousandth the length of a California redwood (the largest living structure), it is about 1 million times longer than a bacterial cell. The vast majority of organisms are far smaller than the human eye. Even some birds and mammals weigh far less than the eye. Neither an ant nor even a mouse could support an organ the size of the human eye. Neither can see as clearly as a man and neither could be creatures of genuine understanding. To see clearly, *Homo sapiens* must be a relatively large organism on the scale of all biological forms.

The Hand

In addition to our brain, our linguistic ability, and our highly developed visual ability, we possess another wonderful adaptation, the ideal manipulative tool—the human hand. No other animal possesses an organ so superbly adapted for intelligent exploration and manipulation of its physical surroundings and environment. Only the great apes, our cousins, come close. Yet the hand of the chimp and gorilla, although possessing an opposable thumb, is far less adapted to fine motor movement and control.[5] Although some chimps are remarkably dexterous,[6] when one sees them attempt even simple manual tasks, they appear clumsy and inept compared to humans. Even a chimp with the intelligence of a human would have considerable difficulty carrying out many of the manipulative tasks that we take for granted, like peeling an apple, tying a knot, or using a typewriter.

One of the earliest and still one of the most fascinating discussions of the adaptive marvel that is the human hand was given by the first-century physician Galen: "To man the only animal that partakes in the Divine intelligence, the Creator has given in lieu of every other natural weapon or organ of defence, that instrument the hand: applicable to every art and occasion."[7] And he continues: "Let us then scrutinise this member of our body; and enquire not simply whether it be in itself useful for all the purposes of life, and adapted to an animal endowed with the highest intelligence; but whether its entire structure be not such, that it could not be improved by any conceivable alteration."[8] The adaptive perfection of the hand was a popular topic among nineteenth-century natural theologians.

In the context of explaining man's biological preeminence on earth, the crucial question is not whether the human hand represents the absolute pinnacle of manipulative capability, but whether any other species possesses an organ approaching its capabilities. The answer simply must be that *no other species possesses a manipulative organ remotely approaching the universal utility of the human hand.* Even in the field of robotics, nothing has been built which even remotely equals the all-around manipulative capacity of the hand.

The hand not only provided man with the ability to manipulate and explore his environment but also with the ability to construct all manner of diverse tools and instruments, the use of which has been crucial to the acquisition of technological and scientific knowledge. It is impossible to envisage man progressing beyond the most primitive technology without the hand.

The hand, like any other organ, does not function in isolation. In fact, its utility is dependent to a large extent on that other crucial and unique adaptation of man, our upright stance and bipedal gait. Without these, the human hand would not be free to execute its manipulative explorations. All the great apes are basically quadrupeds, defined as knuckle-walkers by Owen in the nineteenth century.[9] Only among man's immediate antecedents (known only from fossil remains) is a habitual bipedal posture and gait achieved.

In addition to the above five adaptations, there are other aspects of our biology which have enabled us to be truly *Homo sapiens,* most notably that we are a social animal, a condition of great significance. Being social was not only almost certainly essential to the evolutionary development of language and other key aspects of our intellect, but only a social species could have ever developed an advanced technology through which to further the exploration of nature.

Fire and the Dimensions of the Human Body

In addition to the above adaptations, our ability to handle and manipulate fire is also critically dependent on the basic design and dimensions of the human body being close to what they are.

Our ability to handle fire is no trivial ability because it was only through the use of fire that technological advance was possible. Through fire came metallurgy and metal tools and eventually chemical knowledge. Because metals are the only natural conductors of electricity, the discovery of electromagnetism and electricity, even the development of computers, are all in the last analysis the result of our ancient conquest of fire. That fire is a phenomenon of great significance was perceived from the earliest of times. In many cultures it was invested with mystical and magical significance. Prometheus was condemned because he stole fire from the gods, and in ancient Persia it was worshiped as the manifestation of the Deity.

That fire is itself a remarkable phenomenon has already been noted. That the chemical reaction between carbon and oxygen is manageable at all is the result of the relative chemical inertness of the carbon atom and dioxygen at ambient temperatures. This chemical inertness is not only fit for oxidative metabolism, which provides energy for living systems; its attenuating influence also makes carbon combustion of utility to humans. It is only because of the slowness of the combustion of wood that fire can be handled by a large terrestrial organism on a planet like the earth.

Because the smallest sustainable fire is about 50 centimeters across, only an organism of approximately our dimensions and design—about 1.5 to 2 meters in height with mobile arms about 1 meter long ending in manipulative tools—can handle fire. An organism the size of an ant would be far too small because the heat would kill it long before it was as close as several body lengths from the flames. Even an organism the size of a small dog would have considerable difficulties in manipulating a fire. So we must be at least the size we are to use fire, to utilize metal tools, to have a sophisticated technology, to have a knowledge of chemistry and electricity and explore the world. It would appear that man, defined by Aristotle in the first line of his *Metaphysics* as a creature that "desires understanding," can only accomplish an understanding and exploration of the world, which Aristotle saw as his destiny, in a body of approximately the dimensions of a modern human.

Would an upright bipedal primate much larger than a modern human be feasible? Probably not. The design of a bipedal primate of, say, twice our height and several times our weight would be problematical to say the least. As it is, our upright stance puts severe strain on our lower back, especially on the intervertebral discs. Such a gigantic primate would almost certainly require thicker legs, suffer severe spinal problems, and be less nimble than modern man, and certainly no more capable of building a fire.

Being the size we are is also essential in another way. It is very unlikely that a brain the size of a bee's, which contains less than a million nerve cells, would be large enough to support intelligence remotely like that of man. Although, as Sir Julian Huxley concedes in his book *The Uniqueness of Man*, we have no way of knowing how big a brain built on biological principles out of nerve cells interconnected into a vast synaptic network needs to be to support intelligence, there is every reason to suppose that it must be quite large, as he notes: "The intelligence of a rat would be impossible without brain cells enough to outweigh the whole body of a bee, while the human level of intellect would be impossible without a brain composed of several hundred million cells and therefore reckoned in ounces, outweighing the majority of animals."[10] The fact that all other species exhibiting a degree of intelligence, including porpoises, parrots, apes, seals, etc., have brains close to our own in size, supports strongly the notion that a prerequisite for intelligence is a large brain.

The handling of fire would also be very difficult in an organism without a highly developed sense of vision. And again, only a relatively large organism can possess a high-acuity eye. It turns out, then, that to utilize fire we need to be approximately the size we are for several reasons: to be able to physically manipulate the actual fire itself, to have a brain sufficiently large to support the intelligence required to control that physical manipulation, and to have an eye to see the fire. As well, we need to have manipulative organs somewhat close to the design of arms and hands in modern humans.

Fire and the Size of the Earth

There are some intriguing coincidences related to our biological design and our ability to utilize fire. A carbon-based organism of our size and design possessing an upright bipedal posture is only feasible on a planet of approximately the size and mass of the earth. It is the size of the earth (or more specifically, its total mass) which determines the strength of its gravitational field. This in turn limits the maximum size of large terrestrial organisms like ourselves. If the earth had only twice the diameter, its gravitational field would be eight times stronger and a large upright bipedal creature like ourselves would not be feasible. In a very important sense, then, the earth's size is fit for the design of a bipedal animal of the dimensions of a man and therefore fit for our ability to handle fire.

But this is not all. As we saw in chapter 4, if a planet is to possess a stable hydrosphere and atmosphere fit for life, it must of necessity also possess a mass and consequently a gravitational field very close to that of the earth and undergo the same geophysical evolution. As we saw, its gravity must be strong enough to retain the heavier elements but weak enough to permit the initial loss of the lighter volatile elements, such as hydrogen and helium. Consequently, earth's mass is also fit for the evolution of an atmosphere similar to today's, in density and composition, containing oxygen and therefore capable of sustaining fire.

So the mass of the earth is not only fit for an atmosphere capable of sustaining a complex biosphere and supporting fire, it is also fit for an organism of the weight, size, and dimension capable of utilizing it. The use of fire is of course dependent on additional environmental factors—on the availability of wood, for example, and relatively dry conditions. Unless these additional factors were also favorable, then despite all the physical and mental adaptations which makes us *Homo sapiens* and despite the fitness of the earth as an abode for carbon-based life, neither fire, metallurgy, chemistry, nor any scientific progress would have been possible.

Muscles and Movement

The manipulation of fire necessitates movement. In the case of a large organism the size of a human, this in turn necessitates special structures—muscles—capable of exerting mechanical forces.

Moreover, if muscles are to be fit to give mechanical power and motility to an organism the size of a human, then they must be capable of generating considerable mechanical force, of controlling the generation of this force, and of exerting it repeatedly over short periods of time. It is now known that the muscles of the human body and indeed the muscles of all organisms have the same basic design, consisting of densely packed arrays of contractile elements, and are of approximately the same strength—i.e., they exert the same force per unit volume.[11]

Recent research into the molecular structure of the contractile machinery has shown that each basic working component in the muscle cell is an individual protein molecule consisting of a long tail and a short head rather like an elongated tadpole, and known as a myosin motor. Movement comes about as a result of a sequence of three conformational changes. First, the myosin head attaches itself to another long fibrillar molecule known as actin, indicated as point *a* in diagram 1 below. Second, as shown in 2 below, the head bends suddenly—the power stroke—and this bending causes the myosin molecule and the actin to move in opposite directions. Third, as shown in 3, the head unbends and attaches itself to the actin at point *b*. The sequence is repeated again, and gradually, via a series of small steps, the two molecules slide past each other.

Recent work has also shown that each myosin head moves about 8 nanometers with each power stroke and that the heads are stacked in the

Movement of myosin on actin.

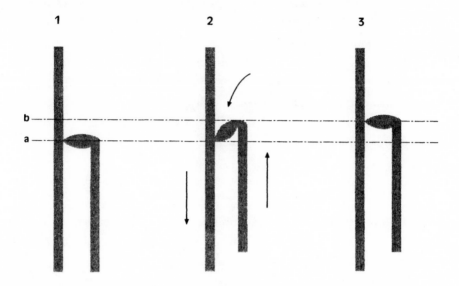

muscle fibrils in a helical conformation about 14 nanometers apart.[12] From consideration of the geometrical constraints consequent on the size and movement of the myosin heads, it is unlikely that further improvement in muscle power could be achieved by increasing the density of packing of the myosin motors.

One hypothetical strategy for increasing the power of muscles might be to envisage increasing the force of the individual power strokes that each myosin head makes as it bends and pushes on the actin fiber. However, recent measurements of the force of an individual power stroke show that this is about 3 piconewtons, and this is already several times greater than the strength of individual weak bonds.[13] Because it is the weak bonds that hold all the cell's constituents together, including the myosin motor and the actin fiber on which it pushes, then it is impossible to increase the force of the power stroke to any significant degree or each stroke would cause damage not only to the myosin motor itself but also to the actin fiber and other delicate components of the contractile machinery.

The movement of muscles is not the only type of biological movement that is based on a sliding fiber design involving a power stroke delivered by a moving head. The same sliding filament system is now known to underlie all biological movement, including the intracellular transport of mitochondria and other organelles in the cytoplasm. (The only biological movement not empowered by the same type of molecular motor is the rotary flagellum system of the bacteria.) The power strokes of the various other types of molecular motors have also been measured, and these are very close to the 3-piconewton level of the myosin motors in mammalian muscle.[14]

Overall, the evidence suggests strongly that, for fundamental reasons, the maximum power stroke of any sort of molecular motor cannot be much greater than it is. And since the packing of the myosin motors in muscle tissue is virtually crystalline and just about as tight as possible, then muscles cannot be designed, on biological principles, to generate any greater degree of power.

If either the tightness of packaging or the power of the motors had to be less for some reason, then organisms of our size and weight would not be feasible, because the muscles would be unable to generate the necessary mechanical forces to lift the body off the ground and hardly any movement of any sort would be possible. As it is, the human body is between 40 and 50 percent muscle, and as every medical student comes to learn when first dissecting the human body at medical school, our limbs are almost entirely composed of muscles. It would be simply impossible to redesign the human body to function with muscles ten times less powerful per unit volume. Indeed, no feasible large terrestrial organisms built on biological principles could be designed to move with muscles ten times less powerful. Even muscles only two or three times less powerful per unit volume would create considerable design problems.

In this context it is interesting to note that the strength of the grip of the human fingers is generated by extrinsic muscles in the forearm and not by the small muscles in the hand itself. Given the existing contractile power of muscle, this placement of the grip muscles in the forearm is not in the least bit gratuitous but of absolute necessity because the muscle bulk necessary to provide the required strength of grip cannot be accommodated in the hand. The fact that it is necessary, even with the strength of muscles as they are, to place the muscle-generating grip in the forearm indicates the tremendous difficulties that would be encountered in attempting to redesign the human frame to handle fire and to inhabit a planet the size of the earth if muscles were even slightly less powerful. It is astonishing that the design of the musculature of the arm of man and even the placement of specific muscle groups can be rationalized to a very large degree from consideration of the force delivered by one individual molecular motor. And it is clear that our existence is critically dependent on that force being almost precisely what it is. Any less, and we would be unable to move; any more, and each power stroke would tear the contractile machinery apart.

It is evident, then, that to make a fire both the power of our muscles and our dimensions must be very close to what they are. A miniature human, one-half or one-third our size, would have considerable difficulty in manipulating logs of more than one kilo in weight. Such a being would be restricted to making fires using small twigs, and whether the heat and sustainability of such fires would have sufficed for the discovery of metals and for the development of metallurgy is open to question. Metallurgy necessitates high temperatures of several hundred degrees.[15] The melting point of gold is 1,064°C, of silver 960°C, of copper 1,083°C, and that of iron 1,535°C. Only tin has a low melting point of 231°C, but tin is far too malleable to be of any great utility in itself for toolmaking.

The strength of muscles is not just relevant to the movement of our limbs and the maintenance of an upright posture. It is muscles which drive the circulation and provide the heart with its ability to pump the blood. It is muscles which move the chest during respiration. If muscles were less powerful, then despite the low viscosity of water, the circulatory system would be impossible. The work of breathing, which necessitates the movement of air through the respiratory passages, is only possible because the density and the viscosity of air is very low. As it is, during periods of maximal ventilation the work of breathing takes up 30 percent of the oxygen consumption of the body. If the power stroke of the myosin motors were somewhat less than it is, it is easy to see that the work of breathing would soon become prohibitive. It is doubtful if any type of large, complex air-breathing organisms would be possible. The circulatory and respiratory systems are only feasible because the viscosity and density of water and air, and the power of the myosin motors, are all very close to what they are.

And this is not all. Not only must the power stroke of each myosin motor exert about the force it does; the energy requirements to drive an individual stroke must also be close to what they are. We have seen that the delivery of oxygen to the human body requires complex adaptations. It is virtually impossible to envisage any sort of radical redesign of either the circulatory or respiratory systems in complex organisms that would double or treble the delivery of oxygen to muscle tissues. As it is, during strenuous activity much of the volume of active muscles is made up of blood capillaries. If the power stroke of molecular motors were only half or a third as efficient—i.e., if it required two or three times more ATP or metabolic energy—then motile complex forms of life would in all probability be impossible.

The Speed of Nerve Conduction

Muscles, no matter how powerful, would be of little biological value unless their movements could be carefully controlled. In the human body the control of muscular movement is carried out by the nervous system.

Catching a ball, rowing a canoe against a current, dodging a wave breaking on the beach, blinking an eye to prevent small objects from impacting on the cornea, handling and manipulating the moving embers in a fire—indeed, manipulating any mobile structures and elements in the environment—all such activities require fast movement and this in turn necessitates rapid reflexes. In an organism the size of a human, rapid movement and reflexes are possible only because the speed of nerve conduction is very rapid. If the maximum possible speed of nerve conduction had been one hundred or one thousand times slower than it is, life as we experience it would be unimaginable and even the simplest of tasks would be full of enormous danger. Constructing and manipulating a fire would be hazardous indeed!

In fact, the speed of nerve conduction imposes an absolute limit on the maximum size that an animal can attain. No animal can be 200 meters long and at the same time nimble. Even at the fastest conduction speeds, in a 200-meter-long organism, a nerve impulse will take four seconds to travel from the brain to its extremities and back.

Among organisms, nerve conduction speeds vary over more than three orders of magnitude, from 10 centimeters per second in simple invertebrates to 120 meters per second along the high-speed myelinated axons in the nervous system of mammals.[16] Consideration of the basic characteristics of nerve impulse propagation suggest that the speed of conduction in the myelinated axons of mammals is close to the maximum possible compatible with the electrical properties and general design of cells. Obviously, fine control and coordination of muscular activity in organisms of our size is only possible because such relatively rapid speeds of nerve impulse conduction are in fact attainable. An organism the size of man could never handle fire or undertake any sophisticated exploration of the world if the maximum speed of nerve conduction was a hundred times less. Indeed, such a creature would probably be unable to think in any way imaginable to us. If nerve conduction speeds were this much lower, only very tiny organisms the size of a protozoan could possess rapid reflexes.

The speed of nerve conduction is itself determined by a number of bio-physical constants, such as the speed of diffusion of sodium and potassium ions across the lipid bilayer membrane. And of course, the existence of the membrane potential is itself inherent in the insulating character of the lipid bilayer that surrounds all animal cells and, as we have seen (in the previous chapter), is the only structure known which is fit to serve as the bounding membrane of the cell.

The Size of Nerve Axons

There is another aspect of the design of the nerve cell which is critical, and that is the diameter of an individual nerve cell axon, or fiber, which carries the nerve signal from the spinal cord to the muscle cell. In man and most mammals the diameter of the high-speed myelinated nerve axons is about 20 microns. Classic physiological studies some decades back showed that the diameter of axons is linearly correlated with conduction velocity up to about 20 microns and that this diameter is optimal for high-velocity con-duction.[17] In fact, this is quite large for a nerve axon because of the layers of myelin—a fatty material—which are wrapped around the axon. But it is still small enough to make it feasible to pack thousands of individual nerve cell axons into a small nerve bundle a few millimeters across—the approxi-mate size of the nerve tracts in the human arm. If individual nerve axons could not be designed to function with diameters as small as 20 microns, the number of nerve axons which could be conveniently carried into the arm would be decreased. If high-speed nerve axons had to be, for some reason, 1 millimeter in diameter instead of 20 microns, then carrying the many thou-sands of axons necessary for the fine motor control of the limbs would ne-cessitate nerve tracts several centimeters in diameter—larger in fact than the limbs themselves. Clearly, the fact that the diameter of the nerve axon can be as small as 20 microns is another critical factor in the design of *Homo sapiens* as important as the necessity for conduction speeds of 120 meters a second!

Without nerve conduction speeds of 120 meters a second, without nerve axons approximately 20 microns in diameter, without molecular motors capable of generating forces of 3 to 5 piconewtons, the whole design of the human musculoskeletal system and our capacity to perform coordinated movements would be impossible. We would not be able to move quickly, if at all, let alone have the strength and capability to construct a fire.

Of course the functioning of the muscular system is also dependent on other adaptations, including the unique characteristics of bone that provide the skeletal framework upon which the muscles work and the unique strength of collagen fibers that form the high-tensile-strength tendons, which transmit the force of muscular contraction throughout the body. An intriguing aspect of the strength of collagen already referred to in chapter 8 is its dependence on the apparently esoteric fact that the amino acid glycine has a very small side group—in fact the simplest possible—consisting of one hydrogen atom that allows the three amino acid helices which form the collagen fiber to twist tightly round each other into a super strong helical cable. Without the very small side group of glycine, the unique super packing of the helices and great tensile strength of collagen could not be achieved, and there is no obvious alternative design to achieve the equivalent strength in a protein fiber. It is an intriguing thought that the functioning of the entire muscular system may be ultimately dependent on the existence of an amino acid with the precise characteristics of glycine.

The Relative Size of Organs

As we have seen, the muscular system necessarily (given the strength of the weak bonds) occupies about 50 percent of the mass of the body. Providing sufficient energy for this muscle mass necessitates in turn a certain mass or volume of tissue devoted to the delivery of adequate amounts of oxygen to the muscles.

In man the proportion of the body that is devoted to the respiratory and circulatory systems is about 20 to 25 percent of the body's volume. Their function is just about as efficient as possible, given the constraints imposed by the solubility of oxygen, the viscosity of water, airway resistance (determined by the density of air), and so forth. It is hard to envisage an organism in which the lungs occupied more than 50 percent of the total volume of the body. Such an organism would be in effect a gigantic air sac! As it is, in many mammals the volume of the respiratory system is already about 50 millimeters for every kilogram of body weight.[18] And in birds, despite the smaller volume of the lungs, the respiratory system as a whole (lungs plus air sacs) occupies an even larger fraction of the total volume of the body.[19] The efficiency of oxygen delivery to muscles could hardly be improved much by increasing the throughput of blood. As we have seen, in highly active muscles much of the volume of the muscles is taken up by the blood capillaries. Increasing the blood volume would only reduce the muscles to a mass of blood capillaries.

Similarly, we have seen that the power generated by muscle per unit of muscle volume can hardly be improved. If efficient oxygen delivery to the muscles had necessitated an oxygen delivery system ten times the weight of the muscle mass, then no large organism would ever have moved. The muscles would be incapable of moving the sheer weight of the oxygen delivery system. Clearly, if a ratio between the mass of muscle and the mass of oxygen delivery system of about 2 to 1 could not have been at least approximately achieved, for whatever reason, then the design not only of man but of all mammals and higher vertebrates would not be feasible.

It is not only the ratio of muscle mass to the mass of the oxygen delivery system which must be very close to what it is. The nervous system, for example, could hardly occupy a volume several times that of muscle. Unless an efficient nervous system could be designed to take up only a fraction of the volume and mass of the muscle, the muscle-nerve ratio would not be fit for life.

It follows that the coherent functioning of the human body and indeed that of all advanced vertebrates is critically dependent on the minimum mass required for the efficient function of each organ system—the circulatory system, the urinary system, the nervous system, the muscular system, and the respiratory system—being very close to what it is. Moreover, the functional efficiency and design of each organ system is largely determined in turn by the laws of nature, by the rate of diffusion of oxygen, by the capacity of transitional metals to reversibly associate with oxygen, by the strength of the weak bonds, by the viscosity of water. If these constants were very slightly different, large complex organisms of design and biology similar to ourselves would be impossible.

Inertia

A further very interesting twist to the deepening teleology in this chain of fortuity is the influence the phenomenon of inertia has on the size and dimensions of man. Inertia is the name we give to the property of things to re-

sist a change in their velocity. An undisturbed body remains at rest and requires the exertion of a force to impart motion to it. A moving car requires
force to slow it down or to make it change direction. Like gravity, inertial
forces are related to mass. It requires more force to make a large object move
or change the direction of its motion than for a small object. The wind may
set a feather in motion but not a boulder.

If inertia had been less, then the wind could well have set a boulder in
motion. In such a world we would be subjected to a continual bombardment by all types of objects in our environment. However, if inertia had
been much greater, then unless the strength of muscles was much greater, we
would have profound difficulty even in starting to move our finger. And
once in motion, control of its direction and speed would be next to impossible. It is clear that the inertia of matter must be very close to what it is for
an animal of our size to function in an environment similar to the earth's.
Extraordinary as it may seem, physicists have proposed that the inertial
forces experienced by objects on the earth are generated by the total combined gravitational attraction of all matter in the cosmos, including the
most distant stars and galaxies. Because most of the matter in the universe is
far from the earth, this means that the greatest contribution to the inertia of
objects on earth is made by the most distant galaxies. As Dennis Sciama
comments in his *Unity of the Universe:*

> The idea that distant matter can sometimes have far more influence than
> nearby matter may be an unfamiliar one. To make it more concrete, we may
> give a numerical estimate of the influence of nearby objects in determining the
> inertia of bodies on the earth: of this inertia, the whole of the Milky Way only
> contributes one ten-millionth, the sun one hundred-millionth, and the earth
> itself one thousand-millionth. . . . In fact, 80 per cent of the inertia of local
> matter arises from the influence of galaxies too distant to be detected by the
> 200-inch telescope.[20]

In a very real sense, then, the existence of beings of our size and mass with
the ability to stand, to move, and to light a fire is only possible because of the
influence of the most distant galaxies, whose collective mass determines the
precise strength of the inertial forces on earth. If this view is correct, then it
means that our existence is critically dependent on both the *mass of the earth*
and the *total mass of the universe* being very close to what they are. There is a
distinct echo in these curious coincidences of the old medieval doctrine of

man the microcosm, which held that the dimensions of the human body reflect in some profound sense the dimensions of the macrocosm.

Alternative to *Homo Sapiens*

It is sometimes claimed that the unique capabilities of *Homo sapiens* could be actualized in a bipedal reptile. This possibility cannot be entirely discounted. However, no known reptile is remotely as intelligent as even a primitive mammal. Moreover, lacking the neocortex of the mammalian brain, the design of the reptilian brain may not permit the evolutionary development of the flexible and adaptable behavior so characteristic of the mammals, especially groups like the primates, cetaceans, and carnivores. Similar constraints may also apply to the evolution of high intelligence in birds. One advantage mammals may possess over reptiles is their highly sensitive skin. This is probably superior to the scaly skin of a reptile for a manipulating device which must be exquisitely sensitive to the texture and form of the objects in its grasp.

Neurological constraints may also mitigate against the evolution of a bipedal marsupial with the cognitive capacities of man. No known marsupial approaches the intelligence of a seal or porpoise. It would appear that the placental mammals have the most advanced brains on earth.

It would seem that no aquatic species could be as fit as *Homo sapiens* to explore and ultimately comprehend the world. The limbs in aquatic vertebrates are adapted for swimming and not suited for grasping and sophisticated manipulative tasks. However, the major problem in envisaging how an intelligent aquatic species could advance and develop a technology is the impossibility of utilizing fire in an underwater environment. And without fire, it is difficult to see how an aquatic organism, no matter how intelligent, could develop a technology or acquire chemical knowledge.

The necessity to derive an alternative humanoid being via a natural evolutionary process imposes additional constraints on the range of possible alternatives. Even if we could specify the design of an intelligent humanoid radically different to man, we might well find that we could not derive it via a plausible evolutionary process. If a computer could be built that was more intelligent than man, this would still not threaten our uniqueness in at least one important sense. The "intelligent computer" would not be a natural form and would not be derivable by natural processes from the materials available on a primitive planetary surface. Even if an intelligent silicon android could be designed, could it be derived by a natural evolutionary process? I suspect the problems would in all probability be insurmountable.

To get from atoms, via molecules, to the cell, and from the cell, via primitive multicellular life forms, to the first mammal, and finally from a primitive mammal to an upright bipedal organism with good eyes, grasping hands, and possessing intelligence and language will surely necessitate a relatively unique evolutionary path. An arboreal stage may be an evolutionary necessity somewhere on the path to *Homo sapiens,* to ensure the development of a grasping hand, high-acuity vision, and perfect coordination between the two. A subsequent terrestrial stage may also have been an evolutionary necessity to ensure the evolution of bipedality.

In a thoughtful analysis of man's evolutionary history and the acquisition of our unique biological adaptations, Sir Julian Huxley concluded:

> Writers have indulged their speculative fancy by imagining other organisms endowed with speech and conceptual thought—talking rats, rational ants, philosophic dogs and the like. But closer analysis shows that these fantasies are impossible. A brain capable of conceptual thought could only have been developed in a human body.[21]

Moreover, as Huxley points out, the evolutionary generation of *Homo sapiens* has come about via a unique path:

> The essential character of man is . . . conceptual thought. And conceptual thought could only have arisen in a multicellular animal, an animal with bilateral symmetry, head and blood system, a vertebrate against a mollusc or an arthropod, a land vertebrate among vertebrates, a mammal among land vertebrates. Finally it could have arisen only in a mammalian line which was gregarious, which produced one young at birth instead of several, and which had recently become terrestrial after a long period of arboreal life.
>
> There is only one group of animals which fulfils these conditions—a terrestrial offshoot of the higher Primates. Thus not merely has conceptual thought been evolved only in man: it could not have been evolved except in man. There is only one path of unlimited progress through the evolutionary maze. The course of human evolution is as unique as its result. It is unique not in the trivial sense of being a different course from that of any other organism, but in the profounder sense of being the only path that could have achieved the essential characters of man. Conceptual thought on this planet is inevitably associated with a particular type of Primate body and Primate brain.[22]

The Human Brain

If the anthropocentric thesis is correct, then the human brain should be the most powerful possible thinking machine—biological or artificial—that can be built out of the atoms of our world. It should be peerless.

As far as biological brains are concerned, unfortunately we still know an insufficient amount about the relationship between intelligence and the structure to be able to judge with any certainty whether or not the human brain represents the most advanced biological brain possible. However, what little knowledge we have seems consistent with the presumption that it is. To begin with, the human brain is one of the biggest in the animal kingdom in terms of the number of neurons it contains and in terms of its gross volume. The brain of a fly is about 1 milligram,[23] small mammals have brains which weigh only a few grams, while the human brain weighs about 1.4 kilograms—more than 1 million times more than that of a fly. Only certain whales, porpoises, and the elephant have larger brains than man.[24] The largest cetacean brain, about 9 kilos (that of the sperm whale) is about six times the size of the human brain, that of an elephant nearly four times larger.[25]

However, brain size alone seems to bear little direct relationship to intelligence. In man, for example, there is no obvious correlation between brain size and intellectual ability.[26] And although the brain of a dolphin may be larger than that of man or any other primate species, its neurons are far simpler and the cortical layer in the dolphin is also only about half the thickness than it is in man.[27] (Moreover, the overall design of the cetacean brain appears to have retained many primitive features.) It seems likely that intelligence is related not only to the sheer size of the brain or number of neurons but to many more subtle factors, including the thickness and convolutions of the cerebral cortex, the complexity of the individual neurons, the density of synaptic connections, and the development of those parts of the cerebral cortex associated with higher integrative functions, such as the frontal lobes. By these criteria the primate brain is the most complex in the animal kingdom.

And among the primates, the human brain is by far the most developed. The human brain is three times larger than that of a chimpanzee and contains absolutely more neurons than any other primate brain and a vastly increased frontal region.[28] Moreover, the neurons in the cortex of humans and other primates are far more complex than those in the cortex of a rat.[29]

Compared with the rat, each neuron in the human brain makes between ten and one hundred times more synaptic connections.[30] Altogether, the human brain contains about 10 million more synapses than the brain of a rat. The compaction of synaptic connections in the human brain is in fact staggering. Each cubic millimeter of the human cortex contains, in addition to 100,000 cells, some 4 kilometers of axonal wiring, 500 meters of dendrites, and close to 1 billion synapses.[31]

If intelligence is related to the total number of nerve cells, the total number of connections between them as well as the density of the connections, then as a recent *New Scientist* article puts it, "on this basis the human brain is the most complex in the animal kingdom." Moreover, as the article continues, "no radical improvement in synaptic density may be possible because of the need to maintain the fine balance between the size and number of neurons and the blood vessels which nourish them. To produce a significant rise in processing power, the axons would have to be wider than they are now to speed up the rate at which they pass signals. This in turn would demand equivalent increases in the amount of insulation along the axons and a better blood supply, which would take up extra space in the brain cavity, leaving less room for axons." As the article puts it, "Humans are about as smart as they are going to get."[32]

The evidence is certainly consistent with the possibility that the human brain does indeed represent the most advanced information-processing device that can be built according to biological principles, that we are indeed "as smart as biological systems can get." It may be that the size of what may be the smartest biological brain, capable of the miracle of understanding the world, is perfectly commensurate with the design and dimensions of the human frame which, as we have seen, is itself wonderfully fit for the exploration and physical manipulation of the world.

Artificial Intelligence

The possibility that the human brain may be the most sophisticated biological brain within the entire realm of carbon-based life naturally raises the far more radical possibility that the human brain may represent the only material form, out of all possible assemblages of atoms, in which genuine cognition and high intelligence can be instantiated, a possibility that would follow from the anthropocentric thesis.

Again, as our knowledge is so preliminary, no final judgment on this issue is possible, but from what we know of the structure and functioning of biological brains, it is not hard to be persuaded that no other alien assemblage of atoms in any other exotic realm of chemistry would come close. To begin with, each one of the basic building blocks of biological brains is a living cell—a veritable molecular microcosm in itself, consisting of a cell body plus a major axon and a vast dendritic tree ending in 100,000 branches. The neuron and its dendritic tree is not a mere frozen network of silicon threads but a living, ever-changing network, learning, reacting, responding, and integrating a vast number of different electronic and chemical signals. In the words of a recent *Nature* reviewer, "The latest work on information processing and storage at the single-cell level reveals previously unimagined complexity and dynamism." We are left with "a feeling of awe for the amazing complexity found in nature. Loops within loops across many temporal and spatial scales."[33]

The enormous problems now being encountered as artificial intelligence (AI) researchers try to create genuinely intelligent computers is consistent with the extreme view—that only in the precise molecular architecture of the human brain can intelligence be instantiated in our world. Although the mechanistic faith in the possibility of AI still runs strong among many researchers in the field, there are also many detractors, including John Searle[34] and Roger Penrose.[35] And there is no doubt that to date, as Penrose argues, no one has manufactured anything which exhibits intelligence remotely resembling that of man.

Final confirmation that the human brain is indeed the most sophisticated thinking machine possible can only come from future advances in the neurosciences and in the field of AI early in the next century. Potential advances that might support the notion could include, for example, evidence that brains built out of biological neurons possess unique properties which cannot be exactly mimicked in nonbiological brains and that self-conscious reflection and genuine cognition is only possible in brains with these particular unique properties. Again, increased knowledge of the various biological design constraints alluded to in the *New Scientist* article cited above could confirm that no further improvements in the information-processing capacity of the human brain is possible. Future research might also reveal that our cognitive abilities are critically dependent on unique neuronal wiring patterns which can only be actualized in the primate brain.

Homo Mathematicus

Our success as a biological species has depended on many factors: on our being smart, on our being terrestrial, on our possessing a body of a dimension and design appropriate to handle fire and explore the environment, on the fitness of the earth's atmosphere to support fire and technological advance. However, there is another intriguing aspect to our success—the mutual fitness of the human mind and particularly its propensity for and love of mathematics and abstract thought and the deep structure of reality, which can be so beautifully represented in mathematical forms. In other words, the logic of our mind and the logic of the cosmos would appear to correspond in a profound way. And it is only because of this unique correspondence that it is possible for us to comprehend the world.

If the laws of nature could not be formulated in simple mathematical terms, it is unlikely that science would have advanced so quickly. It might, in fact, never have advanced at all. The physicist Eugene Wigner, who was much struck by the correspondence between mathematics and the physical world, spoke for many mathematicians and scientists when he remarked:

> It is hard to avoid the impression that a miracle is at work here. . . . The miracle of the appropriateness of the language of mathematics for the formulation of the laws of physics is a wonderful gift which we neither understand nor deserve.[36]

Of course, the fact that nature's laws can be described in mathematical terms is only helpful to minds already fine-tuned for mathematical abstraction. If humans had not had the love and capacity for mathematics and abstract thought, then again no scientific advance would have been possible.

And there are other aspects of the structure of reality which give the impression of having been tailored to facilitate our understanding of nature and ultimately the scientific enterprise itself. On this point Paul Davies comments:

> It is easy to imagine a world in which phenomena occurring at one location in the universe or on one scale of size or energy, were intimately entangled with all the rest in a way that would forbid resolution into simple sets of laws. Or, to use the crossword analogy, instead of dealing with a connected mesh of separately identifiable words; we would have a single extremely complicated word

answer. Our knowledge of the universe would then be an "all or nothing" affair.[37]

That the structure of the world appears to be curiously fit for human comprehension also struck Aristotle. Jonathan Lear comments that for Aristotle "the inquiry into nature revealed the world as meant to be known; the inquiry into man's soul revealed him as a being who is meant to be a knower. *Man and the world are, as it were, made for each other.*[38] (My emphasis.) The stupendous success of science since 1600 is testimony enough to the remarkable fitness of our mind to comprehend the world.

Imperfections

I have argued that the cosmos is fit for only one form of thinking animal—our own species, *Homo sapiens*—and that our biology uniquely equips us with the capacity to comprehend the world. But it does not necessarily follow that the biological design of *Homo sapiens* is ideal or perfect. Such a deduction is unwarranted and in fact absurd. The human body is a wonderfully crafted machine, but its design is not perfect in any absolutist sense.

Our design is constrained due to our evolutionary origin. We suffer spinal problems because the spinal column was not designed originally for an upright stance. Childbirth is painful and difficult in humans because the relative size of the human infant's head at birth is far larger than in the case of any other primate. Because air and food both pass through the same passage; the pharynx, inevitably there is always the possibility of choking. The recurrent laryngeal nerve loops around the aorta and back up to the larynx instead of taking a more direct route.

Moreover, the human body is a material object subject to the laws of nature like everything in the cosmos. And as Plato pointed out, all material objects are imperfect to some degree. Even a geometric form like a triangle can only be imperfectly represented in the world of matter. All material objects from a sand castle to a galaxy are subject to turnover and decay. Nothing lasts forever. And this is true also of the human machine, which ages, runs down, and finally fails at death. The genetic system is a wonderful contrivance, but like all such complex systems, artificial or natural, errors inevitably occur and genetic disease is the result. Similarly, the same tectonic activity that ensures the recycling of the elements also causes earthquakes and volcanoes which are at times massively destructive to life. The cosmos may be uniquely fit for life on earth, but this does not mean that it is so crafted to ensure that every individual living organism will exist in a nirvanalike state of absolute contentment and plenty.

The fact that individuals suffer pain, that individuals die, may raise all manner of questions for a religious believer, but these have no relevance to the fitness of the cosmos for *Homo sapiens* as a biological species. Such imperfections are inevitable in a material world of flux and change. We cannot be material and immortal. The central mystery of human existence is not whether we are here by design but why the design, by its very material and transitory nature, inevitably entails suffering and death. Blake touched on the same enigma when he asked of the tiger, "Did He who make the lamb make thee?"

Conclusion

The evidence that the laws of nature are fit for only one unique thinking being capable of acquiring knowledge and ultimately comprehending the cosmos may not be compelling, but it is eerily suggestive. Is it really just a coincidence that what may well be the most advanced possible biological brain possesses sufficient insight and intelligence to comprehend the world; that a biological brain capable of such feats need not be so large that it would require a clumsy elephantine quadruped to house it, but is of a size fit for an organism of the design and dimensions close to *Homo sapiens*; that this physical design is itself so fit for the manipulation of fire, the key to technology and knowledge; that the muscles provide sufficient power to move the body and limbs; that the speed of nerve conduction is fast enough to permit rapid coordinated movement; that the diameter of the highest-velocity nerve fibers is small enough to efficiently wire the musculature of the body; that a planet of the size of the earth is fit both for a bipedal primate of our size and dimensions and also for an atmosphere capable of supporting fire? The chain of coincidences underlying our existence, our ability to make fire, to develop technology, and ultimately to comprehend the cosmos, is simply too long and the appearance of contrivance too striking.

There is diminishing room in the cosmos for the fantastic alternatives of science fiction. If we want to build out of the matter of the cosmos a creature of understanding, a being possessing the defining characteristics of our species—high intelligence, the capacity to manipulate and investigate the environment with a highly developed visual capacity, the capacity for language and abstract thought, to make fire, to use metals, to do science, and to have power over the natural world, and so on—we will be led via a long chain of fortuity or mutual fitness in the nature of things to an air-breathing vertebrate of about our size and dimensions, and eventually to a gregarious mammal with a highly developed visual sense and endowed with a hand— in other words, toward one unique end—*Homo sapiens.* Moreover, such a being can only come to understand the cosmos, to use fire, make metal tools, and develop a technology on a planet of about the size and characteristics of the earth, with an atmosphere containing between about 12 to 20 percent oxygen, sufficient to sustain a fire and to support oxidative metabolism in advanced, active air-breathing organisms.

What is so striking is that the cosmos appears to be not just supremely fit for our being and for our biological adaptations, but also for our understanding. Our watery planetary home, with its oxygen-containing environment, the abundance of trees and hence wood and hence fire, is wonderfully fit to assist us in the task of opening nature's door. Moreover, being on the surface of a planet rather than in its interior or in the ocean gives us the privilege to gaze into the sky to see the Milky Way. Because of the position of our solar system on the edge of the galactic rim, we can gaze farther into the night to distant galaxies and gain knowledge of the overall structure of the cosmos. Were we positioned in the center of a galaxy, we would never look on the beauty of a spiral galaxy nor would we have any idea of the structure of our universe. We might never have seen a supernova or understood the mysterious connection between the stars and our own existence.

Part 2

EVOLUTION

Chapter   12

The   Tree   of   Life

In which the possibility is considered that the origin of carbon-
based life and the whole subsequent process of organic evolution on
earth has been the result of an immense built-in generative
program. The concept of the tree of life as a natural form whose
evolutionary development was directed and determined by natural
law was familiar to many nineteenth-century biologists. It is
pointed out that DNA is remarkably fit for directed evolution. The
possibility that the direction of evolution may have been partly the
result of an emergent spontaneously generated order as proposed by
Stuart Kauffman is also considered. Also discussed is the growing
consensus that the origin of carbon-based life is built into the laws
of nature and that carbon-based life is therefore inevitable on any
planetary surface where conditions permit it. It is hard to envisage
how life could have originated unless there exist generative laws to
guide a series of self-replicating systems from chemistry to the cell.
The point is also made that, if life's origin is built in, then it is hard
to dismiss the possibility that the whole tree of life may also be built
in. Evidence consistent with the possibility of direction includes the
phenomenon of parallel evolution, the uniformity of molecular
evolution, the speed of molecular evolution, and the rapidity
of the major morphological transitions.

The tree of life, drawn up by Ernst Haeckel in 1866.

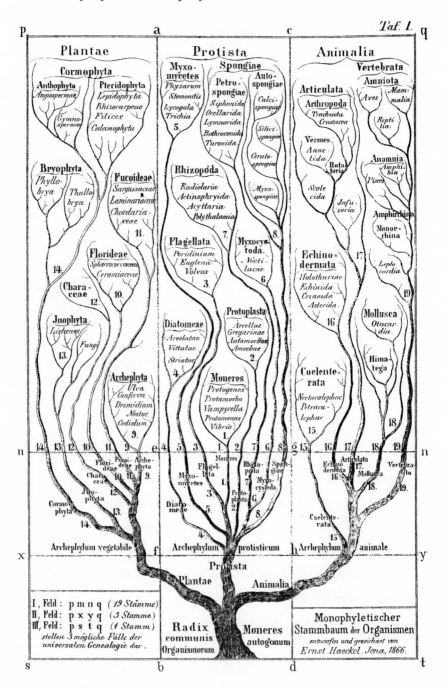

The affinities of all the beings of the same class have sometimes been represented by a great tree. I believe this simile largely speaks the truth. The green and budding twigs may represent existing species. . . . At each period of growth all the growing twigs have tried to branch out on all sides. . . . The limbs divided into great branches and these into lesser and lesser branches, were themselves once, when the tree was young, budding twigs. . . . From the first growth of the tree, many a limb and branch has decayed and dropped off; and those fallen branches of various sizes may represent those whole orders and families which have no living representatives, and which are known to us only in a fossil state. . . . As buds give rise by growth to fresh buds . . . so by generation I believe it has been with the great Tree of Life, which fills with its dead and broken branches the crust of the earth, and covers the surface with its ever-branching and beautiful ramifications.

—Charles Darwin, *On the Origin of Species,* 1859

Nearly everyone is familiar with the story of life on earth from its first primeval stirrings in the ancient Paleozoic ocean to its gradual flowering over the past 4 billion years into many exotic and diverse types of life. From the first simple photosynthetic autotrophs—blue-green algae, which as far as we can tell appeared shortly after the formation of the oceans and thrived in the original anoxic atmosphere—it took more than 3 billion years before sufficient oxygen had accumulated in the atmosphere to support more complex multicellular forms of life. Evolution had to wait until the early Cambrian era, a mere 600 million years ago, before multicellular life forms finally emerged in an explosion of diversity. In a very short period of time, perhaps no more than 25 million years, all the major groups of life were generated, an event we now call the Cambrian Explosion. In the early Paleolithic seas appeared the first representatives of the vertebrates, molluscs, annelid worms, arthropods, echinoderms, and so on. During this short period of time the tree of life underwent a great and never-to-be-repeated burst of creative growth, sprouting all its main branches that were subsequently to grow more sedately down through the geological eras to the present day. Since that great explosion, while the continents formed and re-formed over the past 500 million years, one branch of the tree, which was merely an inauspicious twig in the Cambrian seas, was to flower spectacularly, and to ultimately overshadow all other branches, generating a unique and diverse assemblage of large life forms both aquatic and terrestrial, including such familiar terrestrial forms as dinosaurs and mammals. And it was from one of the mammalian twigs of this great vertebrate branch that in the very latest stages of the drama the human species was born.

As the basic outlines of the story were gradually worked out in the first decades of the nineteenth century, it became increasingly apparent that all the past and present forms of life on earth could be arranged into a vast evolutionary tree. Consequently, it became the major goal of biology to provide an explanation of how this remarkable progression of life forms had come about. Eventually, Darwin's theory of natural selection would come to dominate. But before 1859, and even for a considerable period after the publication of the *Origin,* as Neal Gillespie in his *Charles Darwin and the Problem of Creation* points out, "most explanations invoked some sort of design."[1]

The *Vestiges* and Directed Evolution

An interesting early attempt to provide a comprehensive account of the evolution of life as a process directed by natural law was presented by Robert Chambers in his famous *Vestiges of the Natural History of Creation,* published in 1840 and one of the best-selling books of its day. Chambers proposed that the whole pattern of evolution had been written into the cosmic script from the beginning and that all the laws of nature had been specially arranged or programmed at the original creation to generate the tree of life.

Chambers's view of evolution is worth recounting in some detail because it represents one of the most important attempts in the early nineteenth century to formulate a completely naturalistic interpretation of evolution. Moreover, Chambers's aim to account for evolution by natural law and his view of the tree of life as a natural form correspond closely to the view being presented here. Reviewing critically the creationist position which was the orthodox view in the early nineteenth century, he comments:

> In what way was the creation of animated beings effected? The ordinary notion may, I think, be not unjustly described as this—that the Almighty author produced the progenitors of all existing species by some sort of personal or immediate exertion. . . . How can we suppose an immediate exertion of this creative power at one time to produce zoophytes, another to add a few marine molluscs, another to bring in one or two conchifers again to produce crustaceous fishes. . . . This would surely be to take a very mean view of the creative power—to, in short, anthropomorphise it, or reduce it to some such character as that borne by the ordinary proceedings of mankind. . . .
>
> Some other idea must then be come to with regard to *the mode* in which the Divine Author proceeded in the organic creation. . . . We have seen powerful evidence, that the construction of this globe and its associates, and inferentially of all the other globes of space, was the result not of any immediate or personal exertion on the part of the Deity, but of natural laws which are expressions of his will. . . . More than this, the fact of the cosmical arrangements being an effect of natural law, is a powerful argument for the organic arrangements being so likewise, for how can we suppose that the august Being who brought all these countless worlds into form by the simple establishment of a natural principle flowing from his mind, was to interfere personally and specially on every occasion when a new shell-fish or reptile was to be ushered into

existence on *one* of these worlds? Surely the idea is too ridiculous to be for a moment entertained.[2]

In Chambers's view the "Divine attributes must appear not diminished or reduced in any way by supposing a creation by law, but infinitely exalted." Chambers continues:

If the properties adopted by the elements at the moment of their creation adapted themselves beforehand to the infinity of complicated useful purposes which they have already answered, and may still further to answer, under many such dispensations of the material world, such an aboriginal constitution, so far from superseding an intelligent agent, would only exalt our conceptions of the consummate skill and power that could comprehend such an infinity of future systems, in the original groundwork of his creation.[3]

Chambers saw the origin of life as being analogous to crystallization:

Crystallisation is confessedly a phenomenon of inorganic matter; yet the simplest rustic observer is struck by the resemblance which the examples of it left upon a window by the frost bear to vegetable forms. In some crystallisations the mimicry is beautiful and complete; for example, in the well known one called the *Arbor Dianae*. An amalgam of four parts of silver and two of mercury being dissolved in nitric acid, and water equal to thirty weights of the metals being added, a small piece of soft amalgam of silver suspended in the solution quickly gathers to itself the particles of the silver of the amalgam which form upon it a crystallisation precisely resembling a shrub. . . . Vegetable figures are also presented in some of the most ordinary appearances of the electric fluid. . . . The correspondence here is curious. A plant thus appears as a thing formed on the basis of a natural electrical operation—*the bush* realized.[4]

Chambers was led from his deterministic evolutionary model of the universe to the view that all reality, biological and physical, was in the end one immense interconnected Divine artifact.[5]

One of the most fascinating insights in Chambers's *Vestiges* is the author's analogy between embryology—the development of the individual from an egg cell—and phylogeny—the development of individual species from an original progenitor. This very obvious similarity was taken up by evolutionary biologists later in the nineteenth century and used by biologists such as

Ernst Haeckel as evidence for the fact of evolution, and as a basis for the famous and now discredited law—ontology recapitulates phylogeny.

However, Chambers uses the analogy for a different purpose, one of far deeper significance and one that has subsequently been ignored. Chambers is claiming in effect that the growth of the tree of life is analogous to the growth during development of an individual organism, that the tree of life is in fact a sort of super organism which has grown under the direction of laws of nature that are every bit as determining as those which govern the growth of the individual organism.

Chambers also believed that life existed on many other planets, and, being the product of the same life generating laws as on Earth, it would closely resemble life on Earth.[6]

Chambers's views of the origin of life have a remarkably modern feel, especially in light of the news from Mars. If life arose rapidly on both Earth and on Mars shortly after the planets were formed, as the NASA report implies, then the process can certainly be thought of in Chambers's terms as being analogous to crystallization. And if the origin of life, that is, the transition from chemistry to the cell (biochemical evolution) is programmed into the laws of nature, then why not also the transition from the cell to man (biological evolution) as well. The deduction seems eminently plausible.

The *Vestiges* was mercilessly attacked by the Victorian scientific establishment. As Gavin de Beer puts it in his introduction to a recent reprint of the first 1844 edition: "Adam Sedgwick is on record as saying 'from the bottom of my heart I loathe and detest the Vestiges' and he went on to devote 90 pages of the Edinburgh Review to vent his spleen on it. Huxley also pilloried *Vestiges* unmercifully as 'pretentious nonsense,' 'foolish fancies,' and said that the author knew no more science than can be picked up by reading some popular science journal."[7]

The fact remains, however, that although in de Beer's words: "Chambers's biology was poor, even by contemporary standards. . . [he] had constructed an argument of a forest of loose ends for the erection of a system. . . . It was an incredible amalgam of sound ideas and gratuitous blunders."[8] Nonetheless, read in the light of today's knowledge of cosmology and molecular biology, it has a remarkably modern feel. The *Vestiges* is one of the most remarkable cases of how, in Gavin de Beer's words, "the amateur like Robert Chambers can see a wood, although his detail of the trees may be wrong; the expert will only accept the wood after testing tree by tree."[9]

The basic idea of the *Vestiges* is so immensely attractive that it has simply refused to die. The idea that behind the apparently random ramifications of the evolutionary tree there is direction imposed by the order of nature has been reiterated over and over again since 1844. One of the most recent examples is in Arthur Koestler's *Ghost in the Machine:*

> Several eminent biologists have in recent years toyed with the idea, but without spelling out its profound implications. Thus von Bertalanffy wrote: 'While fully appreciating modern selection theory we nevertheless arrive at an essentially different view of evolution. It appears to be not a series of accidents, the course of which is determined only by the change of environments during earth history and the resulting struggle for existence, which leads to selection within a chaotic material of mutations . . . but is governed by definite laws, and we believe that the discovery of these laws constitutes one of the most important tasks of the future.' Waddington and Hardy have both re-discovered Goethe's notion of archetypical forms; Helen Spurway concluded from the evidence of homology that the organism has only 'a restricted mutational spectrum' which 'determines its possibilities of evolution.'. . .[10]
>
> [Such restrictions may mean that] given the conditions on our particular planet, the chemistry and temperature of its atmosphere, and the available energies and building materials, life from its inception in the first blob of living slime could only progress in a limited number of ways. . . . If this conclusion is correct, it sheds some additional light on man's status in this universe. It puts an end to the fantasies of science fiction regarding future forms of life on earth. . . . [It means]. . . that the evolution of life is a game played according to fixed rules which limit its possibilities but leave sufficient scope for limitless variations. The rules are inherent in the structure of living matter.[11]

Koestler, like Chambers, is viewed with suspicion by the orthodox academic community—another amateur who would presume to tell the professionals something about evolution. Gould pointedly refers to Koestler as a "nonscientist" in a recent review,[12] and Richard Dawkins refers to him pejoratively in the *Blind Watchmaker* as "another distinguished man of letters who could not abide what he saw as the implications of Darwinism."[13] Perhaps, however, even today amateurs may be able to see a "wood" where professionals only see the individual trees.

The idea of directed evolution was popular particularly among paleontologists in the late nineteenth and early twentieth centuries. Just how popular such ideas were is stressed by Bernhard Rensch in his *Evolution Above the Species Level.* Evidence for direction was seen in many phenomena, including parallelism and long-term evolutionary trends. The Russian zoologist and paleontologist Lev S. Berg, for example, believed that the variation of characters in an evolutionary lineage is confined within certain limits, that it follows a "definite course, like an electric current moving along a wire."[15] As evidence for direction in the course of evolution, Berg cited the evolution of plants from the simple mosses through the ferns to the conifers. During this evolutionary sequence a very clear long-term trend is manifested which involves the continual reduction of the sexual form of the plant (the gametophyte). This sexual form is most prominent in the mosses, where the gametophyte is a small self-supporting plant, while in the conifers it is reduced to a few cells.[16] Berg saw evidence for directed evolution in the many long-term evolutionary trends manifested in many vertebrate lineages. As examples, he cited the gradual ossification of the vertebral column, a reduction in the number of bones in the skull, and the transformation of a two-chambered heart into a three- and four-chambered organ associated with a corresponding increase in the complexity of the circulatory system.[17]

The Problem of Direction

A primary difficulty with all such notions of directed evolution, especially in the nineteenth century, was that the *known* laws of nature were not evidently biocentric in any obvious way. Although Chambers cites Whewell's Bridgewater Treatise as providing evidence of nature's biocentricity, the only significant evidence presented by Whewell was the thermal properties of water! Why, if the *known* laws were not obviously biocentric, should there be all manner of *unknown* laws which, according to Chambers in the *Vestiges,* were responsible for directing the course of evolution?

In the nineteenth century there was simply not the slightest justification for viewing the cosmos as biocentric in any way or life on earth as anything other than an inconsequential peripheral thing and certainly not in the least predestined in the order of things. The prevailing view of the cosmos as fundamentally nonbiocentric, governed by lifeless mechanical laws, is strikingly conveyed in this section from Hugh Miller's *Footprints of the Creator* published in 1849:

Nature lay dead in a waste theatre of rock, vapour, and sea, in which the insensate laws, chemical, mechanical, and electric, carried on their blind, unintelligent processes: the creative fiat went forth; and, amid waters that straightaway teemed with life in its lower forms, vegetable and animal, the dynasty of the fish was introduced.[18]

The cosmos of nineteenth-century science, even seen through religious eyes, bore no evidence of a biocentric design. Rather than being "life-giving," the laws of nature are unintelligent, blind, mechanical. There is even a hint of the *sinister* in the descriptive terms used.

The worldview of nineteenth-century science, in which biology was an unnecessary contingent phenomenon divorced from physics, had no room or rationale for providential evolution or biogenic laws. Owen, Lyell, Mivart, Gray, and the many other leading biologists who opposed the Darwinian model and postulated a providential design were simply being true to the tradition of English natural theology. In rejecting the concept of a contingent biology, they were affirming the faith in the wholeness of the cosmos and the connectedness of all things, in an ultimate biocentricity for which they had no convincing evidence. Like Roger Cotes in his introduction to Newton's *Principia,* they were again affirming a faith for which neither nature nor science provided any justification. Their belief in directed evolution was, as Neal Gillespie points out in his *Charles Darwin and the Problem of Creation,* in effect an article of "faith held despite what nature indicated."[19] Even St. George Mivart, one of the most ferocious critics of Darwinism, conceded in his *Genesis of Species* (1871) "that one could not find in nature such evidence of design that no man could sanely deny."[20]

But perhaps an even more fundamental problem facing the proponents of directed evolution was the complete absence of any idea how the supposed "design or direction" could have been executed. Biological knowledge was simply too rudimentary. Neither Chambers nor any other advocate of directed evolution were able to provide any sort of detailed explanation of how precisely the direction of evolution might have come about.[21] If there were undiscovered laws of evolution, no one could imagine how they could be executed.

Compounding the problem was the additional challenge, to all evolutionary theories both directed and undirected, that at a gross morphological level the organic world appears to be markedly discontinuous. There are in-

numerable examples of complex organs and adaptations which are not led up
to by any known or even, in some cases, conceivable series of feasible intermediates. In the case, for example, of the flight feather of a bird, the amni-
otic egg, the bacterial flagellum, the avian lung, no convincing explanation
of how they could have evolved gradually has ever been provided.[22] The
morphological discontinuities and especially organs or adaptations of extreme
complexity, exhibiting what Michael Behe terms "irreducible complexity,"[23]
have, ever since Darwin, provided ammunition for special creationists who
have claimed that these "morphological gaps" could not have been closed
gradually by natural evolutionary processes and that they represent *prima
facie* evidence for Divine intervention in the course of nature.

The Fitness of DNA for Directed Evolution

Today the whole situation with regard to the possibility of directed evolution has been dramatically transformed. There is first the growing evidence,
presented in the previous chapters, that the laws of nature, rather than being
as they were viewed in the nineteenth century as insensate, mechanical, and
lifeless, give every impression of having been preordained for life as it exists
on earth. The concept of directed evolution is therefore no longer an anomaly in a nonbiocentric world. On the contrary, it is merely a logical deduction from a rapidly emerging new teleological worldview. Second, there is
the revolutionary new DNA world revealed by modern genetics, the world
of the genes, a world undreamt of in the nineteenth and early twentieth centuries. And it is a world which provides the basis for relatively detailed and
plausible speculation as to how the whole pattern of evolution might have
been written into the DNA script from the beginning.

We have already seen that every living organism is specified in a precisely
determined way by a set of instructions encoded in the sequence of bases in
its DNA. The fact that all living organisms are now known to be specified in
the linear DNA sequence consisting of a string of several thousand genes has
provided science with a new and utterly different representation of the organic world. These discoveries imply that not only is DNA remarkably fit
for its hereditary role, it is also remarkably fit in a number of different ways
for directed evolution.

One important consequence of the new molecular biological picture of
nature has been the establishment of the principle that biological informa-

Genotypic and phenotypic space.

DNA sequence/genotypic space		Morphological/phenotypic space
DNA	⟶	Protein
Genes	⟶	Organism
Genotype	⟶	Phenotype
Linear DNA space	⟶	3-D morphological space

tion flows in only one direction (see above), from the genes or DNA to the organism, never in the reverse direction. This is known as the central dogma. This unidirectional flow of information from DNA to organism is clearly "fit" for directed evolution. In a world where the central dogma did not hold, where the genetic system was designed on different principles, where, for example, organisms had the ability to intelligently manipulate their DNA sequences at will, or where environmental factors could direct changes in DNA sequences, where information flowed from organism to DNA, it is very difficult to imagine how a long-term evolutionary program based on a programmed succession of changes in the DNA could have been feasible.

The Closeness of All Life in DNA Sequence Space

Over the past twenty years a vast number of DNA sequences drawn from many different species have been determined. The number of known sequences is growing exponentially as sequencing methods continually improve. By the end of the century much of the DNA sequence of the human genome will be determined. Already many large sections of the human genome have been sequenced and the DNA sequence of many regions of the genomes of other mammalian species, such as the chimpanzee, mouse, rat, and cow, have also been determined. In the case of certain microorganisms, the entire sequence has already been determined.

One of the most surprising discoveries which has arisen from DNA sequencing has been the remarkable finding that the genomes of all organisms are clustered very close together in a tiny region of DNA sequence space forming a tree of related sequences that can all be interconverted via a series of tiny incremental natural steps. So the sharp discontinuities, referred to above, between different organs and adaptations and different types of organisms, which have been the bedrock of antievolutionary arguments for the past century, have now greatly diminished at the DNA level.

Organisms which seem very different at a morphological level can be very close together at the DNA level. One of the most dramatic cases of this is that of the cichlid fish species in Africa's Lake Victoria. As Jared Diamond points out in *The Rise and Fall of the Third Chimpanzee:*

> Cichlids are popular aquarium species, of which about two hundred are confined to that one lake, where they evolved from a single ancestor within the last 200,000 years. Those two hundred species differ among themselves in their food habits as much as do tigers and cows. Some graze on algae, others catch other fish, and still others variously crush snails, feed on plankton, catch insects, nibble the scales off other fish, or specialise in grabbing fish embryos from brooding mother fish. Yet all those Lake Victoria cichlids differ from each other on the average by about 0.4% of their DNA studied.[24]

Another example is the very great similarity of the DNA sequences in the human and chimpanzee genomes. In fact, extensive comparisons of long sections of the DNA of man and chimpanzee show that the differences are extraordinarily trivial. Human and chimpanzee DNA sequences differ on average at only one base in a hundred. As far as we can tell, not only are the DNA sequences virtually identical, but every gene identified in the human genome has its counterpart in the chimpanzee genome. So all the morphological differences between man and chimpanzee, involving the form and relative shape of the limbs, the genital organs, sperm morphology, etc., *and all the mental differences* are generated from DNA sequences which are virtually identical. The distance between man and chimp which seems so significant and obvious at a gross morphological level is trivial in DNA sequence space. In fact, the differences between the DNA of man and chimp can be accounted for by simple well-known mutational processes which are occurring all the time in nature at present. In the case of primate DNA, for example, all the sequences in the hemoglobin gene cluster in man, chimp, gorilla, gibbon, etc., can be interconverted via single base change steps to form a perfect evolutionary tree relating the higher primates together in a system that looks as natural as could be imagined. There is not the slightest indication of any discontinuity. Indeed, human and chimpanzee DNA are closer together than the DNA sequences of many so-called sibling species of the fruit fly drosophila, that is, species which are almost indistinguishable in morphological characteristics.

Even more remarkable is the fact that the genetic programs underlying the development of most of the major metazoan phyla, such as the vertebrates, arthropods, and molluscs, which appear so far apart in terms of their fundamental body plan and morphology, are not so far apart in DNA sequence space as might be imagined. As Simon Conway Morris comments, "The story emerging from molecular biology is that what may look very different in anatomical terms can be founded on a basically identical genetic architecture."[25] In the case of organs as dissimilar as the heart in insects and vertebrates, for example, their development may involve common pathways.[26] In short, evolution is far easier to conceive of in DNA sequence space than in morphological or phenotypic space. By analogy, it is far simpler to move from mountain to mountain on a two-dimensional map than it is to move from mountain to mountain in actual three-dimensional space.

From the DNA perspective the whole evolutionary tree of life is in essence nothing more or less than a vast set of closely related DNA sequences clustered close together in the immensity of DNA sequence space, where each individual sequence is capable of specifying a viable life form, and where all sequences are interrelated and ultimately derivable via a series of steps from an original primeval sequence, which was the genome of the first life form on earth.

Escape from Selective Surveillance

DNA sequence space is fit for directed evolution in another important way. Unlike evolutionary change at a morphological level, where it is only possible to move from one adaptation to another through functional intermediates, in DNA sequence space it is possible to move at least hypothetically from one adaptation (position) to another in DNA space via functionless or meaningless intermediate sequences.

This is because a DNA sequence does not have to be functional to survive and be passed on through the generations. In fact, the greater part of all the DNA in nearly all the cells in higher organisms, although it is copied faithfully at each cell division, is never expressed. The genes, for example, specifying the development of the embryo, while present in all the cells of adult humans, are never expressed. These genes may be thought of as being "cryptic" in the adult. It is very easy to imagine how an evolving DNA sequence might be passed silently down through several generations before being expressed. Crucially, while in "evolutionary transit," such DNA sequences are not under any selective surveillance. The fact that DNA sequences can persist and be transmitted over many generations while suffering continuous mutational change which is not subject to selectionist surveillance means that new sequences and hence new evolutionary innovations can be generated, at least hypothetically, via functionless intermediates. Thus, new organs and structures that cannot be reached via a series of functional morphological intermediates can still be reached by change in DNA sequence space.

Overall, the new DNA sequence space is fit for directed evolution in a number of ways: (1) because of the closeness of all life forms at the DNA level and because all known sequences can be interconverted in small natural steps via well-known mutational processes, (2) because information flows only from the genotype to the phenotype, and (3) because functional DNA sequences can be derived via functionless intermediates, a new phenotype or organ system can be generated by saltation.

Directed Mutation and Development

That genes can direct biological change through time is evidenced in the process of development. The development of a complex organism is specified by a genetic program which contains a set of instructions that are deciphered by the organism as development proceeds. One set of instructions may provide information to make a red blood cell, while another may provide information for the laying down of a precise pattern of neuronal connections in the brain. The reading of each set of instructions involves the expression of different genes at different times and places in the embryo. What we have in effect is a fantastic process of biological change from an egg cell to an adult human, from a caterpillar to a butterfly, and in the case of some parasitic life cycles a whole succession of different larval forms, some of which are so dissimilar that for many years it was suspected that they were different species. These changes, directed by the genes, are in many cases quite as dramatic as those changes which occurred during the course of evolution. If genes can direct developmental changes, there is no reason why, at least in principle, they cannot also direct evolutionary change.

During development of an organism from egg to adult form, a variety of genetically programmed gene rearrangements are known to occur. These include, for example, the development of the immune system, where gene segments which are separate within the germ line are somatically rearranged to bring them into new functional relationships. Another example is the insertion of mobile sections of DNA known as transposons, which can change the expression of adjacent genes. In a well-known case in the bacterium *Salmonella typhimurium*, an inversion of the DNA sequence can switch the expression of one gene to another, a change which results in changes to the antigenic properties of the cell. Many other types of programmed genomic reorganization are utilized during development in different species.[27]

These rearrangements are strictly programmed and occur at precisely predetermined times in the development of the organism. There is no compelling reason why similar types of changes could not have been genetically programmed to occur during the far longer time course of evolution. Although most of us have been brought up to be skeptical of any sort of directed evolution, there is no doubt that the analogy here is striking and suggestive. Consider that, first, most genetic change underlying evolution, especially in higher organisms, has been largely a matter of the rearrangement of preexisting genes rather than the emergence of new genes; and second, we know that cells do measure the passage of time during development and count the number of cell divisions that have elapsed since a particular developmental event. So it is premature to reject out of hand the possibility that during the course of evolution specific preprogrammed genetic rearrangements have occurred at specific times.

Directed Sequential Change

Directed sequential change in DNA sequences could conceivably come about from the integration of a host of different genetic and mutational phenomena. The rate and pattern of evolutionary change in DNA sequences is known to be influenced by the sequence itself. Studies of the influence of the local sequence environment in primate DNA, for example, has revealed biases of varying magnitude in the rate of evolutionary substitution of the same base pair in different sequences. The DNA sequences in all organisms are subject to compositional constraints that affect both coding and noncoding sequences, and these largely determine the types of substitution that occur.[28] The proportion of the two base pairs, A-T and C-G, in DNA varies considerably between species and between different regions in the genome in any one species. These variations in sequence can be explained by directional mutational pressure and selective constraints which are inherent in the genome itself.[29]

During the late seventies and early eighties it became apparent that the genomes of nearly all organisms contain so-called gene families, which consist of multiple identical copies of the same gene. Surprisingly, these copies are often identical not only within the genome of one individual but in the genomes of all the individuals in the species. A variety of genetic mechanisms have been identified which act to maintain the sequential *identity between all the copies of the same gene in any one species*. In the early eighties Cambridge geneticist Gabriel Dover suggested that the integrated effect of these various internal mechanisms is potentially capable of causing synchronous genetic changes in all the members of a population. He termed the effect "molecular drive."[30]

It is relatively easy to envisage how such processes could be utilized by a grand instructional program to bring about cohesive directional mutational change during evolution.

Constraints in Sequence Space

Another conceivable mechanism by which evolution could have been directed along highly specific trajectories in the DNA space is if the DNA sequence space had been ingeniously contrived so that it contained preordained, highly restricted, or even unique functional paths. Consequently, an organism at any point on one of these preordained trajectories would have only a few alternative functional pathways available through DNA space.[31] If only certain routes through DNA space are possible, it is relatively easy to explain how directed evolution might have occurred by relatively conventional and quite natural mechanisms. In fact, because of their fundamental nature, living systems are ideally suited to search out the permissible trajectories. Given that living organisms are inevitably subject to mutational changes, and given also that all living things are inevitably also subject to changing environments, which in turn impose ever-changing selection pressures, then it is clear that living systems are in fact compelled to test the DNA space in their immediate neighborhood for trajectories which facilitate their survival.

In short, if indeed a tree of life consisting of a unique branching pattern of permissible or functional trajectories had been written into the DNA space, just so long as islands of function are within short mutational distances, the very nature of living things as self-replicating biochemical automata, subject to mutational change at each replicative cycle and subject to changing survival pressures as their environments gradually change, will inevitably lead to the successive discovery of these preexisting islands of biological function and to the gradual tracing out of the main branches of earth's great tree of life.

Given the fundamental nature of organisms, and given a specially prearranged DNA sequence space, the evolutionary process of tracing out the tree of life becomes a perfectly natural phenomenon; the inevitable unfolding of a preordained pattern, written into the laws of nature from the beginning.

To be viable such a tree would certainly necessitate a very special distribution of biological functions within DNA space. The functional trajectories through DNA space would have to be highly ordered, so that at the base of the tree, where the evolutionary search begins, are clustered functional DNA sequences specifying very simple unicellular plants (autotrophs) from which can be reached, in easy mutational steps, some way up the main trunk, slightly more complex organisms, including simple animals, and so on, as the mutational process reaches upward into new regions in the DNA space. Further, all the life forms recruited as the tree grows would have to be co-adapted and functionally interrelated. In other words, any *interconnected network* of functional islands is insufficient to make a viable tree. Permissible trajectories through DNA space must be preprogrammed so that as the branches of the tree are traced out, a succession of ecologically feasible systems forming a succession of integrated biospheres is generated.

Note in the context of constraints the distinction between directed and undirected evolution begins to blur. Everyone agrees there must be at least some sequential constraints on the types of changes permissible in DNA. Sequential changes are bound therefore to be "directed to some degree." The key issue is the question of the severity of the constraints. If they are very severe, then in effect they are bound to direct evolutionary change along restricted paths. For the teleologist such paths would be preordained in the nature of things; for the Darwinist they are merely contingent.

Other Sources of Direction

In addition to directed mutational processes acting within DNA sequence space, there are other possible sources of evolutionary direction. One source may be the emergent self-organizing phenomena discussed by Stuart Kauffman in his recent book *At Home in the Universe* [32] and in his previous book, *The Origins of Order*. [33] Such phenomena may be responsible for or related in some way to the deeply embedded morphological rules that British biologist Brian Goodwin believes may govern and constrain biological form. [34]

Kauffman's research involves the use of computers to simulate the behavior of complex systems and is basically directed at looking for those biogenic laws that eluded the biologists in the nineteenth century and which might determine the emergence of evolutionary innovations, the general direction of evolution, and the overall pattern of life on earth. According to Kauffman, "we are not precluded from the possibility that many features of organisms are profoundly robust" and that "deep and beautiful laws may govern the emergence of life and the population of the biosphere.

"We can never hope to predict the exact branches of the tree of life but we can uncover powerful laws that predict and explain their general shape. I hope for such laws. I even dare to hope that we can begin to sketch some of them now." [35] If Kauffman is right, his work may have provided the first definite glimpse of key emergent self-organizing processes which have driven and constrained evolutionary change along restricted paths.

Brian Goodwin also believes that the basic form of the tree of life was determined by natural law. He has recently proposed that "all the main morphological features of organisms—hearts, brains, guts, limbs, eyes, leaves, flowers, roots, trunks, branches, to mention only the obvious ones—are the emergent results of morphogenic principles." [36] Such features are therefore not contingent but would recur if the tape of life was rerun. Goodwin cites the example of the spiral patterns which are observed in many flowers and in the arrangement of leaves along a stem or branch. These spiral patterns belong in a great many cases to the mathematical series known as the Fibonacci series. This pattern, like so many other morphological patterns, is clearly not the result of natural selection but rather of mechanical and natural laws. As Goodwin comments, "plants generate this aspect of their form by doing what comes naturally—following robust morphogenetic pathways to generic forms."[37] By this logic we can conclude that wherever in the cosmos there are plants with spiral leaf or flower arrangements we may expect to see this conform to the Fibonacci series. Goodwin raises the possibility of "a logical or a rational taxonomy . . . a theory of biological forms whose equivalent in physics is the periodic table of the elements, constructed on the basis of a theory that tells us the dynamically stable patterns of electrons, protons and neutrons. Biology would begin to look a little more like physics in having a theory of *organisms* as dynamically robust entities that are natural kinds, not simply historical accidents that survived for a period of time. This would transform biology from a purely historical science to one with a logical, dynamic foundation."[38]

In effect, both Kauffman and Goodwin are seeking to identify "directive laws" which would of necessity exist in a cosmos designed for life as we see it on earth and programmed from the beginning to arrive at the life forms we observe. Their work certainly raises the possibility that there exist additional mechanisms by which the course of evolution might have been directed along prearranged paths, by mechanisms which would not have necessitated any sort of specific directed mutation in DNA sequence space. Of course, the two different means of evolutionary direction are not mutually exclusive.

Lamarckian-type Mechanisms

The notion of evolution as directed and the tree of life as a natural form inherent in the nature of the cosmos itself should not be taken to imply that every adaptation in every organism that ever lived is part of nature's grand design. It is hardly conceivable that all the many fascinating and sometimes bizzare adaptations of life, such as those found on isolated islands, were written into life's design from the moment of creation. In such cases it seems we must either assume that their evolution has been the result of natural selection or consider the heretical but tantalizing alternative possibility—that living things may possess some unidentified and mysterious emergent property which endows on them an inventive capacity enabling them to direct their own evolution in a completely autonomous fashion, at least to a limited degree. This was a view that was quite widely held in France in the early decades of this century.[39] Recent studies of adaptive mutations in bacteria (referred to below) which have led some researchers to suggest that micro-

organisms may be able to intelligently alter their DNA sequences in response to various adaptive challenges would, if confirmed, lend support to
the notion that life has inherent inventive capacities.[40] Still, no matter how
appealing such notions may be, there is however to date, no convincing evidence that organisms do possess such abilities and even if such a capacity
does exist, it would have to be severely constrained. Because as mentioned
above, any model of directed evolution leading to the manifestation of a
unique tree of life will work only if genetic determinism is the rule. So that
any capacity for autonomous, intelligent evolution that life may possess
would have to be limited to minor microevolutionary adaptive changes.

The Question of the Spontaneity of Mutation

One of the major obstacles within the biological community in the way of
any widespread acceptance of the idea of directed mutation is the very deeply
held belief in the so-called spontaneity of mutation.[41] According to the
authorities Dobzhansky, Ayala, Stebbins, and Valentine, writing in a standard text on evolution, "Mutations are accidental, undirected, random or
chance events in still another sense very important for evolution; namely
that they are unorientated with respect to adaptation."[42]

The idea of the spontaneity of mutation is taken as a proven fact by a
great many biologists today. And this is the fundamental assumption upon
which the whole Darwinian model of nature is based. If it could be shown
that some mutations, even a small proportion, are occurring by direction or
are adaptive in some sense, then quite literally the whole contingent biology
collapses at once. What is very remarkable about this whole issue is that, as
is typical of any "unquestioned article of faith," evidence for the doctrine of
the spontaneity of mutation is hardly ever presented. Its truth is nearly always assumed. In nearly all the texts on genetics and evolution published
over the past four decades, whenever the author attempts to justify the doctrine of the spontaneity of mutation, he refers back to a series of crucial experiments carried out in the late forties and early fifties on the bacterium *E.
coli* that were associated with the names of Salvador Luria, Max Delbruck,
and Joshua Lederberg.[43]

These experiments were based on the very simple observation that when
bacterial cells are suddenly subjected to a particular selection pressure (for
example, the addition to a culture of cells of an antibiotic which is lethal to
wild-type cells) invariably a small proportion of cells survive because they

contain a mutation that confers resistance to the antibiotic. Ingenious tests were carried out which proved conclusively that the mutations were present in the surviving cells *before the antibiotic was added* to the culture. It was concluded that the mutations were spontaneous events.

But the fact that some mutations in bacteria are spontaneous does not necessarily mean that *all* mutations in *all* organisms throughout the entire course of 4 billion years of evolution have *all been entirely spontaneous.* This very point was made by Max Delbruck himself, who carried out with Salvador Luria some of the crucial experiments proving the spontaneity of mutation. As he conceded at a Cold Spring Harbor Symposium over forty years ago, "One should keep in mind the possible occurrence of specifically adaptive mutations."[44] Recently, John Cairns, a leading microbiologist in the United States, commented in *Nature* on the subject of the spontaneity of mutation: "It seems to be a doctrine that has never been put to the test."[45]

During the course of the past 4 billion years of evolution, countless trillions of changes have occurred in the DNA sequences of living organisms. There is simply no experimental means of demonstrating that they were all spontaneous. And even if all mutations are entirely undirected in themselves, it is still possible to reconcile such a model of mutation with directed evolution by envisaging the existence of prearranged functional paths through DNA sequence space. For as we have seen above, such paths could conceivably have been traced out by an entirely random search, in the same way as an entirely blind trial-and-error search eventually leads to the unique exit from a maze.

The Trees of Life

The postulate of a unique tree does not necessarily imply that the full flowering of the tree would occur on every earthlike planet on which the tree initially took root. As with any real tree, the environment in which it grows will influence its final shape. On a planet entirely covered with water, those branches which lead to terrestrial forms would never appear. A planet like Mars, which has been subject to major climatic changes and contains at present less water than Earth, might only permit the growth of the base of the trunk so that the process of unfolding might only realize very simple unicellular plants and bacteria. Even on Earth different successions of climates and other vagaries of chance would influence growth of the tree. For example, had the meteor strike which is now believed to have wiped out the dinosaurs not occurred, then perhaps the dominance of the mammals that followed the extinction of the dinosaurs might never have occurred. Alternatively, had the dinosaurs died out 10 million years later, then perhaps the small mammals which had already waited through 100 million years during the Jurassic and Cretaceous eras with little change might still have given rise to the same mammalian world we have today. It is also quite possible that many of the branches of the tree never sprouted on earth because the specific succession of environmentally imposed selection pressures required to draw life down those particular trajectories never occurred at the propitious moment.

Nor does the postulate of a unique tree necessarily imply that its form, even in identical environments, would be exactly the same. Just because evolution is determined does not necessarily mean that it was rigidly determined in all details. Even if the major phyla and classes are natural forms and built into the order of the tree, there could still be room for almost infinite microevolutionary variation within each major group.

Marsupial and Other Doppelgängers

It is often claimed by supporters of undirected models of evolution that if the tape of life were played again the pattern that would emerge would be entirely different. On the postulate being advanced here, although the details would be different, the overall form and many of the major types and patterns that would emerge would be the same. Curiously, the evolution tape has been played again, at least in part. This has occurred on several occasions when the fauna on great continental land masses became isolated for millions of years. Two of the most celebrated examples of this phenomenon occurred in South America and Australia, which were isolated from the other continents for most of the past 60 million years.

The diversification of the marsupials in Australia is very instructive. Almost every type of placental mammal has its counterpart among the marsupials. There is a marsupial lion, cat, wolf, mole, anteater, jerboa, and flying squirrel. There was even a giant wombat equivalent to the placental rhino. Only the kangaroo is moderately unique, although it could be thought of as a giant jumping rat! The similarity in some cases is very striking. The skull of the marsupial wolf is amazingly similar to that of the placental wolf.

There are, though, some noticeable absences—there is no marsupial bat or elephant or whale. However, in the case of the whale, it is hard to see how the reproductive system of the marsupial could be adapted for marine life. And in the case of the elephant, perhaps given more time, even the evolution of elephant doppelgängers may have occurred. In the case of the bat, there is some evidence that bats reached Australia shortly after the continent was isolated so the niche available for bat evolution may have been occupied from the beginning of the marsupial radiation.

This remarkable set of doppelgängers is all the more striking considering that the starting point for their evolution was not the same as that of the placentals. Therefore, even from a very deterministic point of view, we should not expect to see an absolutely identical pattern.

The marsupials are not the only example of this phenomenon. Many of the mammals that developed in South America during its time of isolation are also doppelgängers of types that developed elsewhere during the same period. Another example is the parallel evolution that occurred in the various mammal-like reptile lineages over many millions of years. Another example is closer to home. Based on anatomical and behavioral evidence, modern humans and Neanderthals have always been considered to be quite close biologically. Both manufactured quite advanced tools, both used fire, both wore clothes and buried their dead. However, recent DNA comparisons suggest that the lines leading to modern humans and Neanderthals may have diverged 600,000 years ago from a primitive ancestral stock and that the evolution of sophisticated toolmaking techniques and even the evolution of religious belief might have occurred independently in the two different lineages.[46] None of these examples are exact replays of the tape, but they are at least suggestive that evolution may be constrained in very specific ways by as yet unknown mechanisms.

As mentioned above parallelism and long-term evolutionary trends have always struck many biologists, especially paleontologists, as difficult to account for in terms of undirected Darwinian models of evolution.

Molecular Hints of Direction

Although there is no direct evidence that mutational processes were directed during the course of evolution, there are two curious aspects of molecular evolution which strongly hint at the possibility. The first is the curious and surely suggestive fact that the rate of evolutionary substitution is almost equal to the mutation rate. The mutation rate is the number of changes which occur in the DNA sequence over one generation, calculated by counting the number of differences in the DNA sequences between parent and offspring. The evolutionary substitution rate is the average number of changes per generation which have occurred in the DNA since two species separated during evolution, calculated by counting the number of differences in the DNA sequence between two species and then dividing by the number of generations elapsed since their evolutionary divergence.

Comparisons of these two rates, the rate of mutation and the evolutionary substitution rate, have revealed the very surprising fact that the two rates are the same. This remarkable finding implies that *the differences between the DNA sequences of different species have been generated by mutation and that other factors such as natural selection could only have played a relatively minor role.* Which would imply that if all the DNA in the genome is informational, mutational processes pure and unfettered without any surveillance by natural selection must have created biological information.

The discovery of this relationship caused a considerable crisis when it first came to light in the late sixties and early seventies. The most popular explanation, subsequently adopted by most evolutionary biologists, was to suppose that the great majority of the DNA sequences in the genome of organisms was without any specific function and was therefore under no selectional constraints. This line of thought led to the "neutral theory of evolution" and was one of the main observations on which the "junk hypothesis" was based—the hypothesis that the vast majority of DNA is nonfunctional junk. The other observation which supported the junk hypothesis was the finding, during the 1970s, that only a small proportion of the DNA sequence in higher organisms coded for proteins. Most was intronic material, cut out of the initial RNA product of transcription, and discarded. Later the junk hypothesis concept was elevated into a whole new paradigm popularized by Richard Dawkins in *The Selfish Gene*, whereby much of the DNA was viewed as not only nonfunctional, but actually parasitic, perpetrating itself at the expense of the host organism in whose genome it "lived."

If it is true that a vast amount of the DNA in higher organisms is in fact junk, then this would indeed pose a very serious challenge to the idea of directed evolution or any teleological model of evolution. Junk DNA and directed evolution are in the end incompatible concepts. Only if the junk DNA contained information specifying for future evolutionary events, when it would not in a strict sense be junk in any case, could the finding be reconciled with a teleological model of evolution. Indeed, if it were true that the genomes of higher organisms contained vast quantities of junk, then the whole argument of this book would collapse. Teleology would be entirely discredited. On any teleological model of evolution, most, perhaps all, the DNA in the genomes of higher organisms should have some function.

While there is no doubt that at present no specific function can be attributed to most of the DNA in higher organisms, the idea that it is really junk is now under increasing attack. The first evidence that at least some of the noncoding DNA previously classed as junk does contain at least some genetic information is now emerging. Some of this evidence was referred to in a *Science* article entitled "Mining Treasures from Junk DNA" (February 4, 1994) and in a recent editorial in the same journal titled "Hints of a Language in Junk DNA" (November 25, 1994), describing the work of Eugene Stanley of Boston University, who used statistical techniques borrowed from linguistics and found evidence that much of the nonprotein-coding DNA has informational characteristics resembling those of a human language. Further evidence that at least some of the junk may be functional is the recent finding that many nonprotein coding sequences have been conserved over millions of years of evolution.

Another major discovery which arose from comparative studies of the gene sequences in different organisms was the so-called uniformity of molecular evolution. This phenomenon first came to light during the 1960s when it became possible to compare the sequences of genes from different organisms. By counting the number of differences between the sequences of a particular gene in a man and in a mouse, the percentage sequence difference could be determined.

By comparing sequences a curious pattern was observed. For example, in the case of the cytochromes, all the higher organism cytochromes (yeasts, plants, insects, mammals, birds, etc.) exhibit an almost equal degree of sequence divergence from the bacterial cytochrome in *Rhodospirillum*. This means that all their cytochrome genes have changed to about the same degree—in other words, have evolved at a uniform rate.[47]

The same phenomenon of uniform rates of evolution is observed in the case of nearly all the genes coding for proteins that have been examined. There are very few exceptions. The phenomenon raises all sorts of evolutionary questions. As Roger Lewin pointed out in a *Science* article entitled "Molecular Clocks Turn a Quarter Century," although the idea of a clock is "counterintuitive in the sense that anything in evolution might tick in a regular manner, the notion of and evidence for a molecular clock, nevertheless, has become even more pervasive than originally conceived." The development of the idea faced a considerable conceptual barrier, "that of associating the idea of any kind of regularity with the process of evolution." On the whole, however, as Lewin admits, "there is enough data to show that clocks can and do work, even if there appear to be many cogent reasons why they should not."[48]

At present, there is no consensus as to how this curious phenomenon can be explained. Some comprehension of the difficulties in attempting an explanation in selectionist terms can be gained by considering the evolution of the hemoglobins in the higher vertebrates. For example, the hemoglobins of man and salmon are equidistant from those of the hagfish, a primitive vertebrate. From this we may presume that the hemoglobins in the line leading to man and in the line leading to salmon have suffered the same number of substitutions since their common divergence. But since the two lines diverged, the line leading to man has undergone profound physiological and morphological changes, while the salmon remains fairly close in terms of its cardiovascular and respiratory system to its fish ancestor. In the case of the line leading to man, the heart has changed from a simple tubelike organ to a four-chambered efficient pump. The gills and bronchial arteries have been replaced by lungs and the pulmonary circulation. The red blood cells themselves have become completely different. From the large round red cells with a diameter of approximately 20 microns, possessing a nucleus, mitochondria, etc., they have changed into small platelike structures of 8 microns in diameter without nucleus or mitochondria and containing very much more hemoglobin per unit volume. While this dramatic series of changes was going on, the morphological and physiological organization of the cardiovascular and respiratory system on the line leading to the salmon must have remained fundamentally unchanged. Why, under selectionist explanations, has a protein functioning in the basically unchanging physiological environment of the salmon red cell accumulated precisely the same number of changes as a related protein in a line subject to such global adaptational changes?

Explanations of uniform rates of evolution in protein genes in terms of genetic drift of neutral mutations fare no better. The rate of genetic drift in a population is determined by the mutation rate. This is not controversial. Although mutation rates for many organisms are somewhat similar per generation time—10^{-6}/gene/generation—the problem is that generation times are vastly different, so that the rate of mutation per year in, say, yeast, may be 100,000 times greater than in a tree or a mammal such as man or elephant, organisms which have long generation times.

These twin discoveries—that the mutation rate equals the evolutionary substitution rate, and that the rate of change in many genes is regulated by a clock which seems to tick simultaneously in all the branches of the tree of life—may represent the first evidence, albeit indirect, that the mutational processes that are changing the DNA sequences of living things over time are indeed being directed by some as yet unknown mechanism, or more likely, mechanisms. Of course, these discoveries do not prove directed evolution, but it is far easier to imagine them as the outcome of some sort of direction than the outcome of purely random processes. There is no doubt that Asa Gray, Richard Owen, and especially Robert Chambers would have seen these discoveries as greatly supporting the idea that the course of evolution is determined in some way by natural law.

The Origin of Life

Before the tree of life can be manifest, before any sort of evolution can start, life must originate, and explaining how this happened is a major challenge for all models of evolution.

If the cosmos is uniquely fit for life of the carbon-based type that exists on Earth, and if the whole pattern of evolution was indeed written into the cosmic script, then it seems reasonable to suppose that the origin of life—the transition from chemistry to the cell—might be also written into the cosmic script. If it is true, as NASA claims, that carbon-based life—somewhat similar to that on the primitive Earth—arose on both the Earth and Mars shortly after their formation, then this would provide powerful support for the notion that the transition from chemistry to life is built into the cosmic design. As already alluded to in the "Note to the Reader" at the front of the book, many facts—such as the synthesis of carbon and the more complex atoms essential for life in stars throughout the cosmos, the fact that interstellar space contains vast quantities of organic carbon compounds, and the fact that the light of main sequence stars is ideal for photochemistry—makes eminent sense if the becoming of life is in some way programmed into the laws of nature.[49]

But even if it seems very likely that the becoming of life is built in, it has to be admitted that at present, despite an enormous effort, we still have no idea how this occurred, and the event remains as enigmatic as ever.

There have been only two significant developments in this whole area in the past forty years. The first was Stanley Miller's famous spark discharge experiment carried out in 1953. As described in a recent *Scientific American* article, Miller re-created the atmosphere of the primeval earth in a sealed glass apparatus:

> He filled it with a few liters of methane, ammonia and hydrogen and some water. A spark discharge device zapped the gases with simulated lightning, while a heating coil kept the water bubbling. Within a few days the water and glass were stained with a reddish goo. On analyzing the substance Miller found to his delight that it was rich in amino acids. These organic compounds link up to form proteins, the basic stuff of life. . . . Miller's results . . . seemed to provide stunning evidence that life could arise out of simple chemical reactions in the "primordial soup." Pundits speculated that scientists . . . would shortly conjure up living organisms in their laboratories and thereby demonstrate in detail how genesis unfolded. It didn't work out that way.[50]

In fact, the next stage of the process, from a soup of organic compounds to the current cell system, has remained enigmatic. At the heart of the problem lay a seeming paradox—proteins can do many things, but they cannot perform the function of storing and transmitting information for their own construction. On the other hand, DNA can store information, but cannot manufacture anything nor duplicate itself. So DNA needs proteins and proteins need DNA. A seemingly unbreakable cycle—the ultimate chicken-and-egg problem. As Monod put it in *Chance and Necessity*:

> The modern cell's translating machinery consists of at least fifty macromolecular components *which are themselves coded in the DNA: the code cannot be translated except by the products of translation.* It is the modern expression of *omne vivum ex ovo.* When and how did this circle become closed? It is exceedingly difficult to imagine.[51]

And Crick comments about the problem in *Life Itself*:

> An honest man, armed with all the knowledge available to us now, could only state that in some sense, the origin of life appears at the moment to be almost a miracle, so many are the conditions which would have to be satisfied to get it going.[52]

Just about the only real significant breakthrough after Miller's pioneering work was the discovery by Thomas Cech in the early eighties that RNA might have the ability to make copies of itself without the assistance of enzymes. This was very exciting.[53] As the *Scientific American* put it after this new finding: "Some investigators concluded that the first organisms consisted of RNA and that an early 'RNA world' had provided a bridge from simple chemistry to prototypes of the complex DNA-based cells found in modern organisms."[54] When the intermediate RNA world was first proposed back in the eighties, a major problem was the limited set of enzymic activities possessed by RNA molecules—these were insufficient to carry out the very many enzymic activities which would be needed to sustain an RNA world cell. But recent work in this area suggests that RNA molecules might in fact be able to carry out all the catalytic activities needed by any hypothetical RNA cell, thus removing one of the major obstacles to the RNA world hypothesis.[55] The scenario looks promising, although other studies have revealed serious drawbacks:[56] "Tests of the RNA-world hypothesis have shown that RNA is difficult to synthesize in the conditions that probably prevailed when life originated and that the molecule cannot easily generate copies of itself."[57]

And of course, even if the catalytic properties of RNA *were* exploited in some sort of intermediate self-replicating system which led eventually to the emergence of the modern cell, the actual pathway from the RNA world to modern DNA-based life has not been worked out even in outline.

Although many exotic hypotheses far more speculative than the RNA world have been proposed to close the gap between chemistry and life, none are convincing. There is the proposal that organic matter was first synthesized in interstellar space and that life was seeded on earth from space. Others suggest that life originated in the deep oceanic hydrothermal vents. Recently, a German lawyer, Günther Wächtershäuser, has developed a theory which proposes that life arose on the surface of iron pyrite, or fool's gold.[58] Most of these recent models do not merit serious attention, according to Miller. He refers to the organic-matter-from-space concept as "'a loser,' the vent hypothesis 'garbage' and the pyrite theory 'paper chemistry.'"[59] Nonetheless, completely novel and unexpected phenomena which may be highly relevant to the problem are continually coming to light, such as the very fascinating discovery recently reported in *Nature* of a self-replicating peptide.[60]

The problem has been compounded by the possibility that the early atmosphere in which the basic organic precursors of the cell were supposedly synthesized might have been far different from that assumed by Miller in his famous experiment and may not have supported the formation of the various organic compounds he reported. So the mystery may have deepened to include the origin of the basic building blocks themselves.

The mystery is further compounded by the fact that the time interval for life's emergence on earth is now known to be fairly short. In fact, it increasingly appears that life originated on earth shortly after the cessation of the meteor bombardment associated with the formation of the solar system, which ceased about 3.8 billion years ago. It seems that life appeared almost as soon as the planetary hydrosphere had cooled sufficiently to support it. The time available is certainly short—nothing like the supposed thousands of millions of years that was once assumed to be available.

Assuming that life arose as a result of natural processes, and nearly everyone working in the field accepts this assumption, then the very intractable nature of the problem raises the possibility that abiogenesis requires a completely new set of natural phenomena and processes, of which we have at present no idea. The fact that life emerged on the early earth as soon as conditions could support it points to the notion that life's origin was a natural and highly probable event which was inevitable given certain critical conditions. In this context Robert Chambers's notion that the process is analogous to "crystallization" seems remarkably apt, even though the *Vestiges* was written 150 years ago. When we finally hit on the mechanism of life's genesis, it will probably be as Miller confesses: "so damned simple that we'll all say, why didn't I think of that before?"[61]

One phenomenon, already touched on above, which could conceivably have played a role in the origin of life is the surprising tendency of complex dynamical systems to fall into highly ordered states. Spontaneous self-organization is a surprising phenomenon, as Kauffman points out: "Atoms and molecules are always doing their best to randomise themselves into maximum disorder. But on the other hand there are snowflakes, organised weather patterns, recurrent sunspot cycles on the sun . . . order and organisation seems ubiquitous in nature."[62] In 1965, Kauffman carried out a simple experiment in which he simulated on a computer a network of randomly connected interacting "genes." The result was quite counterintuitive. He found that even when the network of interactions was constrained by the simplest of rules, remarkably ordered patterns emerged in the interactions.[63]

As pointed out in a recent *New Scientist* article, "Order for Free," "Complete chaos is what most people would predict from such a system, known as a Boolean network, but instead order emerges. Kauffman calls it order for free."[64]

The notion that the transition to life was directed or facilitated by the laws of nature is perfectly consistent with the biocentric model of nature. Indeed, in a biocentric universe, where all the laws of nature have their ultimate meaning in the existence of life, it is hardly conceivable that the origin of life would have been left to chance. From a teleological perspective the origin of life *must* be viewed as something quite inevitable and built into the laws of nature from the beginning, just as were the properties of water and the mutual fitness of DNA and protein and all the other coincidences in the physical and chemical properties of life's constituents.

Curiously, many biologists are willing to accept the possibility that the origin of life might be built in but not the subsequent path of evolution. For example, Stephen Jay Gould, in a recent article entitled "War of the World Views" in the journal *Natural History,*[65] proposes "that the simplest kind of cellular life arises as *a predictable result* of organic chemistry and the physics of self-organizing systems but that *no predictable directions* exist for life's later development."[66] (My emphasis.) But surely it is far more likely that, if the chemical evolution of the first cell was built in, then the far less complex process—the biological evolution of life—will also turn out to be built in.

The Mode of Evolution

Evidence consistent with directed evolution is also emerging from recent studies of the mode of evolution. It has generally been accepted that the slower the rate of morphological change or the more slowly a new adaptation is acquired during the course of evolution, the more readily the process can be explained by simple nondirected Darwinian mechanisms. Conversely, the more discontinuous the mode of morphological or adaptive change, the more difficult it becomes to explain the process by undirected mechanisms and the more credible the concept of direction becomes. The relationship between saltation and direction is obvious if taken to the limit. The sudden emergence of an entirely new type of organism, or of a functionally perfect novel organ system, would be almost impossible to account for except within some kind of directed evolutionary or teleological framework. Gradualistic models of evolution have therefore always been favored by Darwinists and evolutionary theorists advocating undirected models of evolutionary change. For Darwin, *Natura non facit saltum* was virtually a creed, and for good reason.

Naturally then, when Niles Eldredge and Stephen Jay Gould proposed their theory of "punctuated equilibrium" in 1972,[67] it created some controversy, as it implied that the course of evolution consisted of long periods of stasis during which a species undergoes virtually no change and very short periods of explosive evolution when it suddenly gives rise to one or several new species that appear to burst into the fossil record per saltum.

Despite the considerable controversy surrounding this issue, the growing consensus and the best available evidence suggests that the punctuational mode is in fact the norm. The March 10, 1995, issue of *Science* presented new research on invertebrate paleontology which provided quite unambiguous evidence for the first time that at least in some lineages the evolutionary pattern was one of millions of years of stasis interrupted by periods of no more than 100,000 years of rapid and sudden change.

Accounting for a punctuated model in terms of classical Darwinian gradualism is not so straightforward. As R. A. Kerr, the author of the *Science* article, points out, "One mystery is what would maintain the equilibrium . . . keeping the new species from evolving in spite of environmental vagaries." He continues: "One possibility might be 'adaptive gridlock,' which arises because there are so many conflicting selection pressures pulling in different directions. . . . If a shellfish could reduce the weight of its shell, for example, it might have a better chance of escaping from some fast-moving predator. But that evolutionary route could become closed because a lighter, thinner shell, for example, would also decrease its resistance to other predators that bore into their victims. So the species remains unchanged for millions of years."[68] (The integrative complexity of biological systems and the sort of constraints this is bound to impose against bit-by-bit gradual change is raised again in chapter 14.) But if stability is the rule, and if selection tends to freeze organisms against change, then this raises the question of how selection ever transformed organisms so dramatically: "How do you get from funny little Mesozoic mammals to horses and whales? From *Archaeopteryx* to hummingbirds."[69]

The most celebrated of all evolutionary explosions is of course the sudden appearance of nearly all the major types of animal life in the early Cambrian seas. It has always been accepted that this explosion was compressed into a very short time span, geologically speaking, about 30 million years. However, recent work has revealed that the time span of the explosion may have been far shorter than this. A joint study carried out by Harvard and Russian geologists,[70] has drastically reduced this time span to perhaps as little as 5 million years. As Gould comments: "The entire Cambrian explosion, previously allowed 30–40 million years, must now fit into 5–10 million years and almost surely nearer the lower limit, . . . in other words, fast, much faster than we ever thought."[71] Explosive evolution is not only a phenomenon of animal evolution; the same pattern is seen in plants. Most of the modern flowering plants appeared in a few million years in the middle of the Cretaceous era.

Conclusion

The convincing grounds for interpreting the laws of nature as in some deep sense biocentric completely undermines the contingent *a priori* on which the Darwinian worldview was founded in the nineteenth century. It also provides a perfectly rational sanction for the concept of directed evolution. We have seen that water, the carbon atom, oxygen, the double helix, and many of the other constituents of life possess unique properties which seem so perfectly adapted to the biological ends they serve that the impression of design is irresistible. Many of these adaptations not only serve the end of microscopic life but also give every appearance of having been adjusted to serve the end of macroscopic terrestrial life forms such as ourselves. This raises the very natural but heretical idea, which has been explored in this chapter, that if the cosmos is fit for the being of higher life forms, then surely it is not inconceivable that an evolutionary mechanism for their actualization could also have been written into the order of things and that perhaps the entire process of biological evolution, from the origin of life to the emergence of man, was somehow directed from the beginning. I believe that our current knowledge of molecular genetics sanctions such possibilities.

Chapter 13

The Principle of
Plenitude

*In which it is argued that the diversity of life on earth
approximates to the maximal diversity possible for carbon-based
life. Such a plenitude is precisely what one might expect if the
whole evolutionary process was itself built into the laws of
nature. A variety of lines of evidence are considered. To begin
with, there are those restricted cases where every possible
variation on a particular biological theme is manifest. Examples
cited are the early development of the animal embryo, the
variety of bacteriophages, and the variety of image-forming eyes.
Considering the complex constraints, embryological,
physiological, and evolutionary, the diversity of life manifested
on earth is remarkable. The possibility that life on earth
approximates to the plenitude of all possible biological forms is
perfectly in keeping with the teleological thesis that the cosmos is
uniquely prefabricated for life as it exists on earth.*

The plenitude of nature.

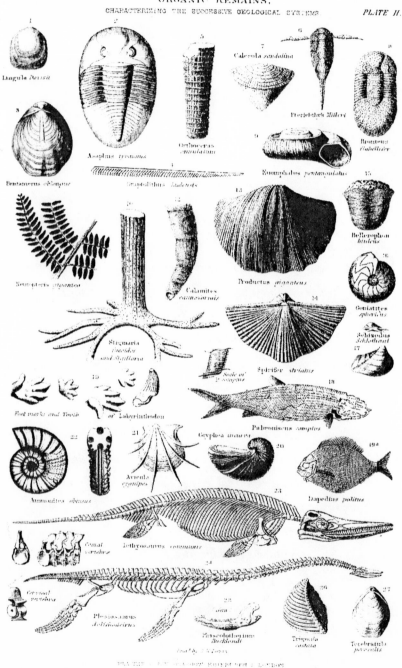

ORGANIC REMAINS,
CHARACTERIZING THE SUCCESSIVE GEOLOGICAL SYSTEMS.
PLATE II.

From Oliver Goldsmith (1876) *A History of the Earth and Animated Nature.*

Nature, inexhaustible in fecundity and omnipotence, has been settled in the innumerable combinations of organic forms and functions which compose the animal kingdom by physiological incompatibilities alone. It has realised all those combinations which are not incoherent and it is these incoherencies, these incompatibilities . . . which establish between the diverse groups of organisms those gaps which mark their necessary limits and which create the natural embranchments, classes, orders, and families.

—Georges Cuvier, *Leçons d'anatomie comparée,* 1835

No doubt we can imagine a greater variety of animals than do actually exist; such are the words of Archdeacon Paley. But what is the fact? Suppose we take the fabled animals of antiquity; not one of them could have existed. But we venture to say that every animal form, not actually existing in nature, but the invention of the artist or poet, would be discovered to have some defect in the balance of the exterior members, or were the exterior and moving parts duly balanced, some internal organ would be found unconformable or displaced.

—George Bell, Bridgewater Treatise, *The Hand,* 1832

It is impossible not to be struck by the enormous functional, structural, and behavioral diversity manifested by life on earth. Is it conceivable that there could be a world of life more varied, a phantasma more diverse than the one existing on our watery planet? From the tiniest bacterial cell to the immensity of the blue whale, from the great sequoias of California to the albatross of the southern ocean, with its wings inches above the waves, gliding perpetually on the eternal westerlies; from the giant squid of the ocean deeps, their bodies ever flickering with a sidereal bioluminescence to the exploding puffball fungi on an autumn evening; from the sinister cacophony of cries and screams as dusk falls across the Ngorongoro crater to the gentle piping of the Australian bellbird and the soft droning of a bumblebee; from the darting flight of the dragonfly to the plodding step of the elephant; from a tyrannosaur to an orb-weaving spider; earth exhibits a diversity of such exuberance that even the most bizarre imaginings of science fiction seem to have found realization in some exotic form of life. Our senses reel before the fantastic panoply of carbon-based life forms which clothes the earth. Is it possible that there could be a world as rich and as multifarious as the spectacular flowering of earth's great tree of life?

Before the rise of Darwinism it was widely believed that all possible living forms had actually been realized in nature. It was argued that an omnipotent Creator who had fashioned all the laws of nature to the end of life and man would surely have so organized these laws to make manifest in material form all possible biological types. This was the view of the leading French biologist of the early nineteenth century Georges Cuvier, who presented it with vigor and clarity in his classic work *Leçons d'anatomie comparée*. As Cuvier put it, nature had realized "all those combinations which are not incoherent."[1]

The idea that all possible organic forms have been actually manifested on earth is an old doctrine termed the Principle of Plenitude by the historian A. O. Lovejoy in his classic *The Great Chain of Being*, which long predates Cuvier and early-nineteenth-century biology. The doctrine was very influential in medieval and early Renaissance thought and remained influential in biology right up to the late eighteenth century. According to Lovejoy, the principle implied "that no genuine potentiality of being can remain unfulfilled, that the extent and abundance of creation must be as great as the possibility of existence and commensurate with the productive capacity of a perfect and inexhaustible source."[2]

The doctrine of plenitude would seem to be an inescapable corollary of the teleological position. For if a program for the evolution of life has been written into the cosmic script from the beginning, and if the earth is ideally fit for its evolutionary manifestation, then life on earth should indeed represent that plenitude that Cuvier envisaged and every possible type of carbon- and water-based life consistent with the laws of nature should have made its appearance on earth. The question, therefore, as to whether or not the pattern of life on earth approaches a theoretical plenitude of all possible forms has a critical bearing on the credibility of teleological claims.

The Diversity of Life

There is no doubt that the diversity of life is stunning. Nowhere is this more obvious than among microbial life. Microbes survive in every conceivable environment: from deep in the crustal rocks, to the frozen deserts of Antarctica, to the hydrothermal vents on the ocean bottom, to the hot springs in Yellowstone National Park. There could hardly exist an ecological niche on earth not filled by some exotic bacterial type. The biochemical diversity of microbial life is no less astonishing than the variety of environments they have exploited. For example, in the case of energy metabolism, bacteria seem to utilize almost every available reaction.[3]

Diversity is just as evident among the higher forms of life, from the protozoa up through the various multicellular groups. Consideration, for example, of the diversity of the unique and distinct bauplans of the major multicellular phyla suggests that at least a considerable proportion of all possible basic body plans have been actualized by life on earth. The basic arrangement of the body compartments in twelve of the more important phyla is shown in the figure below.[4]

Altogether there are currently around seventy known phyla, each of which has a unique and distinct body plan.[5] However, the existence of early Cambrian and Pre-Cambrian fossils of bizarre morphology and unknown affinity suggests that several additional types of body plan may have once existed in the early Paleozoic seas and that the total number of radically different basic animal body plans actualized on earth may be considerably larger than the seventy or so presently known.[6] However, from even a cursory consideration of the radically different arrangements of basic body compartments already realized in the seventy known phyla, it is possible to argue that there could not be a vastly greater number of radically distinct bauplans. The number of different ways in which the basic divisions of the animal body—an outer skin layer, body cavities, the gut, the gonads, the blood system—can be

Arrangements of body compartments in twelve animal phyla.

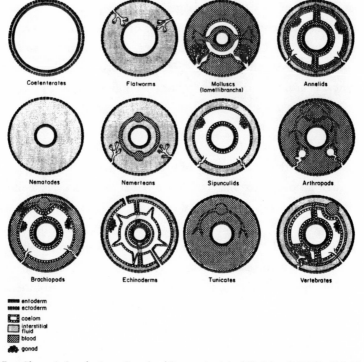

From Ernst Florey, *An Introduction to General and Comparative Animal Physiology;* © 1966 by Holt, Rinehart & Winston and renewed 1994 by Ernst Florey. Fig. 3.1. Reproduced by permission of the publisher.

arranged is limited. It would be surprising if the total number of possible different body plans for carbon-based life were many more than a few hundred.

Diversity within Phyla

Among the phylum Protozoa (the unicellular organisms) the diversity is so spectacular that it is indeed hard to believe that it does not represent a large proportion of all possible forms. As the German zoologist Bernhard Rensch commented in his *Evolution Above the Species:*

> In Protozoa, almost all vital processes show this undirected testing of nearly all imaginable possibilities. Thus, asexual reproduction may occur by simple fission, schizogony (simple separation of cells), or sporogony (spore formation); or there may be sexual reproduction by copulation, conjugation, pedogamy, automixis, or various types of metagenesis and heterogenesis.[7]

Even within small subgroups of the Protozoa such as the ciliates, the diversity of form and function is astonishing. There are about 5,700 ciliate species ranging in size from about 10 microns to 3 millimeters. As one authority put it, "about the same as between a blue whale and a rat."[8]

The diversity of insects is no less remarkable. They crawl, run, fly, swim, hop, and jump. There may be more than 3 million different species, ranging in size from tiny wasps and beetles which weigh only a few micrograms to the largest beetles, which are more than 10 million times heavier. Some dragonflies in the Cretaceous era had wingspans of 70 centimeters. As Rensch notes: "Some are carnivores, herbivores, omnivores, some are even coprophages (feces-eating), bloodsuckers, keratin and wax eaters, xylophages, nectar suckers and pollen eaters, and some that eat nothing during the span of their adult life. The differences are equally manifold as regards display or mating patterns, structures and appendages of genitalia in bumblebees, butterflies, and so forth."[9]

Similarly, within the Vertebrata, among the reptiles and mammals we have carnivores, herbivores, quadrupeds, bipeds, flying and aquatic forms. Among birds, a relatively specialized type, we have flying, terrestrial, and aquatic forms.

Possible Cases of Plenitude?

The question as to what proportion of all possible designs have in fact been actualized in the diversity of insects, vertebrates, or the basic bauplans, is clearly only a matter of subjective judgment. In most cases, it is impossible at present to determine what the theoretical limits might be—for example, what constructional or developmental constraints might apply.[10]

However, there are some cases where the constraints are relatively obvious and where we can be relatively certain that all possibilities have been realized.[11] Bernhard Rensch has suggested some instances, including hibernation strategies in butterflies and the incubation strategy of birds. Regarding the former, he comments:

> There are four possible stages of hibernation in butterflies of the temperate and cold zones: the insect can spend the winters in the stage of an egg, a caterpillar, a pupa, or an adult insect. All these possibilities are realised in nature.[12]

Rensch then goes on to show that in the case of the horns of antelopes the whole range of structural possibilities, apart from those that would be biologically discordant, are actually realized: "straight and smooth, straight with transverse ridges, slightly curved with a smooth surface, slightly curved with transverse grooves and ridges, twisted like a screw with a smooth surface, etc."[13] Likewise, as he shows, the same is true for the range of shells of Gastropoda: "These shells are shaped like a bowl, a cap, a tube, a flat spiral, a more or less tapering cone, a needle, a ball, and so forth."[14] He then considers the possible ways in which the stridulating organs of insects, which produce sound by rubbing body parts together, may be formed. It turns out that in beetles alone there are at least fifteen different ways in which a "pars stridens" can be moved against a "plectrum."[15]

A fascinating case cited by Rensch involves the early development of the egg. Here again, where the total number of possibilities is strictly limited, the evidence strongly suggests that every conceivable possibility has been realized:

> There are equal, unequal, discoid, and superficial cleavage; and there are various intermediate and modified forms (radial, leiotropic [left], or dexiotropic [right] spiral cleavage); and finally there may be a separation of the blastomeres (early embryonic cells) as in polyembryonic forms of development. Hence again we find all possible modes of development.[16]

Another example where all possibilities consistent with biological design may have been realized is seen in the ways by which organisms move. We have, in air, jet propulsion, gliding flight, flapping flight, ballooning; on land, articulated legs; in water, jet propulsion, swimming, and even by propeller in the case of bacteria.

Viruses appear to provide another instance in which there are reasonable grounds for believing that all possible biological forms may have been actualized. For example, all conceivable ways of storing genetic information—using single-stranded RNA, double-stranded RNA, single-stranded DNA, and double-stranded DNA—are found among various types of viruses. Again, of the two possible forms of virus capsule, the cylinder and the icosahedron, which are the only stable hollow structures that can be built up out of single subunits, both occur in nature.

Even among one small subset of viruses, the so-called bacteriophages, which replicate themselves inside bacterial cells, it would appear that all possible forms are actually found in nature. The bacteriophages are of peculiar relevance to the question of whether the actual forms of life represent the limits of the possible, because we are far closer to having a complete description of every aspect of their biology than in the case of any other comparable group of living things. Indeed, in the case of one class of bacteriophages, the so-called RNA phages, which are the simplest of all the viruses, their entire chemical structure has been determined, every gene has been identified, so have virtually all the genetic regulatory devices they utilize during the course of their replicative cycle. In addition, the three-dimensional structure of the viral capsid has been elucidated at a molecular level. This is one area of biology where genetic engineering holds out the fascinating prospect of attempting the creation of completely novel types of organisms quite different from those forms already known, thereby bringing the question as to whether the actual equals the possible into the realm of experimental science. But already, from what we know of the biology and the diversity of these fascinating types of nanoreplicators, it is very difficult to envisage the construction of a bacteriophage radically different from those already existing. Every possible variant seems already to be manifest.

All Possible Eyes?

Another case where it appears that every possibility has been realized is in the design of image-forming optical devices.[17] These include the familiar camera-type of eye found in vertebrates, molluscs, and various invertebrates; the reflecting eye of the scallop pecten and the crustacean *Gigantocypris,* which form an image by reflection from a concave mirror onto a retina situated at the focal point of the mirror; and the three different types of compound eye of the insects and arthropods. One type of compound eye found in diurnal insects is made up of a hexagonal array of tiny lenslets, each of which has its own photoreceptor cell that receives light only from its own lenslet. A second type (the superposition type) is found in nocturnal insects, again made up of a hexagonal array of tiny lenslets which bend the light rays so that light is focused by refraction through many lenslets to one point in the photoreceptor layer. A third type is also a superposition eye, but in this case the light is focused by reflection from a series of tiny square mirror-lined units onto the photoreceptor layer (see the description of the lobster eye in chapter 15). Finally, there is even what appears to be a scanning eye, utilized by a small marine crustacean which scans an image formed by a simple lens by rapidly moving a single photoreceptor back and forth across the image. In addition to the realization of what appears to be all possible image-forming devices, there are of course a near-infinite variety of nonimage-forming simple eyes, from subcellular photosensitive pigment spots in Protozoa to the simple photoreceptor eyes of many invertebrates, such as spiders.

It is also of interest that living things utilize or detect the entire range of electromagnetic radiation reaching the earth's surface from the ultraviolet to the infrared. The human eye, for example, can detect electromagnetic radiation from 0.38 microns to about 0.8 microns. Certain insects detect light in the ultraviolet around 0.3 microns,[18] and the chlorophylls absorb light in the blue (0.35–0.45 microns) and red regions (0.55–0.65 microns); vitamin D synthesis requires ultraviolet radiation near 0.3 microns, and so on.

Although organisms do not utilize infrared radiation (0.8 microns to 2.0 microns) to drive chemical reactions, nearly all organisms, including man, can detect it as warmth on the surface of the body. The warmth of the sun's infrared radiation on the skin is sensed by special cells called thermoreceptors. The precise mechanism by which they detect infrared radiation is not understood. However, they are remarkably sensitive. The thermoreceptors in the heat-sensitive pit organ of the rattlesnake, for example, can detect a change in temperature of as little as 0.003^0C.[19] The thermoreceptors are stimulated by all wavelengths of infrared radiation reaching the surface of the earth, i.e., from wavelengths of 0.8 microns to about 2.0 microns.

It would seem, then, that not only are all possible image-forming devices actualized in some branch of the tree of life but also that the full spectrum of radiant energy reaching the earth's surface is detected or utilized in some way by a variety of biological systems. Moreover, as we saw in chapter 3, radiant energy in the visible and the infrared is the only type of electromagnetic radiation of utility to biological systems.

In addition to their ability to see and detect heat, living things can detect sound over a large range of frequencies, in both air and water. They can detect vibrations transmitted through the ground; they can detect vanishingly small concentrations of a vast variety of chemicals in the air and water; they can detect gravitational fields, magnetic fields, and electric fields.

The Size of Organisms

One area where it is possible to be slightly more objective in judging how close actual life forms approach the limits of the possible is in considering the question of size. The difference in size between the smallest and the largest organism—between the smallest bacteria (the mycoplasma) and the blue whale—is 10^{21}. A blue whale may weigh more than 100,000,000 grams, a mycoplasma cell less than one-tenth of a picogram or 10^{-13} of a gram.[20]

As far as the mycoplasma is concerned, we can safely assume that it is very close to the lower limit of size for an autonomously self-replicating cell. The biochemist Harold Morowitz has speculated as to what might be the absolute minimum requirement for a completely self-replicating cell deriving all essential organic percursors—amino acids, sugars, etc.—from its environment but autonomous in every other way in terms of our current understanding of biochemistry.[21] Such a cell would necessarily be bound by a cell membrane and the simplest feasible would probably be the typical bilayered lipid membrane utilized by all existing cells on earth today. The synthesis of the fats of the cell membrane would require perhaps a minimum of five proteins. Energy would be required, and this might require a further eight proteins for a very simple form of energy metabolism. Altogether, probably a minimum of another hundred proteins would be required for DNA replication and protein synthesis. The size of such a cell, containing perhaps four mRNA molecules, a full complement of enzymes, a DNA molecule about 100,000 nucleotides long and bounded by a cell membrane, would be about one-tenth of a micron in diameter. Morowitz comments: "This is the smallest hypothetical cell that we can envisage within the context of current biochemical thinking. It is almost certainly a lower limit, since we have allowed no control functions, no vitamin metabolism and extremely limited intermediary metabolism."[22]

The physiologist Knut Schmidt-Nielsen considered the question of whether or not the blue whale weighing 100 million grams, the giant redwoods (1 billion grams) and the smallest existing organism, the mycoplasma, also known as PPLO, are close to the actual limits on what is possible and concluded: "There are cogent reasons to believe that the smallest and the largest organisms represent approximate limits to the possible size of animals under the conditions that prevail on our planet."[23]

There are certainly other cases in which there are very good grounds for believing that a particular species possesses the smallest possible body size compatible with its basic biological design. Rensch comments that, as the lower limit of body size is reached,

> organisms usually reduce special structures and special organs and only the indispensable mechanisms are maintained. A good example of this kind is provided by the minute marine snail *Caecum glabrum* (Opisthobranchia), 1 mm long and 2 mm wide. . . . In this species the cells are of about the same size as in larger relatives. . . . Consequently, the intestinal gland of this minute snail consists of two tubules, and the gonads are represented by a single folded tube (while in other snails these organs are made up of quite numerous tubules forming a solid network of glandular elements). Hence, it is quite evident that a further reduction of these organs is impossible. Here is another objective case where the limits of the possible are actualised in a particular form. Moreover in the case of virtually all the main subgroups of insects, vertebrates, molluscs and many other types of organism there is quite convincing evidence that the *actual range of size is close to the possible.*[24] [My emphasis.]

Oxygen Delivery

There are also firm grounds for believing that in the case of certain basic structural and physiological systems, such as oxygen delivery systems, skeletal systems, and excretory systems, all design possibilities have been exhaustively exploited. Consider, for example, the delivery of oxygen to the tissues of a terrestrial air-breathing organism. From first principles there are only two possible ways of achieving this: by the use of a circulatory system to carry dissolved oxygen via small tubes throughout the body, or by the use of a tracheal system of tubes to carry the oxygen gas directly to the tissues. Both these systems are actually exploited by the two major types of macroscopic terrestrial life on earth, the vertebrates utilizing the "circulatory solution" and the arthropods the "tracheal solution."

The vertebrate solution necessitates a lung in which the circulating fluid can be aerated and an efficient pump or heart to force the fluid through the small tubes, or capillaries, and into the tissues where the oxygen is consumed. Further, as we have seen in chapter 6, because of the relatively low solubility of oxygen, it cannot be carried in sufficient quantities in simple solution; consequently, a special oxygen-carrying molecule, hemoglobin, is required, and this in turn (for a variety of reasons already touched on in chapter 2) requires the hemoglobin molecules to be densely packed together in a special cell—the red cell. Thus, we are led from the necessity of delivering oxygen in sufficient quantities to support the needs of combustion in the tissues of a large terrestrial organism to the vertebrate respiratory and cardiovascular systems and even to a molecule with the functions of hemoglobin. As we saw in chapter 9, such a molecule would almost certainly have to be a protein and probably exploit the unique characteristics of the iron atom.

There is nothing in the slightest "accidental" about the fact that it is the larger vertebrates that use the circulatory system, while the tracheal system is utilized by the much smaller arthropods. No system of small air tubes, however modified, permeating the muscles of, say, an elephant or a whale, would be capable of efficient oxygen delivery. Even in the case of large, active insects, the air much be pumped through the tracheal network, because the diffusion of oxygen, although much faster in air than in water, is too slow to supply the needs of the organism. Air sacs which communicate with the tracheal system and which are periodically compressed by the movements of the insect's body are utilized to pump air through the tracheal system. To strengthen the trachea and prevent the tubes collapsing under various pressures exerted on them by the movement of adjacent muscles in the insect's body, many incorporate internal spiral ribs. The largest insects are in fact close to the maximum size possible for an organism obtaining oxygen via a tracheal system.[25]

For small active organisms such as flying insects, the tracheal system has great advantages. In fact, below a certain body size, as Schmidt-Nielsen shows, there are definite deficiencies in a circulatory system when compared to a tracheal system for the delivery of oxygen to metabolically active tissues in small organisms. In a fascinating section in which he discusses the various ways in which physiological constraints impose limits on the size of animals, he notes that the smallest birds and mammals are approximately the same size, between 2 and 3 grams, and asks whether this is the lowest possible weight for these two classes of organism.[26] He continues: "Is there some reason that birds and mammals are not smaller? To produce heat, we need both fuel and oxygen. Hummingbirds get most of their energy from nectar, exactly as do large moths; so fuel supply is an improbable constraint."[27] As he explains, the reason is that below a certain size a circulatory system is increasingly ineffective for oxygen delivery compared with the tracheal system.[28] On the other hand, the tracheal system is remarkably efficient for a small organism. The diffusion coefficient for oxygen in air is some 10,000 times higher than that in water and this ensures an adequate supply of oxygen without the need of blood.[29]

The fact that large insects are able to raise their body temperatures and metabolic rates during flight to that of warm-blooded organisms is testimony to the high functional capacity of the tracheal system.[30] The speed, power, and efficiency of the flight of dragonflies and some of the larger moths is every bit the equal of hummingbirds and small bats.

In passing, it is interesting to note that these two mechanisms of delivering oxygen to the tissues of terrestrial organisms are both critically dependent on the values of a number of key physical constants, including the diffusion rate of oxygen in air, the solubility of oxygen in water, the diffusion rate of oxygen in water, the viscosity of water, the density and viscosity of air, etc. It is fortunate that their values are close to what they are, because terrestrial life would have been impossible or enormously constrained if these values had been even slightly different. As it is, these constants limit the design of respiratory systems to two different designs—the vertebrate and the insect.

A final point in this context is of interest. In the case of the vertebrate lung, there are again two fundamentally different possible types. There is the familiar "bellows type" of lung in which air is drawn in and out via the same passage during respiration. This type occurs in most terrestrial vertebrates, including man. The other, radically different possible design, "the continuous throughput type," is realized in the avian lung, where air is inhaled through one passage drawn unidirectionally and continuously through a system of capillary tubes and then exhaled via another passage. Again, as with the two possible oxygen delivery systems, both possible types of lung have been actualized in nature.

The two basic and radically different types of skeletal system, the endoskeleton and the exoskeleton, have also been actualized in nature in the two major types of higher organism: the vertebrates and the arthropods. Vertebrates have an endoskeleton composed of several internal articulating rods, composed of bone, which is fundamentally a mineralized type of connective tissue. Insects have an exoskeleton composed of a very hard plastic-like polysaccharide, chitin. Again, this difference is not accidental. One can easily conceive of the difficulty of constructing an elephant-sized organism weighing five tons with an exoskeleton or the difficulties of attaching muscles to an articulating endoskeleton in an organism weighing 25 micrograms. The relative merits of the exoskeleton for small organisms and the endoskeleton in large animals are well known and have been discussed in a number of recent publications.[31]

There are surprisingly few simple materials available to living things which are mechanically rigid and hard, with some tensile strength, and therefore suitable for the construction of skeletal parts. The very hard polysaccharides, cellulose and chitin, are used by all plants and a great many invertebrates as the basic building material of their rigid components. Mollusc shells and vertebrate bones contain calcium salts—mainly carbonates in the molluscs, and phosphate in the vertebrates.

It is difficult to see how the vertebrate endoskeleton could be composed out of chitin like the insect cuticle. Chitin is very unreactive, being virtually insoluble in even strong acids and only digestible by enzymes under physicochemical conditions difficult to satisfy in the inside of an animal's body.[32] In this context it may be fortunate that the solubility of calcium phosphate is fit for the formation of the mineralized component in bone in an organism with a pH of 7 because the other readily available skeletal materials chitin and cellulose would be not be suitable for the formation of endoskeletal structures in a vertebrate.

Movement and Legs

Animals, both large and small, must move. Vertebrates have four legs and insects six. Can this difference also be explained, perhaps, by the difference in size? The answer is yes. An insect, having a very small body, is subject to instability caused by gusts of air. Six legs means that even in a fast gait an insect need only have three legs off the ground at any one instance. Calculation shows that this source of instability is significant and an insect with only four legs would be severely disadvantaged. Even the positioning of an insect's legs, well apart on either side of the body, is also related to the necessity for stability to prevent a small organism being destabilized in even a small gust of air.[33]

Virtually every conceivable way of moving on legs that is compatible with fundamental design principles is exploited by some type of terrestrial animal. Humans walk on two legs. Kangaroos hop on two legs. Most mammals walk, run, or amble on four legs. Insects run and walk on six legs, spiders on eight. Wood lice, centipedes, millipedes, and so on use more than ten. Snakes move by sliding without legs.

There would seem to be two basic biological designs for terrestrial macroscopic life, a large vertebrate type, which includes a circulatory system, lungs, heart, endoskeleton, and four legs, and a small insect type, with a tracheal system, exoskeleton, and six legs. These two designs are actualized in terrestrial life on earth, the insect type in organisms from about 25 micrograms to 100 grams and the vertebrate type in organisms from about 2 grams to 10,000 kilograms.

From this very brief consideration of the likely physiological criteria which would have to be satisfied by any type of viable macroscopic terrestrial life, constructed from organic carbon compounds, deriving energy from oxidation, and based in a matrix of water (which as we have seen is probably the only biochemical design capable of replication), it seems likely that only very few alternative basic designs for air-breathing terrestrial life exist. Again, the actual approaches the possible.

The Gaps in the *Scala Naturae*

Those many cases where gaps in the order of nature appear of necessity rather than by accident tend to strengthen the conclusion to plenitude.

Take, for example, the absence of intermediates between the unicellular Protozoa and the various primitive metazoan or multicellular groups (represented by the phylum Porifera, the sponges; the well-known group the Coelenterata, the jellyfishes; the less well-known group the Ctenophora, more commonly known as the comb jellies or sea gooseberries; the nematodes; flatworms; etc.). Collectively, the species comprising these primitive multicellular phyla are very diverse in morphology and behavior. Moreover, they are far from simple in structure and design. They are highly complex organisms made up of most of the basic cell types—muscle, nerve, epidermal, gland, etc.—found throughout the animal kingdom. The Protozoa are also a fantastically diverse group. But between these two groups there is an enormous gap filled only with a few types of simple colonial Protozoa.

That this gap is likely to be necessary is suggested by the difficulty of imagining realistic intermediate types of organism made up, say, of three, four, or five cells leading up to genuinely multicellular life. Precisely what form such organisms would take and what adaptive role their constituent cells might play is exceedingly difficult to imagine. It is not only my own imagination that is lacking here. After a century of intense speculation the evolutionary origin of the Metazoa is still problematical, primarily because no convincing series of functional intermediates between the unicellular and the multicellular level of biological organization has been envisaged. Simple life forms, it seems, can be composed of one cell or many cells but not readily of five or six cells.[34]

In the case of other apparent "gaps," it often turns out that the reason is obvious. There are no marsupial whales or seals. As already mentioned in the previous chapter, this is evidently because the marsupial reproductive system is difficult to adapt to an aquatic lifestyle. As we also saw in the previous chapter, there are no marsupial bats. This may well be because the niche was filled by placentals from the earliest beginnings of marsupial evolution. There are no large mobile terrestrial molluscs; no large terrestrial arthropods; no fish or amphibia capable of powered flight. To modify a frog for powered flight we would need to give it the cardiovascular system of a mammal or bird. To convert a mollusc into a mobile terrestrial form, we would have to give it an endoskeleton, rid it of its shell, clothe it in an impermeable skin—in other words, convert it into a vertebrate.

A great many of the seventy or so major phyla have never generated large complex forms. In many cases this is of necessity. The flatworms, for example, could hardly evolve into anything the size of a mouse. Their basic design prohibits such a prodigious development. Flatworms are flat for good reason—they have no circulatory system. As Huxley points out, "the flatness of the larger flatworms is partly due to the need for having every cell near enough to the surface to be able to get oxygen by diffusion. The elaborate branching of their intestines and all their other internal organs is needed to ensure that no cell shall be more than a microscopic distance away from a source of digested food."[35]

Constraints

In judging to what extent the phantasma of life on earth approaches a complete plenitude of carbon-based forms of life, it is necessary to note that the plenitude we are considering is a plenitude of possible forms, that is, *fully functional living systems that could possibly exist and survive in some conceivable ecosystem on earth.* Consider the fact, for example, that no large organism possesses rotating parts or exploits the wheel as a means of motion.

Wheels are only half as costly as legs in terms of energy consumption, but such a device is not compatible with biological design principles.[36] The reason wheels have not been utilized is because animals must maintain physical connections between their parts. As Stephen Jay Gould asks, "If wheels are so successful an invention, why do animals walk, fly, swim, leap, slither, but never roll?"[37] The problem is that "wheels require that two parts be in juxtaposition without physical connection . . . this cannot be accomplished in creatures familiar to us because connection between parts is an integral property of living systems. Substances and impulses must be able to move from one segment to another."[38]

The incompatibility of wheels with biology is in any case no defect in the scheme of things because of course wheels are only of utility on unnaturally flattened surfaces and are virtually useless on the uneven terrain which covers most of the earth. Advanced robots invariably use articulated legs, which gives them mobility over a far greater range of terrains.

Of course, there are a great many fundamental constraints that impose limitations and restrictions on the range of possible functional biological designs. An elephant with the legs of an antelope is impossible for obvious biomechanical reasons—the legs could never support its weight. Nor can an organism the weight of an elephant, or even a man, fly, because the energy necessary to provide the required degree of lift to make powered flight feasible is simply prohibitive. Even the largest existing flying birds, such as an albatross or a swan, have difficulty getting airborne from rest. The albatross generally takes off into the wind from a hillside or cliff, while a swan often has to run across the surface of a considerable stretch of water. Obviously, a vast number of imaginary organisms are simply impossible for a variety of self-evident biomechanical and other types of design constraints.

Because all the parts and organ systems of an organism are functionally interrelated, constraints on one organ system invariably impose constraints on many of the other organ systems. The need for functional integration and coherence if an organism is to be actualized is bound to restrict the functionally possible to a fantastically small subset of all conceivable organisms. As Schmidt-Nielsen emphasizes:

> The total number of interconnections in the living animal is overwhelming. We can just think of the many steps in supplying oxygen to match the metabolic rate. Structures and functions are all interconnected: breathing, lung size

and area, diffusional pathways, blood flow, heart, haemoglobin function, capillaries, mitochondria, enzyme concentrations, and so on, in a chain of seemingly unending interdependent variables.[39]

In addition to constraints imposed by the necessity of physiological integration, if an organism is to be actualized, it must also be ecologically feasible. A lion or a tyrannosaur without herbivores for prey is impossible. Similarly, herds of herbivores require plant life in abundance.

Evolutionary Constraints

Evolution, whether it is directed or not, can only proceed through functional intermediates, and this is bound to impose additional constraints on what life forms are possible. The origin of life, for example, is difficult to envisage, primarily because of the difficulty of imagining a credible functional sequence of increasingly more complex replicating systems leading from chemistry to the cell. (As was argued in the previous chapter, this suggests perhaps that there may be only one unique route.) A chemist, on the other hand, if he wished to create a living cell, *de novo*, would be free to choose a number of different strategies to synthesize the constituents of the cell and then artificially assemble them into a living whole (there is no reason why this could not be theoretically achieved). Being unconstrained by the necessity to move via a continuous functional series of intermediates, a chemist could at least in theory achieve the same end by far simpler means.

The evolution of the seventy different basic metazoan multicellular body designs from a unicellular ancestor which occurred at the beginning of metazoan evolution is problematical primarily because of the difficulty of envisaging viable intermediates leading from the single-celled ancestral form to a multicellular organism and then the subsequent diversification into the seventy different basic types of life. That all evolutionary transitions must occur through fully functional forms is obviously immensely constraining and suggests that perhaps not all possible fully functional life forms can be generated on a single unique evolutionary tree.

In addition to the evolutionary constraint, i.e., the need for functional continuity, there is another set of constraints which must act to restrict the range of the possible—those associated with the process of development. All multicellular species develop from an egg cell through a complicated and in-

tricate process of embryogenesis. Inevitably, the criteria that must be satisfied to ensure the process is successful are highly constraining.

Consider just one embryological criterion that would have to be satisfied
in the development of a large vertebrate type of organism from its egg cell.
During embryonic development it is essential that all parts of the growing
cell mass are supplied at all times with sufficient oxygen and nutrients. This
will require a cardiovascular and respiratory system. Clearly, not just any sort
of circulatory system will do; only a system which can be continuously transformed and can develop in functional harmony with the growing embryo
will suffice. Circulation must be conserved at every stage of development.
This problem is of course solved in the case of mammalian development, as
every medical student learns, by the expediency of having the system undergo a series of changes from the "first" heart, consisting only of a simple
contractile tube, which then undergoes a gradual transformation into an increasingly powerful pumping system until finally it is converted into the efficient four-chambered pump of the adult mammal. One suspects that there
may be very few alternative ways of continuously changing a circulatory system from simple tube to four-chambered pump while at the same time
maintaining physiological function throughout the process.

In addition to such specific requirements, all developing embryos are
constrained greatly by what two authorities refer to as "generic" physical
mechanisms. As they point out, these include such diverse physical processes
as adhesion, surface tension, and viscosity. Such phenomena may cause
morphological rearrangements of cytoplasm, tissue, or extracellular matrix.
These can sometimes lead to complex forms such as "micro fingers," and to
chemical waves and stripes. They suggest that "major morphological reor-
ganisations in phylogenetic lineages may arise by the action of generic physical mechanisms in developing embryos."[40]

Such physical mechanisms may severely constrain some early events during development such as the formation of the blastula and gastrulation. The
diffusion rate of macromolecular morphogens through an embryo may
limit the size over which a diffusion gradient can be read during development. This limitation taken in conjunction with the viscoelastic properties
of tissues and cells and the small distances over which cells can move in a
short space of time is probably the reason why the major morphogenic
events, including the cell and tissue movements associated with gastrulation

and the specifying of segmentation patterns, occur early in development, when embryos are less than a centimeter across.

Fitness of the Earth

There is a final point to consider regarding the doctrine of plenitude. Only in a uniquely fit environment can a plenitude be actualized. Only in an environment supplied with a reliable and constant source of energy and which is also chemically and physically stable for billions of years and also very diverse could any sort of evolutionary process lead eventually to a manifestation of the full plenitude of life forms. But although these conditions are stringent, the hydrosphere of the earth satisfies them all. For billions of years it has been bathed in a constant radiant energy source (which contains just the type of radiation required for life), and over the vast eons of geological time its chemical and physical stability has been ensured by the various geochemical cycles, including the water and the tectonic cycle. Moreover, although the hydrosphere is remarkably stable, it also contains a great variety of diverse environments—the polar oceans, tropical rain forests, high mountains, hot sandy deserts, arctic tundra, hot springs, the ocean depths, wetlands. That it should be exceedingly stable in terms of its general physical and chemical properties yet at the same time contain very diverse environments is of considerable interest in itself, as this lends further support to the notion of its unique fitness for life. If the earth's hydrosphere had been a monoenvironment, the potential for diverse life forms would have been greatly constrained.

This would seem to be yet another significant coincidence—that the unique environment suitable for carbon-based life, the hydrosphere of a planet of the mass and size of the earth, is also ideally suited for the manifestation of a plenitude of life forms. As we saw in chapter 4, there are convincing grounds for believing that the hydrosphere of the earth (and of any planet of the same size and mass and the same distance from its own sun) is the inevitable end of natural law. In other words, nature would seem to be arranged to generate an environment perfectly fit for the manifestation of what would appear to be the plenitude of all possible carbon-based life forms.

Conclusion

Even though at present we may still be far from having any final answer to the question of plenitude, most of the evidence is nevertheless remarkably consistent with the doctrine. That so many diverse forms of life and basically dissimilar body plans have in fact been actualized during the course of evolution on earth supports the concept that the evolutionary tree of life on earth was generated by direction from a unique program embedded in the order of nature, one that was specifically arranged to generate through a myriad of unique and intricate transformations the fullest possible plenitude of natural biological forms.

Chapter 14

The Dream of Asilomar

In which the challenge posed to undirected evolution by the constraints
inherent in complex systems is examined. In complex systems like a watch
or a living system, all the subsystems are intensely integrated. Engineering
changes in such systems is complex because each change to any one
subsystem must be compatible with the functioning of all the other
subsystems. Any change beyond a trivial degree is bound to necessitate
intelligently directed compensatory changes in many of the interacting
subsystems. In this context it is hard to understand how undirected
evolution via a series of independent changes could ever produce a
radical redesign in any sort of system as complex as a living organism.
It is precisely this integrated complexity which provides a major barrier
to engineering radical change in living things from viruses to mammals.
In the future, if genetic engineers are ever able to radically redesign
living systems from proteins to whole organisms, this will only be via
intelligently directed changes which will almost certainly necessitate
progammed simultaneous change in many of the basic subsystems.
Artificial evolution will be per saltum *and not* per *a succession of*
independent changes. Living organisms not only exhibit an immense
integrative complexity but are also immensely complex in terms of the
sheer number of unique components they contain. In the case of higher
organisms the number of different unique genetic readouts used
throughout the life of the organism may approach several billion.

Three different neurons in the mammalian brain.

Each nerve cell consists of a cell body (c), an axon (a), and dendrites (d). The dendrites receive signals from other nerve cells and transmit them to the nerve cell body. The axons carry the nerve impulses from the nerve cell body to other nerve cells. Nerve cells make between 10,000 and 100,000 connections with other nerve cells. Most axons make highly specific contacts with other nerve cells. Altogether, there are ten trillion nerve cells in the human brain (10^{11}). The total number of connections is about 10^{15}.

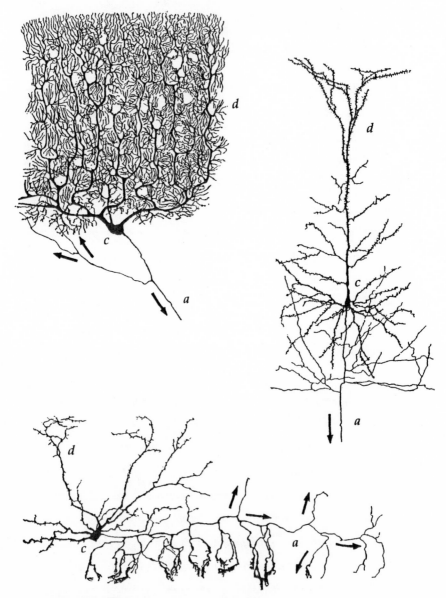

From S. Ramón y Cajal (1909) *System Nerveux,* figs. 8, 9, and 21.)

Breeders habitually speak of an animal's organisation as something plastic which they can model almost as they please . . . [William] Youatt . . . speaks of the principle of selection as "that which enables the agriculturist, not only to modify the character of his flock but to change it altogether. It is the magician's wand by means of which he may summon into life whatever form and mould he pleases." Lord Somerville, speaking of what breeders have done for sheep says, "it would seem as if they had chalked upon a wall a form perfect in itself and then had given it existence."

—Charles Darwin, *On the Origin of Species*, 1859

A handful of sand contains about 10,000 grains, more than the number of stars we can see on a clear night. But the number of stars we can see is only a fraction of the number of stars that are. . . . The cosmos is rich beyond measure: the total number of stars in the universe is greater than all the grains of sand on all the beaches on the planet earth.

—Carl Sagan, *Cosmos*, 1980

Some seventy-five miles south of San Francisco, on the beautiful California coast, beside Monterey Bay, lies the small town of Pacific Grove. It was to this idyllic setting in late February 1975 that 134 of the world's leading biological scientists from the United States and from eighteen other countries gathered for a historic meeting in the Asilomar Conference Center. The meeting was the first example in the history of science of scientists meeting together to discuss the regulation of their activities. The activities which seemed to the participants at the Asilomar Conference so urgently to require regulation concerned experiments using the newly developed experimental techniques that enabled molecular biologists to splice together DNA from two different organisms, creating novel recombinant DNA molecules—that is, molecules of DNA which have never before existed on earth.

Collectively, these new techniques, now generally referred to as genetic engineering, have provided mankind with what is in effect an immense genetic word processor. Just as it is possible with an ordinary word processor to change an individual letter, to delete, to add, or to transpose sections of a text at will, genetic engineering can now be used to create any conceivable DNA molecule, to compose *de novo* any genetic message we may wish and to modify the genetic message in any existing organism in almost any conceivable way. At least, this is true already in the case of microorganisms, and although it is not yet possible to manipulate so readily the genetic text of higher organisms, it seems likely that within a few years such manipulations will also be possible, so that the entire genetic script of any organism will be an open book as accessible and easy to manipulate as the text of an English manuscript using a word processor.

Early Hopes and Fears

The creation of novel recombinant DNA molecules was a cause of widespread concern in the early 1970s. As Nobel laureate Paul Berg pointed out in the now famous "Berg letter" published in the journal *Science* in July 1974:

> Although such experiments [the creation of new recombinant DNA molecules] would facilitate the solution of important theoretical and practical biological problems, they would also result in the creation of novel types of infectious DNA elements, whose biological properties cannot be completely predicted in advance. There is serious concern that some of the artificial recombinant DNA molecules could prove biologically hazardous.[1]

Although the Asilomar Conference was convened to discuss the relatively mundane matter of developing guidelines for researchers using the newly created recombinant DNA molecules, aimed at minimizing the risk of generating a virulent bacterium containing genes harmful to man, the outcome of which might lead, in the words of a *Science* editorial, "to a catastrophe of possibly epidemic proportions,"[2] it was not these immediate practical consequences of genetic engineering that fueled the headlines in the early 1970s.

In those heady days leading up to the Asilomar Conference, the perception was widely shared that the development of recombinant DNA technology represented a historic turning point in the history of science, ushering in a brave new science-fiction era when biologists would indeed possess Darwin's magician's wand to summon up whatever form of life they pleased.

Over the past twenty years articles in glossy magazines, the popular press, and in semipopular and scholarly books with provocative titles such as *Playing God, Man-Made Life,* and *The Ultimate Experiment* have continually proclaimed the theme that fire has finally been stolen from the gods, that man was now creator, that a remodeling of the biosphere was imminent, and that all manner of undreamt-of forms of life were about to leap from the laboratory, conjured up at the whim of the magician's wand.[3]

The scenario of man remodeling the world has not been restricted to the popularizers of science. Even as early as 1972, the distinguished cell biologist Dr. James Danielli, director of the Center for Theoretical Biology at the State University of New York at Buffalo, was widely quoted as claiming that "soon in 20–30 years, but we may well be there in 10 years, scientists will be able to create new species and carry out the equivalent of 10,000,000,000 years of evolution in one year."[4] The scientific community no less than the general public was gripped with what Marie Jahoda described in *Nature* as a sense of "metaphysical awe":

> At the risk of being laughed out of court by these superior minds, I suggest that they were overcome by a metaphysical awe at their own power to fiddle with the very building blocks of life. . . . That metaphysical awe was akin to Oppenheimer's experience in witnessing the first atomic bomb explosion and when it communicated itself to the public, all hell broke loose.[5]

Over the past twenty years the scenario of a biological world remodeled by genetic engineering has been enhanced in the eyes of the general public by a number of widely publicized experiments, some reported in the popular press. For example, *Nature* carried a report in 1982 announcing the first successful transfer of a gene from one species to another.[6] Using a tiny capillary tube culminating in a point one twenty-four-thousandth of an inch in diameter, Richard Palmiter and Ralph Brinster of the University of Washington and the University of Pennsylvania, respectively, injected a DNA molecule containing the rat growth hormone gene plus its promoter sequence (the DNA message which switches the gene on) into the egg cell of a mouse, just after the sperm had penetrated the cell membrane of the ovum. The result of this gene transfer was a so-called transgenic mouse, a mouse containing the gene of another species. Under the alien influence of the rat growth hormone gene, the mouse grew into a giant rat-sized mouse, which gained notoriety in the world press as the "mighty mouse."[7] Another wonder was the sensational "geep."[8] This was a chimera consisting of a mixture of sheep and goat characteristics. The geep was not, strictly speaking, the result of genetic engineering (artificially changing the structure of an organism's DNA), but rather the result of the fusion of embryonic cells from one species with the embryo of another. And during the past year the first successful and widely publicized cloning of a mammal from an adult cell—the sheep Dolly—was announced.

And the wonders are no longer restricted to the laboratory. Since the mid-eighties a number of genetically engineered organisms have been released. One example was the so-called ice-minus microbe, an artificial version of a natural microbe, which is found on the leaves of strawberry plants and which manufactures a protein that acts as a seed for the formation of ice crystals and hence promotes frost formation. Using genetic-engineering techniques, Steven Lindow and Nickolas Panopoulos of the University of California at Berkeley removed the gene which specifies this protein, creating thereby the ice-minus version of the bacterium.[9] In the hope that they would displace their naturally occurring frost-promoting cousins, the ice-minus bacteria were sprayed on strawberry crops in Florida and Southern California.[10] Another artificially engineered organism, created by David Bishop of the Natural Environment and Research Council, Institute of Virology, at Oxford, this time a virus, which naturally infects the pine beauty moth, a serious pest in pine plantations, has been released into the wild. The engineered virus contains new genes, inserted into its DNA coding for insect poisons or insecticides, and has a far more potent destructive effect on the pine beauty moth than the natural virus.

Mere Tinkering

Such events fueled a widespread fear, even hysteria, that the advent of genetic engineering was leading mankind into a genetic hell, a world entirely remodeled, replete with superhumans and all manner of fantastic new types of life. Yet just twenty years later these fears have turned out to be unfounded. The actual achievements of genetic engineering are rather more mundane. The sorts of achievements described above such as the mighty mouse and ice-minus bacteria are far less portentous than they appear. They represent a relatively trivial tinkering rather than genuine engineering, analogous to tuning a car engine rather than redesigning it, an exploitation of the already existing potential for variation which is built into all living systems. An assessment of the achievements of genetic engineering in the agricultural field to 1995 was the subject of a recent *New Scientist* article entitled "Whatever Happened to the Gene Revolution?"[11] As the article points out, although sixty species of plants have been subject to genetic tampering and three thousand field tests of transgenic plants have been conducted worldwide, all of these achievements are relatively trivial and very far from the creation or radical reconstruction of a living organism. Confessed the author of the article, "It isn't what most people expected from genetic engineering."[12]

In fact, genetic engineering does not exist in the usual sense of the word. A mechanical engineer, from his knowledge of the principles of mechanical engineering and of the behavior of materials, can design a suspension bridge on a piece of paper. But no genetic engineer, from his knowledge of the principles of bioengineering and from his knowledge of the behavior and properties of macromolecules, could possibly specify the design of a living system *a priori* and encode the instructions for its assembly in a DNA sequence. Nothing achieved to date by genetic engineering remotely approaches the creation of new living systems from first principles or the radical redesign of an existing organism so that it can compete and survive in a natural environment. The dream has been postponed to some distant future.

Integrative Complexity

The failure to realize the dream of Asilomar, to wave Darwin's magic wand, does not result from our inability to use the DNA word processor. Prometheus in this sense is well and truly unbound. The difficulty in redesigning organisms stems from the fact that living things are immensely complex.

However, the challenge inherent in their complexity resides not primarily in the sheer number of components, which as we shall see below is remarkable enough, but comes from the reality that living systems are such *intensely integrated systems that their components cannot be easily isolated and changed independently*. Consequently, change, even if relatively minor, involves complex compensatory changes. This problem is met with in any attempt to engineer changes in any sort of complex system, such as, for example, a watch, consisting of many richly interconnected component elements.

The watch-organism analogy has of course been one of the most evocative and persistently popular analogies used by philosophers and biologists over the past few centuries.[13] It is useful here, as it very clearly illustrates the challenge of integrative complexity. From a mere cursory examination of the structure of a watch and of the intense functional integration of its various components, it is self-evident that if one cog is to be changed in some way, then if the function of the watch is to be maintained, simultaneous compensatory changes must be made to the entire chain of cogwheels—in effect, the entire watch must be redesigned. It is hard to imagine an object less able to undergo any sort of undirected evolutionary change. Watches are almost infinitely intolerant of any sort of random tinkering or changes in the configuration of any of their components. Change to any part, without intelligently engineered compensatory changes in the other parts, will lead to a complete disruption of the mechanism. The wheels will grind to a halt.

To change or improve the design of a watch or a clock in some way necessitates a total intelligent redesign of the entire system involving compensatory changes to the configuration of nearly all the other components simultaneously. For this reason the historical evolution of watches and clocks occurred in a series of relatively discontinuous steps. Each advance, from the medieval "verge foliot" escapement to the pendulum anchor escapement, was the result of innovative insights on the part of a succession of watchmakers from the twelfth century to the seventeenth, leading to intelligently engineered improvements in watch and clock design. Watches can undergo, and have historically undergone, "directed evolution" but only under the direction of an intelligent engineer. The historical evolution of steam engines, telescopes, car engines, computers, and airplanes conforms to the same discontinuous pattern and for precisely the same reasons.[14]

Before the Darwinian revolution organisms were viewed almost universally as unique wholes, incapable of evolutionary change via a successive series of small independent changes. Just like any other complex system, an organism was "a whole pre-supposed by all its parts," in the view of the early nineteenth-century English poet Samuel Coleridge.[15] This concept can be traced back to the biological philosophy of Aristotle.[16] It was presented forcibly in the first half of the nineteenth century by the leading French comparative anatomist and ardent antievolutionist, Georges Cuvier, whose views profoundly influenced nearly all the leading nineteenth-century biologists in Europe. In Cuvier's own words:

> All the organs of one and the same animal form a single system of which all the parts hold together, act and react upon each other; and there can be no modifications in any one of them that will not bring about analogous modification in them all.[17]

> Every organised being forms a whole . . . a peculiar system of its own, the parts of which mutually correspond, and concur in producing the same definitive action, by a reciprocal reaction. None of these parts can change in form, without the others also changing.[18]

According to this Cuvierian view, because of the intensity of the functional integration, no aspect or component subsystem is isolated or independent. Consequently, any major change in any component subsystem will require of necessity a whole train of *simultaneous* compensatory changes of a highly specific kind in all or many of the interacting components to preserve the functional integration upon which the viability of the system depends. *Thus, gradual change resulting from the accumulation of a succession of minor independent changes is impossible.*

One of the most recent and very scholarly presentations of this principle was given by Stuart Kauffman in his *Origins of Order.* As Kauffman points out, as the number of components in a complex system increases, the constraints against change likewise also increase:

> I believe this to be a genuinely fundamental constraint facing adaptive evolution. As systems with many parts increase both the number of those parts and the richness of interactions among the parts, it is typical that the number of conflicting design constraints among the parts increases rapidly. Those conflicting constraints imply that optimisation can attain only poorer compromises. No matter how strong selection may be, adaptive processes cannot

climb higher peaks. . . . conflicting constraints are a very general limit in adaptive evolution.[19]

Although since 1859 most biologists eventually came to accept the concept of evolution, the idea that the intense functional integration of all the parts of an organism is bound to act as a severe constraint against biological change has been acknowledged almost universally by specialists in every field of biology.[20] The "constraints problem" is a recurring theme in the thinking of many developmental biologists today who acknowledge that the richness of the interconnectedness of living systems is bound to constrain to a large degree the direction of evolutionary change.[21] The same point was made by the Japanese biochemist Susumo Ohno in a *Nature* article defending his notion of saltational evolution by "frozen accidents": "An enzyme seldom functions alone. More often a number of enzymes are functionally coupled together to constitute one metabolic system. Once a reasonably well-functioning system was established, any drastic change in the kinetic property of one enzyme, without concomitant adjustments in the kinetic properties of functionally coupled enzymes, would tend to be disastrous."[22]

In the realm of gene therapy, where genetic engineering has been intensively applied to viral genomes in an endeavor to create safe vectors for the transfer of "healthy genes" into patients with genetic diseases, the problem of the integrative complexity of biological systems is now being directly encountered.[23] The complex and often daunting necessity of having to engineer coordinated and often complex changes in the genomes of viruses to render them capable of efficient or safe gene transfer is at the heart of the problem of gene therapy and one of the major reasons why progress in this area has been relatively slow.

Even Richard Dawkins, one of the staunchest defenders of Darwinian orthodoxy, admits that constraints do exist and would be bound to restrict or channel evolutionary change to some degree.[24] In the context of the above discussion it is ironic that Richard Dawkins should have chosen the title *The Blind Watchmaker* for his recent best-seller. Of all analogies, that of a watch is perhaps the least apt for arguing the case for Darwinism. A watch is the very archetype of a complex integrated system that cannot undergo change other than by intelligent direction because of the stringent demands for simultaneous compensatory change.

The question of how such intensely integrated systems as organisms can undergo continuous change in some part or subsystem without the need for "intelligent compensatory changes" is sidestepped in all discussion of undirected models of evolutionary change. Invariable Darwinian arguments artificially isolate a particular component or organ, such as the eye, from the immensely complex system in which it is embedded. Conveniently isolated from the constraining functional interconnections between organ and organism, it is relatively easy to envisage some organ or structure undergoing gradual change via a long series of hypothetical transitional forms. Thus, Darwinian explanations often appear to be superficially plausible.

For example, it is easy to envisage changing the word MAN via MAT and SAT to CAT via a series of single letter changes when the words are considered in isolation. But to make the same sequence of letter changes while at the same time preserving the meaning of any sentence in which they occur is far more complex, necessitating a number of additional "compensatory changes" to the other words in the sentence.

MAN →	MAT →	SAT →	CAT
THE	THE	HE	THE
MAN	MAT	SAT	CAT
LOOKED	LOOKED	DOWN	SAT
ANGRY	GOOD		DOWN

If an eye or any other organ is to be changed gradually from one state to another via a series of intermediate states, then this of necessity will involve compensatory changes in its biological context.

Dawkins's claim in the concluding paragraph of *The Blind Watchmaker*—"provided we postulate a sufficiently large series of sufficiently finely graded intermediates, we shall be able to derive anything from anything else"—[25] is unrealistic not only because of the functional constraints problem, but also because there are several cases where there are biophysical barriers to particular transformations, and in such cases, no matter how many intermediates we might like to propose, there is simply no gradual route across.

For example, all viral capsids are either cylinders or icosahedrons. The reason is purely biophysical. These are the only two stable forms that can be built up by stacking together a single subunit—the icosahedron and the cylinder. There is no intermediate series of stable forms leading from the cylindrical-shaped viral capsid to the icosahedron. Physics forbids it. Another quite different example regards the two alternative positions of the nervous system within the animal phyla. In invertebrates the nervous system is ventral—situated along the underside of the organism—while in the vertebrates, it is dorsal—situated along the back. No group of organisms exist which have their nervous system on the side, midway between the front and back. It was always hard to imagine how an asymetric intermediate arrangement with the nervous system on the right or left sides could be adaptive. The developmental genetic evidence now suggests there never were such organisms. Recent discoveries have revealed, for example, that the gene specifying which part of the embryo will be dorsal and which ventral is the same in both vertebrates and invertebrates. This in turn suggests that the gene may have suddenly switched its meaning during evolution, causing what was previously ventral to become dorsal. Intermediacy between dorsal and ventral may in effect be excluded, because of the Boolean logic of developmental genetic systems.

Beanbag Genetics

At the beginning of the century, shortly after the rediscovery of Mendel's laws, there was a brief period, the so-called era of beanbag genetics, when individual genes were considered to act separately and independently during development. There was believed to be a simple one-to-one relationship between individual genes and character traits. Given that it was already well established that embryogenesis involved complex phenomena, including highly ordered tissue and cell interactions, it is, from this distance, somewhat difficult to understand how this gross simplification could have had any appeal or how geneticists could have envisaged that a gene could have influenced a particular trait independently of other genes.

Despite the initial appeal of the beanbag concept, as knowledge of genetics and development progressed during the first decades of the century, it became increasingly apparent that most components of an organism are generated by the interaction of very many genes and that most genes influenced more than one character. Just how many components may be affected by the same gene is illustrated by the mutation called "wingless" in domestic fowl. The mutations in this gene cause developmental abnormalities in a wide variety of systems: the wings do not develop properly, the downy cover is underdeveloped, there are multiple abnormalities in the kidney and urinary tract, and the lungs and air sacs are missing.[26] Many other examples could be cited.

Rather than viewing genes as independent entities influencing individual separable character traits, the modern view that has emerged over the past sixty years was summarized by the great evolutionary biologist Ernst Mayr: "Every character of an organism is affected by all genes and every gene affects all characters."[27]

As the molecular structure and organization of the gene in higher organisms was worked out over the past twenty years, one of the reasons the great majority of genes affect diverse characters became clear—because many of the basic functional units in living things are made up of combinations of different gene products—just as words are combined into sentences. (See figure below.) It is generally combinations of gene products which form the key molecular complexes involved in directing and coordinating the development of higher organisms, determining when and where a cell will divide, whether or not a cell will differentiate into another cell type, which genes will be expressed in a particular cell at a particular stage of development, as well as forming the unique cell surface markers by which a cell reads its position in the embryo and signals to other cells its identity. Because the various combinations or complexes in which a particular gene functions may play entirely unrelated biological roles, mutations in any such gene will inevitably lead to a complex pattern of mutation, in which individual anomalies develop without any apparent physiological connection and seem to be distributed in a random manner among very diverse structures and processes.[28]

The fact that many genes are elements in complex combinations which play diverse roles influencing many different aspects of development implies

Gene combination and its consequence, pleiotropy.

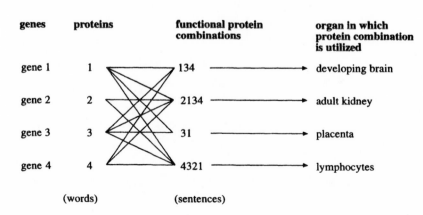

genes	proteins	functional protein combinations	organ in which protein combination is utilized
gene 1	1	134	developing brain
gene 2	2	2134	adult kidney
gene 3	3	31	placenta
gene 4	4	4321	lymphocytes
(words)		(sentences)	

that the process of development is not genetically compartmentalized. Particular processes and organs are not specified by particular sets of genes. Nowhere in the organism is there a set of genes restricted to "making" the brain, an eye, or a leg. No structure or process or organ is genetically isolated; the same genes are involved to a greater or lesser degree in the specifications of all organs, structures, and processes. In terms of the gene interactions which underlie development, higher organisms are indeed richly interconnected systems.

The Genetics and Development of the Nematode

There is no more remarkable illustration of the interconnectedness of living systems than the development of the tiny nematode worm *C. elegans*, which is currently the best understood in terms of its molecular genetics and development of all the multicellular life forms.

The nematodes are tiny cylindrical unsegmented wormlike organisms generally about 1 millimeter long. There are a vast number of different species of nematodes, perhaps as many as 400,000. Normally, they go unnoticed, but they are exceedingly plentiful. A spadeful of garden soil may contain more than 1 million individual nematodes. Most are parasites. The human body hosts at least fifty different parasitic species.

Because they are so small and develop very quickly, and because all their organs and cells can be observed so easily with a microscope, they are an ideal organism for studying in detail the complex mechanisms which direct the development of higher organisms. To exploit the advantages of these tiny worms, the Cambridge biologist Sydney Brenner commenced a long-term project in 1963 to completely describe, cell-by-cell, the entire development of all the 959 cells that make up the larva of this tiny worm.[29]

As a result, we now know the complete developmental history and lineage of every one of the 959 cells in the nematode larva. Thus, it is possible to construct a lineage tree showing the descent of every cell in the mature larva from the egg cell down. In addition, a considerable number of the specific interactions which regulate the development of the worm, including specific cell contacts that control cell fate and movement in the embryo, have been identified. A complete catalog of all the nerve cells has been drawn up, including every single connection made by each individual nerve cell with other nerve cells and other body cells. There is now an extensive catalog of mutants that affect virtually every aspect of the organism's biology, including virtually every mutation that disrupts patterns of development.

As this project got under way, it soon revealed that the assembly of the nematode organs during development was remarkably nonmodular. It is impossible to isolate any part or organ in the nematode and treat it as an independent developmental entity.

Before the detailed analysis of the development of the nematode had been carried out, it might have been predicted that each organ would form separately, perhaps from a separate set of genetic instructions or a separate clone of cells. It turned out, however, that for each organ—the pharynx, the intestine, the nervous system, and the sex organs—the cells composing that organ were not related in any way in terms of lineage. The development of the pharynx of the nematode illustrates this nicely. The cells making up the pharynx are derived from eight completely different cell lines scattered throughout the lineage tree. The same is true of all the organ systems of the nematode; in each case the cells making up a particular organ are completely unrelated in terms of their lineage.

Another curious aspect of the development of the nematode and one that would never have been predicted is that although the organism is bilaterally symmetrical—that is, its left and right halves are mirror images of each other—the equivalent organs and cells on the right- and lefthand sides of the body of the larva *are not derived from equivalent cells in the embryo.* In other words, identical components on the right and left sides of the body are generated in different ways from different and nonsymmetrically placed progenitor cells in the early embryo and have therefore lineage patterns which are in some cases completely dissimilar. This is like making the right and left headlight on an automobile in completely different ways and utilizing completely different processes.

Even individual cells of the same cell type in any one organ, such as, say, the muscle cells, gland cells, or nerve cells of the pharynx, are also derived from different lineages. For example, one particular cell progenitor of the pharynx gives rise to muscle cells, interneurons, gland cells, and epithelial cells. Another progenitor gives rise to muscle and gland cells.

Altogether, there is not the slightest trace of compartmentalization or modularity or logical hierarchy in the assembly of the nematode. The finding was astonishing and completely unpredicted. Before the assembly of the nematode was worked out, "there had been," as a recent editorial in *Science* put it, "a persistent expectation among molecular biologists that the guiding themes of development would somehow be encoded in a genetic program somewhat analogous to the sequential encoding of a protein . . . and Brenner himself expected 'that the nematode would throw light on the logical structure of the program.' . . . Those involved in the project had believed that 'the cells were going to be powers of two, amusing mathematical symmetries, and so on.'" The editorial continues: "One persistent view . . . is . . . that organisms must be partitioned in some kind of molecular fashion, based on anatomical structures, physiological systems or developmental pathways. This modular organisation is then thought to be the basis for molecular genetic representation."[30]

Just as there was not the slightest modularity in organ assembly, the genes likewise showed no sign of a modular order. There was not the slightest evidence for genetic modules—that is to say, the existence of groups of genes involved in the specification of particular parts of the organism, say, the nervous system or the pharynx. No matter which part or organ of the nematode one examined, its development was intimately interconnected with the development of practically all the other organs and parts of the organism.

Brenner acknowledges that the idea that genes might be arranged into functional modules is appealing for both its feasibility for control and its access to ordered evolutionary change. Large computer programs are organized in this manner in order to localize the effects of change: "Thus by analogy it is argued that genes are also arranged in closed logical packets allowing changes to take place in one subsystem without affecting the others. But the analogy has not been borne out."[31]

So tightly "joined" are all the components during nematode development that it would seem a flagrant affront to common sense to presume that any radical change engineered in the structure of any one component, say, the pharynx, would not necessitate compensatory balancing changes in virtually the entire organism. It is safe to say nothing remotely like a radical redesign of the nematode will be achieved for many years to come.

Although the development and genetics of the nematode may be an extreme example of "interconnectedness," as knowledge of the genetic basis of development has advanced over recent decades, the same interconnectedness has been found to some degree in the development of all higher organisms. It may not always be quite as intense, but there is in many instances the same lack of any genuinely independent modules, either genetic or developmental. And it is indisputable that the majority of genes in all higher organisms influence more than one functional or developmental system.

Redundancy

Another very intriguing aspect of development in higher organisms which has become increasingly apparent over the last ten years, and which is bound to impose additional constraints against any sort of bit-by-bit undirected change, is the use of partially or totally redundant components to buffer organisms against random mutational error and ensure reliability, particularly during development. As one authority points out: "The idea that redundancy may be quite common in cell and developmental biology has its origin in Spemann's (1938) idea of double assurance, a term taken from engineering."[32]

The strategy of using several different means to achieve a particular goal, where each of the individual means is sufficient by itself to achieve the goal, is used in all manner of situations to guarantee that the goal will always be achieved, even if one or more of the means fail. Missiles, for example, are often guided to their targets using a number of different automatic guidance systems, including ground-based radar, map matching, inertial guidance, following a graded signal (heat-seeking). Even if one fails, the missile will still home in unerringly on its target. Reliability of information storage on computer discs is increased by encoding the information in two or more different ways. The functional reliability of complex machines such as aircraft and particularly space vehicles invariably involves the use of redundant components.[33] The space shuttle's on-board inertial guidance system, which it uses during boosting into orbit and during reentry, consists, according to the *McGraw-Hill Encyclopedia of Science and Technology*, of "*five redundant computers* and three inertial measurement units. Dual star trackers are used for periodic realignment in space. . . . A radar backup system is provided for safety during launch and landing."[34] (My emphasis.) Another instance where redundancy is exploited to increase reliability is in human and animal navigation, where most often a number of different and individually redundant clues are followed to minimize the risk of navigational error, which might accrue from following only one type or set of clues.[35]

It now appears that a considerable number of genes, perhaps even the majority in higher organisms, are completely or at least partially redundant. One of the major pieces of evidence that this is the case has come from so-called gene knockout experiments, where a gene is effectively disabled in some way using genetic-engineering techniques so that it cannot play its normal role in the organism's biology. A classic example of this came when a gene coding for a large complex protein known as Tenascin-C, which occurs in the extracellular matrix of all vertebrates, was knocked out in mice, without any obvious effect. As the author of a paper commenting on this surprising result cautions: "It would be premature to conclude that [the protein] has no important function . . . [as] it is conserved in every vertebrate species, which argues strongly for a fundamental role."[36] The protein product of the *Zeste* gene in the fruit fly drosophila, which is a component of certain multiprotein complexes involved in transcribing regions of the DNA, can also be knocked out without any obvious effect on the very processes in which it is known to function.[37]

The phenomenon of redundant genes is so widespread that it is already acknowledged to pose something of an evolutionary conundrum. Although in the words of the author of one recent article, "true genetic redundancy ought to be, in an evolutionary sense, impossible or at least unlikely,"[38] partially redundant genes are common. As another authority comments in a recent review article: "Arguments over whether there can be true redundancy are moot for the experimentalist. The question is how the functions for partially redundant genes can be discovered given that *partial redundancy is the rule*."[39] (My emphasis.)

And it seems increasingly that it is not only individual genes that are redundant, but rather that the phenomenon may be all-pervasive in the development of higher organisms, existing at every level from individual genes to the most complex developmental processes. For example, individual nerve axons, like guided missiles or migrating birds, are guided to their targets by a number of different and individually redundant mechanisms and clues.[40] The development of the female sexual organ, the vulva, in the nematode provides perhaps the most dramatic example to date of redundancy exploited as a fail-safe device at the very highest level. A detailed description of the mechanism of formation of the nematode vulva is beyond the scope of this chapter; suffice it to say that the organ is generated by means of two quite different developmental mechanisms, either of which is sufficient by itself to generate a perfect vulva.[41]

It seems increasingly likely that redundancy will prove to be universally exploited in many key aspects of the development of higher organisms, for precisely the same reason it is utilized in many other areas—as a fail-safe mechanism to ensure that developmental goals are achieved with what amounts to a virtually zero error rate. A very high degree of redundancy in the specification of the development of higher organisms is almost certainly not in the least bit gratuitous, but rather of necessity. *Probably no system remotely as complex as a higher organism could possibly function without a large measure of redundancy in many or even every aspect of its design.*

Now, this phenomenon poses an additional challenge to the idea that organisms can be radically transformed as a result of a succession of small independent changes, as Darwinian theory supposes. For it means that if an advantageous change is to occur, in an organ system such as the nematode vulva, which is specified in two completely different ways, then this will of necessity require simultaneous changes in both blueprints. In other words, the greater the degree of redundancy, the greater the need for simultaneous mutation to effect evolutionary change and the more difficult it is to believe that evolutionary change could have been engineered without intelligent direction. Redundancy also increases the difficulty of genetic engineering, as it means that the compensatory changes that must inevitably accompany any desired change must be necessarily increased.

The Complexity of Proteins

The same fantastic interconnectedness and lack of clear modularity which is manifest in the nematode is seen at every level of biological design right down to individual protein molecules. In the late fifties, as the first three-dimensional structures of proteins were worked out, it was first assumed that each amino acid made an individual and independent contribution to the 3-D form of the protein rather in the same way that beanbag geneticists earlier in the century had envisaged that each gene had an independent effect on the organism's phenotype. This simplifying assumption flowed also from the concept of proteins as "molecular machines," which implied that their design should be like that of any machine, essentially modular, built up of a combination of independent parts each of which made some unique definable contribution to the whole.

It soon became apparent, however, that the design of proteins was far more complex than was first assumed. The contribution of each individual amino acid to the configuration of a protein was not straightforward but was influenced by subtle interactions with many of the other amino acids in the molecule. The situation was further complicated by the finding that most proteins could tolerate considerable changes to their amino acid sequence and still maintain the same three-dimensional form and functional properties. After thirty years of intensive study it is now understood that the spatial conformation adopted by each segment of the amino acid chain of a protein is specified by a complex web of electronic or electrochemical interactions, including hydrogen bonds and hydrophobic forces, which ultimately involve virtually every other section of the amino acid chain in the molecule. *It might be claimed with only slight exaggeration that the position of each one of the thousands of atoms is influenced by all the other atoms in the molecule and that each atom contributes, via immensely complex cooperative interactions with all the other atoms in the protein, something to the overall shape and function of the whole molecule.*

Proteins are thus very much less modular than ordinary machines such as watches, which are built up from a set of relatively independent modules or compartments. Remove the cog from a watch, and it still remains a cog; remove the wheel from a car, and it remains a wheel. The parts of a watch do not determine the configuration of the whole watch, nor does the whole configuration of the watch determine the conformation or properties of any of the parts. Proteins are far more holistic than any machine yet built.

Even today protein engineering in the true sense of the word—the specification of entirely new amino acid sequences that will fold into biological proteins with novel functions—has not in any realistic sense commenced. Although it is the Holy Grail of the protein engineer, in the words of Jennifer Van Brunt, "the obstacles are staggering."[42] Max Perutz considers the goal "utopian."[43]

However, attempts to engineer changes in the structure and function of existing proteins are advancing rapidly.[44] Increasingly ambitious transformations are now being attempted. The most complex transformation engineered to date was recently achieved by a group of researchers at Yale who changed one protein conformation into another quite different structure, a major feat which required changing twenty-eight amino acids in the initial starting protein. The way the Yale researchers carried this out is instructive. It was not achieved Darwinian fashion, bit by bit. In fact, all the necessary twenty-eight changes in the amino acid sequence were first worked out theoretically by applying structure prediction algorithms, model building, etc., and then the new amino acid sequence was synthesized in a bacterial expression system. In other words, all the changes were made simultaneously and the conformational change was engineered per saltum in Cuvierian fashion.[45] The magician's wand was waved, but it obeyed the logic of Cuvier, not Darwin. The magic was per saltum, and not via cumulative selection.

No doubt future advances will one day make it possible to radically modify or redesign existing functional proteins on a routine basis. However, from what is now known of the integrative complexity of proteins, and from the work going on in this field, it is clear that any significant engineered change in the fundamental design of a protein—say, a basic change in the folding configuration of part of the polypeptide chain—will necessitate many complex simultaneous changes throughout the molecule to preserve Christian Anfinsen's "harmonic chords of interaction consistent with biological function."[46]

Minor Changes

Despite the rich interconnectedness of their components, living systems are, at levels from organismic to molecular, modular to some extent. Indeed, no sort of evolution would be possible, either directed or undirected, if there was no modularity whatsoever in organisms. My point is not that there is no modularity in any sense—this would be absurd—but that the functioning of the vast majority of identifiable modules, whether an individual gene or a particular developmental cascade, is bound to be so highly constrained that a succession of undirected mutations is unlikely to result in major adaptive advance. This is not to say that organisms are unable to undergo any degree of adaptive evolution via a succession of independent changes. This again would be absurd. The evolution of the finches of Galápagos is a classic example of completely undirected yet adaptive biological change. Evolutionary change of this sort is often referred to as microevolution.

Evidence that organisms are in general intensely constrained against change, while at the same time capable of undergoing minor functional changes in certain directions, is provided by the phenomenon of mutation. The fact that the vast majority of all mutations which have some detectable influence on the functioning of the organism are deleterious suggests that each functional living system is indeed enormously constrained to adaptive changes along only a tiny fraction of all the possible evolutionary trajectories available to it. However, the fact that a small number of mutations are beneficial suggests that there must be at least a degree of modularity and that not every change requires compensatory changes. Not every change need therefore be "intelligently engineered."

Despite the evidence that organisms can undergo microevolutionary change and their components are clearly not quite as constrained as are the cogs of a watch, there is also no doubt that throughout the twentieth century, with each advance in knowledge, the design of living things has been revealed to be increasingly less and less modular and to increasingly approach the watch model or even the holistic nonmodular ideal of Coleridge and Aristotle.[47] This is particularly true of advances made over the past three decades in studies of the molecular genetics of development. Just as the complexity of living things in terms of the sheer number of unique adaptive components has grown relentlessly, so too has their integrative complexity. The studies of the nematode are graphic testimony to this.

The Necessity for Direction

Although organisms are modular to a degree, the modules are intensely interconnected. And in some cases, like the nematode, the integrative complexity exhibits a qualitatively different order of complexity to that realized in any man-made system or machine. Indeed, the order manifest in the development of the nematode or in the chaotic tangle of amino acid chains in a protein is the *very antithesis of the modular order of the kind required by nondirected evolutionary models.* It is an order lacking hierarchy, compartment, division, regularity, rules, grammar, program, symmetry, or logic.

The design of living systems, from an organismic level right down to the level of an individual protein, is so integrated that most attempts to engineer even a relatively minor functional change are bound to necessitate a host of subtle compensatory changes. It is hard to envisage a reality less amenable to Darwinian change via a succession of independent undirected mutations altering one component of the organism at a time.

Perhaps one day organisms will be radically transformed by genetic engineering, and mankind will at last wave Darwin's magic wand. However, given the complexity of life, this will only be by "intelligent" design. In other words, it will be *directed.* A desired change will be selected. The genes or modules involved in its specification will be identified. The changes necessary in these key components will be worked out. Also, the number of compensatory changes necessary in other interacting genetic systems will be identified. And so the process will continue until all the necessary changes have been documented and the engineering project commenced. It all seems plausible. But if the only way we can conceive of artificial evolution is through coordinated change brought about by intelligent direction, then surely the possibility that the process of natural evolution was similarly engineered can hardly be discounted. It may be also that just as the historical development of clocks and other machines has been discontinuous by necessity, so the course of evolution may have also been saltational, at least to some degree, by necessity.

Toward a Third Infinity

Integrative complexity is only one aspect of the complexity of living systems. They are also immensely complex in terms of the sheer number of unique components they contain. In almost every field of biology, as knowledge advances, complexity in terms of the number of unique components grows. Where one gene carried out a particular function ten years ago, now there are a hundred. Where once, not so long ago, there was one cell type in the retina, now there are fifty. Where there was once one neurotransmitter in the brain, now there are hundreds. Biology is now caught up in an ongoing complexity revolution, which is surely one of the most extraordinary events in the history of modern science. The phenomenal nature of the complexity revolution that currently pervades every field of biology is increasingly a source of comment among researchers in various fields. The general reaction is one of amazement at the ever-greater depths of complexity revealed as biological knowledge advances.[48] The process of endless complexification is acknowledged in the amusing titles of some recent review articles in scholarly journals: "With Apologies to Scheherazade: Tails of 1001 Kinesin Motors,"[49] and "1002 Protein Phosphatases?"[50]

Combinatorial Mechanisms

There is no tale of complexification more astonishing in modern twentieth-century biological science than the remarkable story of the gene as it has unfolded over the past twenty years. Only twenty years ago the gene was a relatively simple section of the DNA molecule about a thousand bases long which contained an encoded message for one protein. This was copied into an RNA molecule. The sequence of the mRNA was then decoded by the translational machinery into the amino acid sequence of a protein. Hence, each gene coded for one unique protein. How relatively straightforward it seemed.

However, during the seventies it was shown that in higher organisms the genes are split into noncontiguous sections in the DNA called exons (letters, in terms of our language analogy). And subsequent research revealed that different combinations of the exons of an individual gene are often combined in many different ways to produce different mRNA molecules, which are translated into many different proteins, each having slightly different functional properties (words). In other words, via this combinatorial device each gene could code for many different proteins. On top of this, during the eighties it became apparent that many proteins function in large multiprotein complexes—in other words, in combination with other proteins (sentences).

The total number of combinations that can be generated even from only a few genes by these combinatorial mechanisms is enormous. Recently, one researcher in this field calculated that the 25 G protein genes (proteins involved in transmitting chemical signals across the cell membrane) are probably combined into as many as five thousand different G protein complexes.[51] Another case is that of the sarcomere, which is the contractile unit in the muscle cell. In vertebrates this organelle is produced by the assembly of seven major contractile proteins, each encoded by a multigene family with a minimum of four members. The authors of an article in *Annual Review of Biochemistry* entitled "Alternative Splicing" point out:

> Assuming an average of 5 genes per family, in combination they have the capacity to generate $5^7 = 78,125$ different sarcomeric types. This potential is significantly increased by alternative splicing. To date, more than 3 different exons or pairs of exons are known to be alternatively spliced in sarcomeric contractile genes, raising to *many billions* the number of sarcomeres potentially produced by this limited set of genes. . . . In fact, it is very likely that this maximum potential is never realised because not all genes are concurrently expressed in the same cell. However, even the limited subsets expressed in different muscle types and developmental stages have the potential to generate an impressive number of sarcomeric types.[52] [My emphasis.]

But this is not the end of the story. The G proteins, for example, are always associated in higher-order complexes—in terms of our linguistic analogy, paragraphs—with other elements in the cell membrane, such as the so-called serpentine receptors. There are a large number of these receptors, probably as many as a thousand in the olfactory system alone.[53] To provide the organism with the vast diversity of systems described by Simon as an "apparently bewildering complexity of receptors, heterotrimeric G proteins, and effectors" consisting of "myriads of receptors, isomorphic families of transducers, and multiple effectors" that are "differentially distributed in space and time" and which "interact to generate the appropriate response in different cells"[54] must of necessity require a very large number of unique combinations of these various elements. The possibility that the total number of unique combinations of G proteins and serpentine receptors alone is on the order of a million does not seem out of the question.

Combinatorial strategies are also probably being utilized in the generation of the vast diversity of unique neuronal cell types and axonal branching patterns in the nervous systems of higher organisms. (A few of the different cell types in the mammalian nervous system are shown on page 322.) In a recent paper in the journal *Neuron*, S. L. McIntire and coauthors comment: "Many aspects of the outgrowth of particular neuronal types might be determined by combinations of genes that also function in the outgrowth of other neuron types. In other words, much of the specificity of axonal outgrowth might result from the action of unique combinations of broadly expressed molecules."[55] And this is now a widely held view in neurobiology. Combinations of different neurotransmitters, which are the substances which transmit the nerve impulse from one nerve cell to another, may also be used to generate neuronal diversity in the vertebrate brain. Again, the potential number of biochemically unique cells that could be generated by using combinations of transmitters is very large. The awesome implications inherent in this particular combinatorial expansion is conveyed in the adjectives used in this passage taken from a paper presented at the 1990 Cold Spring Harbor Symposium:

> The *immense* variety of neuronal phenotypes . . . is apparent in considering just the process of chemical transmission. There are approximately 12 known classical neurotransmitters and more than 30 neuropeptides [newly discovered neurotransmitters] thus far identified, and individual neurons simultaneously synthetise, store, and secrete one or more classical transmitters in addition to three or more neuropeptides. The transmitters and peptides are expressed in *an exceedingly large number* of different combinations in different parts of the nervous system. . . . The magnitude of this problem becomes clear if one cal-

culates the number of possible combinations if a neuron is to produce 2 transmitters out of a possible 12 and 3 peptides out of a possible 30. There are *267,960 different potential phenotypes* in this example.[56] [My emphasis.]

Toward a Measure of Complexity

That living things are the most complex objects of which we have any experience is universally accepted. The question naturally arises: Just how complicated an object is a living organism, say, a mammal like a human being? How might we measure it?

A number of approaches might be adopted in attempting to compute the complexity of a higher organism. Perhaps the most conceptually straightforward is simply to count the total number of unique functional gene combinations utilized during the entire process of development, from the fertilization of the egg cell to the final adult form. In the case of a machine, such as a clock, by counting all the unique adaptive components—that is, each component which plays some unique functional role—we can derive some very approximate measure of the complexity of the clock. Similarly, we could count the number of unique sentences in a book. This would again give us a crude estimate of the complexity of the book. Such an approach would provide very much of an underestimate, as the integrative aspect would not be measured.

To count the entire complement of unique gene combinations (each specifying a unique functional multiprotein complex) that conspire together during the development of an organism—a process which in the case of a human results in the production of an organized whole of about 10^{14} cells—would be a titanic task indeed. Such a labor of Hercules would involve enumerating all the gene readouts specifying every single unique molecular switch, device, component, or control signal, etc., from the molecular to the organismic level. Included in this "infinite inventory" would be all the unique molecular signals or devices which cause a particular cell or group of cells to divide at a particular time and place in the embryo throughout the entire period of development; all those myriads of unique signals that turn on a particular gene or groups of genes and cause an individual or a group of cells to start manufacturing a new protein or set of proteins at particular times and positions during development; the entire infinity of molecular markers that tag the surfaces of cells, conferring on them their unique "identity tags" by which cells are recognized by their neighbors and by which cells smell, taste, and touch their ever-changing surroundings in the embryo and by which they also navigate from point to point. Even for a Hercules, this is a hopeless task. The total could easily approach a number in the range of a trillion, or 10^{12}.

The Brain

One aspect of development which could require a vast number of unique gene combinations is the development of the nervous system. This is an area of biology that has always conjured up visions of infinity. Estimates of the total number of connections in the human brain have been possible for more than a century since the famous Spanish neurologist Santiago Ramón y Cajal developed staining techniques that revealed the finest branches of the neuronal dendritic tree. This technique revealed that each cell may make up to 10,000 connections with other neurons. The brain of man, for example, contains about 10^{11} nerve cells, which make between 10,000 and 100,000 connections with other cells, making a total for the whole brain of about 10^{15}, or 1 quadrillion connections. There are certainly more connections in the brain than there are cells in the body.

At present, we cannot answer with any certainty the question as to how many different cells or connections in the human brain might be uniquely specified. But we can still make a tentative guesstimate. We have seen there are 10^{11}, or 100 billion, neurons in the human brain and each connects with about 10,000 other neurons via its dendritic and axonal branches, making a total of about 10^{15} connections. Assuming identifiable subsets of neurons in the human brain contain about 100 cells, this would still mean 1 billion unique, genetically determined cell types (and this is probably an underestimate, as the number of neurons in an identifiable cluster is probably closer to 10 than 100).

But even if we assume that uniquely identifiable classes of neurons in the human brain contain as many as 100 neurons and if we assume that only one-thousandth of the connections are specified—that is, only 10 connections per neuronal equivalence class (again, almost certainly an underestimate)—this would still give 10^{10}, or 10 trillion, uniquely specified connections in the human central nervous system.

To generate such an immense number of unique connections must require unimaginable numbers of cell surface markers and cell signal transducers to guide the movements of the embryonic cells and axons as the order of the brain emerges during development. Even if we can only guess at the total number of uniquely determined connections in the brain, we can be sure that the number of unique genetic readouts involved in the process is phenomenally great and could easily be on the order of 10^{12}.

Attempting to visualize a billion neurons, each a tiny nanoscale navigator, preprogrammed with a unique set of maps and the ability to match each map, at a defined and preprogrammed time, with the unique configuration at a series of unique sites in the ever-changing terrain of the developing brain, all homing in, unerring, toward their target, brings us indeed to the very edge of an "infinity" of adaptive complexity. The unimaginable immensity of "atomic maps," "molecular charts," "nanotimepieces," and other nanodevices used by this eerie infinity of nanorobots which navigate the ocean of the developing human brain, building as far as we can tell the only machine in the cosmos that has genuine understanding, is far greater than that of all the maps, charts, and devices used by all the mariners who ever navigated the oceans of earth, far more even than all the stars in our galaxy, more than all the days since the birth of the earth.

Although neither the number of unique gene combinations utilized in living things nor the number of specified connections in the brain can be estimated with any degree of certainty at present, it is nevertheless clear that *life has been revealed by modern biology to be a thing of phenomenal complexity,* that in terms of the number of unique components utilized in their construction, living things transcend the complexity of our own artifacts by very many orders of magnitude.

And what we have seen already may be only a fraction of what is. In the case of the brain, for example, only 10 percent of its mass is made up of neurons; the rest is composed of the so-called glial cells. There are at least ten times as many glial cells as neurons. For most of the past century these cells have been cast in a supporting role and considered to be a relatively homogeneous mass of relatively inert cells playing little role in the functioning of the brain. But in conformity with the principle of complexification, recent research is revealing signs that this mass of a trillion cells may have important roles to play in information processing in the brain.[57] Similarly, only 1 percent of the genomes code for proteins. All of the complexities of gene expression discovered to date and discussed above involve only this 1 percent;

the remaining 99 percent does not code for protein and has as yet no known function. Further, it has been presumed that it carries no genetic information, and that its role, if any, is merely supportive, like the glial cells in the brain. But again, the first signs are now emerging which suggest that there may well be genetic functions embedded in this vast nonprotein-coding mass of DNA sequences.

The possibilities of informational processing by glial cells and the possibility of genetic functions in the nonprotein-coding DNA could potentially increase the complexity of the nervous system and the genome, respectively, by many additional orders of magnitude.

Then there are the even more radical possibilities, such as the proposal by Stuart Hameroff discussed in chapter 10, that the microtubules in the cytoplasm may be used for computing, providing each individual cell with potentially enormous computing ability. The discovery of entirely new levels of biological order, such as subcellular computing devices, quite unimaginable in terms of our current thinking, could well reveal that the complexity we have uncovered to date is only an infinitesimal fraction of the whole.

The Third Infinity

The concept of the infinite has always been invested with a special kind of reverential awe. It is beyond human understanding. For centuries the church considered it heretical to attribute the infinite to anything but God and consigned Giordano Bruno to the stake in the Roman Piazza del Campo dei Fiori in 1600 for claiming the universe had no end. For the ancient Norsemen the infinite was a challenge too great for any hero to overcome. Even Thor could not drink the sea. It was the unfathomable complexity of the Labyrinth of King Minos that doomed the Athenians and delivered them to the Minotaur.

The infinite stirs many emotions. At the same time, it fascinates, it perplexes, it inspires, it dwarfs, and it terrifies. Who, as a child, asked Rudy Rucker in his *Infinity and the Mind,* "did not lie in bed filled with a slowly mounting terror while sinking into the idea that the universe goes on for ever and ever."[58] Things touched by it are somehow magical or transcendental, reflecting another reality, the realm of the gods. The infinite or measureless are associated with the mysterious in Coleridge's famous poem *Kubla Khan:* "Where Alph, the sacred river, ran / Through caverns measureless to man / Down to a sunless sea." The association of the infinite with things mysterious and beyond understanding is also illustrated by the appearance of the mathematical symbol for infinity, the lemniscus (∞), on Tarot cards in the seventeenth century, shortly after its adoption by mathematicians.

The infinity of the cosmos is an infinity of the very large, the infinity we peer into when we look up at the night sky through a telescope. Another is the infinity we peer into down a microscope, the infinity of the inconceivably small, of the atom and of subatomic particles. But perhaps the most extraordinary infinity of all, conjuring up feelings of paradox and awe every bit as irresistible as those conjured up by contemplating the immensity of the starry heavens or the minuteness of the atom, is the infinity now emerging in modern biology—an infinity of the unimaginably complex. This "third biological infinity" is every bit as awe-inspiring as the previous infinities of the cosmos and the atom.

In effect, modern biology has revealed to us a watch, a watch with a trillion cogs!—a watch which wonderfully fulfills William Paley's prophetic claim in this famous section from his *Natural Theology; or Evidence of the Existence and Attributes of the Deity, Collected from the Appearances of Nature*, published in 1800, that "every indication of contrivance, every manifestation of design, which existed in the watch, exists in the works of nature; with the difference, on the side of nature, of being greater and more, and that in a degree which exceeds all computation."

Chapter 15

The Eye of the Lobster

In which the challenge to undirected Darwinian evolution posed by some complex biological adaptations, is examined. Included is the eye of the lobster, the eye of the scallop, the marsupial frog, and the avian lung. It is argued that such remarkable adaptations are prima facie *evidence that the mechanism of evolution must have involved more than Darwinian processes. The problem of preadaptation is briefly considered in the context of the evolution of the avian lung and the human brain. The question is raised as to whether the evolution of all adaptations such as those very remarkable examples on isolated islands is the result of a built-in plan or whether such cases may be the result of an inherent emergent inventive or creative capacity possessed by all living systems to a small degree.*

The eye of the lobster.

In considering the Origin of Species, it is quite conceivable that a naturalist, reflecting on the mutual affinities of organic beings, on their embryological relations, their geographical distribution, and other such facts, might come to the conclusion that species had not been independently created, but had descended, like varieties from other species. Nevertheless, such a conclusion, even if well founded, would be unsatisfactory, until it could be shown how the innumerable species inhabiting this world have been modified, so as to acquire that perfection and co-adaptation of structure which justly excites our imagination.

—Charles Darwin, *On the Origin of Species,* 1859

Among the most persistent challenges to the Darwinian model of evolution are those many types of complex and unusual adaptations whose evolution is very difficult to account for in terms of a gradual accumulation of successively advantageous changes. The literature of biology is full of examples. The challenge arises because evolution by natural selection can only occur via functional intermediates. Consequently, to get from A to Z by natural selection each step on the path—A to B, B to C, etc.—must be advantageous, and this imposes very stringent constraints on permissible evolutionary paths. Darwin himself spent two chapters of the *Origin* attempting to explain how the origin and evolution of what he called "organs of extreme perfection" may be plausibly accounted for by a gradual accumulation of minor undirected changes. Richard Dawkins has attempted the same in his recent book *Climbing Mount Improbable.* However, despite this "Darwinian apologetic," many biologists have remained unconvinced, finding the "explanations" offered either implausible to some degree or too vague and general to be subjected to critical detailed scrutiny. Moreover, many of these adaptations can be very plausibly accounted for in terms of directed evolution, a possibility which can no longer be dismissed a priori, given the new emerging teleological worldview.

The Eye of the Lobster

There are a great many different types of eye in the animal kingdom, and some are based on very different principles from the well-known vertebrate camera eye. Two of the most remarkable types of eyes found anywhere in the living world are those of the rock lobster and its relatives and of the common scallop.

One of the most striking features of the lobster eye which is immediately obvious even on superficial inspection is that the facets of the eye are perfect squares (see page 352). It is very unusual to meet with perfectly square structures in biology. As one astronomer commented in *Science*: "The lobster is the most unrectangular animal I've ever seen. But under the microscope a lobster's eye looks like perfect graph paper."[1]

The reason for the square facets is that the lobster visual system is based on reflection. Each unit or cell in the eye is a tiny tube of square cross section and plane parallel mirrored sides. The length of each cell is about twice the width. Light which enters the units is reflected off the mirrored sides of the cell wall to points of focus on the retina. The optics of the system were first worked out by Michael Land of Sussex University.[2] The diagram below illustrates the basic principle.

The optical system of the reflector eye of the lobster.

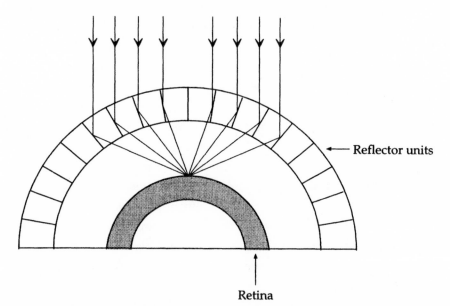

Adapted from M. F. Land (1978), "Animal Eyes with Mirror Optics"; © 1978 by Scientific American, Inc. All rights reserved.

This unique optical system is found in only one group of crustaceans, the so-called long-bodied decapods, which include the shrimps, the prawns, and lobsters. The great majority of crustaceans, and indeed of all invertebrates, have refracting eyes which are based on a completely different design. In these eyes each unit contains a small lens which refracts or bends the light onto the focus on the retina. Moreover, the units are hexagonal or round.

It is generally supposed that the reflecting eye must have evolved from a refracting eye, which are far more common among the Crustacea and of a fundamentally simpler design. The fact that during the development of the lobster—as it changes from the planktonic larval form, which swims in the surface waters of the sea, to the adult form that lives on the sea floor—the larval refracting eye is transformed into the adult reflecting eye would tend to support the idea that evolution followed the same path from refraction to reflection.

However, just what selection pressures may have been responsible and through what intermediate states the reflecting eye evolved is a mystery. The transformation is puzzling because it is very difficult to imagine how the units in some transitional eye—halfway between a hexagon and a square, halfway between a lens and a reflecting surface—could form a better image than the original refracting eye. Consequently, it is difficult to see how those halfway, intermediate eyes would have been selectively advantageous in an evolutionary sense. This is critical, because evolution by natural selection can only follow an evolutionary route from A to B if each step taken on the route to B is adaptively advantageous and confers some increased survival value on the organism.

The mystery is deepened because reflecting eyes of this design can only focus an image if the optics of the system is just right: the units are nearly perfect squares; the length of each unit must be twice its width; the inner surfaces of the units must be flat and mirrored. Deepening the mystery even further is the fact that the remarkable ability of these eyes to form an image is only used by the lobster when the level of illumination is low. At other times, when the illumination is brighter, adjustments are made involving the movement of the opaque pigment so that only those rays directly incident to the units can be seen at the retina.

Why should an organism drop its perfectly functional refracting eyes and start out on the hazardous journey to reflection? Refracting eyes provide organisms with excellent image-forming capabilities, as witness the flight of the dragonfly. Many crustacean cousins of the lobster—crabs, for example—which occupy the same ecological niche as the lobster and have the same predatory lifestyle—have refracting eyes and obviously survive quite well in the same level of illumination.

One would have thought that in the fitness landscape of crustacean eyes the route to an improved or perfected "refraction eye" must be far shorter, less complex, and far more probable than the extraordinary journey from refraction to reflection, from hexagon to square, from curved surfaces to flat surfaces, from lens to mirror, and so forth.

The Eye of the Scallop

The lobster eye is not the only eye that poses this sort of challenge. Another remarkable type of reflecting eye is found in the common scallop, the pecten.[3]

The scallop has about thirty small eyes along the fringe of each mantle, the name given to the two fleshy portions of the scallop which protrude from between the shells. Each eye is small, being only about 1 millimeter across. Each scallop eye contains a large lens in front of the retina. The retina is situated just behind the back of the lens. The back of the eye is formed into a hemispherical reflector surface, and behind this is a layer of brown reflecting pigment. The image is formed as shown by reflection from the hemispheric surface onto the retina.[4]

The eye of the scallop.

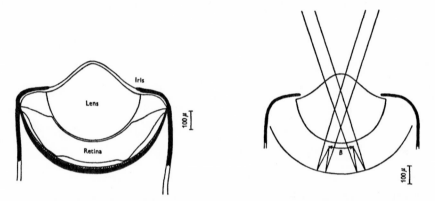

From M. F. Land (1965), "Image Formation by a Concave Reflector in the Eye of the Scallop *Pecten Maximus*," *Journal of Physiology* 179:138–153, fig. 1, p. 138, and fig. 5, p. 147. Reproduced by permission of Michael F. Land.

The visual system is remarkably complex and sophisticated. Amazingly, the scallop has not one but sixty of these tiny image-forming eyes. What is so striking is the apparent gratuity of the whole system. Why has such a simple organism evolved such a complex image-forming eye?

Long before its optical system was understood, the pecten eye was raising evolutionary problems. William J. Dakin, a professor of zoology at Liverpool University before the Second World War and one of the first to describe the eye in detail, had problems accepting the Darwinian explanation. According to Darwin in chapter 6 of the *Origin:*

> When we reflect on these facts . . . with respect to the wide, diversified and graduated range of structure in the eyes of the lower animals; and when we bear in mind how small the number of living things must be in comparison with those which have become extinct, the *difficulty ceases to be very great* in be-

lieving that natural selection may have converted the simple apparatus of an optic nerve . . . into an optical instrument as perfect as is possessed by any other member of the Articulate Class. [My emphasis.]

Commenting on this section, Dakin remarks:

> This is an optimistic view of the problem rather than evidence; it is a view to which I find it very difficult to subscribe in so far as the eyes of the Pectinidae are concerned. Indeed after a careful comparative study of the visual organs of the invertebrates one finds greater difficulty in accepting the principle of natural selection as the dominant factor in their origin than is the case with any other of their morphological features.[5]

Dakin continues:

> Now it is very difficult to conceive of a complex structure, complex as these eyes, being the final result of a sifting by natural selection of a large number of chance variations, stress being laid on external factors. Indeed there is grave doubt as to whether the presence of any variations that might lead to such organs could have any survival value.[6]

Even within the Pectinidae, the lethargic *Pecten maximus,* which has eyes identical to the other pecten species, swims for only short distances, and that infrequently. Another challenge to the plausibility of selectionist explanations of the level of development and diversity of eyes within the bivalves is the curious case of *Spondylus.* As Dakin points out, this genus does not swim but is attached to rocks, yet its eyes are as developed as the actively swimming *Pecten* species. Dakin concludes that the size and complexity of the eyes in Pectinidae cannot be explained by natural selection:

> Whatever may have been the *origin* of the eyes of the *Pecten* group I do not hold that utility explains their evolution . . . in the case of Pectinidae there is no evidence of the elimination of types with less complex eyes as unfit . . . in view of the diverse conditions existing in the Lamellibranchs there is no evidence that a reduction in the efficiency of the eyes of *Pecten* would lead to unfitness. . . . We cannot escape from the conviction that in one particular series of bivalves, all intimately related genetically, a distinct type of visual organ arose, independent of other visual organs, and that apart from adaptation, and apart from utility or advantageousness, it attained a certain extraordinary complexity.[7]

Although some recent studies suggest that the eye of the scallop has some selective advantages over the far simpler eyes of its bivalve cousins,[8] the fact remains that these related species survive perfectly well without the assistance of what is for an organism as simple as a mollusc a fantastically sophisticated eye. All the scallop's close relatives have either small hollowed-out photosensitive pits, or slightly more advanced but still very primitive camera-type eyes consisting of a lens positioned at the front of a spherical hollow lined with photosensitive cells. This is basically the standard molluscan type of eye found in such familiar organisms as the garden snail and the slug. Image-forming eyes within the Mollusca are all variations on the camera theme. The most spectacular are those of the octopus and squid, which are comparable with the vertebrate eye in many ways.

While it is possible to envisage a series of camera-type eyes leading from a photosensitive pit to the sophisticated camera eye of the octopus, it is far more difficult to envisage a transitional series of functional eyes leading from a photosensitive pit to the reflecting image-forming eye of the modern scallop. The fitness landscape of molluscan eyes would seem to lead inexorably downhill from a light-sensitive pit toward the camera type of eye.

The reflecting eyes of the lobster and scallop are only the tip of a vast iceberg of similar examples of adaptations that are difficult to explain in terms of a gradual process of cumulative selection.

The Marsupial Frogs

The marsupial, or egg-brooding, frogs are a group of about sixty species which live in the rain forests and mountains of South America. Although the adults are indistinguishable from ordinary frogs, the development of the egg and the method of reproduction are utterly different. In many species of marsupial frogs the mother carries the developing eggs in a special pouch or brood chamber on her back. The eggs lie in the fluid-filled chamber in intimate contact with the mother's tissue through an organ which resembles the mammalian placenta. Through this organ, mother and embryo exchange gases, fluids, nutrients, and wastes. The jelly layer surrounding the marsupial frog egg is very thin, so as to permit the easy transfer of materials to and from the developing embryo.

But even that is not the most remarkable aspect of the marsupial frog reproductive system. It is the very great difference in the way the marsupial frog egg develops that is so astounding. The details of this were worked out in the 1970s by the Ecuadorian biologist Eugenia M. del Pino.[9] Instead of resembling an ordinary developing frog egg, in the marsupial frog the entire organization of early embryogenesis has been radically transformed and resembles the embryonic development of a mammal. The early cell divisions and the most fundamental processes have been completely transformed. Given the very fundamental nature of early embryogenesis and the great number of genes involved, it is clear that the evolutionary route from the standard pattern to that of the marsupial frog must have involved a complex set of genetic and developmental changes.

The device of incubating the eggs on the mother's back is obviously adaptive in the tropical rain forest, where there is intense competition for breeding sites. Nonetheless, many tree frogs adopt the far simpler strategy of laying their eggs in a small pool of water on a leaf in the forest canopy or even just letting the rain carry the eggs to the forest floor on the chance they may reach a pool of water. So the incubation method is one strategy among many, vastly more complex, but apparently no more effective, than the far simpler methods.

Again, as in the two cases cited above, it is hard to believe that any sort of unguided evolutionary mechanism would have realized such an unusual adaptive end. Moreover, changing the basic organization of an embryo would appear to be far more radical than any of the other changes cited above. And again, for this to happen under the agency of natural selection, each one of the individual steps along the evolutionary route must have been selectively advantageous.

The same phenomenon is seen among the embryos of sea urchins. As Jeffrey Levinton commented recently in another *Scientific American* article: "the embryos of sea urchins are fantastically diverse. The larvae of closely related species have radically different forms—some are adapted for a long life of swimming and feeding on plankton, whereas others are suited for a short nonfeeding period while they are dispersed by currents. These . . . specialisations entail monumental differences in the developmental patterns of the larvae and even in the parts of the embryo used to form adult structures."[10] Yet, as Levinton comments, amazingly, the adult members of these species are virtually indistinguishable. It is fantastically difficult to envisage how an accumulation of tiny selectively advantageous changes could have caused such enormously dramatic changes in embryonic development in the case of organisms virtually indistinguishable in their adult forms.

The Avian Lung

Another spectacular adaptation in a group of very familiar organisms is the avian lung. In all vertebrates except birds the air is drawn into the lungs through a system of branching tubes which finally terminate in tiny air sacs, or alveoli, so that during respiration the air is moved in and out through the same passage (the avian lung has already been briefly described in chapter 13). In the case of birds, however, the major bronchi break down into tiny tubes which permeate the lung tissue. These so-called parabronchi eventually join up again, forming a true circulatory system, so that air flows in one direction through the lungs.

This unidirectional flow of air is maintained during both inspiration and expiration by a complex system of interconnected air sacs in the bird's body that expand and contract in such a way as to ensure a continuous delivery of air through the parabronchi. The existence of this air sac system has necessitated a highly specialized and unique division of the body cavity of the bird into several compressible compartments. No lung in any other vertebrate species is known which in any way approaches the avian system.

Just how such a different respiratory system could have evolved gradually from the standard vertebrate design without some sort of direction is, again, very difficult to envisage, especially bearing in mind that the maintenance of respiratory function is absolutely vital to the life of the organism. Moreover, the unique function and form of the avian lung necessitates a number of additional unique adaptations during avian development. As H. R. Dunker,[11] one of the world's authorities in this field, explains, because first, the avian lung is fixed rigidly to the body wall and cannot therefore expand in volume and, second, because of the small diameter of the lung capillaries and the resulting high surface tension of any liquid within them, the avian lung cannot be inflated out of a collapsed state as happens in all other vertebrates after birth. In birds, aeration of the lung must occur gradually and starts three to four days before hatching with a filling of the main bronchi, air sacs, and parabronchi with air. Only after the main air ducts are already filled with air does the final development of the lung, and particularly the growth of the air capillary network, take place. The air capillaries are never collapsed as are the alveoli of other vertebrate species; rather, as they grow into the lung tissue, the parabronchi are from the beginning open tubes filled with either air or fluid.

The avian lung brings us very close to answering Darwin's challenge: "If it could be demonstrated that any complex organ existed, which could not possibly have been formed by numerous, successive, slight modifications, my theory would absolutely break down."[12]

The avian lung is more efficient than the mammalian because of a special countercurrent mechanism whereby the blood flows throughout the lung in the opposite direction to the flow of air. This allows the blood to take up more oxygen and deliver more carbon dioxide than is possible in, say, the lung of a mammal. As Knut Schmidt-Nielsen points out, it is because of the higher efficiency of the avian lung that "birds have been seen in the high Himalayas flying overhead at altitudes where mountain climbers can barely walk without breathing oxygen."[13] But while this adaptation is clearly advantageous to an eagle soaring in the mountains and to advanced modern birds capable of fast powered flight, it is difficult to believe that it would have been so advantageous in the last common ancestor of all modern birds which lived about 100 million years ago and which was presumably nothing like as accomplished a flier as its modern descendants. Here it is hard not to be inclined to see an element of foresight in the evolution of the avian lung, which may well have developed in primitive birds before its full utility could be exploited.

The idea that an adaptation like the avian lung might evolve before its full utility can be exploited is perfectly consistent with a directed model of evolution.

The Evolution of the Human Brain

There are many other cases of this phenomenon. Perhaps the most celebrated and well-known example is the case of human intelligence. Many have commented on the striking fact that our intellectual capabilities, especially our capacity for abstract mathematical thought, upon which the whole enterprise of science is ultimately based, seems vastly in excess of any conceivable intellectual needs of the small tribe of hunter-gatherers who lived in Africa some 200,000 years ago and were the last common ancestors of all modern humans. What selection pressures on the ancient plains of Africa gifted mankind with musical ability, artistic competence, the capacity for profound abstraction, and ultimately the ability to comprehend the entire cosmos from which we sprang.

Commenting on the evolutionary conundrum posed by our intellectual capabilities in his recent book *The Mind of God,* Paul Davies reminds us "that the success of the scientific enterprise can often blind us to the astonishing fact that science works," and he continues:

> What is remarkable is that human beings are actually able to carry out this code-breaking operation, that the human mind has the necessary intellectual equipment for us to "unlock the secrets of nature."
>
> The mystery in all this is that human intellectual powers are presumably determined by biological evolution, and have absolutely no connection with doing science. Our brains have evolved in response to environmental pressures, such as the ability to hunt, avoid predators, dodge falling objects, etc. . . . John Barrow is also mystified: "Why should our cognitive processes have tuned themselves to such an extravagant quest as the understanding of the entire universe? . . . None of the sophisticated ideas involved appear to offer any selective advantage to be exploited during the pre-conscious period of our evolution. . . . How fortuitous that our minds (or at least the minds of some) should be poised to fathom the depths of nature's secrets."[14]

We might add also, how fortunate it is that we are a terrestrial organism of about the size we are, breathing oxygen in a biosphere containing ample quantities of combustible carbon in the form of wood, which burns so gently and controllably. Only these unique conditions provide an intelligent life form with the ability to handle fire and hence provide access to chemistry and eventually to scientific knowledge. How fortunate also that the speed of nerve conduction is 120 meters per second, providing higher organisms like ourselves, despite our relatively large size, with the ability to carry out fine motor manipulation and hence the ability to handle fire and engage in an exploration of the world.

How very fortunate indeed that evolution should have gifted a mind so fit for the scientific enterprise in a physical form so fit to that same unique end long *before* that enterprise was undertaken.

Can Organisms Direct Their Own Evolution?

Although it seems implausible that such complex adaptations could have resulted from any sort of undirected process, the question arises as to whether or not the direction was built into nature from the beginning or was the result of other secondary phenomena. While it is possible to believe that adaptations such as the eye of the lobster and the avian lung might have been programmed into nature from the beginning, in the case of many other types of adaptations the case for classifying them as natural forms is far less certain.

It is particularly hard to believe, in the case of the many complex adaptations restricted to remote islands, that their blueprint is an integral part of the biocentric design of nature. That they are fundamentally contingent seems to be far more likely. One need only consider the extraordinary morphological and behavioral adaptations of the various species of weta, a type of giant ground cricket found in certain restricted regions of New Zealand, sometimes small islands only ten hectares in area, to see the difficulties of explaining all biological adaptive design in terms of a cosmic blueprint. In some species of tusked wetas, the males have tusks protruding from the front of their jaws which they use in ritual jousting matches with other males. Each dominant male tree weta guards a territory containing a harem of breeding females, and the jousts, as in the case of stags or seals, are basically aimed at preventing another male from gaining access to the harem. As if this were not remarkable enough, the pattern of the call of each individual male tree weta appears to be distinctive; each, as it were, has its own acoustic signature.[15]

In the case of such remarkable and complex adaptations restricted to small isolated geographical regions, it is not easy to envisage them as being pre-programmed into the order of nature and being part of a "grand design." The question naturally arises, how did such adaptations come about? If neither natural selection nor any other sort of undirected evolutionary mechanism seem plausible, then could they conceivably have been the result of the activities of life itself operating via some as yet undefined type of inventiveness inherent in all life? Consideration of the many exotic and complex adaptations that grace the living world led many French biologists in the first half of this century, such as Lucien Cuénot,[16] to propose that life must possess to some degree an autonomous creative ability. As he puts it: "The terms finality, adaptation, organisation have only meaning within the world of living matter. . . . One cannot disregard the analogy between the tools or the artifacts of man . . . and the tools or systems of organised beings; accordingly there must be an analogy between the intelligence and reason of man . . . and some property of living matter. I don't dare to call this intelligence or reason so I call it the inventive power."[17]

The possibility that some degree of adaptive evolution may be the result of an inherent emergent inventive capacity possessed by all living things cannot be ruled out. Such a capacity may be manifest in human consciousness and intelligence as well as in a general capacity for adaptation possessed by all living things. In such a view human creativity, rather than being a thing apart from nature, a gift imparted uniquely to mankind by God, becomes instead a profoundly natural phenomenon shared perhaps in some small degree by all life forms on earth.

For Anglo-Saxon biologists such as myself, schooled within a strictly mechanistic view of life, a view which has, by and large, been adopted by all English-speaking biologists, the possibility of life being more than mechanism, possessing some sort of emergent creative capacity, seems to beckon toward some mystical obscurantist cul-de-sac. However, there are many intriguing phenomena cited in the works of well-known authors such as Rupert Sheldrake and Lyall Watson which suggest that life may be more than our current science admits.[18] And certainly the phenomenon of emergence is itself encountered throughout the natural world. We cannot predict the properties of water, or the speed of nerve conduction, from quantum mechanics. Nor can we predict the social behavior of bees, ants, or indeed any organism from observing the behavior of an individual in isolation. It is because of the problem of emergence that the laws of biology cannot be predicted from the laws of physics and why evidence drawn only from physics and astronomy is bound to be insufficient to secure the biocentricity or anthropocentricity of the cosmos. Moreover, as discussed in chapter 12, there exists the possibility that emergent self-organizing phenomena were involved in the origin of life and the origin of evolutionary innovation.

In the context of a teleological view of the cosmos, even if much of the overall order of organic nature was determined from the beginning, it is surely conceivable that the Creator, to paraphrase Darwin in the last paragraph of the *Origin of Species,* could have gifted organisms not only with the capacity for growth, reproduction, inheritance, and variability,[19] but also with a limited degree of genuine autonomous creativity so that the world of life might reflect and mirror in some small measure the creativity of God.

Conclusion:

The Long Chain of Coincidence

In which it is concluded that after four centuries of spectacular increases in scientific knowledge there is still no direct evidence for the existence of any sort of life other than the carbon-based form with which we are familiar on earth. Moreover, evidence which suggests that the laws of nature are specifically adapted for life as it exists on earth is continually increasing as scientific knowledge grows. The main constituents of life such as water and the carbon atom, and environmental conditions such as sunlight and the hydrosphere of the earth, give every appearance of being ideally and uniquely fit for their biological roles. Although the proposition that the cosmos is a uniquely prefabricated whole with life as it exists on earth as its end and purpose cannot be proven, it is easy to refute. Demonstrate the existence of any one example of a life superior to our own or even of an individual constituent, such as water, which is less than ideally tailored for its biological role, and the whole teleological scheme collapses. It is concluded that the anthropocentric presumption has not only stood the test of four centuries of scientific advance, but it increasingly makes more sense of the cosmos as a whole than does any other competitor theory.

Exotic Life.

"Ammonia! Ammonia!"

Drawing by R. Grossman; © 1962 The New Yorker Magazine, Inc.

In a universe whose size is beyond imagining, where our world floats like a mote of dust in the void of night, men have grown inconceivably lonely. We scan the time scale and the mechanisms of life itself for portents and signs of the invisible. As the only thinking mammals on the planet—perhaps the only thinking animals in the entire sidereal universe—the burden of consciousness has grown heavy upon us. We watch the stars, but the signs are uncertain. We uncover the bones of the past and seek for our origins. There is a path there, but it appears to wander. The vagaries of the road may have a meaning however, it is thus we torture ourselves. . . .

So deep is the conviction that there must be life out there beyond the dark, one thinks that if they are more advanced than ourselves they may come across space at any moment, perhaps in our generation. Later, contemplating the infinity of time, one wonders if perchance their messages came long ago, hurtling into the swamp muck of the steaming coal forests, the bright projectile clambered over by hissing reptiles, and the delicate instruments running mindlessly down with no report.

—Loren Eiseley, *The Immense Journey*, 1957

When I first wrote my treatise about our system, I had an eye upon such principles as might work with considering men, for the belief of a deity, and nothing can rejoice me more than to find it useful for that purpose.

—Isaac Newton, *Principia,* 1687

The defenders of the anthropocentric faith in medieval Europe knew very little, indeed virtually nothing, about the natural world. In a very real sense it was not just the geographical surface of the earth that was largely terra incognita to medieval man but the whole realm of natural phenomena. The nature of such ordinary phenomena as lightning, clouds, stars, infectious diseases, and volcanoes were absolutely mysterious. Moreover, nearly every medieval conception about the natural world was erroneous. The earth was thought to be flat and men could fall off the edge; the alchemists believed that the base metals could be turned into gold; miracles were considered an everyday occurrence; astrology was widely accepted; diseases were thought to be curable by using various herbal and folk remedies, some of which were more harmful than the disease; and mental illness was considered to be the result of demon possession. Given the almost complete absence of any knowledge of the natural world, given also the erroneous nature of so many other far less audacious beliefs, it is all the more remarkable that the most presumptuous of all their beliefs, the central axiom of the Christian faith, on which the whole of medieval civilization was based, has stood the test of time and the critical scrutiny of four centuries of science.

The apparent demolition of the anthropocentric cosmos came about mainly through two great revolutions in thought. The first arose from the discoveries in astronomy in the early seventeenth century, which revealed a cosmos vastly larger than and utterly different in structure from the simple, closed geocentric system conceived of by the medieval theologians, one in which it was increasingly difficult to imagine any teleological place for man and in which there was ample room for many worlds, perhaps inhabited by intelligent beings very dissimilar to ourselves. The second blow that appeared to provide the final *coup de grâce* came in the mid nineteenth century with the rise of Darwinism, which provided what appeared to be an entirely plausible explanation for the apparent adaptive design of living things in terms of a completely undirected process—natural selection. According to this view, all manifestations of life, including our own species, are, in Brian Appleyard's words, "accidents of deep time and chance."[1] With Darwin the process of disenchantment and the secularization of the western mind was completed. However, although these revolutions were based on the findings of science, they were not strictly scientific in essence, but rather philosophical extrapolations from the findings of science which seemed to the scientific community in the seventeenth and nineteenth centuries eminently reasonable.

Other Worlds and Alien Life

Although the existence of a plethora of inhabited worlds full of exotic types of life has always been pure conjecture—no one had actually observed a Jovian, a Martian, or indeed any other extraterrestrial—yet the feeling that the cosmos was inhabited, perhaps by a diverse phantasma of alien types of life and intelligence, arose irresistibly in the minds of the seventeenth-century astronomers as they gazed into the immensity of the sky. This same deep conviction that there is, in Loren Eiseley's words, "life out there beyond the dark" has persisted right down to the present day whenever men have contemplated the enormity of space and time. The concept of extraterrestrial life pervades current culture, both popular and serious, as witnessed in science-fiction movies and television shows such as *Star Wars* and *Star Trek* and in the various serious research projects aimed at detecting radio signals from extraterrestrial civilizations.

The challenge inherent in the existence of extraterrestrial life of a very alien type is self-evident. The claim that the cosmos is specifically designed for the form of carbon-based life that exists on earth can only be seriously defended if the type of life that exists on earth is a unique and peerless phenomenon—the only possible instantiation of the phenomenon compatible with the laws of nature. The existence of extraterrestrial life, especially intelligent life, designed on very different principles to that on earth, would imply that the carbon-based life as it exists on earth is not unique or special in any way and that no one type of biology or intelligence is particularly ordained or prefabricated into the cosmos. Earth's own manifestation of life and intelligence becomes by this doctrine only one possibility among many, interesting to ourselves, no doubt, *but not exceptional in any way and certainly not unique.* And humankind is but one possibility among many equally probable alternatives. If there are indeed exotic forms of extraterrestrial life, including species possessing intelligence vastly greater than our own and perhaps possessing a technology centuries in advance of our own, then one may just as well argue that the cosmos is adapted for any one of these alien life forms such as Christiaan Huygens's long-necked, round-eyed extraterrestrials or Carl Sagan's imaginary gaseous Jovian beings, the size of immense airships, which he named Floaters in his best-seller *Cosmos*[2] (see below), rather than for *Homo sapiens.* Of course, there was no direct evidence for extraterrestrial life or intelligence in the early decades of the seventeenth century. It was not the possible existence of extraterrestrial life in itself that punctured the teleological assumption, but the possible existence of extraterrestrial life of an utterly alien kind. This was the crux of the challenge of the infinity-of-worlds doctrine—the idea of a plurality of extraterrestrial life based on all manner of exotic and utterly alien chemistries. The underlying antipathy between the doctrine of many worlds and the notion of man's uniqueness and his teleological centrality was succinctly captured by Johannes Kepler:

> If there are globes in the heaven similar to our earth, do we vie with them over who occupies a better portion of the universe? For if their globes are nobler, we are not the noblest of rational creatures. Then how can all things be for man's sake? How can we be the masters of God's Handiwork?[3]

However, *no fact* had been uncovered by astronomers in the seventeenth century which compelled belief in other worlds or alien life. The fact that the earth is not the spatial center of the universe has no longer any meaning today, because the cosmos revealed by twentieth-century astronomy has itself no spatial center. Ironically, our relatively peripheral position on the spiral arm of a rather ordinary galaxy is indeed rather fortunate. If we had been stationed in a more central position—say, near the galactic hub—it is likely that our knowledge of the universe of other galaxies, for example, might not have been as extensive. Perhaps in such a position the light from surrounding stars could well have blocked our view of intergalactic space. Perhaps astronomy and cosmology as we know these subjects would never have developed.

There are in fact only two ways to show that the cosmos is not uniquely fit for life as it exists on earth and specifically for the existence of complex higher forms of carbon-based life such as our own species. First, the *straightforward or empirical way*—by directly discovering another type of life based on a completely different chemistry or even more dramatically by directly contacting or discovering a race of beings as intelligent as ourselves but of profoundly dissimilar design and biology to our own. Such discoveries would render hopeless any attempt to interpret the universe as peculiarly fit for life, a designed whole with life and man as its fundamental purpose and goal. Second, there is the *theoretical or indirect way*—by showing from our knowledge of science that nature is at least theoretically fit for the existence of other types of life and other types of intelligence. In other words, that the laws of nature give no indication of their having been arranged specifically for our type of carbon-based life or for the biology of higher forms of life such as ourselves.

The Failure of the Empirical Way

As far as the first way is concerned, it is an extraordinary fact that even as late as 1600—more than a century after the age of exploration had begun with the discovery of the Americas in 1492 and the opening up of the trade routes to Asia around the southern tip of Africa in the early decades of the sixteenth century—it was still conceivable that alien intelligent life very dissimilar to *Homo sapiens,* perhaps even nonmammalian or perhaps even based on an exotic type of biology, might exist in some unexplored region of the globe. In other words, direct demolition of the anthropocentric thesis was still possible by more extensive exploration of our own planet. Myths and ancient legends lent some credence to such a possibility. The legend of the Christian Kingdom of Prestor John beyond the Muslim lands to the east or in Africa and the legends of lost civilizations like Atlantis fueled speculation that the Portuguese caravels might bring back news of an utterly alien civilization in terra incognita. The radical possibility of a highly intelligent nonhuman species extant on earth, members of a civilization perhaps far in advance of sixteenth-century Europe, could not therefore be discounted in 1600. The southern hemisphere had hardly been penetrated, and there was a widespread belief in a great southern land, Terra Australis Incognita, as extensive as Eurasia somewhere east of Africa and south of the Indonesian archipelago. Moreover, the center of the newly discovered continents of North and South America, as well as Central Africa, were still largely unexplored. Such mysterious regions might conceivably have harbored advanced civilizations peopled by nonhuman exotic beings quite unrelated to the biblical Adam and perhaps even of a biology unfamiliar to the Christian Europeans and other cultures of the known world. On the maps of the fifteenth and sixteenth centuries, the interior of these continents are often peopled with a phantasmagoria of strange beasts and semihuman beings. Such imaginings bear witness to the challenging possibility, very real at the time, of intelligent beings very dissimilar to ourselves in the distant unexplored regions of the globe.

Another unexplored realm which held out the possibility of puncturing directly the anthropocentric presumption was the past history of our own planet. Serious scientific exploration of the past through the development of paleontology and archaeology only began in the early nineteenth century. Discovering evidence of nonhuman intelligent activity on the earth before man—for example, complex artifacts in ancient sediments—would pose every bit as significant a challenge as the discovery of extraterrestrial intelligence or St. Augustine's antipodean man. But just as the geographical explorations after 1500 failed to find any nonhuman intelligent races extant in some distant region of the earth, the exploration of the past since 1800 has similarly turned up not the slightest evidence for the existence of intelligent activity on the earth before the advent of man. As far as we can tell, the only life that ever graced our planet was the carbon-based type that is extant today, and no intelligence other than that of *Homo sapiens* has ever left its imprint on the earth in all the 4 billion years that the planet has been capable of sustaining life.

Of course, the earth has, ever since the early seventeenth century, been seen as a <u>mere speck of dust</u> in the immensity of the macrocosm, and it has always been in the stars that the possibility of finding evidence of alien life and intelligence based on a radically different design to our own has seemed the most likely.

Although the concept of extraterrestrial life has been deeply embedded in western culture since the early sixteenth century, it has become particularly popular in the past few decades with the advent of the space age. Almost everyone takes it for granted that the cosmos is teeming with all manner of life forms and that humanity, in Carl Sagan's words, is merely "one voice in the cosmic fugue."[4]

Of the planets in our solar system, Mars has always been considered as one of the more likely candidates for extraterrestrial life. Although the unmanned Mariner spacecraft that flew by Mars in the 1960s and early 1970s and extensively photographed the surface found no evidence of "canals" or any other signs of an extant or vanished civilization, the possibility of there being microscopic life could not be excluded. Consequently, the discovery of at least some microscopic types of life in the Martian soils was very much a possibility when the Viking spacecraft touched down on the Martian surface in the summer of 1976. It carried a vast array of sophisticated instruments for measuring the composition of the atmosphere and seismic activity, for analyzing the chemical composition of the soils, and perhaps most significant of all, a biology lab to carry out experiments designed to test for the presence of life in the Martian soils.

With the imminence of the Viking touchdown on Mars, the summer of 1976 was the culmination of an exciting phase of space exploration. From the successive Mariner missions during the 1960s and 1970s, a fascinating picture of the red planet had emerged. And it was one that was not incompatible with the existence of simple types of microbial life.

Who can recall the first images sent back by *Viking 1* from the plains of Chryse Planitia, in July 1976, and not also recall the mounting excitement of the possible discovery of extraterrestrial life. In the summer of 1976 all mankind stood as they had with Columbus in 1492 and with Cook in 1788 on the shore of a new terra incognita. Moreover, just as was the case with the exploration of "new worlds" on earth, the exploration of this Martian new world could have provided the long feared *coup de grâce* to the man-centered view of the world. When *Viking 1* touched down in July 1976, it was of course already unlikely, judging from the previous observations of the Mariner missions, that any intelligent race would be found on Mars. However, the possibility of the discovery of a completely alien type of life on a planet so close to earth and the very first extraterrestrial world to be examined by humans would have greatly increased the probability of extraterrestrial intelligent life based on completely different principles to those observed on Earth and would have seriously threatened the presumption that the laws of nature are uniquely arranged for life as it exists on Earth.

Even before Viking, the increasing possibility that the planet might prove lifeless was definitely greeted with relief in many conservative Christian quarters. Echoing the fears of the inquisitors of Bruno and Galileo four centuries before, they were, in Sagan's words: "unmistakably relieved. Finding life beyond the earth—particularly intelligent life, although this is highly unlikely on Mars—wrenches at our secret hope that man is the pinnacle of creation. Even simple forms of extraterrestrial life may have abilities denied to us. The discovery of life on some other world will, among many things, be for us a humbling experience."[5]

Although that experience may now be upon us, it may not be as humbling as Sagan implies. Undoubtedly, the evidence of primitive life, detected in a Martian meteor by NASA scientists, would represent, if confirmed, the first genuine scientific evidence of extraterrestrial life and be a defining moment in human history, a moment of great philosophical significance. But it does not threaten in any sense the main claim of this book—that the cosmos is uniquely fit for the specific type of life that exists on Earth. As stressed above, although the discovery of extraterrestrial life *based on dissimilar principles and chemistry* to that on Earth would overthrow immediately the idea that the laws of nature are uniquely arranged for life as it exists on Earth, the discovery of extraterrestrial life *similar to or even indistinguishable from* that on earth tends to reinforce the conception of the cosmos as uniquely fit for life as it exists on Earth. Although the results are only preliminary, a confirmation would imply that ancient Martian life was carbon-based and very closely resembled the earliest life forms on Earth.

If there is, or once was earthlike life on Mars, this would suggest, as planetary systems are probably quite common (see chapter 4), that there may be life similar to that on Earth throughout the cosmos. The discovery also opens up the possibility of there being life on some of the other planets in our solar system and possibly on some of their fifty-four moons.

But even if there is primitive life on Mars or elsewhere in the solar system, it still seems unlikely that advanced life forms, and especially intelligent life, exists anywhere at present in our solar system. The space explorations of the latter half of the twentieth century would seem to have finally laid to rest the visions of generations of dreamers, who from Giordano Bruno to Percival Lowell have envisaged intelligent inhabitants on our near neighbors in space. So while the NASA results open up the possibility of finding in our solar system simple alien life forms based on a different chemistry to our own, the possibility of finding intelligent life based on exotic chemistries is remote.

Of course, outside the orbit of Pluto, outside our solar system, there still lies the unexplored, unimaginable vastness of the cosmos, containing 100 billion galaxies, each containing 100 billion stars. Although the number of stars with planets is unknown, it is now widely assumed that perhaps the majority of stars have planetary systems and that planets rather like Earth may be the inevitable result of the same cosmic processes which lead to the formation of stars. For the most part, this immense terra incognita will remain forever truly incognita to humankind. The planets circling the most distant stars will never be directly explored by man. No spacecraft will ever sniff or taste the soils of a world in another galaxy. Even the Andromeda galaxy, one of the closest, is nearly a million light years away.

Since we cannot seriously contemplate the direct physical exploration of solar systems beyond our own, it would seem that the only hope we have in the near future of obtaining direct evidence from distant regions of the cosmos of sentient extraterrestrial life dissimilar to ourselves is if they contact us, either by physically visiting Earth or by sending a spacecraft advertising their existence and informing us of their biological design—just as our own Voyager spacecraft is presently carrying information about life on Earth deep into interstellar space. Alternatively, they might beam across the void some type of signal capable of traversing the cosmic immensity, perhaps a radio message.

The fact remains that to date no artifact has ever been discovered on Earth which might be interpreted as a "Chariot of the Gods." No structure or piece of machinery has ever been found that might have been constructed by aliens here on earth, or left by ancient star travelers from another world. Invariably, the many intriguing and puzzling phenomena offered as evidence of an alien presence, such as the Nazca lines in the Atacama Desert, corn circles in southern England, the peculiar round stones of Guatemala, the headgear of the Aztec gods, which are often put down at first to the work of aliens, prove to have far more mundane explanations. Similarly, nothing in the solar system, including the supposed Martian Sphinx, the Martian pyramids, or the moons of Mars, provides any evidence of extraterrestrial visitations to our remote corner of space. All such apparent artifacts are either natural objects, or can very easily be interpreted as such. If our solar system was ever inhabited or visited by intelligent beings, they left long ago and left no sign that we can read.

Nor have any radio or optical signals ever been detected that provide evidence of extraterrestrial intelligence. Occasionally, astronomers pick up an unusual signal from some previously unremarkable point in the sky, and for a moment there stirs a faint hope that it might be an intelligent signal from another world. Despite the lack of any evidence, the concept retains a potent force. As Sagan confesses, "There is something irresistible about the discovery of even a token from an alien world."[6] Yet no matter how deeply ingrained the concept of extraterrestrial intelligence, to date neither the direct exploration of Earth nor of our nearest planetary neighbors have provided the slightest evidence for intelligent life beyond the earth. The empirical way has in effect failed. The concept of the cosmos as uniquely fit for our existence and the presumption of our teleological centrality remain intact. After four centuries of ceaseless searching, Earth has yielded no clue, the heavens have remained eerily silent, and even Mars now threatens to disappoint. We still have at present no direct empirical evidence that *the laws of physics might permit the existence of life or of intelligent beings designed along principles fundamentally different from those governing life on Earth.*

The Failure of the Theoretical Way

Curiously, while the sixteenth-century mariners were vastly extending man's knowledge of the earth's surface, their early scientific contemporaries Galileo and Kepler were initiating the far more consequential exploration of the world through science. For in a very real and profound sense, science is an exploration of the cosmos. The analogy is close. This is because the laws of nature are universal and apply everywhere in space and time. Consequently, scientific discoveries on earth in effect carry us to the most distant galaxy and allow us to peer into every corner of the cosmos. Through the abstract eyes of science we can see further and explore realms to which no spacecraft will ever travel. Through science we can know the whole cosmos. The physical and chemical properties of water and carbon dioxide, the characteristics of electromagnetic radiation, the viscosity of silicate rocks—all these are the same in the galaxy of Andromeda as they are on earth. Through science, we can travel in theory to any part of the universe, to any alien planetary surface, and we know that at a particular temperature and atmospheric pressure, oxygen could exist there as a gas or that visible light will activate chemical reactions, that water will expand if cooled below 4°C.

Science has in effect opened up another, theoretical way to disprove the anthropocentric assumption; to provide a convincing blueprint of an alternative form of life, perhaps based on carbon and water or perhaps based on a completely exotic type of chemistry.

Various attempts have been made to envisage life based on exotic chemistries. Gerald Feinberg and Robert Shapiro in their *Life Beyond Earth* discussed in outline a variety of alternative fluids in which an alien life might be based. Water, they conjectured, could perhaps be replaced by liquid ammonia in a low-temperature world. As they point out: "Ammonia may form an ocean when water is hard ice, a kind of rock material in fact, rather like silica in our granite. . . . Ammonia has a good capacity as a reservoir for heat. It dissolves salts and supports reactions between charged substances such as acids and alkalis."[7] Another possible fluid which could serve as the medium of an alternative type of life discussed by Feinberg and Shapiro might be an oily mixture of hydrocarbons that would be liquid at a much lower temperature than ammonia. In a world containing life in oil, the seas would be in effect a giant oil slick, composed of a mixture of hydrocarbons of lower boiling point than those usually carried by oil tankers on earth. They name their hypothetical oil world Petrolia. Yet another possible biosphere considered was one based in liquid silica at a temperature of 1,000°C.[8] In addition to alternative types of chemical life, they also considered the more radical possibility of nonchemical life based on physical rather than chemical ordering systems. They speculate, for example, that a type of electronic organism—a plasmobe—"composed of patterns of magnetic force together with groups of moving charges in a kind of symbiosis" might be possible in the center of stars, where intense pressures and temperatures exclude any sort of molecular or chemical life.[9]

Although most authorities see fluids as the ideal medium for life, some authors, such as Fred Hoyle in his book *The Black Cloud,* have envisaged gaseous life.[10] One of the more exotic scenarios of life in a gaseous medium very different to its earthly manifestation was described by Carl Sagan in *Cosmos:*

> On a giant gas planet like Jupiter, with an atmosphere rich in hydrogen, helium, methane, water and ammonia, you could also be a floater, some vast hydrogen balloon pumping helium and heavier gases out of its interior and leaving only the lightest gas, hydrogen; or a hot air balloon, staying buoyant by keeping your interior warm, using energy acquired from the food you eat. . . . A floater might well eat preformed organic molecules, or make its own from sunlight and air. . . . Salpeter and I imagined floaters kilometers across, larger than the greatest whale that ever was, beings the size of cities. . . . The floaters may propel themselves through the planetary atmosphere with gusts of gas, like a ramjet or a rocket. We imagine them arranged in great lazy herds for as far as the eye can see.[11]

As our knowledge of chemistry is still largely empirical and we cannot predict with any certainty the behavior of chemicals and chemical systems in conditions vastly dissimilar to those with which we are familiar, we cannot rule out completely any of the possibilities raised by Feinberg and Shapiro or even exclude such fantastic possibilities as floaters.

But the fact remains, as Feinberg and Shapiro themselves concede, that no relatively well-developed model providing a detailed account of an exotic type of life has ever been presented. As biologist Norman Horowitz remarks: "It is not possible to evaluate these proposals because they have not been developed in detail. And in the absence of detailed models, all such speculation must be viewed with scepticism."[12] Horowitz's point, however, is critical, because the design of a self-replicating chemical system is bound to pose design problems involving the necessity to satisfy a good many relatively stringent and often conflicting criteria. These will only be revealed on attempting a detailed blueprint. How does alien life originate? How does it evolve? How do alien intelligent beings do science? How did they develop a technology? The questions are endless and unanswered. In our own carbon-based system in many instances, as we have seen, these criteria are in effect already satisfied in the existence of what appear to be a prearranged string of mutual adaptations in many of its basic constituents. It seems more than likely that in developing a detailed blueprint of an exotic biology, it would turn out that in many key instances design problems would prove insurmountable without built-in solutions analogous to those life-facilitating coincidences upon which our own form of life depends.

Despite the optimism of the gurus in the fields of exobiology, artificial life, and nanotechnology, no even remotely detailed blueprint for an alternative feasible self-reproducing system has been worked out. Although the possibility cannot be completely excluded, from the evidence now available it seems increasingly unlikely that life can be realized in any other material system in our cosmos.

Four centuries after the scientific revolution science has provided no significant evidence that any alternative life is possible. The second, theoretical means of disproving the anthropocentric presumption, by showing that the laws of nature are *not specifically fit* for life as it exists on earth, has *failed*. Just as the explorations of the sixteenth-century mariners and all subsequent explorations since have failed to bring back direct evidence to threaten the unique status of life and our own species, so also the scientific exploration has found no token of another life, no shred of evidence for something other than ourselves or of our type of life as it exists on earth. On the contrary, science has revealed a universe stamped in every corner, riven in every tiny detail, with an overwhelmingly and all-pervasive biocentric and anthropocentric design.

Fitness for Life's Being

We may not have final proof that the cosmos is *uniquely* fit for life as it exists on earth—because the possibility of alternative life cannot yet be entirely excluded—but there is no doubt that science has clearly shown that the cosmos is *supremely* fit for life as it exists on earth. For as we have seen, the existence of life on earth depends on a very large number of astonishingly precise mutual adaptations in the physical and chemical properties of many of the key constituents of the cell: the fitness of water for carbon-based life, the mutual fitness of sunlight and life, the fitness of oxygen and oxidations as a source of energy for carbon-based life, the fitness of carbon dioxide for the excretion of the products of carbon oxidation, the fitness of bicarbonate as a buffer for biological systems, the fitness of the slow hydration of carbon dioxide, the fitness of the lipid bilayer as the boundary of the cell, the mutual fitness of DNA and proteins, and the perfect topological fit of the alpha helix of the protein with the large groove of the DNA. In nearly every case these constituents are the only available candidates for their biological roles, and each appears superbly tailored to that particular end.

If these various constituents—water, carbon dioxide, carbonic acid, the DNA helix, proteins, phosphates, sugars, lipids, the carbon atom, the oxygen atom, the transitional metal atoms and the other metal atoms from groups 1 and 2 of the periodic table, sodium, potassium, calcium, and magnesium—did not possess precisely those chemical and physical properties they exhibit in an aqueous solution ranging in temperature from 0°C and about 75°C, self-replicating carbon-based chemical machines would be impossible. And it is not only microorganisms that the cosmic design has "foreseen." Many of the properties and characteristics of life's constituents seem to be specifically arranged for large, complex, multicellular organisms like ourselves. The coincidences do not stop at the cell but extend right on into higher forms of life. These include the packaging properties of DNA, which enable a vast amount of DNA and hence biological information to be packed into the tiny volume of the cell nucleus in higher organisms; the electrical properties of cells, which depend ultimately on the insulating character of the cell membrane, which provides the basis for nerve conduction and for the coordination of the activities of multicellular organisms; the very nature of the cell, particularly its feeling and crawling activities, which seem so ideally adapted for assembling a multicellular organism during development; the fact that oxygen and carbon dioxide are both gases at ambient temperatures and the peculiar and unique character of the bicarbonate buffer, which together greatly facilitate the life of large air-breathing macroscopic organisms.

In short, science has revealed a *vast chain of coincidences which lead inexorably to life* on earth—not just microbial life but all life on earth, including large, air-breathing organisms like ourselves—a chain of adaptations which leads from the dimensions of galaxies, through the physical conditions in the center of stars to the heat capacity of water and the atom-manipulating capacities of proteins, and on eventually to our own species and our ability to comprehend the world. From the inertial resistance we encounter when we move our hand, determined by the mass of the most distant stars, to the radioactive heat in the earth's interior which drives the great tectonic system, thus ensuring a continual replenishing of the vital elements of life—all nature, every facet of reality, is bound together into one mutual self-referential biocentric whole.

What is so particularly impressive and so highly suggestive about these life-giving adaptations is that what at first sight seem to be very trivial aspects of the chemistry and physics of a particular component turns out to be of critical significance for its biological role. Many examples have been cited in earlier chapters, including the decrease in the viscosity of the blood when the blood pressure rises, which increases the blood flow to the metabolically active muscles of higher organisms; the anomalous thermal properties of water, which buffers both the planet and organisms against massive swings in temperature; the curious but critical fact that the hydration of carbon dioxide is quite slow, which prevents a fatal acidosis in the body of higher organisms in anaerobic exercise; the curious fact that it is base sequences in the major groove of the DNA which provide the electrostatic variability that can be recognized by an α helix, and so forth.

It is important also to recall that the vital mutual adaptations are in the essential nature of things and are not the product of natural selection. This was also stressed by Henderson: "Natural selection does but mould the organism without truly altering the primary qualities of environmental fitness."[13] These are antecedent to the existence of life. The precise fit between the α helix and the large groove of the DNA are given by physics; the relationship long predated life. Similarly, the life-giving anomalous expansion of water below 4°C and on freezing and its low viscosity are given by physics. It was given before the first cell appeared in the primeval ocean. The fact that hydrogen bonds and other weak bonds have sufficient strength to hold proteins and DNA in "metastable" conformations at ambient temperatures; the fact that the majority of organic compounds are relatively stable below 100°C; the fact that the reactivity of oxygen, the only feasible terminal oxidant for carbon, is relatively unreactive below 50°C; the fact that the solubility of oxygen in water, the unique matrix for life is relatively low; the fact that carbon dioxide is a gas, that bicarbonate has such excellent buffering capabilities—all these unique coincidences are in effect laws of nature, universals no less than the constants of physics. Commenting on Henderson's arguments, the great biologist Joseph Needham stressed the same point: "Since the properties of water and the . . . elements antedate the appearance of life . . . they can be regarded philosophically as some sort of preparation for life. Purposiveness, then, exists everywhere, it permeates the whole universe. . . . Restricted teleology melts away in the immensity of that discussed by Lawrence Henderson."[14]

Fitness for Becoming

The evidence that life's becoming is also built into nature, presented in the second part of the book, is admittedly not as convincing as the evidence presented in the earlier chapters. But it is consistent with the possibility. The curious equality of mutation rates and evolutionary substitution rates and the just as curious uniformity of protein evolution which have caused endless discussion over the past twenty years have not proved easy to reconcile with Darwinian explanations. And although in no sense can either of these two phenomena be claimed as evidence for design, they are suggestive of something more in the evolutionary process than purely random mutation. Again, the current picture of the origin of life is also compatible with the concept of a uniquely ordained path from chemistry to the cell. The growing evidence that evolution is jumpy and that major evolutionary transformations have occurred rapidly is again suggestive. The more saltational the course of evolution, the easier it is to envisage it as being the result of a built-in program. The enormous diversity of the pattern of life on earth may not represent a full plenitude of all life forms, but it appears to approach closely this ideal. The very great complexity of life, and especially its quite fantastic holistic nature, which seems to preclude any sort of evolutionary transformations via a succession of small independent changes, is perfectly compatible with the notion of directed evolution. The ease with which the evolution of the very many complex adaptations such as the eye of the lobster and the avian lung can be explained in terms of design lends further support to the notion of directed evolution.

The Argument for Design

The strength of any teleological argument is basically accumulative. It does not lie with any one individual piece of evidence alone but with a whole series of coincidences, all of which point irresistibly to one conclusion. It is the same here. Neither the thermal properties of water, nor the chemical properties of carbon dioxide, nor the exceptional complexity of living things, nor the difficulties this leads to when attempting to give plausible explanations in Darwinian terms—none of these individually counts for much. Rather, it lies in the summation of all the evidence, in the whole long chain of coincidences which leads so convincingly toward the unique end of life, in the fact that all the independent lines of evidence fit together into a beautiful self-consistent teleological whole. The evolutionary evidence is similar; it compounds. In isolation, the various pieces of evidence for direction, the speed of evolutionary change, the fantastic complexity of living things, the apparent gratuity of some of the ends achieved, are perhaps no more than suggestive, but taken together, the overall pattern points strongly to final causes.

Reinforcing further the teleological position is the fact that its credibility has relentlessly grown as scientific knowledge has advanced throughout the past two centuries. In the early part of the nineteenth century when chemistry was just beginning, the only biocentric adaptations that Whewell was able to cite in his Bridgewater Treatise as evidence for a biocentric design were a few of the thermal properties of water. But by Henderson's time in the first decade of the twentieth century, while ironically the last vestiges of teleology were being exorcised from mainstream biology, advances in physiological and organic chemistry had revealed an additional and highly significant series of mutual adaptations in life's constituents which provided for the first time a significant body of evidence consistent with the view that our own carbon-based life is unique and that the laws of nature are specifically tailored to that end. Once again, during the past fifty years advances associated with molecular biology have, as we have seen, revealed yet another set of unique mutual adaptations at the heart of life in key constituents such as DNA and protein. And over the same period advances in cosmology and astrophysics have indicated that the overall structure of the universe and the constants of physics seem also to be fine tuned for our existence.

Note also that theories or worldviews are most often accepted not because they can explain everything perfectly but because they make sense of more than any competitor does. Evolution was accepted in the nineteenth century not because it explained everything perfectly but because it accounted for the facts better than any other theory. Similarly, the teleological model of nature presented here is far more coherent and makes far more sense of the cosmos than any currently available competitor. The idea that the cosmos is a unique whole with life and mankind as its end and purpose makes sense and illuminates all our current scientific knowledge. It makes sense of the intricate synthesis of carbon in the stars, of the constants of physics, of the properties of water, of the cosmic abundance of the elements, of the existence throughout the cosmos of organic matter, of the fact that the two adjacent planets Earth and Mars appear so similar, that the atom-building process continues to uranium. No other worldview comes close. No other explanation makes as much sense of all *the facts.*

Falsification

It is sometimes claimed by critics of the design hypothesis that the universe is bound to look as if it is designed for our existence because we could only be here if the universe was adapted for our existence. There is obviously an element of truth in this line of argument, for indeed the universe must be adapted to some degree for our existence if we are to be here as observers. However, the conclusion to design is not based on evidence that the laws of nature are adapted to *some degree* for life but rather on the far stronger claim that the cosmos is *optimally adapted* for life so that every constituent of the cell and every law of nature is uniquely and ideally fashioned to that end.

It is important to note that the design hypothesis is in fact very easy to refute. Any number of observations could potentially refute the claim that the cosmos is uniquely fit for life and overthrow the whole teleological conception of nature. If the laws of nature had permitted another type of life comparable in every way to our own (a possibility that now seems very remote), then the entire argument would collapse. In the seventeenth century it was the mere likelihood that the cosmos might contain a plurality of alternative worlds, some perhaps superior to our own, which threatened the whole anthropocentric worldview. In a sense, for the seventeenth-century scientific community the design hypothesis had been *refuted empirically.* When Kepler, for example, contemplated the immensity of the heavens, he could not imagine a connection between the newly revealed vastness of the cosmos and life on earth.

But the design hypothesis can, of course, be refuted by far less dramatic evidence than the discovery of an exotic type of extraterrestrial life. For example, the discovery of an alternative liquid as fit as water for carbon-based life, or of a superior means of constructing a genetic tape, better than the double helix, of alternatives superior to oxidation, superior to proteins, superior to the bilayer lipid membrane, to the cell system, to bicarbonate, to phosphates, and so on. The creation of a machine with an intellectual capacity superior to that of man would also effectively demolish the argument that the universe is contrived with mankind and human intelligence as its primary end. Just one clear case where a constituent of life or a law of nature is evidently not unique or ideally adapted for life, and the design hypothesis collapses.

If refutability is the hallmark of a scientific theory, as claimed by Karl Popper, then the hypothesis that "the cosmos is uniquely fit for life" might be classed as a perfectly ordinary scientific hypothesis. According to Popper, no hypothesis can be finally proved. All we can do with the hypothesis is attempt to refute it. The longer it resists our attempts, the better the theory. Consistency with the facts is the best we can hope for, even in the most powerful scientific theory. By the criteria of the Popperian philosophy of science, the design hypothesis is demonstrably an exceedingly robust hypothesis. Even the most rigorous skeptic must surely concede that the hypothesis is at least consistent with the facts.

The traditional way of avoiding the teleological conclusion is of course the classic "appeal to chance" which, given an infinite period of time, will generate even the most improbable result. This has been used throughout western history to counter the argument for design. This strategy was first used by the atomists in classical times. It was used specifically for this purpose by Lucretius in his great poem *De rerum natura:*

For verily not by design do the first beginnings of things station themselves each in his right place, occupied by keen sighted intelligence, . . . but because after trying motions and unions of every kind, at length they fall into arrangements, such as those out of which this our sum of things has been formed. . . .[15]

The same line of reasoning was used by David Hume in his famous *Dialogues on Natural Religion,*[16] and again very recently by the Oxford chemist P. W. Atkins in his book *The Creation* to avoid concluding to design.[17]

According to this tradition, the order of the cosmos is ultimately a matter of chance and we need seek no further explanation. This line of reasoning is of course impossible to refute. This is not a strength but rather a serious defect. For in terms of the Popperian view of knowledge, irrefutable claims are outside the realm of science. Whatever else the appeal to infinity may be, it is not a scientifically refutable hypothesis. Whether we can consider it seriously as a valid strategy to avoid the teleological conclusion is therefore open to debate. Whatever may be the philosophical status of the design hypothesis, unlike the appeal to infinity, it is certainly capable of refutation. But as this book has shown over and over again, new evidence which could potentially have refuted the hypothesis has only ended up confirming it.

I believe that Henderson's verdict on the chance hypothesis—that "the mind baulks at such a view" and "there is no greater [improbability than] that these unique properties should be without some cause uniquely favourable to the organic mechanism"[18]—is the only verdict compatible with a strictly scientific and commonsense approach.

Whether one accepts or rejects the design hypothesis, whether one thinks of the designer as the Greek world soul or the Hebrew God, there is no avoiding the conclusion that the world *looks* as if it has been uniquely tailored for life: it *appears to have been designed.* All reality *appears* to be a vast, coherent, teleological whole with life and mankind as its purpose and goal.

Are We Alone?

If the cosmos is uniquely fit for the being and becoming of our type of life, then earthlike life should arise and flourish on any planet where the conditions are similar to those on Earth. Moreover, the evolution of life on any such planet should result in many life forms similar to those generated during the evolution of life on Earth. If the evolutionary constraints are very stringent, then extraterrestrial life forms may be as identical to those on earth as Australian marsupials are to the placentals elsewhere.

A key question is how many earthlike planets might exist? From the evidence of our own solar system, which contains at least one other planet— Mars—that is very similar in many ways to the Earth and may even have had oceans and glaciers at times in the past, earthlike planets cannot be that rare. There are about 10^{11} stars in a galaxy and a total of 10^{11} galaxies in the universe, which makes 10^{22} stars in all. Since most stars probably have solar systems, the number of planetary systems is simply unimaginable. Even if only one solar system in a billion were like our own, this would still imply that there might be 10^{13} planets like Earth.

Because we cannot judge how likely the route to life, it is difficult to know how many would harbor life. The existence of life on Mars would provide strong evidence that the route to life is highly probable. But even if the route to life is somewhat tortuous and requires stringent conditions, given the number of planets, it is hard not to be inclined to the view that a vast number of planets do in fact harbor life.

As to the question "How many planets might harbor intelligent life?", again it is difficult to judge. To get from a single cell to *Homo sapiens* has taken about 4 billion years on Earth. This is a significant fraction of the entire history of the universe. Moreover, our planet has been struck many times by meteors, which have on several occasions nearly wiped out all life. If the Cretaceous meteor, credited by many with having eliminated the dinosaurs, had been only a few kilometers bigger in diameter, it could easily have boiled the oceans, effectively wiping out all life, not just the dinosaurs. Perhaps only a few planets are lucky. Perhaps on only a few does life survive for so long.

Then there is the difficulty of knowing how stringent the evolutionary constraints may be in moving from a cell to *Homo sapiens*. Perhaps the cosmos abounds in trees of life, but perhaps only one in a million trees grows at all like our own on Earth to reach the higher primates and eventually a species like *Homo sapiens*. Perhaps only in a cosmos of the size and age of our own is there a probability of one that *Homo sapiens* will arise. Science cannot yet say.

Conclusion

In the discoveries of science the harmony of the spheres is also now the harmony of life. And as the eerie illumination of science penetrates ever more deeply into the order of nature, the cosmos appears increasingly to be a vast system finely tuned to generate life and organisms of biology very similar, perhaps identical, to ourselves. All the evidence available in the biological sciences supports the core proposition of traditional natural theology—*that the cosmos is a specially designed whole with life and mankind as its fundamental goal and purpose, a whole in which all facets of reality, from the size of galaxies to the thermal capacity of water, have their meaning and explanation in this central fact.*

Four centuries after the scientific revolution apparently destroyed irretrievably man's special place in the universe, banished Aristotle, and rendered teleological speculation obsolete, the relentless stream of discovery has turned dramatically in favor of teleology and design, and the doctrine of the microcosm is reborn. As I hope the evidence presented in this book has shown, science, which has been for centuries the great ally of atheism and skepticism, has become at last, in these final days of the second millennium, what Newton and many of its early advocates had so fervently wished—the "defender of the anthropocentric faith."

Epilogue

It is not sufficient any longer to listen at the end of a wire to the rustlings of a galaxy: it is not enough even to examine the great coil of DNA in which is coded the very alphabet of life. These are our extended perceptions. But beyond lies the great darkness of the ultimate Dreamer, who dreamed the light and the galaxies. Before act was, or substance existed, imagination grew in the dark. Man partakes of that ultimate wonder and creativeness. As we turn from the galaxies to the swarming cells of our own being, which toil for something, some entity beyond their grasp, let us remember man, the self-fabricator who came across an ice age to look into the mirrors and magic of science. Surely he did not come to see himself or his wild visage only. He came because he is at heart a listener and a searcher for some transcendent realm beyond himself.

—Loren Eiseley, *The Unexpected Universe*, 1970

If the scientific evidence is consistent with the traditional teleological view of the cosmos as an anthropocentric whole with our own race, *Homo sapiens*, as its fundamental end and purpose, then this surely raises the further possibility that the acquisition of scientific knowledge itself and even the actual historical sequence of scientific and technical discoveries which led to modern science and eventually to the revelation of our centrality may also have been prearranged in the nature of things.

A hint that this might be so is the fact mentioned previously that our intellectual capacity and particularly our mathematical and aesthetic sense seem remarkably adapted for the scientific enterprise. There is, for example, the very curious fact which has fascinated philosophers since Plato—that the order of nature is mathematical and that it is primarily because the laws of nature can be described in simple mathematical forms that nature is inherently decipherable. As we saw in chapter 11, Aristotle was also struck by the correspondence between the human mind and the natural world.[1]

But in itself the mutual fitness of the human mind and the underlying structure of nature, although a necessary condition for the scientific enterprise, is clearly insufficient. For no matter how intelligent, no matter how much the deep structure of reality is fit for scientific understanding, no matter how much the human brain is adapted for the scientific enterprise, science is impossible without sophisticated tools, and these in turn are impossible without metals, and these in turn are impossible without wood. For without wood there can be no fire, and without fire, no metallurgy, and without metals, no technology and certainly no science. A race restricted, like the Eskimo, to a treeless tundra would be unable to develop any sort of sophisticated technology no matter how intelligent or manually dexterous.

In short, if the scientific enterprise is to succeed, the environment must also be fit. The major breakthroughs which ultimately made science possible—particularly the discovery of fire and the discovery of metals—have been possible only because of certain unique environmental conditions on the surface of the earth. Fire, which is the oxidation of carbon, is a remarkable phenomenon in itself. It is virtually the only known chemical reaction that is relatively nonviolent while at the same time generating vast quantities of heat. The controlled fire utilized by early man is only possible in turn because the oxygen level in the earth's atmosphere is approximately 20 percent and because of the availability of trees, which provide the carbon in the form of wood. Without trees there would have been no fire and certainly no metallurgy, and human advancement would have been forever frozen somewhere between the Stone Age and the civilization of the Aztecs. But metallurgy is itself possible only because of the existence of various geophysical processes which concentrate metal atoms in certain types of rock, because these metal-bearing ores are relatively common, and because the heat required to extract the metals is not prohibitively high and thus within the easy reach of a wood fire. Without all these favorable coincidences there would be no metallurgy, and no technologically sophisticated society would ever have developed.

The historical path that led humanity from the Stone Age hunter-gatherer to the dawn of science may have had its vagaries, but its general direction was not a matter of contingency. For fire must come before metallurgy and metallurgy before wheels (for wheels can only be easily manufactured with metal tools). Thus, the American Indians, who had only a rudimentary knowledge of metals, never developed the wheel. Again, the route from villages, via the development of agriculture and the domestication of animals, to the construction of cities, a route taken by societies in both the Old World and the Americas, is of necessity. The specific temporal sequence from the initial manufacture of stone tools via the control of fire to the discovery of metals and the development of metallurgy to the manufacture of the wheel and so on down to the scientific revolution was largely of necessity. Even the succession from copper to iron was of necessity, determined by the relative ease of extraction of copper compared with iron.

It is often claimed that chance played a large part in the process of discovery. But this is only true in the immediate sense. The classic case of Hans Christian Oersted's chance finding, during a student lecture, that an electric current in a metal wire held over a magnet could cause the magnet to move, one of the great discoveries in nineteenth-century science[2] and which, by indicating a link between electricity and magnetism, led eventually to the dynamo, electric motors, and the whole modern twentieth-century world of electrotechnology, occurred only because metal wire was freely available, because metals are conductors of electricity, and because magnetism is a natural phenomenon which had been known and used since before classical times. It seems more than likely that the discovery would have been made in the early nineteenth century if not by Oersted then by at least one of the many other physicists who were interested in the connection between electricity and magnetism. Mendel's laws were discovered independently on two occasions within the space of forty years. Differential calculus was discovered simultaneously in the seventeenth century by Newton and Liebnitz.

The fact that the scientific revolution occurred in Europe in the sixteenth century was again hardly a matter of chance. The scientific revolution could only have occurred in a technologically advanced society, skilled in the use of metallurgy, capable of constructing complex tools and artifacts, having a knowledge of mathematics, carrying out trade and commerce in manufactures. In other words, a society very similar to that which existed in Europe in the sixteenth century. Although the relative importance of the various factors which led to the advent of science in Europe at that time are controversial, there is general agreement among most historians (not only among Marxists) that given the level of technological development and the chronic shortage of labor, the rapid growth of a mercantile class anxious to expand trade and apply labor-saving technologies, the political liberty consequent on the breakdown of the feudal state, and the rediscovery of classical science and rationalism, the advent of science was virtually inevitable.

There is, I believe, every justification for viewing our planetary home with its oxygen-containing atmosphere, large land masses covered in trees, with its readily available and well scattered metal-bearing rocks as an ideal and perhaps unique environment for the use of fire and the development of metallurgy and ultimately the emergence of a technologically advanced complex society similar to that of sixteenth-century Europe. Any social animal endowed with our mental and physical attributes, with the capability of language, the ability to preserve and transmit knowledge across several generations and an innate sense of curiosity would be bound to follow the same progressive path. From the camp fires of our Neolithic ancestors we were led inevitably to copper, to iron, to toolmaking, to the wheel, to the lathe and eventually to the level of technological development of sixteenth-century Europe and from there to the scientific revolution.

And so it would seem that that same handful of about thirty atoms, which seem so perfectly fit for the construction of self-replicating chemical systems, which have in other combinations during the evolution of the earth generated a planetary environment supremely fit for life, have also possessed a myriad of properties in other combinations that have proved of very great utility to man and have facilitated greatly the development of a sophisticated technology, without which science would have been impossible and the revelation of our centrality forestalled. And so in perfect concordance with teleology, we are led to view the emergence of science and its revelation of the centrality of man as no less the inevitable and determined end of things than our biological emergence and the original emergence of life.

We have come far from the long dawn of the Paleolithic, when our ancestors huddled by wood fires, gazed wonderingly out into the night, divining imaginary messages and meanings in the pattern of the constellations, far from those distant days when a roughly hewn ax head was our only technological accomplishment. We have traveled far from the July night when the Chinese watched in uncomprehending awe a strange new light in the evening sky; we have come far from the birth of science, from the early seventeenth century, when Galileo first glimpsed the rings of Saturn.

But although the journey was long, the route often slow and tortuous, the evidence increasingly suggests that the end was never in doubt, that we followed a path already charted to an end foreseen and that our success was not in the least a matter of contingency. Like pilgrims seeking the source of their own transcendence, we have been drawn along a predetermined path from the discovery of fire to the birth of science to the revelation of our own centrality in the order of nature. We have deciphered the meaning of the constellations, and in science the cosmos has called us home.

Appendix

Miscellaneous Additional Evidence of the Fitness of the Constituents of Life

In which the properties of a variety of important constituents of the cell—sugar, glycogen, lipids, phosphates, acetic acid, and the bicarbonate buffer—are examined and shown to be uniquely fit for the biochemical roles they perform in living systems. Some of the adaptations which enable proteins to recognize particular sequences of DNA are also examined.

1. Sugar and Glycogen

One of the major molecular fuels used in all living systems are the sugars. The figure below shows the chemical structure of the five-carbon sugar arabinose.

Examples of a fully reduced carbon compound (a hydrocarbon), a partially reduced compound (a sugar arabinose), and the fully oxidized carbon compound (carbon dioxide).

fully reduced	partially oxidized	fully oxidized

```
        H                    H - C = O
        |                        |
      H - C - H              HO - C - H                  O
        |                        |                       ||
      H - C - H  ───────►    H - C - OH  ───────►        C
        |                        |                       ||
      H - C - H              H - C - OH                   O
        |                        |
        H                    H - C - OH
                                 |
                                 H
```

(the sugar, arabinose)

In chemical terms, the sugars represent a halfway stage in the oxidation of carbon between the lipids, $C_{18}H_{36}O_2$ (almost fully reduced carbon) and carbon dioxide, or CO_2 (fully oxidized carbon). The sugars are quite reactive compounds. They have a tendency to oxidize spontaneously, but this reactivity is attenuated in the case of the five- and six-carbon sugars by their characteristic and relatively stable ring-shaped structure. (This structure is known as the hemiacetal structure.) The attenuation of the reactivity because of this hemiacetal ring structure is particularly marked in the case of glucose. As David Green and R. F. Goldberger comment:

> The glucose ring is puckered and has both axial and equatorial groups bonded to the carbon atoms of the ring. The unique structural feature of glucose can now be fully appreciated. In glucose, all the large bulky groups are equatorial. No other six-carbon sugar has this special feature. All other six-carbon sugars have at least one large axial group. This means that glucose is the most stable six-carbon sugar possible.[1]

And as A. E. Needham points out, the stability of the hexoses (the six-carbon sugars) combined with their intrinsic reactivity:

> no doubt accounts for the outstanding biological role of the hexoses. In crystalline form, or in solutions too concentrated to be attacked by living organisms, they decompose very slowly. On the other hand, once activated they oxidise rapidly, even explosively, and are ideal fuels for ready use.[2]

On top of its basic chemical nature, which fits glucose so perfectly for its fundamental biological role as the "current coin" of the cell's energy system, glucose and the other hexoses have the additional very necessary characteristics of being nonvolatile (hence not lost by evaporation), very soluble in water and small enough to diffuse rapidly throughout the cell. On top of this, the breakdown of glucose generates many small molecules of great value for synthetic and other purposes.

The sugars have another property that contributes further to their fitness for their biological role and that is their capacity to polymerize into relatively insoluble complex-branched macromolecules, the polysaccharides, such as starch in plants and glycogen in animals. The molecular characteristics of polysaccharides such as glycogen, shown in the figure below, are perfectly suited to act as a readily available store of glucose to meet the ever-changing needs of the cell for energy.

The fitness of the branched structure of glycogen is commented on by Green and Goldberger:

The molecular structure of glycogen.

The black circles represent sugar molecules, the black lines chemical bonds holding them together.

From H. A. Harper, V. W. Rodwell, and P. A. Mayes (1979) *Review of Physiological Chemistry* (Englewood Cliffs, N. J.: Prentice-Hall), fig. 8.24. Reproduced by permission of V. W. Rodwell.

The structure of glycogen is not just *a piece of fanciful design by nature: it is uniquely suited for the role of glycogen as a storehouse of glucose in the animal organism.* The storage of thousands of glucose molecules in one big macromolecule accomplishes three related purposes. First, being a large molecule, glycogen cannot diffuse across the cell membrane and is thus a stable source of glucose. Second, the storage of many glucose units in a single macromolecule forestalls the osmotic problem which a high concentration of free glucose units would entail for the cell. Finally, the localisation of glucose units within a macromolecule simplifies enormously the logistics, both of commandeering glucose when the concentration of free glucose is low and of storing it when the concentration of free glucose is high. [My emphasis.]

Moreover, as Green and Goldberger continue:

By virtue of the branched structure, the outer surface of the glycogen molecule presents a high concentration of substrate to the enzymes that regulate glycogen synthesis and breakdown, although in molar terms glycogen is present in very low concentrations in the cell. The lower degree of branching in starch is no disadvantage to plant cells, since plants have a much lower metabolic rate than animals.[3]

There is another characteristic of glucose which contributes further to its biological fitness, and this is seen in the process of glycolysis, where, as Needham points out, energy is released:

without an external supply of oxygen by intramolecular changes—a mild version of what happens in some explosive molecules. The virtue of this carbohydrate-halting stage in biosynthesis, with considerable oxygen still in the molecule, is therefore obvious for there are situations in which energy is required but free oxygen is not available. Provided the acid products are not allowed to accumulate, glycolysis may continue for long periods.[4]

The hexoses are perfectly fit, in a number of crucial ways, for their role as the primary fuels of the cell.

2. The Lipids

The fatty acids most commonly occurring in lipids have chain lengths between 16 and 18 carbon atoms long. This number is dictated by a number of factors. As Green and Goldberger explain:

Fatty acids with more than eighteen carbon atoms are so nearly insoluble in water that it is impossible to use them in an aqueous medium. Fatty acids with less than 16 carbon atoms are too soluble. At high concentrations they rapidly disrupt the delicate membranes of the cell. (The chains are held in orientation by the London-van der Walls attractions of neighbouring molecules and this is effective only within a certain range of chain lengths, namely C16–C36, . . . beyond this length the molecules topple and tangle while shorter chains have insufficient attraction.) Thus the exact length of the fatty acids that are selected for use as a source of energy is a compromise between the potentially dangerous, more soluble acids and the unmanageable, less soluble acids. Nevertheless, one may ask why fatty acids are utilised, and not fatty alcohols, or fatty amines? Two chemical advantages of the fatty acids over alcohols or fatty amines are decisive: these are their greater solubility in water and higher reactivity, particularly after thioester formation.[5]

Chain lengths of 16 to 18 carbon atoms are ideal for other reasons as well. Fortuitously, fatty acids of these chain lengths are fluid or near fluid over the temperature range in which most metabolic processes occur in living things. In this section from his *Uniqueness of Biological Materials*, Needham comments on this interesting point:

> Lipid also forms a good cushion and shock absorber, and the viscera of mammals are usually well surrounded by fat. . . . In all cases the lipid is also, if not primarily, a reserve fuel . . . so that cushioning is a gratuitous asset . . . the high viscosity of lipids [compared with water] reduces their rate of flow under shearing forces, and there will be less displacement of the organs of the body during locomotion . . . than if water were the packing fluid. It is of course essential that the lipid should be fluid at body temperature, and this is found to be true. [Cold-blooded animals] have fats of lower melting point, mainly due to a larger percentage of unsaturated fatty acids. . . . Since their body temperature is very near that of the environment, the amount of unsaturated fat increases with latitude within the same species. . . . It appears that the melting point of body fat of [warm-blooded animals] also varies with the distance from the surface. . . . In man the temperature gradient is considerable, the skin being as cool as 24^0C compared with the maximum of 37^0C.[6]

The subcutaneous lipid of warm-blooded animals acts as a heat insulator preventing heat loss. The extreme example of this is the Cetacea with a layer of blubber up to 15 inches thick, which allows it to thrive in the polar seas.[7] It is fortunate for whales that carbon is lighter than oxygen so that most lipids are lighter than water. In fact, the low density of lipids is exploited universally among aquatic life forms to provide buoyancy. Needham comments:

> Oil drops give buoyancy to some Protozoa, siphonophores, embryos of Crustacea and fishes, and other plankton. . . . In adult marine fish the fat content of the body is fairly closely related to the height in the water in which they normally swim.[8]

It seems that the viscosity of just that class of lipids which for other reasons are ideally suited within the cell for constructional, metabolic purposes and energy storage would seem to be also ideally suited for buffering the organs of higher organisms against shearing forces. This is another instance in which the viscosity of one of life's constituents has a critical bearing on its biological role. Previously, we saw that the viscosity of water and ice also have a critical bearing on their respective biological roles.

Because of its hydrophobic properties the lipid bilayer has another characteristic—that of an electrical insulator. This is because, as Needham explains,

> most of the molecule is hydrocarbon, non-ionising and bearing only weak electrostatic charges . . . most electrical activity in living organisms depends on ions rather than electrons and the insulating properties of such lipid structures as the myelin sheath of nerve fibres are very great. They have a high resistance, and lipid therefore also acts as a good dielectric medium for condensers of high potential and low capacity; this type is believed to play a part in the generation of the sudden large changes in electrical potential which accompany the propagation of a nerve impulse. For such condensers a low dielectric constant is required and lipids can satisfy this requirement admirably.[9]

And in addition to its insulating characteristics the lipid bilayer makes another vital contribution to the generation of the membrane potential. As Bruce Hendry puts it in *Membrane Physiology and Cell Excitation:* "the lipid bilayer is vital as it provides the appropriate environment in which membrane proteins can reside and function. . . . The proteins endow the membrane with its specific ionic permeability."[10] Some of these proteins span the membrane. Hendry continues: "Such proteins are clearly well suited to providing a means by which ions may cross the membrane without passing through the bilayer . . . the importance of these membrane proteins for excitability is that they give the membrane the ability to pump ions into or out of the cell and to exhibit selective ion permeabilities."[11]

3. Phosphates

The energy released by oxidation is carried throughout the cell by a special class of energy-rich phosphate compounds. The figure on page 405 shows the structure of adenosine triphosphate (ATP), the main energy-rich phosphate utilized in the cell.

The biochemist F. H. Westheimer, writing in a recent *Science* article, comments that phosphates play a dominant role in the living world:

> Most of the coenzymes are (phosphates). The principal reservoirs of biochemical energy (adenosine triphosphate—ATP, creatine phosphate, and phosphoenolpyruvate) are phosphates. Many intermediary metabolites are phosphate esters, and phosphates or pyrophosphates are essential intermediates in biochemical synthesis and degradations.[12]

However, as Westheimer points out, organic chemists invariably use quite different compounds when carrying out analogous reactions to those carried out by phosphates in living things; for synthetic reactions, chlorides, bromides, iodides, tosylates, triflates, trialkylamines, sulfoxides, and selenoxides among others; for activating molecules for reaction, compounds such as carbodiimides. Chemists need to use reactive intermediates or at least intermediates which react at only moderately raised temperatures. While these compounds may well suit the organic chemist, living things could not tolerate reactive compounds, such as alkyl halides or dialkyl sul-

The chemical structure of ATP.

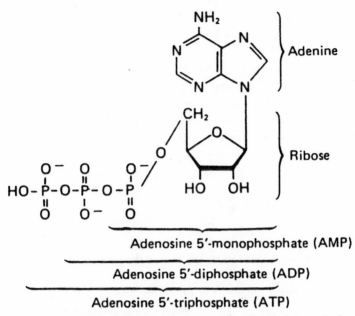

Adenine

Ribose

Adenosine 5′-monophosphate (AMP)

Adenosine 5′-diphosphate (ADP)

Adenosine 5′-triphosphate (ATP)

From Robert K. Murray et al., eds. (1996) *Harper's Biochemistry,* 24th ed. (Stamford, Conn.: Appleton & and Lange), fig. 35.12. Reproduced by permission of V. W. Rodwell.

fates, as they would alkylate enzymes and metabolites and inactivate the delicate machinery of the cell.

The energy-rich activating compounds used in the cell are phosphates, such as ATP and GTP. These are far more stable and far less reactive than their equivalents used in organic chemistry, but still sufficiently labile and reactive to fulfill these roles in the cell. In fact, the chemical characteristics of the phosphates are exactly those required of an energy-rich molecule to drive the biochemistry of the cell. Westheimer comments:

> In sharp contrast to [other energy-rich compounds] the phosphoric anhydrides are protected by their negative charges from rapid attack by water and other nucleophiles so that they can persist in an aqueous environment even though they are thermodynamically unstable, and thus can drive chemical processes to completion in the presence of a suitable catalyst (enzyme). This remarkable combination of thermodynamic instability and kinetic stability was noted many years ago by Lippmann, who correctly ascribed the kinetic stability to the negative charges in ATP. A citric acid anhydride would not survive long in water and could not serve as a convenient source of chemical energy.[13]

Interestingly, the phosphates have another key biological role. As we saw in chapter 7, they link together the nucleotide bases in the DNA. As Westheimer points out, in constructing a "tape" from small molecules, the connecting groups must be at least bivalent in order to supply one connection to each of the two adjacent nucleotides. Further, because the DNA helix functions in an aqueous environment and as water tends to cause hydrolytic breakdown of ester bonds—that is, the $-0-$ bonds in the DNA which link the phosphates to the sugars (see figure on page 142)—it is also an advantage, perhaps even essential, that the connecting groups carry a negative charge. The phosphate groups in the DNA do in fact carry a negative charge, and this negative charge greatly retards the rate of hydrolysis of DNA.

What other sorts of simple compounds possess the capacity to form two chemical bonds and remain negatively charged at the same time and might therefore be substituted for phosphate? Among the possible candidates, including citric acid, glutamic acid, ethylenediaminemonoacetic acid, arsenic acid, and silicic acid, none of them are as fit as phosphate to function as the joining group in the genetic tape. For example, silicic acid and arsenic esters hydrolyze too rapidly, and in the case of citric acid, although hydrolysis is less rapid than in the case of silicic or arsenic acid because of the geometry of the molecule, the negative charge is too weak to confer sufficient stability for citric acid to function as the joining molecules in a genetic tape.

Without the unique properties of phosphate, there could be no DNA double helix, perhaps no self-replicating biochemical system, probably no life. Westheimer, commenting on the role of phosphate in linking the nucleotides in DNA, remarks that any such compound must be at least divalent, it must also possess a negative charge, and the charge must be physically close to the two ester bonds to protect them against hydrolysis: "All of these conditions are met by *phosphoric acid and no other alternative is obvious.*"[14] (My emphasis.) No other compounds possess the correct mix of properties to drive the chemical machinery of the cell.

4. Acetic Acid

One individual compound that plays a central role in the metabolic system is acetic acid. It is nature's choice for building many of the larger molecules in the cell. This is again almost certainly no accident, because there is no other obvious candidate available. As Green and Goldberger comment:

> The arithmetic for the synthesis of long chain fatty acids takes the form of the series $2+2+2$ . . . rather than $1+1+1$ . . . or $3+3+3$. . . . The numbers refer to the numbers of carbon atoms in the fatty acid. Formic acid, the one carbon atom acid, can be disqualified on each of several important chemical grounds. An essential metabolic feature of a fatty acid is its terminal methyl group, and this is missing in formic acid. Thus it would be difficult to build up larger saturated molecules by successive condensations of units of formic acid. The three carbon acid is too unreactive chemically for purposes of condensation. The two carbon molecule of choice could be an acid (CH_3COOH), an al-

cohol (CH_3CH_2OH), or an aldehyde (CH_3CHO). Why was the acid selected as the starting point for synthesis? The alcohol is too unreactive and the aldehyde, although reactive, is somewhat unstable. We may conclude that chemical considerations were paramount in the selection of acetic acid as the starting point for the synthesis of larger molecules. *No other compound comes close to acetic acid in respect to properties excellently suited for building molecules by condensation reactions.*[15]

5. Buffers

The acidity of a solution is determined by the concentration of H^+ ion. The greater the concentration of H^+ ions, the more acid the solution. Pure water contains only a very low concentration of H^+ ions—about one H^+ ion to every 200 million molecules of water, or one 10-millionth of a gram of H^+ ions per liter. A common way of expressing the concentration of H^+ ions is as the negative logarithm of the concentration. Therefore, pure water, which has a concentration of H^+ ions of 10^{-7} grams per liter has a pH of 7. The diagram below gives the pH scale and corresponding H^+ ion concentration.[16]

The pH values of various fluids.

	H^+ CONCENTRATION (g/liter)		pH	BODY FLUIDS	SOLUTIONS
↑	10^0	1.0	0		
	10^{-1}	0.1	1		0.1N HCl
				Gastric	
	10^{-2}	0.01	2	Juice	
Acidic	10^{-3}	0.001	3		
					0.1N H_2CO_3
	10^{-4}	0.0001	4		0.0001N HCl
	10^{-5}	0.00001	5		
↓	10^{-6}	0.000001	6	Urine	
				Saliva	
Neutral	10^{-7}	0.0000001	7		Pure Water
				Blood	
↑	10^{-8}	0.00000001	8	Bile	
				Intestinal Juice	
	10^{-9}	0.000000001	9		
	10^{-10}	0.0000000001	10		
Basic	10^{-11}	0.00000000001	11		0.001 NaOH
	10^{-12}	0.000000000001	12		0.1N NH_4OH
	10^{-13}	0.0000000000001	13		0.1N NaOH
↓	10^{-14}	0.00000000000001	14		

From M. Toporek (1968) *The Basic Chemistry of Life;* © 1968 by Appleton & Lange, Stamford, Conn.

At every pH value from 1 to 14 a fraction of water molecules dissociate into H^+ (hydrogen) and OH^- (hydroxide) ions:

$$H_2O = H^+ + OH^-$$

The concentration of these two radicals varies inversely: when the concentration of H^+ ions goes up, the concentration of OH^- ions goes down. The diagram below shows the way the concentration of these two radicals varies over the complete pH range.

Note that the pH at which the concentration of these two charged radicals is minimum is 7. At pH 7 there are about two of these radicals for every 200 million molecules of water, while at pH values markedly lower or higher than 7 there is a dramatic increase in the number of these radicals. For every 200 million molecules of water at a pH of 1, there are 10 million H^+ ions, while at a pH of 14, there are 10 million OH^- ions.

The concentration of hydrogen and hydroxyl ions at various pH values.

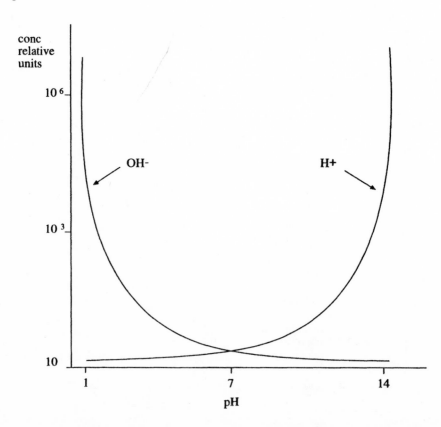

Unfortunately, both these ions are highly reactive, interacting in a variety of ways with practically all of the most important organic chemicals in the cell, with sugars, proteins and with the constituents of DNA and RNA, etc. High levels of either of these two reactive radicals causes the rapid hydrolytic breakdown of most organic compounds and are therefore incompatible with cellular life. And even slight increases in their concentration interfere in all manner of subtle ways with the finely tuned chemical activities of the cell and are therefore inimical to life. This was already well known in Henderson's day, as he remarks:

> The hydrogen ion concentration exerts a marked influence upon the rate of progress of chemical reactions. Thus for example [the hydrolysis of cane sugar] into glucose and fructose is commonly accomplished by warming a solution . . . to which a little acid has been added. . . . This process depends upon the strength of the acid, or, according to the modern view, upon the concentration of hydrogen ions. . . . Reactions of this type in which carbohydrates, fats, proteins, and other substances take part, make up a large if not the largest fraction of all the processes of metabolism. . . . In the body, to be sure, such reactions are under the control of enzymes, but the concentration of hydrogen and hydroxyl ions is not less, rather more important for that reason. Besides retaining their direct influence upon the reaction, the ions exert an influence on the enzymes themselves.[17]

By maintaining the pH of their body fluids close to 7, living systems can carry out their chemical activities with minimal interference from these two highly reactive ions. Consequently, a pH of 7, which is the pH of pure water, is the most fit for life. The further the pH is from 7 (either higher or lower), the greater the deleterious influences of the H^+ and OH^- ions on the vital activities of the cell. Not only are most of the organic constituents of the cell most chemically stable in aqueous solutions around pH 7, but the weak chemical bonds which hold together the complex 3-D architecture of the cell are also most effective at pH values close to neutrality. DNA, for example, which is stabilized by hydrogen bonds, is most stable at around this pH. Those critical activities involving the reduction and oxidation of water that occur in oxidative metabolism and photosynthesis and which involve transitional metal atoms and electron currents are also optimal close to pH 7. Also, the vital properties of the calcium and phosphate ions can only be utilized at pH values near neutrality. Bone cannot be formed at pH values below 5, while at pH levels much above neutrality the insolubility of many calcium compounds, but particularly calcium phosphate, becomes prohibitive.[18]

Life based on the sophisticated manipulation of organic compounds is impossible in a strongly acid or alkaline condition—i.e., at very low or high pH levels. In such conditions the delicate structures of the cell would suffer rapid hydrolysis and breakdown. As Fraústo da Silva and Williams comment: "Virtually all biological cells have a cytoplasm which operates at pH = 7; in almost any environment, it is as if nature had selected a buffer with as low an OH^- and H^+ concentration as possible."[19] The choice of pH 7 is therefore no accident. It is to a large extent of necessity.

To maintain a pH close to 7 and ensure that chemical activities can proceed in optimal conditions necessitates the use of substances known as buffers. Buffers are therefore also an essential part of life's design.

A buffer is merely a compound which tends to resist changes in the level of acidity or H^+ ion concentration in a solution. To understand how a buffer works, in simple terms, we may think of the buffer as having two forms, an *acid form* and an *alkaline, or basic, form.* (Chemists refer to these two forms as the conjugate acid and the conjugate base.) When the level of H^+ ions rises as the solution becomes more acid, the alkaline form of the buffer soaks up the H^+ ions:

$$H^+ + Buffer^- = Buffer.H$$
$$\text{(basic form)} \quad \text{(acid form)}$$

Conversely, when the level of H^+ ions falls, the buffer gives off H^+ ions into the solution and the reaction moves to the left.

$$H^+ + Buffer^- = Buffer.H$$

Thus, through the activities of buffers, changes in the concentration of H^+ ions can be "buffered."

6. The Bicarbonate Buffer

The major buffer in the body is bicarbonate. Bicarbonate is an excellent buffer mainly because of the volatility of the gas carbon dioxide (CO_2). When acid accumulates and the concentration of H^+ ions increases, bicarbonate (the basic form) combines with the H^+ ions forming H_2CO_3 (carbonic acid—the acid form), which then dissociates into the two absolutely innocuous substances water (H_2O) and carbon dioxide (CO_2). Thus, the reaction below tends to move toward the right, driving up the concentration of CO_2 which leaves the body via the lungs. It is as if, almost by magic, the excess acid (H^+ ions) were simply drawn out of the body in the lungs.

$$H^+ + HCO_3^- = H_2CO_3 = H_2O + CO_2$$

If CO_2 were not a gas which can leave the body, its concentration would relentlessly increase, and eventually the reaction would tend to run in the reverse direction.

The bicarbonate buffer only works because carbon dioxide can be exhaled in the lungs. In effect, because of the volatility of CO_2, the acid is simply drawn out of the body via the lungs. Thus, by respiration the reaction can be moved permanently to the right.

$$H^+ + HCO_3^- = H_2CO_3 = H_2O + CO_2$$

By this wonderfully clever device even a large and potentially fatal accumulation of H^+ ions can be almost instantly removed from the body. Because in effect the H^+

ions are simply breathed out of the body, the speed and ability of this remarkable system to handle increases in the concentration of H+ ions is unrivaled. However, there is an additional and marvelously adaptive feature of the bicarbonate buffer system. To grasp its significance, first we need to recall that the H+ ion concentration or acidity of solutions varies over a very large range—from very high in acidic solutions to very low concentrations in alkaline solutions. The range is 14 orders of magnitude or 10^{14} (see diagram on page 407).

There are a vast number of different buffers known to chemists. Each buffer works best at a particular level of acidity, or H+ ion concentration. One buffer may function optimally in an acid solution with a pH value of 3. Another might work best in an alkaline solution at a pH of 10, another in a solution of pH 5.5 and so on.

At the H+ ion concentration, or pH, where a particular buffer functions optimally, the basic and acidic forms of the buffer are present in equal concentrations— they are in equilibrium. The optimal pH for a buffer is known as its pK_a value. The pK_a values for a number of buffers are given in the table on page 414.

As we have seen in the case of the bicarbonate system, the acid form is H_2CO_3 (carbonic acid), and the basic form is HCO_3^-, or bicarbonate, and the H+ ion concentration (pH) at which these two forms are in equilibrium is about 6.4 in pure water and close to 6.1 in blood and other body fluids.

To function as a buffer in the body, ideally the concentration of the acid and basic forms of a buffer should be in equilibrium—i.e., should be present in equal concentrations at the level of acidity in the body fluids, which are close to pH 7. From this it would appear that the bicarbonate system is not ideally adapted to buffer the body fluids because it functions optimally at a pH level of 6.1, which is considerably lower than pH 7. This appears to be an anomaly but it isn't.

First, because of the volatility of CO_2 and the ease with which it can be eliminated from the body, the system can still function with great efficiency even at a pH of 7. In fact, as B. D. Rose points out in his *Clinical Physiology of Acid-Base and Electrolyte Disorders,* calculation shows that because of the ease with which the carbon dioxide (and with it, in effect, the hydrogen ions) can be breathed away, the buffering capacity of the bicarbonate system is in effect increased by between ten and twenty times (compared with an ordinary buffer) and is far more efficient than an ordinary buffer working at its pH optimum.[20]

There is yet another twist to this intriguing story, arising from the fact that the pK_a value of the bicarbonate buffer is approximately 6.1 in the body. It turns out that this pK_a value, rather than being "non-ideal," is in fact perfectly suited to defending the organism from the major challenge to pH homeostasis, which nearly always comes from an accumulation of acids rather than alkalis. The production of acids and the consequent generation of H+ ions is an inevitable result of the oxidative metabolism of organic compounds because many of the intermediates on the path from sugar to CO_2 are acids. In fact, the first part of the main catabolic pathway involves oxidative rearrangements in the intermediary compounds, which can occur in the absence of oxygen, and when an organism is deprived of oxygen for any length of time, a considerable buildup of acid is bound to occur. Some organisms derive all their energy from this first part of the catabolic pathway; indeed, catabolism in the absence of oxygen, known as anaerobic metabolism, is vital even in organisms such as mammals, which derive most of their energy from the complete oxidative catabolism of carbon to H_2O and CO_2. Moreover, as Henderson noted: "In the main the foodstuffs are neutral substances, but their principal end products, except water, are almost exclusively acid compounds, . . . phosphoric acid, sulphuric acid, uric acid."[21]

Because the pK_a of the bicarbonate system is close to 6.1 in blood and body fluids, the organism is able to maintain a far higher concentration of bicarbonate ion in its body fluids than would be possible if its pK_a was actually a 7, and this in turn allows the organism to maintain a larger reserve of bicarbonate ion to soak up the acids generated during metabolism.

To understand why this is so, recall that at the H^+ ion concentration (pH) at which a buffer works with maximal efficiency, i.e., its pK_a value, the concentration of its acid and basic forms are equal. In the case of the bicarbonate system this occurs at a pH of 6.1.

However, at a pH of 7 the equilibrium is forced to the left and the relative concentration of bicarbonate is about twenty times greater than the concentration of carbonic acid.

This relatively high concentration of bicarbonate is precisely what is required to defend the body from the accumulation of acids arising from the metabolism of food or during anaerobic exertion. That the bicarbonate levels can be maintained at such a high level to soak up any excess acids is only possible because the pH optimum of the bicarbonate buffer is 6.1.

It turns out, therefore, that the bicarbonate system is exquisitely adapted to defend the body against increases in acidity. Because its optimum pH is considerably lower than 7, this allows a buildup of bicarbonate ions in the body to a much higher concentration than would be possible if the pH optimum of the system was 7. This is just what the body needs for defense against the accumulation of acids. However, this advantage can only be exploited in turn because, as we have seen, unlike an ordinary buffer, when the level of acid increases, the bicarbonate base is converted into the neutral gas carbon dioxide, which can be easily excreted from the body.

The bicarbonate buffer system is therefore anomalous on two counts: it functions far from its optimal pH, and on soaking up acid it generates a neutral gas which can be readily excreted from the body. Both these two anomalies are essential to the design of the whole system. If carbon dioxide was not a gas, the system would fail. If the pH optimum of the bicarbonate system was 7, the system would again fail. The system works only because the pH optimum of the system is very close to 6.1 in body fluids and only because the acid form is in equilibrium with the gas carbon dioxide.

Because the pH optimum of the bicarbonate buffer system is 6.1 rather than 7, this raises the amount of bicarbonate available to soak up acid tenfold or more, which, together with the ten-to-twentyfold increase in its efficiency over ordinary buffers consequent on the volatility of CO_2, provides a buffering system of unparalleled efficiency and one wonderfully fit to maintain the hydrogen ion concentration in the body fluids of a large terrestrial organism close to neutrality.

What is really astonishing about this ingenious buffer system is that there are few if any buffers which function optimally close to pH 7 suitable to replace the bicarbonate system in living organisms. (See table below, which lists the pH optima, i.e., the pK_a values, of a number of buffers). Note that of the few candidate buffers that have a pH optimum close to 7 and might conceivably be utilized by living things such as oxalic acid, benzoic acid, etc., nearly all can be excluded for various reasons.

Phosphoric acid has a pH optimum in the right range and is in fact utilized as a buffer by living organisms, but for a variety of reasons only a small proportion of the buffering can be handled by phosphate because many phosphate compounds are insoluble and levels of phosphate much higher than those which occur physiologically would lead to the precipitation of these compounds with various deleterious effects. We are led inexorably to the conclusion that bicarbonate is the only buffer available and, as with so many of the other constituents of life, is also ideally adapted for this very specific and absolutely critical role.

7. DNA Recognition by Proteins

Individual α helices are incapable of tight binding to a unique DNA sequence because the number of weak interactions between an individual α helix and a 4-base-long section of DNA, which is generally about 5 or 6, are insufficient to stabilize the binding. The recognition α helix which fits into the large groove of the DNA is generally about 10 amino acids long. The key recognition interactions usually involve about 3 of the amino acids in the recognition helix and these make a total of about 5 or 6 specific weak interactions, mainly hydrogen bonds with the bases in the DNA.

Strong binding between a protein and DNA requires approximately 10 to 18 weak interactions. Thus, from first principles it would seem that only by using a combination of 2 or more α helices can this number of weak bonds be achieved and a protein be constructed to bind firmly to a particular sequence of the DNA. And this is precisely what is found.

As Suzuki and Yagi point out:

> An α helix can bind to no more than five base pairs because of the curvature of the major groove; it can only access one side of the DNA. To recognize more than five base pairs, two or more helices are used in combination, essentially by relating the two by a twofold symmetry axis or repeating them in tandem. The classic helix turn helix proteins . . . use the symmetric arrangement, while the Zn Finger proteins, use a tandem arrangement.[22]

The ionization constants and pK_a values of a number of buffers.

TABLE AI-3. IONIZATION (DISSOCIATION) CONSTANTS AND pK_a VALUES OF SOME WEAK ACIDS

Conjugate Acid	MW	Conjugate Base	K_a	pK_a ($= -\log K_a$)
Acetic acid	60.05	Acetate^{-1}	1.75×10^{-5}	4.76
Ascorbic acid	176.12	Ascorbate^{-1}	8×10^{-5} (K_{a_1})	4.1 (pK_{a_1})
Ascorbate^{-1}		Ascorbate^{-2}	1.6×10^{-12} (K_{a_2})	11.79 (pK_{a_2})
Benzoic acid	122.12	Benzoate^{-1}	6.30×10^{-5}	4.20
Boric acid	61.84	Borate^{-1}	5.8×10^{-10}	9.24
n-Butyric acid	88.10	Butyrate^{-1}	1.5×10^{-5}	4.82
Carbonic acid	62.03	Bicarbonate^{-1}	4.31×10^{-7} (K_{a_1})	6.37 (pK_{a_1})
Bicarbonate^{-1}		Carbonate^{-2}	5.6×10^{-11} (K_{a_2})	10.25 (pK_{a_2})
Citric acid	192.12	Citrate^{-1}	8.7×10^{-4} (K_{a_1})	3.06 (pK_{a_1})
Citrate^{-1}		Citrate^{-2}	1.8×10^{-5} (K_{a_2})	4.74 (pK_{a_2})
Citrate^{-2}		Citrate^{-3}	4.0×10^{-6} (K_{a_3})	5.40 (pK_{a_3})
3,6-Endomethylene-1,2,3,6-tetrahydro-phthalic acid,	182.2		5×10^{-5} (K_{a_1})	4.3 (pK_{a_1})
"EMTA"			1×10^{-7} (K_{a_2})	7.0 (pK_{a_2})
Formic acid	46.03	Formate^{-1}	1.77×10^{-4}	3.75
Fumaric acid	116.07	Fumarate^{-1}	9.3×10^{-4} (K_{a_1})	3.03 (pK_{a_1})
Fumarate^{-1}		Fumarate^{-2}	3.4×10^{-5} (K_{a_2})	4.47 (pK_{a_2})
Glycerophosphoric acid	172.08	Glycerophosphate^{-1}	3.4×10^{-2} (K_{a_1})	1.47 (pK_{a_1})
Glycerophosphate^{-1}		Glycero-phosphate^{-2}	6.4×10^{-7} (K_{a_2})	6.19 (pK_{a_2})
Hippuric acid	179.17	Hippurate^{-1}	2.3×10^{-4}	3.64
Hydrocyanic acid	27.03	Cyanide^{-1}	4.9×10^{-10}	9.31
Hydrofluoric	20.01	Fluoride^{-1}	1×10^{-3}	3.00
Hydrogen sulfide	34.08	Hydrosulfide^{-1}	5.7×10^{-8} (K_{a_1})	7.24 (pK_{a_1})
Hydrosulfide^{-1}		Sulfide^{-2}	1.2×10^{-15} (K_{a_2})	14.92 (pK_{a_2})
Hydroquinone	110.11	Hydroquinone^{-1}	1.1×10^{-10}	9.96
N-2-hydroxy-ethylpiperazine-N'-2-ethane-sulfonic acid,				
"HEPES"	238.3		2.82×10^{-8}	7.55
Itaconic acid	130.10	Itaconate^{-1}	1.46×10^{-4} (K_{a_1})	3.84 (pK_{a_1})
Itaconate^{-1}		Itaconate^{-2}	2.8×10^{-4} (K_{a_2})	5.55 (pK_{a_2})
Lactic acid	90.08	Lactate^{-1}	1.39×10^{-4}	3.86
Maleic acid	116.07	Maleate^{-1}	1.0×10^{-2} (K_{a_1})	2.0 (pK_{a_1})
Maleate^{-1}		Maleate^{-2}	5.5×10^{-7} (K_{a_2})	6.26 (pK_{a_2})
Malic acid	134.09	Malate^{-1}	4×10^{-4} (K_{a_1})	3.40 (pK_{a_1})
Malate^{-1}		Malate^{-2}	9×10^{-6} (K_{a_2})	5.05 (pK_{a_2})
Malonic acid	104.06	Malonate^{-1}	1.4×10^{-3} (K_{a_1})	2.85 (pK_{a_1})
Malonate^{-1}		Malonate^{-2}	8.0×10^{-7} (K_{a_2})	6.10 (pK_{a_2})
2-(N-morpholino)-ethane sulfonic acid, "MES"	195.2		7.06×10^{-7}	6.15
Nitrous acid	47.02	Nitrite^{-1}	4×10^{-4}	3.40
Oxalic acid	126.07	Oxalate^{-1}	6.5×10^{-2} (K_{a_1})	1.19 (pK_{a_1})
Oxalate^{-1}		Oxalate^{-2}	6.1×10^{-5} (K_{a_2})	4.21 (pK_{a_2})
Phenol	94.11	Phenolate^{-1}	1.3×10^{-10}	9.89
Phosphoric acid (H_3PO_4)	98.00	$H_2PO_4^{-1}$	7.5×10^{-3} (K_{a_1})	2.12 (pK_{a_1})
$H_2PO_4^{-1}$		HPO_4^{-2}	6.2×10^{-8} (K_{a_2})	7.21 (pK_{a_2})
HPO_4^{-2}		PO_4^{-3}	4.8×10^{-13} (K_{a_3})	12.32 (pK_{a_3})

From I. H. Segal, *Biochemical Calculations;* © 1968 by John Wiley & Sons, New York. Table *AI-3.* Reprinted by permission of the publisher.

The diagram below illustrates the two different ways in which combinations of helices are used to recognize a DNA binding site.

The symmetrical arrangement exploits the symmetry inherent in the DNA double helix. Note that the sequence looked at from the right is identical to that looked at from the left. As Mark Ptashne puts it in his short monograph *A Genetic Switch:* "a tiny demon standing at the middle of the target sequence facing right and then left would see identical corridors of chemical groups."[23] The proteins which recognize these symmetrical target sequences are invariably dimers consisting of two identical subunits or monomers. One subunit recognizes via its recognition helix the base sequence on the left-hand side of the target sequence, and the other recognizes the identical sequence in the right half of the target.

In the symmetrical arrangement the recognition helix of one subunit might bind to the bases GCAT in the large groove of the DNA on the left side of the target while the helix of the other subunit will bind to the identical bases GCAT in the large groove on the right side of the target. In addition to possessing a recognition

The symmetrical arrangement of two recognition α *helices.*

The tandem arrangement of recognition α *helices.*

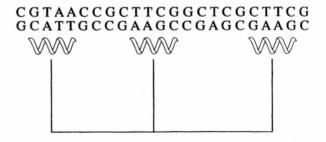

helix which recognizes and binds to the DNA, each subunit also possesses the capacity to recognize and bind to another subunit forming the active dimer. The 2 dimers exhibit cooperativity when binding such that the binding of one subunit enhances the strength of the binding of the other subunit—so the dimer binds more strongly than either of its constituent monomers individually. Thus only 1 identical protein is required to recognize what are in effect 2 different but sterically identical binding sites placed back-to-back in the DNA.

As mentioned above, effective binding between a protein and DNA necessitates about 10 to 18 weak bonds, and the use of 2 or 3 α helices can achieve this number. Much more than about 18 weak bonds and the binding is too strong. This means that the longest DNA sequence that can be recognized by an individual protein recognition system is about 15 to 16 bases long. As Mark Ptashne comments in *A Genetic Switch*, attempting to double the size of the DNA-protein recognition complex will not work. By doubling the size of the DNA sequence and its recognition protein we have increased the specificity of binding by many orders of magnitude. But now we run into another problem—the absolute strength of binding is now so high that the recognition proteins spend most of their time bound nonspecifically to random DNA sequences, i.e., on nonspecific sites. Calculation shows that our hypothetical oversized protein will never find its target sequence during a bacterial cell generation of 2.5 hours. And there is another problem with our oversized repressor. Its binding is so strong that once it has bound it will stay on virtually forever. Because the energy of binding would be so large, the repressor would have to be drastically altered while on the operator to remove it from the operator.[24]

The fact that the longest DNA sequence to which a protein can reversibly bind is about 15 bases long is intriguing because a simple mathematical calculation shows that in the genome of a mammal ("genome" is the term used for the complete DNA sequence of an organism, containing all its genes and hereditary information), which is approximately 3 billion bases long—about one meter in length if pulled out into a long string—sequences which will occur by chance only once are about 15 bases long.

Note that DNA sequences 5 bases long occur by chance once in a sequence about 4^5 or 1,000 bases long, DNA sequences 10 bases long occur by chance once in a sequence about 4^{10} or 1 million bases long, and DNA sequences 15 bases long occur by chance once in a sequence about 4^{15} or 1 billion bases long. The significance of this intriguing coincidence is that if a DNA sequence is to function as a unique target sequence somewhere in the genome, then that sequence must be long enough to ensure that no other similar sequence will occur by chance.

The binding of a protein to a particular sequence in the DNA is the key event which leads to the expression of the genes in adjacent sections of the DNA. Unwanted, random binding of proteins to the DNA interferes with the enormously complex and intricate mechanisms that regulate gene expression and would have disastrous effects. The proper functioning of the whole genetic data bank is absolutely dependent on the recognition proteins, binding strongly *only to their proper target sequences.*

If each target sequence used to label or address particular regions of the genome were not unambiguously unique, then chaos would inevitably ensue. The genome would resemble a filing cabinet with the same labels on different drawers. Hence the necessity that target sequences in the DNA of higher organisms like mammals be 15 to 16 bases long, for only sequences of this length will not occur again in the genome by chance, causing unwanted binding of the recognition protein to a non-target area of the DNA.

The use of the four bases in DNA means that the required length of 15 bases for a unique label can be met even in the 3-billion-base-long genome of a mammal. From these considerations it is clear that in a theoretical mammalian genome 3 billion bases long, constructed out of DNA composed of 2 bases, where unique target sequences would have to be, of necessity, 20 to 30 bases long (which is twice as long as in DNA composed of four bases), given the existing energy levels of weak bonds, functional repressors designed to recognize such superlong sequences would not be feasible, as they would bind irreversibly to the DNA. Clearly, a hypothetical two-base system would therefore be of little utility for protein-DNA recognition, certainly less than the existing four-base system.

A unique target sequence 15 bases long in a theoretical genome constructed out of only 2 bases would occur once by chance in about 130,000 bases—the length of the genomes of many viruses. This means that to use proteins as devices for recognizing unique DNA sequences in a 2-base genetic system we will be restricted to genomes ten thousand times smaller than that of a mammal—too small to construct organisms of any complexity.

Ptashne's comment raises again the significance, discussed in chapters 5 and 8, of the energy levels of noncovalent bonds. If these had been, say, twice as strong, then proteins designed specifically to bind to unique sequences of DNA 10 to 15 bases long—i.e., long enough to function as unique target sequences in the genome— would bind to their target sequences irreversibly and would have been of no utility to the cell. This would mean that the regulation of gene expression, which is dependent on the ability of proteins to recognize and bind reversibly to unique DNA recognition sequences adjacent to a gene, would be greatly constrained.

Here is another case where the actual energy level of the weak interactions are critical to an absolutely vital biological function. Not only are they set just right to confer on proteins their unique "metastability" and their consequent ability to undergo allosteric transitions, but they are also set at precisely the level needed for the reversible binding of proteins to unique target sequences between 10 and 15 bases long in the DNA composed of four bases.

A 2-base genome would be disadvantageous in other ways too. As we have seen in chapter 8, an α helix can feel only 4 contiguous bases in the DNA. As we also saw, a 4-base system provides 256 unique quadruplets for a helix recognition. A 2-base system would provide only 16 different quadruplets for a helical recognition, a number surely far too small to allow anything remotely approaching the sophistication of the genetic regulation possible with the existing system.

We have already considered the protein coding consequences of constructing DNA of 6 instead of 4 bases. As we saw in chapter 7, the use of 6 bases to code for 20 amino acids would necessitate what would appear to be a number of less elegant alternative solutions to the amino acid coding problem. What might be the consequences for protein-DNA recognition of having six bases instead of four?

In a large mammalian genome 3 billion bases long composed of 6 bases, a unique sequence will still need to be about 12 bases long, which would still require the same number of α helices, approximately 2 or 3 for protein recognition. As an α helix can only feel a DNA sequence 4 bases long, the additional 2 bases would provide only a very slight advantage over the existing system. And against any very minimal advantage that might be gained, a 6-base system would require the additional burden and complexity of synthesizing and maintaining a readily available pool of 6 rather than only 4 bases for the construction of DNA.

Notes

Note to the Reader

1. P. C. W. Davies (1982) *The Accidental Universe* (Cambridge: Cambridge University Press). See also J. D. Barrow and F. J. Tipler (1986) *The Anthropic Cosmological Principle* (Oxford: Oxford University Press).
2. Davies (1982); see Preface.
3. P. C. W. Davies (1995) "Physics and the Mind of God," the Templeton Prize Address, *First Things*, August-September, pp. 31–35.
4. P. C. W. Davies (1995) *Are We Alone?* (London: Penguin Books), pp. 70, 85.
5. Ibid.; see p. 25.
6. P. C. W. Davies (1992) *The Mind of God* (London: Penguin), p. 232.
7. F. Hoyle and C. Wickramasinghe (1996) (London: Orino Books); see chap. 4.
8. S. L. Miller and L. E. Orgel (1996) *The Origins of Life on the Earth* (Englewood Cliffs, N.J.: Prentice-Hall); see chap. 15.
9. S. V. W. Beckwith and A. I. Sargent (1996) "Circumstellar Discs and the Search for Neighbouring Planetary Systems," *Nature* 383:139–144.
10. W. Paley (1807) *Natural Theology* (London: Faulder & Son).
11. L. J. Henderson (1958) *The Fitness of the Environment* (Boston: Beacon Press).
12. D'Arcy W. Thompson (1952) *On Growth and Form*, 2nd ed. (Cambridge: Cambridge University Press).
13. G. Wald (1964) "The Origins of Life," *Proceedings of the National Academy of Sciences of the United States of America* (hereafter *Proc. Natl. Acad. Sci. USA*), 52:594–611, see pp. 600–601.
14. A. E. Needham (1965) *The Uniqueness of Biological Materials* (Oxford: Pergamon Press), pp. 9–10.
15. C. F. A. Pantin (1968) *The Relations Between the Sciences*, eds. A. M. Pantin and W. H. Thorpe (Cambridge: Cambridge University Press); see Appendix 1 entitled "Life and the Conditions of Existence," pp. 129–154, and see pp. 148–152. See also C. F. A. Pantin (1951) "Organic Design," *Advancement of Science* 8(29):138–150.
16. S. Kauffman (1995) *At Home in the Universe* (New York: Oxford University Press).
17. Ibid., p. 112.
18. Ibid., p. 92.
19. C. de Duve (1995) *Vital Dust* (New York: Basic Books).

20. Ibid., p. 301.
21. K. E. Yandell (1986) "Protestant Theology and Natural Science in the Twentieth Century," in *God and Nature,* ed. D. C. Lindberg and R. L. Numbers (Berkeley: University of California Press), pp. 448–471; see pp. 468–469.
22. A. Peacocke (1979) *Creation and the World of Science* (Oxford: Oxford University Press). See also A. Peacocke (1993) *Theology for a Scientific Age* (London: SCM Press); and D. J. Bartholomew (1984) *God of Chance* (London: SCM Press).
23. Peacocke (1993), p. 119.

Prologue

1. A. J. Gurevich (1985) *Categories of Medieval Culture* (London: Routledge & Kegan Paul), pp. 57, 61.
2. Ibid., p. 57.
3. From Bacon's *De sapientia veterum,* cited in J. D. Barrow and F. J. Tipler (1986) *The Anthropic Cosmological Principle* (Oxford: Oxford University Press), p. 48.
4. B. V. Subbarayappa (1989) "Indian Astronomy: An Historical Perspective," in *Cosmic Perspectives,* ed. S. K. Biswas, D. C. V. Mallik, and C. V. Vishveshwara (Cambridge: Cambridge University Press), pp. 25–39; see p. 25.
5. W. Theodore de Bary, W. Chan, and B. Watson (1960) *Sources of Chinese Tradition* (New York: Columbia University Press), pp. 518–519.
6. Barrow and Tipler, op. cit., pp. 92–93.

Chapter 1: The Harmony of the Spheres

1. C. Sagan (1985) *Cosmos* (New York: Ballantine Books), p. 192.
2. J. D. Barrow and F. J. Tipler (1986) *The Anthropic Cosmological Principle* (Oxford: Oxford University Press), see chap. 1.
3. H. Ross (1989) *The Finger of God* (Orange, Calif.: Promise Publishing Co.), p. 127.
4. P. C. W. Davies (1982) *The Accidental Universe* (Cambridge: Cambridge University Press), p. 118.
5. Ibid.
6. V. Trimble (1977) "Cosmology: Man's Place in the Universe," *American Scientist* 65: 76–86.
7. Davies (1982), p. 39.
8. J. Boslough (1985) *Stephen Hawking's Universe* (New York: Quill), p. 101.
9. Ibid.
10. For a discussion of the sorts of universe that would result if the constants were different, see J. R. Gribbin and M. J. Rees (1989) *Cosmic Coincidences* (New York: Bantam Books), chap. 10, pp. 241–269. See also Trimble, op. cit.
11. Davies (1982), Preface.
12. S. J. Dick (1982) *Plurality of Worlds* (Cambridge: Cambridge University Press), p. 61.
13. I. B. Cohen (1958) *Isaac Newton's Papers and Letters on Natural Philosophy* (Cambridge: Cambridge University Press), pp. 360–361.
14. P. C. W. Davies (1987) *The Cosmic Blueprint* (London: Penguin), p. 203.
15. S. J. Gould (1989) *Wonderful Life* (New York: Norton), p. 291.
16. Ibid., p. 320.
17. Ibid., p. 323.

Chapter 2: The Vital Fluid

1. I. B. Cohen (1958) *Isaac Newton's Papers and Letters on Natural Philosophy* (Cambridge: Cambridge University Press), pp. 381–382.
2. See A. E. Needham (1965) *The Uniqueness of Biological Materials* (Oxford: Pergamon Press), pp. 9–10. See also N. V. Sidgwick (1937) "Molecules," *Science* 86:335– 340, for discussion of the conditions for life.
3. J. Von Neumann (1966) *Theory of Self-reproducing Automata,* ed. W. A. Burks (Urbana: University of Illinois Press); see p. 82.
4. W. Paley (1807) *Natural Theology* (London: Faulder & Son), p. 401. See also Paley's discussion on p. 406, which illustrates the difficulty encountered at the time in alluding to properties of water that were specially beneficial to life.
5. W. Whewell (1871) *Astronomy and General Physics Considered with Reference to Natural Theology,* 8th ed. (London: Bohn).
6. Ibid., pp. 70–72.
7. Ibid., p. 78.
8. Ibid., p. 79.
9. Ibid., pp. 123–125.
10. L. J. Henderson (1958) *The Fitness of the Environment* (Boston: Beacon Press).
11. J. Needham (1929) *The Sceptical Biologist* (London: Chatto & Windus), pp. 211–218.
12. H. J. Morowitz (1987) *Cosmic Joy and Local Pain* (New York: Scribner), pp. 99–107.
13. Henderson, op. cit.; see Preface.
14. Ibid., pp. 99–100.
15. Ibid., p. 106. See also F. Franks (1972) "Water, the Unique Chemical," in *Water: A Comprehensive Treatise,* vol. 1 (New York: Plenum Press), p. 488.
16. Henderson, op. cit., pp. 86–89.
17. Ibid.
18. Ibid., p. 105.
19. Ibid., p. 106.
20. Ibid., pp. 126–127.
21. A. E. Needham, op. cit., p. 11.
22. Franks, op. cit., p. 20.
23. Henderson, op. cit., p. 111.
24. Franks, op. cit., p. 20.
25. Henderson, op. cit., pp. 112–115.
26. Ibid., pp. 113–115.
27. A. E. Needham, op. cit., p. 23.
28. Henderson, op. cit., p. 79.
29. A. E. Needham, op. cit., p. 12.
30. K. Schmidt-Nielsen (1975) *Animal Physiology* (Cambridge: Cambridge University Press), p. 671.
31. H. Davson and J. F. Danielli (1952) *The Permeability of Natural Membranes* (Cambridge: Cambridge University Press), pp. 51–52.
32. H. Stern and D. L. Nanney (1965) *The Biology of Cells* (New York: Wiley), p. 77.
33. Schmidt-Nielsen, op. cit., p. 671.
34. As M. W. Clark (1948) *Topics of Physical Chemistry* (Baltimore: Williams & Wilkins), p. 128, explains, "The slowness of diffusion over long distances and its great rapidity over short distances is, as the physiologist A. V. Hill who carried out pioneering work on diffusion in the thirties pointed out: 'the basis of the capillary circulation and therewith the whole design of the larger animals.'"

35. Ibid., p. 146.
36. Schmidt-Nielsen, op. cit., p. 143.
37. Ibid., p. 44.
38. M. Reiner (1959) "The Flow of Matter," *Scientific American* 201(6):122–137.
39. G. Ranalli (1987) *Rheology of the Earth* (Boston: Allen & Unwin), p. 71. A. Holmes (1965) *Principles of Physical Geology* (London: Nelson), pp. 61–62.
40. R. C. Weast and M. J. Astle (1980) *CRC Handbook of Chemistry and Physics,* 61st ed., (Boca Raton, Fla.: CRC Press). The densities cited are all taken from this source.
41. Morowitz, op. cit., pp. 152–153.
42. Ibid., 154.
43. A. E. Needham, op. cit., p. 22.
44. Henderson, op. cit., pp. 130–131.

Chapter 3: The Fitness of the Light

1. C. Sagan (1985) *Cosmos* (New York: Ballantine), p. 199.
2. Ibid., p. 199.
3. I. M. Campbell (1977) *Energy and the Atmosphere* (London: Wiley), pp. 1–2.
4. G. Wald (1959) "Life and Light," *Scientific American* 201(4):92–108.
5. K. L. Coulson (1975) *Solar and Terrestrial Radiation* (New York: Academic Press), from fig. 3.1, p. 40.
6. Campbell, op. cit., p. 1.
7. *Encyclopaedia Britannica* (1994), 15th ed., vol. 18, p. 200, fig. 5.
8. Ibid., from fig. 3, p. 198.
9. Ibid., p. 198.
10. Ibid., p. 203.
11. J. A. Maclaughlin, R. R. Anderson, and M. F. Holick (1982) "Spectral Character of Sunlight Modulates Photosynthesis of Previtamin D3 and its Photoisomers in Human Skin," *Science* 216:1001–1003.
12. K. L. Bushaw et al. (1996) "Photochemical Release of Biologically Available Nitrogen from Aquatic Dissolved Organic Matter," *Nature* 381:404–407.
13. K. Ya. Kondratyev (1969) *Radiation in the Atmosphere* (New York: Academic Press), p. 123.
14. T. Fenchel and B. J. Finlay (1995) *Ecology and Evolution in Anoxic Worlds* (Oxford: Oxford University Press). See also N. R. Pace (1997) "A Molecular View of Microbial Diversity and the Biosphere," *Science* 276:734–740.
15. H. B. Barlow (1964) "The Physical Limitations of Visual Discrimination," in *Photophysiology,* ed. A. C. Giese, vol. 2, pp. 163–202; see esp. 187–197, and table on p. 189 and discussion on p. 197.
16. H. B. Barlow (1981) "Critical Limiting Factors in the Design of the Eye and the Visual Cortex," *Proceedings of The Royal Society of London, Series B* 212:1–34; see p. 4.
17. J. R. Brobeck (1979) *Best and Taylor's Physiological Basis of Medical Practice* (Baltimore: Williams & Wilkins), pp. 8–67.
18. M. D. Levine (1985) *Vision in Man and Machine* (New York: McGraw-Hill); see p. 61.
19. S. Duke-Elder (1958) *System of Ophthalmology* (London: Henry Kimpton), pp. 450–451.
20. Barlow (1981), p. 5. See also Brobeck, op. cit., pp. 8–71.
21. M. A. Ali and M. A. Klyne (1985) *Vision in Vertebrates* (New York: Plenum Press), p. 153.
22. Barlow (1981), pp. 4–5.
23. A. Despopoulous and S. Silbernagl (1991) *Color Atlas of Physiology* (New York: Thieme Medical Publishers), p. 306.

24. B. Alberts et al. (1989) *Cell,* 2nd ed. (New York: Garland Publishing); see pp. 1104–1107.

25. Despopoulos and Silbernagl, op. cit.

26. Alberts et al., op. cit.

27. N. Henbest and M. Marten (1983) *The New Astronomy* (Cambridge: Cambridge University Press). M. A. Mitton (1977) *The Cambridge Encyclopaedia of Astronomy* (London: Jonathan Cape). See also J. M. Pasachoff and M. L. Kutner (1978) *University Astronomy* (Philadelphia: W. B. Saunders).

28. *Encyclopaedia Britannica,* vol. 18, p. 203.

29. Ibid., pp. 196–197.

30. Henbest and Marten, op. cit., p. 8.

Chapter 4: The Fitness of the Elements and the Earth

1. J. J. R. Fraústo da Silva and R. J. P. Williams (1991) *The Biological Chemistry of the Elements* (Oxford: Oxford University Press), pp. 3–4. P. A. Cox (1995) *The Elements on Earth* (Oxford: Oxford University Press).

2. Fraústo and Williams, op. cit., p. 5.

3. C. Ponnamperuma (1983) "Cosmochemistry and the Origin of Life," in *Cosmochemistry and the Origin of Life,* ed. C. Ponnamperuma (Dordrecht, Holland: Reidel), chap. 1, fig. 6.

4. J. T. Edsall and J. Wyman (1958) *Biophysical Chemistry,* vol. 1 (New York: Academic Press), chap. 1, fig. 2.

5. Cox, op. cit., pp. 183–186.

6. S. Levy (1993) *Artificial Life* (London: Penguin), pp. 87–120.

7. F. Press and R. Siever (1986) *Earth* (New York: W. H. Freeman), p. 11.

8. Ibid., p. 366.

9. Ibid., p. 367.

10. Ibid., p. 366.

11. Ibid., pp. 11–12.

12. Ibid., pp. 13–14.

13. Ibid., p. 14.

14. Ibid., pp. 367–368.

15. H. Rymer (1996) "Book Reviews," *Nature* 383:684.

16. Ibid., p. 122.

17. Yi-Fu Tuan (1968) *The Hydrologic Cycle and the Wisdom of God* (Toronto: University of Toronto Press), p. 4.

18. Ibid., pp. 4–5.

19. Press and Siever, op. cit., p. 479.

20. W. D. Parkinson (1983) *Introduction to Geomagnetism* (Edinburgh: Scottish Academic Press), pp. 356–357. M W. McElhinney (1973) *Paleomagnetism and Plate Tectonics* (Cambridge: Cambridge University Press), pp. 146–147.

21. N. C. Brady and R. R. Weill (1996) *The Nature and Properties of Soils* (Englewood Cliffs: Prentice Hall), pp. 242, 270.

22. Ibid., p. 241.

23. Ibid., p. 270.

24. C. F. Ugolini and H. Spaltenstein (1992) "Pedosphere," in *Global Biogeochemical Cycles,* ed. S. S. Butcher et al. (London: Academic Press), pp. 123–153; see p. 128.

25. A. Holmes (1965) *Principles of Physical Geology* (London: Nelson), p. 63.

26. J. E. Fergusson (1982) *Inorganic Chemistry and the Earth* (Oxford: Pergamon Press); see chap. 7.

27. J. G. Hering and W. Stumm (1990) "Oxidative and Reductive Dissolution of Minerals," *Reviews in Mineralogy* 23:427–465; see p. 456.

28. R. Siever (1983) "The Dynamic Earth," *Scientific American* 249(3), pp. 30–39.

29. R. A. Berner (1995) "Chemical Weathering and Its Effect on Atmospheric CO_2 and Climate," *Reviews in Mineralogy* 31:565–583; see pp. 567–568.

30. Ibid., p. 570. As Berner points out: "The importance of mountain uplift to weathering of silicates has been emphasized recently. . . . The idea is that uplift results in rugged relief, and cold temperatures at high elevation. The rugged relief enhances physical erosion and the removal of protective covers of highly weathered clay residues, allowing greater exposure of primary silicates to chemical weathering. Cold temperatures result in greater physical weathering due both to freeze-thaw and to the grinding where glaciers are present. The enhanced physical weathering exposes more surface area of the primary minerals to the weathering solutions. In addition, mountains can bring about enhanced rainfall due to orographic effects resulting in greater flushing of rocks by water. All these factors should have brought about greater weathering of silicate minerals during geologic periods when the extent of high mountains was globally more important. An example is the late Cenozoic when the uplift of the Himalayan/Tibetan system occurred."

31. J. E. Lovelock (1987) *Gaia: A New Look at Life on Earth* (Oxford: Oxford University Press); see Preface.

32. Ibid., p. 34.

33. D. Attenborough (1995) *The Private Life of Plants* (London: BBC Books), p. 70.

34. E. Pennisi (1995) "The Secret Language of Bacteria," *New Scientist*, September 16, pp. 30–33.

35. Press and Siever, op. cit., p. 4. See also G. Wald (1964) "The Origins of Life," *Proc. Natl. Acad. Sci. USA* 52:594–611; see pp. 600–601. In Wald's words: "Those conditions almost surely involve a planet somewhat resembling the Earth, of about this size and temperature, and receiving about this quantity of radiation from its sun. To mention a few points of the argument: a much smaller planet could not hold an adequate atmosphere, a much larger one might hold too dense an atmosphere to permit radiation to penetrate to its surface. Too cold a planet would slow down too greatly the chemical reactions by which life arises; too warm a planet would be incompatible with the orderly existence of macromolecules. The limits of temperature are probably close to those at which water remains a liquid, itself almost surely a necessary condition for life."

36. Press and Siever, op. cit., p. 4.

37. Ibid.

38. J. S. Kargel and R. G. Strom (1996) "Global Climatic Change on Mars," *Scientific American* 275 (5):80–85; see p. 80.

39. Ibid., p. 82.

40. A. Henderson-Sellers (1986) "The Evolution of the Earth's Atmosphere," in *The Breathing Planet*, ed. J. Gribbin (Oxford: Basil Blackwell), pp. 19–26; see p. 21.

41. Ibid., pp. 21–22.

42. J. Davies (1995) "Searching for Alien Earth," *New Scientist*, May 13, pp. 24–28. See also *Science* 267 (1995):1273, and G. A. H. Walker (1996) "A Solar System Next Door," "News and Views," *Nature* 382:23–24.

43. Noam Stoker cited by M. Chown, *New Scientist* 155, no. 2091 (1997): 21. See also S. V. W. Beckwith and A. I. Sargent (1996) "Circumstellar Disks and the Search for Neighbouring Planetary Systems," *Nature* 383:139–144.

44. C. Sagan (1980) *Cosmos* (New York: Ballantine); see p. 177.

45. See "Worlds Around Other Stars Shake Planet Birth Theory," in the "Research News" section, *Science* 276:1336–1339.

46. Ibid.; see p. 144.

47. G. W. Wetherill (1995) "How Special is Jupiter?" *Nature* 373:470. See also G. W.

Wetherill (1993) "Our Friend Jove," *Discover,* July, p. 15. See also M. A. Corey (1995) *The Natural History of Creation* (Boston: University Press of America); see p. 69.
48. Wetherill (1993).

Chapter 5: The Fitness of Carbon

1. R. E. D. Clark (1961) *The Universe: Plan or Accident?* (London: Paternoster Press), p. 98.
2. Ibid., p. 119.
3. H. T. Pledge (1966) *Science Since 1500* (London: Her Majesty's Stationery Office), pp. 124–125.
4. W. Prout (1855) *Chemistry, Meteorology, and the Function of the Digestion,* 2nd ed. (London: Bohn), p. 6. Prout was well-known in his day as the first to propose the notion that the atomic weights of all the elements were multiples of the atomic weight of hydrogen, the first to divide foods into sugars, fats, and proteins, and as the discoverer of hydrochloric acid in the stomach.
5. L. J. Henderson (1958) *The Fitness of the Environment* (Boston: Beacon Press), pp. 193–194.
6. N. V. Sidgwick (1950) *The Chemical Elements and their Compounds,* vol. 1 (Oxford: Oxford University Press), p. 490. As Sidgwick explains, the reason for the stability of carbon compounds is that "in the first place the typical four-covalent state of the carbon atom is one in which all the formal elements of stability are combined. It has an octet, a fully shared octet, an inert gas number, and in addition, unlike all the other elements of the group, on octet which cannot increase beyond 8, since 4 is the maximum covalency possible for carbon. Hence the saturated carbon atom cannot co-ordinate either as donor or as acceptor, and since by far the commonest method of reaction is through co-ordination, carbon is necessarily very slow to react and even in a thermodynamically unstable molecule may actually persist for a long time unchanged. More than 50 years ago Victor Meyer drew attention to the characteristic inertness (*Tragheit*) of carbon in its compounds, and there is no doubt that this is its main cause."
7. Ibid.
8. Ibid.
9. G. Wald (1964) "The Origins of Life," *Proc. Natl. Acad. Sci. USA* 52:595–611; see p. 603: "Silicon . . . forms looser, less stable compounds . . . (and) silicon chains . . . are susceptible to attack by molecules possessing lone pairs of electrons, in part because of their more open structure but still more because silicon, a third period element, possesses $3d$ orbitals available for further combination. . . . Silicon however has another fatal disability, its failure to form multiple bonds." As Wald explains, silicon dioxide molecules bond with each other, forming the long polymers which make up quartz, the major constituent of most rocks. Silicon is "fit for making rock," while carbon is "fit for life."
10. Sidgwick, op. cit., p. 490. A. E. Needham (1961) *The Uniqueness of Biological Materials* (London: Pergamon Press), p. 32.
11. J. B. S. Haldane (1954) "The Origin of Life," *New Biology* 16:12–27.
12. Needham, op. cit., p. 30.
13. Ibid., pp. 32–33.
14. Henderson, op. cit., pp. 220–221, 235–237.
15. J. Yudkin (1985) *The Penguin Encyclopaedia of Nutrition,* (London: Penguin), p. 98.
16. T. Hoyem and O. Kvale (1977) *Physical, Chemical, and Biological Changes in Food Caused by Thermal Processing* (London: Applied Science Publishers), pp. 185–201.
17. H. R. White (1984) "Hydrolytic Stability of Biomolecules at High Temperatures and Its Implication for Life at 250°C," *Nature* 310:430–432. See also H. Bernhardt, D. Lude-

man, and R. Jaenicke (1984) "Biomolecules Are Unstable Under Black Smoker Conditions," *Naturwissenschaften*, 71:583–586.

18. S. L. Miller and L. E. Orgel (1974) *The Origins of Life on the Earth* (Englewood Cliffs, N.J.: Prentice-Hall); see chap. 9 on the stability of organic compounds.

19. H. Eyring, R. P. Boyce, and J. D. Spikes (1960) "Thermodynamics of Living Systems," in *Comparative Biochemistry*, vol. 1, ed. M. Florkin and H. S. Mason (New York: Academic Press), pp. 60–62.

20. Clark, op. cit., p. 59.

21. Wald, op. cit., p. 605.

22. L. M. Lederman (1989) *From Quarks to the Cosmos* (New York: Scientific American Library), p. 152.

23. F. Hoyle (1954) "Ultrahigh Temperatures," *Scientific American* 191(3): 145–154.

24. The bonds are: ionic bonds, van de Waals forces, hydrogen bonds, and the hydrophobic force. A detailed description of these bonds can be found in any major textbook of biochemistry.

25. J. Walker (1981) "The Physics and Chemistry of the Lemon Meringue Pie," *Scientific American* 244(6):154–159; see pp. 154–155.

26. G. N. Somero (1995) "Proteins and Temperature," *Annual Review of Physiology* 57:43–68; see p. 61.

Chapter 6: The Vital Gases

1. T. Fenchel and B. J. Findlay (1995) *Ecology and Evolution in Anoxic Worlds* (Oxford: Oxford University Press). See also N. Pace (1997) "A Molecular View of Microbial Diversity and the Biosphere," *Science* 276:734–740.

2. Fenchel and Findlay, op. cit. See also Pace, op. cit. One interesting group of bacteria, the methanogenic bacteria, derive energy from the reduction of carbon dioxide by hydrogen to produce methane, i.e., $CO_2 + H = CH_4 = H_2O$.

3. Fenchel and Findlay, op. cit.; see chap. 2, pp. 62–63, and chap. 5.

4. N. V. Sidgwick (1950) *The Chemical Elements and Their Compounds*, vol. 1 (Oxford: Oxford University Press), pp. 1124–1129.

5. L. J. Henderson (1958) *The Fitness of the Environment* (Boston: Beacon Press), pp. 247–248.

6. J. E. Lovelock (1987) *Gaia* (Oxford: Oxford University Press), p. 71.

7. Ibid.

8. B. Halliwell and J. M. C. Gutteridge (1990) *Methods in Enzymology* 186:1–88; see p. 1.

9. M. J. Green and A. O. Hill (1984) *Methods in Enzymology* 105:1–21.

10. J. Needham (1970) *The Chemistry of Life* (Cambridge: Cambridge University Press), pp. 30–33.

11. L. L. Ingraham (1966) "Enzymic Activation of Oxygen," in *Comprehensive Biochemistry*, ed. M. Florkin and E. H. Stotz, vol. 14 (Amsterdam: Elsevier), pp. 424–446; see p. 424.

12. Sidgwick, op. cit., p. 490.

13. *Van Nostrand's Scientific Encyclopedia* (1995), 8th ed., vol. 2, p. 2321. G. L. Pollack (1991) "Why Gases Dissolve in Liquids," *Science* 251:1323–1330; see p. 1323. A. Krogh (1941) *The Comparative Physiology of Respiratory Mechanisms* (Philadelphia: University of Pennsylvania Press); see p. 12, table 5.

14. Schmidt-Nielsen, op. cit., pp. 676–677. Krogh, op. cit., pp. 5–6.

15. G. N. Ling (1967) "Effects of Temperature on the State of Water in the Living Cell," in *Thermobiology*, ed. A. H. Rose (New York: Academic Press), pp. 5–24; see fig. 2, p. 10. L. Watson (1988) *The Water Planet* (New York: Crown Publishers); see p. 132.

16. I. Fridovich (1976) "Oxygen Radicals, Hydrogen Peroxide, and Oxygen Toxicity" in *Free Radicals in Biology,* ed. W. A. Pryor, vol. 1 (New York: Academic Press), pp. 239–277.
17. Ibid., pp. 239–240.
18. V. B. Mountcastle (1968) *Medical Physiology,* vol. 1 (St. Louis: C. V. Mosby), p. 629.
19. Ibid., p. 631.
20. P. B. Bennett and D. H. Elliott (1969) *The Physiology and Medicine of Diving and Compressed Air Work* (London: Bailliere, Tindall & Cassell); see chap. 22, pp. 508–509.
21. Pollack, op. cit., p. 1324.
22. A. Naqui, B. Chance, and E. Cadenas (1986) "Oxygen Intermediates," *Annual Review of Biochemistry* 55:137–166.
23. Fenchel and Findlay, op. cit., p. 237.
24. A. Henderson-Sellers (1983) *The Origin and Evolution of the Planetary Atmospheres* (Bristol: Adam Hilger); see chaps. 4 and 5, and p. 164.
25. J. B. West (1979) "Mechanics of Breathing," in *The Physiological Basis of Medical Practice,* 10th ed. J. B. Brobeck, ed. (Baltimore: Williams & Wilkins), pp. 636–653.
26. Ibid. V. B. Mountcastle (1968) *Medical Physiology,* vol. 1 (St. Louis; C V. Mosby), pp. 622–626. *Encyclopaedia Britannica* (1994), 15th ed., vol. 26, p. 745.
27. Bennett and Elliott, op. cit.; see chap. 4, pp. 76–109; p. 81.
28. D. R. Lide (1995) *CRC Handbook of Chemistry and Physics,* 76th ed. (Boca Raton, Fla.: CRC Press), pp. 6–17.
29. Lovelock, op. cit., p. 78.
30. J. W. Drake (1970) *The Molecular Basis of Mutation* (San Francisco: Holden-Day), p. 171.
31. A. E. Needham (1905) *The Uniqueness of Biological Materials* (Oxford: Pergamon Press), p. 35.
32. Henderson, op. cit., pp. 139–140.
33. Ibid., p. 153.
34. J. T. Edsall and J. Wyman (1958) *Biophysical Chemistry,* vol. 1 (New York: Academic Press), p. 550.
35. I. B. Cohen (1958) *Isaac Newton's Papers and Letters on Natural Philosophy* (Cambridge: Cambridge University Press), p. 361.
36. Edsall and Wyman, op. cit., p. 554. As the authors point out: "The hydration of CO_2 to H_2CO_3 is a process requiring a rearrangement of the valence bonds, the two C-O bonds of CO_2, 180 degrees apart and 1.15 A long, being transformed to the three C-O bonds of H_2CO_3, approximately 120 degrees apart and not far from 1.3 A long. We shall not attempt to comment here on the details of the electronic rearrangements that must be involved in the process, and indeed little is known of them. It is not surprising however that a process such as this should require an appreciable time, in contrast for example to a process such as the hydration of NH_3 to NH_4OH in which the hydration process simply involves the formation of a hydrogen bond between the unshared electron pair in the ammonia molecule."
37. Henderson, op. cit., p. 141.
38. Ibid., p. 138.
39. Ibid., pp. 266–267.
40. Ibid., p. 272.

Chapter 7: The Double Helix

1. J. Von Neumann (1966) *Theory of Self-Reproducing Automata,* ed. A. W. Burks (Urbana: University of Illinois Press).
2. C. G. Langton (1989) "Artificial Life," in *Artificial Life,* ed. C. G. Langton, Proceedings

of an Interdisciplinary Symposium held in September 1987 in Los Alamos, New Mexico (Redwood City, Calif.: Addison-Wesley), pp. 1–48; see p. 1.

3. C. Schneiker (1989) "Nano Technology with Feynman Machines: Scanning, Tunneling, Engineering, and Artificial Life," in *Artificial Life*, ed. C. G. Langton, Proceedings of an Interdisciplinary Symposium held in September 1987 in Los Alamos, New Mexico (Redwood City, Calif.: Addison-Wesley), pp. 443–500.

4. Ibid., p. 449.

5. K. E. Drexler (1987) *The Engines of Creation* (New York: Anchor Press). See also K. E. Drexler (1992) *Nanosystems: Molecular Manufacture and Computation* (New York: Wiley).

6. A. K. Dewdney (1988) "Computer Recreations," *Scientific American* 258(1):88–91.

7. V. Tartar (1961) *The Biology of Stentor* (London: Pergamon Press); see chap. 7, pp. 105–134.

8. H. F. Judson (1979) *The Eighth Day of Creation* (New York: Simon & Schuster), pp. 173–175.

9. Ibid., p. 175.

10. F. Crick (1974) "The Double Helix: A Personal View," *Nature* 284:766–769.

11. W. Saenger (1984) *Principles of Nucleic Acid Structure* (New York: Springer-Verlag), p. 8.

12. "News and Views" (1997) *Nature* 389:231–233.

13. G. G. Simpson (1960) "The History of Life," in *Evolution of Life*, ed. Sol Tax (Chicago: University of Chicago Press), pp. 117–180; see p. 135.

14. A. A. Travers (1989) "DNA Conformation and Protein Binding," *Annual Review of Biochemistry* 58:427–452; see p. 428. See also A. A. Travers (1990) "Why Bend DNA?" *Cell* 60:177–180.

15. Saenger, op. cit., pp. 220–241.

16. D. E. Draper (1995) "Protein-RNA Recognition," *Annual Review of Biochemistry* 64: 593–620; see. p. 596.

17. Ibid. See also L. Gold et al. (1995) "Diversity of Oligonucleotides," *Annual Review of Biochemistry* 64:763–797.

18. "News and Views" (1995) *Nature* 376:548. M. Bolli, A. Micura, and A. Eschenmoser (1997) "Pyranosyl-RNA: Chiroselective Self-Assembly of Base Sequences by Ligative Oligomerization of Tetranucleotide −2',3'-Cyclophosphates," *Chemistry and Biology* 4:309–320. A. Eschenmoser (1993) "Towards a Chemical Etiology of the Natural Nucleic Acids," in *40 Years of the DNA Double Helix* (Houston: Robert A. Welch Foundation), pp. 201–235. See also L. E. Orgel (1992) "Molecular Replication," *Nature* 358:203–209.

19. A. Eschenmoser (1997) personal communication. See also A. Eschenmoser, "Towards a Chemical Etiology."

20. A. Rich (1963) "On the Problems of Evolution and Biochemical Information Transfer," in *Horizons in Biochemistry*, ed. M. Kasha and B. Pullman (New York: Academic Press), pp. 103–126; see p. 120.

21. J. D. Bain et al. (1992) "Ribosome-Mediated Incorporation of a Nonstandard Amino Acid into a Peptide Through Expansion of the Genetic Code," *Nature* 356:537–539. See also J. Piccirilli (1990) "Enzymic Incorporation of a New Base Pair into DNA and RNA Extends the Genetic Alphabet," *Nature* 343:33–37.

22. Saenger, op. cit., see chap. 5.

23. Ibid., p. 114.

24. W. Saenger (1997), in a personal communication, summarized the fitness of DNA thus: "The Watson-Crick base pairs are ideally suited for the [biological function] of DNA as (1) they have the same overall dimensions so that a regular double helix can be formed, (2) the hydrogen bonds can be opened and closed at a rate that permits rapid read-out and replication, and (3) the ribose rings of the sugars have sufficient flexibility to permit conformational changes from the A to the B form. If you modify the bases chemically, it

is still possible to form selective base pairs so that the specificity is retained, but you will change the strength of the hydrogen bonds so that the kinetics of read-out and replication will be altered. This is because any chemical modification will change the pK-values of the bases so that the hydrogen-bonding strength will be influenced. As to the sugar moieties, the riboses are never planar but have envelope or twist conformations so that the DNA backbone has a certain flexibility. This would be impossible with six-membered sugar rings which are rigid and cannot confer flexibility that is necessary for biological functioning of nucleic acids. . . . one could also speculate on the phosphodiester link that connects adjacent ribose units. It could be replaced by a peptide or a sulphate diester or some other link which, however, is not found. It appears that the negative charge of the phosphate is necessary to maintain the solubility of the nucleic acids, and a certain flexibility and geometry to provide the properties of the nucleic acids."

25. A. Rich, op. cit., pp. 119–120.
26. D. Maxime, M. D. Frank-Kamenetskii, and S. M. Mirkin (1995) "Triplex DNA Structures," *Annual Review of Biochemistry* 64:65–95.
27. D. K. Gifford (1994) "On the Path to Computation with DNA," *Science* 266:993–994.
28. T. Kaeler (1995) "Designing Molecular Components," in *Prospects in NanoTechnology*, ed. M. Krummenacker and J. Lewis (New York: Wiley), pp. 53–66; see p. 65.

Chapter 8: Nanomanipulators

1. J. Monod (1972) *Chance and Necessity* (London: Collins), p. 64.
2. M. F. Perutz (1969) "X-Ray Analysis: Structure and Function of Enzymes," *European Journal of Biochemistry* 8:455–466.
3. Ibid., p. 462.
4. See "News and Views," *Nature Structural Biology* 4 (1997):424–427.
5. J. Watson (1976) *The Molecular Biology of the Gene*, 3rd ed. (Menlo Park, Calif.: W. A. Benjamin), p. 100. Chap. 4 contains a discussion of the role and biochemical significance of weak bonds.
6. Ibid., p. 65.
7. I. Hirao and A. D. Ellington (1995) "Re-creating the RNA World," *Current Biology* 5:1017–1022.
8. G. J. Narlikar and G. Herschlag (1977) "Mechanistic Aspects of Enzymic Catalysis," *Annual Review of Biochemistry*, 66:19–59.
9. G. Stix (1996) "Waiting for Breakthroughs," *Scientific American* 274(4):78–83.
10. Ibid., p. 81.
11. Ibid.
12. Ibid., p. 82.
13. Ibid.
14. Ibid., p. 83.
15. C. O. Pabo and R. T. Sauer (1984) "Protein DNA Recognition," *Annual Review of Biochemistry* 53:293–321; see pp. 313–314. See also Y. Cho et al. (1995) "Crystal Structure of a p53 Tumor Suppressor-DNA Complex: Understanding Tumorigenic Mutations," *Science* 265:346–355; see p. 353.
16. Ibid., p. 314.
17. N. P. Pavletich and C. O. Pabo (1991) "Zinc Finger-DNA Recognition: Crystal Structure of a Zif 268-DNA Complex at 2.1 A," *Science* 252:809–817; see p. 816.
18. M. Suzuki and N. Yagi (1994) "DNA Recognition Code of Transcription Factors in the Helix Turn Helix, Probe Helix, Hormone Receptor and Zinc Finger Families," *Proc. Natl. Acad. Sci. USA* 91:12357–12361. See also "History," *Nature Structural Biology* (1998) 5:100.
19. M. Ptashne (1986) *A Genetic Switch* (Palo Alto, Calif.: Blackwell Scientific Publications).

Chapter 9: The Fitness of the Metals

1. C. Sagan (1985) *Cosmos* (New York: Ballantine); see p. 198.
2. R. J. P. Williams (1985) "The Symbiosis of Metal and Protein Function," *European Journal of Biochemistry* 150:231–248; see p. 232.
3. Ibid., p. 247.
4. E. Frieden (1974) "Evolution of Metals as Essential Elements," in *Protein-Metal Interactions,* ed. M. Friedman (New York: Plenum Press), pp. 1–31; see p. 11.
5. J. J. R. Fraústo da Silva and R. J. P. Williams (1991) *The Biological Chemistry of the Elements* (Oxford: Oxford University Press).
6. Ibid., p. 107.
7. E. Baldwin (1964) *An Introduction to Comparative Biochemistry,* 2nd ed. (Cambridge: Cambridge University Press), p. 81.
8. N. N. Greenwood and A. Earnshaw (1984) *Chemistry of the Elements* (Oxford: Pergamon Press), pp. 1276–1277.
9. Baldwin, op. cit., p. 81.
10. Frieden, op. cit., pp. 20–21.
11. Ibid., p. 19.
12. Ibid.
13. Ibid., p. 22.
14. R. Gennis and S. Ferguson-Miller (1995) "Structure of Cytochrome *c* Oxidase, Energy Generator of Aerobic Life," *Science* 269:1063–1064.
15. Fraústo da Silva and Williams, op. cit., pp. 411–435. See also E. I. Stiefel (1977) "Molybdoenzymes: The Role of Electrons, Protons, and Dihydrogen," in *Bioinorganic Chemistry,* ed. K. N. Raymond (Washington D.C.: American Chemical Society), pp. 353–388; see p. 388 for reasons for the choice of molybdenum.
16. Ibid., p 427.
17. Williams, op. cit., p. 238.
18. Ibid.
19. M. Calvin (1962) "Evolutionary Possibilities for Photosynthesis and Quantum Conversion," in *Horizons in Biochemistry,* ed. M. Kasha and B. Pullman (New York: Academic Press), pp. 23–57; see p. 53. For discussion of the unique properties of Mg in chlorophyll, see also J. Katz (1973) "Chlorophyll," in *Inorganic Biochemistry,* vol. 2, ed. G. L. Eichhorn (Amsterdam: Elsevier), pp. 1022–1066; see pp. 1025–1026.
20. G. Wald (1959) "Life and Light," *Scientific American* 201 (4):92–108. See p. 97.
21. Williams, op. cit., p. 247.
22. Ibid., p. 246.

Chapter 10: The Fitness of the Cell

1. V. Tartar (1961) *The Biology of Stentor* (London: Pergamon Press); see chap. 7, "Regeneration," pp. 105–135.
2. D. Small (1986) *The Physical Chemistry of Lipids* (New York: Plenum Press); see first page of Preface.
3. D. E. Green and R. F. Goldberger (1967) *Molecular Insights into the Living Process* (New York: Academic Press), p. 25.
4. A. E. Needham (1961) *The Uniqueness of Biological Materials* (London: Pergamon Press), p. 77.
5. Ibid., p. 78.
6. J. P. Trinkaus (1984) *Cells into Organs* (Englewood Cliffs, N.J.: Prentice-Hall), p. 53.
7. Ibid., pp. 51–52.

8. Needham, op. cit., p. 78.
9. B. Hendry (1981) *Membrane Physiology and Cell Excitation* (London: Croom Helm), pp. 18–21.
10. Trinkaus, op. cit., p. 69.
11. A. Kotyk and K. Janacek (1977) *Membrane Transport: An Interdisciplinary Approach* (New York: Plenum Press), p. 100.
12. G. I. Bell (1978) "Models for the Specific Adhesion of Cells to Cells," *Science* 200:618–627; see p. 624. J. M. Baltz and R. A. Cone (1990) "The Strength of Non-covalent Biological Bonds and Adhesion by Multiple Independent Bonds," *Journal of Theoretical Biology* 142:163–178. See p. 172.
13. T. P. Stossel (1993) "On the Crawling of Animal Cells," *Science* 260:1086–1094.
14. Ibid., pp. 1086–1087.
15. D. A. Lauffenburger and A. F. Horwitz (1996) "Cell Migration: A Physically Integrated Process," *Cell* 84:359–369. T. Oliver, J. Lee, and K. Jacobson (1994) "Forces Exerted by Locomoting Cells," *Seminars in Cell Biology* 5:139–147. P. A. DiMilla, K. Barbee, and D. A. Lauffenburger (1993) "Mathematical Model for the Effects of Adhesion and Migration on Cell Migration Speed," *Biophysical Journal* 60:15–37.
16. B. Alberts et al. (1989) *The Molecular Biology of the Cell,* 2nd ed. (New York: Garland Publishing), p. 308. See also D. M. Woodbury (1974) "Physiology of Body Fluids," in *Physiology and Biophysics,* vol. 2, ed. T. C. Ruch and H. D. Patton (Philadelphia: W. B. Saunders), pp. 450–479.
17. Ibid.
18. Alberts et al., op. cit., p. 304.
19. *Encyclopaedia Britannica* (1994) 15th ed., vol. 23, p. 650.
20. J. C. Waterlow, P. J. Garlick, and D. J. Millward (1978) *Protein Turnover in Mammalian Tissues and in the Whole Body* (Amsterdam: Elsevier), see chap. 14.
21. H. C. Berg (1990) "Bacterial Microprocessing," *Cold Spring Harbor Symposium on Quantitative Biology* 55:539–544; see p. 539.
22. H. S. Jennings (1962) *Behavior of the Lower Organisms* (Bloomington: Indiana University Press); see pp. 15–18.
23. S. Hameroff (1988) "Molecular Automata in Microtubules: Basic Computational Logic of the Living State, in *Artificial Life,* ed. C. G. Langton (Redwood City, Calif.: Addison-Wesley), pp. 521–553; see p. 543.
24. Ibid.
25. Ibid.
26. C. Pantin (1951) "Organic Design," *Advancement of Science* 8(29):138–150; see p. 149.
27. R. Penrose (1994) *Shadows of the Mind* (Oxford: Oxford University Press), p. 357.
28. J. Brown (1994) "Tell Me Where Consciousness Is Bred," *New Scientist,* Nov. 19, pp. 46–47; see p. 47. Penrose, op, cit., p. 366.
29. D. Bray (1995) "Protein Molecules as Computational Elements in Living Cells," *Nature* 376:307–311.
30. R. F. Goldberger (1967) *Molecular Insights into the Living Process* (New York: Academic Press), pp. 24, 35–36. See also Needham, op. cit., pp. 43–44.
31. F. H. Westheimer (1987) "Why Nature Chose Phosphates," *Science* 235:1173–1178. See also comments in D. E. Green and R. F. Goldberger (1967) *Molecular Insights into the Living Process* (New York: Academic Press), p. 27.
32. G. Wald (1964) "The Origins of Life," *Proc. Natl. Acad. Sci. USA* 52:594–611; see discussion on pp. 607–608.
33. Ibid., p. 608.
34. C. Pantin (1951) "Organic Design," *Advancement of Science* 8(29):138–150; see pp. 143–144.

35. J. E. Gordon (1980) "Biomechanics: The Last Stronghold of Vitalism," *Symposia of the Society for Experimental Biology* 34:1–11; see p. 1.
36. Pantin, op. cit., p. 145.

Chapter 11: Homo Sapiens: *Fire Maker*

1. G. G. Simpson (1967) *The Meaning of Evolution* (New Haven: Yale University Press), p. 288.
2. P. Lieberman (1975) "On the Evolution of Language: A Unified View," in *Primate Functional Morphology and Evolution,* ed. R. Tuttle (The Hague: Mouton Publishers), pp. 501–540; see pp. 504–510.
3. Ibid., pp. 508, 536.
4. Aristotle, *Metaphysics* 1.1,980a21–7.
5. R. D. Martin (1990) *Primate Origins and Evolution* (London: Chapman & Hall), pp. 496–497.
6. R. M. Yerkes and A. W. Yerkes (1929) *The Great Apes* (New Haven: Yale University Press), p. 346.
7. J. Kidd (1952) *The Bridgewater Treatise on the Physical Condition of Man,* 6th ed. (London: Bohn); see chap. 3 on the hand, p. 26.
8. Ibid., pp. 29–31.
9. R. Tuttle (1975) "Knuckle-Walking and Knuckle-Walkers: A Commentary on Some Recent Perspectives on Hominoid Evolution," in *Primate Functional Morphology and Evolution,* ed. R. Tuttle (The Hague: Mouton Publishers), pp. 203–211; see p. 203.
10. J. Huxley (1941) *The Uniqueness of Man* (London: Chatto & Windus), p. 147.
11. K. Schmidt-Nielsen (1975) *Animal Physiology* (Cambridge: Cambridge University Press), pp. 514–515.
12. M. S. Block (1996) "Nanometers and Piconewtons: The Macromolecular Mechanisms of Kinesin," *Trends in Cell Biology* 5:169–175. See also R. A. Crowther, R. Padron, and R. Craig (1985) "Arrangement of the Heads of Myosin in Relaxed Thick Filaments from Tarantular Muscle," *Journal of Molecular Biology* 184:492–439; and B. Alberts et al. (1994) *Cell* (New York: Garland Publishing), p. 851.
13. R. Simmons (1996) "Molecular Motors: Single-Molecule Mechanics," *Current Biology* 6:392–394. See also Block, op. cit. For strength of weak bonds, see Alberts et al., op. cit., pp. 90–92. For energy levels of kJ of myosin cross bridges, see W. F. Harrington (1979) "On the Origin of the Contractile Force in Skeletal Muscle," *Proc. Natl. Acad. Sci. USA* 76:5066–5070. For energy levels of affinity bonds composed of multiple weak bonds, see J. M. Batz and R. A. Cone (1990) "The Strength of Non-covalent biological Bonds and Adhesions by Multiple Independent Bonds," *Journal of Theoretical Biology* 142:163–178; and F. Amblard et al. (1994) "Molecular Analysis of Antigen-Independent Adhesion Forces Between T and B Lymphocytes," *Proc. Natl. Acad. Sci. USA* 91:3628–3632.
14. Simmons, op. cit.
15. A. J. Wilson (1994) *The Living Rock* (Cambridge: Woodhead Publishing); see pp. 10–16.
16. Schmidt-Nielsen, op. cit.; see p. 625, table 13.2.
17. W. A. H. Rushton (1951) "A Theory of the Effects of Fibre Size in Medullated Nerve," *Journal of Physiology* 115:101–122.
18. Schmidt-Nielsen, op. cit.; see p. 53.
19. Ibid.
20. D. W. Sciama (1959) *The Unity of the Universe* (London: Faber & Faber), pp. 118–119.
21. Huxley, op. cit., p. 8.
22. Ibid., pp. 15–16.
23. V. G. Dethier (1964) "Microscopic Brains," *Science* 143:1138–1145.

24. E. J. Slijper (1962) *Whales* (London: Hutchinson); see pp. 245–246.
25. Ibid.
26. W. E. Le Gros Clark (1969) *The Antecedents of Man,* 3rd ed. (Chicago: Quadrangle Books), p. 260.
27. C. Wills (1993) *The Runaway Brain* (New York: HarperCollins); see p. 7.
28. G. A. Shariff (1953) "Cell Counts in the Primate Cerebral Cortex," *Journal of Comparative Neurology* 98:381–400.
29. Ibid.; see p. 263. J. DeFelipe and E. G. Jones (1988) *Cajal on the Cerebral Cortex* (New York: Oxford University Press); see chap. 5 and chap. 7, fig. 34, p. 69.
30. Ibid.; see p. 263.
31. See "News and Views," *Nature* 385 (1997): 207–210.
32. M. Ward (1997) "End of the Road for Brain Evolution," *New Scientist* 153, no. 2066:14.
33. *Nature,* op. cit., p. 210.
34. J. Searle (1987) *"Minds and Brains Without Programs,"* in *Mindwaves: Thoughts on Intelligence, Identity and Conciousness,* ed. C. Blakemore and S. Greenfield (Oxford: Basil Blackwell), pp. 209–233.
35. R. Penrose (1990) *The Emperor's New Mind* (London: Vintage).
36. E. P. Wigner (1960) "The Unreasonable Effectiveness of Mathematics in the Natural Sciences," *Communications on Pure and Applied Mathematics* 13:1–14.
37. P. C. W. Davies (1992) *The Mind of God* (London: Penguin); see p. 157.
38. J. Lear (1988) *Aristotle: The Desire to Understand* (Cambridge: Cambridge University Press), p. 230.

Chapter 12: The Tree of Life

1. N. C. Gillespie (1979) *Charles Darwin and the Problem of Creation* (Chicago: University of Chicago Press); see chap. 5, "Providential Evolution and the Problem of Design."
2. R. Chambers (1969) *Vestiges of the Natural History of Creation* (New York: Leicester University Press), pp. 152–154.
3. Ibid., p. 158.
4. Ibid., pp. 165–167.
5. Ibid., pp. 250–251.
6. Ibid., pp. 163–164.
7. Ibid., Introduction.
8. Ibid.
9. Ibid.
10. A. Koestler (1970) *The Ghost in the Machine* (London: Pan Books), p. 174.
11. Ibid., pp. 174–175.
12. S. J. Gould (1972) "Zealous Advocates," *Science* 176:623–625; see p. 625.
13. R. Dawkins (1986) *The Blind Watchmaker* (London: Longman Scientific), p. 291.
14. B. Rensch (1959) *Evolution Above the Species Level* (New York: Wiley), pp. 57–58.
15. L. S. Berg (1969) *Nomogenesis* (Cambridge: MIT Press), p. 110.
16. Ibid., pp. 118–120. Re: the reduction of the gametophyte, Berg comments: "We may thus trace the entire process of the reduction of the gametophyte, commencing with its flourishing condition in mosses, and proceeding with its gradual decline in the seed ferns until its complete disappearance in the conifers. . . . A definite course of evolution is here strikingly exemplified."
17. Ibid., pp. 121–124.
18. H. Miller (1869) *Footsteps of the Creator,* 11th ed. (Edinburgh: Nimmo), pp. 293–294.
19. N. C. Gillespie (1979) *Charles Darwin and the Problem of Creation* (Chicago: University of Chicago Press), p. 85.

20. Ibid., p. 104.
21. Gillespie, op. cit.; see chap. 5.
22. M. J. Denton (1985) *Evolution: A Theory in Crisis* (London: Burnett Books).
23. M. Behe (1996) *Darwin's Black Box* (Chicago: Free Press).
24. J. Diamond (1992) *The Rise and Fall of the Third Chimpanzee* (London: Vintage); see p. 23.
25. S. Conway Morris (1995) "Book Reviews," *Nature* 376:736.
26. R. P. Harvey (1996) "NK-2 Homeobox Genes and Heart Development," *Developmental Biology* 178:203–216.
27. B. John and G. Miklos (1988) *The Eucaryotic Genome in Development and Evolution* (London: Allen & Unwin), p. 112.
28. G. Bernardi and G. Bernardi (1986) "Compositional Constraints and Genome Evolution," *Journal of Molecular Evolution* 24:1–11; see p. 1.
29. N. Sueoka (1992) "Directional Mutation Pressure, Selective Constraints, and Genetic Equilibria," *Journal of Molecular Evolution* 34:95–114.
30. G. Vines (1982) "Molecular Drive: A Third Force in Evolution," *New Scientist,* December 9, pp. 664–665; see p. 665.
31. We can envisage such a contriving or tampering of the DNA space to be analogous to rearranging the structure of the English lexicon to permit the evolution of a particular word tree, which could grow from a single beginning to include a galaxy of long complex words. As the lexicon is structured at present, most English words over ten letters long are completely isolated and cannot generally be transformed via single letter changes via functional intermediates to nearby words. Consequently, it is impossible to go from a simple starting word such as "a," to reach complex English words more than ten letters long. However, by playing God and restructuring the lexicon we would be able, if we wished, to arrange a vast word tree within the letter space, so that all functional words were clustered together in a highly ordered manner in the space and so that starting from one unique letter string we would be led inevitably by the necessity to move in single-letter steps via functional intermediates to find all functional words and trace out all the branches of the tree.
32. S. Kauffman (1995) *At Home in the Universe* (New York: Oxford University Press).
33. S. Kauffman (1993) *The Origins of Order: Self-Organization and Selection in Evolution* (New York: Oxford University Press).
34. B. Goodwin (1995) *How the Leopard Changed its Spots* (New York: Simon & Schuster).
35. Kauffman (1995), p. 23.
36. Goodwin, op. cit.; see p. 168.
37. Ibid., p. 131.
38. Ibid., p. 114.
39. M. P. Schutzenberger (1996), personal communication.
40. J. W. Drake (1991) "Spontaneous Mutation," *Annual Review of Genetics* 25:125–146. N. Symmonds (1991) "A Fitter Theory of Evolution," *New Scientist,* September, 21, pp. 30–34.
41. Dawkins, op. cit., p. 313. J. Monod (1972) *Chance and Necessity* (London: Collins), p. 114. E. Mayr (1976) *Evolution and the Diversity of Life* (Cambridge: Harvard University Press), p. 32.
42. T. Dobzhansky et al. (1977) *Evolution* (San Francisco: W. H. Freeman), p. 65.
43. Ibid.
44. M. Delbruck (1947) *Cold Spring Harbor Symposium on Quantitative Biology* 11:154.
45. J. Cairns, J. Overbaugh, and S. Miller (1988) "The Origin of Mutants," *Nature* 335:142–145; see p. 145.
46. "Research News," *Science* 277 (1997):176–178.

47. M. J. Denton (1986) *Evolution: A Theory in Crisis* (Bethesda, Md.: Adler & Adler), p. 249.
48. B. Lewin (1988) "Molecular Clocks Turn a Quarter of a Century," *Science* 239:561–563; see p. 561.
49. F. Hoyle and C. Wickramasinghe (1996) (London: Orino Books); see chap. 4.
50. J. Horgan (1993) "In the Beginning," *Scientific American* 264 (2):101–109; see p. 101.
51. Monod, op. cit., p. 135.
52. F. Crick (1981) *Life Itself* (New York: Simon & Schuster), p. 88.
53. Horgan, op. cit., p. 103.
54. Ibid., p. 102.
55. I. Hirao and A. D. Ellington (1995) "Re-creating the RNA World," *Current Biology* 5:1017–1022.
56. Horgan, op. cit.
57. Ibid.
58. Ibid., p. 106.
59. Ibid., p. 102.
60. "News and Views," *Nature* 382 (1996):496–497.
61. Ibid., p. 109.
62. M. M. Waldrop (1990) "Spontaneous Order, Evolution, and Life," *Science* 247:1543–1545; see p. 1543.
63. R. Lewin (1993) "Order for Free," *New Scientist* 137, no. 1860, Supplement on Complexity: pp. 10–11; see p. 10.
64. Ibid., p. 10.
65. S. J. Gould (1996) "War of the World Views," *Natural History* 105:22–33.
66. Ibid., p. 30.
67. N. Eldredge and S. J. Gould (1973) "Punctuated Equilibria: An Alternative to Phyletic Gradualism," in *Models in Paleontology*, ed. T. J. M. Schopf (San Francisco: Freeman, Cooper & Co.), pp. 82–115.
68. R. A. Kerr (1995) "Did Darwin Get it Right?" *Science* 267:1421–1422. For evidence that avian evolution conforms to the same pattern, see A. Feduccia (1995) "Explosive Evolution in Tertiary Birds and Mammals," *Science* 267:637–638.
69. Ibid.
70. R. A. Kerr (1993) "Evolution's Big Bang Gets Even More Explosive," *Science* 261:1274–1275.
71. S. J. Gould (1994) "In the Mind of the Beholder," *Natural History* 103(3):14–23.

Chapter 13: The Principle of Plenitude

1. W. Coleman (1964) *Georges Cuvier, Zoologist* (Cambridge: Harvard University Press), pp. 171–172.
2. A. O. Lovejoy (1953) *The Great Chain of Being* (Cambridge: Harvard University Press); see p. 52.
3. N. Pace (1997) "A Molecular View of Microbial Diversity and the Biosphere," *Science* 276:734–740. See also T. Fenchel and B. J. Findlay (1995) *Ecology and Evolution in Anoxic Worlds* (Oxford: Oxford University Press).
4. E. Florey (1966) *An Introduction to General and Comparative Animal Physiology* (Philadelphia: W. B. Saunders), p. 39.
5. S. Conway Morris (1993) "The Fossil Record and the Early Evolution of the Metazoa," *Nature* 313:219–225. Morris lists seventy-one different phyla in all, twenty-nine of which are extinct; see fig. 2, p. 221.

6. S. J. Gould (1989) *Wonderful Life* (New York: Norton); see chap. 3.

7. B. Rensch (1959) *Evolution Above the Species* (New York: Wiley); see p. 66.

8. A. R. Jones (1974) *The Ciliates* (London: Hutchinson), p. 17.

9. Rensch, op. cit., p. 67.

10. Ibid., p. 59.

11. Ibid.

12. Ibid.

13. Ibid., p. 60.

14. Ibid., p. 61.

15. Ibid., p. 62.

16. Ibid., p. 66.

17. M. F. Land and R. D. Fernald (1992) "The Evolution of Eyes," *Annual Review of Neuroscience* 15:1–29.

18. E. T. Burtt (1974) *The Senses of Animals* (London: Wykeham Publications), p. 115. See also G. Wald (1959) "Light and Life," *Scientific American* 201 (4):92–108.

19. E. A. Newman and P. H. Hartline (1982) "The Infrared 'Vision' of Snakes," *Scientific American* 246 (3):98–107.

20. K. Schmidt-Nielsen (1984) *Scaling* (Cambridge: Cambridge University Press), pp. 1–2.

21. H. J. Morowitz (1966) "The Minimum Size of Cells," in *Principles of Biomolecular Organisation*, G. E. W. Wolstenholme and M. O'Connor (London: Churchill), pp. 446–459.

22. Ibid., p. 456.

23. Schmidt-Nielsen, op. cit., p. 213.

24. Rensch, op. cit., p. 171.

25. K. Schmidt-Nielsen (1975) *Animal Physiology* (Cambridge: Cambridge University Press); see section on insect respiration, pp. 61–68. See also A. D. Imms (1964) *A General Textbook of Entomology*, pp. 133–150; see p. 144 on diffusional constraints. The tracheal system and the size of insects is also discussed in R. McNeil Alexander (1971) *Size and Shape* (London: Edward Arnold), pp. 21–22.

26. Schmidt-Nielsen (1984); see discussion on pp. 204–208.

27. Ibid., p. 207.

28. Ibid., pp. 207–208.

29. Ibid., p. 10.

30. Ibid., p. 205.

31. J. D. Curry (1970) *Animal Skeletons* (London: Edward Arnold). See pp. 5–8 for a discussion of the comparative merits of exo- and endoskeletons. An exoskeleton, for example, is far superior to an endoskeleton in regard to failure by buckling and bending, the sorts of stresses likely to be encountered by a small organism. However, an endoskeleton is far more resistant to external forces of impact because the soft tissues can absorb a great amount of energy without serious damage whereas the hard, stiff exoskeleton is unprotected. See also Schmidt-Nielsen (1984), pp. 52–53: "The entire kinetic energy is absorbed on impact, and for a fast-moving large animal, the forces impacting on a hard exoskeleton are likely to cause local failure."

32. S. A. Wainwright et al. (1976) *Mechanical Design in Organisms* (London: Edward Arnold). On Page p. 239 the authors note: "Vertebrates must have an endoskeleton . . . but sclerotised cuticle has a great disadvantage—it is extremely resistant to enzymes . . . invertebrates overcome this problem by shedding their cuticle as they grow . . . bone on the other hand, although stiff and seemingly immutable, is in a dynamic state of erosion and deposition the whole time; therefore remodelling necessitated by growth is easily brought about."

33. Ibid., pp. 49–51.

34. J. Huxley (1941) *The Uniqueness of Man* (London: Chatto & Windus), pp. 134–135.

35. Ibid., p. 141.
36. Alexander, op. cit.; see sec. 5.2 on animal legs.
37. S. J. Gould (1981) "Kingdoms Without Wheels," *Natural History* 90 (3):42–48.
38. Ibid., pp. 47–48.
39. Schmidt-Nielsen (1984), p. 212.
40. S. A. Newman and W. D. Comper (1990) "Generic Physical Mechanisms of Morphogenesis and Pattern Formation," *Development* 110:1–18; see summary, p. 1.

Chapter 14: The Dream of Asilomar

1. P. Berg et al. (1974) "Potential Biohazards of Recombinant DNA Molecules," *Science* 185:303.
2. "News and Comments," *Science* 190 (1975):1175.
3. J. Goodfield (1977) *Playing God* (London: Hutchinson); see pp. 4–5.
4. Ibid., pp. 58–59.
5. M. Jahoda (1982) "Once a Jackass," *Nature* 295:173–174.
6. J. G. Williams (1982) "Mouse and Supermouse," in "News and Views," *Nature* 300:575. See also I. Wilmut, J. Clark, and P. Simons (1988) "A Revolution in Animal Breeding," *New Scientist* 119, no. 1620:56–59.
7. A. Wyke (1988) "A Survey of Biotechnology," *Economist,* April 30, pp. 5–10; see p. 7.
8. Ibid., p. 17.
9. Ibid., p. 6.
10. Ibid., p. 20.
11. K. Schmidt (1995) "Whatever Happened to the Gene Revolution?" *New Scientist* 145, no. 1959:21–25; see p. 22.
12. Ibid.
13. G. Cuvier (1854) *Animal Kingdom* (London: W. Orr). See p. 18: "Life then presupposes organisation in general, and the life proper to each being presupposes the organisation peculiar to that being, just as the movement of a clock presupposes the clock."
14. K. E. Drexler (1987) *Engines of Creation* (Garden City, N.Y.: Anchor Books). K. E. Drexler (1988) "Biological and Nanomechanical Systems: Contrasts in Evolutionary Capacity," in *Artificial Life,* ed. C. G. Langton (Redwood City, Calif.: Addison-Wesley), pp. 501– 519; see pp. 509–510.
15. P .C. Ritterbush (1972) "Organic Form: Aesthetics and Objectivity in the Study of Form in the Life Sciences," in *Organic Form: The Life of an Idea,* ed. G. S. Rousseau (London: Routledge & Kegan Paul), pp. 25–59.
16. W. Coleman (1964) *Georges Cuvier, Zoologist* (Cambridge: Harvard University Press); see Introduction, p. 2, and pp. 38–43.
17. G. Cuvier (1812) *Reserches sur les ossements fossiles de quadrupèdes, Discours préliminaire,* English trans. by R. Kerr (1813), entitled *Essay on the Theory of the Earth* (Edinburgh and London), pp. 94–95. Also referred to in Coleman, op. cit., p. 108.
18. G. Cuvier (1829) *Revolutions of the Surface of the Earth* (London: Whittaker, Treacher & Arnot), p. 60.
19. S. A. Kauffman (1993) *The Origins of Order* (Oxford: Oxford University Press); see pp. 53–54.
20. D'Arcy W. Thompson (1952) *On Growth and Form,* vol. 2, 2nd ed. (Cambridge: Cambridge University Press), p. 1019. A. G. Cairns-Smith (1982) *Genetic Takeover and the Mineral Origins of Life* (Cambridge: Cambridge University Press), p. 78. R. Lewontin (1978) "Adaptation," *Scientific American* 219(3):212–231; see p. 231.
21. P. Alberch (1980) "Ontogenesis and Morphological Diversification," *American Zoologist* 20:653–657.

22. S. Ohno (1973) "Ancient Linkage Groups and Frozen Accidents," *Nature* 244:259–262.

23. J. D. Harris and N. R. Lemoine (1996) "Strategies for Targeted Gene Therapy," *Trends in Genetics* 12:400–405; see p. 401.

24. R. Dawkins (1986) *The Blind Watchmaker* (London: Longman Scientific), pp. 85–86, 311.

25. Ibid., pp. 317–318.

26. E. Hadorn (1961) *Developmental Genetics and Lethal Factors* (London: Methuen); see p. 196.

27. E. Mayr (1970) *Populations, Species, and Evolution* (Cambridge: Harvard University Press), pp. 162–164.

28. C. Q. Doe et al. (1988) "Expression and Function of the Segmentation Gene *Fushi Tarazu* During *Drosophila* Neurogenesis," *Science* 239:170–175.

29. R. Lewin (1984) "Why Is Development So Illogical?" *Science* 224:1327–1329; see p. 1327.

30. Ibid.

31. Ibid.

32. L. Wolpert (1992) "Gastrulation and the Evolution of Development," *Development,* Supplement, pp. 7–13.

33. *McGraw-Hill Encyclopedia of Science and Technology* (1992), vol. 17, p. 163.

34. Ibid., vol. 6, p. 243.

35. K. P. Able (1980) "Mechanism and Orientation, Navigation and Homing," in *Animal Migration, Orientation, and Navigation,* ed. S. A. Gauthreaux (New York: Academic Press); see chap. 5, quote from p. 327. T. H. Waterman (1989) *Animal Navigation* (New York: Scientific American Library); see pp. 59, 60–61.

36. H. P. Erickson (1993) "Tenascin-C, Tenascin-R, and Tenascin-X: A Family of Talented Proteins in Search of Functions," *Current Biology* 5:869–876; see p. 869.

37. M. L. Goldberg, R. A. Colvin, and A. F. Mellin (1989) "The Drosophila *Zeste* Locus is Nonessential," *Genetics* 123:145–155.

38. J. Brookfield (1992) "Can Genes Be Truly Redundant?" *Current Biology* 2:553–554; see p. 553. See also J. H. Thomas (1993) "Thinking About Genetic Redundancy," *Trends in Genetics,* 9:395–399.

39. P. W. Sternberg (1993) "Intercellular Signaling and Signal Transduction in *C. elegans,*" *Annual Review of Genetics* 27:497–521; see p. 512.

40. S. W. Wilson (1993) "Clues from Clueless," *Current Biology* 3:536–539.

41. C. Kenyon (1995) "A Perfect Vulva Every Time: Gradients and Signaling Cascades in *C. elegans,*" *Cell* 82:171–174; see p. 173.

42. J. van Brunt (1986) "Protein Architecture: Designing from the Ground Up," *Bio/technology* 4:277–283; see p. 277.

43. M. F. Perutz (1985) "The Birth of Protein Engineering," *New Scientist* 106, no. 1460: 12–15; see p. 14.

44. M. Mutter (1985) "The Construction of New Proteins and Enzymes—A Prospect for the Future," Angewandte Chemie (International Edition in English) 24:639–653.

45. S. Dalal, S. Balasubranian, and L. Regan (1997) "Protein Alchemy: Changing β-Sheet into α Helix," *Nature Structural Biology* 4:458–552.

46. C. B. Anfinsen (1964) "On the Possibility of Predicting Tertiary Structure from Primary Sequence," in *New Perspectives in Biology,* ed. M. Sela (New York: Elsevier), pp. 42–50.

47. G. S. Orsini (1977) "The Ancient Roots of a Modern Idea," in *Organic Form: The Life of an Idea,* ed. G. S. Rousseau (London: Routledge & Kegan Paul); see pp. 8–12.

48. M. I. Simon (1992) "Summary: The Cell Surface Regulates Information Flow, Material Transport, and Cell Identity," *Cold Spring Harbor Symposium on Quantitative Biology* 57:673–688. E. R. Kandel (1983) "Neurobiology and Molecular Biology: The Second

Encounter," *Cold Spring Harbor Symposium on Quantitative Biology* 48:891–908; see p. 904.

49. L. S. B. Goldstein (1993) "With Apologies to Scheherazade: Tails of 1001 Kinesin Motors," *Annual Review of Genetics* 27:319–351.

50. H. Charbonneau and N. K. Tonks (1992) "1002 Protein Phosphatases," *Annual Review of Cell Biology* 8:463–469.

51. Simon, op. cit., p. 678.

52. C. W. J. Smith, J. G. Patton, and B. Nadal-Ginard (1989) "Alternative Splicing in the Control of Gene Expression," *Annual Review of Genetics* 23:527–577; see p. 564.

53. Ibid., p. 676.

54. Ibid., p. 687.

55. S. L. McIntire et al. (1992) "Genes Necessary for Directed Axonal Elongation or Fasciculation in *C. elegans*,"*Neuron* 8:307–322; see p. 307.

56. H. Nawa, T. Le. Yamamori, and P. H. Patterson (1990) "Generation of Neuronal Diversity: Analogies and Homologies with Hematopoiesis," *Cold Spring Harbor Symposium of Quantitative Biology* 55:247–253; see p. 247.

57. "Glia: The Brain's Other Cells," in "Research News," *Science* 266 (1994):970–972.

58. R. Rucker (1983) *Infinity and the Mind* (New York: Bantam); see p. 2.

Chapter 15: The Eye of the Lobster

1. J. R. P. Angel (1979) "Lobster Eyes as X-ray Telescopes," *Astrophysical Journal* 233:364–373. See also B. K. Hartline (1980) "Lobster-Eye X-ray Telescope Envisioned," *Science* 207:47.

2. M. F. Land (1976) "Superposition Images Are Formed by Reflection in the Eyes of Some Oceanic Decapod Crustacea," *Nature* 263:764–765.

3. M. F. Land (1978) "Animal Eyes with Mirror Optics," *Scientific American* 239(6):88–99.

4. Ibid.

5. W. J. Dakin (1928) "The Eyes of *Pecten, Spondylus, Amussium,* and Allied Lamellibranchs, with a Short Discussion on Their Evolution," *Proceedings of the Royal Society of London, Series B* 103:355–365; see pp. 359–360.

6. Ibid., p. 361.

7. Ibid., p. 364.

8. M. F. Land (1966) "Activity in the Optic Nerve of *Pecten maximus* in Response to Changes in Light Intensity, and to Pattern and Movement in the Optical Environment," *Journal of Experimental Biology* 45:83–99.

9. E. M. del Pino (1989) "Marsupial Frogs," *Scientific American* 260(5):76–84.

10. J. S. Levinton (1992) "The Big Bang of Animal Evolution," *Scientific American* 267(11):52–59; see p. 59.

11. H. R. Dunker (1978) "Development of the Avian Respiratory and Circulation Systems," in *Respiratory Function in Birds, Adult and Embryonic,* ed. J. Piiper, (New York: Springer-Verlag), pp. 260–273.

12. C. Darwin (1962) *The Origin of Species,* 6th ed. (New York: Collier Books), p. 182.

13. K. Schmidt-Nielsen (1975) *Animal Physiology* (New York: Cambridge University Press), p. 61.

14. P. C. W. Davies, (1992) *The Mind of God* (London: Penguin), p. 149.

15. G. Gibbs (1994) "The Demon Grasshoppers," *New Zealand Geographic,* January–March, pp. 90–117.

16. L. Cuénot (1944) "L'anti Hasard," *Revue Scientifique,* pp. 339–346.

17. Ibid.; see p. 345, trans. M. P. Schutzenberger.

18. See L. Watson (1973) *Supernature* (London: Hodder & Stoughton). Also R. Sheldrake (1981) *A New Science of Life: The Hypothesis of Formative Causation* (London: Blond & Briggs). And see also the short note in *New Scientist,* July 26, 1997, p. 39, reporting recent experiments carried out by Sheldrake on a "mysterious sixth sense."
19. Darwin, op. cit., p. 484.

Conclusion: The Long Chain of Coincidence

1. B. Appleyard (1992) *Times Saturday Review,* April 25, p. 12.
2. C. Sagan (1985) *Cosmos* (New York: Ballantine), p. 30.
3. S. J. Dick (1982) *Plurality of Worlds* (Cambridge: Cambridge University Press), p. 61.
4. C. Sagan (1985) *Cosmos* (New York: Ballantine). "One Voice in the Cosmic Fugue" is the title of chap. 2.
5. J. S. Shklovskii and C. Sagan (1977) *Intelligent Life in the Universe* (London: Pan Books), p. 22.
6. Sagan, op. cit., p. 242.
7. G. Feinberg and R. Shapiro (1980) *Life Beyond Earth* (New York: Morrow); see p. 247 and pp. 246–250 for discussion of life in ammonia.
8. Ibid., pp. 252–256.
9. Ibid., pp. 382–384.
10. F. Hoyle (1957) *The Black Cloud* (London: Heinemann); see chap. 10.
11. Sagan, op. cit.; see pp. 29–30.
12. Feinberg and Shapiro, op. cit., p. 235.
13. Ibid., pp. 274–275.
14. J. Needham (1929) *The Sceptical Biologist* (London: Chatto & Windus), p. 217; see pp. 210–218 for a review of Henderson's *Fitness.*
15. H. F. Osborne (1894) *From the Greeks to Darwin* (New York: Macmillan), p. 61.
16. N. K. Smith (1935) *Hume's Dialogues Concerning Natural Religion* (Oxford: Oxford University Press), pp. 224–226.
17. P. W. Atkins (1981) *The Creation* (San Francisco: W. H. Freeman), pp. 36, 123, 125.
18. L. J. Henderson (1958) *The Fitness of the Environment* (Boston: Beacon Press), pp. 275–276.

Epilogue

1. J. Lear (1988) *Aristotle: The Desire to Understand* (Cambridge: Cambridge University Press).
2. *Encyclopaedia Britannica* (1994), 15th ed., article entitled "Electricity and Magnetism," in vol. 18, pp. 189–193. See p. 191 for Oersted's discovery while lecturing students.

Appendix: Miscellaneous Additional Evidence of the Fitness of Earthly Life

1. D. E. Green and R. F. Goldberger (1967) *Molecular Insights into the Living Process* (New York: Academic Press), p. 24. Note that because of its closed-ring hemiacetal form, glucose has the lowest frequency free-aldehyde conformation and the slowest rate of Schiff base formation. Consequently, glucose is the most stable sugar in the presence of protein and other amino-bearing groups such as nucleoproteins.
2. A. E. Needham (1965) *The Uniqueness of Biological Materials* (Oxford: Pergamon Press), p. 43.
3. Green and Goldberger, op. cit., pp. 35–36.

4. Needham, op. cit., pp. 43–44.
5. Green and Goldberger, op. cit.; see p. 25.
6. Needham, op. cit., p. 77.
7. Ibid., p. 78.
8. Ibid.
9. Ibid.
10. B. Hendry (1981) *Membrane Physiology and Cell Excitation* (London: Croom Helm); see p. 18.
11. Ibid., pp. 19–21.
12. F. H. Westheimer (1987) "Why Nature Chose Phosphates," *Science* 235:1173–1178; see p. 1173. See also comments in Green and Goldberger, op. cit., p. 27: "The P-O-P bonds of ATP represent a convenient packet of chemical energy in the sense that it is sufficient to drive all the chemical reactions for which it is required while not being so large that its power is wasted. Another important prerequisite that a molecule must meet as a satisfactory energy store is stability. There are many compounds with 'energy rich' bonds which are highly unstable in water at body temperature. Such compounds would not be very useful. The P-O-P bonds of ATP are remarkably stable under physiological conditions; thus ATP poses no problems of storage."
13. Westheimer, op. cit., p. 1176.
14. Ibid., p. 1178.
15. Green and Goldberger, op. cit., pp. 25–26.
16. M. Toporek (1968) *Basic Chemistry of Life* (Englewood Cliffs, N.J.: Prentice-Hall); see table 1, p. 137.
17. L. J. Henderson (1958) *The Fitness of the Environment* (Boston: Beacon Press), pp. 159–160.
18. W. S. Hoffman (1970) *The Biochemistry of Clinical Medicine* (Chicago: Year Book Medical Publishers); see chap. 12, esp. pp. 548–549.
19. J. J. R. Fraústo da Silva and R. J. P. Williams (1991) *The Biological Chemistry of the Elements* (Oxford: Oxford University Press), p. 138.
20. B. D. Rose (1977) *Clinical Physiology of Acid-Base and Electrolyte Disorders* (New York: McGraw-Hill), p. 176.
21. Henderson, op. cit., p. 158.
22. M. Suzuki and N. Yagi (1994) "DNA Recognition Code of Transcription Factors in the Helix Turn Helix, Probe Helix, Hormone Receptor and Zinc Finger Families," *Proc. Natl. Acad. Sci. USA* 91:12357–12361.
23. M. Ptashne (1986) *A Genetic Switch* (Palo Alto, Calif.: Blackwell Scientific Publications).
24. Ibid.; see Appendix 1, pp. 109–115, esp. p. 112: "Consider a repressor that binds to its operator with a dissociation constant of 10^{-10} M (the dissociation constant is a measure of the strength of binding between two molecules, the lower the figure the greater the intensity of binding) and to a random DNA sequence with a dissociation constant of 10^{-4} M. Now double the size of the repressor and the operator, so that twice as many . . . contacts are made. The larger version, to a first approximation, would bind to operator and to random DNA with a dissociation constant of 10^{-20} M (ten orders of magnitude stronger) and 10^{-8} M respectively. (Twice as many contacts implies twice the energy [-DG] and recall that the dissociation constant is related to DG exponentially: Dissociation constant = $e^{-DG/RT}$. For every 2.8 kcal change in DG, the dissociation constant changes 100 fold.)"

Index

Page numbers in *italics* refer to illustrations.

Mercury
Venus
Earth
Mars
Jupiter
Saturn
Uranus
Neptune
Pluto

Printed in the United States
1485000004B/166-213